RECEVED F

DR. PAUL CHEN

12-26-19

THIS BOOK BELONGS

TO JARED

1-10-26

[illegible]

READ CHAPTER 13

FOR MY PARTICIPATION IN THE

P.O.W. RIOTS-

The Hijacked War

THE HIJACKED WAR

THE STORY OF CHINESE POWS IN THE KOREAN WAR

David Cheng Chang

STANFORD UNIVERSITY PRESS
Stanford, California

STANFORD UNIVERSITY PRESS
Stanford, California

This book has been partially underwritten by the Stanford Authors Fund. We are grateful to the Fund for its support of scholarship by first-time authors. For more information, please see www.sup.org/authorsfund.

Printed in the United States of America on acid-free, archival-quality paper

Library of Congress Cataloging-in-Publication Data
Names: Chang, David Cheng, 1974– author.
Title: The hijacked war : the story of Chinese POWs in the Korean War / David Cheng Chang.
Description: Stanford, California : Stanford University Press, 2019. | Includes bibliographical references and index.
Identifiers: LCCN 2018021585 (print) | LCCN 2018022756 (ebook) | ISBN 9781503605879 | ISBN 9781503604605 | ISBN 9781503604605 (cloth : alk. paper)
Subjects: LCSH: Korean War, 1950-1953—Prisoners and prisons, Chinese. | Korean War, 1950-1953—Personal narratives, Chinese. | Repatriation—China—History—20th century. | Repatriation—Taiwan—History—20th century. | Communists—China—History—20th century. | Nationalists—China—History—20th century. | United States—Foreign relations—1945-1953. | China—History—Civil War, 1945-1949.
Classification: LCC DS921.2 (ebook) | LCC DS921.2 .C43 2019 (print) | DDC 951.904/27—dc23
LC record available at https://lccn.loc.gov/2018021585

Typeset by Kevin Barrett Kane in 10/13.5 Adobe Garamond

Cover design: Angela Moody

Cover photograph: G. Dimitria Boria, MacArthur Memorial Archives

To the more than twenty-one thousand Chinese prisoners of war who returned to China, went to Taiwan, or chose neutral nations

and

to the several hundred Chinese prisoners who perished in UN prison camps or north of the 38th parallel.

Contents

Maps, Tables, and Figures

MAPS

TABLES

FIGURES

Note on Transliteration

For Chinese and Korean personal names, I have followed the order of family surname first and the given name second, except for Syngman Rhee and Wen Chao Chen. All Chinese personal and place names are rendered in pinyin with the exceptions of Sun Yat-sen, Chiang Kai-shek, Chiang Ching-kuo, Taipei, Tsinghua, and the Yangtze River.

For Korean personal and place names, I follow the historian Allan Millett's practice of adopting the *Herald-Times* system, a simplified version of the McCune-Reischauer system without the diacritical marks. This system had been widely used since the 1940s until the South Korean government introduced a markedly different system in 2000. Therefore, to be consistent with names appearing in historical records, I use Pusan instead of Busan, Cheju instead of Jeju, Koje instead of Geoje, Uijongbu instead of Uijeongbu, Yongdungpo instead of Yeongdeungpo, and so on.

MAP 1. China, 1945–1950

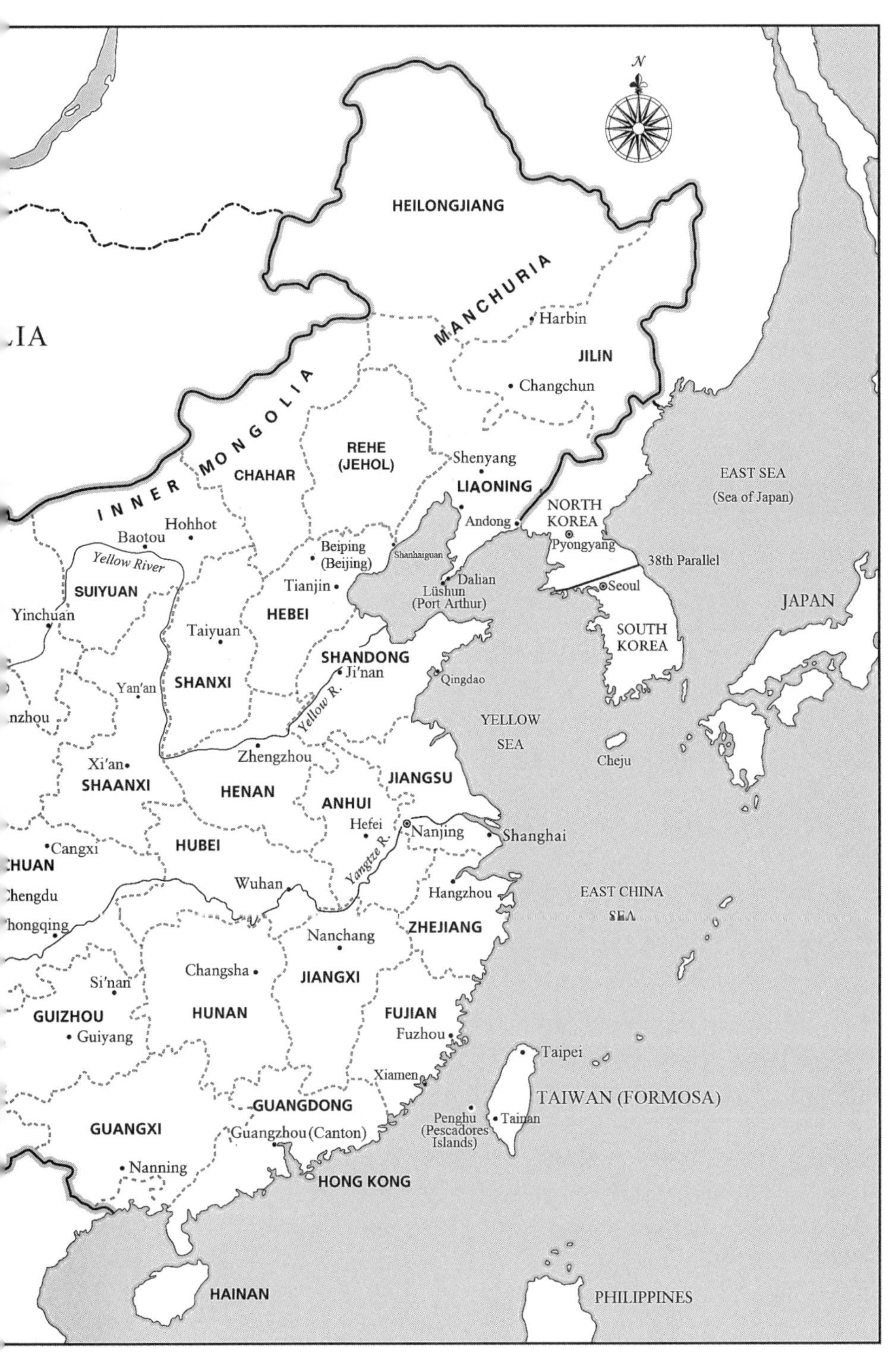

N
HEILONGJIANG
MANCHURIA
Harbin
JILIN
Changchun
INNER MONGOLIA
REHE
(JEHOL)
CHAHAR
Shenyang
LIAONING
NORTH
KOREA
Andong
Pyongyang
EAST SEA
(Sea of Japan)
Hohhot
Baotou
Yellow River
Beiping
(Beijing)
Shanhaiguan
38th Parallel
Dalian
Lüshun
(Port Arthur)
Seoul
Tianjin
SUIYUAN
Yinchuan
HEBEI
JAPAN
Taiyuan
SOUTH
KOREA
SHANDONG
Ji'nan
Yan'an
SHANXI
Qingdao
Yellow R.
YELLOW
SEA
Cheju
Zhengzhou
Xi'an
SHAANXI
HENAN
JIANGSU
ANHUI
Hefei
Nanjing
Shanghai
Cangxi
HUBEI
Yangtze R.
Wuhan
Hangzhou
EAST CHINA
SEA
Nanchang
ZHEJIANG
Changsha
JIANGXI
Si'nan
GUIZHOU
HUNAN
FUJIAN
Guiyang
Fuzhou
Taipei
Xiamen
GUANGDONG
TAIWAN (FORMOSA)
GUANGXI
Penghu
(Pescadores
Islands)
Tainan
Guangzhou (Canton)
Nanning
HONG KONG
HAINAN
PHILIPPINES

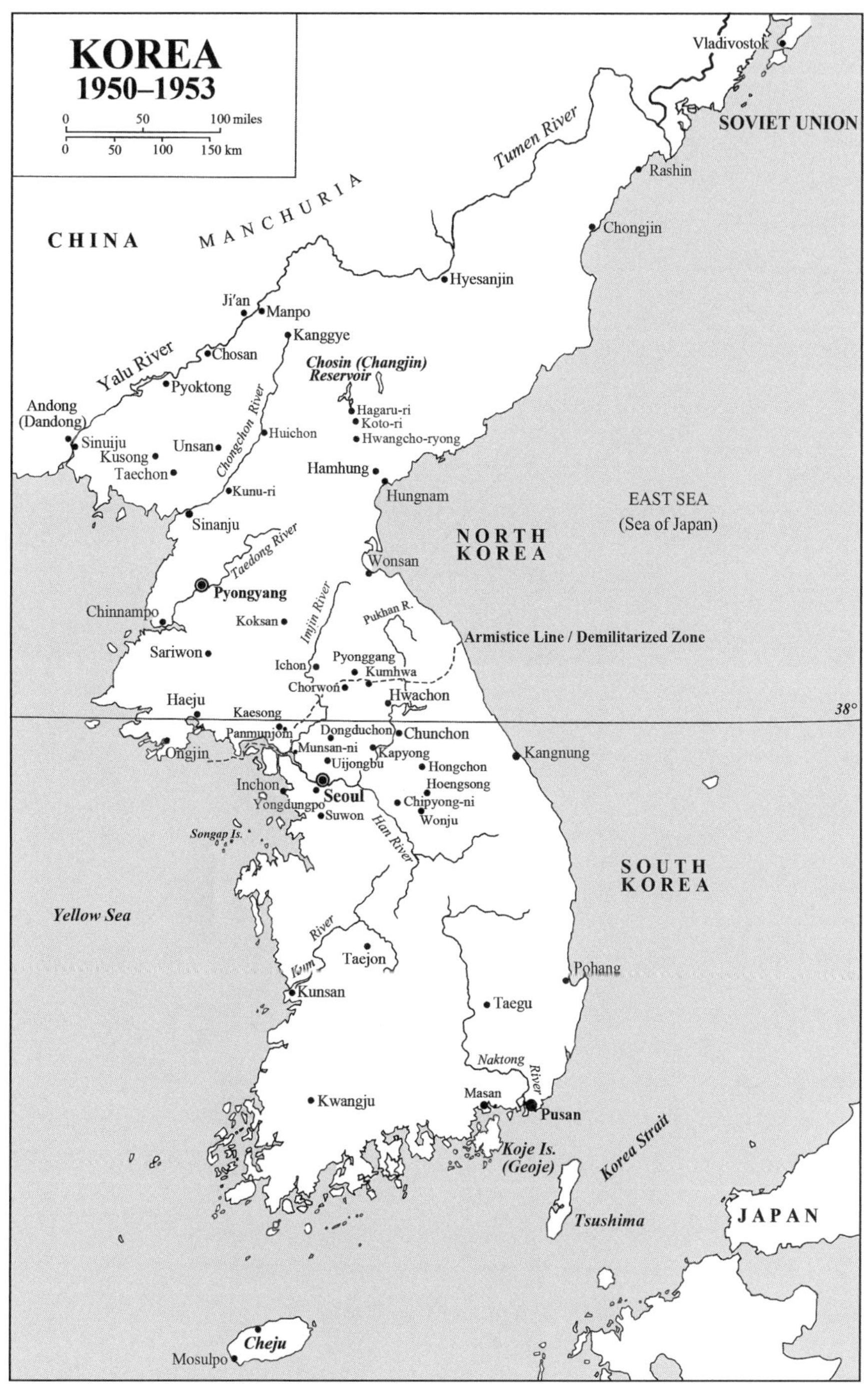

MAP 2. Korea, 1950–1953

THE HIJACKED WAR

Introduction

ON THE MORNING OF JANUARY 20, 1954, a blaze of red, white, and blue emerged on the distant horizon at the 38th parallel, Korea. Along the frozen dirt road from Panmunjom to the southern boundary of the Demilitarized Zone (DMZ), a contingent of Chinese prisoners of war (POWs) marched in columns of five, holding Chinese Nationalist "Blue Sky, White Sun, and Red Earth" flags and portraits of Sun Yat-sen and Chiang Kai-shek. As the marching feet drew closer to the newly erected Freedom Gate that separated the DMZ from South Korean territory, the prisoners' singing of the Nationalist anthem grew louder.[1]

"Here they come," US Marines waiting near the gate muttered. "Everybody get back and keep this road clear!" their captain shouted. "These guys have been waiting a long time for this."[2] Indeed, these former Chinese Communist troops had been held in United Nations Command (UNC) prisons for two to three years or more. Their refusal to return home to China had prolonged the Korean War for fifteen months and extended their own captivity for another 180 days after the armistice agreement was signed on July 27, 1953.

"Dear Anti-Communist Heroes (*fangong yishi*), we have come from Taiwan to welcome you," a Chinese Nationalist officer announced over a loudspeaker as the prisoners reached the gate at 8:52 a.m. "You are free now. Congratulations!" The POWs and the welcoming crowd erupted into jubilant cheers. Dozens of smartly dressed Nationalist officers, civilian dignitaries, and reporters greeted the prisoners with salutes and handshakes, with a giant portrait of Chiang Kai-shek smiling approvingly in the background.[3]

"Attention! Follow the UNC's orders," boomed a loudspeaker, "and fully cooperate with the American troops."[4] The prisoners were promptly guided to a loading area nearby, where hundreds of ten-wheel GMC trucks stood ready, and a US Army band played march music.

At 9:31 a.m. the first convoy, carrying 421 men, led by a jeep of the US Eighth Army, rumbled down the winding road toward Seoul and then Inchon, where fifteen US ships awaited. Braving frigid winds, exuberant prisoners pulled down the trucks' canvas covers so that they could wave flags, sing songs, and shout cheers to throngs of South Korean and Chinese diaspora well-wishers lining the route. This scene was repeated over the next eighteen hours until the last of the 14,220 Taiwan-bound prisoners left the demilitarized zone at 2:45 a.m. on January 21.[5]

Zhang Yifu, a veteran Communist army doctor, reached Freedom Gate shortly after 4:00 p.m. First he saw the word "Welcome" in English and Chinese painted on the gate and then broadly smiling Nationalist officers and military policemen. "Words cannot describe my joy," Zhang recalled. "My three-year prison life finally came to an end."[6]

FIGURE 0.1. More than fourteen thousand CPV prisoners carry Nationalist flags and portraits of Sun Yat-sen and Chiang Kai-shek as they march out from the demilitarized zone at Panmunjom, January 20, 1954. US National Archives.

As daylight gave way to darkness, hundreds of bonfires were lit in empty gasoline drums placed every sixty feet along the road from Panmunjom. "It was a spectacular sight, just like an airstrip illuminated at night," marveled Chen Juntian, a young Nationalist military school cadet in the welcoming delegation and the painter of the giant Chiang portrait. As the night wore on, fierce wind and drizzling rain put out many bonfires; in their place, dozens of US jeeps and trucks were deployed with headlights beaming onto the road.[7]

In sharp contrast to the festive mood in the sunny morning, the prisoners now were walking or loping, weighted down with anxiety and fear. "They didn't know what might happen after dark," Chen reasoned, "as the Communists had threatened to sabotage their release." Chen and fellow officers walked past the gate into the DMZ to comfort the POWs. When some prisoners saw the Nationalist emblem on Chen's cap up close, they embraced him and broke into sobs, "We haven't seen our officers for so long!" Chen could feel their tears and sweat despite the icy temperature. "Don't be afraid," he reassured them. "You're safe now. Come this way."[8]

FIGURE 0.2. Behind a row of barbed wire and US Marines, a giant portrait of Chiang Kai-shek bearing the slogan "Long Live President Chiang" greets POWs. The painter Chen Juntian, a Nationalist political school cadet, stands on a makeshift platform waving a Nationalist flag. US National Archives.

"The entire operation has gone extremely smoothly, and no untoward events are expected," the Nationalist embassy in Seoul cabled Taipei in the early afternoon of January 20. "A decisive victory has been won in this political battle," it declared.[9] Generalissimo Chiang Kai-shek agreed. "The Communists dare not intervene," he recorded in his evening diary entry with calm brush strokes. He noted, "Upon its completion, this event will amount to a major victory for the anti-Communist coalition."[10]

At 8:05 a.m. the next day, the first batch of five tank landing ships (LSTs) carrying 4,686 prisoners left Inchon harbor for Taiwan with the high tide, followed by a second batch of 4,517 men an hour later. The last group of 4,875 men set off at 3:45 p.m.[11] To prevent a possible naval attack, US 7th Fleet warships escorted the convoy and the 5th Air Force provided air cover. As it turned out, the 900-mile, 88-hour voyage was uneventful—other than the accidental drowning of one man on the high seas.[12]

While they were on the East China Sea en route to Taiwan, at one minute after midnight on January 23, General John E. Hull, the UNC commander in chief, announced that these former prisoners "now have civilian status" and are "free men."[13] Although the Armistice Agreement specified that January 22, 1954, was the last day that the Neutral Nation Repatriation Commission (NNRC) had legal custody over prisoners refusing repatriation, the NNRC, led by India, had returned two days ahead of schedule 14,220 Chinese and 7,574 North Korean prisoners to the UNC, which immediately transferred them to the governments of Taiwan and South Korea.[14] On January 23, the UNC formally completed the transfer ex post facto in a ceremony in Seoul.[15] On the same day, 142 seriously ill and wounded Chinese POWs were flown to Taipei.[16]

The total number of Taiwan-bound Chinese POWs reached 14,342 as of June 1954.[17] In the other direction, 7,109 men and one woman were repatriated to China, including 1,030 sick and wounded exchanged during the "Little Switch" in April 1953, 5,640 who were returned during the "Big Switch" in August and September, and 440 who were originally classified as non-repatriates but sought to return in the "Explanation" process from October to December 1953 and during the final release in January 1954.[18] Among the last group of 440 men, 70 were those who asked the Indian Custodian Forces for repatriation to China on January 20 and 21, 1954. Also on these two final days, 12 other Chinese prisoners along with 74 North Koreans and 2 South Koreans chose to go to neutral nations.[19]

Events on January 23, 1954, marked the denouement of the two-year ideological, diplomatic, and military contest over the repatriation of prisoners, which had dominated the Korean War since early 1952 and continued for another 180 days after the armistice. The United States prevailed in upholding the policy of voluntary repatriation (or non-forcible repatriation) despite vehement opposition from the Chinese Communists. In the end, two-thirds of some 21,000 Chinese prisoners went to Nationalist Taiwan (the Republic of China, or the ROC), and only a third returned to Communist China (the People's Republic of China, or the PRC).

More than 14,000 anti-Communist POWs went to Taiwan under the slogan of "Returning to Taiwan!" Among them, however, only two were Taiwanese; coincidentally, among the 7,110 repatriates to China, one was Taiwanese. Why did the Chinese prisoners make such starkly different choices? Why did some 14,000 men reject home and "return" to a place to which they had never been? Who were these men? Under what circumstances did they make their choices? Did they actually have a free choice as the term "voluntary repatriation" suggests? This book seeks to answer these questions.

The consequences of the Chinese prisoners' choices and US policies were grave. In the last two years of the war, 12,300 Americans and at least 90,000 Chinese soldiers were killed in Korea, and at least 140,000 North Korean civilians died from escalated American bombings.[20] It may be argued, although in an imprecise fashion, to secure one Chinese prisoner's "freedom" not to return home but to go to Taiwan, nearly one American GI lost his life. On the other side, to deny such a "right" to one individual Chinese prisoner, more than six Chinese soldiers, ten North Korean civilians, and an unspecified number of North Korean troops were killed. These unsettling equations have apparently never entered the collective memories of Americans, Chinese, Taiwanese, or Koreans in the past six decades.

Remembered and Then Forgotten

Chiang Kai-shek woke up one hour later than usual on the morning of January 24, 1954. Apparently comforted by a flow of good news, he had enjoyed "the soundest sleep in recent years"—a decent nine hours for the sixty-seven-year-old, who had been troubled by insomnia for years.[21] Following Chiang's morning prayers, his son Ching-kuo—Taiwan's de facto intelligence chief—came to report the safe arrival of the sick and wounded prisoners by air and the reception he had arranged for those coming by sea.

Over the next three days, 14,077 men completed their odyssey and disembarked at the port of Jilong.[22] A rapturous reception was staged for these so-called "Anti-Communist Heroes," one so grand and emotional that "only the V-J Day celebration of 1945 could match," remarked General Lai Mingtang, who oversaw the prisoner transfer from Korea to Taiwan.[23]

Leading the welcoming crowd was Chiang Ching-kuo, the mastermind of the entire prisoner defection operations dating back to early 1951. In a mass rally on the dock, the prisoners presented to him seventeen Nationalist flags painted with their own blood. Chiang raised the flags and called out through a loudspeaker, "Treasure these flags painted with blood! Take them back to Nanjing! Take them back to Beiping!" The prisoners responded in unison, "Fight our way back to the mainland!"[24] The Generalissimo's son was seen wiping tears from his eyes.[25]

Chiang Kai-shek noted in his diary that the arrival of the prisoners constituted "a major victory in the struggle against Communism in the past two years." In his "reflections of the week," Chiang upgraded his assessment to "a significant psychological victory in the struggle against the Russians in the last five years."[26] He further elevated his claim in a cable to US president Dwight Eisenhower, calling it "the first significant victory of the democracies in their ten-year struggle against international Communism."[27]

Chiang's glowing assessment found an echo in Washington. In a National Security Council meeting on January 21, Allen Dulles, head of the Central Intelligence Agency (CIA) and the younger brother of Secretary of State John Foster Dulles, remarked that the release of prisoners "constituted one of the greatest psychological victories so far achieved by the free world against Communism. Conversely, it amounted to a great loss of face for the Communists, particularly in light of their threats and warnings prior to the event."[28]

Facing this humiliating outcome of the Korean War, the Chinese Communists could do nothing but fume with rage. In an editorial entitled "The Utter Failure of American 'Psychological Warfare'"—with no irony intended—the Communist mouthpiece *People's Daily* blustered: "The American aggressor's barbarity and cruelty have far exceeded that of its predecessors, the German fascists. Now no one has any doubt about that." It predicted that "since mankind's court of justice did not spare the German fascists, certainly it will not spare the more vicious American aggressor."[29] Two days after the completion of the prisoners' transfer to Taiwan, Premier Zhou Enlai issued a statement condemning the "complete political and moral bankruptcy of the United States." He vowed, "No matter where these prisoners are forcibly detained, as long as the Americans do not retrieve them, we will not give up our prosecution of this crime!"[30]

Indeed, Beijing continued to pursue the issue well into the spring of 1954, when a conference was convened in Geneva to settle issues on the Korean peninsula and in Indochina. Zhou repeatedly raised the demand of retrieving POWs from Taiwan and South Korea, but found no sympathy among friends and foes alike. The North Korean foreign minister Nam Il—formerly the Communist chief delegate during the armistice talks at Panmunjom—made only perfunctory mention of the prisoners in his lengthy speeches.[31] Coming to terms with the futility of their demand to reopen this issue, Chinese diplomats dropped the matter for good. Domestically, the Korean War prisoners, once prominently featured in official media between 1952 and early 1954, soon thereafter disappeared as if they had never existed.[32] For a regime that has systematically used "national humiliation" (*guochi*) to mobilize the masses, Beijing decided not to remind its people of this particular case of indignity. Apparently, even for the master propagandists in Beijing, the history and memory of the Korean War prisoners have been too difficult and too sensitive to handle.

For Chinese Communist leaders, especially Zhou, however, the outcome of the war over prisoners was painful to swallow and too humiliating to forget. When US president Richard Nixon made his historic visit to China in 1972, his remark about North Vietnam's detention of American POWs touched off Zhou's outpouring of bitter memories. "In talking about prisoners of war," Zhou interjected, "I want to mention something." He reminded Nixon, who was Eisenhower's vice president in the final year of the Korean War, that "the number of our prisoners who were coerced to go to Taiwan was not in [the] thousands, but up to ten thousand or more." He pointed out that "we could have made a big issue . . . but we tolerated that" because "we thought it was not good to insist that the war continue over the question of prisoners"—a disingenuous claim that the North Koreans would certainly disagree with, as Chapter 10 will demonstrate. "It is a matter of history," Zhou concluded, "but something very much in our hearts."[33] This apparently spontaneous emotional outburst from the premier, who was known for his steely self-discipline, reveals the severity of this unspeakable wound.

On the other side of the Taiwan Strait, Chiang Kai-shek—"the deadly enemy of the Chinese people" in Communist lingo—emerged victorious from the Korean War. The rise of Chinese anti-Communist prisoners in Korea enabled Chiang to play a pivotal role in the war without contributing a single troop on the ground. As it turned out, Taiwan became the main beneficiary of a war with no clear winners. Chiang's once bankrupt and moribund regime was revitalized and renewed. The "defection" of 14,000 Communist prisoners to Taiwan provided a much-needed shot in the arm, boosting morale among the population and adding legitimacy to Chiang's claim that the ROC was the only lawful government of China.

"These stout-hearted made history when they rejected Communism in favor of freedom at the risk of their lives," Chiang said in a statement welcoming the "fourteen thousand brethren coming back from Korea." Their choice "leaves no room for doubt," he asserted. "Were the people on the mainland given the same chance, they, too, would not hesitate to fight for their freedom in the same heroic manner as has been demonstrated by these compatriots."[34] Nationalist foreign minister George K. C. Yeh made a similar case in the UN General Assembly in September: "That 80 percent of the Chinese prisoners of war should have decided to choose freedom at the risk of their own lives and those of their families is the strongest attestation of how the puppet Communist regime in Peiping is repudiated by the Chinese people behind the Iron Curtain."[35]

This large-scale "defection" of Communist soldiers was a spectacular propaganda coup. Referring to them as "Fourteen Thousand Anti-Communist Heroes" or "Fourteen Thousand Witnesses" (of Communist tyranny), the Nationalist government repeatedly cited this episode to justify its UN representation in place of Communist China. For Beijing, it was not merely "a great loss of face," but a major setback to its claim to legitimacy and popular support. Moreover, the Chinese Communists' winning streak against the Nationalists ended here. "This is the one battle the Communists did not win," Yeh declared.[36] To remind its population of this victory, the Nationalist government made January 23 the "123 Freedom Day." Throughout the Cold War, this day was commemorated each year with much fanfare in Taiwan.

In the United States, however, this supposedly moral victory went uncelebrated and was summarily forgotten. When the anti-Communist prisoners were released in January 1954, other than a short proclamation by UN commander General Hull in Tokyo praising these men as "living symbols providing hope of freedom to millions who still suffer under Communist oppression," the US government was conspicuously silent.[37] President Eisenhower and Secretary of State John Foster Dulles made no public statement. The aforementioned celebratory assessment by CIA chief Allen Dulles was unpublicized.

In the voluminous memoirs of President Harry S. Truman and Secretary of State Dean Acheson—the ultimate advocates of the voluntary repatriation policy—no mention was made of the prisoners' final release.[38] Their silence is puzzling especially given Truman's self-righteous declaration in May 1952 that forcible repatriation "would be repugnant to the fundamental moral and humanitarian principles which underlie our action in Korea. . . . We will not buy an armistice by turning over human beings for slaughter or slavery."[39] Truman's insistence on giving Chinese and North Korean prisoners the choice of not returning home effectively foreclosed any prospect of a timely armistice, prolonged the war, and eliminated any hope for his reelection. The stalemate in Korea devastated the Truman presidency, but in the end, his lofty principle prevailed. U. Alexis Johnson, then deputy assistant secretary of state for Far Eastern Affairs, lauded Truman's stand as "one of the greatest acts of moral courage" he had "witnessed in any President."[40] If so, why didn't Truman celebrate—or at least acknowledge—this final moral victory? Given the fact that over 12,000 GIs had been killed since negotiations began and the only visible winner of the prolonged war was Chiang Kai-shek, Truman perhaps did not wish to be remembered for this final outcome of the war.

Neither did Truman's successor Dwight Eisenhower claim victory in January 1954. Half a year earlier, however, he nearly did so. On the evening of July 26, 1953, Washington time—July 27 in Korea—Eisenhower made a radio and television address announcing the armistice. He first paid tribute to killed and wounded American soldiers who had sacrificed to "keep freedom alive upon the earth." Then he went on to speak of American POWs: "Our thoughts turn also to those other Americans wearied by many months of imprisonment behind the enemy lines. The swift return of all of them will bring joy to thousands of families." The next paragraph in his original prepared statement continued: "We think, too, of the enemy prisoners in our hands. We have steadfastly sustained their right to choose their own future, to live in freedom if they wish." These last two sentences, however, were omitted from the actual address for unexplained reasons.[41] Most likely, Eisenhower was advised to delete any reference to enemy prisoners that might lead the American public to perceive voluntary repatriation as an "exchange of Chinese lives for American lives."[42] Unfortunately, that very exchange is precisely what happened.

Admiral C. Turner Joy, senior delegate of the UNC armistice delegation, admitted in his 1955 memoir that the US policy of "voluntary repatriation" had "placed the welfare of ex-Communist soldiers above that of our own UNC personnel in Communist prison camps, and above that of our UNC personnel still on the battle line in Korea."[43] Had this realization dawned on the American public, not only would their support for the war have collapsed much earlier, but they would have questioned the entire war effort and the postwar commitment to Korea.

The US government chose not to remind the American people of the fact that enforcing voluntary repatriation had prolonged the war by fifteen months and increased its cost in terms of casualties of American and other UNC troops—45 percent of all American casualties occurred in the last two years—and longer captivity of UNC prisoners in enemy hands, during which more UNC prisoners died.[44] Any suggestions linking enemy prisoners' freedom to American prisoners' extended captivity and additional casualties had to be avoided. This aversion is most clearly manifested in what was deleted from Eisenhower's speech. It is also palpable in the suppression of Joy's revelatory book on the Panmunjom negotiations, as General Matthew B. Ridgway, UNC commander in chief and Joy's direct superior during the truce talks, observed that "there occurred an apparent concerted effort severely to limit public distribution and particularly to curtail its circulation among policy-makers in the Executive branch of our government."[45] In a supposedly democratic society with a free press, the US government managed to obscure the true *casus belli* for the second half of the war. Perhaps not coincidentally, the Korean War became "the forgotten war."

The limited Western scholarship on Korean War POWs consists mostly of diplomatic history accounts relying on US diplomatic and military documents, while the Chinese and Korean prisoners themselves—the central subject in the second half of the war—remain nameless, faceless, and characterless masses. Only in recent years, the works of Sheila Miyoshi Jager, Tessa Morris-Suzuki, and Monica Kim began to give more focus to the prisoners.[46]

The prisoners have fared no better in Chinese, Taiwanese, and Korean scholarship. The POW issue has remained off limits to scholars in the PRC as Beijing has regarded it as a major humiliation, even to this day. In authoritarian Taiwan and South Korea, the POW issue was also too sensitive to be freely examined. In the post-democratization era, it has largely been forgotten as a subject of the bygone era of Chiang Kai-shek and Syngman Rhee.

This scholarly neglect is a reflection of a larger amnesia: the Korean War over prisoners has been virtually forgotten by all belligerent countries, politicians, and scholars alike. Is this historical amnesia a result of the Korean War having become a "forgotten war?" Or has the war over prisoners been willfully forgotten, and perhaps even the very reason why the war became forgotten? This book suggests the latter. Forgetting, Nietzsche remarked, "is rather an active and in the strictest sense positive faculty of repression."[47]

Most ironically, the United States and the PRC—the two sworn enemies in the Korean War and the ensuing Cold War—were unwitting accomplices in creating and maintaining this amnesia through their respective obfuscations, distortions, cover-ups, and censorship. The only place where the anti-Communist prisoners were once remembered was Taiwan under Chiang Kai-shek and his son Chiang Ching-kuo, but that memory was also tightly managed and censored.

Two Korean Wars: The First over Territory, the Second over Prisoners

In Korean War historiography the POW issue is invariably identified as the central bone of contention in the second half of the war, but surprisingly little attention has been paid to this half of the war. Many scholars have examined the origins of the war, yet the vast majority of both scholarly and popular history books concentrate on the first half—from the outbreak of the war to China's intervention, and to General Douglas MacArthur's dismissal—as epitomized by David Halberstam's *The Coldest Winter*, whose narrative ends with the Truman-MacArthur controversy.[48] Bruce Cumings has noted that American historians' varying interpretations of the war largely agree on a split verdict: "the first Korean War, the war for the south in the summer of 1950, was a success. The second war, the war for the north, was a failure."[49] This understanding—leaving out the last two years of the war—highlights a collective amnesia.

This book suggests a new two-war formulation. The first Korean War was fought over territory, including the war for the south from June 25 to September 1950, the war for the north from October to December of 1950, and the war above and below the 38th parallel from January to June 1951. The second Korean War was fought over prisoners from late 1951 to July 1953—a period of negotiating while fighting, as the fate of the POWs quickly emerged as the main stumbling block in the armistice negotiations.

The Korean War lasted for three years, one month and two days, but the armistice negotiations occupied more than two of those years, from July 10, 1951, to July 27, 1953. In the last two years, after 575 meetings at the negotiating table and a tremendous number of casualties on both sides, the final armistice line barely budged a few miles north or south from the battle line of July 1951. What prevented an agreement for so long was the deadlock over the repatriation of the 21,000 Chinese prisoners, especially the some 14,000 anti-Communist prisoners. The North Korean POWs, numbering some 150,000, were less of an issue, as Kim Il-sung had begun to seek an end to the hopeless war in early 1952, only to be overruled by Mao Zedong and, ultimately, Joseph Stalin. If not for the Americans' insistence on voluntary repatriation—or more precisely, their inability to return a sufficiently large number of Chinese prisoners to Communist China—the war most likely would have ended by early or mid-1952. In early February 1952, Acheson belatedly realized that POW repatriation "will shortly become the sole remaining fundamental issue in the Korean armistice negotiations."[50]

From late February 1952, when Truman made his final decision to uphold voluntary repatriation, to early June 1953, when both sides signed the Terms of Reference on prisoner exchange, fifteen months of war—and the sudden death of Stalin in March 1953—were required to force the Chinese Communists to accept voluntary repatriation.

To justify the extension of the war and its resultant additional costs in lives and treasure, Secretary of State John Foster Dulles asserted after the war that the United States and its allies had fought for two principles in Korea: "to throw back the aggressor to his original boundaries or beyond; and the non-forcible repatriation of prisoners and political asylum for those not wishing to return."[51] The first objective had been accomplished by mid-1951, but it took fifteen months to impose the second principle on the Communists and another 180 days to grant the prisoners political asylum.

Contrary to the Communist allegation of an American conspiracy, the two final outcomes of the war over prisoners—the fifteen-month extension of the Korean War and the "defection" of some 14,000 Chinese POWs to Taiwan—were unintended and unplanned by Washington. Instead, they were the result of major policy blunders made by the Truman-Acheson administration and inherited by Eisenhower. There was no American conspiracy, as conspiracies would have required substantial knowledge, foresight, and planning, all of which were largely absent from US POW policies—from their conception to implementation and conclusion.

The Truman-Acheson administration's arrogance, ignorance, and negligence led the United States to adopt inherently self-contradictory policies. While the US government was seeking peace through the Panmunjom talks, two other policies at cross purposes were being implemented: prisoner reindoctrination and voluntary repatriation. These two policies—the first being covert and the second overt—were separately conceived, but became fatefully intertwined.

The US government became hostage to its own moralistic but ultimately hypocritical policy of voluntary repatriation and to Chinese anti-Communist prisoners, whose ascendancy in UNC prison camps was the direct result of the runaway "success" of American psychological warfare programs. By the time top US officials belatedly realized the gravity of the prisoner issue, the United States found itself riding a tiger of its own making, from which it was impossible to dismount. In the end, only Chiang Kai-shek could tame the tiger by taking it to Taiwan in triumph. In a sense, the brightest minds of the mightiest power on earth were taken captive by the captives—a reality so embarrassing that the US government had to hide it from the American people.

The curious history of the policy of voluntary repatriation has been scrutinized by a handful of scholars.[52] Less studied are the prisoner reindoctrination and exploitation programs as part of the larger US psychological/political warfare project against the Soviet bloc.[53] The interplay of the two policies remains unexamined, but it is the key to the question of how the United States dug itself into such an inextricable hole on the prisoner issue.

Predating the voluntary repatriation policy, the prisoner reindoctrination program was a natural offshoot of the political/psychological warfare programs that American Cold War architect George F. Kennan and China Hand John Paton Davies had advocated since the late 1940s. In early September 1950, it became a national policy mandated by National Security Council (NSC) document 81/1 as a corollary policy of the rollback strategy to unify Korea and also a part of the global psychological war against Communism. It was drafted mainly by the State Department, approved by Truman, enthusiastically supported by Acheson, and energetically implemented by MacArthur and his successors, Matthew B. Ridgway and Mark W. Clark.

President Truman approved NSC-81/1 on September 11, 1950, four days before the Inchon landing (see Chapter 4) and well before the Chinese intervention in late October. The prisoner reindoctrination/exploitation program's original targets were the North Koreans. However, the program was expanded in spring 1951 to cover Chinese POWs—a decision arrived at as if by default and supported by both military and civilian leaders, including Acheson. It was only after MacArthur's dismissal in April 1951 that the prisoner reindoctrination program was implemented on a large scale and included Chinese POWs. So effective was the program in converting prisoners into "avowed anti-Communists" that the majority of Chinese POWs refused repatriation and demanded to be sent to Taiwan—a logical outcome anticipated by none of the policymakers in Washington.

The greatest surprise in the second half of the Korean War came in April 1952, when some 19,000 Chinese POW were interviewed, more than 14,000 declared that they would violently resist repatriation. While Communist negotiators were stunned by the result and cried conspiracy, the Americans were equally shocked but feigned nonchalance in public, lest their surprise betray their ignorance, miscalculation, and mismanagement of the prisoner issue.

Remarkably, American, Chinese Communist, and Nationalist intelligence sources independently arrived at the same estimate that 3,000 bona fide Chinese anti-Communist prisoners dominated and controlled the rest of the alleged anti-Communist prisoners. What can explain the fact that this small core of anti-Communist prisoners defeated more than 7,000 Communist Party and Youth League members, and dominated the Chinese camps?[54]

The Chinese Prisoners Who Hijacked the Korean War

One popular explanation is that most Chinese prisoners were former Nationalist troops captured by the Communists and pressed into the People's Liberation Army (PLA) during the Chinese Civil War from 1945 to 1949. When Mao sent these conscripts to Korea as cannon fodder, it was thought they would naturally attempt to escape, and their capture or surrender in Korea would present a rare opportunity. In fact, Nationalist military service history did not dictate prisoners' repatriation outcome. Prisoners with similar experiences made divergent choices.

Conspiracy was the Communists' explanation. They consistently alleged that the United States plotted with Taiwan and South Korea to intimidate and coerce Communist prisoners. The Americans had "made use of the Chiang Kai-shek and Syngman Rhee special agents to perpetrate all kinds of criminal activities in the prisoner-of-war camps," Chinese negotiator Chai Chengwen charged in Panmunjom.[55] Assuming the worst of the Americans, Chai asserted that "the only possible explanation" for the insistence on voluntary repatriation was an American scheme to use it "as a guise" to retain prisoners and to "turn them over to the Chiang Kai-shek brigands on Taiwan . . . for the purpose of enlarging the war and get[ting] more cannon fodder."[56]

From the Chinese Communists' perspective, judging from the sequence of events, this conclusion made perfect sense. They could neither believe in Truman's desire for peace nor appreciate the predicament he was facing. This book will demonstrate, however, that Truman made his decision on voluntary repatriation independently, without considering the US Army's psychological warfare proposal dated July 5, 1951, five days before the armistice negotiations commenced, whose timing naturally raises suspicions of a conspiracy. The proposal's defining feature—the disposition of some Chinese prisoners to Taiwan—was never discussed by Truman or Acheson at any point throughout their tenure, even though Taiwan was the only possible destination for a large number of Chinese anti-Communist prisoners. This absence of any discussion on the final disposal of Chinese anti-Communist POWs was one of the most striking absurdities of Truman-Acheson policy making.

This book demonstrates that, contrary to conspiracy theories, the lack of American planning and foresight was the very reason for the rise of anti-Communist prisoners. First and foremost, Truman and Acheson's visceral antipathy for Chiang Kai-shek precluded the possibility of an American conspiracy to send Chinese prisoners to Taiwan, as doing so would only vindicate their Republican critics. The American chief negotiator Joy once observed that the Chinese Communists' hatred of Chiang was "so intense as to border on psychotic."[57] Yet the same remark could also apply to Truman and Acheson's loathing of the Generalissimo. In fact, precisely because of Washington's aversion to being associated with Chiang, throughout the war the United States made no promise to prisoners that they would be sent to Taiwan. Therefore, a bizarre phenomenon emerged: while on the one hand, the United States was carrying out a rigorous prisoner reindoctrination program designed to convert POWs into "avowed anti-Communists," on the other, it planned, as least initially, to send these new converts back to China, with an eye on their "future use as a nucleus for democratization."[58]

Such contradictory policies put all Chinese prisoners in an increasingly precarious situation. All prisoners feared Communist reprisal after repatriation, including not only hardcore anti-Communists, who had risked their lives to defect on the battlefield, but also Communists and neutrals, who had been coerced by anti-Communist prisoners to participate in anti-Communist activities. Impelled by this fear, many Communist and neutral POWs opted to go along with the dominant faction, taking a chance on their uncertain future in UNC prisons and thereafter.

In the end, the very success of US psychological warfare—symbolized by the "defection" of 14,000 Chinese prisoners to Taiwan—gave a new lease on life to Chiang Kai-shek's regime, whose demise Truman, Acheson, and Davies had long predicted and, in fact, eagerly anticipated. That is one of greatest ironies in the history of US-China relations and the Korean War.

Second, the policy of voluntary repatriation had largely dominated the war agenda by early 1952, three months after Truman first indicated his preference for it in late October 1951. Strangely, at no time during 1952 did Truman and his advisors discuss the obvious contradictions inherent in this policy. The very concept of prisoners making free choices is self-contradictory by definition. Needless to say, prison is not a democratic institution where individuals can freely express their will. Chinese negotiator Chai rightly challenged the Americans: "Under your military control, how could there be the conditions for expression of free will and purpose?" He went on to assert, "I think that in your hearts you yourselves are also aware that your proposition is in no way justifiable." Chai's suspicion was not unwarranted. UNC chief negotiator Joy conceded after the war: "To require prisoners to make a highly important and permanent choice under the conditions of imprisonment was to ask of them a decision they were probably not best prepared to make."[59] Similarly, General Boatner, an Old China Hand and the UNC prison commandant in summer 1952, considered it "unrealistic to expect a free and voluntary decision from men being held prisoner by those they had been fighting only a few months earlier," and all the more so when these men "had never had the experience of choosing a political leader or a form of government."[60] When prisoners were totally dependent on their captors for food and survival, their decisions were highly susceptible to influences from the prison authorities, whose own position was far from neutral. Yet, no documentary evidence indicates that Truman's advisors alerted him to these obvious complications, even though some of them were aware of the endemic coercion, violence, and anarchy in UNC prisons.

Truman's lack of intellectual curiosity and his penchant for simplistic moralizing, coupled with the inattentiveness and subservience of his advisors, Acheson in particular, led him to adopt a self-righteous moralistic policy that, once announced, immediately became irrevocable. By the time top officials in the State and Defense departments realized the complexity and gravity of the issue, it was already too late to reverse course. Rather than informing Truman of the unpleasant truth and admitting their neglect and miscalculation, these officials withheld key facts from the president. Nor did Truman ask for details. Shielded from the stark facts in UNC prisons, Truman was spared the agony of facing the moral dilemma that full knowledge would have thrust upon him. With ignorance and certitude substituting for evidence and analysis, Truman upheld voluntary repatriation.

By framing the prisoner repatriation issue as a matter of moral principle, the US government sought to extract a propaganda victory—as a substitute for a military victory—out of a morass emanating from a series of blunders, as historians Barton Bernstein, Rosemary Foot, and Charles Young have argued.[61] To impose America's will on the Chinese Communists, Truman and Eisenhower brought America's military might to bear on Communist troops and North Korean civilians. While ostensibly promising freedom to Communist prisoners, voluntary repatriation mainly served to cover up US policy predicaments. It not only prevented the early return of American and other UNC prisoners, but also resulted in horrendous casualties on all sides, especially among North Korean civilians. All these tragic consequences, however, were unnecessary and could have been avoided had Truman and Acheson understood the Chinese Communists' extreme sensitivity to the POW question and the residual appeal of the Chinese Nationalists among a significant minority of the Chinese population. Ironically, Truman's National Security Council staff dismissed the prisoner issue as an unimportant, nonpolitical question from the outset.[62]

This book reveals the reality beneath historical fiction: the US policy of voluntary repatriation promised freedom to Chinese prisoners, but it actually denied the right of many to return home. In peace talks, Washington's initial toying with voluntary repatriation quickly hardened into an irreversible moralistic principle; on Koje Island, prisoner reindoctrination enabled some 3,000 Chinese diehard anti-Communists to hijack fellow POWs. The lopsided screening results in April 1952 presented Washington with a fait accompli that it found impossible to disown. In May Truman presented this fait accompli to the Communists, who in turn rejected it. In short, to the Americans' great surprise and chagrin, the mighty US government's control over the war agenda was wrested away by a bunch of prisoners and Chiang's tottering regime in exile. The Chinese anti-Communist prisoners had thus effectively hijacked the Korean War.

Sources

This book's two main sources are archival documents and oral history interviews. The US National Archives' extensive collection of diplomatic, military, and intelligence documents related to Korean War prisoners includes the complete rosters of 21,000 Chinese POWs, in-depth interrogation reports of more than a thousand individual Chinese prisoners, and dozens of investigation reports on incidents including murders, assassinations, and riots. Multiple archives in Taiwan are a rich source of diplomatic and military documents that shed light on the clandestine operations waged by Chiang Kai-shek and his agents in Korea.

In the PRC, though archive access remains extremely restricted, nonofficial sources have proved to be a treasure trove. Repatriated prisoners have published extensively since the 1990s. The most valuable source is an unpublished three-volume document compiled by a former senior editor of the *PLA Literature and Art*, containing the dossier entries and oral histories of approximately four hundred Communist prisoners, including all the leaders, all of whom have passed away.[63]

Since 2007, I have interviewed eighty-four former prisoners, including twenty-nine in the PRC, fifty in Taiwan, one in the United States, and four in Argentina and Brazil (one Chinese and three North Koreans). I have also interviewed a former interrogator in Taiwan and a translator and a prison guard in the United States. Many interviewees also shared letters, diaries, memoirs, and photos.

For eighteen of the eighty-four interviewed former prisoners, I have full interrogation records produced by the UNC between 1950 and 1952. Upon careful comparison, I found their recent oral history accounts highly consistent with their interrogation narratives. The possibility of a former prisoner producing consistently false narratives sixty years apart is slim.

Benefiting from multiple sources for most interviewees, these oral history accounts provide meaningfully detailed substantive information. Interviewees include eyewitnesses to several major incidents: the collapse of the Chinese 180th Division and its commanders' cowardly escape in May 1951, the murder of a former college student and pro-Communist on the eve of the prisoner screening in April 1952, and the bloody crackdown on Communist demonstrations on October 1, 1952, which resulted in fifty-six deaths, as told by Private Patrick Vigil, who had fired into the crowd.

The history of Chinese POWs in the Korean War grows out of several interconnected stories. First is the tale of young men caught up in the Civil War on mainland China between the Nationalists (KMT) and the Communists (CCP) that waxed and waned for more than two decades, beginning in the late 1920s—with an uneasy interlude of a united front during the Anti-Japanese War of Resistance from 1937 to 1945—and reaching its apogee in the years immediately following World War II. Second is the story of the troubled relationship between the United States and China during and after World War II, culminating in the defeat of the Nationalists and triumph of the Communists in 1949 and the latter's intervention in the Korean conflict a year later. Third is the development in the United States of a psychological warfare strategy designed to undermine support for Communism abroad in the midst of the escalating Cold War struggle with the Soviet Union, manifesting in the form of prisoner reindoctrination programs—or brainwashing, American style. Finally, there is the story of a flawed decision-making process in Washington that produced an ill-informed, misguided policy on the disposition of Korean War prisoners known as "voluntary repatriation."

This story of Chinese POWs unfolds shortly after VJ Day.

1

Fleeing or Embracing the Communists in the Chinese Civil War

SECOND LIEUTENANT YANG XINLIN and his fellow paratroopers emerged from American transport planes after landing at the Guangzhou (Canton) airport one day in early September 1945. Outfitted with US-made uniforms, helmets, .45-caliber pistols, and M1 carbines, these troops were not typical Chinese soldiers. They were the cream of the crop of the Nationalist army—members of the recently formed Chinese Army Commando Force trained by officers of the US Office of Strategic Services (OSS). They had flown from their base in Kunming as the advance unit to take over Guangzhou from surrendering Japanese forces.[1] Their second mission was to serve as honor guards for the formal surrender ceremony scheduled to take place on September 16.[2]

When the paratroopers' jeeps rolled down the streets of Guangzhou, firecrackers went off, and the crowd cheered and applauded. Since the city's fall in October 1938, residents for the first time saw Chinese troops—smartly dressed, splendidly equipped, proud, and confident. The once arrogant Japanese Imperial Army officers and soldiers stood at attention, saluted, and bowed to their Chinese victors. "Probably these Japanese had never seen a carbine before," Yang thought.[3]

For the twenty-three-year-old Yang, it had been a rollercoaster journey. Born into a well-off landlord and merchant family in Cangxi County in northern Sichuan, Yang was once a carefree adolescent. Constantly running afoul of his teachers, he was expelled from the local middle school, after which he failed in another one in the provincial capital Chengdu, and then in 1942 dropped out of the 18th class of the Central Military Academy (the Whampoa Academy). After joining the Youth Expeditionary

Force in early 1944, he was flown to India, where he was trained by the Americans and became a wireless operator in the 12th Artillery Regiment. Yang fought in the savage battle in Myitkyina, Burma, twice survived Japanese banzai attacks at night, and finally participated in the liberation of northern Burma in early 1945. Once back in Kunming, he changed his name and jumped ship for better pay and higher rank in the newly established commando force. After an intensive two-month training that included four parachute jumps, Yang participated in a Sino-US joint special operations attack on the Danzhu airfield in Guangxi in late July 1945.[4]

At this moment of triumph, even Yang himself could hardly believe his transformation from a mischievous teenager to a battle-tested soldier and patriot. He did not anticipate what lay ahead: soon after the victory over Japan, Yang and his war-torn country were to be swept into a civil war and his life was to become dominated by a force totally foreign to him—the Chinese Communists. All he knew about the Communists was that when the Red Army occupied his hometown in the mid-1930s, he didn't go to school for two years.[5] After 1945, he fought the Communists, first as a commando, then as a wireless specialist. He was captured twice and escaped both times. Eventually he was drafted by the Communists to fight in Korea against the Americans—his former instructors and comrades. He defected to the UN side and became an anti-Communist prisoner leader. Most unexpectedly, the US Army's special operations Unit 8240 selected him to parachute into North Korea as an intelligence agent. How could anyone endure all these ordeals and survive?

Some of the first Americans to arrive in Guangzhou were US Office of War Information (OWI) personnel, who had arrived by August 30.[6] Also present in Guangzhou was US Army Major Monta L. Osborne, a China theater psychological warfare officer who was there to study Japanese psychology.[7] Six years later, he would design a psychological warfare program whose subjects were Chinese POWs in Korea, some of whom had been his erstwhile comrades in arms in World War II, including Yang.

Some four hundred miles northwest of Guangzhou, Brigadier General Haydon L. Boatner, deputy commander of the Chinese Combat Command, represented the United States at the first surrender talks on August 21, when Japanese representatives flew to Zhijiang, Hunan, to discuss surrender terms.[8] A West Pointer, a fluent Chinese speaker with a master of arts in Chinese history, and former chief of staff to Joseph W. Stilwell, Boatner once led the Sino-American joint attack on Myitkyina, where Yang had fought. The victory over Japan brought peace to the Americans, but only for five years. In late 1951, Boatner returned to the front lines in Bloody and Heartbreak Ridges in Korea, fighting the Chinese People's Volunteers (CPV) (the Chinese army in the Korean War), whose troops included many men once trained and led by him in the China-Burma-India theater (CBI) in World War II. Precisely because of his reputation as a China Hand, he was called to restore order at the UN

POW camp on Koje Island after its commandant was kidnapped by prisoners. Boatner cracked down forcefully, but his success was short-lived and disorder returned after his promotion to major general and departure from Korea. The PRC labeled him "executioner Boatner."[9]

The conflict in the UN prison camps in Korea took the form of small civil wars between pro- and anti-Communist prisoners, both Korean and Chinese. The seeds of conflict among the Chinese prisoners had been sown in the 1945–1949 Civil War, during which the Nationalists' popularity declined while the Communists won many supporters. The Communists were particularly successful in attracting two groups of converts: "the poor and suffering people" (*qiongku renmin*) and idealistic students. Despite the Nationalists' eventual defeat on the mainland, some young people, especially children of the rich and conservatives, still identified with the old order and rejected Communist ideology and methods. In the face of advancing Communist forces, some embraced them; others fled hundreds and even thousands of miles until they were captured. Their divergent choices reflected their differing assessment of the Communists and of their own prospects under the new regime. Although suppressed under a surface of conformity in the newly established PRC, tension exploded into life-and-death struggles in the UN prison camps in Korea.

Largely in chronological order, this chapter examines the Civil War experiences of a number of future prisoners. In 1949 these individuals of vastly different backgrounds converged in Sichuan, either as Nationalist or Communist soldiers, guerrillas, or refugees. In 1950 most of them became soldiers of the CPV 60th and 12th Armies, which suffered the heaviest casualties in Korea in spring 1951 and contributed nearly half of the 21,000 Chinese soldiers captured by UN forces.

The First Prisoners of the Civil War, October 1945

Two weeks after V-J Day, on August 28 Mao Zedong flew from his base in Yan'an to Chongqing, China's wartime capital. Repeatedly pressured by Stalin, Mao reluctantly agreed to take his first plane ride—with his safety guaranteed by US ambassador Patrick Hurley, who was also on board. After weeks of negotiations and public relations activities, the Nationalists and the Communists announced their "October Tenth Agreement"—in fact, merely a "summary of conversations"—promising peace and collaboration with a view to implementing democracy and Dr. Sun Yat-sen's Three People's Principles.

While the leaders were talking about peace and democracy, fierce battles raged in North China, where the Nationalist and Communist forces fought to secure Japanese-occupied territories. Before flying to Chongqing, Mao had told Generals Liu Bocheng and Deng Xiaoping, who later became China's paramount leader in the 1980s, before they were flown to southern Shanxi on an American plane: "Pull no punches in battle. The better you fight, the safer I will be in Chonqging and the better I can negotiate."[10] The day after Mao's return to Yan'an on October 11, the entire Nationalist 19th Army was annihilated by Communist forces led by Liu and Deng, concluding the month-long Battle of Shangdang. Among the thousands of prisoners were General Shi Zebo and a fifteen-year-old paramedic, Zhang Yifu. They were the first prisoners in the undeclared Civil War.

Zhang Yifu was born in a peasant family in southeastern Shanxi, an area contested by Japanese, Nationalist, and Communist forces and frequently harassed by bandits during World War II. In 1943, Zhang's family fled to Nationalist-controlled southwestern Shanxi, where he joined the 19th Army under the strongman Yan Xishan. Zhang experienced firsthand the absurd three-way war: while Yan's forces clashed with the Japanese in certain areas, they also collaborated in attacking the Communists in other areas. Zhang's unit, however, never caught a single Communist guerrilla. Instead, Zhang was taken prisoner by the Communists in 1945. He became a medic in a Communist guerrilla unit that eventually grew into the PLA 179th Division. His division fought numerous battles in southern Shanxi, and eventually went on to "liberate" the provincial capital of Taiyuan in April 1949. It marched on to Xi'an, Shaanxi, in June, and Chengdu, Sichuan, in December.[11]

While the Communists incorporated captured Nationalist soldiers, low-ranking officers, and technical specialists such as medical and artillery personnel, they strategically released high-ranking officers for united front purposes—or psychological warfare in American parlance. After two years in prison, General Shi Zebo was released in 1947. When he and other released prisoners returned to Taiyuan, they were urged to tattoo "Anti-Communism" (*fangong*) and "Eliminate Communism" (*miegong*) on their arms to demonstrate their loyalty to Yan Xishan, who set up an "Avenging Humiliation Battle Group" for the returnees.[12] This peculiar practice of tattooing political slogans was common in Yan's army, but was shunned by the Communist army despite its absorption of many former Yan troops. It, however, later resurfaced in the UN prison camps in Korea, as anti-Communist prisoners of Shanxi origin used tattoos to demonstrate their own ideological zeal and to prevent fellow prisoners from returning to China.

Three Taiwanese Recruits' Odyssey to the "Motherland," 1945–1948

Among the 21,000 Chinese prisoners in the Korean War, only three were Taiwanese, and two of them returned home to Taiwan. Chen Yonghua became the symbol of the anti-Communist prisoners' rallying cry "Return to Taiwan." Wang Yingchang, obscure throughout his prison term, also returned home. Chen Qingbin, who had become a Communist on the mainland, chose to "return" to the PRC. Perhaps coincidentally, their divergent repatriation choices—in a 2-to-1 ratio—coincided with that of the 21,000 Chinese prisoners.

In November 1945, three months after the end of Japan's fifty-year colonial rule in Taiwan, sixteen-year-old farm boy Chen Yonghua volunteered to join the victorious Chinese Nationalist army, which had barely landed in Taiwan. Chen, the youngest of four siblings in a poor family in Tainan, had been working on the farm and tending cattle since finishing elementary school. He was attracted to the army's recruitment offer, which included a decent salary plus four *dou*, or about twenty-eight kilograms, of rice per month. Chen secretly picked the lock on his father's drawer with a piece of wire and found the seal. With his father's "seal of approval," Chen joined the 95th Division, 62nd Army.[13]

Chen Qingbin, a fifteen-year-old boy in Yilan on the northeastern tip of the island, stole his mother's most valuable coat, sold it to a pawnshop, and ran away from home. But the money did not last long. He enlisted in the Nationalist 70th Army on November 17. The Chen family had once enjoyed modest prosperity from their poultry vending business. All of their six children could eat chicken drumsticks everyday—which was very rare at the time.[14] During the Pacific War, the Japanese colonial police—or the "Four Legged" (beasts) as the Taiwanese called them in private—imprisoned Chen's father in Taipei for tax evasion. In an Allied bombing raid in 1944, he was killed in a locked prison cell, as the prison guards had fled. The once-prosperous family quickly fell into ruin. Soon his elder brother died in an accident. Qingbin became the eldest son and had to help support the family. He joined a local Japanese army unit, but came home within half a year, stricken with malaria. When the Chinese army arrived, Qingbin was enticed by its promised benefits, but was forbidden by his mother from joining the army again. Finally, he ran away from home and responsibilities. "He was hungry!" his younger sister Guimei explained. "That's the reason he left us."[15] A month later, Wang Yingchang, a twenty-year-old fisherman from the Penghu (Pescadores) Islands, also volunteered for the 70th Army.[16]

The Nationalist army scattered Taiwanese recruits in various units, with each squad receiving two or three. "Initially the mainlanders gave us a hard time," Chen Yonghua recalled. The first shock was the mess culture. The mainlanders "started with their first bowl of rice half-full, poured soup on top, then dumped it all down their throat." Then they rushed to get a second bowl of rice, which was compressed hard and filled to the rim. By the time the Taiwanese finished their first bowl at the normal speed, there was "not a single grain of rice left," and they had to go hungry. Chen later found out why: because officers embezzled money, soldiers ended up having not enough food, so they had to fight over whatever there was to eat.[17] Chen and his fellow Taiwanese were certainly not alone in experiencing this race-to-eat mess culture. The practice was common in the Nationalist army, and it was a major source of discontent among the troops.[18]

Chen Yonghua and his unit guarded the Tainan airport for only two or three months before being transferred to Taidong in southeastern Taiwan for training. Rumors were rife that the unit was about to go into the war on the mainland. To deal with desertion, mainland soldiers were assigned to monitor Taiwanese troops closely. Taiwanese were never assigned to sentry posts, lest they escape. Before boarding ships at Jilong, controls were further tightened. Without the presence of their squad leader, soldiers were not allowed to leave their barracks. In September 1946, troops of the 62nd Army boarded freight ships at Jilong. After landing at Qinhuangdao, Hebei, they boarded trains for Beiping (Beijing). A few days later, they moved to the front line in central Hebei to "suppress Communist bandits."[19] Immediately Chen was thrown into the vortex of the escalating Civil War.

Soon Chen gave up his original given name Yanzhan and renamed himself Yonghua, meaning "forever Chinese." Having only studied Japanese in colonial schools, he could barely understand his mainlander comrades. However, he overcame the language barrier quickly and soon became a reconnaissance man in his unit.[20] Evidently Chen had a gift for languages—he eventually mastered several mainland Chinese dialects; in UN prison camps in Korea he picked up some English as well.[21]

In September 1946, Chen Qingbin's 75th Division, 70th Army, also departed from Jilong, but it landed in Shanghai. Immediately the troops boarded trains heading to Yutai in southwestern Shandong.[22] In January 1946, Wang Yingchang's 139th Division, 70th Army, followed suit and arrived in Xuzhou in northern Jiangsu, near the Shandong border.[23] This area soon became the site of some of the fiercest battles of the Civil War.

In 1946 and 1947, the balance of military power was in favor of the Nationalists, who outnumbered and outgunned the Communists. Chen Yonghua recalled that his rifle could fire five bullets in one burst, while the Communists' could only fire one shot at a time. Initially the Communist guerrillas "fled immediately when they saw us" and went into hiding in a maze of tunnels under the North China plain. To force the guerrillas out, Chen and his men burned wheat straw at tunnel entrances in a village—only to see smoke wafting out in the distant wheat field. In this cat and mouse game, the Nationalist forces could not fully exploit their superiority in weaponry. More frustrating than the army's failure to subdue the enemy was the abuse Chen Yonghua suffered at the hands of his superiors. Chen deserted the 62nd Army but was soon apprehended and pressed into the 43rd Division of the 94th Army in Tianjin. The unit moved to Manchuria in August, but surrendered to the PLA in October. However, Chen escaped to the city of Shenyang, where he joined the Nationalist Youth Army's 207th Division.[24]

Desertion and forcible conscription, the twin bugbears plaguing the Nationalist forces, contributed to the army's reputation as corrupt and ineffective. When soldiers deserted, headcounts were not adjusted, and, based on "ghost headcounts," commanding officers often continued to receive the same amount of overhead, effectively embezzling funds. Consequently, Nationalist units' strength was endemically inflated. Before major operations or inspections from above, various units would scramble to add recruits to fill their quota. In times of relative peace and order, recruitment was presented as a job opportunity. In times of turmoil and war, it often degenerated into outright press-ganging, grabbing young men from the streets and fields. Chen Yonghua had experienced both, the former in Taiwan and the latter on the mainland.

The enemy Chen faced in Manchuria in 1948 was no longer Communist guerrillas scurrying through tunnels, but General Lin Biao's elite troops of the PLA Northeastern Field Army. Before the Soviet occupation forces withdrew in the spring of 1946, they had transferred a large quantity of captured Japanese arms to the Communists. And the Soviet Union continued to provide arms and technical assistance.[25] After a series of battles, by early 1948 the PLA in Manchuria had expanded to nearly one million strong and controlled 97 percent of the land, 86 percent of the population, and 95 percent of the railroads.[26] The Nationalist forces were isolated in three unconnected pockets around the cities of Changchun, Shenyang, and Jinzhou.

When he escaped from his Communist captors and returned to the Nationalist army in October 1947, Chen Yonghua apparently thought the Nationalists would prevail. In a year Chen found out that he had bet wrong. As a soldier with limited contact with the outside world, Chen was probably oblivious to the sea change taking place in China at the time. The relative strength of the Nationalists and Communists had reversed, not just militarily, but also in terms of popular support. Idealistic students and intellectuals were among the first to embrace the Communists.

A Tsinghua Student's Journey from Sichuan to Beiping and Back, 1946–1948

When Taiwanese teenagers Chen Yonghua and Chen Qingbin embarked for the mainland in September 1946, seventeen-year-old Sichuan native Zhang Zeshi boarded a Minsheng Company steamship in Chongqing.[27] As the young Taiwanese were sailing into an unknown war on an unknown land, Zhang began his journey to his dream university—Tsinghua (often dubbed China's MIT), the top university funded by the Boxer Indemnity Fund that had been returned to China by the US government. Within two years, Zhang was transformed from an apolitical youth to an ardent Communist. His conversion illustrates the intellectual and emotional appeal of Communism, which promised to solve China's ills once and for all.

Zhang hailed from a well-educated middle-class family. He studied in an American missionary elementary school and the Oberlin Shansi Memorial School, which was established in 1907 by H. H. Kung (Kong Xiangxi)—who later became Chiang Kai-shek's brother-in-law and the prime minister—and Oberlin College to commemorate the thirteen missionaries slain in Shanxi during the Boxer Rebellion in 1900. Taught to "save the nation through science," Zhang decided to major in physics at Tsinghua.[28]

Zhang's trip to Beiping got off to a bad start. When his ship arrived in Hankou, he learned that the railway to Beiping had been interrupted by Communist insurgents. Zhang and fellow students went downriver to Shanghai, where they boarded a British collier heading to Qinhuangdao, where Chen Yonghua's army also landed. Zhang then took the train to Beiping, where he began his university life at Tsinghua.[29]

In winter 1946, while Chen Yonghua was fighting Communist guerrillas on the North China plain, Zhang Zeshi was enjoying physics classes taught by China's foremost scientist, Zhou Peiyuan, and literature lectures by noted writer Zhu Ziqing. Chen hid in icy water on a reconnaissance mission; Zhang swam in an indoor pool on campus. Continuing his interest in singing first developed in missionary schools, Zhang joined a folk song ensemble.[30] Thus far, Zhang had studied and lived in American-run schools and a prestigious university, a world sheltered from the poverty and war experienced by ordinary Chinese. The quiet and picturesque campus, however, soon became a hotbed of protest and revolt.

Christmas 1946 was a turning point in the lives of Zhang Zeshi and many other students across China. On Christmas eve, Shen Chong, a Peking University preparatory student, was raped by two US Marines in downtown Beiping—merely a few blocks away from the house where Zhang and fellow Christian students were singing carols. Two days later, protest posters emerged in Tsinghua. On December 30, thousands of college students, including Zhang, took to the streets in Beiping, shouting slogans and waving banners that read "Get out, US Army! Go back home, US Army!"[31] Although it started spontaneously, the movement was quickly seized by the Communists to fan anti-American and anti-Nationalist government sentiment. The Communist Party Center in Yan'an ordered all party branches to escalate the protests. It cautioned, however, "in order to win broader sympathy [for our movement], our propaganda should be in a sad and indignant tone, not a blithe one."[32] It also directed its underground cells to recruit potential members: "As many new activists have emerged in this movement, our party should help these activists to organize as the core for a sustained movement."[33] Zhang was a perfect candidate.

After the protest on December 30, Zhang's class president invited him and several other protesters to join a secretive "reading group," which was a typical peripheral organization of the Communist underground. Their meeting took place in the courtyard house of Tsinghua professor Wu Han, a well-known historian of the Ming dynasty, who pointedly compared the current state to the final years of the Ming. Wu recommended the *Communist Manifesto* as the subject of the next meeting. When the group studied the *Manifesto*, the leader made an impassioned speech, detailing his intellectual journey from nationalism to Communism. The eighteen-year-old Zhang was deeply moved, feeling as if Karl Marx's voice was thundering: "The genius of the communism is now hovering in your Asia [*sic*]!"[34]

As the Civil War raged, inflation soared. Students like everyone else felt the impact of rising food prices. They launched an "anti-hunger, anti–civil war" demonstration in Beiping and Tianjin on May 20, 1947. After the protest, Zhang was shocked to learn that a high school friend, who was attending the Catholic Fujen University, had joined the Communist Party and was leaving for the Communist area the next day. Another unexpected impetus came in June. Zhang's eldest brother, who had volunteered for the Youth Expeditionary Army to fight the Japanese in Burma during World War II, deserted to avoid fighting in the Civil War. He asked Zeshi for help getting to the Communist areas. Facilitated by Professor Wu, his brother made it.[35]

While Zhang was rapidly moving toward Communism, his best high school friend tried to pull him back. A strong skeptic of the Communists, he argued that the Shen Chong rape case should be treated as an isolated incident, not as a cause for an anti-American movement. He claimed that his eldest brother had studied in the Soviet Union, but had come back resolutely opposed to Communism. He warned Zhang that all revolutions end in power struggles and dictatorship. "In the end, those destroyed by revolution were the naïve idealists obsessed with their dreams." But it was too late for Zhang. There was no turning back. He became a probationary party member in August 1947; his sponsor and only contact person was his roommate, who had been secretly observing and cultivating him for a year.[36] The world around Zhang pulled him irrevocably toward the Communists.

As the PLA made headway in North China, the CCP leadership envisioned advancing to the south. On June 2, 1948, sophomore Zhang Zeshi assumed the identity of a shop apprentice and bid farewell to his university. After passing through several Nationalist checkpoints, he arrived at his destination: Bo Township, Cang County, Hebei. Zhang and his fellow students received a four-week-long "training course for work behind enemy lines," which entailed intensive political indoctrination but only two days of hands-on weapons training. Trainees were prohibited from revealing their identities to each other. In certain classes, instructors taught behind a cloth curtain and students wore masks. In early August, Zhang returned to Beiping, and then headed to Tianjin, where he boarded a ship to Shanghai. It took him another eight days on the Yangtze to reach Chongqing.[37] Ostensibly returning home to escape the war in the north, Zhang had been dispatched on a mission to prepare for the final "liberation" of Sichuan, which took place a year later.

In less than two years, Zhang Zeshi was transformed from a college freshman to a Communist underground agent. Situated in Beiping, the boiling center of the student movement, it was nearly impossible for any hot-blooded young man not to protest against the government's corruption and ineptitude, which were evident to everyone. The most energetic and progressive student groups were often front organizations of the Communist underground. As one of the youngest students in his class, Zhang was eager to be accepted and recognized. He found gratification and meaning in propaganda work for these student groups. Intellectually and emotionally, Zhang's embrace of Communism was a love feast with fellow idealists.

After Zhang's return home in September 1948, he learned for the first time that his father had joined the Socialist Youth League, a Communist student organization, during his college days in Beiping, but had questioned the morality of class struggle—the central tenet of Communism. He told Zeshi the story of a former Red Army officer who was stranded in the province of Xikang (a territory consisted of today's western Sichuan and eastern Tibet), during the Long March (1934–1935) and worked in his factory. He had been expelled from the party and demoted for his "sentimentalism." During the radical land reform in Jiangxi between 1931 and 1934, when a landlord family of seven was being buried alive by the Communist-led Poor Peasant Association, this officer rescued a suckling baby at the final moment. Zeshi countered that this type of extreme cruelty was not in accordance with "the party's policy." Shifting to his propagandist mode, he asserted, "History has proved that only Communism could awaken the masses in Russia to overthrow the Tsar's dynasty and create a Soviet Republic, where exploitation and repression have been eradicated." Moreover, "History will prove that only Communism can enable the Chinese nation to regenerate."[38]

Zhang had certainly become well versed in Communist propaganda. But his faith in Communism was based largely on theory and imagination. His contact with the world outside the university campus was very limited, and his visit to the "liberated areas" was brief and tightly controlled. The 19-year-old was naïve in many ways.

Two Whampoa Cadets Flee from Manchuria to Sichuan, 1945–1948

While Zhang embraced Communism as the panacea for all of China's ills, other young people fled from it in horror. Yu Rongfu and Gao Wenjun were two of those who escaped from the Communists in Manchuria. When Japan announced its surrender on August 15, 1945, sixteen-year-old Yu Rongfu was a student in a vocational school in Dalian, which had been under Japanese rule since 1905. As the school was soon disbanded, he returned home in Pulandian, forty miles north. Soon the Soviet Red Army arrived. "They burned, killed, pillaged, and raped. . . . They removed all machinery from factories," Yu recalled. "There was no evil deed that they did not perpetrate."[39]

At the time, another sixteen-year-old, Gao Wenjun, lived on a farm near Shenyang (Mukden). As he recalled, the Russians forced Japanese women to serve as "comfort women" and raped Chinese. Local women cut their hair short like men's and wore men's clothes. The Soviet soldiers, in response, groped people's chests to check their gender. Even good-looking men were raped. Gao's sisters and female relatives hid in their homes for months on end and dared not step out.[40] The Soviet Union that Yu and Gao came to know firsthand bore no resemblance to the repression-free socialist paradise that Zhang Zeshi had romanticized.

The Chinese Communists appeared on the heels of the Soviet Red Army. In mid-September, a Soviet military plane transported top Communist leaders Peng Zhen and Chen Yun from Yan'an to Manchuria. They arrived in Shenyang and stayed at the "Marshall's mansion," the former residence of warlord Zhang Zuolin.[41] On October 4, Peng and Chen informed Yan'an that the Soviets had made their final decision to "open wide the front door and leave all domestic business to us." The Soviets strongly urged the CCP to immediately send its best forces from all other base areas to Manchuria. The CCP acted immediately. At the time, the Nationalist government did not have a single soldier there.[42]

By the end of 1945, nearly 110,000 Communist troops had swarmed into Manchuria from Shaanxi, Shanxi, Suiyuan, Chaha'er, and Hebei by land, and from Shandong by sea. Luo Ronghuan, Lin Biao's future right-hand man, took a steamboat that landed north of Dalian on November 8, and then camped out at Pulandian overnight.[43] Some of the strangers passing through Yu Rongfu's town soon became top leaders of the new Communist order in Manchuria.

On January 14, 1946, the Communist Northeastern Democratic United Army (*Dongbei minzhu lianjun*) was formally established. With the support and acquiescence of the Soviet Union, this 270,000-man army quickly occupied nearly half of Manchuria.[44] Overcoming their lack of modern transport, the Communists had moved with great efficiency on foot or by boat. In contrast, the Nationalist forces transported by US naval ships did not make their first forced landing at Qinhuangdao, Hebei, until mid-October 1945, and did not attack Liaoning until mid-November. However, once the US-equipped and battle-tested Nationalist armies began pushing north along the Bo Sea coast, the Communist forces were swept out of major cities. The Nationalists took Shenyang on January 15, 1946.[45]

As the Nationalist armies were largely confined to their city bases, the Communists took control of the countryside and its population. Pulandian, Yu's hometown, was one of the many towns the Nationalist forces never reached. Yu had never experienced Nationalist rule before fleeing to Shenyang in 1946. The first Chinese government he encountered was the Communists'. Soon after their arrival, they launched class struggle in the name of "account-settling" (*qingsuan*). The rich were ordered to attend mass meetings, where the poor denounced them for their alleged crimes and exploitation. After the meetings, crowds flocked into the homes of the denounced and looted them. "The mob were not Communists," Yu recalled, "but local thugs and ruffians who were mobilized by them." The Yu family-owned grocery store was emptied by the mob. Even his bicycle was not spared. Luckily, his family members were not beaten and they were allowed to keep their house, while the wealthiest families were evicted from their homes. Compounding these miseries, the old currency became worthless, and people had to sell their valuables at fire-sale prices to obtain the new currency issued by the Russians, the so-called Red Army notes (*hongjunpiao*). They also bartered with each other for essential goods.[46] Yu's family lost their store and their livelihood.

In early 1946, two types of Communist "United Armies" (*lianjun*) appeared. One group, presumably Korean, began to conscript local youths. In desperation, Yu's father took him, the eldest son, to escape to Shenyang, leaving behind his mother, three younger brothers, and two sisters. With refugee students in mind, the Nationalist government had set up a "Training and Education Center for Youths from Dalian and Port Arthur," which offered classes off and on. In these despondent days, Yu "just lived there and filled his stomach" (*hunfanchi*).[47]

In contrast to Yu's refugee experience, Gao's life in his village near Shenyang was more stable, at least for the first three years after V-J Day. Under the Soviet occupation, although schools remained closed, teachers who had been imprisoned by the Japanese for their anti-Japanese beliefs returned. They offered informal instruction to eager students. Gao was greatly influenced by these patriots. When the Nationalist army recovered Shenyang, schools were reopened. Gao began boarding at Shenyang No. 1 Middle School. A Nationalist official served as the school principal and two teachers who had survived the dreaded Japanese Kempeitai prisons taught history and civics.[48] Gao's education in his formative years had a lasting impact: he became a loyal Nationalist.

In June 1948, the Central Military Academy came to recruit cadets in Manchuria for the second time. Out of the 6,000 applicants, 600 were admitted, including Gao and Yu. Gao's parents were reluctant to let him go, as there was no other young male left in his family. At the time the Communist forces were closing in on Shenyang, and the rich and well-connected had begun fleeing south. Gao's family had been farmers for generations, and it was impossible to sell their land and run away. Getting into Whampoa presented an opportunity for their son to escape the war. One morning in August, his parents saw him off at the train station. That was their last sight of him.[49]

As most railroads had been disrupted by the Communists, Gao and other future cadets were flown from Shenyang to Jinzhou, where troops were busy building fortifications for the looming showdown. They took a train to Qinhuangdao, where they boarded a ship for Shanghai. From there, they reached Chongqing by riverboat. After boot camp, they formally enrolled in the academy in December 1948.[50]

In the same month that Gao Wenjun traveled to Chongqing on the Yangtze River, Zhang Zeshi, the Tsinghua dropout and Communist agent, also returned to Chongqing by boat. Zhang returned home to Sichuan with the express purpose of overthrowing the Nationalists. Gao and Yu left home in Manchuria to escape the Communists. A year later the Whampoa cadets would become the final defenders of the Nationalist regime on the mainland, and prisoners of the Communists.

The Capture of Three Taiwanese in Three PLA Campaigns, 1948–1949

Gao and Yu left Shenyang just in time to escape the final collapse of the Nationalists in Manchuria. On September 12, 1948, the Communists launched the Liao-Shen Campaign to eliminate the Nationalist forces then isolated in three cities—Changchun, Jinzhou, and Shenyang. Changchun fell in late October, and Shenyang on November 2. At the end of the 52-day campaign, the Nationalists had lost 472,000 men, including 56,800 killed or wounded and 324,300 captured.[51]

Chen Yonghua, the Taiwanese who had escaped from his PLA captors a year earlier, was recaptured by the same PLA 116th Division, 39th Army, in Shenyang. He did not have the same luck twice. "By this time, all of Manchuria was under Communist control," Chen recalled. "Even the civilians were incorporated into their organizations. There was simply no place to hide. Escapees were quickly apprehended." The captives were put through a two-week indoctrination course, where political officers "brainwashed prisoners with Marxism, Leninism, and Mao's Thought." Soon they were integrated into the PLA.[52]

Chen noticed one major difference between the Nationalist and Communist armies: "The PLA was better disciplined." While the Nationalist troops often robbed and harassed civilians, such misconduct was "absolutely prohibited" in the PLA. When PLA troops entered a village, they were sent to each household to help with household chores, such as carrying water from the well and sweeping the yard. Not surprisingly, "the PLA was much more popular." Chen concluded, "The PLA could easily mobilize a large number of militia to assist with logistics or launch 'human-wave attacks.'"[53]

In December, Lin Biao's army swept across the Great Wall and encircled Beiping and Tianjin. Chen Yonghua's 39th Army attacked and captured Tianjin. In January 1949, Fu Zuoyi, the Nationalist commander in Beiping, negotiated a surrender partly through his daughter Fu Dongju, an underground Communist who had aided Zhang Zeshi's escape from Beiping to Tianjin in August 1948.[54] Fu's quarter-million troops laid down their arms.

Lin Biao's forces—now renamed the 4th Field Army—kept marching south. "We fought through Shandong, Anhui, Hubei, Hunan, Guizhou, Guangxi, and all the way to Zhennanguan" on the Sino-Vietnamese border, Chen Yonghua recalled. It was done "all on foot!"[55] As a "liberated soldier" (*jiefang zhanshi*, a term for former Nationalist troops integrated into the PLA), Chen Yonghua literally helped "liberate" half of China.

While Chen Yonghua was fighting, the idea that troops on the other side of the battlefield might be fellow Taiwanese probably crossed his mind. However, "there was absolutely no chance to think about this possibility," Chen recalled. "If anyone hesitated to follow orders, he would be arrested immediately." Every evening each squad held "criticism meetings" to examine each soldier's actions—and thoughts—during the day. Poor performers were segregated for reeducation. "Everyone just followed orders and tried his best to perform, and dared not think too much."[56] The difference between the Communist and Nationalist armies was not simply about disciplining the body, but also controlling the mind.

From November 6, 1948, to January 10, 1949, the PLA dealt a fatal blow to Chiang Kai-shek's regime in the Huaihai Campaign in East China, where the Nationalists lost 555,000 troops, including 320,000 captured, 35,000 surrendered, and 28,000 defected.[57] Taiwanese Wang Yingchang of the 70th Army was captured at Xuzhou, the epicenter of the campaign. He was integrated into the PLA 3rd Field Army, which crossed the Yangtze River on April 21, took Nanjing the following day, and conquered Shanghai on May 27. Wang deserted in June, but was quickly apprehended. He was sent back to his unit and continued to battle Nationalist remnants in Zhejiang and Jiangsu.[58]

Taiwanese Chen Qingbin, also of the Nationalist 70th Army, escaped from the Huaihai battle zone to Shanghai, where he joined the cavalry company of the 45th Division. When the division evacuated to Taiwan in May, Qingbin's company was transferred to Jiangxi, where he was finally taken prisoner by the PLA on June 20. After two weeks of indoctrination, he joined the PLA 2nd Field Army.[59]

Life hung on a thin thread for the three Taiwanese soldiers. What separated them from those who safely evacuated to Taiwan was a random unit assignment. What lay between returning home and being captured was a chance decision made by someone above. Fate seemed to take them farther and farther away from their homes. Now they were PLA soldiers in three different field armies heading in three directions in their unfamiliar "motherland." In fact, they were experiencing the greatest social upheaval in the history of China. Their new ruler, Mao Zedong, would dominate their lives for the next two years, and in Chen Qingbin's case, three decades.

1949: To Flee or Embrace the PLA?

When the PLA began crossing the Yangtze River on April 21, 1949, Mao issued a "March to all China" order: "Charge ahead valiantly. Resolutely, completely, thoroughly, and totally annihilate all Nationalist reactionaries who dare to resist."[60] Mao mapped out plans for his four field armies. The 3rd Field Army under Chen Yi and Su Yu was to advance to Zhejiang and Fujian along the coast. Lin Biao's 4th Field Army was to sweep south along the central north-south axis to conquer Hubei, Hunan, Guangdong, and Guangxi. Once Shanghai was taken, and if the Americans did not intervene, the 2nd Field Army under Liu Bocheng and Deng Xiaoping was to go westward along the Yangtze River to capture Guizhou and Sichuan. Finally, the 1st Field Army was to split into two groups. Peng Dehuai would advance to the northwest, and He Long would attack Sichuan from Shaanxi. Mao instructed the 2nd Field Army to flank Sichuan from the south to cut off the Nationalist forces' escape route to Yunnan and capture as many enemy troops as possible, lest they flee to the mountains in Yunnan, Tibet, or Burma.[61]

Mao was not simply a military strategist, but also a political visionary. On January 8, 1949, he predicted that, from a military point of view, the Nationalist regime would be largely overthrown by the spring. He turned his attention from destroying the old order to building a new one, using the same tools: his party and his army. Mao issued two orders in the following weeks enjoining the PLA to "transform the army into work teams." Noting that the 53,000 cadres assigned to go south (*nanxia*) were "grossly insufficient" to govern "nine provinces and dozens of large cities," Mao declared, "the PLA is a school. The 2.1 million-strong field army is equivalent to thousands of universities and middle schools." The PLA must become "adept in mobilizing and organizing youths, uniting and training cadres in newly liberated areas." Under the new regime, "all cadres should be provided by the army itself."[62] Former Nationalist personnel were to be purged. The PLA became the main channel for upward social mobility.

As the PLA advanced south, many youths looked forward to joining its ranks, including some longtime Communist sympathizers, such as the twenty-one-year-old Tang Yao. Born into a small merchant family in hilly Lanxi County in central Zhejiang, Tang had no interest in inheriting his family-run paper and firecracker shop. He became a clerk in the local government in 1946, but was heavily influenced by an uncle, a writer and underground Communist, who induced him to "join the revolution." When the PLA approached in May of 1949, Tang Yao guided the army to "liberate" Lanxi. Soon he joined the 12th Army as a clerk in the HQ's Security Department, writing documents related to internal security and discipline. Tang's literary talent and prudent character led to his promotion to the commander's secretary dealing with confidential materials (*jiyao mishu*), with a rank equivalent to a platoon leader.[63] It appeared that Tang was on a fast track to a promising career.

On October 1, 1949, Mao proclaimed the founding of the PRC. Standing beside Mao atop Tian'anmen Gate were his top lieutenants, including Liu Bocheng and Deng Xiaoping. As a much-feared American intervention did not occur, Liu and Deng soon returned to Nanjing and launched the long-planned march to Sichuan. The Nationalist government moved from Guangzhou to Chongqing in mid-October. Chiang Kai-shek flew from Taiwan to Chongqing with his son Ching-kuo on November 1, hoping for a repeat of the miraculous survival of his government in Sichuan, just as had happened in the Anti-Japanese War of Resistance (1937–1945). This time, however, the idea proved to be wishful thinking. A million battered and tattered Nationalist troops were no match for spirited PLA forces engulfing this mountainous redoubt from three directions.

The PLA 12th Army departed from its bases in Anhui and marched toward Chongqing through Hubei.[64] As Nationalist defense crumbled in Hubei, the provincial government evacuated to Sichuan, taking along more than two thousand refugee students, who were mostly the children of landlords and the rich (*difu zidi*). The governor hurriedly created a hodgepodge 3rd Army Group, including a training regiment for half of the students. Yan Tianzhi, a fifteen-year-old boy from the Xianfeng County in southwestern Hubei, was one of them. By the time the unwieldy army of students embarked, the Communists had already blocked the main road to Sichuan. The students had to trek across the mountains by circuitous routes in western Hubei and eastern and northern Sichuan. They reached Chengdu in November, where their exodus came to an abrupt end.[65]

On the morning of November 30, Chiang Kai-shek made a last-minute exit from Chongqing's airport to Chengdu. Hours later, the PLA 2nd Field Army took the city. It continued to march west and south, rapidly outflanking Chengdu from the south. In the meantime, Nationalist General Hu Zongnan's army group belatedly began retreating south toward Chengdu from Shaanxi. Behind them in hot pursuit was He Long's PLA 18th Army Group. Various PLA units were deployed to encircle the Nationalists on the Chengdu plain and annihilate them.

In his final days in Chengdu, Chiang headquartered on the Central Military Academy campus. Cadets were posted as sentries. Manchurian Yu Rongfu and Gao Wenjun both remembered that Chiang made roll calls and gave a speech to the cadets.[66] As the commandant of all Whampoa cadets, Chiang was known to be partial to them. He devised an exit plan for the nearly twenty thousand cadets and staff.[67]

At 2:00 p.m., December 10, Chiang's plane left Chengdu for Taiwan. A week later, the academy abandoned its plans to defend Chengdu in street fighting; instead, more than fifteen thousand cadets evacuated toward Dayi County, west of Chengdu.

Gao Wenjun's artillery column rolled out of Chengdu, and cadets took turns riding in vehicles. Other columns marched. Gao's semi-motorized column first arrived in the walled city of Dayi, which came under mortar attack after midnight. A shell exploded in Gao's unit, killing a cadet instantly.[68] The next morning Yu's column arrived at the gates of Dayi and came under attack by defected Nationalist troops. Enemy snipers mainly aimed at officers dressed in khaki uniforms, sparing cadets in gray. Soon cadets ran out of bullets and two officers were killed. Fortunately, these skirmishes did not escalate into an all-out battle.[69] While being pressed by the PLA from the north, the remaining loyal Nationalist troops found that their escape routes to the west were cut off by defected Nationalist units. Adding desperation to confusion, several Whampoa units also declared they were joining the Communists "in an uprising."[70]

At this critical moment, the acting commandant appeared to rally the cadets, vowing to live and die with them, but he secretly flew to Taiwan that night. Hu Zongnan, Chiang's favorite general, had flown to Hainan Island one day earlier. In desperation, Gao's column commander, Li Yunzhong, led cadets toward the Xinjin airport, hoping to catch a flight to Taiwan, but they were turned back by bullets fired by Hu's troops guarding the airstrip. With their last hope of escape dashed, the cadets dropped their arms and ran back to Chengdu.[71]

On December 25, Hu Zongnan's main units were annihilated west of Chengdu. The Hubei governor and his ragtag army surrendered to the PLA's 180th Division on the following day. Standing before the young student-soldiers, he conceded that there was no other option but to surrender. Many students wept, Yan Tianzhi recalled. On December 30, Gao Wenjun read in a local newspaper the surrender announcement by his column commander Li. Gao and fellow cadets broke down in tears.[72]

The Communists had won the Civil War. It was a tearful moment for Gao Wenjun and Yan Tianzhi. Yet, for others, it was a moment of joy and hope.

The Homecoming of a "Liberated Soldier"

More than 50,000 troops of the victorious PLA 18th Army Group paraded into Chengdu on December 30, 1949. He Rui, a seventeen-year-old PLA soldier, marched with great pride, joyously singing and shouting slogans. His return to Chengdu was a homecoming of the best kind. This moment was his. He sincerely believed he was coming back to liberate fellow "poor and suffering" people in Sichuan. He grew up in a well-off family in a market town in southwestern Sichuan. When he was fourteen, however, his father died of illness and the family's fortunes rapidly declined. He went to Chengdu to work as an unpaid apprentice in a machine shop, where he was treated roughly. He returned home, only to find that the government was press-ganging young men. To avoid conscription, a neighbor even chopped off his own index finger. When the police and militia came to seize him, He Rui pulled out a hammer hidden in his coat and smacked the face of a policeman. But he was overpowered and arrested.[73]

In the next few months, He was confined in various conscript training centers. For a failed escape attempt, a draftee received forty strokes of a bamboo shoulder pole and nearly died. He Rui was so terrified that he did not even contemplate escape. As was the case for Taiwanese Chen Yonghua in the Nationalist army in Taiwan, food was in perpetual short supply in He's experience. Meat dishes only appeared twice a month. Living conditions were horrendous. Conscripts were not allowed to take a bath for months on end. "With each swat, I could catch one or two fleas," He recalled. Draftees quickly contracted scabies and sores festered. Yet no treatment was available.

In the winter of 1948, eighty-seven conscripts in He's company marched on foot from Chengdu to Shaanxi. By the end of the twenty-nine-day trek, hunger, disease, and exhaustion had claimed the lives of eight men. One day, an eighteen-year-old collapsed on the road and soon died. He was stripped of his uniform and tossed into a roadside ditch unburied. The unit just marched on. To make up for the lost headcount, the guards captured random men ranging from their teens to forties, forcing them into the ranks at gunpoint. He Rui was assigned to the Nationalist 38th Army, a "Central Army" (*zhongyangjun*) under Hu Zongnan. Food was sufficient, but life was no better. Only a few days after his arrival, He was beaten for misplacing the cap on a machine gun barrel. Ordered to prostrate himself on the ground, He received eight blows with a wooden truncheon administered by his squad leader. Then his platoon leader denied him lunch. That was He's first taste of the regular Nationalist army.

He's unit fought a series of losing battles against the PLA. In summer 1949, He's defeated unit fled into the Qinling Mountains in southern Shaanxi. When a straggler stumbled back to his unit, a tempestuous officer shot him from behind point-blank. The victim fell, rolling on the ground, his mouth wide open and gasping. This senseless murder once again convinced He of the wickedness of the Nationalists.

On August 30, while guarding their mountain positions, He's unit was overrun by the PLA in broad daylight. Hiding in a pillbox, He heard the Communists speaking for the first time: "We are the Chinese People's Liberation Army. We don't beat or insult people (*bu daren, bu maren*). Come out and surrender." Another man shouted, "You are all sons of the working people. We are going to liberate all of China, so poor people will suffer no more." He Rui was touched. "I am here!" He jumped out of the trench. A PLA soldier warmly greeted him, "Hey, little guy (*xiaogui*), come over here. You haven't eaten, right? Have some food and water." An officer patted his head and spoke as if he knew him, "You've suffered. We are going to liberate your hometown."

He Rui immediately felt an affinity for the Communists. He ripped the Nationalist emblem off his cap, tossed it away, and became a PLA soldier.

The next day, He's company leader handed him a rifle. He and his squad captured six Nationalist stragglers in the same afternoon. In their evening group meeting, the officers praised He effusively. Whereas he received nothing but verbal and physical abuse in the Nationalist army, he received proper recognition for the first time in his adult life. Moreover, food was a vast improvement. Before their final invasion of Sichuan, PLA troops enjoyed excellent food: a different menu each day, four dishes and one soup per meal, meat dishes three times a day. Sundays were dumpling days. He ate 120 of them the first time! The contrast between the two armies was like night and day.[74]

Another major difference was how discipline was enforced. In the PLA, "thought work" (*sixiang gongzuo*), or persuasion and indoctrination, was the main method; the Nationalist army relied on corporal punishment and verbal abuse. He Rui ran afoul of PLA regulations in December 1949. While on march pursuing Hu Zongnan's forces, He spotted his former Nationalist squad leader limping among other POWs. He confronted him, yelling at him. Before He could strike the prisoner, his PLA squad leader stopped him and reminded him of the "Three Main Rules of Discipline and Eight Points for Attention," which specifically prohibited mistreating prisoners. As He Rui "violated discipline by breaking ranks and berating a prisoner," he had to make a self-criticism at the "squad affairs meeting" that night. The PLA was serious about discipline and its promise to protect civilians and prisoners.

He Rui found group meetings, the hallmark Chinese Communist approach to disciplining soldiers, more civilized and effective than the Nationalists' crude methods of physical punishment. Even sixty years later, He still fondly remembered the "Three Major Democracies" practiced in the PLA: political, economic, and military democracies. Certainly, the meaning of "democracy" in the Chinese Communist lexicon is fundamentally different from how democracy is understood in the West. The Chinese Communists often equate "democracy" with a "democratic [work] style" (*minzhu zuofeng*), i.e., allowing people to speak and participate in activities sanctioned and directed from above. This is premised on the denial of the rights of certain elements of the population, who are excluded from the body of "the people" or "the masses." This kind of "democracy," however illiberal, was a novelty for individuals like He, who had rarely experienced dignity in their lives, not to mention opportunities for participation. The Communists invited such individuals to join "the people" and encouraged them to speak up. Even if their participation was heavily guided, they felt empowered. The sense of belonging and solidarity was profoundly powerful. Six months later, He became a Communist Party member. A year later in Korea, he led suicide attacks on American tanks with hand grenades.

If university student Zhang Zeshi's conversion to Communism was a classic example of the intellectual and emotional appeal of Communism to idealistic students, He Rui was a textbook case of how the CCP and the PLA attracted "poor and suffering people" and converted them into highly disciplined and motivated soldiers. His personal experience of family tragedy, financial hardship, forced conscription, and abuse in the army was common for many people in the final years of the Nationalist regime. That partly explains the popularity and strength of the Communists.

New Recruits, 1949–1950

The experience of Chengdu native Zhong Junhua is another case of how poor youths were attracted to the Communists and the PLA. Born in the outskirts of Chengdu in 1933 and abandoned by his derelict father, Zhong and his younger brother were single-handedly raised by their mother, who earned a meager income as a seamstress and laundress for the rich. Zhong's childhood memories were dominated by hunger. Each day the family "had only two meals, which consisted of rice porridge and bean curd dregs cooked with wild vegetables." At the age of eleven, Zhong began working as an apprentice. In 1949, trying to avoid conscription, Zhong went into hiding in the barracks of the local 95th Army where his cousin was an officer. As the PLA 60th Army absorbed the 95th Army in 1950, a PLA officer asked Zhong if he would like to work in the medical team, an offer he gladly accepted. In the "old society" such an opportunity to learn professional skills was inconceivable for someone like him.[75]

Zhong described his days as a paramedic trainee as "fantastic." When his mother came to take him home, he refused. Soon he became a Youth League member. In November 1950 Zhong was decorated with an Extraordinary Merit for his service in tending smallpox patients. At home, his mother was appointed director of the local residents' committee. "That was the happiest time in my mother's entire life," Zhong recalled. For the first time, Zhong felt he and his family were "treated like human beings." He attributed all these positive changes to the Communists, with whom he wholeheartedly identified.[76]

The circumstances of Zhong's induction into the PLA were unusual, as in the early 1950s youths with little education were not the typical PLA recruit. The Communists were already saddled with nearly a million surrendered former Nationalist troops in Sichuan, most of whom were uneducated and unreliable. The ideal candidates for the new army were educated youths, whom the Communists planned to train as future cadres to govern the country. Because educated youths were mostly from middle- or upper-class families, political indoctrination became a top priority. The Attached School of the Western Sichuan Military Region was set up in Chengdu immediately after the victory over the Nationalists. Some 1,200 students between the ages fourteen and thirty, whose prior education ranged from junior high school to college, enrolled.[77]

Attached School student Cai Pingsheng was born in Beiping in 1932—and named Pingsheng ("Beiping-born")—to a painter-craftsman father and a Manchu mother. Fleeing the ever-advancing Japanese army, the family went from Beiping to Jiangxi, then to Wuhan. En route to Chongqing, his bother was born on the boat. When his father got off the boat at Yichang to buy food for the newborn, the boat departed before his return. The family remained separated throughout the war. His mother raised the two boys in Shaanxi, working as a seamstress. Pingsheng went to school, but also worked after school as a peddler at a train station. After V-J Day, the family finally was reunited in Chengdu.[78]

A few days after Chengdu's "liberation," Cai went to apply for admission to the PLA Attached School, which promised a tuition-free three-year curriculum. The officer sized up the skinny Cai and warned him, "This is an army school. It's very tough. We may go to the front line, and there will be casualties. Now it's not too late to change your mind." Cai replied, "I've thought it over already, and I will not back out." Two months after his enrollment, Cai was inducted into the Youth League, thanks to his proletarian family background and his own diligence, and soon became the leader of his class. The eighteen-year-old Cai, for the first time in his life, felt that his future would be "smooth sailing" (*yifan fengshun*) and "a walk in the clouds" (*pingbu qingyun*).[79]

While Cai could rightly claim he was from a proletarian family, his schoolmate Lin Mocong's family history was complicated. His father, Lin Chunhua, was one of China's pioneers in stenography and once worked as Sun Yat-sen's shorthand assistant during the Nationalist Party's First National Congress in Guangzhou in 1924. Chiang Kai-shek selected Lin as his aide and arranged for his enrollment in the third class of the Whampoa Academy. Lin served Chiang until 1931, and then became an instructor at Whampoa.[80] Born in Nanjing in 1934, as a toddler Lin Mocong had to flee with his family before Japan attacked the capital city in late 1937. After a perilous three-year journey, Lin rejoined his father in Chengdu, where the Whampoa Academy had relocated. Lin came to know several important Nationalist military and intelligence figures, including Deng Wenyi and Kang Ze, who had served along with his father as Chiang's aides. His father, however, loathed spymaster Dai Li, calling him a ruthless man who "ate people without spitting out the bones." In Lin's memory, his father had become disillusioned with the regime well before his death in 1946.[81]

After his father's death, the whole family relied on his elder sister, who taught at the military academy's attached high school. Enrolled in the same school, Mocong became influenced by leftist teachers, who were probably underground Communists. Lin was also appalled by the Nationalists' corruption and violence. At the age of six, en route to Sichuan he had witnessed an officer beating a sick soldier to death. In high school, he saw the Nationalist army executing a deserter on his campus. He concluded,

"What the Nationalists practiced was exactly opposite to what they preached. Not just me, but most people in my family lost confidence."[82]

After the Communist victory, Lin's elder sister was sent to a PLA school for indoctrination, leaving the family without an income. Partly because of this, both Lin and his younger sister decided to join the PLA. Mocong was admitted to the Attached School and his younger sister joined a medical unit. Lin quickly learned various musical instruments and began dabbling in composing. When his elder sister completed her reindoctrination and received a good job placement, she tried to take her siblings home. Both refused. "Life here is like the immortals' (*shenxian yiyang*)! Why should I go home?" Mocong reasoned.[83] Lin, who was from an insider family of the Nationalist regime, approved of the Communists and enthusiastically accepted what they had to offer.

After witnessing the Nationalists' rigid hierarchy firsthand, Lin was greatly impressed by the Communists' egalitarianism. He especially enjoyed the democratic atmosphere in his school, where "everything had to go through democratic discussions." However, he did notice the limits of this "democracy." In a special meeting to discuss Youth League membership nominations, the teacher told the students to nominate a particular student, claiming "that is the upper-level's intent. We should be of one heart with the party." Feeling "very uncomfortable," Lin wondered, "What kind of democracy is this?" However unwillingly, he still raised his hand to support that nomination. Lin also sensed a gradual tightening of control. After running into a series of small troubles, he learned to be "docile" (*xueguai*). Nonetheless, Lin still believed in the overall superiority of the Communists.[84] This belief would sustain him after his capture in Korea.

Like Lin Mocong's sister, many other girls also joined the PLA's propaganda or medical units. Yang Yuhua, later the only known Chinese female prisoner in Korea, joined the PLA paramedic school in Chengdu in November 1950. Yang was raised by her grandmother, who worked as a domestic helper for a landlord family and saw to it that Yuhua graduated from junior high school. Just like Cai Pingsheng, who joined the army without telling his parents, Yang ran away from home and applied to the school. A few days after her admission, Yang, together with twenty other female and forty male students, was assigned to the 180th Division's medical unit, where they were told to "learn by actual work." A month later, the division left Sichuan for the battlefield in Korea.[85]

Zhang Zeshi, the Tsinghua student-turned-underground agent, also joined the PLA in 1950—not as a student, but as guerilla fighter. Ordered by the Communist underground to quit Tsinghua University and return to his home province in the summer of 1948, he engaged in the Communist-led student movement at Sichuan University. When the Nationalist government cracked down, he fled to the countryside to join Communist guerrillas in western Sichuan. After Liberation, Zhang was told to join the PLA to continue the revolution, as educated cadres were needed to carry out land reform and "bandit suppression" campaigns. Instead of fulfilling his dream of resuming studies at Tsinghua, Zhang, along with his girlfriend, a fellow college-student-turned-guerrilla, became a PLA propaganda officer. The couple belatedly learned that they were not allowed to marry, as marriage was an entitlement exclusively enjoyed by battalion-level officers and above in the PLA.[86]

Zhang and his girlfriend, however, had a serious row in the spring of 1950 that attracted wide attention and drew an official reprimand. In frustration, Zhang decided to return home so he could go back to Tsinghua in the fall. One early morning in June, when Zhang, dressed as a civilian, tried to pass through the city gate, the guards recognized him and asked: "Propaganda Team Leader, what's going on?" Zhang admitted, "I want to quit the army." He was duly arrested. Soon he was expelled from the party for "deserting the revolution." However, instead of being discharged from the army, he was demoted to a company as a cultural instructor.[87] Mao had famously said, "Revolution is not a dinner party." In sharp contrast to the Nationalist Party and army, the Communist Party and army were much more difficult to join and—almost impossible to quit.

The experiences of Zhong, Cai, Lin, and Yang demonstrate the powerful political and emotional appeal of the Chinese Communists, especially for people who were neglected or oppressed under the Nationalist regime. They were not necessarily all from the working class, but they shared similar sufferings, such as poverty, social discrimination, or government oppression. Perhaps, by more than pure coincidence, many of the pro-Communists mentioned above grew up in broken families. They suffered not only the loss or absence of the father or both parents but also the resultant social discrimination. In a sense, the Communist government was an ideal fatherly figure that provided order, discipline, care, and purpose. During their imprisonment in Korea, their emotional attachment to family and home was fused with their identification with the Communist Party. All these emotions were merged and transformed into an intense fighting spirit in their struggle against the anti-Communist prisoners and the prison authorities.

Even though most recruits understood there were certain risks involved in joining the army, they were accustomed to the image of the Communists claiming victory after victory. Few could anticipate fighting an enemy as strong as the United States in a conflict as brutal as the Korean War. It is true they volunteered to join the army, but they did so before the outbreak of the Korean War. "It was fashionable to join the PLA. It was cool. Some people even cried when they were rejected," Lin Mocong remarked.[88] They did not know what was coming.

2

Reforming Former Nationalists

AT TEN IN THE MORNING of December 30, 1949, General He Long led more than 50,000 troops of the PLA 18th Army Group parading into Chengdu. Some 300,000 residents poured into the streets. Tanks rumbled in first, followed by columns of artillery, infantry, and cavalry. Weapons were well maintained. Troops appeared well nourished and high-spirited, singing songs such as "The East Is Red" and "The Sky in Liberated Areas Is Bright." Amid the sound of firecrackers, the crowd cheered: "Long live Chairman Mao!" "Victory!" and "Liberation!"[1]

While "liberated soldier" He Rui marched triumphantly in the ranks of the PLA, 3,000 former Whampoa cadets and faculty stood in the welcoming crowd. As the Nationalist Central Military Academy Marching Band blared the "March of the PLA," Yu Rongfu, still in his gray cadet uniform stripped of its Nationalist emblem and insignia, somberly watched this Communist show of force. He finally registered, "The Nationalist regime has collapsed for sure."[2]

Thought Reform Policies

By the end of the Southwest Campaign, which culminated in the fall of Chengdu on December 27, 1949, the PLA held 932,600 captured, surrendered, and defected Nationalist troops from more than 100 different units. The size and composition of the ex-Nationalists presented a daunting challenge to the Communists, whose army was 600,000 strong in the region.[3] By the end of 1950, after a year-long indoctrination, or "thought reform," ex-Nationalist personnel seemed to have completely surrendered to their captors, physically, emotionally, and for some, intellectually as well. While the Communists' ideology and methods won some converts, others remained unconvinced. To survive, however, these dissenters had to hide their misgivings under the guise of complete submission.

How to reform and ingest nearly a million former enemy troops was extremely complex and politically delicate. Deng Xiaoping, then the top leader of the Southwest Military Region, which controlled Sichuan, Guizhou, and Yunnan provinces, warned his officers that the "battle" was not over yet.[4] In fact, Mao had asserted in early 1949: "We should not think that once the counterrevolutionaries submit to us, they will become revolutionaries. . . . That is absolutely not the case." While some might be reformed, others might be "made redundant," Mao declared. "Die-hard counterrevolutionaries will be suppressed"—meaning physically liquidated.[5] Under this overarching principle, the Communists adopted nuanced approaches in practice.

The Southwest Military Region divided defected (*qiyi*) and surrendered (*toucheng*) Nationalist troops into four categories and treated them differently.[6] Three features stand out. First, irrespective of which category a Nationalist unit fell into, the inevitable final outcome involved careful screening, thorough reindoctrination, and complete integration into the PLA. The only difference was a matter of schedule. Second, the policy in a nutshell was: "soldiers were to be integrated into the PLA, and officers were to be educated in special schools."[7] The officers were segregated from their units and re-indoctrinated in various "officer prisoners' units" or regional military and political universities, which were essentially PLA-run reindoctrination camps. In the end, few high- and mid-ranking officers were retained; most low-ranking officers were inducted into the PLA, but were demoted.

Third, the Communists took pains to keep undesirables—whom they labeled hooligans (*liumang*) and vagrants (*youmin*)—in the PLA instead of letting them loose to join the insurgents. The Communists had learned a lesson from the Nationalists' failure in Manchuria in 1946 when former Manchukuo puppet troops under the Japanese were disbanded and ended up joining the Communists.

The PLA dispatched "representative teams" to take control of various Nationalist units. The PLA 60th Army was tasked with reorganizing eighty-eight Nationalist units, the largest being the defected 95th Army with 1,531 officers, 11,189 soldiers, and 1,685 family dependents.[8] From December 1949, the 95th Army, with its designation intact, joined the PLA in fighting Nationalist insurgents in "bandit-suppression campaigns" in western Sichuan.[9] Then, in March 1950, PLA "representatives teams" took over the army. First, the teams established "military committees" at all levels to replace the old chain of command. Then, the army's personnel were completely reshuffled. High-ranking officers were mostly transferred out, company-level officers and above were segregated for reindoctrination, and officers' dependents were organized to undergo "education through study, production, and labor."[10]

To many Nationalist rank and file, the Communist program of "three democracies"—political, economic, and military—seemed refreshing. Beating and berating soldiers were no longer allowed; embezzlement through "ghost headcounts" was outlawed; and soldiers' living standards were improved. Representative teams mobilized soldiers to "air grievances" (*suku*) against the old society and the old army.[11]

What truly impressed the former Nationalist soldiers was not Marxist social theory, but the tangible differences between the Communists and the Nationalists. The PLA's discipline was vastly superior, as were its relations with civilians. It was free of the corruption that plagued the Nationalists. The quality and quantity of food were a cut above. More importantly, the Communist army also seemed democratic, in its own peculiar way. Although the "three democracies" were strictly guided and carefully choreographed by experienced PLA officers, most soldiers for the first time in their military life, if not their adult life, were encouraged to speak up and participate in public affairs. In sharp contrast to the Nationalists' rigid hierarchy, PLA officers and soldiers appeared to be equal, as they wore the same kind of uniform and addressed each other as "comrades." Most importantly, officers did not beat or berate their men. For troops who were used to abuse from their superiors, this single feature of the PLA won many hearts. Many men like He Rui were genuinely impressed and felt empowered by the Communists.

Even if some former Nationalists were not necessarily converted to the cause of revolution, they were still attracted to the Communists. Again, social class had much to do with their assessment of the Communist regime. People of poor, neglected, or "oppressed" family backgrounds tended to identify with the new order.

Mao had a point, however, that former Nationalist officers and military academy graduates and cadets, especially those with close ties to Chiang Kai-shek, were the most "poisoned by counterrevolutionary ideas" by virtue of their extended service in the Nationalist army. Their ideological conversion was the most difficult—if it was possible at all—despite their outward submission. Thought reform, as a never-ending process, served the purpose of ferreting out "die-hard counterrevolutionaries," who were to be imprisoned or liquidated. Reforming officers and cadets required separate institutions and more intense programs, such as the military and political universities.

Reforming Whampoa

After their units disintegrated during the failed retreat on the Chengdu plain in late December 1949, cadets Gao Wenjun and Yu Rongfu ran back to their campus in the city, only to find that it had been looted by mobs. The faculty and officers had either disappeared or failed to take charge.[12] While the Sichuan natives went home, people like Gao and Yu had nowhere to go. Unable to speak the local dialect, they could hardly hide in the local population. While Gao and Yu chose to wait and see, a small number of daring cadets went to Chongqing and took riverboats downstream, and eventually reached Taiwan via Hong Kong. Another group of some 200 cadets fled south to Xichang on the border with Yunnan, but were captured by the PLA and sent back to their former units.[13]

Soon, a former officer of the academy led a small group of PLA officers to campus. Despite their friendly appearance, Gao found their frequent use of the title *tongzhi* (comrades) distasteful, "giving me goose bumps." Two weeks later, two Nationalists-turned-PLA officers arrived. They took inventory of the remaining weapons and created rosters of all the cadets. Once the weapons problem was taken care of, the "representatives" wasted no time in issuing orders. Then a full contingent of PLA officers arrived. All cadets were reshuffled into new units, and all former officers were relocated.[14]

Days after New Year, 1950, cadets and faculty were "enrolled" in the 18th Army Group's Attached School, which was renamed the Western Sichuan branch of the Southwest Military and Political University (*Junzheng daxue*, or *Junda*) in June.[15] The student body consisted of more than 8,000 ex-Nationalist personnel and civilians, including 15 general-grade and 985 field-grade officers (faculty of the academy), 3,500 company-grade officers and cadets of the academy, some military policemen, and 1,500 civilians. A cadet recalled that 7,000 Whampoa cadets were organized into 7 battalions. The 8th Battalion was composed of 1,000 ex-military policemen. The 9th consisted of 1,000 civilian students who had completed at least two years of senior high school and passed the entrance examination. Student recruits included men like Cai Pingsheng and Lin Mocong. In addition, about 100 women students were also admitted and formed a female student company. Another cadet reported that each of the 9 battalions had about 700 students.[16]

The PLA carefully selected 30 instructors, many of whom were Nationalist defector-turned-PLA officers.[17] Gao's company leader was a graduate of Whampoa's 14th class.[18] The curriculum was entirely political. "No military tactical training or field training was given since graduates were all scheduled for assignment to rear echelon units," one student reported, believing that "they were not trusted to supervise or command front line units." Their so-called military training consisted of lectures on the history of the PLA, discipline, operating procedures, and the like.[19]

All lectures were given outdoors in the morning to each battalion. Without the benefit of any broadcasting equipment, "students had difficulty in hearing them" but "took copious notes." Textbooks included the works of Mao and other ideologues, such as the *History of Social Development* and the *Basic History of the Chinese People's Revolution*. In the afternoon, students in each squad met for supervised debates on subjects chosen by the instructors. Typical subjects included "Pros and cons of partnership with the Soviet Union," "The reason for anti-American feeling in China," and "Opinions on Chiang Kai-shek." Under the instructors' watchful eyes, "naturally participants in the debates usually hid their feelings, spoke evil of capitalism and praised communism," recalled a student.[20] They learned quickly to police their own actions and words.

Cadets noted that some of the Communist instructors were less educated than themselves. Gao found his company commissar particularly crude. In his regular two-hour lectures, the commissar repeatedly admonished the students to "make a clean break with the Nationalists" and "work hard to redeem past crimes." Gao simply did not believe he had committed any crime. The instructor often disparaged Chiang Kai-shek for fighting the Communists but not the Japanese during World War II, and praised the Soviet Union as China's "big brother." Gao, a Manchurian who had witnessed Soviet atrocities, was appalled but dared not argue. Moreover, Gao was repeatedly pressed to explain why he had fled Manchuria just before Liberation and joined Chiang's military academy.[21]

Thought Reform Methods

If Communist ideology held no appeal for Gao, its methods alienated him even further. Gao summarized the methods as a three-step strategy. First, the party divided students into three groups: active, middle, and backward elements. Then it "fully utilized the active elements and united with the middle elements to isolate and rescue the backward elements." If the "backward" students refused to admit guilt, they were ruthlessly attacked by the whole class. Initially, the Communists encouraged everyone to speak freely. Activists were instructed to take the lead in the "tell the truth" movement. Everyone was led to speak publicly about his family history from generations back. Then each individual was assigned a "family origin" (*jiating chengfen*) label. In addition to being a "counterrevolutionary" (as an ex-Nationalist), Gao's second crime was his family origins (from the "exploiters' class"). Gao and fellow students had to perform properly and play the game according to the instructors' rules. Deep inside, however, Gao resented the programs and hated the Communists. He recalled that this hatred did not subside until he was converted to Catholicism many years later in Taiwan.[22]

One of the most striking features of the Communist methods was the extraordinary number of meetings and discussions troops had to go through at various levels. "We were always kept busy, and everyone was under great pressure to participate actively," a prisoner remarked.[23] Virtually no personal time or space was allowed. Former Nationalist officers were university students in name, but prisoners in fact. They had to comply and participate actively. This kind of forced participation and performance was Mao's hallmark invention.

Former Nationalist captain Wang Zunming described his typical day in the Liangshan branch of the Southwest Military and Political University in eastern Sichuan, which illustrates the psychological intensity of the indoctrination regimen.[24]

5:00 A.M.	Get out of bed, and immediately divide into small groups of four or five persons to resolve good behavior for the day. For example, "We must work hard and study hard. We must not let our heads nod in class."
5:20	Twenty-minute rest period
5:40	Breakfast
6:00	Big Class. A two-hour lecture on the current subject matter. Students must take voluminous notes.
8:00	Twenty-minute rest period
8:20	Small Class. Students in small groups read their notes from the Big Class and discuss the topic for three and a half hours. Everyone participates actively.
12:00 P.M.	Lunch
12:15	Fifteen-minute rest period
12:30	Small group discussion. Questions asked about aspects of the current topic that are still not understood.
1:00	Big Class
3:00	Small Class
5:00	Supper
5:15	Folk dance. Everyone participates.
5:45	Thirty-minute rest period
6:15	Small Cell discussion. Four or five students report to each instructor. Personal criticism and the leader indicates where improvement can be or has been made. Sample topic: how to become eligible for the Communist Party.
6:45	Ten-minute rest period
7:00	Small Class. Three cells with a total of twelve persons. Criticism of daily behavior. For example, "You carried only forty sacks of rice."
7:30	Singing session. All songs have an ideological content.
8:30	Roll call. As names are called, the leader gives praise or blame to the student for his behavior during the day.[25]

Meetings were held throughout the day at various levels. First, there were subsquad small groups (*xiaozu*), each led by a party or Youth League member. Luo Shiqing, a clerk in the 95th Army, recalled, "Small Group Discussion Meetings were frequently held for 5 to 30 minutes whenever there was spare time. Such meetings were sometimes held four or five times a day." At the squad level, self-criticism and mutual criticism meetings were held every night for approximately twenty minutes after supper. All issues and complaints had to be raised in meetings. Men were told not to talk "behind the backs" of others.[26]

Each week, Squad Affairs Meetings were held for one or two hours "to give individuals an opportunity to confess mistakes in their conduct during the week." If anyone failed to confess or attempted to hide a "mistake," other members were expected to expose it and criticize the malefactor. "If a man failed to mend his way after being criticized three times at Squad Affairs Meetings, he was subject to public criticism at the Platoon Affairs Meetings," and the same review of work, public self-criticism, and mutual criticism were performed all over again.[27] Such repeated self-denigration and public humiliation created psychological pressure and fatigue so intense that few could resist. These intense and pervasive psychological control methods produced their intended result: conformity and participation.

However, as "the incessant meetings and discussions . . . took up practically all their leisure time," they "sharply annoyed many men and 'made them mad,'" Luo reported. While party and Youth League members "liked these meetings because it gave them an opportunity to display their abilities," nonmembers and shy persons disliked them. Luo concluded that these meetings produced very few true converts to Communism. Instead, "[a] few became obstinate non-believers but the majority were either indifferent or pretended to believe what they were taught."[28]

Another distinct Communist method involved a system of dossiers, which included detailed autobiographies, confessions, self-criticism statements, and responses to accusations. In contrast to the Nationalist Party, which did not carefully check the background or social network of its members, the Communists had a sophisticated dossier system, perfected in Yan'an during the dreaded "cadre investigation" and "purge of counterrevolutionaries" campaigns from 1942 to 1945. Now they applied the same techniques to Nationalist officers. Permanent dossiers were created and would haunt them throughout their lives.

Certainly not unique to Sichuan, this dossier system was implemented across China. At the Military and Political University in Beijing (formerly Beiping), three weeks were devoted to the "scrutiny of ideology," during which each student wrote a detailed personal history since age six.[29] Students were required to write their views of the Nationalist and the Communist Parties. At the Western Sichuan branch, each month students had to give their opinions of Communist ideas.[30] The instructors enjoined the students not to hide anything and assured them that the Communist government would forgive their past mistakes if they would come clean. Students, however, were keenly aware of the fact that all these statements were added into their ever-growing dossier files. If one made a confession, he effectively dug a hole for himself. If one tried to hide certain past deeds, other students might still betray him in their criticism statements. Then he would have to defend himself or confess more. It was a trap with no way out. While normally the instructors did not use explicit threats to force students to confess, in the end most men cracked and confessed. With a person's past wrongdoings or "crimes" on record, he was completely at the mercy of the regime.

At the time, few at the military and political universities knew that the process they were undergoing had been experienced by the Communists a few years earlier. During the Yan'an Rectification Campaign (1942–1944), Mao had perfected thought reform methods, which the historian Gao Hua describes as the "melding of theoretical inculcation with brute intimidation, which, when accompanied by powerful organizational measures, imposed a formidable force on Party members in general and on intellectuals in particular. The repeated shock waves caused them to slough off the 'old self' and replace it with an entire new spirit."[31]

When the Communists applied the same methods to Nationalist officers and cadets in 1950, the system was extraordinarily effective in subjugating its targets, just as it had been in Yan'an. Most initially headstrong Nationalists soon caved in, confessed their "crimes," and vowed to become "new men." One prisoner later remarked, "In this way they could kill without having the victim's blood on their hands."[32] Indeed, in line with Mao's dictum that the bourgeoisie should be won over by "bloodless struggle," the Communists subdued these former Nationalists without relying on overt violence, although the threat of violence always lurked in the background.

The Communists' intense indoctrination and thorough investigation uncovered among Whampoa cadets 340 Nationalist secret agents and 346 conspirators plotting to kill their Communist instructors.[33] Gao recalled the execution of three cadets from his 23rd class for alleged conspiracy.[34] Student recruit and future pro-Communist POW Lin Mocong vividly remembered the public trial on September 8, 1950, two days before "graduation day." Four alleged members of a "Three People's Principle Restoration Alliance," including two Whampoa instructors and two cadets, were paraded onto the stage and made to kneel before more than ten thousand students and personnel of the university. Representatives from all nine battalions, Whampoa cadets themselves, went on the stage to denounce the conspirators. In the end, the commissar declared, "These men committed heinous crimes. They deserve execution." When they were dragged off stage, one man completely collapsed. They were shot by a firing squad nearby. In the evening, students had to discuss the case and continue to denounce the executed. That was the only public execution he witnessed, Lin recalled.[35]

Resistance was suicidal. Most men chose to submit. Submission, however, did not necessarily mean a change of heart, as Mao had warned. Perhaps the Communists did not really expect ideological conversion. The military and political universities had fulfilled their purpose of subduing ex-Nationalists and putting their dossiers in place. Thought reform would continue elsewhere throughout their lifetime. Therefore, once the Communists had broken the ex-Nationalists' psychological resistance, destroyed their social network, and rendered them atomized and powerless, students could "graduate" from the "university."

The length of study at the Western Sichuan branch averaged about eight months, depending on individual progress. However, it could "be extended indefinitely at the discretion of instructors."[36] One cadet reported that early graduation was granted to about a thousand "over-aged (over 30) and physically weak students," who were discharged in May 1950. But PLA historian Chen Yu claims that half the cadets were discharged and sent home. From June to November, 7 battalions, or more than 3,000 students, were deployed to build the Chengdu-Chongqing Railway.[37] After Mao decided to intervene in Korea in early October, graduations were accelerated.

Korea-Bound Whampoa Cadets

In November, while other battalions remained in Chengdu, the entire 3rd Battalion, consisting of roughly 700 former cadets, was assigned to the PLA 60th Army and set out for Hebei Province, where the army was ordered to conduct "strategic maneuvers," a cadet reported.[38] According to Chen Yu, some 400 cadets were selected to join the 60th Army's Training Regiment. After repeated vetting in Hebei, only around 150 men were deemed sufficiently trustworthy to go to Korea.[39] They were mostly assigned posts as cultural instructors, whose job was to teach illiterate soldiers to read and sing. A small number of the other cadets with technical expertise became staff officers.

The Korea-bound ex-cadets, representing only 2 percent of the roughly 7,000 cadets who had been captured by or surrendered to the PLA, were presumably the most trusted by the Communists. However, one of them, Kou Weicheng, after his capture in Korea, told his American captors that most cadets remained loyal to the Nationalists, while only "approximately 20% of graduates were converted" to the Communist cause.[40]

The degree to which cadets had been converted to the Communist cause influenced their repatriation choice in the POW camps in Korea. And, as pointed out earlier, their conversion to Communism was largely determined by two factors: family background and their life experience under the Nationalists and their indoctrination experience under the Communists. The two best-known pro-Communist cadet prisoners in Korea were from poor families.

Yang Wenhua, who was brutally murdered by anti-Communist POWs in April 1952, was born into a small merchant family in Shaanxi. As his father was an itinerant merchant, Yang was raised by his mother. Driven by poverty, he quit middle school at fifteen and enlisted in the Nationalist army. Later he entered the 23rd class (1949) of the Central Military Academy. Under the Communists, Yang was one of the first Whampoa cadets to be admitted to the Youth League. After indoctrination, he became a radio operator at the 180th Division HQ—a highly sensitive position and hence one indicating he had the trust of the Communists.[41] Guo Naijian, also in the 23rd class, was born to a peasant family in Liaoning. After finishing elementary school he worked as a grocery store apprentice.[42] Although there is no information on their families' experiences after 1949, it is reasonable to assume that the Yang and Guo families, like most other poor people, welcomed the social changes brought by the Communists, or *fanshen*, literally meaning "turning over." Yang and Guo might not have had contact with their families during their reindoctrination in Sichuan, but they probably had good reason to believe their families would benefit from the revolution. Furthermore, their humble family origins also enhanced their political standing among the students. Such men were more likely to emerge as activists.

On the other hand, cadets from richer families were more likely to have the opposite experience. Being members of the "exploiters' class," they became the target of frequent and intense criticism. Such psychological pressure naturally caused resentment and resistance, which in turn drew more criticism. How could Communist indoctrination break this vicious cycle of criticism and resistance? The experiences of Gao Wenjun and Yu Rongfu demonstrate the near impossibility of true ideological conversion. Despite their ostensible submission, they were deeply embittered.

Just as Gao learned to conform, Yu also learned the game quickly. When students held their daily criticism meetings after dinner, "each was closely watched by the instructors and fellow classmates. Even one's facial expressions could not escape their notice." Each day every student made a self-criticism, then others criticized his conduct or utterances that day. Yu found that "the really smart people acted dumb, and talkative people often got into trouble." Yu knew he could only talk with impunity about minor issues, such as food. Despite his participation, Yu concluded, "it was impossible to reform people's minds. What people said and what people thought were entirely different."[43] Even though the eight months at the Sichuan branch was decidedly unpleasant, both Gao and Yu survived unscathed. Having passed repeated vetting and tests, they had apparently deceived their Communist captors.

Since cadets were very young, their alleged "crimes" were either of birth or association. They were too young to have "the people's blood," especially the Communists', on their hands. However, that was not the case for many Nationalist officers, who had served in the military long enough to have killed Communists. Not surprisingly, their reform process was even more thorough, intense, and even life-threatening. Captain Wang Zunming lived under such a precarious situation for nine months.

A Future Anti-Communist POW Leader

When a group of American social scientists interviewed Wang Zunming in Korea in 1953, he was described as "a vigorous man of action; he is also unusually lucid and articulate. He is tall, with an impressive military bearing, and speaks with an air of authority and conviction."[44] At the time of the interview, Wang had established himself as one of the top anti-Communist prisoner leaders. At the peak of his power, he controlled more than 8,000 prisoners in Compound 86 on Koje Island. Three years earlier, however, Wang was a subdued and humiliated prisoner caged by the Communists. Deep down, nevertheless, he was not crushed. Instead, he "developed a bitter-end will for revenge."[45] Wang's emergence as an anti-Communist POW leader had a great deal to do with his experiences under the two regimes.

Wang was born in 1926 in Shenmu in northern Shaanxi. His father was a local official and his eldest brother a police chief. His family owned a cloth shop and ten mu of land (about sixteen acres). In 1938, two years after their arrival in northern Shaanxi, the Communist forces expanded to Shenmu, threatening the local government. Many rich families sent their sons to military schools in Nationalist-controlled areas. Even though Wang was only twelve, his parents asked a Nationalist officer friend to take him away. In the next few years during World War II, Wang moved about in North China with this officer.[46] Wang's extensive travel experiences later became an asset in the prison camps, aiding him in dealing with men from various provinces.[47]

By V-J Day, Wang had studied for two years at a military-run senior high school. He passed an examination to become a warrant officer in the Civilian Service Team, which organized anti-Communist militias. After four months of training, Wang was posted as a political indoctrinator to villages in Jiangsu and Shandong, where the Communists and the Nationalists—including Chen Qingbin and Wang Yingchang's 70th Army from Taiwan—were mired in seesaw battles. Wang Zunming became familiar with Communist methods of control and mobilization. His description of account-settling struggle sessions was strikingly similar to Yu Rongfu's experience in Manchuria. Wang claimed that he saw through the Communists' good discipline and "love the people" act, a veneer over their master plan to demolish the "traditional moral code and loyalties" and substitute loyalty to Mao and the CCP, even before loyalty to one's family.[48]

Wang joined the Nationalist Youth League in 1947 and received further political training in Nanjing in early 1948. Upon graduation, he requested to serve in his native province of Shaanxi and became a company political officer in the 90th Army, Hu Zongnan's crack force. Stationed in southern Shaanxi, Wang claimed that he "thoroughly enjoyed fighting the Communists," especially since the 90th Army initially enjoyed military superiority over the Communists. As the balance of power reversed, Wang's regiment was annihilated in October 1948. Wang escaped and was promoted to company leader. He became a member of the Nationalist Party in 1949, when the regime was on the brink of collapse.

When the PLA finally crushed Hu Zongnan's armies on the Chengdu plain in late December 1949, the 90th Army was one of the last units to surrender. When the commanding general finally ordered his army to surrender on December 27, Wang refused to follow orders and led his men in an attempt to break out, only to be captured by defected Sichuan units—most likely from the 95th Army. After repeated failed attempts to lead his men to escape, he was incarcerated for "seven days and nights in a dark room." Apparently, he was more staunchly anti-Communist than his commanders. As a "die-hard reactionary," his reeducation was destined to be especially intense.

In January 1950, Wang's unit was transferred to Liangshan, where Wang and forty other officers were segregated in a compound not far from their former troops. What the troops experienced was similar to the reform of the Nationalist 95th Army. Initially the unit was not disbanded; only a small team of PLA representatives came to give lectures. Most comforting was that the food was excellent, with "meat everyday—even better than [what] the Communist army" had. In the next two months, however, the PLA officers quietly interviewed individual soldiers and obtained a thorough knowledge of all officers and troops. Then the grievance-airing campaign began. Selected officers were struggled against, and "reactionary elements" were systematically purged.

Officers like Wang were transferred to the Southwest Military and Political University, Liangshan branch, in March. In the first two weeks, students, mostly captured Nationalist officers, were surprised to be "given complete freedom." They conducted their own elections and disciplined themselves; there was "no coercion and no indoctrination." Many students had received little education before, and "they thought now they would get a college education." Even Wang was impressed, "ready to give them the benefit of the doubt and make the best of it." Two weeks later, however, students were divided into smaller classes and the real indoctrination began. After the first few weeks of lectures and discussion on Communist ideology came the grievance-airing movement, during which students were required to engage in self-criticism and mutual criticism. Then they were repeatedly required to write detailed personal histories. They also had to write responses to others' accusations and criticism. All these writings went into their dossiers, which would follow them like a rap sheet.

Initially Wang tried to hide certain aspects of his past, especially regarding the question "How many Communists have you killed?" Although Wang had bayoneted several Communists in battle, he claimed he didn't know if he had killed anyone because all fighting and firing had been at a distance. Instead, he exaggerated the number of prostitutes he had visited and invented incidences of rape, since "the

Communists believed that all Nationalists had committed rape." Under pressure, he even fabricated cases of homosexual acts. In addition, officers always confessed to having killed chickens, ducks, and other domestic animals. Their instructors knew many of these confessions were false, but "they didn't mind because it went on the record and it could be used against a man in the future." The prisoners' tricks did not fool their captors.

Wang's psychological defense finally cracked in April. One day four officers purportedly from his home province came to demand his return to face land reform struggle sessions, which he knew was tantamount to a death sentence. Wang recalled his reaction: "I was struck with a great fear. This was the first time I really realized the danger I was in." He desperately begged the four Shaanxi officers and his instructors to give him a second chance at the university, and asked classmates to speak on his behalf. What eventually saved him, however, was a letter he wrote to his former troops, whom he had earlier led to escape. Now he told them he had totally given up all his old thinking and vowed to become a new man. He urged them to do the same. By doing so, Wang lost all his credibility among his men. He could no longer organize any resistance among his old troops. He had no choice. He had to save his own life first.

Believing that "the school authorities engineered this whole thing," Wang concluded that the Communists were "diabolically clever." By breaking down the resistance of commanding officers, the Communists used them as an example "to educate others in the school and among the troops back in their old units." Soon his troops began criticizing him ruthlessly, and some even made false charges. Wang felt he had fallen into a death trap:

> They wanted physical and mental liquidation of oneself by oneself, so that no one could say they had done it, but rather the person had brought it upon himself by the nature of his previous actions. In this way they could kill without having the victim's blood on their hands.

In June 1950, Wang and the other officers were sent to a hard labor unit in Wan County. No matter how hard he worked, his instructors refused to praise him. As everyone else had been reviewed positively, Wang became frightened, knowing that praise was "insurance that you are secure." In a desperate attempt to rescue himself, instead of carrying his usual load of 50-pound rice bags, he carried the heaviest ones weighing over 150 pounds up the mountain slope, until he collapsed and spat blood. Finally his instructor praised him: "Today you demonstrated the true spirit of the proletariat." Having "won evidence of security," Wang felt relieved. He at last confessed that he had killed a Communist soldier in battle. The instructors accepted this admission as "showing improvement and progressiveness." However, that was not enough. At the end of the three-month indoctrination in Wan County, while a hundred prisoners were released because of their relatively old age, Wang was sent to another location, near Chongqing, for three more months of thought reform.[49]

One may wonder why Wang did not attempt to escape during the nine months of unbearable indoctrination. In fact, none of the three schools Wang attended was walled or fenced, but guards were posted and students were not allowed to leave. The only time they went outside was to attend public trials of class enemies. Had they escaped, they had no money. Their monthly stipend was so small they could not buy more than half a pound of local tobacco. Wang knew of three students who escaped from Liangshan. If caught, Wang believed, they would have been executed.[50] As the Communists tightly controlled all of society, prisoners knew they could not run far before being captured.

Physical punishment, endemic in the Nationalist army, was largely unnecessary since discipline was reinforced by mutual criticism and surveillance. That is not, however, to suggest that the Communists did not use outright violence. In fact, the threat of violence constantly loomed large and occasionally struck hard publicly. Early on in Liangshan, Wang was made to witness the execution of two of his comrades in arms, his former regiment and battalion commanders. When they were put on a show trial before the entire school, all the students had to acknowledge the correctness of the charges and vote for their execution. The Communist officers asked all who voted "yes" to their deaths to raise their hands. "Gradually the hands were raised higher and higher," Wang recalled, "as the leaders on the platform closely watched the actions of everybody. Everyone knew they were condemning their friends to death, but they had no alternative." Then the leaders announced, "You voted their execution." The two men were shot right in front of the group. Wang had to "hold back the tears and smile" during the process. The bodies were buried next to the students' quarters "under only six inches of earth." It was a scene that Wang would never forget.

Wang described his condition throughout his indoctrination, especially the last two schools, as "constant physical and mental exhaustion." There was "never time for relaxed conversation" with anyone, as no one could be trusted. Some men committed suicide, and some went insane. When one of the students in an adjoining class suffered a mental breakdown, the instructor asserted the cause was that "he did not reveal everything in his reactionary past." Despite the nerve-wracking pressure, Wang survived. He claimed, "I fortified myself repeatedly with an old historical story that gave me faith in the future, that made me believe that I could preserve myself, escape Communism, and eventually get revenge."

Indeed, Wang's outward compliance and internal resistance enabled him to survive nine months of brutal indoctrination. In December 1950, Wang and some students were assigned to the PLA 12th Army, while others were sent to Xinjiang to open up the northwestern frontier. Tapping Wang's technical expertise, the PLA made him a drill instructor with a rank equivalent to a platoon leader. In late March 1951, the 12th Army crossed the Yalu River and entered Korea.[51]

Perhaps the experience of Wang Zunming was representative of only a small minority of former Nationalist personnel. Wang fit all the most undesirable labels in Communist society: a reactionary for being the son of a landlord and a Nationalist government official, a counterrevolutionary for being an army officer with the Communists' blood on his hands, and a moral derelict for his rapist and homosexual past (although confessed under duress). In contrast, there were many other former Nationalist personnel, especially enlisted men, who had fewer undesirable labels, or even had good ones. Some had good family origins, such as poor peasants, craftsmen, and workers, or the urban poor. Some were too junior to have killed any Communists. Their experiences under the Communists could be decidedly different. The PLA called these former Nationalist troops "liberated soldiers," and some of them, such as He Rui, truly felt liberated by the Communists.

After their capture in Korea, divergent ideological beliefs compounded by personal hatred escalated into a life-and-death mini–civil war in POW camps. Both Communist and anti-Communist prisoners would build similar organizations and employ similar methods. As many future anti-Communist POW leaders had experienced Communist indoctrination and control methods firsthand, they applied those same methods to control Communist prisoners to crippling effect.

3

Desperados and Volunteers

BEFORE DAWN on November 14, 1950, twenty-two-year-old Guizhou native and former policeman Cheng Liren bade farewell to his parents and left his home village of Xujiaba for the Si'nan County seat ten miles away. He rushed to see his close friend Wen Beihai—a former Nationalist policeman retained by the new Communist regime—and asked him to join the Communist army along with him. The two men went straight to see the PLA commander in the small city and offered themselves for military service. "If you want to join the army, get on the truck right now!" the officer told them, as the unit was decamping. Cheng and Wen climbed onto a truck. Soon the convoy rumbled down the mountain road for Chongqing, 260 miles away. Eight days later, Cheng's unit, the 31st Division, 12th Army, departed from Chongqing for North China. In March 1951, the 12th Army entered Korea. In May Cheng deserted and became a UN prisoner. "Finally, I broke loose from them!" Cheng recalled in a calm, understated voice, sitting in his comfortable home in Buenos Aires, Argentina, in 2014.[1]

A week before Cheng's enlistment, Deng Xiaoping, the top leader of the Southwest Military Region, cabled Mao and the CCP Center, detailing his plan to supply reinforcement troops to Korea: "We will first send three armies replenished to full strength with additional personnel, and three more are to follow."[2] The first three armies—the 12th, 15th, and 60th, then scattered across Sichuan and Guizhou in "bandit-suppression" campaigns—immediately began to withdraw and reassemble. From Guizhou, the 540th Regiment of the 60th Army rushed to its base in Chengdu, and the 91st Regiment of the 12th Army raced back to Chongqing. Cheng Liren's account of joining the PLA on the spot was entirely plausible.

As the Korea-bound armies had to leave behind some personnel for local garrison duties in Sichuan, they absorbed a number of new recruits and "liberated soldiers."[3] Cheng was one of them. At the time, he had no clear idea what the slogan "Resist America and Aid Korea, Protect Our Country and Safeguard Our Home" (*Kangmei yuanchao, baojia weiguo*) entailed.[4] He soon found out: he had become a Chinese People's Volunteer on his way to Korea.

The Chinese People's Volunteers Army

On October 8, 1950, Mao ordered the formation of the Chinese People's Volunteers Army (CPV). The term "volunteer" was a misnomer artfully chosen to camouflage China's strategic intentions and lure the Americans into underestimating China's commitment and strength in Korea. The CPV was made up of PLA units, which retained their designation, but the troops' badges and patches were removed. In the first two Chinese offensives from late October to late November, the CPV achieved near complete surprise, thanks to the massive but surreptitious night movement of a quarter million men into Korea. These troops were no volunteers, as they only learned of their mission days before crossing the Yalu River. Similar strict secrecy rules were also imposed on the second batch of CPV units, the 19th and 3rd Army Groups, which entered Korea in February and March 1951 respectively, and launched the disastrous Fifth Offensive in late April and May. By June, the number of Chinese prisoners soared to 17,182—equivalent to 82 percent of the total number of Chinese POWs in the entire war.[5] Thus, the vast majority of Chinese prisoners came from the first two batches of CPV units. Most of these troops had joined the PLA before the war broke out in June. If they were volunteers in any sense, they had volunteered for the PLA, not the CPV.

CPV troops consisted of PLA veterans, "liberated" former Nationalist troops, and some new recruits. They had no choice but to follow orders. Admittedly, many wrote "patriotic pledges" (*juexinshu*) vowing to resist America and aid Korea, when their officers inspired and pressured them to perform such rituals. When the order came, however, all troops in Korea-bound units, regardless of whether they had made the pledge, had to go. Deserters were severely punished, often dragged along to the front line, as this chapter will show. Therefore, strictly speaking, few of the Chinese prisoners under discussion in this book were volunteers.

The CPV also added new personnel to bring its units up to full strength before entering Korea. To be sure, the Communists' recruitment methods were an improvement over the Nationalists' frequent practice of press-ganging. Nonetheless, deception and implicit coercion were often employed. As two recruits featured in this chapter found out belatedly, "job training" turned out to be a cruel conscription hoax.

Finally, some individuals like Cheng Liren indeed volunteered for the army, regardless of whether their unit was going to Korea. Under the new Communist regime, many similarly desperate individuals joined the army, voluntarily or involuntarily, as the alternatives were even more perilous. For men facing imminent persecution at home, joining the PLA offered a final chance of redemption and survival, even at risk of fighting and dying in Korea. For certain daring individuals, Korea might present a chance to escape. In the first year of the People's Republic, these men had become "enemies of the people." They were desperados in New China.

"Kill Three Per Thousand" in Guizhou

On October 10, two days after Mao ordered the formation of the CPV, he made another equally momentous decision: to launch the Campaign to Suppress Counterrevolutionaries (*zhenfan*). Now three mass campaigns—the anti-American war, land reform, and mass suppression—would go hand in hand. Mao saw the timing as a rare opportunity that "occurred only once in a thousand years" (*qianzai nanfeng*).[6] Freed from earlier inhibitions and restraints, the Communists used the war to accelerate their continuous revolution by liquidating internal enemies, real or imagined.

Counterrevolutionaries were loosely defined as people in one or another of five categories: (1) bandit leaders; (2) secret agents; (3) local despots (*eba*); (4) key personnel (*gugan*) in the Nationalist Party, Youth League, military, government, police, and military police; (5) secret society leaders.[7] In line with the Maoist tradition, none of these terms were clearly defined, leaving much latitude to local officials. Yet for the accused, the consequences could be a matter of life or death. A former minor Nationalist official or low-ranking officer might not qualify as "key personnel" in a large city, but probably would qualify as such in a small town, and definitely would in a village. When the Nationalist government collapsed, many former officials returned to their hometowns or villages to seek refuge, inadvertently offering themselves as counterrevolutionaries, a prize in the eyes of zealous local Communist cadres.

"Our revolution doesn't look like a revolution without killing the counterrevolutionaries," Mao told Luo Ruiqing, the Public Security minister entrusted to run the campaign. "It is necessary to physically liquidate some of them," declared Liu Shaoqi, the CCP's second in command, giving an economic rationale, "so that we can save a little bit of millet." Luo laid out the task: "Specifically speaking, (our program) is to kill people (*sharen*), to kill people according to plan (*youjihua de sharen*)."[8] As Mao was deliberately vague when it came to details, regional leaders were required to come up with killing plans. The southwest under Deng Xiaoping soon reported that nearly 10,000 had been executed and estimated that 20,000 to 30,000 more would be killed.[9] Praising this as "very good," Mao circulated Deng's plan among regional leaders as a model.[10] Thus a terror campaign was underway.

In January 1951, buoyed by the CPV's routing of American forces in Korea, Mao became impatient with the speed and magnitude of domestic killings. "It is time to seize the opportunity presented by the double climaxes of the anti-American [war] and the land reform." He exhorted his underlings to "strike steadily (*wen*), strike accurately (*zhun*), and strike ruthlessly (*hen*)." Provinces that had not killed many should "kill in a big way (*dasha yipi*); must absolutely not stop the killings too early." He added, "the bourgeoisie may howl. Just ignore them."[11] In February, Mao handed down an execution quota of one per thousand persons, "half of which should be killed for starters."[12] A frenzy of killing was unleashed in the ensuing four months.

Zealous cadres at all levels had every incentive to err on the side of excess. The southwestern provinces had killed over 80,000 by the end of March, exceeding the original plan's upper limit of eradicating 30,000 within weeks. As the killing rate quickly approached one per thousand, Deng Xiaoping attempted to rein in the frenzy, but found it difficult as his underlings were "in the heat of killing." Another 50,000 people lost their lives in late March and April.[13] By the end of April, the killing ratio in western and eastern Sichuan, Guizhou, and Xikang had all exceeded two per thousand.[14] By September, the Southwest had killed 160,000, including 10,000 within the PLA, and imprisoned 240,000; the Central-South Military Region under Lin Biao, including Henan, Hubei, Hunan, Jiangxi, Guangdong, and Guangxi provinces, had killed 220,000 and imprisoned 340,000.[15] In terms of killing ratio, the Southwest topped all other five regions (each consisted of several provinces). It repeatedly received lavish praise from Mao for its ruthless efficiency.

In western Sichuan, where the PLA 180th Division was garrisoned until December 1950 when it left for Korea, 17,795 people, or 2.19 per thousand, were killed by April 1951.[16] In Wenjiang Prefecture, where the 538th Regiment was based, the killing ratios in eight out of twelve counties exceeded three per thousand, with some reaching four per thousand. After receiving the order to suspend the killings in late April, one county party secretary, the number one in command, still gave the go-ahead to his police chief: "You can take a look and pick a few [to kill]." In the ensuing three days, fifty-three people were shot by firing squads in seven townships, right before Workers' Day on May 1.[17]

In Guizhou, the number of executed shot up from 500 before August 1950 to 13,143 by March 1951.[18] Yet the provincial leaders requested permission to kill another 20,000 to 25,000, arguing that "unless we kill three per thousand, we are not adhering to the principles of 'strike accurately and ruthlessly.'" Even Mao found it excessive for a province of ten million people. He suggested a compromise: "We can allow them to kill an additional 10,000 or slightly more. So that the ratio is capped at two per thousand." The some 10,000 spared prisoners could be condemned to life imprisonment and hard labor. In the end, Mao conceded that his two-tiered approach was "very cumbersome, not as pleasing and crisp (*shuangkuai*) as 'killing them off' (*shadiao*)."[19]

All in all, by the end of 1953, at least 712,000 people, or 1.24 per thousand of the population, had been killed nationwide.[20] According to a source within China's Public Security Bureau, 75 percent of the killings occurred in the eleven months following October 1950, when more than half a million people were "suppressed."[21] In contrast, during the entire Civil War from 1945 to 1949, the number of PLA troops killed was about 260,000.[22] The Communists took revenge on their enemies, killing twice as many and more.

The Party Center believed all these killings were "completely necessary," proclaimed Luo Ruiqing. He cited Mao: "If we don't chop off (*kandiao*) these Little Chiang Kai-sheks, there will be earthquakes, and we cannot sit securely." Who were the Little Chiang Kai-sheks? In addition to counterrevolutionaries, the Public Security minister also included "bad elements, landlords, rich peasants, and bureaucratic capitalists" as the Communists' enemies, altogether fifty million strong, or one out of every twelve people in China. By 1956 the counterrevolutionary suppression and other campaigns had either killed, or imprisoned, or monitored 10 percent of these enemies, or more than five million people. Among them 770,000, or 1.3 per thousand of a 600 million population, had been executed.[23] Certainly, there was no honeymoon, but only bloodshed in the early years of the PRC.

Against this bloody backdrop, some of the future POWs joined the PLA/CPV in late 1950, voluntarily or involuntarily. Joining the army alone, however, might not have provided much protection. In fact, the PLA was an even more dangerous environment. By April 1951, nationwide 140,000 PLA troops were imprisoned and destined for labor camps.[24] In the southwest alone, 10,000 military personnel had been executed by September 1951. Assuming the troop strength in the region was one million, roughly one out every hundred PLA troops was executed, a killing ratio several times higher than that of the general population.

Only units in the Korea-bound 3rd Army Group escaped the most savage domestic killings in spring 1951, as they had left Sichuan in December 1950 and January 1951. Having escaped the sea of terror, however, they had to face the American "sea of firepower" in Korea in the same spring. Incredibly, some newly enlisted Sichuan and Guizhou natives escaped both carnages and survived.

Cheng Liren: From Policeman to Desperado to Volunteer

Cheng Liren came from "probably the richest family" in Si'nan, a mountainous county in northeastern Guizhou. His grandfather built a successful business trading tung oil, which had become a major export commodity in World War II. After finishing high school in the provincial capital of Guiyang, Cheng was admitted to the Chongqing branch of the Central Police Academy in 1947. With the Nationalist regime crumbling in 1949, the class was given an early graduation in May. Cheng returned to Guizhou and worked as a Nationalist police officer for three months in Zhenyuan County, where his high school teacher had become the county mayor. Before the PLA reached Zhenyuan, Cheng returned home to Si'nan, which soon fell without a fight.[25]

Peace and calm only lasted two months. Popular insurgencies erupted across the southwest immediately following the Chinese New Year in mid-February. Protesting against exorbitant grain taxes, a bewildering mix of groups, including surrendered Nationalist soldiers, local power holders, peasants, bandits, and ethnic minorities, took up arms and attacked Communist cadres and troops. The number of armed "bandits" soon reached 277,000 in the three provinces in the Southwest Military Region (Sichuan, Guizhou, and Yunnan), including 110,000 in Guizhou alone.[26]

The woefully undermanned Communist garrison forces in Guizhou were quickly overrun. By April, insurgents had occupied 31 of the 79 county seats in the province, including Si'nan.[27] Cheng Liren told his UN interrogators in 1951 that he had joined the guerrillas in February 1950 and fought the Communists sporadically for several months, until the insurgents' leader was captured and executed by the PLA in July.[28] In 2014, however, he denied his involvement, adding, "How dare I oppose the Communists?"[29] Probably he did.

According to the *Si'nan Gazetteer*, the Communists were forced to abandon the county in early April. When PLA reinforcements arrived, the first major battle took place in no other place than Xujiaba, Cheng's hometown, resulting in the capture of some two hundred rebels.[30] As Cheng was in town during this period of mass rebellion, it would have been highly unlikely that he, a former Nationalist police officer and the son of a local elite family, could have completely stayed out of the fray.

In fact, the timeline Cheng provided to his American interrogators in Korea closely matches the gazetteer's chronology. Between July and September 1950, the PLA's "iron encirclement" crushed the insurgency, and rebel leaders were killed in three rounds of public executions. By the year's end, in Si'nan alone, 37 "bandit leaders" and 362 followers had been killed in battle or executed; 44 leaders and 2,379 followers were captured. With this, the "bandit suppression" operations had formally come to an end, but the ruthless purge continued unabated. Captured "bandits" were interned, interrogated, indoctrinated, and screened. Curfews were imposed; mass searches and arrests were launched twice in the city. In the countryside, "Peasant Associations" were set up to man checkpoints and hunt escaped "bandits."[31] Under such circumstances, someone like Cheng was unlikely to survive; further resistance would have been suicidal.

When the Campaign to Suppress Counterrevolutionaries was launched in mid-October, Cheng could have been easily labeled a "counterrevolutionary" given his past as a Nationalist police academy graduate and a police officer, and possibly a one-time insurgent. In Si'nan, the first major victim of the campaign was Cheng Tianxiang, the former head of Xujiaba Township, who was shot by a firing squad in public.[32] More shocking news came from neighboring Zhenyuan County, where the mayor, Cheng's former teacher, was executed. "Eight people were shot in one go!" Cheng recalled.[33] In fact, his teacher was only one of the 81 former Nationalist county mayors in Guizhou; all were executed.[34] The Red terror was closing in on Cheng Liren. His remark "how dare I oppose the Communists?" was perhaps an after-the-fact reflection of the overwhelming danger he once faced.

By the end of 1950, the Southwest government announced that 558,000 "bandits" had been "annihilated"—meaning killed or captured—in the three provinces, though the actual number was nearly 850,000. Deng Xiaoping reported to Mao that twenty-five PLA divisions had been mobilized in the first phase of the Bandit Suppression Campaign that focused on Sichuan. In September, four divisions were sent to reinforce Guizhou.[35] One was the 31st Division, which Cheng Liren joined.

When Cheng and Wen climbed onto the army truck in early November 1950—one month after the terror campaign was launched—they escaped the probable fate of being killed as "counterrevolutionaries." Wen, the holdover policeman, had "realized that he was in a precarious position." Cheng concluded, they "had no alternative but to volunteer" for the PLA. In fact, they barely escaped. Years later, Cheng learned from his family that less than one hour after his departure from home, the local Communists came to search for him. "If you had left one hour later, you wouldn't have made it," he was told.[36]

As a former Nationalist captain, Wang Zunming had realized death was almost certain if someone with a counterrevolutionary history was taken back to his hometown to face a mass trial. The only way out was to redeem oneself in the PLA. Similarly, Cheng Liren saw joining the army as his last hope. He did not know if he would be sent to Korea; in fact, he did not have the time to think about it. He had to leave immediately. By joining the army, at the minimum he could escape local persecution. If he was lucky, he might have a chance to redeem himself through good service. Finally, there might be a chance, albeit remote, of escape.

Yang Shuzhi: From Paratrooper to Escapee to Truck Driver

Also in November 1950, twenty-eight-year-old Yang Shuzhi was summoned to take a driver's test in Chongqing, the capital of the Southwest Military Region. He started the engine and pushed the accelerator, but the truck jerked and stalled. "Have you ever driven before?" asked the visibly irritated examiner. Yang said no. "If so, why are you here to take the test?" Yang replied, "The police commissar told me to come." He was motioned off the truck. As he walked out of the testing ground, Yang ran into

Zhao Mingyu, a former comrade in the Nationalist airborne unit and now a PLA driver. Zhao asked: "Yang Xinlin, you didn't go to Taiwan?" Yang Shuzhi was none other than Yang Xinlin, the paratrooper who had flown to Guangzhou to receive the Japanese surrender in September 1945. Five years later, Yang had assumed a new name and a new identity.[37]

Yang's paratrooper unit left Guangzhou in late September 1945 and was stationed for two months in Shenzhen, then a tiny village on the border with Hong Kong. Later the unit moved to Kowloon and waited for two months before embarking for Nanjing via Shanghai in early 1946.[38] In 1947, the Nationalists combined the airborne and armored units to create the Rapid Force (*Kuaisu zongdui*), which fought a series of losing battles against the Communist forces in southern Shandong, northern Jiangsu, and Henan.[39]

In early 1948, Yang was transferred to the Ministry of Defense's Second Bureau (G-2 intelligence). He received advanced wireless training one-on-one in a secret location near Sun Yat-sen's mausoleum, where the trainees were required to wear masks to hide their identity on those rare occasions when they saw each other. In August, Yang was promoted to captain and posted to the Advanced Headquarters (HQ) of the Nationalist forces in Xuzhou, the epicenter of the looming Huaihai Campaign. When the final showdown began in early November, Yang was dispatched to General Huang Baitao's 7th Army Group, which soon came under siege. Tormented by the sight of his army of 100,000 men being annihilated by overwhelming PLA forces, General Huang committed suicide on November 22.

Wearing civilian clothes and claiming to be truck drivers, Captain Yang and another wireless operator surrendered to the PLA. A friendly female commissar invited the two "drivers" to join her for lunch. Afterwards, she immediately put their skills to work by having them fix captured vehicles. Yang scavenged for parts and soon got a jeep running again. The cadre was overjoyed, and POW Yang became her chauffeur. Two days later, Yang and his fellow "driver" escaped south under the cover of darkness.

Once back in Nanjing, Yang found that the Ministry of Defense had already decamped. He joined a Nationalist training regiment, which was soon incorporated into the Temporary 1st Army. When the PLA poured across the Yangtze River in late April, his new outfit was guarding Chongming Island at the mouth of the Yangtze. In an eleventh-hour withdrawal, much of the army boarded ships for Taiwan.[40] Yang was one of those unlucky souls stuck behind.

When he returned to Nanjing, Yang, completely oblivious of Communist ideology and policy, bought a used truck and started a transportation business. Having completed only two round trips to Hangzhou, he was arrested by the Communists for "illegal profiteering." After spending two days in jail writing detailed autobiographical confessions, Yang was brought to the interrogation room. He was astonished to meet the police chief—who was the squatter that had lived in his courtyard house in Nanjing, claiming to be a refugee from northern Jiangsu. Out of sympathy, Yang had let the man and his teenage daughter stay for free and twice bailed him out when he was arrested by the Nationalist police for stirring up riots. Yang had been fooled all along.

"Your confession is not thorough enough," the police chief sternly said. After a long pause, he asked: "What about this? Do you want to go back to your hometown?" Yang nodded yes. A travel permit had been prepared. It read: "Former Chiang Kai-shek Army Captain Yang Xinlin is permitted to travel from Nanjing to his hometown in Cangxi, Sichuan. Please allow safe passage."[41] In a rare display of sentimentalism, this former Communist underground agent repaid Yang's kindness, letting a Nationalist officer off the hook. His truck, of course, became state property.

Yang and his nephew began their thousand-mile journey to the west in the fall of 1949, coinciding with the Liu-Deng 2nd Field Army's campaign to "liberate" the southwest. After trekking for two weeks, they reached Changde, Hunan, where a truck carrying student recruits of the Southwest Service Corps had broken down. Offering his help, Yang got the truck fixed. Then the women cadres asked him to drive the truck for the group. They reached Chongqing in early December, shortly after its "liberation."[42] Yang did not proceed to Cangxi immediately, as the PLA 60th Army had just launched an attack on northern Sichuan from Shaanxi.

When he finally returned home after the Chinese New Year, Yang hid in the countryside for two weeks. His elder cousin, an MP (military police) officer who had enlisted him in 1940, had been arrested, tortured, and driven to commit suicide by jumping into a river. His uncle, the Nationalist officer who had helped him enroll in the Whampoa Academy, had been brought back from Chengdu and executed. Too many people knew his past. He could become the next victim.

His mother sought help from another of his cousins, who had joined the Communist underground and was now the deputy county head. The cousin produced a travel permit for Yang with a new name—"Yang Shuzhi"—and a new occupation, "driver." With his past wiped clean, Yang was a new man.

Yang immediately left Cangxi for Chongqing, a large city where few people knew him. Being carefree and ignorant of Communist ideology, Yang invested all his money in a small garment factory and became a "capitalist," unwittingly adding another potential "crime" on top of his Nationalist past. Under the new regime, everyone had to register with the police and a detailed dossier was created. After Mao made the decision to enter the Korean War, a nationwide campaign to mobilize drivers began. "Comrade Yang, you should take this driver's test," the local police officer told him, claiming that the Southwest Transportation Bureau was hiring. Yang, however, was suspicious. So he faked clumsiness and failed the test. On his way out, he ran into his former comrade Zhao from the World War II days. "This test is not for 'Resist America and Aid Korea'!"

insisted Zhao, now a PLA driver. "In fact," he added, "you're are not qualified to join the People's Volunteers, even if you wanted to!" Zhao took the hesitant Yang back to retake the exam. Driving a ten-wheel GMC truck was effortless for Yang, who had first learned from the Americans in Ramgarh, India, in 1944. The examiner gave him a score of 95 percent and remarked, "Earlier you acted really well."

As it turned out, the unit Yang joined was the Southwest Military Region's Technical Corps, a semi-military organization with more than two hundred newly recruited drivers. Although strictly speaking they were not soldiers, they were confined to their training ground and living quarters, a requisitioned ancestral hall in the town of Lijiatuo, a few miles west of Chongqing. They were allowed only half a day off—from noon to five in the afternoon on Sundays. As buses were few and unreliable, Yang often ended up walking to Chongqing to meet his girlfriend, a two-hour journey each way.

The Sunday before the Chinese New Year (February 6, 1951), driver Chen Yulin returned to the unit two hours late. A struggle meeting was staged immediately. Brushing aside Chen's explanation that he had missed the bus, the commissar challenged him, "In that two extra hours, you could have robbed a bank or contacted enemy agents!" Then Chen's disreputable past was dug out and paraded. A dozen fellow drivers attacked Chen; no one spoke up for him. The accused was unable to prove his innocence. Without any evidence, the commissar charged Chen with "contacting enemy agents" and asked the crowd: "What should we do with him?" Several activists, party members, and probational party members raised their arms, shouting *qiangbi!* (have him shot). Under the stern watch of the commissar, who was taking careful notes, all two hundred drivers raised their hands, one by one, to support Chen's execution. "I raised my hand, too," Yang recalled. "I had no choice."

Soon after dawn the next morning, Chen was declared a counterrevolutionary in a mass trial and dragged to the bank of the Yangtze River. A PLA rifleman took aim at the back of his head only three feet away and killed him instantly. His body was tossed into a nearby pit that had been freshly dug. Made to watch the scene, Yang was unfazed. Having witnessed executions of bandits in Cangxi when he was a child, and experienced carnage in Burma and the Civil War, he coolly observed that "the Nationalist executioners usually aimed at the heart from the back, but the Communists shot in the back of the head." Nevertheless, he sensed that the killing was a precursor to events in Korea: "The Communists were killing one to dissuade a hundred" from deserting. In fact, Yang and his girlfriend had discussed escaping to Hong Kong.

As Yang had feared, a few days after Chen's execution, his unit was ordered to "immediately go to Beijing to receive new Russian-made trucks and drive them back." When their train reached Beijing, however, it did not stop; instead, it sped all the way to Shenyang, Manchuria. The drivers finally reached Andong on the Yalu River, where they received the new trucks. On March 2, Yang's unit drove into Korea. On April 14, he and several other drivers would surrender to the UN side near Kaesong. He would become one of the earliest anti-Communist leaders in the UN prison camps.

Undeniably, Yang Shuzhi felt cheated by the Communists. He had to admit, however, that his conscription had probably saved his life and given him a chance to escape. Had he stayed in his hometown or Chongqing, he could hardly have survived the terror campaign. In late 1950, the Cangxi government uncovered an alleged regional headquarters of the Sino-American Cooperative Organization (SACO), an intelligence agency co-established by the Office of Strategic Services (OSS) and Chiang Kai-shek's secret police. More than fifty people were arrested.[43] Yang would have made a perfect suspect.

Li Da'an: Insurgent, Prisoner, Escapee, and Truck Driver

Li Da'an, who later became known as the "devil incarnate" and was probably the most notorious anti-Communist Korean War prisoner, had little choice but to serve as a driver in February 1951. Born in Andong, Liaoning, in 1927, Li had four and a half years of education under the Japanese occupation, and began working as a truck driver in 1943. When the Soviet forces transferred Andong to the Communists in late 1945, Li joined anti-Communist guerrillas. In 1946, the Nationalist forces took Andong, and Li resumed his work as a chauffeur and truck driver. In summer 1947, Li followed the retreating Nationalists to Shenyang. Later he decided to return to join his wife and daughter in Andong. Although he had received a covert agent assignment from the Nationalists, he had not initiated any contact in Andong before his arrest in July 1948.[44]

As he readily confessed, Li initially was not beaten. Before long, however, his captors charged him with hiding a gun. Li was "suspended in mid-air" and "beaten half dead" (*siquhuolai*) several times. He asked his wife to bring him poison so that he could commit suicide, but she refused. He tried to hang himself with his belt, but his cellmate stopped him. He was sent to another prison, where he "never ate his fill" for six months, subsisting on nothing but vegetables and soybean cake (*doubing*), the leftovers from extracting oil and normally used as animal fodder. Corporal punishment was frequently meted out for frivolous infractions, such as taking too long to relieve himself or not speaking loudly enough to the wardens. After two years in prison, Li was finally released in September 1950, but could not find a job under the new regime.

Soon Li was conscripted as a civilian truck driver for the CPV. After completing four trips to the Chosin Reservoir in Korea, Li deserted and wandered to Shenyang. Unable to find a job, he had no choice but to return to the truck unit.[45] Li recrossed the Yalu River on February 27, 1951, and defected on March 24. Once in UN prison camps, Yang and Li would become the founding leaders of the first anti-Communist POW organization.[46] The Communists had underestimated these truck drivers.

Victims of Hoax: Rich and Poor Peasants

To be sure, the Chinese Communists did not press-gang men into military service as the Nationalists did. They recruited soldiers with great finesse and propaganda fanfare, promising material benefits and bestowing honor on the recruit and his family. In many cases, however, the threat of coercion was ever present. Prospective recruits often had no alternative but to join the army. Moreover, to fulfill their conscription quota, local cadres also employed various dubious methods to dragoon young men into the army.

One of the most fabled, and resented, recruitment hoaxes employed a "hot earthen bed." In much of North China, the heated earthen bed (*kang*) was the place where a peasant family slept at night and ate and socialized during the day, especially in winter. During recruitment drives, cadres summoned young men to meetings without telling them the exact purpose. Sitting on warm earthen beds, candidates were served sweetened hot water, a treat for villagers. After a couple of rounds, the cadres announced that now it was their precious chance to volunteer for the army. Usually, no one volunteered. However, the earthen bed became increasingly hot, as other cadres kept adding fuel to the stove. As the villagers' buttocks were being burned and their bladders were about to burst, the first person who moved his butt or raised his hand to ask for permission to relieve himself would be immediately applauded by the cadres, and fellow villagers, for "volunteering to join the army."[47] The hapless and helpless young man unwittingly became a "volunteer."

While there were no earthen beds in South China, Communist cadres came up with other inventive hoaxes, as Sichuanese Huang Changrong and Zhejiang native Jin Yuankui discovered.

Huang Changrong was born in 1930 in Anyue County in central Sichuan. As the eldest child among four siblings in a peasant family, he had to quit school after the sixth grade to work on the farm. His family owned some land, but also rented rice paddies from a landlord, who was friendly and reasonable, as Huang recalled. Rural life was strenuous, but the Huangs had achieved a modicum of success—they had a spacious courtyard and could afford meat occasionally—which would earn them the class label of "rich peasant" under the Communists. Despite the chaos in the last days of Nationalist rule, Huang was spared the draft. This was because his two brothers were very young, and thus the rule of "one draftee out of three eligible males" in a family did not apply.

After the arrival of the Communists, however, Huang was made to join the militia. "It was impossible to resist," he recalled. "Dozens of PLA troops were billeted in our house, and the cadres nagged me about joining their work team day and night." When he still refused, they told him, "You'll be drafted by the army and go far away." He relented. Since the local militia job was full-time but unpaid, the family actually lost out financially.[48]

In November 1950, cadres had Huang undergo three months of "training" in a neighboring county, promising a job in the local government afterward. Once the candidates reached the town of Tongliang, they were locked in a stone turret and ordered to shed their civilian clothes for PLA uniforms. "I realized I was entrapped by the Communists!" Huang broke into tears. On the third night, Huang pretended he was going to the latrine and escaped, but was caught half a mile down the road. Some other escapees were lucky enough to make it home, but were soon apprehended and returned by the local authorities. "No one could escape," Huang reflected.[49] Any attempt to escape was futile under the Communist regime, where surveillance and mutual surveillance were ubiquitous and travel restrictions were near watertight—something unimaginable under the Nationalists or in a Western society.

The PLA scattered the local draftees, including Huang, in the 180th Division, 60th Army—a practice similar to that experienced by Taiwanese Chen Yonghua under the Nationalists. During the army's thousand-mile move from Sichuan to Hebei, the Sichuanese were at first watched by northerner veterans. Once in North China, the southerners were assigned to monitor the northerners.[50] Stationed in villages in Qing County, Huang's unit feasted frequently and ostentatiously, gobbling up dumplings, pork, and vermicelli before the jealous eyes of the villagers, who could rarely afford meat. "It was a trick to lure the villagers into volunteering for the army," Huang reckoned. He was equally unmoved by "revolutionary comradely acts" of officers and activists, including some "liberated soldiers," such as carrying extra loads for him on marches or washing and rubbing his blistered feet with hot water at night.

Instead, Huang was disgusted by the nightly two-hour squad meetings, where all twelve members had to engage in endless self-criticism and mutual criticism, and competed to report selfless acts that sometimes bordered on the absurd. For example, one soldier got up at three in the morning to carry water from the well to fill the vat of his billet host. Soldiers were not allowed to chat in private, as everything had to be discussed "in the open" in meetings. Feeling cheated, suffocated, and homesick, Huang often shed tears at night. He wrote many letters to his parents, as the PLA encouraged troops to write home. But all envelopes had to be left unsealed and submitted to superiors to be mailed, supposedly. None of his letters reached home, as Huang found out four decades later.[51] In fact, a Communist officer admitted that encouraging troops, especially former Nationalists, to write letters home was a method to verify their home addresses and to see if they had lied about their past.[52]

Resentful of the Communists' deception and control, the apolitical Huang would later join the first batch of prisoners in Korea to tattoo anti-Communist slogans on their own bodies—an act tantamount to signing one's own death warrant in the event of repatriation. In nabbing Huang the CPV managed to add a "volunteer," but utterly failed to win his allegiance.

About a thousand miles to the east in Shaoxing, Zhejiang, the birthplace of leftist literary icon Lu Xun, Jin Yuankui was born in 1930 to a poor peasant family. During the Japanese occupation, Jin's mother died giving birth to his sister. Soon after V-J Day, his father died of illness, leaving him and his sister orphaned. Jin began working for a landlord tending cattle at the age of ten, and at seventeen he became a hired long-term farmhand (*changgong*).[53] If Huang Changrong hailed from a "rich peasant" family, Jin fit the Chinese Communist definition of a member of the rural proletariat, the very people the CCP sought to liberate. Jin, however, shared Huang's revulsion.

After the "liberation," like Huang, Jin was pressured to join the militia. Wearing a red armband, Jin had to stand guard during mass trials, which usually ended in a summary execution. Former Nationalist officials and landlords were paraded onto a stage and forced to kneel before hundreds or thousands of people, their heads bowed and their hands tied behind their backs. After denouncing their crimes, the leading Communist cadres invariably asked the crowd: "What should we do with these criminals?" Planted activists immediately raised their arms, shouting, "Have them shot!" Then the entire crowd called for execution. The accused were dragged off the stage and shot immediately nearby. "That's what they called 'the people's will,'" Jin recalled. "It was such a sham."[54]

Jin can never forget the trial of the former township head and his wife, and three other men. After the PLA firing squad shot them, the masses were told to take a closer look at the killed "for their education." Jin walked over and saw a horrific scene: their heads had exploded, and their brains were splattered all over. Only the woman was spared this gruesome death—she was shot in the heart. "They were all shot at point-blank range," Jin explained. "The Communists told us that to kill one person, they only use one bullet. Two would be a waste." Jin was sickened. He went home, nauseated and unable to eat. He pleaded with his commander not to assign him to public trial duties again. He wanted to quit. "Although the Communists treated me fairly well," Jin recalled, "I was disgusted by their killings. I disagreed with them, but I dared not speak out."

When the Communists completed their terror campaign and carried out land reform, they sent Jin to the city for further training, promising him a job. On Chinese New Year's Eve, February 5, 1951, he was sent off to a collection point, where recruits underwent a health check. After roll call the next morning, they were trucked away. Realizing that the training was a hoax and they had been drafted, some began to weep. Several married men escaped, only to be brought back soon. Jin was resigned to his fate. He took the last chance to go to a local temple, kowtowed to the Bodhisattva, and made a pledge: "As a soldier, I will do good deeds and not abuse civilians."

A week later, Jin and the other conscripts boarded trains in Shaoxing and embarked on a five-day journey to Manchuria. Jin was one of the 10,000 recruits from East China transported to Korea to replenish the CPV 9th Army Group.[55] During their training near Andong, Jin hated the nightly squad meetings, where each soldier had to speak. On one occasion, Jin refused to talk; so did other recruits. Calling them "sons of bitches," their squad leader threatened, "If you don't talk, you don't eat." Jin and the other recruits kept their heads down, said nothing, and did not eat. Jin felt deceived, especially since "even the Nationalists did not conscript me, an orphan."

Tan Xingdong: Veteran Communist, Deserter, and Future Traitor

Born in northern Jiangsu in 1923, Tan Xingdong joined the local Communist forces in 1941, but soon deserted. Half a year later, he "was picked up" and reassigned to another unit. In 1942, his unit marched to Shandong and was integrated into the Communist New 4th Army's 2nd Division. After V-J Day, his unit departed for Jilin Province in Manchuria in September 1945, and later became part of the PLA 38th Army, the "Tiger Army," the best of the best under General Lin Biao's command. It swept from the northeast all the way to Guangxi in the southwest in 1949. Tan was promoted to assistant battalion commander in August 1950.[56] His future looked bright.

Tan, however, had a track record of "thought problems," which had first manifested in his desertion in 1941–1942. Between June and July 1946, Tan was "given a special indoctrination lecture because of [his] hostile attitude toward Communist doctrine." On August 9, 1950, Tan "went AWOL, after receiving news his rich parents were killed by the Communists." He was captured at home in Jiangsu the next month and was escorted to Manchuria. By the time he reached Manchuria, his unit had crossed the Yalu. "Still under guard," Tan "headed south to catch up with his outfit." After passing through Pyongyang and Seoul, he finally rejoined his unit in February 1951, but was demoted to assistant platoon leader. Soon Tan led three men to defect near Seoul on March 12, 1951.[57] Citing the persecution he and his family had suffered, Tan became the most effective anti-Communist propagandist in the POW camps.

Nationalist Past, Class, or Other Explanations?

To account for the lopsided outcome of repatriation choices that favored Chiang Kai-shek and the Nationalists in Taiwan, one common but specious explanation is that most of the Chinese prisoners were former Nationalist troops captured by the Communists and integrated into the PLA during the Civil War. They were sent to Korea as cannon fodder. Naturally, it is often supposed, these former Nationalist soldiers would attempt to escape from Communism.

Undoubtedly, the CPV contained a large number of former Nationalist troops. Wang Shunqing, an anti-Communist prisoner leader, claimed that as many as 80 percent of the men in his unit—the 354th Regiment, 40th Army—had served in the Nationalist army.[58] Premier Zhou Enlai reported that for the PLA as a whole, the ratio had reached 65 to 70 percent in early 1949 and grew to 70 to 80 percent by June 1950.[59] Among the prisoners eventually sent to Taiwan, two-thirds (66.7 percent) had once served in the Nationalist army.[60]

As we have seen, past Nationalist affiliation did not necessarily lead a soldier to identify with the Nationalists, nor did it dictate a prisoner's future repatriation choice in the POW camps in Korea. Many former Nationalist officers, such as Wang Zunming, were unmoved by Communist indoctrination and remained anti-Communist deep down; by contrast, some others came to favor the Communists. Likewise, former Whampoa cadets experienced indoctrination differently and made divergent repatriation choices. While many former Nationalist foot soldiers, especially those from poor families, such as He Rui, were attracted to the Communists, others remained unmoved, and some became embittered.

In fact, a divergence in attitudes toward the Communist regime was common in other groups as well. Many educated youths were attracted to the Communists because of their discipline, purposefulness, and efficiency; others were appalled by thought control and the loss of individual freedom. While most Communist officers had no choice but to remain faithful to the party, a small number became disillusioned and looked for an opportunity to escape. Therefore, Nationalist affiliation did not predetermine one's ideological inclination or repatriation choice.

Class is another plausible explanation. To a certain degree, class was a major factor influencing one's attitude toward the regime. Rich peasants, landlords, and capitalists were more likely to suffer under the Communists. People of the "exploiting classes" and "counterrevolutionaries" were the first to be persecuted, often brutally. Although service in the Communist army did provide some protection for the individual soldier, it did not prevent one's family from being struggled against at home. If a soldier's or officer's family were persecuted and family members killed in land reform or other political campaigns, naturally he would doubt and resent, if not hate, the Communists. Wang Zunming's case was among the most extreme.

In practice, the Communists carried out land reform and other political campaigns in various locations on different schedules. Before the troops went into Korea in 1950 and early 1951, some landlord families, especially those in the south, had not yet suffered severe persecution. Even if they had, news would not have reached their sons in the army quickly and easily. For example, Yan Tianzhi, a refugee student who had no choice but to join the PLA, had lost contact with his landlord family since late 1949. As a PLA soldier, he was dispatched to carry out land reform in villages in Sichuan, where he witnessed the torture and execution of landlords and their family members. He assumed the same thing must be happening to his family in neighboring Hubei. Once captured in Korea, he decided not to return to Communist China.[61]

Certain violent methods employed by the Communists not only alienated people of the "exploiting classes," but also some of the "exploited classes." The cases of Huang Changrong and Jin Yuankui demonstrate that individuals' judgments were not necessarily dictated by their class, as class itself was a constructed concept that required much indoctrination to take hold, and class labels were often arbitrarily given. In a sense, Huang and Jin saw the diabolic side of the Communists, and so they wanted to escape. That was probably true for many prisoners who later emerged as anti-Communists.

Therefore, in addition to the early victims of class struggle or political suppression—landlords, rich peasants, and "counterrevolutionaries"—individuals of other class backgrounds could also be alienated by Communist programs and methods. They did not identify with the Communists and they wished to escape. The Korean War gave them such an opportunity.

In contrast, most young people had lived under the Communists only for a year or so and had not yet experienced or witnessed the brutal side of Communist rule. To young people from poor families such as Zhong Junhua and Cai Pingsheng, Communism meant that the poor could finally enjoy dignity, respect, and security. To idealistic youths like Zhang Zeshi, Communism promised a stronger China. To propaganda soldier Lin Mocong, Communism was songs, plays, and music. They had witnessed mostly the best side of the Communists and saw their future in China. When captured in Korea, they became pro-Communist activists in the POW camps and strenuously fought to return home.

4

Chiang, MacArthur, Truman, and NSC-81/1

CHIANG KAI-SHEK, accompanied by his son Ching-kuo and a small entourage, evacuated his temporary headquarters in the Whampoa Building at the Central Military Academy in Chengdu at 2:00 p.m. on December 10, 1949. Chiang boarded his C-54 *Sino-American* for Taiwan, leaving behind more than 900,000 Nationalist troops in Sichuan, including some 10,000 Whampoa cadets. Without radio guidance, his pilots managed to fly the plane to Taiwan by "dead reckoning."[1] Beneath the dark clouds, Chiang saw the vast territory that had been taken over by the Communists: Sichuan, Guizhou, Hunan, Guangdong, and Fujian. Chengdu, the Nationalists' last bastion on the mainland, finally fell on December 27. As Whampoa cadet Yu Rongfu observed, the Chiang Kai-shek era had truly come to an end.

"Fate of Taiwan Sealed"

Yu Rongfu was not alone in coming to terms with the end of the Chiang era; many governments were also ready to write Chiang off as a thing of the past. India recognized the newly founded PRC on December 30, 1949. On January 5, 1950, US President Harry S. Truman announced the US government's hands-off policy on Taiwan, stating that his government "will not provide military aid or advice to Chinese forces on Formosa" and "will not pursue a course which will lead to involvement in the civil conflict in China."Emphasizing that the United States "has no predatory designs on Formosa," Truman in effect assured Beijing that it would not intervene if the Communists invaded Taiwan.[2]

On the same day, Secretary of State Dean Acheson rebuffed Senator William F. Knowland's call for the United States to defend Taiwan, maintaining that "Formosa was not of vital importance from a strategic standpoint." Adding insult to injury, Acheson promised that Washington would "continue to supply the needs of the island for fertilizer and to carry on the rural rehabilitation program." However, "anything further than that by way of increased military assistance or military advice is regarded as unnecessary on our part and would be defeative of the principles of non-intervention."[3]

On January 6, the British government declared its recognition of the PRC as the de jure government of China and made clear its readiness to establish diplomatic relations.[4] Facing this stark reality, Chiang believed that Washington would "certainly follow suit" and recognize Beijing. In that event, "the Chinese Communists would certainly join the UN without preconditions, and our representatives would be expelled from the international community." He lamented, that outcome "had been decided" (*yidingzhiju*).[5]

These developments had come as no surprise to Chiang. He saw them as additional steps taken by the Truman-Acheson administration to "destroy Chiang and sell out China" (to the Russians) (*hui Jiang mai Hua*), a refrain that dominated his diary entries in the tumultuous years between 1948 and 1953. However, his most vehement resentment was reserved for General George C. Marshall. Chiang painfully recalled that in spring 1946, when Nationalist elite forces were poised to crush Communist general Lin Biao's troops near Harbin, Marshall demanded an immediate cease-fire, threatening to end American aid.[6] In Chiang's mind, that had been the final opportunity to defeat the Communists militarily.

To get Chiang's government to reform, Washington had repeatedly threatened it with an arms embargo and suspension of economic aid. Although these policies succeeded in pressuring Chiang to back down, at least temporarily, Washington failed to achieve any of its major policy objectives, including its wishful goal of forging a Nationalist-Communist coalition government. Following a series of Nationalist military debacles, Washington ratcheted up the pressure to depose Chiang. "Chiang Kai-shek or American aid" became the stark choice. In January 1949, Chiang stepped down from the presidency, relinquishing the position to Vice President Li Zongren. Chiang, however, retained de facto control over the military and the Nationalist Party. Acting President Li's peace appeals were ignored by the victorious Communists. In late April the PLA crossed the Yangtze River and took Nanjing. Although the Nationalist government had fled to Guangzhou, US ambassador John Leighton Stuart remained in Nanjing for another three months, until early August—a curious contrast to the Soviet Union's removal of its embassy to Guangzhou with the Nationalist government. Apparently, Washington was trying to forge ties with the Communists while preparing to abandon the Nationalists.

Sensing China's imminent fall to the Communists, Truman and Acheson authorized the compilation of the *China White Paper, August 1949*, an attempt to counter Republican criticism by arguing that the Nationalists' defeat could not be attributed to US policy. One year earlier, Secretary of State Marshall had rejected the very idea of issuing a white paper on the grounds that it would amount to a coup de grâce for Chiang, but now his successor Acheson proceeded to sound the death knell: "The unfortunate but inescapable fact is that the ominous result of the Civil War in China was beyond the control of the government of the United States." Acknowledging the Soviet Union's influence, Acheson asserted, "In this case, however, the foreign domination has been masked behind the façade of a vast crusading movement which apparently has seemed to many Chinese to be wholly indigenous and national." Therefore, the fall of China to Communism "was the product of internal Chinese forces, forces which this country tried to influence but could not." He concluded: "The Nationalist armies did not have to be defeated; they disintegrated. History has proved again and again that a regime without faith in itself and an army without morale cannot survive the test of battle."[7] Making such claims, the US government was attempting to wash its hands of the Nationalist defeat and lay all the blame on Chiang Kai-shek, who was to be remembered as "the man who lost China."

The *White Paper* had predicted, and perhaps also precipitated, the fall of the entire mainland to the Communists. In November 1949, Acting President Li fled to the United States for "medical treatment." On December 10, Chiang Kai-shek fled Chengdu for Taipei. In his refuge in Taiwan, Chiang was despairing. "A state of anarchy befell our government, military, party, and society," he lamented. "From any perspective, the future of our [Nationalist] revolution was absolutely hopeless. There was no way out for the nation and the people but to wait to die."[8] Against this grim backdrop, Chiang resumed the presidency on March 1, 1950, and took a number of measures to reform the Nationalist Party and government.

Chiang's formal return to power won him neither friends nor influence in Washington. On March 7, 1950, Acheson wrote to Secretary of Defense Louis A. Johnson to interdict a shipment of twenty-five M-4 Sherman tanks and twenty-five F-80 fighter jets to Taiwan. Even though the jets would be paid for by the Nationalist government with its own funds, Acheson offered a rather tenuous rationale, citing British concern about "the possibility that such equipment might fall into the hands of the Chinese Communists through defection or capture and thus be available for use . . . against Hong Kong."[9] It was as if the British had the will to put up a fight to defend Hong Kong. As John Foster Dulles, the Republican then serving as a special advisor to the State Department, later observed, the British government had "its tongue in its cheek," although its leaders "appeared to feel that their position in Hong Kong was immune so long as they could persuade the Chinese Communists that they were trying to get Formosa back for them."[10] Apparently, the British were ready to sell Chiang out.

The situation in Taiwan continued to deteriorate, as observed by US intelligence operatives. Although the CIA did not rule out the possibility of a "somewhat longer survival" of the Nationalist regime, an appraisal it made in March 1950 concluded that the fall of Taiwan before the end of 1950 "still seems the most likely course of future developments." In late April, the Nationalist forces abandoned Hainan Island in the face of an overpowering PLA invasion. "Each mainlander now believes the days of Taiwan are numbered, that loss . . . of Taiwan is matter of time," US chargé d'affaires in Taipei Robert C. Strong reported to Washington.[11]

In mid-May, taking the Communists by surprise, Chiang Ching-kuo administered a well-planned and orderly retreat from the Zhoushan Archipelago off the coast of Zhejiang Province, thus effectively reduced Taiwan's exposure to attack. Strong interpreted the situation quite differently, coldly concluding that the "fate of Taiwan [is] sealed, [a] Communist attack can occur between June 15 and end July."[12] Two days later, the State Department decided to issue an evacuation notice to American citizens in Taiwan by registered mail.[13] Charles M. Cooke, a retired US admiral and Chiang Kai-shek's private advisor, received his evacuation notice dated May 22, which "strongly advise[d]" Americans "to withdraw as soon as possible," as "there can be no assurance that the United States Government will be able to provide transportation facilities in any emergency that may arise."[14]

While the Americans were making their exit, Washington did not completely forget its erstwhile ally. "It will not leave a good taste if we allow our political problems to be solved by the extermination of our war allies," reasoned Dean Rusk, the assistant secretary of state for Far Eastern Affairs. "That was the Russian solution of General Bor's Polish Army," Rusk quipped, referring to the German massacre of Polish non-Communist resistance fighters in Warsaw in 1944, during which Stalin's armies stood by and watched the carnage from outside.[15] Washington certainly did not relish the thought of seeing Chiang captured by the Communists. But instead of offering him refuge in America, the State Department sounded out the Philippines. President Quirino flatly said that Chiang would not be welcome; his foreign minister added that if Chiang came to the Philippines he would be given 24 hours to get out.[16]

What options were left? After lengthy discussions among State Department officials, UN trusteeship emerged as the preferred solution: "The Gimo [Generalissimo] would be approached, probably by Dulles in the course of his trip to Japan on June 15, with the word that (a) the fall of Formosa in the present circumstances was inevitable, (b) the US would do nothing to assist Gimo in preventing this, (c) the only course open to the Gimo to prevent the bloodshed of his people was to request UN trusteeship."[17] In a nutshell, "Chiang Kai-shek or American aid" was the only choice, once again. Chiang's fate seemed sealed.

Dulles flew to Tokyo on June 21, but he never made the ultimatum-delivery trip to Taiwan. On June 25, North Korea attacked the South.

God-Sent Korean War

Hours after the outbreak of the Korean War, the UN Security Council unanimously passed Resolution 82, condemning the North Korean aggression. This result was enabled by the Soviet representative's absence, ostensibly in protest over the Chinese Nationalists' seat in the UN. On June 27, Truman announced the United States had decided to intervene in Korea under the aegis of the UN, effectively declaring war without congressional approval. He also called for the "neutralization" of Taiwan.

> I have ordered the Seventh Fleet to prevent any attack on Formosa. As a corollary of this action, I am calling on the Chinese Government on Formosa to cease all air and sea operations against the mainland. The Seventh Fleet will see that is done. The determination of the future status of Formosa must await the restoration of security in the Pacific, a peace settlement with Japan, or consideration by the United Nations.[18]

While pro-Chiang American officials, including Secretary of Defense Johnson, lauded the deployment of the Seventh Fleet, the Nationalists' reaction to Truman's statement was mixed. There were misgivings about the restrictions on Nationalist military actions against the mainland. More importantly, Truman's reference to "the future status" of Taiwan amounted to a glaring challenge to the Nationalist government's claim of sovereignty over Taiwan.[19] Wellington Koo (Gu Weijun), the Nationalist ambassador to Washington, noted in his diary, "The language of the statement in regard to Formosa is abrupt, almost brutal, seldom seen in official statements regarding another friendly power."[20] Even Dulles conceded to Koo that "the language used was blunt and discourteous."[21] Koo warned Taipei that the new policy in effect questioned the legitimacy of the Nationalists' rule in Taiwan.[22] Indeed, Truman and Acheson had not laid aside the idea of getting rid of Chiang, although by then they had reversed course and intended to keep the island out of the hands of the Communists.

Despite the insult, Koo advised Chiang to focus on the positive and not to raise the issue regarding Truman's wording. Chiang acquiesced. Nationalist foreign minister George Yeh (Ye Gongchao) issued a statement on June 28 announcing that "the Chinese Government has accepted the U.S. proposal regarding the defense of Taiwan in principle, and has ordered its navy and air force to suspend attacks on the mainland." However, this statement also added that Truman's announcement had no effect on China's sovereignty over Taiwan.[23]

Chiang poured out his pent-up rage in his diary on July 27: "The US government disregards our sovereignty over Taiwan, and it prohibits our military from attacking our mainland territories occupied by the Communist bandits. We are treated even worse than a colony. This is a most painful humiliation."[24]

On the next morning, when Chiang just completed his morning prayers, air sirens blared. Government officials ran to shelters for safety. Assuming it was a Communist attack, the Nationalist air force dispatched fighters to intercept the invading planes. Soon it was discovered they were in fact US reconnaissance planes.[25] "The US Navy and Air Force entered Taiwan's sea or airspace without notifying us," Chiang remarked in his diaries. "The US treats us not only as a conquered territory but also as an enemy!"[26]

Soon Taiwan's authorities found out from Tokyo that the twenty-eight planes had been sent by the Seventh Fleet to survey military installations in Taiwan. Tokyo had cabled the US naval attaché in Taipei, who, however, had gone out to golf for the day. So the telegram sat on his desk all day.[27] This bizarre incident vividly reveals the inadequacy of communication channels between Taipei and Tokyo. As *Time* magazine observed, the most senior military representative was "an Army lieutenant colonel assisted by a staff of three other officers and barely enough enlisted men to answer phones, drive staff cars." Evidently none of staff "had the rank or authority to provide the liaison so urgently required with the U.S. Seventh Fleet" or Tokyo.[28]

With MacArthur commanding US forces in the Far East and the Seventh Fleet ordered to protect Taiwan, the establishment of direct military liaison links between Taipei and Tokyo would have been a logical move. Acheson and the State Department, however, abhorred such contact. Chiang noted: "While American military policy toward Korea, Taiwan, and the Pacific has changed fundamentally, the State Department has continued to insult us in the most extreme fashion." He added, "Its evil intention of agitating the Taiwanese to oppose our government remains unchanged." He fulminated against Acheson: "Why did God create this bad egg (*huaidan*) so he could harm us China to such a degree!"[29]

Had Chiang known what actually transpired at two Blair House meetings on June 25 and 26, he probably would have been even more enraged and perhaps frightened. Although Acheson first proposed neutralization of the Taiwan Strait on the evening of June 25, he also emphasized that the United States "should not tie up with the Generalissimo." Truman agreed, "We were not going to give the Chinese 'a nickel' for any purpose whatever." He added, "All the money we had given them is now invested in United States real estate." Perhaps the most consequential suggestion Acheson made was that the future status of Formosa might be determined by the UN. "Or by the Japanese Peace Treaty," Truman interjected. Truman even suggested "taking Formosa back as part of Japan and putting it under MacArthur's Command." He reckoned that "the Generalissimo might step out if MacArthur were put in."[30] With the deployment of the Seventh Fleet, Taiwan, or Formosa as US policymakers preferred to call it, became secure from Communist attack. Chiang Kai-shek, however, was in greater danger of being deposed by his former ally. Chiang's visceral perception that Washington was treating him like an enemy turned out to be accurate.

Having reversed its hands-off policy on Taiwan, Washington shifted to a new policy of denying Taiwan to the Communists without getting "tied up" with Chiang. In order to reconcile the objective of retaining Taiwan and the wish to depose Chiang, Truman and Acheson came close to the novel solution of a military coup from within or an outright US invasion from without. With a new war breaking out in Korea, the first reactions of Truman and Acheson included plans to eliminate a former ally in a third country, as if the United States had too many resources and too few enemies. Their personal loathing of Chiang had taken US policies to an absurd extreme of being simultaneously anti-Communist and anti-Nationalist.

Truman's policy shift only represented a change of policy toward the island of Taiwan, but not a change of heart toward Chiang. Acheson followed up to make sure that this point was well understood by US diplomats. Four days after the June 27 announcement, Acheson reminded US diplomats that the neutralization should be "taken as immediate security measure to preserve peace in Pacific and without prejudice to pol[itical] questions affecting Chi[nese] Govt." He emphasized, "No change anticipated in relations" between the United States and Taiwan.[31]

The famed American architect of the Cold War, George Kennan, shared Acheson's distrust of Chiang and his contempt for the Chinese: "The Nationalist forces on the island must, in view of their national temperament, their past experiences and their unfortunate leadership, be regarded as wholly unreliable."[32]

Not surprisingly, Chiang's offer to provide 33,000 troops to fight in Korea was first entertained but eventually declined by Truman because Acheson vehemently objected.[33] Clearly, in no way did Truman and Acheson want to take Chiang Kai-shek back into the American embrace.

MacArthur Comes to the Rescue

The outbreak of the Korean War alone did not save Chiang's tottering regime, but events were to take an unexpected turn. MacArthur's bursting on the Taiwan scene was as enigmatic as the man himself. "Before 1950 General MacArthur had neither shown nor expressed interest in Formosa," Acheson recalled sourly, citing a *New York Times* report in which the general made no mention of Taiwan in his discussion of "our line of defense . . . against Asiatic aggression."[34] But that was March 1949, when the Nationalist government still ruled half of China, including Taiwan. After the fall of the Chinese mainland by the end of 1949, the situation had changed.

In the first Blair House meeting on June 25, Secretary of Defense Johnson jumped the gun by asking Omar Bradley, chairman of the Joint Chiefs of Staff (JCS), to read

MacArthur's memorandum entitled "On Formosa" dated June 14, which Bradley had just brought back from Tokyo. MacArthur declared, "Formosa in the hands of the Communists can be compared to an unsinkable aircraft carrier and submarine tender."[35] However, his plan included neither the removal of Chiang nor a US takeover of Taiwan. In fact, he had resisted Washington's suggestion of removing Chiang with a coup.[36]

MacArthur's memorandum concluded that he "should be authorized and directed to initiate without delay a survey of the military, economic and political requirements to prevent the domination of Formosa by a Communist power."[37] In fact, such a fact-finding mission had been recommended twice by the JCS, as early as December 23, 1949, and May 4, 1950. After the Korean War broke out and the Seventh Fleet patrolled the Taiwan Strait, MacArthur informed the JCS that he had planned "a brief reconnaissance" of Taiwan. While suggesting MacArthur should "go later yourself" in view of Washington's evolving political deliberations, the JCS conceded: "However, if you feel it necessary to proceed personally on the 31st, please feel free to go since the responsibility is yours."[38]

On July 31, MacArthur, the supreme commander of Allied Powers in Japan (SCAP), and commander-in-chief of both the Far East Command and the UN Command flew to Taipei, accompanied by the entire top echelon of military officers in the Far East, including his chief of staff Major General Edward M. Almond, intelligence chief Major General Charles A. Willoughby, commander of the Seventh Fleet Vice Admiral Arthur D. Struble, US Navy commander in the Far East Vice Admiral Charles Turner Joy, and US Air Force commander in the Far East Lt. General George E. Stratemeyer.[39] Evidently, this star-studded delegation was more than a simple survey team. Whether intentionally or inadvertently, MacArthur threw his and the United States' prestige behind Chiang Kai-shek, who in return welcomed him like a head of state.

"How do you do, Generalissimo," MacArthur greeted Chiang on the tarmac, giving him his famous "number-one" handshake—right hands clasped, his left hand holding Chiang's right elbow. "It was nice of you to come down and meet me."[40] In fact, the entire Nationalist political and military leadership showed up at the Taipei Songshan Airport. MacArthur and his officers immediately plunged into conferences with the Chiangs and Nationalist generals.

Having refused to allow his State Department–appointed political advisor William J. Sebald to tag along, MacArthur left the State Department completely in the dark. Chargé Strong complained to Acheson from Taipei, "Absolutely no information given . . . on talks or on decisions made." To his chagrin, Strong noted that the visit became a major morale booster for the Nationalists. "Press looking forward to large military mission from SCAP, demanding military aid as a right, and predicted early world war and return to mainland." Chiang's regime seemed to "feel situation well cared for in hands of MacArthur, who will straighten out U.S. policy. . . . Formosa seems to be on verge of joining close cooperation" with MacArthur in Tokyo.[41]

Taiwan media effusively praised the meeting of the "two great men." Local reporter Huang Tiancai recalled, "I believe at the time in Taiwan the seven to eight million people's affection and admiration for General MacArthur was unrivaled."[42] While MacArthur promised "effective military coordination between the Chinese and American Forces," Chiang pronounced that "now that we can again work closely together with our old comrade-in-arms," victory was assured.[43] Years later MacArthur would fondly recall that "it was a great pleasure for me to meet my old comrade-in-arms of the last war," whose "indomitable determination to resist Communist domination aroused my sincere admiration."[44] More consequentially, Chiang and MacArthur found themselves to be kindred spirits in their shared loathing of Truman and Acheson.

Acheson was startled and incensed to read in the press about MacArthur's visit and his kissing Madame Chiang's hand.[45] Moreover, under the erroneous impression that MacArthur had ordered fighters to move to Taiwan, Acheson "naturally went through the ceiling," Bradley recalled.[46] A horrified Truman immediately dispatched W. Averell

FIGURE 4.1. General MacArthur arrives in Taipei to meet President Chiang Kai-shek during a two-day visit. July 31, 1950. US National Archives.

Harriman, his roving envoy, and Matthew B. Ridgway, the army's deputy chief of staff, to Tokyo to rein in MacArthur. In two sessions on August 6 and 8, Harriman "explained in great detail why Chiang was a liability" and suggested that "perhaps the best way would be through the medium of the UN to establish an independent government." MacArthur concurred with Harriman that Chiang's ambition to retake the mainland could not be fulfilled. He offered a novel solution—"it might be a good idea to let him land and get rid of him that way"—that was a joke. Showing his faith in Chiang, MacArthur argued the situation in Taiwan could improve, both politically and economically. He then turned the tables, admonishing those "kicking Chiang around." He hoped that "the President would do something to relieve the strain that existed between the State Department and the Generalissimo."[47] MacArthur had become Chiang's champion.

MacArthur was "especially ardent about Formosa," recalled Ridgway, who would soon become MacArthur's subordinate and eventual successor. "Should the Chinese Communists be so foolhardy as to attack the island," MacArthur promised, he would rush there and assume command, and "deliver such a crushing defeat it would be one of the decisive battles of the world—a disaster so great that it would rock Asia, and perhaps turn back Communism." He doubted they would be so foolish, but he added, "I pray nightly that they will—would get down on my knees." Ridgway reflected years later that MacArthur's "vision of himself as the swordsman who would slay the Communist dragon" probably "did add luster to his dream of victory" in his drive to the Yalu River two months later.[48] As it turned out, MacArthur's prayer was answered—the Chinese Communists did attack, although the site was not Taiwan, although Korea.

"In an extension of his famous 'divide and rule' tactics, the Generalissimo is playing the Tokyo end of the United States Government for all it is worth," Strong reported following his recall to Washington. Noting that Chinese Nationalist officials frequently visited Tokyo without informing the US embassy in Taipei, Strong indicted MacArthur as an accomplice: "Encouragement to the Generalissimo in this game has been given unwittingly by General MacArthur, who has played a lone hand with the National Government to the complete exclusion of the Embassy in Taipei."[49]

If MacArthur had single-handedly moved to protect Chiang in the Far East, Washington also played a lone hand at the UN in defending its intervention in the Taiwan Strait. American allies' stance was in sharp contrast to Washington's fear of losing Taiwan to the Communists: "The Canadians and, to a lesser extent, the UK delegation seemed to assume that there was only one possible answer . . . namely, the handing over of Formosa unconditionally to Communist China."[50] On the question of UN representation, while Washington officially "opposes the seating of Chi[nese] Commie reps in the UN," it was in fact ready to "accept the normal parliamentary majorities . . . on this matter and will accept the result if a majority decides to seat the reps" of Communist China.[51]

Besides placating the allies, who were hard enough to accommodate, Acheson also felt compelled to mollify a fuming Beijing. In a secret telegram to the US embassy in India dated August 3, 1950, intended for relay to Kavalam Panikkar, the Indian ambassador in Beijing and the conduit between Beijing and Washington, Acheson wrote, "You may in [yo]ur discussion point out that obvious lack of preparation on part of So[uth] Korean army and US armed forces for war in Korea must in itself constitute clear evidence to the Chi[nese] auth[oritie]s in Peiping that US has no aggressive intentions in Asia."[52] It was as if Washington was begging Beijing for understanding.

MacArthur took a swipe at Acheson's line of thinking in an open letter to the Veterans of Foreign Wars (VFW) Convention in Chicago on August 26. Highlighting Taiwan's importance as "an unsinkable aircraft carrier," MacArthur made a thinly veiled attack on Acheson's Asia policy, deriding "the hypocrisy and the sophistry which has confused and deluded so many people distant from the actual scene." He declared, "Nothing could be more fallacious than the threadbare argument by those who advocate appeasement and defeatism in the Pacific [that] if we defend Formosa we alienate continental Asia." He went on, "Those who speak thus do not understand the Orient." He argued that "it is in the pattern of the Oriental psychology to respect and follow aggressive, resolute and dynamic leadership—to quickly turn on a leadership characterized by timidity or vacillation."[53]

MacArthur's outburst lit a political firestorm in Washington. "Who is the President of the United States?" Acheson cried out.[54] Truman ordered MacArthur to withdraw the statement; MacArthur complied. But the "officially withdrawn" letter had been released to the press. Truman considered the relief of MacArthur, but the conclusion was not to do anything at that time.[55] Instead, Johnson was sacked—the last straw being his attempt to "weasel out" of sending the order to MacArthur to retract his VFW letter.[56]

George C. Marshall was sworn in as the new secretary of defense on September 15, hours after MacArthur launched his daring amphibious landing at Inchon, Korea. In fact, one of the reasons Truman decided not to relieve MacArthur immediately was that he had approved the landing, which he called "a bold plan worthy of a master strategist."[57] MacArthur's gamble paid off spectacularly. "The swiftness and magnitude of the victory were mind-boggling," effused an awed Bradley. "In hindsight," he conceded, "the JCS seemed like a bunch of nervous Nellies to have doubted" MacArthur, who was now "deservedly canonized as a 'military genius.'"[58] Not surprisingly, MacArthur's victory eclipsed the need for an immediate settling of political accounts.

At the end of 1950, Chiang Kai-shek would look back and thank God for "making the Communist Bandits join the Korean War, thus entrapping themselves" and "making the United States side with justice, fight Communism, and not forsake the

Far East, thus turning the whole situation around."[59] Indeed, the Korean War and MacArthur saved Chiang and the Nationalist regime on Taiwan.

What Chiang Had to Offer—Intelligence

The Inchon landing precipitated a total collapse of North Korean forces. Within a month, more than 60,000 North Korean soldiers were captured.[60] About 30 percent of them carried psychological warfare leaflets promising them safety if they surrendered.[61] On September 29, Seoul was restored as the capital of the Republic of Korea. And on the same day UNC and ROK forces approached the 38th parallel, and Truman approved MacArthur's plan to advance into North Korea. On October 1, ROK troops crossed the line and UNC troops followed a few days later.

At 12:30 a.m. on October 3, Zhou Enlai, Chinese premier and concurrently foreign minister, summoned Indian ambassador Panikkar and issued a warning to be relayed through Indian prime minster Nehru to the United States and the UK. If the US Army were to cross the 38th parallel, the message stated, China "will not simply sit and watch." Over the next two days, at an enlarged Politburo meeting, Mao prevailed over his reluctant generals, and the Communists decided to intervene. On October 8, Mao issued the order to assemble the Chinese People's Volunteer Army (CPV), and the only top general who strongly supported Mao's belligerent stance, Peng Dehuai, was named the commander. In the meantime, Zhou's warning via India went unheeded in Washington, Tokyo, and New York. On October 7, the UN General Assembly passed a resolution authorizing UN forces to cross the 38th parallel. While MacArthur's troops were racing toward Pyongyang, Zhou Enlai conferred with Stalin on October 11 at a resort in the Crimea, haggling over how much armament and air cover the Soviets would provide to the Chinese ground forces once they were in Korea.

Ominously, most of the intense diplomatic and military maneuverings on the Chinese and Russian side went unnoticed by American intelligence for a very simple and incredible reason. "We were not reading Red Chinese radio traffic at all," recalled Colonel James H. Polk, an intelligence officer in Tokyo. "One reason was that they employed the Mandarin dialect. We had no Mandarin linguists."[62] Willoughby explained that "the whole linguist units had been previously deactivated" in the post–World War II retrenchment, and so "valuable intelligence on Manchurian, Chinese and Soviet participation may never be recovered."[63]

Now Chiang Kai-shek came to the rescue. The Nationalists were reading the traffic and shared intelligence with the US military attaché and MacArthur's liaison officers in Taipei. The Nationalist-produced intelligence constituted "a substantial percentage" of that from MacArthur's headquarters, which in turn accounted for about 90 percent of the US intelligence, observed JCS chiefs Generals Bradley and Collins.[64]

As early as August 27, a G-2 intelligence summary contained a "miscellany of highly suggestive and completely ominous reports from Chinese Nationalist channels." It was reported that a high-level meeting was held in Beijing, Chinese Communists were ordered by the Soviets to assist North Korea, Soviet officers were to command combined Communist forces, and Taiwan and Indochina were to be invaded. The report also hedged its bet with the plausible observation that "Chinese Communists [were] reluctant to undertake further adventures."[65] Taiwan's alarmist intelligence, which frequently predicted the outbreak of a Third World War, however, found a receptive audience in neither Tokyo nor Washington. "No one trusted what they produced," Polk recalled, "because it was invariably biased or self-serving." To remedy the situation, Polk tried to bring Nationalist specialists to Korea to work under American code breakers, but Washington rejected his request.[66]

"The Chinese Would Not Attack. . . . We Had Won the War"

Apparently unperturbed by his intelligence handicap, on October 14 MacArthur flew 1,900 miles to Wake Island in the western Pacific to meet President Truman, who flew "14,404 [miles round-trip] . . . to reach an understanding face to face" with MacArthur on a host of issues in the aftermath of the VFW affair and the Inchon landing. Truman felt he was going to "talk to God's right-hand man," as he wrote in-flight to his cousin.[67] Conspicuously absent from Truman's large entourage were the secretaries of state and defense. Finding the whole idea "distasteful," Acheson "begged to be excused." While MacArthur "had many of the attributes of a foreign sovereign," Acheson found it unwise to "recognize him as one."[68]

When Truman's plane *Independence* landed at 6:30 on the morning of October 15, MacArthur and John J. Muccio, the US ambassador to Korea, had been waiting at the airstrip. Truman found his "Great General" his usual self, "with his shirt unbuttoned, wearing a greasy ham and eggs cap that evidently had been in use for twenty years."[69] Instead of saluting his commander in chief, MacArthur gave Truman his number-one handshake, like the one he gave Chiang Kai-shek several weeks earlier, heartily booming, "Mr. President!" Truman warmly replied, "How are you, General? I am glad you're here. I've been a long time meeting you, General." MacArthur answered, "I hope it won't be so long next time, Mr. President."[70] That was the first and the last time the two men met.

Truman and MacArthur climbed into a battered Chevrolet and went to a Quonset hut for a private breakfast meeting that lasted half an hour. Truman recorded that MacArthur assured him that "the Chinese would not attack, that we had won the war and that we would send a Division to Europe from Korea in January 1951." Then MacArthur brought up the subject of his VFW statement about Formosa, saying that "he was sorry if he had caused any embarrassment."

Truman told him, "I consider the incident closed." MacArthur concurred, "I also considered it as closed."[71]

The general meeting for Truman's and MacArthur's parties lasted from 7:36 to 9:12 a.m.—an hour and thirty-six minutes. Apparently assuming that victory was at hand, the first question Truman asked was not about the ongoing war, but the rebuilding of Korea, leading to a discussion that dominated almost half of the meeting. MacArthur first replied that rehabilitation could not occur until military operations had ended. He believed that "formal resistance will end throughout North and South Korea by Thanksgiving," and hoped to "withdraw [the] Eighth Army to Japan by Christmas." He mentioned that "we now have about 60,000 prisoners in compounds," who were "well-fed and clean" and were "the happiest Koreans in all Korea." Ambassador John Muccio suggested that US policy should "emphasize the mental and psychological rehabilitation more than the economic." He reported that sound trucks were "very, very effective." Truman laughed and said, "I believe in sound trucks. I won two elections with them."[72]

Halfway through the meeting, the president finally asked the big question: "What are the chances for Chinese or Soviet interference?" "Very little," MacArthur answered. "Had they interfered in the first or second months it would have been decisive. We are no longer fearful of their intervention. We no longer stand hat in hand." He went on to note that although the Chinese had 300,000 men in Manchuria, "only 50/60,000 could be gotten across the Yalu River." MacArthur, a believer in air power, stressed, "They have no Air Force. . . . If the Chinese tried to get down to Pyongyang, there would be the greatest slaughter." Dismissing the possible combination of Chinese Communist ground troops and Russian air cover as something that "just wouldn't work" and asserting that "we are the best," MacArthur ended his succinct analysis on the war in Korea. Neither Truman or JCS chair Bradley pursued the topic. The entire discussion on Chinese or Soviet interference amounted to roughly 320 words—probably no more than five minutes of talking time.[73]

In the remaining time Truman rushed through a long list of issues: policy on war criminals in Korea, the peace treaty with Japan, getting the Eighth Army back to Japan by Christmas, sending troops to Europe, and Indochina. Watching Truman "whizzing through" his agenda so quickly, a "fidgeting" Rusk feared that the whole meeting could finish "in about thirty minutes." He passed a note to Truman asking him to slow down, "to lend a note of seriousness to the meeting." Truman scribbled on the note: "Hell, no! I want to get out of here before we get into trouble!"[74]

After a brief discussion on the Philippines, Truman declared: "General MacArthur and I have talked fully about Formosa. There is no need to cover that subject again. The General and I are in complete agreement." Apparently Truman was trying to preempt any discussion of Formosa, lest it ruin the studied cordial atmosphere. Concluding the meeting at 9:12 a.m., Truman announced, "No one who was not here would believe we have covered so much ground as we have been actually able to cover."[75]

Having completed the meeting several hours ahead of schedule, Truman and MacArthur signed a communiqué announcing their agreement "as if they were heads of different governments," noted a *New York Times* reporter. He added, Truman was "like an insurance salesman who has at last signed up an important prospect while the latter appeared dubious over the extent of the coverage." An "abstracted" MacArthur declined the president's invitation to lunch, claiming that he had to get back to war as quickly as possible.[76] In fact, he had been planning his second amphibious landing—this time at Wonsan on the northeast coast of Korea.

On the airstrip, Truman decorated MacArthur with his fifth Distinguished Service Medal. He told reporters, "I have never had a more satisfactory conference since I've been President." MacArthur bid farewell to the president: "Goodbye, sir. Happy landing. It has been a real honor talking to you." Five minutes after Truman's plane took off, MacArthur's departed for Tokyo.[77] His parting words to reporters were: "Come up to Pyongyang. It won't be long now."[78]

At the time on Wake, MacArthur's confidence, if not arrogance, seemed warranted. Four days later, on the October 19, UN forces took Pyongyang and continued their simultaneous advance on both coasts toward the China–North Korea border in a pincer formation. On the same day, however, three full-strength Chinese armies began crossing the Yalu into Korea. Both MacArthur and the CIA failed to detect this crucial development.

Upon close examination of the conference transcript, it is striking how little time Truman, MacArthur, and the other participants spent on the war itself, and how much attention they paid to postwar recovery, especially "psychological rehabilitation," including that of POWs. MacArthur's analysis of the war situation was embedded in his answer to Truman's first query on "the rehabilitation situation." The only military-related question Truman asked was about "the chances for Chinese or Soviet interference." Although Truman's overconfidence in an imminent victory may account for his lack of interest in military matters, that doesn't explain the preoccupation with "rehabilitation," which seemed to involve extensive "educational and information" activities or, in other words, propaganda and psychological warfare.[79]

This peculiar preoccupation was even more pronounced in a separate discussion between Dean Rusk and Ambassador Muccio. Rusk recommended "reorientation" of POWs, that is, putting them through "a one or two weeks' course of psychological decontamination before releasing them." Muccio replied that his men had been doing that for refugees and had plans to include prisoners. Rusk emphasized that

"American re-orientation activity should operate as intensely as possible during the military phase of the Korean operation" before future UN interference made access to prisoners difficult. Muccio promised to create "as large and as quick an educational program as could be put together."[80]

It strains credulity to believe that President Truman, General MacArthur, and other top officials flew thousands of miles to a little island in the Pacific for the main purpose of discussing "rehabilitation" and "reorientation" of Korean refugees and prisoners. The meeting makes little sense unless considered along with NSC-81/1, which remained classified until 1975.

NSC-81/1's Twin Conclusions: Crossing the 38th Parallel and Reindoctrinating POWs

NSC-81/1, "United States Courses of Action With Respect to Korea," was approved by Truman on September 11, 1950, four days before the Inchon landing and one month before the Wake Island meeting. It is best known as "a masterpiece of obfuscation," in General Bradley's words, as it authorized MacArthur to advance north of the 38th parallel "in pursuance of a roll-back," provided there was no indication of major Soviet or Chinese intervention.[81] The consequence of this decision is well known: MacArthur's forces marched into a massive trap set up by the Chinese and suffered a humiliating defeat.

The crossing of the 38th parallel and the rollback, however, were Washington's policy. Acheson had argued in late August, long before the Inchon landing, that UN troops "could not be expected to march up to a surveyor's line and stop. . . . As a boundary it had no political validity."[82] The historian Bruce Cumings argues, "rollback was not MacArthur's policy, nor his fault (even though he favored it)." In fact, this policy "stimulated the broadest coalition in Washington behind any Korea policy in the postwar period. It stretched from unreconstructed anticommunists on the Right to liberals like John Vincent and O. Edmund Clubb." In the State Department, John Foster Dulles, Acheson, Rusk, John Allison, Deputy Director of Far Eastern Affairs, and John Paton Davies had adopted a hawkish stance on crossing the 38th parallel.[83] The pivotal role of NSC-81/1 in leading the United States into a disastrous war in North Korea has been well established.

Little studied, however, is its prisoner reindoctrination component, which later became intertwined with the policy of voluntary repatriation. Together the two policies inadvertently encouraged the rise of Chinese anti-Communist POWs and consequently nearly doubled the length of the war.[84] Paragraph 21 of NSC-81/1's conclusion stipulates that the US government, especially its military and embassy in Korea, should make an "immediate" and "intensive" propaganda effort to "turn the inevitable bitterness and resentment of the war-victimized Korean people away from the United States and to direct it toward the Korean Communists, the Soviet Union, and, depending on the role they play, the Chinese Communists, as the parties responsible for the destructive conflict."[85] Ominously, the reference to China was written more than two months before China's intervention in late October.[86]

The main target of this propaganda drive, however, was not North Korean civilians but POWs. Paragraph 22 established the principle that in order to "effect the reorientation of the North Korean people, to cause defection of enemy troops in the field," the treatment of POWs, "after their transfer to places of internment, shall be directed toward their exploitation, training and use for psychological warfare purposes." It mandated the UNC to "set up immediately on a pilot-plant scale an interrogation, indoctrination and training center for those POW's now in our hands in Korea."[87]

The substance of NSC-81/1's conclusions was transmitted to MacArthur on September 15, the day of the Inchon landing.[88] On the 27th, the JCS explicitly directed MacArthur to cross the 38th parallel and to "set up on a pilot-plant scale interrogation, indoctrination and training centers."[89] In General Bradley's plain words, the instructions to MacArthur included: "He should make an all-out propaganda effort, blaming the war on the communists. He should attempt to *brainwash* North Korean POWs."[90] This was brainwashing American style.

In the following weeks, a flurry of orders flew from Washington to MacArthur in Tokyo, mandating prisoner reindoctrination. MacArthur acted on Washington's orders with alacrity. In October, while UNC troops were racing toward the Yalu River, a pilot project for five hundred North Korean prisoners at Yongdungpo near Seoul was set up and formal instruction began in November.[91]

American civilian officials were no less enthusiastic. In compliance with the NSC-81/1 requirement that both the field commander and the US embassy in Korea "augment their present propaganda and information programs," Ambassador Muccio waxed lyrical in a telegram to Acheson on October 9, four days before his Wake Island trip, declaring that the "liberation" of North Korea "places upon us a moral commitment of the first magnitude to remold the thinking of the Korean people along democratic lines." One of the American objectives was to "restore the Korean people to sanity."[92]

The civilian centrality—especially Acheson's centrality—in the rollback decision has been well established.[93] Likewise, the civilian centrality in prisoner reindoctrination decisions is plain. That explains the preoccupation in the Wake Island meetings with "rehabilitation" and "reorientation," which had become a national policy of the United States shortly before the Inchon landing. Like the rollback decision, the prisoner reorientation policy was not conceived by MacArthur, even though he supported it and implemented it with gusto.

Acheson and the State Department were mainly responsible for the two key components of NSC-81/1. The first decision led to a lost war over North Korean territory, from October 1950 to summer 1951, and the second caused a stalemated war over prisoners, from early 1952 until June 1953. The paramount role of NSC-81/1 in nearly doubling the length of the war has hitherto not been recognized, partly because it remained classified until 1975, and partly because of Washington's suppression of any suggestions linking the stalemate to its muddled and bungled POW policies.

5

Defectors and Prisoners in the First Three Chinese Offensives

HAVING ACHIEVED "complete unity in the aim and conduct of our foreign policy" in his conference with MacArthur on Wake Island, Truman embarked on a leisurely trip back to Washington, making stops in Hawaii and San Francisco. "I have seldom seen him in better spirit," General Bradley recalled, adding that "it was a great relief to all of us that the Korean War would soon be over." Truman and his top advisors were all eager to revert their attention to building the North Atlantic Treaty Organization (NATO) in Europe.[1]

Truman did not forget to send Beijing another peace signal in his speech in San Francisco: "We seek no territory or special privileges in Korea or anyplace else. We seek no aggressive design in Korea or in any other place in the Far East or elsewhere. And I want that to be perfectly clear to the whole world."[2] However, with General MacArthur's forces closing in on the North Korean capital of Pyongyang and racing toward the Sino-Korean border along both coasts, Truman's declaration must have sounded hollow and disingenuous to Mao and his generals.

A more genuine-sounding statement would have made no difference, as Mao and the Politburo had decided on October 4 and 5 to intervene in Korea. Between October 15 and 18, exactly the same period when Truman returned from Wake Island to Washington, the first wave of CPV units were transported to three crossing points along the Yalu in a massive operation involving 74 trains and 1,979 railcars. When Truman's plane landed in San Francisco on October 16, some 2,500 troops of the CPV 370th Regiment of the 124th Division, 42nd Army, had begun crossing the Yalu from Ji'an, Jilin, to Manpo, marking the first entry of a regular CPV unit into Korea, despite its official designation as a "reconnaissance unit."[3]

After a fierce two-day battle, General Paik Sun Yup's ROK 1st Division captured Pyongyang, the North Korean capital and the general's hometown, by nightfall on October 19.[4] At the same time, some 100 to 150 miles to the north, twelve infantry and two artillery divisions of the CPV began pouring across the Yalu at three points under cover of a dark, drizzling night.[5] This massive movement went undetected by US intelligence.

As noted in Chapter 4, MacArthur declined the president's lunch invitation on Wake, claiming that he should return to Tokyo to direct his X Corps' amphibious landing at Wonsan, after which the corps would attack westward and "take Pyongyang in one week."[6] The second half of the plan never materialized. In a major anticlimax, the X Corps did not land until October 26, after being stranded at sea for a week while struggling with a heavily mined harbor. More embarrassingly, the ROK 3rd and Capital Divisions, which moved overland from the 38th parallel, had captured Wonsan on October 10, robbing the landing of any drama. MacArthur's hope of repeating his Inchon glory was dashed. The botched Wonsan landing did not portend well—MacArthur's luck had run out.

The CPV First Offensive, October 25–November 7, 1950

On October 24, MacArthur issued a new order removing all restrictions on the use of US and other UN ground forces south of the Manchurian border, and instructed his troops to press forward toward the Yalu in force. An alarmed JCS immediately asked MacArthur to explain his move, as it violated the JCS directive of September 27 prohibiting non-Korean troops from approaching the Sino-Korean border. MacArthur replied that he "felt he had enough latitude under existing directives to issue the order, and furthermore, the whole subject had been covered in the Wake Island Conference." The JCS acquiesced. UN forces, including US forces and the 27th British Commonwealth Brigade, were authorized to proceed to the Yalu. "Everything is going just fine," reported Eighth Army commander Walton H. Walker on October 25.[7]

On the same morning, however, the Chinese 360th Regiment of the 120th Division, 40th Army, ambushed the ROK 1st Division at Unsan in the northwest, firing the CPV's first shot in the Korean War. Some 70 air miles to the east, the CPV 42nd Army attacked the ROK 3rd Division at Hwangcho-ryong south of the Chosin Reservoir.[8] The CPV's First Offensive was launched on the eastern and western fronts simultaneously. "Chinese stagehands had raised the curtain on the Battle of Unsan," ROK 1st Division commander General Paik Sun Yup recalled, "and a bitter battle it proved to be."[9]

On the first day of battle, at 11:44 a.m., the first Chinese prisoner in the war was captured by Paik's division. Paik, a Mukden Military Academy graduate and former officer in the Japanese-led Manchukuo Army, immediately conducted an interrogation in Chinese. The prisoner readily admitted that he was Chinese, not an ethnic Korean living in China, and that 10,000 Chinese soldiers had taken positions in the surrounding mountains and 10,000 more to the east nearby. Paik promptly brought General Frank W. Milburn, commander of the I Corps, to see the prisoner. Paik told Milburn that he had examined enemy dead and determined they were Chinese, adding that there were "many, many Chinese."[10]

The prisoner was taken to the US Eighth Army advance command in Pyongyang for further interrogation. By mid-afternoon the next day, three more Chinese prisoners were brought to Pyongyang. They all "looked Chinese, spoke Chinese, and understood neither Korean nor Japanese." They were interrogated intensively, even with a lie detector.[11] On October 27, Eighth Army G-2 reported the capture of two prisoners who "candidly boasted" that the Chinese forces had "massively intervened in North Korea." But MacArthur's G-2 chief Willoughby decided that their stories were "unconfirmed and thereby unaccepted."[12] Tokyo GHQ insisted these prisoners were ethnic Koreans in China who volunteered to fight in their fatherland.[13]

The first four prisoners taken to Pyongyang most likely included Li Xinlin and "Syng Chong San." Li, a thirty-three-year-old from Hunan, deserted the CPV 360th Regiment before it attacked the ROKs on the morning of October 25, and finally managed to surrender at six in the evening. A Nationalist soldier since 1939, Li was captured by the PLA on Hainan Island in April 1950. After crossing the Yalu on October 18, he heard a rumor that Chiang Kai-shek's forces were on the UN side, and "he wished to rejoin them." Li said that approximately 60 percent of the 30,000 men of the 40th Army were former Nationalists and that morale was low.[14] Although he had been in the PLA/CPV for six months, Li remained loyal to the Nationalists and defected at the first opportunity. Some of the earliest Chinese prisoners were defectors like Li.

By contrast, Syng Chong San, a twenty-nine-year-old ammunition bearer of the 40th Army, was apparently not a defector. He was captured near Unsan on October 25, when his unit came under attack and dispersed. Illiterate and apolitical, he reported that "although having low morale," the troops were "willing to fight because they have been told that when the U.S. Forces crossed the 38th parallel, it was the sign of U.S. intentions to invade China." He added, while "most of the troops do not care about Communism . . . , the individual is satisfied if his needs are adequately met." However, he was not completely forthcoming. He gave a strange unit code below the army—"the 3rd Branch Unit"—which was most likely a hoax.[15]

Before dawn on October 28, twenty-five-year-old rifleman Yan Shuzheng deserted the 199th Division, 40th Army, near Unsan, and surrendered to ROK troops at seven in the morning. Immediately interrogated, he claimed that he "wished to rejoin the Chinese Nationalist Army (CNA) and thought the ROK would return him to CNA

Forces." He stated, quite accurately, that both the 39th and 40th Armies, with a combined strength of 60,000 men, had entered Korea on October 20.[16] Yan's account was apparently dismissed. The I Corps reported two days later, "There are no indications at this time to confirm the existence of a CCF organization or unit, of any size, on Korean soil." Similarly the Eighth Army HQ concluded that there were "no indications of open intervention on the part of Chinese Communist Forces."[17]

The Eighth Army on the west coast and the X Corps on the east continued to capture more Chinese prisoners in small numbers. In the west, eleven Chinese had been captured by October 31.[18] In the east, on October 29 an ROK unit took sixteen Chinese prisoner, all members of the 370th Regiment, which had first crossed the Yalu on October 16. General Edward (Ned) Almond, X Corps commander and concurrently MacArthur's chief of staff, flew to Wonsan to interrogate the prisoners the following day. The captives reported that roughly 70 percent of the men in the 124th Division had been Nationalist troops until their surrender in Beiping in early 1949.[19] Almond made these exhausted men, who had not eaten for three days, do some close-order drills. He was not impressed. These "Chinese laundrymen" were not very intelligent, he quipped.[20] Nevertheless, he immediately sent a detailed radio message to MacArthur alerting him to Chinese presence in his zone.[21] Willoughby flew in. Although he could no longer deny they were Chinese, he casually branded them as "stragglers" or "volunteers."[22]

"Meeting a New Foe"

Despite mounting evidence of a massive Chinese intervention, MacArthur and Willoughby doggedly dismissed much of the early interrogation results. One US regimental commander recalled, "We had interrogators who were part Chinese, who spoke Chinese. There was absolutely no question that these prisoners were Chinese. . . . But nobody back at the division, or higher echelons, believed they were Chinese."[23] Ambassador Muccio later remarked, "Willoughby had a disdain of the capability of the Chinese, of all classes, and his appraisal of Chinese capabilities was based on the little that he knew about China years prior to the advent of the Communists." Because he was the intelligence chief, Willoughby's willful neglect filtered down throughout the intelligence apparatus, thus "prevent[ing] MacArthur from getting the intelligence that he had to have in order to make the right decisions."[24] Others believed MacArthur was to blame as well. Almond's staff officer Jack Chiles remembered, "MacArthur did not *want* the Chinese to enter the war in Korea. Anything MacArthur wanted, Willoughby produced intelligence for. In this case, Willoughby falsified the intelligence reports."[25]

Just as Willoughby told MacArthur what he wanted to hear, the Eighth Army HQ minimized the strength of the Chinese, lamely citing the lack of "confirmation." Dismissing multiple defectors' accounts of large-scale intervention as a Communist bluff designed to deny MacArthur the full glory of an early victory, Americans from MacArthur down to G-2 analysts consciously and unconsciously bought into the "volunteers" fiction.

The Chinese ruse worked for several reasons in addition to MacArthur's arrogance. First, the number of Chinese prisoners was very small: in the Eighth Army zone, 11 were captured by October 31; 55 by November 2; 84 by November 20; and 96 by November 23, Thanksgiving Day, when MacArthur resumed the final drive toward the Yalu. Second, while the defectors frankly poured out all they knew, other prisoners stuck to fake unit designations that were recently adopted to confuse the Americans, who assumed that the reported 54th, 55th, 56th, 57th, and 58th Units were small units. In fact, each represented a full-strength 30,000-man-strong army.[26]

Third, before entering Korea, Chinese troops had removed all insignia and items that might identify their nationality, including letters and papers. To ensure secrecy, even the term "Chinese People's Volunteer" was forbidden initially. Two days before launching the first attack, Mao ordered all scout units to disguise themselves as members of the Korean People's Army (KPA).[27] Regular troops also wore KPA uniforms. Prisoners from the 38th, 39th, and 40th Armies reported that all troops in their units had changed into KPA uniforms before crossing the Yalu.[28] Yang Wanfu of the 125th Division, 42nd Army, also recalled that his unit switched into KPA uniforms.[29]

FIGURE 5.1. X Corps commander Almond talks to the first group of Chinese prisoners captured in Korea. Unimpressed, Almond called them "Chinese laundrymen." October 30, 1950. US National Archives.

American troops found killed Chinese carrying no official identification, but noticed that officers' uniforms had "a vertical red piping" on pants and jacket—unmistakable signs of the more elaborate KPA uniforms.[30]

Mao, a master manipulator of human psychology, succeeded in confusing the Americans, especially MacArthur and his subordinates, who were willfully inclined to see these Chinese troops as mere stragglers or "Manchuria-bred Koreans." As Walker put it, "After all, a lot of Mexicans live in Texas."[31]

MacArthur finally changed his tune in early November, admitting that UN forces "are meeting a new foe" in "certain areas of Korea." Reporting that thirty-five Chinese troops had been captured, MacArthur noted that "elements" of the 38th, 40th, and 42nd Armies were "presently in hostile contact," leaving out the 39th Army.[32] The 39th Army's presence had been reported on October 29 by a deserted cook, who claimed that it had 45,000 to 50,000 troops.[33] Apparently his account had been rejected.

Believing, or wishing, that only elements of these Chinese armies were in Korea, MacArthur and his command grossly underestimated Chinese strength. Their estimates steadily grew from "no positive evidence" on October 31 to 16,500 on November 3, to 34,500 on November 7, and to 76,800 on the 14th.[34] In fact, the initial batch of Chinese forces consisted of four elite armies (including twelve full-strength infantry divisions, each at least 10,000 strong) and three artillery divisions. On their heels came six divisions of the 66th and 50th Armies. The CPV poured 290,000 troops into the First Offensive.[35] G-2 underestimated Chinese strength by a factor of four or more.

American generals and G-2 analysts had little appreciation of their adversaries, who were not the "Chinese laundryman" of their racist imagination. They were the cream of the crop of the PLA: the strongest units of the 4th Field Army, which had swept from Manchuria to Hainan Island in the Civil War.

The Chinese First Offensive did not dent MacArthur's hope for a quick and complete victory. Making no attempt to hide his contempt for the enemy, he branded the Chinese intervention as "one of the most offensive acts of international lawlessness of historic record"—an expression reminiscent of Chiang Kai-shek's "Communists bandits."[36] Chiang had learned a bitter lesson in China; MacArthur would soon learn his in Korea.

The First Chinese Prisoners

In hindsight, MacArthur's G-2 consistently distrusted defectors' honest reports of the CPV's strength, while it often believed false intelligence supplied by prisoners giving fake unit names that suggested ad hoc small units. At the time, however, it was difficult to distinguish honest defectors from lying prisoners. With little understanding of or interest in Chinese politics, the UNC made no effort to screen or segregate defectors from regular prisoners. Most defectors erroneously assumed that the United States was still Chiang Kai-shek's ally. By surrendering, they thought, they would be sent to Taiwan. The Americans, however, harbored absolutely no such plan. The defectors would soon discover the fate of unrequited affinity: they were treated indiscriminately as prisoners of war.

Ma Yufu, a twenty-two-year-old medic of the 112th Division, 38th Army, surrendered to UN forces near Huichon, sixty miles south of the Yalu, on November 2, because he was "sick at heart under the CCF and also that he might be able to join up with his older brother, who is with the CNA at Formosa." His interrogator noted: "Since the U.S. Gov't and Nationalist China were friends, PW maintained such ideas when he surrendered." Captured by the PLA in Shenyang in 1948, Ma claimed that he "would very much rather live under" the Nationalists. He offered a list of eleven reasons, including that the Communists allowed little freedom of speech or movement, discriminated against and closely monitored former Nationalists, and lied about taking care of soldiers' dependents. And, perhaps most importantly, "he was happy" in the Nationalist army.[37] Repeatedly interrogated, Ma became one of the only three Chinese prisoners whose names appear in an official US Army history of the Korean War.[38]

Sharing Ma's distinction was Wang Futian, a thirty-two-year-old rifleman of the 372nd Regiment, 124th Division, 42nd Army. Wang surrendered to the US 1st Marine Division at Hwangcho-ryong on November 7.[39] He was "a large man with a forceful personality," observed American social scientists in 1953, when they interviewed him as a major leader among anti-Communist prisoners.[40] Born in a poor peasant family in Hebei, Wang had only a year and a half of education. At the age of fourteen, he went to Shenyang (Mukden) and apprenticed in a Japanese ordnance factory for several months. Three years later he joined General Fu Zuoyi's Nationalist 35th Army as a messenger in Suiyuan (today's central Inner Mongolia). After the Sino-Japanese War broke out in 1937, he was transferred to a cavalry regiment, which later became a Sino-American Training School and Special Forces unit (*Zhong-Mei xunlianban biedongjun*).[41] Soon after V-J Day, his unit took over the city of Baotou but came under attack by the Communists. Reorganized as the Transport Police Corps, the US-armed unit defended the Beiping-Baotou railroad. In December 1948, Wang was captured by the PLA.[42]

After a three-month indoctrination, former Master Sergeant Wang was pressed into the PLA as a private in the 124th Division, which fought in Hebei, Henan, and eastern Sichuan until late 1949. Like other Nationalists described in Chapter 3, Wang was embittered by relentless indoctrination, being forced to "call black white and white black." When his political instructor asserted that "the Communists deserved all the credit for the eight-year Anti-Japanese War and that the Nationalists did not do a single thing against the Japanese," an indignant Wang "jumped up," disputed the claim, and asked, "Do the Communists have any conscience?" He was jailed for a week as a "reactionary." Although he never witnessed any public execution, Wang often had nightmares. He became completely antagonized. Later he reflected: "All of us in the Communist army were just like puppets. Although you have eyes, you cannot see; although you have ears, you cannot hear anything; although you have a mouth, you cannot say anything."[43]

Twice Wang deserted, only to be captured, returned to his unit, struggled against, and jailed. When the PLA launched the "Resist America and Aid Korea" propaganda drive, he was secretly delighted, knowing that he "was going to get a chance to escape pretty soon." However, he was arrested once again, because he challenged the platoon leader's claim that America was a mere "paper tiger," pointedly highlighting that the reason "we couldn't liberate Taiwan is because the American Imperialist Seventh Fleet is there." He was only released in October, just before his unit embarked for Korea.[44]

To boost morale, Communist officers told troops that Chiang Kai-shek had dispatched 33,000 men to "invade" Korea along with the Americans, implying that these troops could be as easily defeated as they had been in the Civil War. For men like Wang, this rumor had the opposite effect: "This was a chance for me—maybe I could meet the Nationalist soldiers."[45] Wang did not know that Truman had rejected Chiang's troop offer four months earlier.

In the First Offensive, the CPV 124th Division was deployed to hold blocking positions on two overlooking hills at Hwangcho-ryong, where the US 1st Marine Division trudged uphill along the deep valley toward the Chosin Reservoir. After a hellish six-day battle from November 2 to 7, the Marines broke the Chinese resistance, largely thanks to "feverish" attacks by Marine aircraft. The CPV division was nearly depleted, down to about 3,000 men. On November 6, Peng Dehuai ordered a retreat on the following day. During the night, a US artillery and mortar barrage "caused crippling casualties in the 372d Regiment," leaving many dead and wounded. Wang survived and surrendered.[46]

"Because of his acquaintanceship with Americans" while serving in the Sino-American Training School in World War II, Wang believed that America's POW policy promised "better treatment than that of the Oriental countries." He added that he hoped "to be sent to Formosa to fight for Chiang Kai-shek's forces."[47]

Among the first hundred Chinese prisoners in the Korean War, Wang Futian, Ma Yufu, Li Xinlin, and Yan Shuzheng were not the only defectors. One fact confirmed by their interrogation records is that they all shared the desire to escape Communist China to rejoin the Nationalists in Taiwan. They risked their lives to desert, as defectors would be shot on sight. Crossing battle lines to surrender was by no means a simple task. It required heart, smarts, guts, and, most of all, luck.

The Second Offensive, November 25–December 24, 1950

After ten days of fighting, the CPV succeeded in driving the Eighth Army back to the Chongchon River, 65 miles south of the Yalu, and delaying the X Corps' advance toward the Chosin Reservoir. As the Eighth Army halted its advance and became well entrenched and the CPV 42nd Army was outnumbered and outgunned by the X Corps, Mao promptly ordered the end of the First Offensive on November 5 in the western sector and on November 7 in the east.[48]

Apparently under pressure from MacArthur, Walker pledged on November 6 to launch a large-scale attack "as soon as conditions permit."[49] In response to the UNC's probing, the CPV initially fought back resolutely and then, from November 17 and on, ended resistance and broke off contact, leaving behind scenes of "hasty retreat." On November 18, the CPV released 103 UN POWs, including 27 Americans, who were told that the Chinese were returning to China due to food shortages.[50] As abruptly as they had first appeared, the Chinese disappeared like a phantom.

Mao's ruse worked, again. MacArthur and the Eighth Army staff increasingly saw this eerie lull as a sign of Chinese weakness and timidity. They interpreted the previous Chinese offensive as a measure to protect power plants along the Yalu River. Their estimate of Chinese strength in Korea actually dwindled from 76,800 on November 14 to a range between 46,700 and 70,000 by November 24.[51] MacArthur gave an even lower estimate to Ambassador Muccio on November 17: "25,000 and certainly no more than 30,000 soldiers." A larger force was improbable. He argued: "If they had moved in the open, they would have been detected by our Air Force and Intelligence."[52] A believer of modern air power, MacArthur could not imagine how a low-tech enemy could hoodwink him.

November 24 was set as the D-day of the UNC's final attack toward the Yalu. The order reached the frontline units by November 23, Thanksgiving Day, when GIs enjoyed a sumptuous turkey dinner. Some had a hot shower and a change of uniform.[53] It turned out to be the last hot meal and hot shower for many.

MacArthur and his top brass flew from Tokyo to the Sinanju airfield, seventy miles south of the Yalu, on the morning of November 24 to "fire the starting gun." During his inspection, reporters heard him saying to a general: "If this operation is successful, I hope we can get the boys home by Christmas." He repeated this to 24th Division commander John Church: "I have already promised the wives and mothers that the boys of the 24th will be back by Christmas. Don't make me a liar. Get to the Yalu and I will relieve you." The final push became known as the "end-the-war offensive" or the "home-for-Christmas drive."[54]

When his plane took off, MacArthur ordered his pilot to fly north so he could survey the full length of the Yalu River. The flight ran over the airspace later known as the Mig Alley, but met no enemy planes or flak. Refusing to wear a parachute,

MacArthur smoked his pipe and gazed into the mountainous wilderness covered in snow 5,000 feet blow. "All that spread before our eyes was an endless expanse of utterly barren countryside, jagged hills, yawning crevices, and the black waters of the Yalu," wrote MacArthur. He found no military concentration south of the river. However, as he later admitted, "if a large force or massive supply train had passed over the border, the imprints had already been well-covered by the intermittent snowstorms of the Yalu Valley."[55] That was exactly what had transpired days and weeks before MacArthur's eyeball intelligence-gathering.

In fact, not until November 21 did MacArthur order the Air Force to conduct intensive reconnaissance of the mountainous area between the two coasts. By then, most of the Chinese forces had already stealthily assumed attack positions.[56] MacArthur thought that the Chinese "could not possibly have got more [than 30,000 men] over with the surreptitiously covert means used."[57] Yet they had done just that. Calling the CPV "a phantom which cast no shadow," military historian S. L. A. Marshall noted it "moved only by night, preserved an absolute camouflage discipline during . . . daytime rests and remained hidden to view. . . . Air observation saw nothing of this mass maneuver."[58]

The Chinese trap sprang the day after MacArthur inaugurated the "end-the-war offensive" on November 24. The CPV launched its Second Offensive at dusk, attacking the IX Corps east of the Chongchon River. It struck at the I Corps west of the Chongchon River on the night of the 25th and the X Corps at the Chosin Reservoir on the 27th. More than 380,000 Chinese troops poured out of the mountains, and soon overwhelmed and demoralized the UN troops. The Eighth Army began to pull back on the 27th and withdrew on the 29th, but was enveloped and ambushed by rapid-moving CPV units.[59] The 2nd Infantry Division was the worst hit and suffered 4,940 casualties in the Battle of Kunu-ri.[60] The Eighth Army's defense unraveled and units began fleeing. Pyongyang was abandoned on December 5. By the 16th, the entire Eighth Army had retreated south of the 38th parallel, almost 130 miles south of where the battle started.[61]

In Communist military history, the Second Offensive is vaunted as "the most brilliant campaign" that "struck the enemy the hardest" in the first year of the war.[62] For Americans, it was a major humiliation. Acheson's assessment that it was "the worst defeat of U.S. forces since Bull Run" was certainly not an exaggeration.[63]

Despite the overall disaster, there was one saving grace: while the X Corps at the Chosin Reservoir and the IX Corps to the east of the Chongchon River suffered heavy losses, the I Corps to the west of Chongchon—consisting of the US 24th and ROK 1st Divisions, and the British 27th Brigade—escaped intact.[64]

Coincidentally, several Chinese defectors surrendered hours before the attack. At five in the afternoon of November 24, medic Wang Shunqing of the 40th Army brought three American POWs to the UNC lines. At six the next morning, Captain

Liu Bingzhang of the 66th Army defected. At eight on November 26, porter Qi Zhenwu of the 50th Army abandoned the ammunition he was carrying and deserted.[65] They were lucky since they defected during the calm before the storm, half a day or a day before their units went on the offensive. The intelligence they provided might have caused the I Corps to halt its advance and begin to retreat, thus possibly altering the course of the war and saving the lives of thousands of American, British, South Korean, and Turkish soldiers.

Future Anti-Communist Leader Wang Shunqing

At dusk on November 24, one day before the CPV opened its Second Offensive by striking the IX Corps east of the Chongchon River, Wang Shunqing of the 40th Army defected with a UN Safe Conduct Pass in hand. His interrogation report noted:

> PW, a medic, was left to care for 3 U.S. soldiers (2 wounded) captured during the engagement. PW decided to desert the CCF, and, with 4 CCF soldiers (who did not know the PW's intention of surrendering), brought the 3 wounded soldiers through CCF lines and surrendered.[66]

This seemingly unbelievable episode was apparently true, as the three rescued American prisoners made a special request to "extend the best treatment possible" to Wang. He was wearing a scarf and a worn-out olive drab US uniform with a parka, which had "obviously been given to him in gratitude." Wang's uncanny ability to hoax four fellow Chinese soldiers to bring wounded Americans to the UN side attests to his leadership skills. Equally unusual was Wang's language ability—"part of the interrogation was performed in English." This probably had to do with his twelve years of education in Qingdao, Shandong, and his former occupation as a teacher.

Before he was captured by the PLA on Hainan Island in June 1950, Wang was a deputy company leader in the Nationalist 63rd Army, which fought the final battle of the Civil War.[67] He concealed his rank and his English skills, and most likely forged his personal history, so that he was spared the intensive indoctrination required for Nationalist officers. He became a medic in the PLA 40th Army. Five weeks after crossing the Yalu on October 19, Wang defected. He outwitted the Communists, twice.

Claiming to be a devout Christian and staunch anti-Communist, Wang reported that his mother and two brothers were killed by the Communists during the land reform in 1948. From his capture in Hainan in June 1950 to his surrender in November, Wang's experience under the Communists was the shortest compared to that of other prisoners. But his hatred was most intense. He later became one of the most powerful anti-Communist POW leaders, a role that earned him the epithet "Little Caesar."

Future Anti-Communist Leader Captain Liu Bingzhang

On October 24, Mao cabled General Peng, authorizing the plan to launch the Second Offensive on the following day.[68] At three the next morning, Captain Liu Bingzhang, a twenty-six-year-old staff officer of the 590th Regiment, 66th Army, deserted his unit in Taechon, sixty miles southeast of the Yalu. Liu walked three miles south, and surrendered to the ROK 1st Division at 6:00 a.m.

Through a Chinese-speaking Korean interpreter, Liu stated that "he intended to surrender since he first crossed the border." Judged to be "of above average intelligence," he "spoke freely and was very cooperative." He divulged "details of the tactical situation," especially the CPV intention to entrap UN forces: the 66th Army's three divisions were deployed to allow the enemy "to advance toward Kusong [roughly forty miles southwest of the Yalu], through Taechon, and then conduct an encircling movement with the 39th army and elements of the 50th Army." Liu was recommended for further interrogation.[69]

Roughly twelve hours after Liu's surrender, the CPV launched the Second Offensive, attacking east of the Chongchon—the IX Corps zone. The 39th and 40th Armies struck at the US 2nd Division, while the 38th and 42nd Armies attacked the ROK 7th and 8th Divisions.[70] However, the 66th and 50th Armies' attack on the I Corps west of the Chongchon did not begin until the evening of November 26, which meant there were thirty-six hours between Liu's defection and the CPV attacks. The battle plan Liu revealed was accurate. When the CPV 66th and 50th Armies sprang into action, they found their prey—the ROK 1st Division and the US 24th Division—had withdrawn.[71] The I Corps became the only corps that survived the Second Offensive largely unscathed.

Over the next few days and weeks, Liu passed lie detector tests and was interrogated repeatedly. His evaluation was superlative: "PW is unusually alert and excellent for details. As he is well educated by ordinary standards in the Orient and has had a great deal of military training and experiences, he is able to comprehend the many military activities that he had an opportunity to participate in. Information is considered to be very accurate and reliable."[72] Although there is no evidence indicating that Liu's intelligence had any direct impact on the I Corps' course of action, one thing can be said with certainty: Liu must have been gratified to see UN troops escaping the deathtrap set by his former unit.

From the outset, Liu claimed that he was "a loyal supporter of the KMT and expressed eagerness to serve the interest of anti-communist forces in any capacity." He asserted that he "surrendered to UN forces on the chance that he might be sent by them to rejoin the Chinese Nationalist Army." Liu's strong pro-Nationalist sentiment was probably inculcated during the Anti-Japanese War. In 1941, he left his hometown in Tai'an, Shandong, which was then under Japanese occupation, and went to Nationalist-controlled Anhui to attend high school. Afterward he attended two Central Military Academy branches, first in Hubei and then in Shaanxi. Upon graduation in 1946, he was commissioned as a second lieutenant in the 92nd Army. With Beiping's peaceful "liberation" in 1949, Liu had no choice but to surrender and join the PLA.[73] The nearly two years under the Communists did not transform but embittered him. He resented the fact that the Communists confiscated 21 out of 24 mu of land owned by his family in Shandong. Liu lamented, "People with education are not respected by Communists and are held up to public ridicule at their pleasure."[74]

Apparently surprised by Liu's strident anti-Communism, his interrogators asked him to explain the Communist victory. The principal reason, Liu argued, was "due to the Communist mob organization of the lowest elements of the Chinese people who had nothing, never had anything, and who for the most part would never be able to own anything because of their ignorance." Moreover, the "sheer number" of the mob demoralized the Nationalists' supporters. Then he proceeded to offer his list of recommendations as to how to defeat the Communists: cut supply lines by occupying Sinuiju; strike quickly with superior strength; and "use poison gas," as the Communists "have no gas masks."[75]

Among early defectors and prisoners, Liu was clearly the most articulate, knowledgeable, cooperative, and committed anti-Communist. He was so valuable that he would be flown to Tokyo in February 1951, where he would be interrogated for almost four months.[76]

"An Entirely New War"

"We face an entirely new war," declared MacArthur in a desperate message to the JCS on November 28. Interrogation reports and other intelligence had established that enemy strength was near 200,000. In an about-face, MacArthur asserted that China's "ultimate objective was undoubtedly a decisive effort aimed at the complete destruction of all UN forces." He kicked the ball back to Washington by stating that "this command has done everything humanly possible within its capacities but is now faced with conditions beyond its control and its strength."[77]

MacArthur cabled Washington the following day: "the Chinese Nationalist armies on Formosa represented the only source of potential trained reinforcement available for early commitment to the war in Korea," and they could be combat ready within fourteen days. He trusted his friend Chiang so much that he assured Washington that "much larger forces than had been previously offered would undoubtedly be made available if desired." Therefore, he "strongly recommended" that he be authorized to negotiate directly with Chiang regarding the incorporation of Nationalist units under the UN Command.[78]

In Washington, however, the very notion of re-engaging that "old crooked Chiang Kai-shek" was almost as horrifying as losing the war in Korea.[79] At an NSC meeting in the White House, Secretary of Defense Marshall advocated a limited war. Although it was clear to him that "the Chinese Communist action is dictated in large measure by the [Soviet] Politburo," the United States should not "publicly hold the USSR responsible now." Instead, it "should use all available political, economic and psychological action to limit the war." He argued emphatically, "We should not go into Chinese Communist territory and we should not use Chinese Nationalist forces. To do either of these things would increase the danger of war with the Chinese Communists."[80] Marshall spoke as if the troops who were thrashing the Americans were not Chinese. Compounding the irony, at the UN Security Council meetings in New York around the same time, the Communist general-turned-diplomat Wu Xiuquan harangued the United States for its aggression against China, and demanded a settlement on Taiwan and the PRC's admission to the UN as preconditions for a cease-fire in Korea.[81]

Contrary to Marshall's contention that it was "possible to hold a line," UN forces were driven south toward the 38th parallel in hasty retreat.[82] Eighth Army troops fled south even before seeing the enemy. "Look around here," lamented Colonel Paul Freeman, commander of the 23rd Regiment, 2nd Division. "This is a sight that hasn't been seen for hundreds of years: the men of a whole United States Army fleeing from a battlefield, abandoning their wounded, running for their lives."[83]

Washington was staggered. Truman, when queried by reporters on November 30, said that "there has always been active consideration" of the use of atomic bombs. "It is a matter that the military people will decide." He added, "I am not a military authority that passes on these things. . . . The military commander in the field will have charge of the use of weapons, as he always has."[84] This statement, in effect suggesting that MacArthur had the discretion to use nuclear bombs, immediately caused a worldwide uproar. The White House issued a clarification on the same day: "by law, only the President can authorize the use of the atom bomb, and no such authorization has been given."[85] But it was too late.

Although it was Truman who made a colossal gaffe in his A-bomb talk, Acheson asked Truman to stop MacArthur from talking about a naval blockade and aerial bombing of China. He suggested "censorship in the Far Eastern Command immediately" and named Willoughby in particular.[86]

Truman's A-bomb talk did not deter Chinese forces. The seven battered US divisions were vastly outnumbered and overrun by twenty-six Chinese divisions, which MacArthur described as "fresh, completely organized, splendidly trained and equipped and apparently in peak condition for actual operations." On December 3, MacArthur told Washington that his "small command . . . is facing the entire Chinese nation in an undeclared war." He pleaded for reinforcements in this "entirely new war against an entirely new power of great military strength and under entirely new conditions."[87] Marshall finally realized that the "situation looked very bad indeed." Bradley concluded, "not more than 48 to 72 hours would elapse before it reached a crash state."[88]

Both Tokyo and Washington were devising an exit from Korea and weighing its consequences. At that moment the debate was not so much on whether to cut and run but whether ROK troops should also be evacuated. In a Pentagon meeting, Acheson came to terms with the possibility of the United States being driven out of the Far East: "There is danger of our becoming the greatest appeasers of all time if we abandon the Koreans and they are slaughtered; if there is a Dunkirk and we are forced out it is a disaster but not a disgraceful one."[89] Bradley feared that Indochina and Formosa would be lost next. In Europe, the Germans "are already saying we have proved that we are weak. Appeasement is gaining."[90] The situation looked bleak across the globe.

In the critical 48 to 72 hours after Bradley spoke of "a crash state," Truman and Acheson were obliged to entertain British prime minister Clement Attlee who, alarmed by the A-bomb talk, invited himself to Washington. While Truman, Acheson, and company were alleged "appeasers" in the eyes of the Republicans, in contrast, to Attlee they appeared unmistakably hawkish. In a State Department preparation meeting George Kennan, now called back from Princeton University, advocated a hard-line policy, asserting that "we owe China nothing but a lesson."[91]

"The only way to meet communism is to eliminate it," Truman told Attlee, as if lifting a line directly from MacArthur. Attlee disagreed, suggesting that by handing over Chiang Kai-shek to the Communists the Korean problem would disappear. "It is hard to believe," Acheson countered, "that if we give them Formosa and make other concessions, they would then become calm and peaceful." Truman tried to draw Attlee's attention to Chinese threats to British assets: "After Korea, it would be Indochina, then Hong Kong, then Malaya."[92]

In his defense of American policy on Taiwan, Marshall inadvertently exonerated Chiang Kai-shek, whose regime Attlee deemed "rotten and corrupt" and who should be "take[n] off."[93] Marshall explained that he "held Chiang free from personal corruption but his followers and party were corrupt." When Marshall remarked that he could not contemplate a Taiwan without Chiang, Truman suggested "a UN Trusteeship."[94] Undoubtedly Truman remained fixated on the idea of getting rid of Chiang.

While UN soldiers were running for their lives in Korea, the two-day marathon meeting at the White House lapsed into an intellectual debate on whether Mao and his men were Communists or nationalists. Attlee asked, "When is it that you scratch a Communist and find a nationalist[?]" Truman deferred to Marshall, who recalled several meetings he had with Mao and many more with Zhou Enlai when he was mediating the Chinese Civil War in 1946. He remembered Zhou saying to Mrs. Marshall that the Chinese Communists were true "Marxist Communists" and they resented being referred to as "merely agrarian reformists." Attlee retorted, "Tito was also a full Communist."[95] Attlee clearly still thought that Mao was another Tito, and the West could drive a wedge between Mao and Stalin by sacrificing Chiang.

Perhaps alarmed by Marshall's softness on Chiang, Acheson wrote to Marshall on December 5, reiterating his disapproval of using Chiang's troops in Korea.[96] In a memorandum to US diplomats around the world, Acheson defended his China policy while acknowledging observers' fear of "extremist demands of Amer[ican] supporters of Chiang Kai-shek."[97] No doubt, one of such demands was MacArthur's repeated requests to use Nationalist troops in Korea and to lift restrictions on aerial bombing and a naval blockade of China. "If these restrictions were withdrawn," MacArthur claimed on December 7, "and if he could use 50,000–60,000 Chinese Nationalist troops," he could hold a line across Korea. Otherwise, UN forces should evacuate Korea.[98]

On December 16, the day when the Eighth Army retreated south of the 38th parallel, Truman declared a nationwide state of emergency. On December 21, MacArthur asked for all four US National Guard divisions to be sent to the Far East, but was rebuffed.[99] A few days later, the CIA gave a negative assessment of his proposed use of Chiang's troops.[100] The JCS concluded that "the time had come for withdrawal."[101] On December 30, MacArthur made a last-ditch effort, proposing to: (1) blockade China's coast; (2) bomb China's industrial complex; (3) use Nationalist troops in Korea; (4) unleash Chiang's forces to attack the mainland.[102] While Truman and the NSC deliberated over a rebuttal, Seoul was lost on January 4, 1951. On the 9th, the JCS cabled MacArthur to reject all his proposals, concluding that when "evacuation is essential to avoid severe losses of men and material you will at that time withdraw from Korea to Japan."[103]

MacArthur's desperation and the JCS's fatalism could have been avoided had they studied prisoners' interrogation reports that revealed the limits of Chinese capabilities.

Future Communist Leader Captain Sun Zhenguan Captured at Chosin

While eighteen CPV divisions with 230,000 men in the west sent the Eighth Army reeling 130 miles to a line below the 38th parallel in three weeks, twelve fresh CPV divisions of the 9th Army Group with some 150,000 troops attacked the X Corps in the Chosin Reservoir area for two weeks, but ultimately failed to crack it. Led by the 1st Marine Division, the X Corps broke through the encirclement in a methodical and cohesive fashion. CPV official history boasts that it inflicted "annihilation-quality damage" (*jianmiexing daji*) on the enemy. But in fact, other than the destruction of the US Army 32nd Regiment, 7th Division, that resulted in 2,760 killed, wounded, and missing, the 1st Marine Division's casualties were limited: 393 killed, 76 missing in action, and 2,152 wounded. Frostbite casualties were much higher.[104]

During its withdrawal south—or "advancing in a different direction" in the words of 1st Marine Division commander Oliver P. Smith—UN forces captured a number of Chinese prisoners and took them along in a seaborne evacuation to Pusan.[105] One of them was Captain Sun Zhenguan, a battalion commissar of the 180th Regiment, 60th Division, 20th Army.

On the morning of November 27, General Almond flew in by helicopter to the 1st Marine Division command post at Hagaru-ri, four miles south of the Chosin Reservoir. He told the cautiously moving Marines: "We're still attacking and we're going all the way to the Yalu." He added, "Don't let a bunch of Chinese laundrymen stop you." Little did the Americans know that their enemy in the First Offensive, the 42nd Army, had already been replaced by three fresh, over-strength armies—the 20th, 26th, and 27th, each with four divisions.[106]

The temperature plunged to zero degrees Fahrenheit on the night of November 26, and further dropped to 20 below zero on the 27th.[107] By nightfall, the CPV launched its Second Offensive near the Chosin Reservoir. Four divisions of the 20th Army swung south to cut off the Marines' only supply and retreat route at various points. Sun Zhenguan's 60th Division marched in snow toward Koto-ri, ten miles south of the Hagaru-ri. The next day, units of the 58th and 60th Divisions occupied two hills overlooking Koto-ri on each side of the road, creating a ten-mile gauntlet for any retreating or relieving forces. This spot was to be remembered as Hell Fire Valley, where the 1,000-man-strong British-American Task Force Drysdale suffered 300 casualties on November 29 and 30, and 237 men surrendered to the Chinese.[108]

As the X Corps began withdrawing south, Chinese forces quickly moved to take blocking positions along the ten-mile hairpin road between Koto-ri and the valley below, as Mao personally directed on December 4. Sun's 20th Army was relieved by the newly arrived 26th Army at Koto-ri, and it moved south to occupy Hwangcho-ryong around the Funchilin Pass to block relief forces from the south.[109]

On the night of December 8, the temperature plummeted to 40 degrees below zero. The poorly equipped and thinly clothed CPV troops, who had been fighting for ten days without rest or resupply, were powerless to stop the 1st Marine Division from breaking out. When the sky cleared on the morning of the 9th, the Marines attacked the mountain pass south of Koto-ri, only to find the frozen corpses of Chinese defenders.[110] As the Marines' convoy of more than a thousand vehicles snaked south toward Funchilin Pass, a relief force—the 1st Battalion of the 1st Marine Regiment—had been attacking from the south toward the pass for a day. After a "stiff battle," the relief force captured Hill 1081 and soon joined forces with the main convoy.[111]

The defenders of the pass were none other than Sun's 180th Regiment and one battalion of the 179th. After fighting the Marines from both directions for two days, "the majority of the 180th regiment were killed or wounded by enemy fire or the freezing temperature."[112] Captain Sun was one of the ten to twenty survivors captured by the Americans, who found Chinese soldiers' stamina under such extreme conditions bewildering. One standard interrogation question asked if "narcotics or stimulants" were used to "provoke fanaticism in attacks."[113]

By the time Sun's unit was ordered to occupy Hwangcho-ryong, his entire 3rd Battalion had been decimated.[114] When all able-bodied soldiers were assembled, it was found that there were enough to fill only two platoons. They tried to dig trenches and foxholes overnight in the frozen earth. After daybreak, their position was bombarded by artillery and air strikes.[115] Sun and two soldiers rushed from their rear post to check the front positions, only to find American tanks and troops there. As Sun turned around and ran, his eyeglasses became fogged from his breath. He stumbled to a machine gun position, only to be seized by American soldiers. The entire hill had been overrun.[116]

Captain Sun had a pistol, a notebook, and binoculars. To hide his identity as an officer, he hid the notebook in the snow. When he tried to put his glasses in his pocket, a GI yanked them away and smashed them. Sun identified himself as a clerk carrying the pistol and binoculars for the company leader, who had picked up better ones from dead Americans.

When the prisoners arrived in the coastal city of Hungnam in the afternoon, Sun's heart sank. "Where will the Americans take us? Will they send us to work as slave labor in Southeast Asia as the Japanese had done? Or send us to Taiwan?" In any case, "there is no way I can come out alive." Sun thought of committing suicide. "As a Communist Party member and cadre, I should never have allowed myself to be taken prisoner." A captured platoon leader comforted him: "There are Communists everywhere, even in Southeast Asia." Meanwhile, some former Nationalists were quickly emboldened to taunt their ex-superiors. Sun's identity was exposed.[117] Long-suppressed Communist-Nationalist rivalry reemerged barely hours after Sun's capture.

On Christmas Eve, 1950, the X Corps completed its evacuation from Hungnam, leaving the port city in smoke as abandoned supplies and facilities were blown up. Chinese and North Korean troops immediately entered the ruined city, marking the end of the Second Offensive.

Also evacuated from Hungnam to Pusan were 86,000 refugees, including the parents of Moon Jae-in, the ROK president elected in May 2017, and a number of prisoners, including Sun. When UN prison authorities assigned serial numbers beginning with 700001 to Chinese POWs, Sun was number 700101, suggesting that he was one of first hundred Chinese prisoners.

The Third Offensive, December 31, 1950–January 8, 1951

The Eighth Army's commander Walton Walker was killed in a jeep accident north of Seoul on December 23, and Matthew B. Ridgway, US Army deputy chief of staff, was named as his successor. Ridgway arrived in Tokyo before midnight on Christmas Day. "The Eighth Army is yours, Matt," MacArthur told him, giving him full command of all forces in Korea, including the X Corps.[118]

On New Year's Eve, the CPV and the KPA launched the Third Offensive on a 100-mile-wide front along the 38th parallel. ROK units quickly unraveled. Troops fled with "just one aim—to get as far away from the Chinese as possible." Ridgway tried in vain to stop them. Soon the Eighth Army also fell back, though "in good order and with almost all its equipment," Ridgway recalled.[119]

Potential CPV defectors must have found it exceedingly difficult to cross the line to surrender, as UN forces were mostly in quick retreat in the first week of 1951. Nevertheless, Wei Shixi, a heavy machine gun instructor, managed to defect the day before the offensive began—nearly an exact replay of Captain Liu Bingzhang's escape on the eve of the Second Offensive. Wei, also formerly a captain in the Nationalist 92nd Army before its surrender to the PLA in Beiping in 1949, was retained by the PLA 66th Army for his technical expertise. While Liu, with the 197th Division, defected near Taechon on November 25, 1950, Wei's 196th Division fought UN forces for two hours at the same location two days later.[120] Apparently Wei had no chance to escape then.

Shortly before the Third Offensive, Wei was reassigned to a stretcher-bearer platoon as its deputy leader—a move laying bare Communist distrust of former Nationalists. Before dawn on December 29, Wei's unit arrived at Sachang-ni near Hwachon in central Korea. Wei escaped at four in the morning and surrendered to ROK troops 28 hours later at Chichon-ri, ten miles to the southeast.[121] He defected roughly 40 hours before the Third Offensive began.

After he reached the ROK lines, Wei was evacuated to Seoul on December 31.[122] Meanwhile, the 66th and 42nd Armies overwhelmed ROK units, resulting in 3,200 ROK casualties. They captured Chunchon and Kapyong on January 2 in a flanking movement threatening Seoul, 35 miles to the west. Soon Seoul fell.[123]

If Liu Bingzhang was lucky to take the first opportunity to defect, Wei probably seized the last. Had Wei hesitated, he probably would not have had a second chance. The 66th Army would return to China in early March, permanently closing the window of opportunity.[124]

On January 3, Ridgway ordered a general withdrawal from Seoul. The CPV 116th Division of the 39th Army, 149th Division of the 50th Army, and KPA 1st Corps fought their way into the city the next day.[125] Chinese troops raised a North Korean flag over the city hall, marking its third change of hands.[126]

Fang Xiangqian, a twenty-year-old cultural instructor in the 150th Division, 50th Army, entered Seoul with his unit sometime after dark. The ancient city gate was still burning and the devastated city was blanketed in choking smoke. Fang's unit rushed straight to an enemy depot, where hungry troops carried away as many sacks of wheat flour and cans of C-rations as they could. Private Lu Xuewen of the same unit recalled, "Each soldier carried away at least twenty pounds of rice." Then they marched out of the city. There was no time for a victory march or celebration.[127] Within 24 hours, the 50th Army crossed the frozen Han River in hot pursuit of UN forces. It took Suwon on January 7th. Fang and Lu's 150th Division occupied an area 10 to 15 miles above the 37th parallel.[128] That was probably the southernmost point reached by the CPV in the entire war.

By the end of the offensive on January 8, the Communists had pushed UN forces some 50 to 70 miles south—from the 38th parallel to a line near the 37th.[129] The Third Offensive was the last major campaign in which the CPV achieved a clear victory. In retreat, the UNC captured few prisoners. The number of Chinese POWs grew from 1,245 in December 1950 to 1,360 in January 1951—an increase of only 115 men in the entire month of January.[130]

"Advance to Taegu! Advance to Pusan!" The *People's Daily* celebrated the capture of Seoul with an exhortation: "If the American aggressors refuse to withdraw, drive them into the sea!" Dismayed by such exuberance, General Peng Dehuai remarked, "If the enemy retakes Seoul, how am I supposed to explain it to the people?"[131] That feared eventuality would come about much sooner than Peng—and the Americans—had anticipated.

Puzzled by conflicting reports from MacArthur in Tokyo and Ridgway in Korea, the JCS dispatched Generals Lawton Collins and Hoyt Vandenberg to Korea and Japan in mid-January 1951. On the 17th they reported to Washington, "Eighth Army in good shape and improving daily under Ridgway." Upon receiving the news, General Bradley noted, "you could almost hear the sighs of relief" throughout the upper levels of the US government in Washington.[132]

While Ridgway would have "absolutely no talk about" possible evacuation, MacArthur doggedly continued his debate with Washington, arguing that not taking Chinese and Korean prisoners to the United States in case of a withdrawal would be "a sign of weakness." Finding the idea abhorrent, Acheson asserted, "This was a sign of weakness which, if it got to the point of evacuation, we would have to show." He recommended simply leaving the POWs on an offshore island.[133]

That worst-case scenario never came to pass. The tide was about to turn.

6

Ridgway's Turnaround, MacArthur's Exit, and Taiwan's Entry

BRUSHING ASIDE OBJECTIONS from the North Koreans and their Soviet advisors, General Peng Dehuai ended the Third Offensive on January 8, 1951. "Without rest and replenishment, without improved transportation and supply," he warned Mao, his army "could hardly continue to fight."[1] By this time, the CPV had been fighting continuously for more than two months in freezing weather. Its supply lines had become so overextended that its archaic logistics system consisting of trucks, pack animals, and human porters could no longer support any meaningful offensive. The CPV general headquarters made plans for a two- to three-month recuperation period before mounting a spring offensive.[2] General Matthew Ridgway, however, permitted his foe no such luxury.

Ridgway Turns the Tide

Various Communist units had barely reached their designated rest areas between January 12 and 14 when, on the 15th, Ridgway ordered a probing attack, Operation Wolfhound. In the western sector, the I Corps sent combined tank and motorized infantry units to harass CPV outposts, meeting only pockets of resistance. Having confirmed the absence of large enemy forces south of Suwon, Ridgway launched Operation Thunderbolt on the 25th, mobilizing 250,000 troops. A reconnaissance in force quickly escalated into a full-fledged general attack.[3]

The UNC recaptured Suwon on January 26. The heaviest fighting occurred on the 27th near Kumnyangjang-ni, a few miles to the east, where the 1st Cavalry Division killed at least 300 men of the CPV 150th Division, to which Fang Xiangqian belonged.[4] Captured CPV soldiers identified only two divisions of the 50th Army across a thirty-mile-wide front.[5] For the first time in the war, the CPV enjoyed no numerical advantage over its enemy. It was vastly outnumbered south of the Han River, where it deployed only one army (the 50th Army) plus two divisions (the 112th of the 38th Army and the 125th of the 42nd Army).[6] The 50th Army faced off with the I Corps, comprising the US 3rd and 25th Divisions, the ROK 1st Division, the British Commonwealth 29th Brigade, the Turkish Brigade, and the IX Corps's US 1st Cavalry Division.

At this juncture, more than a hundred Chinese and North Korean generals and leaders, including Peng Dehuai and Kim Il-sung, were holding a conference to assess their first three offensives. Caught off guard by UN forces' swift turnaround, Peng changed the agenda and ended the conference early. He cabled Mao on January 27 suggesting a limited cease-fire and a tactical withdrawal. Having rejected the UN proposal of "a ceasefire first and negotiations second" ten days earlier, Mao was in no mood for an about-face. Instead, he ordered: "The CPV must immediately launch a fourth offensive with the goals of annihilating 20,000 to 30,000 US and ROK troops" and occupying areas north of the 36.5th parallel. Mao commanded that Seoul, Inchon, and beachhead positions south of the Han must be defended. Upon receiving Mao's directive, Peng fell into a long silence. Poring over the situation maps and shaking his head, Peng finally said, "On what basis has Beijing made this decision? Given the fact that the enemy counteroffensive is so ferocious, how can we advance south?" Stalin, however, weighed in to endorse Mao's plan on January 30.[7] In the ensuing weeks, Communist generals and troops would find out how wildly unrealistic Mao's ambitions were.

Peng had no choice but to follow the order. Nevertheless, he made clear the difficulties his troops were facing: "The Third Offensive already overstrained us (mainly fatigue)," but the new offensive "entails a greater level of overstraining." Without the usual numerical advantage enjoyed by the CPV, he warned, "If our main thrust is blunted, we could temporarily lose the initiative."[8] Peng's fear soon became reality, even before his troops were fully deployed for an offensive.

The CPV 50th Army, having been under constant attack since January 15, bore the brunt of the UNC offensive along the Suwon-Seoul axis. Pushed out of two successive defensive lines, it had lost nearly half of its troops by February 4.[9] Private Lu Xuewen's company of 220 men was reduced to fewer than 40. It received reinforcements three times, but these were untrained men aged from fifteen to sixty. "They were supposedly litter-bearers. But now they were handed rifles and ordered to charge." One night in a foxhole, a middle-aged Shandong native kept sobbing and saying how much he missed home and his mother. The next morning, he was blown to pieces by a shell.[10]

CPV troops with small arms took blocking positions on snowy hills, where they were pulverized by UNC firepower. When barrages rained down at night, many wounded men wailed, "Help! Anyone! You're my father. Help!" Yet no one was able or willing to move out from his foxhole to help. Having lost much blood, the wounded swallowed snow to quench their thirst, and in doing so merely hastened their death, which often came within half an hour. "Dead people were scattered everywhere on the hill. It was horrific," Lu recalled. "We hated Mao. He sent us there without supplies, simply as pigs to take bullets."[11]

Having suffered nearly 50 percent casualties, the 50th Army finally crossed the thawing Han River on February 7, but left behind its 450th Regiment to defend the southern beachhead, along with a reinforced 38th Army and four KPA battalions. With their backs against the river, the remaining troops resisted UN forces for another eleven days and nights.[12] In one of the battles, Fang Xiangqian, the cultural instructor now turned ammunition bearer of the 450th, saw "enemy fire everywhere, from airplanes, tanks, and swarming infantry." When the heavy machine gunner's eyes were blown out by artillery shrapnel, Fang, whose only prior training involved firing a test burst back in Manchuria, bellowed, "Let me do it!" He clutched the handle grips of the Maxim gun, and fired with a vengeance, until the gun gave out.[13] Finally, all Communist units in the western sector withdrew north of the Han on February 16 and 18.[14]

On February 17, just hours before the CPV's final retreat across the river, twenty-year-old Wu Jiansheng of the 50th Army's transportation company deserted. He surrendered to the US 25th Division near Kwangju the following day. The son of a former mayor of Linsen County, Fujian, Wu joined the Nationalist army in 1948 and was captured by the PLA on Hainan Island in April 1950. He told his interrogator that he "abhorred the CCF because with all his education, [his] assigned duty was horse tender."[15] Having missed the chance to flee to Taiwan from Hainan a year earlier, Wu now seized the opportunity to escape.

The Communist retreat was necessitated by a major setback in the central sector, where the CPV concentrated its attack. Despite its initial success in routing three ROK divisions near Hoengsong (50 miles east of Seoul) between February 11 and 13, in the subsequent three days 20 miles to the west, four CPV divisions from three different armies—the 39th, 40th, and 42nd—failed to crack the defensive perimeter held by Paul Freeman's US 23rd Regiment and a French battalion at Chipyong-ni. Peng called off the siege and ordered a retreat, thus ending the offensive phase of the campaign merely five days after it began.[16] Ridgway saw that the US forces had "substantially regained the confidence lost during the distressing withdrawals of December and early January."[17] The war had reached a turning point.

Prisoners and Defectors in the Fourth Offensive, January 27–April 21, 1951

Giving his retreating enemy no respite, Ridgway swiftly launched Operation Killer on February 21. In the next two weeks, the UNC pushed north slowly but steadily, meeting only scattered, occasional but strong resistance. Thanks to unseasonable rainfall that made the UNC advance "a plodding affair," the CPV had a "head start in withdrawing." Ridgway's primary objective of destroying enemy forces was "only partially achieved."[18] Nevertheless, the UNC's first major counteroffensive created opportunities for potential defectors.

Taiwanese Chen Yonghua surrendered on February 27. Chen's 116th Division of the 39th Army enjoyed the unique distinction of having both led the attack in the CPV's first victory at Unsan on November 1–3, 1950, and spearheaded the capture of two capitals—Pyongyang on December 6, 1950, and Seoul on January 4, 1951. Its winning streak came to an end at Chipyong-ni, where it suffered staggering losses.[19] During the withdrawal, Chen and two other scouts accompanied a staff officer to reconnoiter UNC positions on February 23. After dusk, Chen "escaped northward" and then "went southward," managing to elude detection. Four days later, he passed through UNC lines and surrendered to the US 1st Marine Division in Hoengsong. He claimed that he had planned to defect "ever since he picked up his first surrender leaflet at Seoul."[20]

Since his capture by the PLA in Shenyang, Manchuria, in November 1948, Chen had followed the 39th Army in its campaign to "liberate half of China," sweeping from Manchuria in the northeast all the way to the Sino-Vietnamese border in the southwest. He was promoted to assistant squad leader in the reconnaissance company attached to the divisional headquarters—a highly sensitive position. Apparently, Chen's performance had earned the Communists' trust. After biding his time for more than two years, he finally outsmarted his captors. But it would be two years before his homecoming to Taiwan.

Facing a distressing situation, General Peng rode a jeep overnight to Andong, and then flew to Beijing on February 21. He rushed to the Jade Spring Mountain resort, pushed aside Mao's bodyguards, barged into his bedroom, and woke him up. Peng told Mao that a quick victory was impossible. Highlighting the fact that some frontline soldiers were fighting barefoot in the snow, Peng warned, "Without effective transportation and logistic support, we cannot fight a protracted war." After a long pause, Mao relented and said, "Win a quick victory if you can; if you can't, win a slow one." In the following ten days, Peng conferred with Zhou Enlai and other leaders, seeking to boost logistic support. In a meeting at the PLA General Staff Headquarters, Peng became so frustrated with bureaucratic foot-dragging that he pounded the table, stood up, and exclaimed: "So many of our young soldiers have starved or frozen to death on the front line. Were they pigs? Why can't you overcome some difficulties back home?" On March 9, Peng returned to the CPV GHQ in Korea, only to find that the enemy had launched another offensive two days earlier.[21]

Before dawn on March 7, the US 25th Division fired the opening salvo of Operation Ripper by raining fire on the north bank of the Han River. Then three infantry regiments made a crossing nearly unopposed, and tanks forded or were ferried north.[22] Fang Xiangqian and two comrades of the heavy machine gun company, 450th Regiment, exhausted and dead asleep in a bunker overlooking the river, were woken up by the rumble of tanks. "Look! The enemy is already here!" shouted the squad leader, "Fire!" As the heavy machine gun opened up, Fang loaded ammo. A UNC tank promptly returned fire. A shell blew their machine gun asunder and shattered the makeshift bunker made of railway track beams, pine tree branches, and dirt. Stunned, Fang and his comrades climbed out and surrendered. "Until that moment, I had never thought of being captured," recalled Fang. Ironically, he had been trained to capture Americans. Six decades later he still remembered these three English lines: "Drop your guns! You will not be killed. You will get better treatment."[23]

FIGURE 6.1. Captured Chinese soldiers, including some teenagers, are questioned by ROK and US officers north of the Han River. March 8, 1951. US National Archives.

CPV official history claims that on March 7 several companies lost every man, their troops having "died heroically defending their positions."[24] In reality, some survived and were captured. The US 25th Division took 213 prisoners that day, the largest number captured in a single day by any division in the offensive.[25] Some of these POWs were defectors. Xiao Lixing, a cultural instructor in the 450th Regiment, escaped with three men before dawn. Soon he was aboard a helicopter with loudspeakers, calling on his former comrades to surrender. A student refugee from Hubei, Xiao was captured by the PLA in Sichuan in December 1949. He defected with the hope of being sent to Taiwan.[26]

When a tank shell hit the position manned by Lu Xuewen and three others, a fifteen-year-old boy was shredded into gore and bone splinters. Lu and two survivors ran into a tunnel for cover. Soon they were flushed out by a search squad firing into the tunnel. When Lu crawled out, the GIs fired again, sending bullets flying over his head. He was searched and then told to go down the hill. "They're not going to kill us here, but will do it down there," Lu feared. Instead, he was taken to a POW stockade and was interrogated.[27]

On March 9, merely a few hours after his return to his GHQ, Peng ordered a gradual withdrawal with delaying actions, effective on the night of the 10th.[28] Just hours after the retreat began, acting platoon leader Tan Xingdong of the 113th Division, 38th Army, escaped with three men and surrendered to UN forces east of Seoul on March 11. Tan, the former assistant battalion commander demoted for desertion, had long been waiting for this chance.[29]

On March 14, as the badly mauled 50th and 38th Armies withdrew north, the Communists abandoned Seoul—and would never reclaim it. About the same time, in the central sector four soldiers of the 124th Division, 42nd Army, deserted as they pretended to look for drinking water during retreat. From their hiding place, they wrote a letter addressed to "Dear Comrades of the UNC":

> Thank you for your hard work! We had served in the Chinese Nationalist Army, but were unfortunately captured during the final battle in Shenyang in October 1948. In the Communist bandit army, we lay low and bided our time. Now four of us have been safely hiding in a villager's house for more than a week, waiting for your rescue. The Communist bandit army withdrew two days ago. We guarantee it is all safe now. Please advance without hesitation. Salute!
>
> [signed] Tang Jusheng, Shi Wenxuan, Yuan Pengying, Wang Qiming[30]

On March 20, they surrendered to advancing UN units near Hongchon.[31]

In the western sector, a twenty-four-year-old doctor, Meng Ming, of the 26th Army finally reached UNC lines on March 26, after trekking alone for more than ten days from the rear.[32] Meng hailed from a well-off family of traditional medicine practitioners in Tianshui, Gansu, in northwestern China. In 1944, he answered Chiang Kai-shek's call to fight the Japanese, joining the Youth Army, which was largely composed of high school and college students. After V-J Day, Chiang kept his promise and decommissioned former students on June 3, 1946—hence the day became Youth Army Day. Meng enrolled in military-sponsored high schools and training regiments, and prepared for the college entrance examinations, but failed twice. In October 1949, he was captured by the PLA in Xiamen, Fujian, barely missing the last chance to flee across the Taiwan Strait. Given his education and family background, the Communists selected him for medical training. He became a medical officer.

Meng's 14th Artillery Regiment, part of the 9th Army Group from eastern China, was spared frontline action in the clashes at the Chosin Reservoir in late 1950. While the 20th and 27th Armies were decimated and put out of action until May 1951, the 26th Army and its attached 14th Artillery participated in the Fourth Offensive by relieving the 50th Army.[33] As his unit was taking up defensive positions north of Seoul, Meng came under suspicion in "thought examination" meetings, especially after he was found secretly studying an English dictionary in his bunker. He and fifty other suspects were removed from the front and sent to rear units. Embittered, Meng began plotting to defect. He tried to persuade a former Youth Army friend to escape with him, but was rejected.

As UN forces pushed north, one night when Meng's rear unit decamped, he pretended to have to relieve himself and escaped into the dark forest. He raced up two hills. After making sure his pursuers had given up, he found himself soaked with sweat. On his way south, he made a daring gamble: he walked during the day and rested at night, the opposite of the CPV pattern. One day he ran into a former superior, who pointed his pistol at him, asking, "What are you doing here?" Meng said that he was sent to the front line to pick up the wounded. The officer lowered his gun and cautioned him, "Be careful! Watch out for enemy soldiers and agents!" Meng managed to cheat fate.

Meng finally approached the UNC lines near Dongduchon, 35 miles north of Seoul. Two days earlier, the US Airborne 187th Regiment and the 3rd Division had joined forces and pushed into this area, where the 26th Army, Meng's outfit, had fiercely resisted.[34] When he finally saw UN troops, Meng waived a white towel and shouted in English, "Surrender! Surrender!" Surprised to see a lone enemy defector, GIs searched him thoroughly. Reaching into a hidden pocket of his tattered jacket, Meng produced three old photos showing him in Nationalist uniforms. The Americans called in a helicopter and flew him to Seoul.

Ten miles to the east in the Pochon area, truck driver Li Da'an defected on March 24, less than a month after crossing the Yalu River.[35] A hagiographic account published in Taiwan in 1955 dramatized Li's defection: After unloading ammunition, Li sped toward the UNC lines. With one hand on the steering wheel, Li swung a hammer onto the head of his dozing co-driver. "Blood gushed out like water bursting from a faucet."[36] However, in his confession made to the Communists after his recapture in 1953, Li admitted that he, his assistant, and four others escaped from their bivouac on foot. Guided by a local Korean woman, they absconded into the woods.[37]

By the end of March the UNC offensive had reached the 38th parallel. On the western end of this new battle line lay Kaesong, which ROK patrols reached in mid-April.[38] On April 14, three CPV truck drivers surrendered: former Nationalist paratrooper Captain Yang Shuzhi, his assistant Du Wenpu, and former New 1st Army Captain Yin Ruliang. After they were drafted in Chongqing in late 1950, Yang, Yin, and some two hundred drivers were sent to Andong in February 1951. One month after crossing the Yalu River on March 3, Yang's truck, loaded with seventy crates of meat, broke down at a bridge destroyed in an air attack. Yang told Du, "We are stuck. We might as well go to the UN side." They hid in a villager's home for eleven days until anti-Communist guerrillas took them to safety. Expressing his "liking for Americans because of the past relation while attending school in India under American instructors" in World War II, Yang asked his interrogators to send him to Formosa to rejoin the Nationalists.[39]

Between January 25 and April 21, when the Fourth Offensive ended, the Communist forces had retreated from a line near the 37th parallel to the 38th. The offensive turned out to be a misnomer, as the main attack did not begin until February 11 in the central sector and was already thwarted within four days. In the western sector the CPV was on the defensive throughout. In fact, in Communist parlance, it was simply called the Fourth Campaign (*Disici zhanyi*).

The 87-day campaign with extensive troop movements created many opportunities for escape. The number of Chinese prisoners, however, grew by only roughly 2,000 in three months, or 23 a day.[40] Despite being put on the defensive, the CPV methodically implemented a three-phased defense and retreat. As unit cohesion was maintained, it was very difficult for troops to escape. To prevent defection, the CPV moved some suspects to the rear. Suspects remaining on the front line were closely monitored, and some were stripped of weapons. Former Nationalist Zheng Zheng'an, a litter bearer in the 26th Army, had to turn in his two grenades—the only weapons he carried—when his unit went into battle. He managed to escape in early April.[41]

In many cases, defectors took extraordinary risks to escape from places far behind the front line. They either had to hide and wait for days, if not weeks, before surrendering—if UN forces had advanced far enough north to reach them at all—or they walked south, and had to elude capture along the way. They often needed help from sympathetic Korean villagers or partisans. Had anything gone wrong, they would not have made it to the UNC lines. Moments before surrendering, they could still be killed or maimed by landmines or crossfire in no-man's-land. For each successful defector, several others might have failed. Aside from their sheer luck, these defectors demonstrated certain traits: determination, bravery, intelligence, and leadership. In the UN prison camps, truck drivers Yang, Yin, and Li, doctor Meng, horse tender Wu, cultural instructor Xiao, and Communist veteran Tan would soon emerge as anti-Communist leaders.

MacArthur's Dismissal

In a matter of two to three months, Ridgway miraculously turned around the badly beaten Eighth Army and reversed the tide in Korea. His success with existing UN forces discredited MacArthur's claim that without additional troops or expanding the war to China, the UNC could not hold a line in Korea. MacArthur's earlier repeated warnings of a Dunkirk-like evacuation now sounded like scaremongering.

In sharp contrast to MacArthur, Ridgway was low-key, no-nonsense, and, most importantly, on the same wavelength with Washington, sharing its aim of limiting the war. The JCS continued to send messages to MacArthur, but as Omar Bradley noted, "there was a feeling that MacArthur had been 'kicked upstairs' to chairman of the board and was . . . mainly a prima donna figurehead who had to be tolerated."[42]

MacArthur's legendary pride, already wounded by the CPV in the winter of 1950, suffered further injury as his subordinate's victories called into question his judgment and competence. "The only possible means left to MacArthur to regain his lost pride and military reputation," Bradley put it bluntly, "was now to inflict an overwhelming defeat on those Red Chinese generals who had made a fool of him. In order to do this he was perfectly willing to propel us into an all-out war with Red China and possibly with the Soviet Union, igniting World War III, and a nuclear holocaust."[43]

With his penchant for histrionics, MacArthur had developed a pattern of appearing on the scene in Korea to "fire the starting gun" at the beginning of major operations, including his disastrous "home-by-Christmas" advance to the Yalu in late 1950. Now he routinely capped his tours with inflammatory remarks or communiqués suggesting a wider war to punish the Chinese and roll back Communism—in direct violation of Washington's gag order issued in December.

On January 28, 1951, MacArthur flew to newly recaptured Suwon. As he stepped off the plane, he declared to Ridgway, "This is exactly where I came in seven months ago to start this crusade," referring to his visit on June 29, 1950, four days after the North Korean invasion. He added, "The stake we fight for now, however is more than Korea—it is a free Asia." Having played no part in planning the counteroffensive, MacArthur was eager to be seen directing the war—a potentially larger war—much to the consternation of London and Washington.[44]

On February 20, MacArthur descended on Wonju, where Ridgway briefed him on the imminent Operation Killer. After the meeting, MacArthur "calmly" announced to the press corps: "I have just ordered a resumption of the offensive." An appalled Ridgway concluded that MacArthur, who wasn't involved in the planning at all, sought to steal back the limelight just to "keep his public image always glowing."[45]

On the opening day of Operation Ripper, March 7, MacArthur flew to Suwon several hours after the offensive had begun, heeding Ridgway's request. After touring the front, MacArthur held a news conference. He predicted, rather accurately, that given "the existing limitation upon our freedom of counter-offensive action," without "major additions" to his forces, "the battle lines in the end will reach a point of theoretical stalemate," which would be followed by "savage slaughter."[46] Dubbed the "die for tie" statement, the speech had a demoralizing impact on UN troops. "'Stalemate' connoted defeat, not victory," the historian Clay Blair noted. Ridgway "stewed and fumed" for five days and then called his own news conference. "We didn't set out to conquer China. We set out to stop Communism," he declared. "If China fails to drive us from Korea, she will have failed monumentally." For the UNC to reach the 38th parallel, he stated, it would be a "tremendous victory."[47] Three days later, UN forces entered Seoul unopposed.

As UN forces were fast approaching the parallel again, the JCS notified MacArthur of Truman's plan for a peace feeler on March 20. Four days later, before flying to Korea, MacArthur issued a communiqué that ostensibly offered to "confer in the field" with the enemy commander to arrange a cease-fire. However, it read like an ultimatum. MacArthur first taunted China for its "exaggerated and vaunted military power," as it lacked the "industrial capacity" to produce arms that were "essential to the conduct of modern war." He then ridiculed Chinese soldiers' "fanatical" bravery and their leaders' "most gross indifference of human loss." Contrary to his earlier defeatist predictions, he now claimed that "even under the inhibitions" placed on his command, China had "shown its complete inability to accomplish . . . the conquest of Korea." He ominously threatened, "[A] decision of the United Nations to depart from its tolerant effort to contain the war to the area of Korea through expansion of our military operations to his [China's] coastal areas and interior bases would doom Red China to the risk of imminent military collapse."[48] A livid Truman called MacArthur's act "deliberate, premeditated sabotage of U.S. and UN policy."[49] He later told his daughter, Margaret, "I was ready to kick him into the North China Sea at that time."[50] He didn't have to wait long.

MacArthur lobbed "another political bomb" on April 5, when Republican minority leader Joseph Martin read the general's reply to his letter on the House floor. MacArthur wrote, "Your view with respect to the utilization of the Chinese forces on Formosa is in conflict with neither logic nor this tradition" of "meet[ing] force with maximum counterforce." Repeating the criticism he made in his VFW letter in August 1950, he impugned Truman and Acheson's Eurocentrism: "It seems strangely difficult for some to realize that here in Asia is where the Communist conspirators have elected to make their play for global conquest. . . . If we lose the war to Communism in Asia the fall of Europe is inevitable, win it and Europe would most probably avoid war and yet preserve freedom." He concluded with his famed one-liner: "We must win. There is no substitute for victory." To Truman, this act of "rank insubordination" was "the last straw." He wrote in his diary that "our Big General in the Far East must be recalled."[51]

As if exacting bitter revenge for the VFW affair, during which Truman learned of MacArthur's letter through a hostile newspaper, "which had been *accidentally* sent" to his pressroom, this time around Truman called an extraordinary press conference at 1 a.m., April 11, lest a leak reach MacArthur before Army Secretary Frank Pace could deliver the message in person.[52] MacArthur received the news from his wife Jeannie, who was informed by an aide who had heard it on the radio. "Jeannie, we are going home at last," MacArthur said.[53]

Ridgway, now named MacArthur's successor, flew to Tokyo on April 12. He saw his former boss "entirely being himself—composed, quiet, temperate, friendly, and helpful," and there was "no trace of bitterness or anger in his tone."[54] Ridgway was being polite in his memoirs. In fact, MacArthur told him that Truman "would be dead in six months," citing an "eminent medical man."[55] He deeply resented the manner of his sacking. He asserted, "No office boy, no charwoman, no servant of any sort would have been dismissed with such callous disregard for the ordinary decencies."[56]

Upon learning the news, Chiang Kai-shek immediately instructed his representative in Tokyo to seek an audience with MacArthur and solicit "his advice on Taiwan, myself, and other on-going business." In a personal letter, the Generalissimo invited the general to go to Taiwan to "aid Asia's fight against Communist aggression."[57] None of the proposals came to pass. As MacArthur's plane lifted off from Tokyo on April 16, his era in the Far East drew to a close.

Ridgway was no fan of Chiang nor did he have confidence in Chiang's troops. The discussion of using Nationalist forces ceased altogether. Throughout his tenure in the following thirteen months, Ridgway did not bother to pay a visit to Taipei. Before leaving for Europe to succeed General Eisenhower as the NATO commander in May 1952, he raised a touchy question with the head of the Nationalist mission in Tokyo: were there any alternative leaders to Chiang, and were there any outstanding generals? In Chiang's view, Ridgway belonged to the Marshall faction, whose bias against him and desire to depose him remained deep-rooted.[58]

Already "feeling extremely low" over MacArthur's dismissal, Chiang Kai-shek became alarmed by the impending arrival of Major General William C. Chase as the head of the newly established Military Assistance Advisory Group. Chiang was reminded of his traumatic relationship with General Joseph W. Stilwell during World War II, when Stilwell with the full backing of Washington sought to take control of China's military. "Gimo, who is sensitive as ever regarding sovereignty, feels that subject of advisory group should have been discussed with him prior to ordering," reported the naval attaché in Taipei.[59]

US Senate hearings on MacArthur's recall, held from May 3 to June 27, quickly lapsed into a rancorous partisan debate on China policy. When Marshall was attacked by "Chiang Kai-shek Republicans," Truman denounced one of them in his diary as an "official mudslinger and Goebbels liar . . . trying another Nazi-Communist trick."[60] Equally emotional, Chiang Kai-shek vented his anger in his diary. When Acheson testified, Chiang wrote, "Acheson was put on trial." Chiang bitterly relived the betrayal and slight he had suffered between 1946 and 1949 on the mainland. Compounding his pain, his World War II allies reached a peace treaty agreement with Japan in June 1951, excluding Nationalist China from the negotiations. Tormented by the worst insomnia in two years, Chiang fulminated, "If God truly believes in love, why were idiots (*chuncai*) like Acheson and Truman created?"[61]

To Chiang's dismay, MacArthur's immense popularity soon fizzled out, as the Senate hearings dispelled the general's aura of infallibility and Ridgway's resounding victory in May once and for all obliterated the myth that MacArthur was indispensable. Bradley scathingly accused MacArthur of trying to drag the country into "the wrong war, at the wrong time, and with the wrong enemy."[62] The American people were in no mood for a bigger war with China. Just as MacArthur had promised in his oration before a joint session of Congress, the old soldier soon faded away.

The Communists missed no opportunity to mock the aging general. On the front lines, CPV psychological warfare loudspeakers blared in English, "MacArthur is right. Old soldiers never die, but the younger ones always do."[63]

The Prisoner Reindoctrination Program Revived

At the core of the Truman-MacArthur controversy was MacArthur's persistent call to widen the war to China and to use Chiang's troops for that purpose. In the end, MacArthur was fired by the American president, with whom he had conferred for two hours on Wake Island, for defending the Chinese Nationalist president, whom he had met for two days on Taiwan. Chiang praised MacArthur for "having built an indestructible bridge foundation for the United States . . . in the hearts of the Asian people."[64] Literary flourish aside, neither Chiang, nor MacArthur, nor anyone else, suspected at the time that MacArthur had indeed inadvertently laid the foundation for an extended war over prisoners by reviving the prisoner reindoctrination program and hiring interpreters from Taiwan shortly before his dismissal.

Eight days before his firing, MacArthur ordered the revival of the prisoner reindoctrination program in the UN prison camps.[65] As discussed in Chapter 4, psychological warfare and prisoner reindoctrination had been mandated by NSC-81/1. When NSC-81 was formulated in August and September 1950, the whole idea of reindoctrinating North Korean POWs was predicated on the assumption that the entire Korean peninsula would be unified under the UN's aegis. When China entered the war, however, the same assumption did not hold for Chinese prisoners, as Washington never planned to invade China or roll back Communism there. Prisoner reindoctrination should not have included the Chinese in the first place. By early 1951, when Washington had for all intents and purposes given up the goal of unifying Korea, the basis for prisoner reindoctrination had vanished. The entire program should have been abandoned. Instead, Washington doubled down by intensifying and expanding the program to include Chinese POWs—a seemingly incomprehensible move that was largely driven by policy inertia and ignorance of Chinese Communism.

A JCS directive of September 27, 1950, instructed MacArthur to set up a pilot interrogation and indoctrination program. The Eighth Army inaugurated a program for 500 North Korean prisoners at Yongdungpo near Seoul on November 23, the day before MacArthur launched the "home-by-Christmas" offensive. When the CPV crushed UN forces and swept south toward Seoul, the program was terminated on December 8, and the "test students" were hastily evacuated to Pusan.[66] The program lasted only sixteen days.

The Department of the Army's Office of the Chief of Psychological Warfare, however, did not forget this program. It made "numerous telecom inquiries on the status" of the suspended program but received no reply from Tokyo. Finally, MacArthur's GHQ replied on February 28, 1951, arguing that should Washington decide to resume the project, it would be "impracticable" for "a field army engaged in combat" (i.e., the Eighth Army) to operate the program. Instead the GHQ argued it should be placed under the Civil Information and Education Section (CIE) of the Supreme Commander for the Allied Powers (SCAP) in Tokyo.[67] Dubbed by the historian Toshio Nishi as the "American Ministry of Japanese Education," the CIE was MacArthur's brainchild conceived to democratize Japanese society through propaganda and education. As a part of the "political reorientation of Japan," the CIE played a pivotal role in the US occupation authorities' effort to "write into Japanese daily life such ideals as 'individuality,' 'liberty,' 'freedom,' and 'equality.'"[68]

On March 22, the Department of the Army issued an instruction prepared by its psychological warfare chief General Robert A. McClure, directing MacArthur "to reestablish on a Pilot-Plant Scale Interrogation, Indoct[rination] and T[rai]ng Cen[ter] for these PW now in your hands in Korea, to include Chinese Communists." Since the purpose of the program was "to cause defection of enemy troops in the field," McClure concluded that it "should specifically include Chinese Communist POWs."[69] While Tokyo had made no mention of Chinese prisoners, Washington specifically included them for indoctrination.

On April 3, MacArthur issued General Orders 8, directing the establishment of a CIE section under the UNC with the mission "to initiate, organize and operate an orientation and education program for North Korean and Chinese" POWs. His dismissal on April 11 did little to hinder the psychological warfare machinery that had been set in motion. On April 16, his successor Ridgway made a request of the "highest priority" for the "immediate recruitment" of a number of Chinese and Korean language and education specialists. The CIE recommended contacting the "boards of foreign missions and Harvard University (Yen Ching University Institute)" for possible candidates. Monta L. Osborne, who had been active in the pilot program, became the CIE director.[70] As a US Army major and China theater psychological warfare officer, Osborne had studied the psychology of surrendered Japanese in Guangzhou in 1945 (see Chapter 1).

On April 23, the day after the CPV launched its Fifth Offensive, Ridgway ordered the CIE to set up a pilot program. Its objective, among other things, was to "develop such knowledge, understanding, and attitudes among North Korean prisoners of war as will influence them toward participation in and support of an independent, unified Korean nation."[71] By this time, however, it should have been abundantly clear to Ridgway that the unification of Korea—the original goal of NSC-81/1—had been tacitly removed from Washington's agenda. What then was the purpose of reindoctrinating North Korean POWs in preparation for a unified Korea? Facing a massive Chinese strike, Ridgway perhaps paid little attention to the nuances of a directive prepared by his staff, who were not privy to high-level discussions and had no incentive to question a standing order.

The JCS's new directive a week later left no room for doubt: "You should make an intensive effort using all info media available to you to initiate and maintain a psychological offensive." Specifically, "you should initiate and maintain a *comprehensive* program for interrogation, indoctrination, and reorientation of POWs with a view toward their eventual utilization as *avowed anti-Communists*." This order, buried in a long "compilation and condensation of existing directives," was repeated to Ridgway on May 31. Truman gave his "final clearance" on July 10, following the recommendations of Acheson, Marshall, and the JCS.[72] In essence, while Washington had abandoned the rollback component of NSC-81/1, it retained its psychological warfare and prisoner exploitation components. In fact, it broadened the mandate to create a large-scale program with the express goal of converting prisoners into "avowed anti-Communists." This psychological warfare objective had become a substitute for a rollback victory.

From a moral perspective, the very act of reorientation entailed an implicit commitment to the safety of prisoners, particularly those who had surrendered voluntarily and cooperated with the UNC. Why would they want to be converted into "avowed anti-Communists" one day, and then sent back to China or North Korea the next to be executed or imprisoned? Perhaps this prospect did not occur to policymakers; or if it did, they did not care. The ultimate goal of the program was the POWs' "future use as a nucleus for democratization on return to their native countries." The implicit assumption of their post-repatriation safety and use was based on the experiences of German and Italian POWs interned in continental United States in World War II. "Such circumstances surrounding WWII practice may not exist or be applicable in respect to conditions in Korea at this time," psychological warfare officials admitted. But they still recommended POW reindoctrination in Korea.[73] West Germany and Italy became democracies and US allies after World War II. China and North Korea would remain Communist and adversaries of the United States after a future truce. The circumstances were entirely different. And the consequences for prisoners could be deadly.

From a practical perspective, this program was fraught with unexamined assumptions about its effectiveness. What was the purpose of reindoctrinating prisoners? If the goal was to turn them into anti-Communists, how could the US government actually "utilize" them? How could ideological conversion in the POW camps possibly cause defections on the battlefield? Without the promise of asylum, which Washington had absolutely no intention of giving, why would enemy troops defect in the first place? Without the promise of asylum, why would prisoners welcome anti-Communist indoctrination, which would only endanger their lives after their repatriation? There is little evidence indicating that policymakers debated these questions in the spring of 1951.

On June 1, the CIE inaugurated its reorientation instruction in Korean Compound 63 on Koje Island. Its instructors, however, were "chosen from among qualified POWs."[74] The CIE was woefully ill prepared for its lofty but nebulous mission. The beginning did not bode well.

On MacArthur's watch, the short-lived pilot program involved no Chinese. The program for Chinese POWs was mandated by Washington immediately before his sacking, but was not implemented until August 6, almost four months after his departure.[75] Subsequent political polarization and unrest in the POW camps emerged under Ridgway. Nonetheless, MacArthur, by virtue of his position as the UNC commander, set in motion a train of events that few foresaw at the time.

The Arrival of Nationalist Interpreters

MacArthur's second legacy was his policy of hiring Chinese interpreters from Taiwan—a seemingly ordinary decision that had an unexpectedly far-reaching impact on the course of the war. The UNC and Taiwan initially collaborated in two areas: intelligence gathering and psychological warfare—both involving prisoners. Psychological warfare was designed to cause defection; prisoner interrogations, in turn, yielded intelligence. Both functions required Chinese linguists, but the UNC had few.

As explained in Chapter 4, Washington initially rejected Tokyo's request to hire linguists and code breakers from Taiwan. This handicap only prolonged the UNC's intelligence woes and probably contributed to its disastrous defeat in the first three Chinese offensives, as UN forces marched right into enemy traps with their eyes and ears closed. When Ridgway assumed command of the Eighth Army, all his G-2 could show him was "a big red goose egg out in front of us, with '174,000' scrawled in the middle of it." Apparently, detailed intelligence provided by the hundreds of Chinese already captured was not properly utilized. A frustrated Ridgway flew in a two-seat spotter plane twenty miles into enemy territory to see it for himself. Similar to what MacArthur had observed along the Yalu on November 24, 1950, Ridgway saw "no sign of life or movement. No smoke came from the chimneys, and nothing moved either on or off the roads, neither vehicles, men nor animals."[76] Not surprisingly, this type of eyeball air reconnaissance yielded little insight into the enemy.

Washington relented eventually. The Armed Forces Security Agency, the precursor of the National Security Agency, hired a "limited" number of Nationalists to help with radio interception and translation. Later the UNC praised this operation for providing "an outstanding intel[ligence] source for MacArthur and Ridgway." To remedy the shortage of Chinese linguists, the Air Force began teaching airmen Chinese through a program at Yale University.[77] This was, however, too little and too late.

The main source of tactical intelligence came from prisoner interrogations. With very few Korean-English or Chinese-English translators in service, the UNC had to improvise. Relying on Japanese-speaking Koreans and Japanese-English bilingual speakers, mostly Nisei (second-generation Japanese-Americans), G-2 instituted "a tedious system where Korean documents were translated into Japanese and then into English." To interrogate prisoners, Willoughby recalled, "A three-man system was set up whereby questions by an English-Japanese speaking interrogator were relayed to the informant through a Japanese-Korean speaking medium."[78] Rapid and accurate interrogation was impossible, especially given the large number of North Korean prisoners.

When Chinese prisoners appeared, the already cumbersome three-way translation set-up became even more unwieldy. The "need for English-speaking Chinese has been one of the top intelligence problems in Korea," noted a reporter, who had witnessed an extreme case where a Turkish officer interrogated a Chinese near the front line. The Turk's questions in German were translated into English by a German-speaking correspondent who happened to be present. Then a Korean interpreter translated them into Korean for another Korean who spoke Mandarin Chinese. The reporter concluded, "It is difficult to find a Korean who speaks

Chinese and virtually impossible to find one who is trained in interrogation and exact translation."[79]

One might expect that the shortage could have been relieved by tapping into the sizable Chinese population in the United States. Most Chinese Americans, however, spoke Cantonese and did not understand Mandarin well, not to mention various other dialects.

The only source of qualified interpreters was Taiwan. During World War II, the Nationalist Central Military Commission's Foreign Affairs Bureau recruited thousands of university students and trained them as interpreters for US forces in the China-Burma-India (CBI) theater. Some three hundred of these highly educated and experienced interpreters lived in Taiwan as of early 1951.[80]

Moreover, a number of Chinese air force pilots were trained in the United States during and after World War II. Fighter pilot Gao Qingchen became one of the first linguists hired by the UNC. Gao recalled that, in response to Willoughby's request for linguists, Taipei decided in late December 1950 to supply 22 men to the UNC. The Ministry of Defense's Second Bureau (G-2) first selected 26 candidates. Only eighteen passed the interview by US military attachés on February 2, including eleven from the army, three from the navy, two from the air force, and two from the Foreign Ministry. Nationalist deputy chief of staff Guo Jiqiao and G-2 director Lai Mingtang gave them instructions on the 11th. Although Gao divulged no details, most likely the two generals instructed the men to gather intelligence for Taiwan while working for the UNC. On February 12, the 18 men were sworn in as US Department of Army Civilians (DACs) at the US embassy, promising not to reveal their identities or make any contact with the Nationalist government during their service. In the next twelve months of their employment, they were supposed to appear as if they were American citizens hired by the US Army. That night, they boarded a DC-4 plane and departed for Tokyo.[81]

Once in Tokyo, these interpreters learned that their unit was the Allied Translator and Interpreter Section (ATIS) under G-2, Far East Command, whose responsibilities included translating enemy intelligence and interrogating prisoners. The ATIS's Tokyo headquarters retained six interpreters and assigned twelve, including Gao, to Korea. The interpreters were issued DAC uniforms, which had no insignia of rank other than brass plates with two letters "US" on the lapels and cap. While they looked no different from other Chinese-American DACs, the eighteen men had many ties with Nationalist personnel in Tokyo. They telephoned their friends in the Chinese mission, which was the de facto embassy until a peace treaty between Japan and Nationalist China was signed in Taipei in 1952. Then they asked to go out to visit the mission. Their American superiors initially refused permission, but soon relented.[82] The prohibition on contact with the Nationalist government broke down a week after the swearing-in. The US military simply could not control the private lives of its civilian employees the way the Communists controlled their men. The DACs would have ample opportunities to transmit information to the embassies if they chose to do so.

Soon the UNC asked Taiwan for 55 additional interpreters.[83] These new hires—half were army and air force officers and the other half had been CBI interpreters in World War II—arrived in Korea in three batches, bringing the total number to 73.[84] The last group of twenty left Taipei on March 9, and "completed quota of 75 requested by GHQ, FEC," a State Department cable reported. The discrepancy of two was negligible. The State Department through the military attachés in the Taipei embassy was fully involved in the vetting of the linguists. The cable noted that half of the 75 men were Nationalist officers and the remainder were either employed by other military agencies or had a record of government service, which enabled the Nationalist Ministry of Defense to "guarantee unconditionally their loyalty and political stability." The salary of US$170 a month, more than ten times the local salary in Taiwan, attracted a large number of applicants. The selected group represented the "cream of Interpreter material presently available," the cable concluded.[85]

There is little doubt about the caliber of these interpreters. Huang Tiancai, one of the twenty men who left Taipei on March 9, had interpreted for Americans twice for a total of 3 years. In January 1945, Huang, then a sophomore at National Chengchi College (Political College), volunteered for the army. He interpreted in an armored vehicle unit and then in a US field hospital. After the war, he resumed his university studies and graduated in 1947. Huang subsequently interpreted for the US Military Advisory Group in Fengshan, Taiwan. When the Americans pulled out in late summer 1949, Huang became a reporter for a small news outlet in Taipei. In February 1950 he received an official letter inviting former army interpreters for an interview. Out of more than one hundred applicants, only twenty were selected in his batch.[86]

In addition to the 73 or 75 interpreters, a small number of psychological warfare personnel were hired from Taiwan. According to Chu Songqiu, Chiang Ching-kuo's former student and assistant in the Ministry of Defense's Political Department, Ching-kuo had received requests for propagandists from Tokyo as early as November 1950. For various reasons, however, Chu and other "information specialists," including painters and writers, did not arrive in Tokyo until June 1951.[87] The Voice of the United Nations radio in Tokyo hired five top announcers and editors from the Broadcasting Corporation of China (*Zhongguang*) in June.[88]

On the ground in Korea, however, the Eighth Army had no Chinese-speaking psychological warfare specialists. It secretly contacted the Nationalist embassy in Pusan for help in early February 1951. Ambassador Shao Yulin happily obliged, dispatching military attaché Du and secretary Chen to the Eighth Army HQ in Taegu.

Du and Chen designed leaflets with photographs and composed messages and songs for airborne loudspeakers. Du even personally flew on planes to broadcast messages around the Chinese New Year on both the eastern and western fronts, resulting in the surrender of a number of former Nationalist troops. Shao cabled Chiang Ching-kuo, "We must take this opportunity to have one foot (*chazu*) in anti-bandit propaganda operations and to infiltrate."[89] On February 21, two Eighth Army officers visited the embassy, asking for help with screening candidates from the local Chinese diaspora for psychological warfare operations. Shao reported that fourteen English-speaking students had been selected and sent to Taegu, and that the UNC was looking to hire more Chinese linguists in Hong Kong.[90] Undoubtedly, the Eighth Army desperately needed Chinese linguists. It is doubtful, however, that these young students would be useful.

To the Eighth Army's great relief, well-trained linguists soon arrived. After learning that twelve of the first eighteen interpreters had arrived in Pusan on February 22, the Eighth Army made an urgent request to ATIS to borrow them to interrogate Chinese prisoners and translate documents captured during and after the UNC victory at Chipyong-ni. Gao and eight others were sent to Taegu on February 25. When a new batch of Nationalist interpreters arrived in Taegu, Gao returned to the ATIS interrogation center at Pusan on March 10. In the following eleven months, he would interrogate 877 Chinese prisoners, including the mayor's son-turned-horse tender Wu Jiansheng, and produce more than 800 detailed intelligence reports.[91]

Prisoners-Interpreters-Taipei Nexus

Given Washington's deep aversion to open collaboration with Chiang Kai-shek, the UNC hired Nationalist personnel as individual civilians. To avoid the impression that Chiang was intervening in Korea, which would certainly consternate US allies, the hiring was kept secret. Some Nationalist officers adopted pseudonyms. When queried by the press, both the UNC and Taipei denied the existence of such cooperation.[92] Such measures, however, were self-deceiving.

No doubt most DACs were loyal Nationalists, and some performed intelligence work for Taiwan. Even those who were not agents in a strict sense identified with Nationalist Taiwan as their own fate hinged on Taiwan's survival. Many DACs kept frequent contact with the Nationalist mission in Tokyo and the embassy in Korea, often in the most innocuous forms, such as weekend dinners and poker or mah-jong sessions at the embassy. A prisoners-interpreters-Taipei nexus soon emerged.

The earliest recorded contact between Taiwan personnel and prisoners occurred in Tokyo. According to an official Nationalist account, Captain Liu Bingzhang, who had defected in November 1950 and been under "nearly daily interrogation" for two months in Pusan, was whisked off to Tokyo in February 1951—coinciding with the arrival of the first eighteen Nationalist interpreters. Guo Zheng, an army officer and one of the six men retained by the ATIS HQ, acted as Liu's interpreter during the four months of interrogations that followed. Guo did his work while keeping an arm's length from Liu. However, on the last day before Liu's return to Korea, Guo approached Liu quietly, addressing him as a "Nationalist comrade." A delighted Liu asked, "Have you been dispatched by Taiwan?" Guo replied rather accurately, "No. I've been hired by the UNC, but I'm from Taiwan." Guo gave Liu a farewell present, a copy of Sun Yat-sen's *The Three People's Principles*, which was later hand-copied by anti-Communist prisoners in POW camps until the arrival of large quantities of literature for CIE programs.[93]

If Guo Zheng was discreet in his interaction with prisoner Liu, other DACs were more audacious. Li Da'an, the CPV truck driver who defected on March 24, was soon flown to Taegu, where he was questioned by two interrogators from Taiwan. Li later claimed that one interrogator told him to investigate Communist prisoners' activities once he arrived in the POW camps.[94] Li's account is plausible, as nine Nationalist officer interpreters had arrived at the Eighth Army headquarters in Taegu on February 25 to engage in interrogation, psychological warfare, and counterintelligence.[95]

From Pusan, South Korea's wartime capital and the site of the POW interrogation center, Nationalist ambassador Shao Yulin dispatched to Taipei on May 7 a top secret "List of Communist Officer Prisoners" compiled by "our personnel working in UNC POW camps." It contained information on each prisoner: name, serial number, capture date and location, CPV and previous Nationalist army unit numbers, political party affiliation, and so on. Among the 105 listed officers were Sun Zhenguan, Liu Bingzhang, Wei Shixi, Tan Xingdong, and Meng Ming.[96] Such a comprehensive and detailed list could only be produced by an insider working in the ATIS interrogation center in Pusan, which, coincidentally, had just completed the registration of all Chinese prisoners on May 3. Gao Qingchen, in charge of the task, had developed a system highlighting prisoners' ranks and won his American boss's praise.[97] Evidently, the officers' list was transmitted to the embassy over the weekend, and then promptly forwarded to Taipei on Monday, May 7.

In addition to diplomatic channels, certain DACs enjoyed direct contact with Chiang Ching-kuo, Taiwan's de facto intelligence chief. Only twenty days after he arrived in Tokyo as an "information specialist," Chu Songqiu asked a friend to hand-carry an envelope to his mentor Chiang. Enclosed were two items: a letter written by six POWs, former Nationalist troops, being held at the UNC headquarters in Tokyo; and the interrogation report of a prisoner who had recently left.[98] Perhaps it was not a pure coincidence that the UNC headquarters' command report noted that "six Chinese POWs arrived in Japan in May 1951 to participate in a special G-2 FEC project involving psychological warfare leaflets."[99] Most likely the six men included Wang Futian, who surrendered in the First Offensive near Chosin, and Wang Shunqing, who defected on the eve of the Second Offensive. Both Communist and anti-Communist prisoners recalled the two Wangs were removed from the Pusan camps in May 1951.[100] The prisoner who had recently left was probably Liu Bingzhang. The three men later became major anti-Communist POW leaders.

The State Department's Role

MacArthur has often been blamed for the prisoner reindoctrination program, much as he has been scapegoated for Washington's disastrous decision to cross the 38th parallel to "liberate" North Korea. But, as we have noted, it was NSC-81/1 that mandated rollback and psychological warfare, including prisoner reindoctrination. The prisoner reindoctrination program was not MacArthur's "private venture . . . sanctioned after the fact by the army," as some scholars have assumed.[101] In fact, prisoner reindoctrination was one of the very few policies on which MacArthur and Washington agreed.

The State Department supported psychological warfare and prisoner reindoctrination from its inception. NSC document 59/1, entitled "The Foreign Information Program and Psychological Warfare Planning" made the secretary of state responsible for the "formulation of national psychological warfare policy" in times of peace and war and the "coordination of policies and plans for the national foreign information program and for overt psychological warfare with the Department of Defense" and other government agencies, including the CIA. In the immediate aftermath of the North Korean invasion, the department transferred information specialists from its embassy in Korea to MacArthur's G-2.[102] The State Department, far from being an innocent bystander, as Ambassador Muccio later seemed to suggest, was directly involved in prisoner indoctrination and interrogation.

As discussed in Chapter 4, the Truman-MacArthur conference on Wake Island on October 15, 1950, devoted much of its attention to postwar rehabilitation, especially the reorientation of the Korean people. Dean Rusk urged Muccio to operate "as intensely as possible" a reorientation program that included POWs. Muccio pledged to create one "as large and as quick[ly]" as possible.

In November, the State Department drafted a "Reorientation Plan for Korea"—a unified Korea. On November 27 and 28, officials from the State Department, US Information Service (USIS)-Korea, GHQ Far East, the CIE, and the Department of the Army met to finalize the plan. They decided to create an information and education program "conducted . . . by State Department personnel but is not be identified as a US program"—i.e., it should appear under the UN aegis. While no military or civilian personnel in MacArthur's GHQ would be available for this program, a "ten-man State Department team" was "available in the US and will be airlifted to

Korea" within three days.[103] However, the CPV's surprise, massive Second Offensive derailed the plan for good.

When MacArthur suggested and received approval for putting the revived prisoner reindoctrination program under the CIE in spring 1951, there seemed no need for the State Department to reinvent the wheel, as a ready-made organization like the CIE could easily replicate its operations in Korea. Having ceded leadership in prisoner reindoctrination to the UNC, the State Department nevertheless maintained its own prisoner interrogation operations, whose mission was to gather political, social, and economic intelligence on China. Acheson cabled Muccio on April 13: "Dept urgently required prepare immediate estimate on current public opinion in China, including morale Chi Commie forces."[104] However, just as the military lacked Chinese linguists, the embassy apparently had no one capable of interrogating Chinese prisoners, until the arrival of a thirty-year-old foreign service officer in April 1951.

Philip W. Manhard was dispatched by the State Department's Bureau of Intelligence and Research, an offshoot of the Office of Strategic Services' Research and Analysis Department. A graduate of the University of Southern California, Manhard studied Chinese in Peiping/Beijing from March 1948 to October 1949, and then served as a vice consul in Tianjin until April 1950, when he and several other US diplomats made the final exit from China.[105] In Pusan, Manhard led an interrogation team that included two interpreters on loan from USIS offices in Hong Kong and Taipei. From Hong Kong was Larry Wu-tai Chin (or, Jin Wudai), a Communist mole who was not exposed until 1985 in a high-profile espionage case.[106] Ironically, the US prisoner exploitation projects were infiltrated by Chinese agents left and right, Communist and Nationalist.

While Larry Chin's impact was grossly exaggerated by US prosecutors in 1985, the ramifications of the first seventy-some interpreters from Taiwan were far more consequential, as the following chapters will demonstrate. The hiring of Nationalist personnel was done under MacArthur, apparently with the State Department's knowledge and acquiescence. When MacArthur requested the second group of fifty-five interpreters from Taiwan in February 1951, an official in the office of Chinese affairs warned that they "would assuredly be in the service of the KMT secret police."[107] The State Department, however, did not countermand MacArthur's move, as the need for Chinese linguists was genuine and urgent, and no one except Taiwan could help.

Two decades later, Ambassador Muccio claimed in an oral history interview, "Willoughby sent down to Taipei and got some seventy-five camp guards, or whatever terms you want to use. There's no doubt in my mind that those men were all . . . Chiang Kai-shek's Gestapos."[108] As this chapter has shown, while it is true that some interpreters collected and transmitted intelligence for Taiwan, not all of them, contrary to what both Muccio and the Communists alleged, were necessarily Chiang's secret agents.

Muccio's claim that these men were "camp guards" was patently false. The interpreters arrived in Tokyo and Korea in February and March 1951, when Chinese prisoners numbered about 1,500. There was simply no need for 75 "camp guards" from Taiwan. Evidently, Muccio conflated the interpreters and anti-Communist prisoner trusties, whose rise will be discussed in subsequent chapters. At the time, no one could have foreseen the explosion of the Chinese POW population three months later and their repatriation becoming the sole issue preventing an armistice some ten months later. When MacArthur hired interpreters from Taiwan, no one could have possibly imagined a conspiracy to use prisoners as a substitute for victory. Had someone other than MacArthur been in command, the hiring would have still occurred. Given the NSC's mandate and the UNC's abject shortage of Chinese linguists, MacArthur had few options but to hire Nationalist interpreters. Driven by sheer necessity, this policy would have unexpected, far-reaching consequences.

The number of Chinese POWs would surge more than tenfold to over 17,000 in May and June, when the CPV Fifth Offensive, the largest in the entire war, became its largest debacle. When the influx of Chinese prisoners entered UN prison camps, they would soon realize that the Nationalists had already one foot in the game.

7

The Fifth Offensive Debacle

> Valiant and fearless,
> We cross the Yalu River.
> To preserve peace and protect the motherland,
> To safeguard our home,
> The fine sons and daughters of China unite as one heart.
> Resist America, aid Korea.
> Defeat the American imperialist jackals!

Leading the valorous tune of the "Battle Hymn of the Chinese People's Volunteers Army," twenty-one-year-old Zhang Zeshi and his propaganda team of the 538th Regiment, 180th Division, marched across the Yalu River at dusk on March 21, 1951. Zhang and his comrades stopped on the steel bridge moments before stepping onto Korean soil. They looked back and shouted, "Farewell, loved ones. Wait for the news of our victory!"[1] At this moment, Zhang and his comrades were unaware that UN forces had recaptured Seoul a week earlier.[2] They had no inkling of what lay ahead of them—the biggest military defeat suffered by the CPV.

The Second Wave of CPV Units

Zhang's 180th Division was one of the eighteen fresh divisions pouring into Korea in February and March 1951. The second wave of CPV units consisted of the 19th Army Group from the northwest, including the 63rd, 64th, and 65th Armies, and the 3rd Army Group from the southwest, comprising the 12th, 15th, and 60th Armies. On November 7, 1950, Deng Xiaoping, the top leader of the southwest, cabled Mao, promising to immediately provide Korea with three armies. These units, then scattered across Sichuan, Guizhou, and Yunnan in "bandit-suppression" campaigns, promptly reassembled and reorganized. From early December 1950, they were transported north. The 60th Army departed from Chengdu for Shaanxi by truck, and then continued toward Hebei by train. The 12th Army embarked from Chongqing downstream along the Yangtze River by steamships and wooden boats. After passing through the Three Gorges and reaching Wuhan, it switched to trains for Hebei.[3]

The CPV 3rd Army Group was not an organic unit, even though it inherited the designation from the PLA 3rd Army Group, to which only the 12th Army belonged. The 15th Army was from the 4th Army Group then based in Yunnan and southern Sichuan; the 60th Army belonged to the 18th Army Group then in western Sichuan. It was not until on February 18, after the arrival of the three armies in Hebei, that the Central Military Commission ordered the formation of the CPV 3rd Army Group. Its headquarters was not established in Beijing until March 16, two days before the three armies began crossing the Yalu. Exacerbating the disorganization, the army group's commander and concurrently the commissar, Chen Geng, who had recently returned from Vietnam after serving as Ho Chi Minh's military advisor, suffered leg pains so severe that he had to pass his command to deputy commander Wang Jinshan. Wang came from the original 3rd Army Group but was unfamiliar with the army group HQ staff, who were from the 4th Army Group.[4]

Similar reshuffling occurred at lower levels as well. The CPV 60th Army consisted of the 179th and 180th Divisions of the PLA 60th Army and the 181st Division of the 61st Army. Wei Jie, the commander of the 61st Army, was named to lead the CPV 60th Army. While Wang was only familiar with one army under his command, Wei knew only one division well. On top of the leadership change, some veteran officers had been assigned to local garrison or government duties. The 180th Division faced a peculiar problem: the top positions of divisional commander and commissar remained vacant. Deputy commissar Zheng Qigui was hastily promoted to division commander—an unusual move given his lack of combat command experience. Political Department director Wu Chengde—ranked fourth in the chain of command—became the acting commissar.[5]

At the regimental level, the 538th had a new commissar from the army HQ, Zhao Zuoduan. Conscious of his own lack of combat command experience, Zhao later admitted that he felt diffident before the regimental commander.[6] The 540th's regiment and battalion commanders were ordered to stay in Sichuan and were replaced by their deputies; at the company level, the reverse took place, as many deputy leaders stayed behind.[7] Later Wei complained about his predecessor's selfishness in removing many of his ablest officers from the army.[8] No doubt, the army's combat effectiveness had been severely compromised.

Another detriment was the high concentration of former Nationalist troops—so-called "liberated soldiers." Commissar Zhao reported that 60–70 percent of the enlisted men in his 540th were such. The number in itself was not extraordinary, as the overall figure for the PLA had reached 70–80 percent by June 1950, according to Premier Zhou.[9] The 60th Army was somewhat unusual in that as it had "integrated" (*hebian*) the entire Nationalist 95th Army after the latter's defection in December 1949. Former Nationalist officers became deputies to Communist officers at various levels, and the troops were mixed. Shortly before departing for Korea, however, former Nationalists serving at the regimental level or above were removed, including the 538th's deputy commander.[10]

After the purge of unreliable former Nationalists and the reassignment of some veteran Communist officers, the three armies from the southwest reached full strength by hastily adding "liberated soldiers," militiamen, and students in various PLA schools, such as the Southwest Revolutionary Military and Political University and medic schools.[11] As discussed in Chapter 2, among the more than 14,000 surrendered former Whampoa cadets and instructors, roughly 150 cadets, including Gao Wenjun and Yu Rongfu, were selected to join the CPV 60th Army.[12] Student recruits in the university, such as Cai Pingsheng and Lin Mocong, also hastily "graduated" and joined the 60th Army as cultural instructors. From the PLA medic school, Yang Yuhua also "graduated early" and joined the 180th Division's medical team.

Militiaman Huang Changrong was coerced into joining the 60th Army, as mentioned in Chapter 3. To escape local persecution, former Nationalist policeman Cheng Liren volunteered for the 12th Army, probably without fully revealing his past (see Chapter 3). He became an ammunition bearer in the 12th Army.[13] Sun Xiuhe, a former clerk and high school graduate from the same town, also joined Cheng as a coolie.[14]

The 12th, 15th, and 60th Armies arrived in Hebei in January 1950. Troops received Soviet-made small arms to replace the motley collection of Chinese, Japanese, and American-made weapons. Billeted in several counties along the Beijing-Shanghai railroad, troops underwent "the necessary, urgent military training" and political mobilization.[15] Cheng Liren recalled, "It was all political study, no military training."[16] Dr. Zhang Yifu of the 179th Division reported that the temperature dropped so low that many southerners were unable to perform any meaningful training; some stayed indoors and wept.[17] Posted as a sentry in the bitter cold, Huang Changrong was overwhelmed by crushing homesickness and broke into tears.[18] Given the large number of unarmed personnel serving propaganda and logistics functions in the Communist army, the troops' lack of combat training was not surprising.

Nevertheless, certain combat personnel undertook training, especially in anti-tank and anti-air tactics. In the 180th Division, Huang's unit dug deep camouflaged tank traps. Li Yueming dug trenches day and night until his hands bled, as the earth froze and became as hard as concrete. Ox-drawn carts were used as tank mockups. In the 179th Division, He Rui was selected to receive specialized if crude anti-tank explosives training. He practiced blowing up tanks both by throwing Soviet-made anti-tank grenades and by a more dangerous method: rushing the tank, climbing up to the turret, opening the hatch, and dropping a hand grenade inside. Soon he would carry out such a suicidal mission in Korea.[19]

Most new recruits, like propaganda officer Zhang Zeshi, however, had no actual combat experience. The few battles they had fought in were mostly lopsided "bandit suppression" operations. They were told that the Americans were "spoiled brat troops" who "put a blanket on the ground before getting into a shooting position" and that the extent of damage caused by the atomic bomb was merely some shattered glass.[20] The very subject of being captured was never broached in any of these mobilization meetings, and any thought of being taken prisoner was too dangerous to be entertained.[21] Most Chinese "volunteers" could not imagine being captured merely two months later.

From the Yalu to the 38th Parallel

After departing from Hebei at midnight on March 11, the 3rd Army Group arrived at the Sino-Korean border on the 18th.[22] Having heard a rumor that American airplanes were "as numerous as crows," troops now witnessed with their own eyes planes swarming in North Korean airspace south of the Yalu. To defuse fear, some officers told their troops: "What is the chance of getting hit by crow shit? Very little. If so, why should you be afraid of American bombs?"[23] Such daft analogy probably convinced very few men.

Soon after the 12th Army's 92nd Regiment reached the border, the firing pins on four anti-aircraft (AA) machine guns went missing. After fourteen hours of nonstop interrogation of everyone in the newly established AA machine gun company, two squad leaders finally owned up to removing the pins and hiding them in their cotton-padded jackets. Fearing that AA fire would attract deadly aerial attacks, they had disabled the guns in hopes the company would be disbanded and they would return to infantry units. These two veteran Communists were promptly expelled from the party and demoted to ammo bearers.[24] Less fortunate was ex-Nationalist Yang Dengyun, who was accused of intentionally damaging a heavy mortar and a rifle. He had also allegedly plotted with others to blow up the train en route from Hebei to Andong and to defect in Korea, a plan that did not materialize. He was court-martialed and sentenced to death. Wu Chengde, the 180th Division's acting commissar, acted as the judge advocate general and signed off on the sentence.[25] On the eve of crossing the Yalu, the Communists made Yang an example for other potential defectors, especially former Nationalists.

From March 18 to 28, the 60th and 15th Armies crossed the Yalu at Andong and the 12th Army crossed at Changdian. In the next 16 to 19 days, troops force-marched approximately 250 miles until they reached Ichon, a major road junction in central Korea and a historical staging point for attacks on Seoul.[26] Documents later captured by the UNC reveal that the 60th Army averaged 18 miles a day. In a nine-day stretch, Zhang Zeshi's 538th Regiment covered 215 miles—24 miles a night on average. Impressed by the "precision and discipline," the US Far East Command remarked, "this march was a major military accomplishment" and "the troops concerned displayed superior stamina and courage." The military historian Roy Appleman marvels, "the Roman legions could do no better."[27]

This type of long-distance march with full gear and supplies was unprecedented, even for Communist veterans. Each infantryman carried nearly 90 pounds of weapons and supplies on his back, including a rifle, 200 rounds of ammunition, four grenades, sometimes two mortar shells or Bangalore torpedoes, a short shovel, a long tube sack of roasted wheat flour (*chaomian*) and biscuits weighing 15 to 30 pounds, and a poncho. To reduce weight, many troops ditched their bedrolls and used their cotton-padded coats for blankets. Zhang, the propaganda newspaper editor, carried a mimeograph plate, a stencil, and waxed papers in place of a rifle. Young propaganda soldier Lin Mocong carried his beloved violin.[28]

For the first time in Chinese Communist military history, mess and hot water were not served, as any smoke would give away the location of troops—making them sitting ducks for American bombers. Troops had to make do with eating roasted flour mixed with cold water. No meat, cooking oil, rice, or vegetables were available.[29]

To evade air raids, troops trekked at night without flashlights. During the day, they rested in woods or individual foxholes dug with shovels. When it rained, foxholes became mud puddles. Some soldiers put on ponchos and tied themselves to tree trunks and went to sleep.[30] One morning, Zhang was wakened by the sudden explosion of a delay-action bomb. Watching a heavy tree branch snap and fall right before him, he felt his heart nearly pounded out of his chest. Then he wet his pants. Since there was no dry place to change in the heavy rain, Zhang simply dozed off again, still tied to the tree.[31]

While the delay-action bomb was probably the most hated American weapon, napalm was definitely the most feared.[32] Marching in a valley one night, Zhang's unit heard air raid warning shots. Troops immediately dispersed from the main road and took cover in woods or behind rocks. First, a string of flares was dropped, slowly descending under large, white parachutes. The sky was lit up so bright that many soldiers recalled, "Even if there was a needle on the ground, one could find it."[33] Then a bomber dived into the illuminated valley, strafing vehicles, horses, and mules. The frightened animals broke loose and bolted. The next bomber took aim at the animals and sprayed napalm. A blinding flash of pinkish flame gushed down from the sky.

Engulfed in giant fireballs, horses and mules galloped away like mad. A tender hiding under a horse caught fire. Instinctively he tumbled and rolled on the ground, trying to put out the fire, only to catch more burning jellied gasoline. Howling in pain, he struggled to stand up, trying to rip off his burning jacket. But the fire quickly consumed his face and head. Slowly he crumpled to the ground, shaking violently in a death spasm, and burned until his body became a charcoaled mass. Zhang and other comrades could do nothing but watch in helpless agony.[34]

Soon after the 60th Army arrived at Ichon, a veteran Communist staff officer blew himself up with a hand grenade in his foxhole. It was reported that he had been paranoid about his safety after witnessing comrades being killed by napalm or wounded by strafing planes. The same evening, he was declared "a traitor to the party and the country." He was expelled from the party and the army posthumously; his family back home was stripped of military family status. To the Communists, suicide and self-mutilation were acts of treason.[35] So was being taken prisoner, it went without saying.

While American bombing struck fear into the hearts of many, it also stoked indignation and nationalist fervor. Staff officer Ma Furui was appalled by the indiscriminate destruction of North Korean cities and villages, where "not even a 50-meter bridge was spared." He figured, "Even an atomic attack could not have done such a thorough job." He later recalled, "We hated the Americans so much that we felt that once we got our hands on them, we would slice them to pieces." Ma, a former Whampoa cadet and son of a Manchurian landlord family, was nevertheless inspired by earlier Chinese victories over the Americans.[36] His patriotism was genuine and spontaneous.

Another former Nationalist, Tao Shanpeng of the 12th Army, was struck down by malaria soon after crossing the Yalu, and became a straggler. He continued trekking south alone, determined to reach the front lines. "I ran wherever there was gunfire," Tao explained. "Had I had a chance to survive under the Communists, I would not have risked my life for freedom." Born in 1927 to a landlord family in Anhui, Tao fled the Japanese occupation and joined the Communist Anti-Japanese Resistance University (Kangda) in Yan'an in early 1943, but escaped three months later. He went to a Nationalist military academy in Xi'an and rose to the rank of a captain under General Hu Zongnan by 1949. Captured by the Communists in the final battle in Sichuan, Tao was assigned to the Training Regiment of the 35th Division, 12th Army. As a sick straggler in Korea, he begged, scavenged, and stole food for almost twenty days, until he finally found his unit at Yonchon near the 38th parallel. Given his genuine illness and his determination to catch up, Tao was allowed to rejoin the ranks as the 12th Army was making final preparations before launching the Fifth Offensive.[37] The opportunity Tao had been waiting for was about to arrive.

Ambitious Goals

The 19th Army Group had reached their staging areas in central Korea in March, but the 3rd Army Group did not arrive until mid-April.[38] In anticipation of the arrival of all the second-wave units, Peng Dehuai held an expanded party conference at Shangganling (Triangle Hill) near Kumhwa on April 6. Nearly all the commanders and commissars at the GHQ, army group, and army levels were present. Notably absent were the 3rd Army Group's commander and commissar, who were represented by their deputies. Also missing was the 60th Army's commander.[39]

Peng laid out the objectives of the Fifth Offensive: "To annihilate several enemy divisions in order to smash the enemy's plan [for an amphibious landing in the rear] and to regain the initiative." He warned, "It will be a ferocious, major battle. It may cost us several tens of thousands of casualties."[40] Given that the CPV had never annihilated any US division in the past and the largest enemy units it had destroyed were below regimental size, Peng's objective was wildly ambitious.[41] The goal had been set by Mao, who informed Stalin on March 1 that the CPV's second-wave units aimed to eliminate "several tens of thousands of American and ROK troops."[42]

"Commander Peng, there is no problem for my army group to annihilate one American division," boasted Wang Jinshan, the 3rd Army Group's deputy commander, nicknamed "Madman Wang" (*Wang fengzi*). He added, "I guarantee that we will also capture 5,000 American prisoners." Observing Wang thumping his chest, Yang Di, deputy director of the CPV GHQ's Operation Division, became concerned about Wang's "blind optimism," as he knew the entire CPV had only captured 5,300 UNC troops thus far.[43]

However irrational it might have appeared, Wang's exuberance was abetted by Peng, who desperately needed a major victory to "regain the initiative." Other commanders with combat experience in Korea, including CPV deputy commanders Deng Hua, Hong Xuezhi, and Han Xianchu, and the 9th Army Group commander Song Shilun, were reluctant to dampen Wang's enthusiasm. Only Deng gingerly suggested that the US forces were qualitatively and quantitatively much stronger than the Chinese Nationalist forces in the Civil War. But Wang would have none of it. Other generals kept their mouths shut.[44]

Wang's contempt for the Americans was probably influenced by Mao. In November 1950, Mao sent a cable to all military regions in China, calling for a "Strike the Americans" mobilization campaign. "The Americans can be defeated," Mao declared, "as their forces are actually weaker than some battle-tested units under Chiang Kai-shek."[45] The logic was that since the Communist forces had trounced the US-armed Nationalists, they could also defeat US troops in Korea. This kind of morale-boosting talk failed to convince some Chinese soldiers, as discussed earlier, but it apparently convinced General Wang.

As the top Communist commanders were conferring, UN forces had recrossed the 38th parallel, arriving in the Iron Triangle area anchored on the towns of Chorwon, Pyonggang, and Kumhwa. As UNC planes menaced the conference site from above, artillery rumbled in the distance. The CPV GHQ soon evacuated to Ichon, more than 30 miles to the northwest. Upon his arrival on the morning of April 9, Peng suffered a near miss. A US plane strafed his new quarters, riddling his cot with bullets, and then blew up the house from which he had been dragged out by his aide-de-camp moments earlier.[46]

By mid-April, all second-wave units had arrived in central Korea. An urgent cable from the 60th Army to the CPV GHQ reported that certain units were suffering from food shortages and some troops had bartered their winter coats and towels with Korean civilians for food. "What's going on?" an incensed Peng questioned Hong Xuezhi, CPV deputy commander in charge of logistics. Hong assured Peng that the report was false but promised to investigate it anyway. Unconvinced, Peng secretly dispatched his aide-de-camp to visit the 60th Army overnight, who vindicated Hong. The army's commanders offered a rather tenuous explanation: when some troops bartered clothes with villagers for chickens and pickled vegetables, their commanders became alarmed by the breakdown of discipline and low stocks of food, which could last only three days. Therefore, they asked the GHQ for more supplies before the coming battle. Upon learning this, Peng had to apologize to Hong.[47] This bizarre incident was by no means trivial. On the eve of a major offensive, the 60th Army bypassed the 3rd Army Group to make a flippant request directly to the GHQ, causing commotion in the top echelon. Its mortified commanders would not dare break the chain of command again, even if future battlefield exigencies warranted or even demanded it.

The Fifth Offensive, First Phase, April 22–29, 1951[48]

With the infusion of second-wave units, the CPV had amassed nearly 800,000 troops in Korea. The number of CPV armies doubled to fourteen, artillery divisions nearly tripled from four to eleven, and four tank regiments were introduced, the first time the CPV deployed tanks.[49] On the front line north of the 38th parallel, the CPV deployed thirty-three infantry and four artillery divisions, totaling 548,000 troops, thus enjoying a numerical advantage of two to one over the UNC. In addition, three North Korean corps with nine divisions were ready to join the offensive.[50] Mao and Peng apparently believed that one million men could achieve their ambition of destroying several US divisions.

On April 18, Peng outlined the directions and objectives of the Fifth Offensive. Concentrating his strike forces in the western sector above Seoul, Peng ordered the newly arrived 19th and 3rd Army Groups, and the 9th Army Group, which had

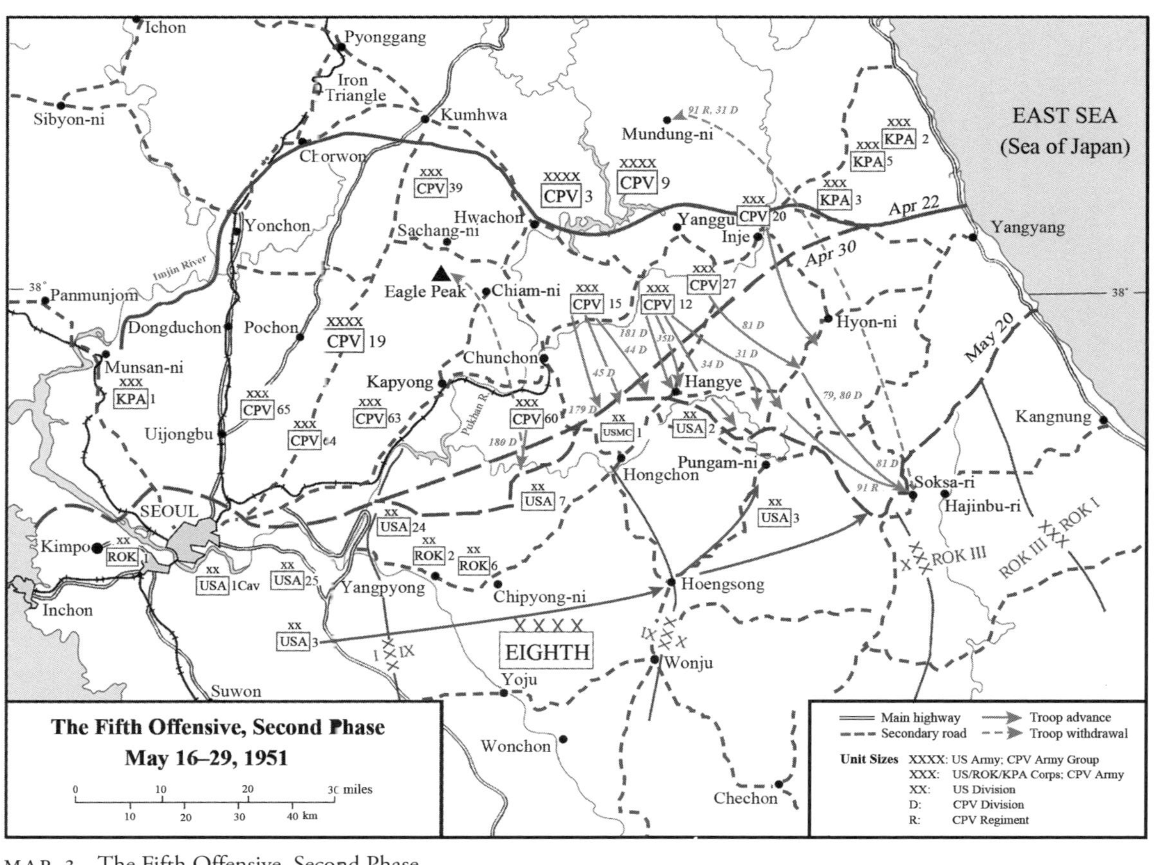

MAP 3. The Fifth Offensive, Second Phase

recovered following the brutal Second Offensive at the Chosin Reservoir, to attack UNC positions along a line slightly above the 38th parallel. Their objective was to "annihilate three US divisions, one British and one Turkish brigade, and two ROK divisions north of the Han River." The next day, the GHQ further instructed each army to annihilate one to two enemy regiments. In the afternoon of April 21, Peng finally ordered the offensive to be launched at dusk the following day.[51]

To prevent enemy interception of radio signals, Peng's final order was "only transmitted orally to division commanders and above."[52] However, the UNC had learned of the plan. By April 20, recently captured Chinese prisoners from the newly arrived 60th, 64th, 63rd, and 27th Armies had reported an imminent offensive, some accurately specifying the 22nd as the D-day. Although it "generally recognized" this intelligence, the US Eighth Army was unsure if the CPV troop movements presaged a general offensive or simply a delaying action to prevent the UNC from seizing the Iron Triangle. UNC patrols continued their probing attacks to the north. On the morning of the 22nd, the Turkish Brigade captured a CPV artillery survey team attached to the 12th Army. Two officer prisoners confirmed that the Fifth Offensive was to begin that night. This vital intelligence was quickly relayed "throughout the army units on line."[53]

At dusk on April 22, the Chinese and North Korean forces launched the Fifth Offensive—almost like a replay of the Third Offensive, but the result was vastly different. While the 3rd Army Group made a frontal assault on the US 3rd Division and the Turkish Brigade along the Chorwon-Seoul axis, the 19th and 9th Army Groups made flanking movements on the west and east, aiming to envelop and destroy the US 24th and 25th Divisions before capturing Seoul.[54] However, the operation was botched from the start. On the west, when the 64th Army commander, Zeng Siyu, received the attack order, his artillery unit had barely reached its positions, but the infantry units had not arrived. He immediately telephoned the army group commander Yang Dezhi, requesting extra time. "Just follow the order. Don't ask why," replied Yang and then hung up. What ensued was chaos: when CPV artillery units showered UNC positions with a preparatory barrage, some infantry units were still miles away, running toward the front. By the time they reached their attack positions, the artillery fire had been extended to the second line of UNC defense as scheduled.[55] The 12th Army had the opposite problem. When it launched its attack, only a third of its attached artillery had arrived to provide the preparatory shelling. Infantrymen mounted massed attacks in the face of intense Turkish fire.[56]

As half a million Chinese troops crowded onto a 50-mile-wide front stretching from the Imjin River in the west to the Hwachon Reservoir in central Korea, the 3rd Army Group's front in the middle was less than 10 miles wide, and the 60th Army's front was half of that.[57] Such dense troop deployment not only caused traffic congestion but also provided easy targets for the UNC's aerial and artillery fire. Since its humiliating rout in November and December 1950, the US Eighth Army had undergone a transformation under Ridgway, who had been promoted to replace MacArthur and was succeeded by James Van Fleet a week before the Fifth Offensive. Under Van Fleet, overwhelming artillery firepower was employed to inflict maximum casualties on the attacking Chinese troops.

Knowing that CPV troops carried individual rations that could sustain them for no more than seven days, UNC units, when coming under heavy attack, made several methodical phased retreats roughly 18 miles each—exactly the distance Chinese soldiers could march per night—and then adopted well-fortified new defensive lines, from which they inflicted further casualties on the tired attackers.[58] Facing a reinvigorated enemy, the CPV continued to rely on its tried-and-true tactics of "penetrating, dividing, encircling, and destroying"—only to find itself no longer able to tear up the UNC's defensive lines as it had in late 1950. Similarly, without the element of surprise, massed—or "human wave"—attacks became less effective against UNC units that had become psychologically prepared and made sure their positions were well fortified against such assaults, even in nighttime close combat. The military historian Xiaobing Li has noted that the CPV offensive "was conducted with a stupefying lack of flexibility and creativity, from the most senior marshal down to regimental levels."[59] Peng had run out of tricks and out of luck.

From April 22 to 29, in what Allan Millett considers "the most widespread and intense fighting of the Korean War," the CPV managed to push the UNC back roughly 35 miles in the western sector above Seoul and about twenty miles in the central sector.[60] After crossing the 38th parallel on April 24, the CPV occupied Uijongbu, ten miles north of Seoul, on the 27th, but it failed to trap any UNC units as planned. The 3rd Army Group reached the Han River on the 28th and 29th, cutting the Seoul-Chunchon road.[61] The 180th Division, a reserve unit of the 60th Army, arrived at the north bank of the Han without much fighting. Optimistic talk of recapturing Seoul was still in the air. Some soldiers claimed they could see the smoke emanating from the city's train station.[62]

Seoul was in sight but beyond reach, as Van Fleet's defense perimeter promised a killing field for the CPV, a spent force whose primitive logistics could only sustain "week-long offensives." As the offensive ground to a halt, Peng called it off on April 29, exactly a week after it had started.

The 179th Division's 537th Regiment, however, continued to fight, because it did not receive the withdrawal order until the next day. By three in the morning of April 29, it had fought its way to Kuleung-san, a hill only eight miles east of the Seoul city center. As US planes destroyed the division HQ's radio, two batches of messengers were dispatched to the regiment, but were killed en route. The third and fourth messengers arrived after midnight on the 30th. The 537th finally withdrew, having lost more than half of its men. The 1st Battalion was almost entirely destroyed and its 1st Company had lost every man, it was believed.[63] In reality, however, the company assistant commander, Chen Shihuan, a former Nationalist military academy graduate and captain, survived and surrendered at 11:00 a.m. He claimed that he "had had the intention of deserting since he entered Korea, but did not have the opportunity" until his battalion was decimated by UNC artillery. He recalled a UNC loudspeaker message: "Officers and soldiers of Chinese Army, the United States and China were as one family."[64] It apparently struck a chord with him.

Another former Nationalist captain, Tao Shanpeng, had deserted on April 22, when his 12th Army was departing from Chorwon for the front line.[65] As the CPV advanced south, leaving Tao farther away from the UNC lines, he saw his chance of successful defection diminishing, unless the UNC were to repel the Chinese offensive and counterattack.

The Lull, April 30–May 15, 1951

The Chinese offensive so far—which became known as the first phase of the Fifth Offensive—had largely been a failure. The CPV once again approached Seoul but fell short of retaking it. Although it boasted of the "annihilation of 23,000 enemy troops," the figure most likely included a large number of wounded and escaped ROKs. Most critically, instead of destroying five enemy divisions and three brigades and killing "several tens of thousands of Americans" as Mao had hoped and Peng and his generals had promised, the Communists only managed to kill 314 and wound 1,600 Americans in the weeklong offensive, while the CPV suffered 75,000 to 80,000 casualties, including 13,349 known deaths and 23,829 estimated deaths. In addition, 246 men were captured.[66]

In analyzing the failure, Peng criticized the "disorder, cowardice, and the lack of coordination and mutual support" among army commanders. The 3rd Army Group's 12th and 60th Armies were singled out for their disorderly command. Peng also blamed poor communications between the GHQ and various levels. Walkie-talkies either failed to connect or there was no one who knew how to use them. Most critically, US planes routinely bombed CPV command posts, killing or wounding commanders, breaking down communications, and generating widespread fear. Peng stressed that the normal chain of command should be bypassed in case of emergency.[67]

Resigned to the reality that the CPV could no longer dislodge UN forces from Seoul as it had in January, Peng decided to shift CPV forces from the west to the east to mount another strike. To ensure surprise, Peng sent burn-after-reading orders to the commanders of the CPV 19th Army Group and the KPA 1st Corps: feign an attack on Seoul in order to pin down the US I and IX Corps in the west. The 3rd and

9th Army Groups would make a surreptitious lateral movement to the east. The 9th Army Group's three armies and three KPA corps were tasked with accomplishing the main objective of the second-phase offensive: to annihilate three or more ROK divisions near Hyon-ni, 78 miles east of Seoul. To maximize the strike force, Peng transferred the 3rd Army Group's 12th Army to the 9th Army Group, whose 26th Army had retired to the rear. Wang Jinshan's 3rd Army Group—now stripped of the 12th Army, the only army Wang had commanded previously, but reinforced by the 39th Army—would tie down the US 1st Marine, 2nd, and 7th Infantry Divisions in the central sector, preventing them from moving east to relieve the ROK divisions. The 60th Army would penetrate south along the Chunchon-Hongchon road to prevent UNC reinforcements moving from west to east.[68]

From May 9 to 15, fifteen CPV divisions—more than 150,000 men—moved from the west and central sectors to the east largely undetected. In the opposite direction, Van Fleet had earlier shifted UN forces, placing most of his strength and all US divisions in the west and central sectors, as he expected Peng to repeat the assault on Seoul.[69] Almond's X Corps, in the central sector, however, noticed the CPV concentration around Chunchon. James Polk, formerly of Willoughby's GHQ G-2 section and now the X Corps G-2, gathered good intelligence from intercepted electronic communication and line crossers—agents posing as civilians or Communist soldiers. He concluded the CPV's main target was the X Corps, not Seoul. But nobody in the Eighth Army believed him.[70]

On May 10, the Eighth Army obtained its first precise intelligence on the enemy's secret move to the east from a Chinese prisoner. With two surrender leaflets in hand, thirty-one-year-old doctor Zhang Wenxing of the 12th Army defected to the US 3rd Division 12 miles above Seoul. A former Nationalist medical officer since 1942, he was captured by the PLA near Chengdu in 1949. Zhang reported that the 12th Army and two other armies would begin a four-day march to the east for 72 kilometers (45 miles) and then strike the US 2nd and ROK divisions. Zhang, the 92nd Regiment's chief doctor, was privy to top-secret troop movement plans, as doctors had to make medical preparations before major operations. His information was remarkably accurate. Yet once again, the US military left this crucial intelligence unexploited.[71]

As of May 16, the US Eighth Army still doubted that the CPV had shifted as far east as Chunchon.[72] In fact, Chunchon was on the western edge of the main offensive of the second-phase attack, which began that evening.

The Fifth Offensive, Second Phase, May 16–21, 1951

At 6:00 p.m. on May 16, under overcast and rainy skies, Communist forces launched the second-phase attack with a brief artillery barrage on the eastern front. The CPV

15th, 12th, 27th, and 20th Armies and three KPA corps attacked the US X Corps and the ROK 3rd and 1st Corps—in all, two US divisions (the 1st Marine and the 2nd Infantry Divisions) and six ROK divisions—on a 50-mile front stretching from Chunchon to the east coast. The main objective was to establish three concentric layers of encirclement around Hyon-ni, thus completely cutting off the escape routes of the ROK divisions and annihilating them.[73]

The CPV 20th and 27th Armies easily crushed the ROK 5th and 7th Divisions and encircled Hyon-ni, but the 12th Army met stubborn resistance from the US 2nd Division and its attached French Battalion.[74] While the 34th and 35th Divisions launched costly head-on assaults on US positions, the 31st Division made a flanking movement to form the outer layer of the encirclement in the southeast. The 31st Division's 91st and 92nd Regiments quickly smashed the ROK units, but soon ran into well-fortified US positions. Braving tank fire, waves of Chinese charged forward, "exploding mines and setting off trip flares." Shortly before dawn, the Chinese finally gave up, leaving behind more than 450 bodies strewn across the minefields or hanging in the barbed wire.[75] The division commander decided to bypass US positions and head south. Pressed for time, the 92nd Regiment marched in broad daylight.[76] When US planes approached, the troops put on abandoned American helmets and kept running in a scattered formation, giving the appearance from above of defeated ROK soldiers fleeing south. The ruse worked. Several planes hovered above for some time but held back from firing, political officer Xie Zhiqi recalled.[77]

Spearheading the division's thrust, the exhausted 92nd Regiment reached Pungam-ni, an important road junction, on May 18. General Peng soon ordered, "Continue to advance south day and night; make bold flanking movements to isolate enemy units in order to encircle and annihilate them all." On the morning of May 20, the 91st Regiment took Soksa-ri, forty miles from the Soyang River where the offensive had begun, and continued its drive to the southeast. At dusk, the main force of the 31st Division also arrived at Soksa-ri.[78] The 91st Regiment won the distinction of being the CPV unit that made the deepest thrust south in the Fifth Offensive. Its victory proved fleeting, however.

The rapid collapse of the ROK divisions and the deep penetration of the CPV 31st Division prompted Van Fleet to move the US 3rd Division from west to east. A reinforcement unit dashed across the peninsula overnight and arrived on May 18 to plug the holes left by fleeing ROK units. On May 21, the 3rd Division dislodged the CPV 31st Division from Soksa-ri, one day after the Chinese takeover.[79] The sudden appearance of a US division at this critical juncture turned the CPV attack on its head. The 91st Regiment's retreat route was cut off.

In the west, the 19th Army Group, now stretched out from Uijongbu to Kapyong, launched holding attacks on the US I and IX Corps. In the central sector—the west flank of the main offensive—the 3rd Army Group's 60th Army crossed the Pukhan River near Chunchon during the night of May 16–17 and advanced toward Hongchon. Its objectives were twofold: to tie down the US 1st Marine and 7th Infantry Divisions, preventing them from moving east to rescue the ROKs, and to cut the east-west link between UNC units, which soon proved to be a quixotic task given the rapid lateral redeployment of the US 3rd Division. The 180th Division's initial advance, however, was swift and eerily unopposed, until it approached Hongchon, where the 1st Marines stood firm.

East of the 60th Army, the 15th and 12th Armies' frontal attack on the US 1st Marine and 2nd Infantry Divisions was met with a sea of fire. On May 17, Van Fleet authorized artillery ammunition expenditures at five times the normal rate—later known as the "Van Fleet rate of fire." Appleman has noted, "The curtain of steel laid down at some designated targets . . . was more than human flesh could bear."[80] As the two armies suffered staggering casualties, their offensive faltered. The 3rd Army Group hastily transferred the 60th Army's 179th Division to reinforce the 15th Army on May 18; the next day, the CPV GHQ transferred the 181st Division to the 12th Army.[81] The 60th Army now only had the 180th Division under its command, defending a twelve-mile-wide front stretching from Kapyong to Chunchon.

Retreat

On May 20, Generals Song Shilun and Wang Jinshan, commanders of the 9th and 3rd Army Groups respectively, jointly cabled Peng, pleading for an end to the offensive. Citing the fact that "the US forces have shifted east, the ROK units have collapsed and withdrawn, and especially that our food supplies have been nearly depleted and troops in certain units have begun to starve," they argued that the opportunity to destroy UN forces had been lost. The next day, Peng ordered a general retreat: the three CPV army groups were told to pull back toward the Iron Triangle along a line slightly above the 38th parallel, or back to square one (pre–Fifth Offensive). That night, Peng cabled Mao, admitting that the CPV had failed to overcome UNC resistance at Hongchon—without naming the two attacking units: the 15th and 60th Armies. As CPV soldiers' seven-day rations could only sustain five to six days of combat, Peng called for an end to the campaign, despite having failed to destroy any US regiments. Mao concurred.[82]

Peng and his GHQ apparently did not anticipate any UNC counterattack in force. He instructed each army group to deploy merely "one division to one army as the rearguard to conduct mobile defense." He explained: "Certainly the enemy will pursue us. But its speed will be determined by the size of its forces and the effectiveness of our mobile defense. The depth of its advance remains to be seen." His sketchy withdrawal plan, however, betrayed his assumption of a minimal UNC counterattack. The 3rd Army Group in the central sector was ordered to leave one army to form a line from Kapyong to Chunchon. East of Chunchon, the most heavily engaged 9th Army Group would deploy one division to cover the entire front. At this point, however, the 3rd Army Group was fighting east and south of Chunchon, and the 9th Army Group was further in the east.[83] To execute Peng's order, both army groups' rearguard units had to make a lateral movement westward along the front line, exposing them to attack.

Peng's absurdly optimistic assumptions were probably based on his past experience: the UNC did not launch a counterattack immediately after any of the previous four offensives and the first phase of the Fifth Offensive. But this time, it was different. "This was the first time in the Korean War that the UN forces had been able to resume the offensive so quickly after a major enemy attack," notes Appleman.[84] In fact, the counteroffensive had already begun.

On May 19, Ridgway toured the front and visited every corps and division command post. He ordered Van Fleet to launch a full-scale counteroffensive on the west and central fronts to relieve pressure in the east. On May 20, the US I and IX Corps sprang into the offensive along a line stretching from the west coast to Chunchon. East of Chunchon, the X Corps's reserve unit, the 187th Airborne Regiment, entered the fight on May 22. It quickly blocked the 27th Army, the 9th Army Group's designated rearguard, from moving west. On May 23, the entire X Corps went on a counteroffensive.[85]

In the extreme east, the 91st Regiment of the CPV 12th Army had become isolated, as the US 3rd Division had blocked its retreat route at Soksa-ri on May 21. The regimental commander made a bold decision to proceed east to cross the Namhan River and then swing north. His gamble paid off. By taking a route so far east, passing through the rugged Taebaek Mountains, the 91st encountered only scattered ROK units, which were unfamiliar with the CPV and unprepared to fight. On May 29, the 91st finally rejoined the 31st Division at Mundung-ni, some sixty miles north of Hajinbu-ri, where the retreat began. Peng was so relieved that he immediately sent a commendation cable to the regiment.[86]

The 91st's circuitous breakout created opportunities for deserters, including three men of the heavy mortar company. Drill instructor Wang Zunming, a former Nationalist captain captured by the PLA in the final battle near Chengdu in December 1949 (see Chapter 2), surrendered to UNC troops on May 25.[87] Four days later, ammunition bearers Cheng Liren and Sun Xiuhe turned themselves in near Hyon-ni, apparently on the 91st's retreat route. They were given consecutive POW numbers, 715261 and 715262. Sun reported that he "deserted [his] unit during a UN aerial attack" on May 22, and "hid in the mountains with another soldier."[88] The other man was fellow Guizhou native Cheng. Later Cheng recalled his escape: "It took us a whole day to climb up the huge mountain, where we hid. How could our unit come to find us?" Out of food, they subsisted on fruits and berries for days. Despite the hunger, Cheng, the former Nationalist policeman, was greatly relieved. "Finally, we broke loose from them [the Communists]," he recalled six decades later.[89]

That the 91st Regiment was able to escape unharrassed by US forces was in large measure thanks to the 92nd and 93rd Regiments, which tied down the pursuing US 3rd Division. From May 21 to 25, the decimated 92nd Regiment held the enemy for five days, giving the 91st precious time to escape north.[90] On May 23, Chen Qingbin, the Taiwanese assistant platoon leader in the 92nd (see Chapter 1), surrendered as he was unable to withdraw due to a high fever. However, three months later he told interrogators that he had "decided to use [the] UN surrender leaflet, which he had secretly kept," and he "walked over to UN lines" with ten other soldiers.[91]

When Chen's superior, Xie Zhiqi, heard the rumor that Chen had defected soon after the offensive was launched, he was appalled, considering that Chen was promoted in November 1950 after receiving the only Extraordinary Merit Award (*tedenggong*) in the entire 31st Division for his performance in railroad construction. Before long, Xie himself was also captured. Wounded in his right leg, Xie was carried on a stretcher for half a day to an "army field hospital," a wooded valley filled with litter cases. Left abandoned and untreated for days and strafed by UNC planes occasionally, Xie finally collapsed. When he woke up, he found himself in an American field hospital. A woman doctor cut open the blood-clotted bandage on his leg, and then poured a bottle of antiseptic onto his festering wounds. As frothy bubbles oozed, maggots fell off in droves. "Can my leg be saved?" Xie wondered.[92]

In hasty retreat, not only the frontline CPV units abandoned their wounded, but so too did army HQs. Tang Yao, the twenty-three-year-old volunteer from Zhejiang and a clerk in the 12th Army HQ (see Chapter 1), was struck down by diarrhea after wading the Soyang River. During the retreat, fifty-one wounded and sick were left uninformed and unattended in a cave, where they were captured by the French Battalion on May 26.[93] Under similar circumstances, Gao Jie, a former college student, veteran of the China-Burma-India theater in World War II, and the leader of the 12th Army's Enemy POW Work Unit, was captured in a cave. Suffering from typhoid fever, Gao had yielded his spot to the more severely wounded, who were transported to the rear by the only available truck. Gao's subordinate Feng Zequn, another college-educated interpreter who also fell sick, escaped and fled north on foot. But he was finally captured on May 31. Both Gao and Feng had handled UN prisoners, and Feng had released four on the front line. Now they themselves were prisoners.[94]

Unable to muster enough trucks, the CPV frequently ordered those not critically wounded to trek to the rear on their own. Jin Yuankui, the poor peasant orphan who was deceived by local cadres in Zhejiang to join the army on Chinese New Year's

Eve (see Chapter 2), was wounded and told to walk to the rear. Jin was one of the 48,000 replenishment troops, including 10,000 recruits from East China, that joined the 9th Army Group.[95] After two months' training in Manchuria, Jin was assigned to the 27th Army and crossed the Yalu River in late April. In the Fifth Offensive, Jin's anti-aircraft machine gun company did not shoot down any US planes; instead, it was bombed. Hit by shrapnel, Jin's face bled. Unable to treat him, his boss told him to walk to the rear. Jin wandered about in the mountains until he fell asleep in exhaustion. When he awoke, his unit was nowhere to be found. "I don't care," Jin thought. "You go on fighting. I'll live." He went to a farmer's house, asked for some rice, and boiled gruel in his water bottle. Suddenly, a US soldier appeared, checked his wound, and then handed him a stick as a cane. Soon Jin was transferred to a US field hospital for treatment. He remembered the date, May 27, the day he finally broke away from the Communists.[96]

The Lone Rearguard—The 60th Army, May 22–24

According to Peng's retreat order of May 21, all units would begin to withdraw on the night of May 23. On May 22, however, Peng bypassed the 3rd Army Group to directly order its reserve unit, the 39th Army, to withdraw immediately "in order to avoid traffic congestion."[97] Peng's precipitate move to first pull out the only unused army in the second phase, instead of deploying it to relieve severely battered frontline units or to take blocking positions to protect the retreat route, betrayed his assumption of an easy withdrawal and his lack of a contingency plan.

Also on May 22, the 3rd Army Group, without seeking the GHQ's approval, ordered its 15th Army to withdraw one day ahead of schedule.[98] With the 39th Army in its rear and the 15th Army on its east flank retreating north early, the 60th Army became the army group's rearguard responsible for the entire central front—by default. It, however, had only the 180th Division under its command, as the 181st and 179th Divisions had been reassigned to the 12th and 15th Army, respectively. Once the retreat began, the two divisions were ordered to return to the 60th Army. Within a few days, they had to make lateral movements back and forth across rugged terrain—another indication of poor command. The 181st Division was 25 miles—or a two-day march—in the east of the 60th Army HQ. The 179th Division, which was adjacent to the 180th Division, however, was ordered by the 15th Army to cover its retreat before returning to the 60th Army. While nearly all other units were moving north, the two divisions had to move west. Blocked by an aggressive UNC counteroffensive, they would not be able to join the 180th Division.[99]

At 5:00 pm May 22, the 60th Army received the withdrawal order from the 3rd Army Group HQ.[100] It accordingly planned to move north of the Pukhan River on May 23 and establish a defensive line in the mountains northwest of Chunchon. However, at 8:00 a.m. on the 23rd, the 3rd Army Group ordered its three armies to halt their retreat and stand their ground until all wounded troops were transported to the rear. As the 12th Army had 5,000, the 15th Army had 2,000, and the least engaged 60th Army had over 1,000 wounded stranded south of the river, it seemed logical to order the 60th Army to cover the withdrawal.[101] Since the 15th Army had begun its retreat the night before and the 12th Army was far to the east, carrying out the order effectively fell on the 60th Army's shoulders alone.

Due to communication delays and prolonged debates at the 60th Army HQ, it did not send out its new order of halting retreat to divisions until 6:00 p.m. on May 23, by which time the 180th Division—following the initial order—had pulled back from the front line and was preparing to cross the Pukhan River that night. Now the 179th and 180th Divisions were ordered to dig in the south of the river for five days—an arbitrary number not specified in the army group's order—and the 60th Army's front widened from twelve to more than eighteen miles, as a result of the early withdrawal of the 15th Army.[102]

On the 60th Army's western flank, the 63rd Army's 189th Division moved north without notice on the night of May 23, leaving a twelve-mile gap in the CPV's line. Shocked, the 60th Army commander Wei ordered the 180th Division to widen its defensive line westward.[103] Having made the initial mistake of making the 180th Division stay put for five days, Wei stretched the division's already thin defense wider and thinner in a futile attempt to plug the gaping hole. By this point, the CPV command structure had fallen into disarray. Chinese military leadership at all levels—from Peng's GHQ to Wang's 3rd Army Group and Yang's 19th Army Group to Wei's 60th Army—had been arbitrary, careless, and disorderly.

Exacerbating the CPV's command chaos, US aircraft—guided by electronic intelligence—accurately bombed CPV radio stations, causing widespread communication breakdowns at all levels.[104] During the 3rd Army Group HQ's withdrawal on the afternoon of May 23, an air raid destroyed two trucks carrying radios. In the following two critical days, the 3rd Army Group command could not be reached. The 60th Army cabled the army group at 9:00 p.m. on May 23, and again at 11:30 a.m. the next day, but received no reply.[105] While waiting for more than two days in vain for the army group to respond, the 60th Army commanders—perhaps still smarting from their earlier indiscretion of breaking the chain of command—made no direct contact with the CPV GHQ. Equally inexplicable, Peng's GHQ did not reach out to the 60th Army, despite having lost contact with the 3rd Army Group for two days.

Facing off against the 180th Division were three divisions of the UNC IX Corps—the US 24th, ROK 6th, and US 7th Divisions, from west to east. On its east flank, the 179th Division faced the formidable US 1st Marine Division. Further to the east, the 181st Division confronted the US 2nd Infantry Division. After the UNC counteroffensive got off to a slow and cautious start on May 20 to 21, Van Fleet reprimanded the 24th and 7th Divisions for failing to advance aggressively. On May 23, as the 1st Marine and 2nd Infantry Divisions joined the general counterattack, the 24th Division's tank task force captured Kapyong, which had been abandoned by the CPV 63rd Army.[106] Having been denied the last opportunity to withdraw north as its neighboring units had, the 180th Division was now threatened on both flanks, with its back against the river.

On the morning of May 24, the IX Corps commander Bill Hoge ordered the 7th Division's commander Claude Ferenbaugh to lead a fifteen-mile armored drive from Hongchon to Chunchon. Task Force Hazel, consisting of a reconnaissance company, a tank platoon, and a squad of engineers, advanced north but came under heavy rifle and machine-gun fire at a twisting mountain pass near Sinjom-ni, eight miles below Chunchon. Without anti-tank weapons, the 180th Division's 539th Regiment was unable to stop the tank column. Although the jeeps and trucks were turned back, eleven tanks sped through the gauntlet and reached Chunchon at 5:05 p.m.[107]

From the 60th Army's HQ perched on a hill overlooking Chunchon, commander Wei Jie saw columns of smoke and dust rising in the south. About twelve miles to the west, the US 24th Division continued its drive north of Kapyong and dislodged the CPV 540th Regiment from Songhwangdang, threatening to cut off the 60th Army's retreat route. About twelve miles to the southwest, the ROK 6th Division captured Kangchon, depriving the Chinese of the main ferry site on the Pukhan River. As the 60th Army's repeated desperate cables to the 3rd Army Group remained unanswered, Wei finally made an independent decision and ordered the 180th Division to move north of the river, the 179th Division to move adjacent to the 180th Division, and the 181st Division to break contact with the enemy and withdraw to Hwachon.[108]

Before its pullout, the 539th Regiment almost captured US 7th Division commander Ferenbaugh. At 4:30 p.m., the Chinese ambushed the general's party of two jeeps on the Chunchon-Hongchon Road, killing two escorts. Ferenbaugh and his aides escaped into thick foliage and hid until 9:00 p.m., when another tank column, overcoming intense small-arms fire, arrived to their rescue.[109] Apparently the Chinese could not have imagined that a US general would venture into the battle zone unprotected. Had they sent a search squad and captured Ferenbaugh, the 180th Division would be remembered for seizing the greatest prize in the entire war, not for its subsequent humiliations.

Alarmed by loss of contact with Ferenbaugh, Task Force Hazel returned south to Hongchon. Its foray into Chunchon, however, had unknowingly liberated nineteen American POWs. The eighteen Marines and one soldier, who had been captured by the CPV at Koto-ri near the Chosin Reservoir the previous December, were selected as part of the CPV's "releasing enemy POWs on the front line" program. They marched from their camp at Pyoktong on the Yalu River to Pyongyang and then to Chunchon, a distance of more than 220 air miles. The 180th Division HQ dispatched a team to escort the Americans to the front line. After wading across the Pukhan River, the group hid in a roadside village. When American tanks suddenly appeared, the Chinese packed up their gear and ran off. But the prisoners were not discovered until the next morning, when a spotter plane pilot noticed a ground panel of wallpaper spelling out: "POW's—19—rescue." When tanks reappeared, "tears actually rolled down my cheeks," recalled one of the prisoners. Their seven-month-long captivity had finally come to an end.[110] However, some of the Chinese who escorted the Americans to freedom, including Cai Derong, the deputy division commander's bodyguard, would themselves end up being captured.[111]

The 180th Division Entrapped, May 24–26

The 180th Division crossed the Pukhan River from late night May 24 until early morning the next day. As the main fords had been occupied by the UNC, it had to cross from less hospitable locations. A week earlier, when the division first crossed the river from the north, the water had been knee to waist deep and calm, and the UNC had not intervened.[112] After days of rain, the water now had risen to chest level—or chin level for shorter people. Guided by spotter planes, UNC artillery shells rained down on the Chinese, exploding in the river, creating massive waves. Lit by flares as bright as daylight, the river flowed red with blood.[113]

Clutching one of the three cables placed across the river, troops waded into the roaring current. Some shorter men and women nurses clung to the tails of horses or mules. To protect the wounded, some brave litter bearers lifted the stretchers above their heads. A shell exploded near Zhang Zeshi, sending shockwaves through the water. When Zhang emerged from the bloody water, the stretcher before him was gone, and the two carriers had been swept far away. The nurse beside him was scrambling and sinking. Zhang reached out to her, but only caught her cloth cap. More than 600 men and women were lost in the crossing.[114]

Once on the northern shore, the 180th Division battled UNC units in the mountains between Kapyong and Chunchon. In the center, the ROK 6th Division's 19th Regiment attempted to block the Chinese from escaping north along the mountain ridges. In the west, the 17th Regiment of the US 24th Division advanced north along the Kapyong–Chiam-ni road. In the east, the 21st Regiment of the US 7th took Chunchon and continued to drive north toward Chiam-ni and Hwachon. The three UNC regiments aimed to pen the 180th Division in a rough triangle formed by the two roads on both flanks and the ROK baseline in the south. By dark on May 25, the two US regiments were within six miles of each other near Chiam-ni.[115] Luckily for the Chinese, US forces halted and rested at night, as usual. This six-mile gap on the night of May 25–26 was their final chance to escape.

Having not received any supplies since the beginning of the second phase offensive nine days earlier, the 180th Division was largely out of food. After making repeated desperate requests for instructions, the 180th Division finally received a withdrawal order from the 60th Army at dusk on May 25. With the 540th Regiment serving as the rear guard, the 538th and 539th were to move northeast to Mapyong-ni in the direction of Hwachon. The 538th and the 539th's 3rd Battalion set out. Within half an hour, however, another order arrived, reversing the earlier one. Brushing aside his regimental officers' vehement protests, division commander Zheng Qigui ordered the 538th to return to join the 540th to dig in on Mount Kadok. The 539th was reassigned to transport the wounded. The 538th Regiment dutifully turned back. The 539th's 3rd Battalion, however, did not, as it had lost contact with higher units soon after setting out. Thanks to this communication breakdown, the battalion barely escaped encirclement before the opening was sealed.[116]

The U-turn had been prompted by the restoration of the 3rd Army Group's radio after a two-day lapse. At 6:50 p.m., the army group finally responded to the 60th Army's cable sent thirty-one hours earlier. It ordered the 60th Army to have one division, the 180th Division by default, establish a defensive line from Kapyong to Chunchon along the north bank of the Pukhan River. The situation on the ground had deteriorated so much that the order was wholly obsolete, as both towns had been lost and the division had moved miles north of the line. Instead of challenging this blatantly untenable order, General Wei "mechanically" forwarded it to the 180th Division with a minor adjustment. The defensive line was moved northward roughly eight miles, but right below the Kapyong–Chiam-ni road, which had been occupied by the UNC. This order effectively locked the division in a death trap.[117]

The night of May 25–26 was "the most critical" since it determined the life or death of the 180th Division, recalled Yang Di, operation section chief, CPV GHQ. After receiving the 60th Army's report, the GHQ immediately cabled the army, ordering the 180th Division to cross the Kapyong–Chiam-ni road that night.[118] It is unclear if that cable reached the 60th Army at all. One cannot help but wonder why the GHQ did not directly cable the 180th Division, given the widespread communication breakdowns and delays. The GHQ bypassed the 3rd Army Group to contact the 60th Army; it might as well have bypassed both to reach the division directly. In any event, the 180th Division did not cross the road that night.

Before dawn on May 26, the 180th Division HQ climbed up Mount Kadok. After daybreak, the US 17th and 21st Regiments resumed their advance. The Chinese watched enemy tanks and mechanized infantry moving rapidly on the roads below. Although rain and heavy clouds prevented UNC airplanes from flying all day, tank and artillery fire pounded the Chinese mercilessly. Early in the morning, the two

US regiments from both flanks joined forces at Chiam-ni, thus "plac[ing] the cork in the bottle."[119]

The 180th Division's commanders looked northeast, desperately searching for any sign of the promised rescue force—the 179th Division—which, in fact, was stuck five miles away at Mapyong-ni, a CPV depot guarded by two battalions of the 536th Regiment.[120] Around ten in the morning, the US 7th Division's tank-infantry unit appeared across the river from the 536th's position. The 3rd Battalion's commander ordered the explosives squad to take out the tanks. Squad leader He Rui grabbed two Soviet-made anti-tank grenades, slung a submachine gun over his shoulder, and ordered two men, "Follow me!" The team charged downhill, and then dashed onto a pontoon bridge. UNC machine guns opened up, blue and red tracer bullets whizzing and streaking toward them. Seconds after landing on the south bank, He felt a heavy thud in his chest; blood gushed onto his face. A large-caliber machine gun bullet had pierced his chest and exploded in his upper arm, shattering the humerus. He fell to the ground and blacked out.[121]

The capture of Mapyong-ni completely cut off the 179th Division from the 180th, quashing the latter's hope of rescue. The May 25 order to "stand firm and wait for reinforcements" had become unfeasible. The 180th Division's strength was down to 3,000 men and the situation was deteriorating hourly. At noon, the division held a Communist Party Committee meeting. Most divisional and regimental officers advocated an immediate breakout. Division commander Zheng reluctantly agreed but insisted on obtaining approval first. The 60th Army HQ approved Zheng's request and ordered the division to break out to the northwest. The HQ promised: "After crossing the road, you will reach our defensive lines" on Eunbong (Eagle Peak). In the meantime, it ordered the 179th and 181st Divisions to fight their way toward Eagle Peak. Soon after, however, the army HQ learned of the plight of the 179th Division and canceled its mission. Due to radio transmission and decoding delays, the 181st Division did not receive its order until 9:30 p.m., when it was engaged in heavy fighting near Hwachon, eleven miles east of Eagle Peak. At midnight, the division began a forced march westward in heavy rain. But it was blocked by the UNC the next morning. It never made contact with the 180th Division.[122]

At 6:00 p.m. on May 26, in heavy rain the 180th Division began its breakout toward Eagle Peak. First, troops descended from 2,800-foot-high Mount Kadok to the valley, where they had to cross the Kapyong-Chiam-ni road, which was guarded by enemy tanks and infantry. Then they had to climb the 4,700-foot-high Eagle Peak. The distance was only six miles, but it was a daunting task for troops who had been without food for days. Soldiers had been eating grass and roots, and some had been sickened or even killed by poisonous herbs. Some even ate snakes.[123] Before the breakout, all heavy equipment, including howitzers and mortars, and documents were destroyed or buried. As pack animals were no longer needed, deputy division commander Duan proposed slaughtering for their meat, but was overruled by commander Zheng, who considered them "revolutionary comrades." Hundreds of horses and mules were set free. As horses whinnied and lingered, horse tenders broke into tears.[124]

More heart-wrenching was the decision to abandon wounded comrades. "Our unit had never abandoned the wounded since the Anti-Japanese War," recalled Nan Yangzhen, a company commissar of the 538th, which was tasked with spearheading the breakout. After crossing the road, only a dozen or so in Nan's heavy machine gun company survived.[125] Illuminated by flares, Chinese troops were pummeled by UNC artillery, and many were killed. Several rear echelon units were cut off and never crossed the road.[126]

At dawn on May 27, the survivors of the 180th Division—less than a thousand—finally approached the summit of Eagle Peak. Contrary to the army HQ's information, the peak had been occupied by the UNC. Remnants of the 539th and 540th Regiments managed to take the peak, but fighting continued in surrounding mountains throughout the day.[127]

At six in the evening, the division made its final contact with the army HQ via walkie-talkie. Army commander Wei Jie ordered the division to break out toward Sachang-ni, roughly five miles downhill, northwest of Eagle Peak. Afterward, the 180th Division could not be reached again. CPV commander Peng later lambasted Zheng for ordering the destruction of the radio transmitter. CPV deputy commander Hong asserted that the order was driven by the fear of electronic detection and bombing.[128] However, 60th Army commander Wei only accused Zheng of ordering the burning of codebooks, an account confirmed by two members of the division HQ wireless section. Other survivors reported that the radio was destroyed by enemy artillery or bombing.[129] Regardless of the exact circumstances of the radio's destruction, the divisional commanders probably felt relieved, as it had repeatedly transmitted orders to impede the division's breakout, exacerbating its predicament. Now the 180th Division was completely on its own.

In retrospect, the May 26 order to climb Eagle Peak made little sense. Wei should have told the division to go around the peak and move directly to Sachang-ni, which was under CPV control until the morning of May 28. The division made the mistake of "mechanically" following the order, lamented chief of staff Wang Zhenbang.[130] Another crucial day had been squandered, and the UNC's snare had tightened.

"Disperse and Break Out," May 27

At dusk on May 27, the 180th Division HQ organized 400 available troops into three companies before the final breakout. Commander Zheng and Acting Commissar Wu led the vanguard company; Deputy Commander Duan and Chief of Staff

Wang immediately followed. This setup reflected the decision made at the party committee meeting earlier in the afternoon: in case of failure to break out as a unit, officers and men were to break out in dispersed groups (*fensan tuwei*).[131] Peng Dehuai later berated Zheng for "ordering each regiment to organize its officers to break out, abandoning nearly ten thousand troops," a charge Wu Chengde vehemently denied when interviewed in 1985. The interviewer Wu Jinfeng, a 20th Army veteran of the Fifth Offensive and the deputy chief editor of the *PLA Literature and Art*, regarded Wu Chengde's denial spurious. "Breaking out in dispersed groups" was a play on words. In effect, the order was "to disperse and escape," concluded Wu Jinfeng. As amply demonstrated in Wu Jinfeng's "Andeshe Notes," a compilation of post-repatriation confessions and interview records, many officers escaped first, abandoning their troops, not to mention the wounded.[132] Du Gang, the 538th Regiment's deputy chief of staff, received a telephone instruction: "You should control a portion of the men as the backbone force (*gugan*) for your protection in case of emergency." The 540th Regiment's commissar told officers to ensure that cadres and party members could escape to safety. Tian Fangbao, a company commissar of the 540th, understood the disperse order as "cadres abandon their units."[133]

The 180th Division disintegrated in an appalling fashion from May 27 and on. Instead of leading the troops into battle, the four divisional commanders fled in the front pack of the escape party. For their protection, the best portable arms were gathered, and the reconnaissance company was reassigned to the HQ. Each top commander received two additional bodyguards and two scouts. Guo Zhaolin, the division's artillery section chief (a regimental-level officer), was teamed with the divisional flag bearer, two scouts, and two interpreters. While high-ranking officers were informed of the breakout plan, troops were left in the dark. Cultural instructor Li Zhenghua recalled that troops of the 539th regimental HQ assembled and waited for four or five hours on the night of May 27, assuming that officers were in meetings to plan the breakout. In reality, they had absconded. After learning that the divisional commanders had "escaped under disguise," Wei Lin, the 539th's deputy chief of staff, and the commissar hastily left a note to the regimental commander, and then ran off with their bodyguards. When stragglers attempted to join the party of four, they were rebuffed.[134]

Without a bugle call or signal, the final breakout began under the cover of darkness. As a confused mass of men crowded onto narrow mountain paths and rushed downhill to the north, UNC artillery and machine-gun fire rained down on them, exacerbating the chaos. Guided by Japanese maps from the 1930s, the vanguard company went in the wrong direction. It had to make a U-turn, only to find that Eagle Peak had been lost. Firing from vantage points above and from the road below, UN forces blocked all the paths to Sachang-ni. On the morning of May 28, the Chinese, entrapped in the woody foothills below Eagle Peak, heard the sound of battle from the direction of Sachang-ni, which soon fell into UNC hands. Utterly demoralized, the 180th Division's commanders resorted to plan B: to disperse and escape.[135]

The four divisional commanders, along with other key officers and bodyguards, slipped into a valley, where they heard wounded men crying for help in a deep gully. Wu ordered the 538th Regiment's commander Pang Kechang to deal with them. "That's impossible," Pang balked, arguing, "We have no manpower." Pressured to hurry up by an impatient Commander Zheng, Wu told Zheng to leave first and he would catch up shortly. The main party immediately left. When Pang finally agreed to attend to the wounded, Wu had fallen behind the main group. Tired and hungry, Wu was dragged and pushed by his bodyguards up and down the hills. At dawn on May 28, Wu ran into another group of more than 400 sick and wounded men lying or sitting in a valley, begging for help. "The division commander and deputy commander had walked past us," some cried. "They abandoned us, but you cannot leave us!" Wu relented. While he was trying to organize the group, Pang caught up. Again, Wu ordered Pang to lead the wounded to safety. "You're a divisional leader," Pang flatly said. "This is your business, not mine." He added, "But if you want to break out, I can take you along." Some of the wounded pleaded with Wu, "Wherever you go, we'll go with you!" An emotional Wu raised his voice, "I won't leave you. We will live together and die together!" While Wu was speaking, Pang disappeared.[136] Knowing perfectly well that there was little chance he could lead the wounded to safety, Wu made the fateful decision to stay.

The other three divisional commanders forged ahead. When they ran into enemy blocking forces, they ordered whatever units at hand to launch diversionary attacks, so that they could slip through quietly. On May 28, deputy divisional commander Duan Longzhang ordered a platoon of the 538th to defend a hilltop near his hideout. The platoon repelled four waves of attacks until their machine gun gave out, only to discover that the top officers had left long before. The surviving troops immediately fled.[137]

Under cover of a morning mist on May 29, the divisional commanders' group waded across a river, but soon came under fire. Two bodyguards returned the fire to attract the enemy's attention; the commanders ran in a different direction and escaped. One bodyguard was instantly killed. Another was wounded and captured. He was none other than Cai Derong, Duan's bodyguard, who had released nineteen American prisoners at Chunchon on May 24.[138]

In the following few days, the three top commanders returned to CPV lines; so too did Pang Kechang, the 538th Regiment commander who twice snubbed Wu. Many other officers and troops, however, did not have such luck.

Cowards, Heroes, and Many In Between

Days before Pang reaching the CPV lines, his commissar Zhao Zuoduan had been captured. On the night of May 26, before the 180th Division set out for Eagle Peak, Pang refused to let Zhao join him in the front pack. Once the breakout began, rear units rushed to the front, jamming the escape routes. Since Zhao carried one of the few flashlights in his unit, his bodyguards, scouts, and several officers followed him. Simmering with rage over being dumped by Pang and filled with the fear of getting killed or captured, Zhao made a mad dash in the dark wilderness dense with boulders, brush, and trees. Soon he found himself alone and lost. The next morning he was captured without a firing a shot.[139] Zhao became the highest-ranking Chinese prisoner up to this point in the war.

Following the example of their commanders, officers at all levels gathered the best small arms and best-trained men, and sometimes doctors, for protection, while abandoning their troops, especially the untrained and unarmed, such as propaganda and paramedical personnel. Many officers resorted to threats and deception to prevent troops from joining or following them.

On May 28, more than twenty men of the 539th Regiment's 92 mm mortar company failed to break out. The commissar ordered the men to stay in a hut and wait for him and the deputy leader to return. The unsuspecting bugler, messengers, and cultural instructors went in and waited. Their officers never returned.[140]

When two straggling male nurses of the 538th's medical unit found their leader in a valley, they were told, "Comrades, we should go separate ways. Large groups are easily detected by the enemy. If that happens, none of us can survive." Unconvinced, the two nurses continued to shadow the officer until he told them, "If you follow me, I'll kill you!" The two men finally gave up, thinking, "Even the enemy hasn't hurt us so far. What's the point of getting killed by you?" They went to sleep in a hut, waiting to be captured. At the first sight of UNC troops, they surrendered. Similarly, several male nurses of the 540th Regiment were turned away at gunpoint by an officer, who threatened, "I'll execute anyone who follows me!" The men had to stop and wait until the officer was out of sight.[141]

Feeling betrayed, some men took revenge. On May 28, several members of the 540th Regiment medical unit were hiding in the brush, waiting for the chance to cross a road. When UNC troops randomly fired into the thicket, a paramedic coughed. The chief pharmacist, already resentful of unwanted followers, warned: "If you cough again, I'll kill you with this grenade!" Minutes later, the paramedic darted out and turned himself in. The officer, having no other weapon, soon put away his grenade, walked out of the thicket, and surrendered.[142]

Messenger Li Shaoliang of the 539th followed his deputy company leader for two days. When they met another officer, however, the officers ganged up and told Li to get lost. Li later joined five unarmed stragglers. At daybreak, they ran into a group of pistol-toting officers of the 538th, who forced them to go away from their hiding spot. When these disgruntled men were captured, they informed on the officers. "They used to preach that officers love and care about their men, but now no one cares about us," Li groused. "They turned us away and we got caught. If we die, we should die together! So I fingered them," Li explained.[143]

In sharp contrast to their top commanders' cowardice, some Chinese officers and men fought heroically despite hopeless circumstances. Jiang Ruipu, an eighteen-year-old cultural instructor with little combat training, volunteered for a suicide attack on May 27. Eighteen Chinese rushed American tanks blocking the mouth of a valley. Half of the men were immediately knocked out by the tanks. The rest jumped into a ditch, only to be pursued. Soon Jiang became the sole survivor. He debated if he should commit suicide with the last bullet in his Russian-made Mosin Nagant rifle. While he fidgeted with his rifle, pointing the long barrel against his abdomen, a GI approached. Jiang fired at him, smashed the rifle, and then dashed toward the hills. When GIs seized him, Jiang burst into tears, crying, "Everything is over."[144] His interrogator later noted, "PW was firmly indoctrinated with Communist ideology."[145]

On May 29, former Whampoa cadet Ma Furui witnessed a Communist officer leading forty to fifty volunteers, all party members carrying small arms, in a suicidal charge against tanks. Hiding in the hillside, Ma's boss Guo Zhaolin, director of the divisional artillery section, told him to go down to investigate the result. Before reaching the battle scene, Ma took cover behind a large boulder. As US troops approached, he waved a white towel on a tree twig and surrendered. When he was escorted to the main road, Ma saw the attackers' bodies—they had been crushed, maimed, or flattened by tanks. As many prisoners gathered, Ma noticed Guo, who had changed into an enlisted man's uniform. Guo signaled Ma to keep his mouth shut. Ma realized, "Perhaps Guo had decided to surrender when he sent me away."[146] In the POW camps, Ma became an anti-Communist, but he never betrayed his boss.

Most captives were neither cowards nor heroes. They surrendered simply because they had been out of food, weapons, or ammunition; and some had been wounded. Zhao Yingkui, a messenger of the 538th Regiment HQ, initially followed Commander Pang. While marching in the darkness, he fell into a ten-foot-deep ravine. Landing on his head, he bled profusely and passed out. When he woke up, he found himself in a US Army hospital on Koje Island.[147] Cultural officer Zhang Zeshi fell off a boulder and blacked out on May 27. He was kicked awake by steel-heeled boots. "This fellow is alive," a GI shouted, "Get up!" The first thing that came to his mind was, "It's over. Everything is over. Why didn't I die from the fall?"[148] Cai Pingsheng of the 179th Division was also captured on May 27, while dead asleep from exhaustion. His first thought was: "How could I become a prisoner? This is the end of everything in my life."[149] Being taken prisoner was shameful. The CPV soldier's role models were the legendary World War II Five Heroes of Mount Langya, who purportedly jumped off a cliff to avoid capture by the Japanese. But suicide was rare. On May 27–28, the US 24th Division alone captured 4,411 Chinese, the vast majority of them from the 180th Division.[150]

It is noteworthy that despite—or perhaps because of—the total disintegration of the 180th Division, there was no wholesale surrender or mass defection. CPV officers and men surrendered as individuals or in small, scattered groups. The only known exception took place two days before the final debacle. On May 24, two platoons of the 540th Regiment defending Mount Kekwan north of the Pukhan River became surrounded by the ROK 6th Division. The company commander, a veteran Communist, told a platoon leader to negotiate a surrender. The platoon leader, in turn, ordered private Zhang Qize to go down the hill to meet the ROK soldiers. Brandishing his submachine gun, he threatened, "Go! If you don't, I'll kill you!" Zhang went downhill and was captured. Soon the deputy platoon leader Yang Guocheng, formerly of the Nationalist 95th Army, descended to liaise with the ROKs. Not long after, more than thirty men surrendered without firing a shot. In the ensuing interrogations, Zhang tried to evade answering the questions, claiming he didn't know the officers. The ROKs slapped him. Watching on the sidelines while smoking a cigarette and eating cookies, Yang admonished Zhang, "This is not your [Communist] world anymore. You'd better be forthcoming!" Before long, Yang began teaching the prisoners to sing the Nationalist anthem. "You must sing. If you don't," warned Yang, "watch out!"[151]

Former Nationalists

"Former Nationalists made up the majority of those who defected, surrendered, and deserted," asserted Du Ping, the CPV's political department director, at the post–Fifth Offensive conference in September 1951. He lambasted the 180th Division for its "most serious internal impurity," as "many bad guys, who had sneaked into the division, instigated others to surrender."[152] In reality, however, former Nationalists had little to do with the division's collapse or the defeat of the Fifth Offensive. Their surrender and desertion were a result of the collapse, not the cause of it. Du's claim was typical of the Maoist practice of blaming "internal impurities/enemies" for the Communists' own failures.

As detailed above, the only known case of organized surrender occurred under the command of veteran Communist officers, although a former Nationalist facilitated it. Equally remarkable, there was only one known incident of former Nationalists turning their guns against the Communists. The 540th Regiment's acting commander Liu Yaohu was shot from behind and severely wounded. The gunman, rumored to be a Nationalist 95th Army veteran, fled and was never captured. Liu later died in a UNC hospital.[153]

Certainly, for some men, especially some former Nationalists, surrender was more than just an option, but a dream come true, or a nightmare (under the Communists) brought to an end. At the first opportunity, they defected or surrendered. Liu Ruyu, former Whampoa artillery major graduate and CPV staff officer of the 179th Division, had secretly tucked surrender leaflets inside his quilted cotton jacket several days before his defection on May 25, 1951. He followed the instructions: "Leave your unit after dark and hide in a secure place overnight. Walk on main roads to surrender the next day." Once he was on the UNC side, Liu went on the radio to persuade fellow soldiers to surrender.[154]

Until the 180th Division's collapse on May 26–27, very few former Nationalists managed to defect. They surrendered en masse along with other CPV soldiers only after the disintegration. Strictly speaking, they were not defectors. Yu Rongfu, former Whampoa cadet and cultural instructor in the 540th regiment, followed the confused mass of men escaping north on mountain paths on the night of May 25. Somehow the path ended abruptly at the edge of a precipice. Unable to gauge the depth of the descent in the dark, desperate men nevertheless slid down the slope. To protect themselves, some

FIGURE 7.1. Standing near loudspeakers, two female members of the Eighth Army Psychological Warfare Section don parachutes in a C-47 aircraft equipped to broadcast surrender appeals to Chinese troops. April 20, 1952. US National Archives.

men sat on tree branches and slid downhill, only to find the road had been blocked by UNC troops. Hundreds of men, including Yu, surrendered on May 26.[155]

Wen Chuanji, another former Whampoa cadet and cultural instructor in the 540th, surrendered on May 30, along with his boss Li Zhiyuan and two others. Li recalled that only four stragglers—exhausted, hungry, and unarmed—were left in their party by May 29. As the sound of battle moved increasingly distant up north, their chances of breaking out diminished. "What if we fail to cross the line?" Wen asked "in a wavering tone." Li replied, "We're all officers. If we're captured, we'll be killed. Don't ever talk like this!" Falling silent, Wen dropped to the ground and dozed off. At dawn the next day, they ran into a UNC search squad. No one put up any resistance.[156] Wen was captured two days after the majority of the 180th Division's troops had surrendered. He could have easily escaped from his unarmed boss and comrades, but he did not defect. A few months later, however, this Sichuanese would reveal where his heart truly lay, telling his interrogator that his home address was "China, Formosa."[157]

Gao Wenjun, the Whampoa classmate of Wen and Yu and an artillery staff officer of the 538th, initially tried to follow his boss during the final escape, but was soon shaken off during an enemy shelling. Secretly feeling relieved, Gao turned to the southwest. He picked up some surrender leaflets, including one falsely claiming

FIGURE 7.2. Using a loudspeaker, a captured Chinese prisoner urges his comrades to surrender. September 1951. US National Archives.

that three Nationalist divisions were fighting in Korea, he recalled. When he finally surrendered to the Americans near Kapyong on May 29, Gao immediately asked: "Where are my Nationalist brothers?" The interpreter, a defector himself, retorted in irritation: "You go find them, and then tell me!" There were no Nationalist forces in Korea. Realizing that there was no guarantee he could go to Taiwan, Gao felt cheated.[158]

Like Gao, several other men defected or surrendered on the assumption that there were three Nationalist Divisions, led by General Bai Chongxi, fighting on the UN side. In fact, CPV officers had spread the "news" that the Nationalists were battling in Korea. They asserted that Bai, who had missed his chance to defect in the Civil War, would do so at the first opportunity. Another practical reason for the belief was that many illiterate soldiers simply could not distinguish between the UN forces (*lianheguojun*) and the Nationalist Army (*guojun*), which sounded very similar, especially through airborne loudspeakers.[159]

Slow-flying planes hovered over the mountains, dropping leaflets and calling for surrender. Propaganda soldier Yan Tianzhi heard a voice booming from the sky, "Comrades, you are encircled. There is no way you can escape."[160] Zhao Yingkui heard: "Brothers

FIGURE 7.3. Chinese prisoners captured near the Hwachon Reservoir wait for chow at the 21st Regiment HQ, 24th US Infantry Division. May 29, 1951. US National Archives.

of the Chinese Communist Army, you are former troops of President Chiang Kai-shek. President Chiang has a message for you: Don't die for the Communists. Take a leaflet and return to our side. Americans will treat you well."[161] Guo Shigao of the 179th Division claimed that he even heard the promise of repatriation to Taiwan.[162]

Heavy machine gunner Yu Dehai was one of those blaring surrender messages from airplanes. A Nationalist veteran of World War II, Yu was captured and pressed into the PLA in December 1949. When the 180th Division collapsed, Yu and two fellow machine gunners became stragglers. When a ROK squad approached the gully where they were hiding, they decided to kill the South Koreans, who were notoriously cruel to prisoners.

Their machine guns opened up from three directions, killing all the ROKs. Having eaten only once in three days, the three starving men finally walked out and surrendered to the Americans on May 27. The GIs immediately gave them a loaf of bread and cigarettes. After interrogation, Yu was kept by the US unit, where he enjoyed regular meals of chicken and rice and unlimited milk and coffee. When asked to broadcast the surrender message in place of UNC personnel, Yu happily obliged. Aboard a helicopter, he announced through loudspeakers: "The UN forces treat

FIGURE 7.4. Wounded Chinese prisoners being treated at the 21st Regiment, 24th US Infantry Division collection station. May 29, 1951. US National Archives.

prisoners very well. They won't abuse you. Don't worry. Many men have come over, and they are doing well." Yu broadcast twice a day for a week, thirty minutes per session. "It was an easy job," Yu reminisced with a grin in 2014.[163]

The JCS later admitted that US psychological warfare leaflets and broadcasts "promised safety and asylum to those Chinese and North Korean military personnel who would voluntarily surrender."[164] However, no plans had been made to provide asylum. Moreover, it would not be surprising if psychological warfare personnel and the Chinese prisoners they drafted made improvised, unauthorized promises. Induced by such promises, some Chinese defected, but they were treated as regular POWs, not as asylum seekers who expected protection. When he was handed a POW tag, Liu Ruyu's heart sank. His hope of going to Taiwan was "half dashed."[165] Liu and Gao, like many others, had their first taste of American unscrupulousness and irresponsibility. And it was not their last.

The Final Tally

On May 31, Mao cabled Peng: "What is the 180th Division's status? [I am] very concerned." Peng replied: "The 3rd Army Group has suffered major losses. Troops are fleeing in all four directions. Many are trying to escape back to China. Units have been dispatched to intercept them."[166] In one of the largest humiliations in Chinese Communist military history, the 180th Division was annihilated. It was "the first [major] loss suffered by the CPV in the entire war," conceded Peng in his autobiography, noting the division suffered 3,000 casualties.[167] The 3rd Army Group's commander, Wang Jinshan, however, reported more than 7,000.[168] The 180th Division later provided a detailed breakdown: it lost 7,644 men, including one divisional- (Wu Chengde, who was captured 14 months later in July 1952), and 9 regimental-, 49 battalion-, 201 company-, and 394 platoon-level officers.[169] More than 2,000 were killed or wounded, and more than 5,000 were captured.[170] The 4,000 survivors included those who escaped enemy encirclement but also those in rear units that had not gone into battle in the first place.[171]

Peng blamed the loss on "poor command" without specifying which level of command. "The 60th Army is particularly weak," Peng said. "The basic cause was that too many middle- and lower-ranking officers had been transferred out." Peng admitted his "serious neglect in failing to make careful withdrawal plans after achieving a great victory"—which was not an unequivocal admission of guilt.[172] Mao offered a similarly half-hearted reassessment: the CPV's mistakes were "somewhat too hasty, somewhat too ambitious, and somewhat too deep" in prosecuting the offensive.[173] Nonetheless, Mao correctly identified a major issue with Peng's command structure: "Layers of command should be reduced; the army group should be eliminated."[174] The Fifth Offensive became the first and the last campaign where the army groups operated.[175]

Despite the humiliating loss, the Communists again boasted of victory in public, claiming that they had "annihilated 23,000 enemy troops" during the second phase—exactly the same number as in the first phase. During the retreat, they "annihilated" another 36,000. The Fifth Offensive as a whole, they claimed, inflicted 82,000 casualties on the UNC at the cost of 85,000 Communist casualties.[176] The UNC put Communist casualties at 105,000 for the second phase, including 17,000 killed and 10,000 captured. The estimates of enemy killed in action submitted by field commanders came to a total so high that Ridgway found it difficult to accept. The ratio of wounded to killed was "probably not less than 3 to 1," Ridgway reported. Contrary to the CPV's fanciful claims of enemy casualties, the UNC reported that only 745 American, 1,221 ROK, and 71 other UNC troops were killed in May.[177]

To boost the Communists' badly damaged morale, the CPV GHQ exhorted the troops to "properly view the victory of the Fifth Campaign." It asserted that the campaign was prosecuted "correctly throughout, except for a flawed tail end (*shouwei*)." "We can only say," it concluded, "this is an imperfect victory." In explaining the losses, the GHQ contended "many misconceptions (*cuojue*) at many levels and various factors" came together to produce "unnecessary losses."[178] No one took direct responsibility.

FIGURE 7.5. Chinese prisoners are inspected by James Van Fleet, Eighth Army commander; William Sebald, the de facto US ambassador to Japan; and Matthew Ridgway, UNC commander. May 29, 1951. US National Archives.

Wang Jinshan, the 3rd Army Group commander who had promised to capture 5,000 Americans but instead gave the enemy almost twice as many Chinese POWs, was not punished. Wei Jie, the 60th Army commander whom Peng chastised for doing little more than "simply forwarding telegram orders," was transferred back to China. Zheng Qigui, the 180th Division's commander whom Peng had initially threatened to court-marshal, was merely demoted by one rank and transferred to the army group HQ. No one was court-martialed for the debacle.[179]

While the Communists were in denial, Ridgway reported to Washington: "The enemy has suffered a severe major defeat." However, instead of advocating an advance above the 38th parallel, he suggested that the situation offered "optimum advantages in support of . . . diplomatic negotiations."[180] When the armistice talks began in July 1951, 83 percent of the eventual total of more than 21,000 Chinese prisoners had been captured. Among them, 15,510 CPV soldiers were captured in April, May, and June.[181]

Unusual Prisoners: A Japanese, a Taiwanese, and a General

On May 24, Matsushita Kazutoshi, a Japanese blacksmith serving in the Mountain Gun Regiment, 58th Division, 20th Army, surrendered to the ROK Capital Division on the east coast. During the Ichigo offensive in World War II, Matsushita was captured by Chinese Nationalist guerrillas in Hunan and pressed into their service. In the ensuing Civil War, he served in the Nationalist 74th Division and was captured by the PLA. After entering Korea in December 1950, he deserted near Hwachon on May 11, 1951, five days before the second phase attack. He hiked in rugged terrain for two weeks, "hoping to make his way to the Sea of Japan, then escape by water to Japan," until he reached Chahang-ni near Pyongchang, some fifty air miles from Hwachon.[182] He became the only Japanese POW in the Korean War.

On May 27, Tao Shanpeng, the former Nationalist captain who had deserted the 12th Army on April 22, the first day of the Fifth Offensive, finally surrendered to advancing UNC units near Chorwon. He had been hiding in the mountains for more than a month.[183] On June 10, Wang Yingchang, the Taiwanese fisherman from the Penghu/Pescadores Islands and ammunition inspector of the 17th Artillery Regiment, 20th Army, surrendered to the UNC near Hwachon. He had deserted on May 15, the day before the second phase attack, and then had hidden out for twenty-five days.[184] Had the CPV offensive succeeded in pushing the UNC south, Tao and Wang could never have been rescued.

On July 12, 1952, 410 days after he made the fateful decision to stay behind to lead wounded troops, Wu Chengde, the 180th Division's acting commissar, was finally captured. Wu and his bodyguards had hidden behind enemy lines, surviving on food scavenged or stolen from Korean farmers and UNC units. While their desperately anticipated sixth offensive never materialized, they "fail[ed] in repeated attempts to cross [the] line to [the] north." Wu claimed he was a cook named Wu De, befitting his relatively old age of thirty-eight. However, the 308th US Counter Intelligence Corps (CIC) established his identity when he was interned at Kimpo, where Wen Qingyun, the 180th Division's cryptographic section chief, who was captured twenty days before Wu, was also interned.[185] In a telegram from the US embassy to Secretary of State Acheson, incredulity was palpable: "Highest ranking Chi[nese] POW to date (approx equivalent major gen). This officer claims to have been straggler behind UN lines for over one year prior capture."[186]

Despite noting that Wu was "indoctrinated deeply with Communist ideology and propaganda," Wu's interrogators claimed, "PW did not want to return to Communist China. He wanted books to read in order to reindoctrinate himself in democratic ways."[187] Regardless of the veracity of the claim, Wu certainly did not appreciate the "democratic ways" that followed. Transferred to Pusan, Wu was frequently interrogated by G-2 and the State Department Intelligence Team. The interrogator was a Chinese civilian "from Formosa and in frequent contact" with the Nationalist embassy.[188] Wu claimed that he was routinely tortured by anti-Communist prisoners during the process. One of his tormentors, Wang Qian, later received a "Special Award" in Taiwan for "beating Wu Chengde black and blue all over his body until he revealed his secrets."[189]

The US embassy believed that, despite his "evasive and uncooperative" attitude, Wu was "of high potential value for poli[tical] as well as milit[ary] background info, and well worth later attempt at exploitation for propaganda matching Commie handling" of General William F. Dean, the US 24th Division commander captured by the North Koreans in August 1950.[190] However, by the time of Wu's capture, Chinese anti-Communist prisoners had defeated the Communists in their civil war in the prison camps on Koje and Cheju Islands. They had hijacked the war agenda. The Americans were at a loss as to what to do with the POWs. Wu's capture was left unexploited.

Sun Zhenguan

Zhang Zeshi

Lee Hak Ku (Lee Hak-koo)

FIGURE 00.1. Mug shots of Chinese POW leaders Sun Zhenguan and Zhang Zeshi and North Korean leader Lee Hak-koo at the time of their arrest following General Boatner's crackdown in Compound 76. US National Archives.

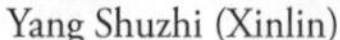

Yang Shuzhi (Xinlin)

Chen Yonghua

Cheng Liren

Gao Wenjun

Yu Rongfu

Meng Ming

FIGURE 00.2. Major Chinese anti-Communist prisoners. Courtesy of Yang Shuzhi, Cheng Liren, Gao Wenjun, Yu Rongfu, Meng Ming, and Kuomintang Archives, Taipei.

FIGURE 00.3. Major Chinese Communist prisoners. Courtesy of Wu Qingpu, Lin Mocong, Jiang Ruipu, Fang Xiangqian, Cai Pingsheng, Zhong Junhua, Wu Chunsheng, Xie Zhiqi, and Zhang Maolin.

8

Civil War in the POW Camps

WHEN THEY ARRIVED in Pusan, Chinese prisoners could not help but notice the huge presence of North Korean POWs, with whom they initially had to share space. Whereas the bulk of the 21,000 Chinese prisoners were captured in May and June 1951, the majority of the near 150,000 North Korean POWs and civilian internees had been captured soon after the Inchon landing in September 1950. The North Koreans were better organized and indoctrinated. With their unit structure largely left intact, the Korean Communist leadership in the POW camps was active in staging protests and planning uprisings, acting in direct response to instructions transmitted from the North through grapevine communication channels supported by guerrilla networks in South Korea. In contrast, the Chinese POWs were like heaps of loose sand. With their officers busy concealing their own identities, Communist leadership was nonexistent. But not for long. Both Communist and anti-Communist prisoner leaders emerged. The Chinese Civil War continued behind the barbed wire. In fact, long before the surge of prisoners from the disastrous Fifth Offensive, the battle had begun in Pusan.

The First Battle: Li Da'an Versus Sun Zhenguan in Pusan

When truck driver Li Da'an arrived at the Fifth POW Enclosure in Pusan (the transit depot) in April 1951, Yu Qingde, a Chinese prisoner working in the processing section, saw "a slender and tall man with a rather pale complexion, who appeared to be easygoing and didn't look like a rough man (*curen*)." Fang Xiangqian, who was captured on March 7 and now worked in the section, however, found

Li "thin, not physically strong, but pugnacious." Still riding high on his successful defection on March 24 and subsequent friendly interrogation by the Eighth Army G-2 at Taegu, Li was ruffled by the very idea of POW registration. "I was released by the Communists from prison and sent to drive a truck for them. I drove down to the UNC lines with a truckload of ammo in an uprising. I'm not a prisoner," Li protested vociferously, demanding to see the American officer in charge. He declared his hatred of the Communists because they had murdered his parents.[1] "Don't forget that you are a Chinese," warned a bespectacled colleague of Fang and Yu. He added, "Soon prisoners will be exchanged. You must consider your own future." Li shot back, "Give me a break! I surrendered voluntarily. You must be a Communist troublemaker!"[2]

The man was Sun Zhenguan, the battalion commissar of the 20th Army, captured near the Chosin Reservoir and the highest-ranking Chinese prisoner until the arrival of regiment-level officers in June 1951. Sun had an uncanny ability to charm his captors and befriend them.[3] When he was first interrogated in Humhung, the port city south of the Chosin, Sun found out that the interpreter, Chen, was Shanghainese; he deftly switched to the local dialect to build rapport. Chen in return told him privately how to deal with G-2 officers' questions. When white officers were away, Sun claimed, he often turned interrogations into information and propaganda sessions on New China.[4] After his arrival in the Pusan hospital for frostbite treatment in December 1950, Sun linked up with the North Korean prisoners' underground leadership. In late February 1951, G-2 got wind of the North Korean plots. When interrogated by Master Sergeant Wu, Sun denied all charges. In early March, Sun was discharged from the hospital and transferred to the transit depot, where he stayed to work thanks to arrangements made by the North Korean underground.[5]

Fang Xiangqian, who spoke some English, was also selected for the processing section. His boss, a KPA officer prisoner who had lived in Shanghai, quizzed Fang in fluent Chinese: "Is Kim Il-sung good? Is Mao Zedong good?" Without hesitation, Fang said, "Kim Il-sung is good. Mao Zedong is good. Really good!" The Korean prisoners extended their hands, saying "Chinese comrade, you're good!" A bond was formed instantly.[6] As Korean Communist and anti-Communist prisoners were secretly battling for control of the transit depot, the Korean comrades welcomed Sun and Fang. This was where they encountered their future nemesis Li Da'an.

In the evening, Li Da'an led US guards to Sun and Fang's tent, pointed his finger at Sun, and said, "This Communist officer is anti-UNC." Sun denied the charge and rebuked Li: "How dare you, a traitor, be so shameless!" The US officer ordered Sun to pick up his personal belongings, consisting of a blanket, a rice bowl, and a pair of chopsticks, and leave. Before he left, Sun told Fang, "When you return to our motherland, and if you don't see me, please tell my superiors and comrades that I died in prison, and I didn't betray our country." Sun, Fang, and their Korean comrades were all in tears, assuming the worst.[7] This first clash between Li and Sun ended in victory for Li.

With the arrival of a natural leader like Li, willing followers came out of hiding, showing their anti-Communist true colors. Tang Jusheng, the former Nationalist soldier who had led three others to defect in March, told Li, "The [South] Korean interrogator Lee told us earlier not to fight with the Communists until we have more people. Now you guys are here. It's time."[8] Li had found his power base.

According to Li's confession after his recapture by the Communists in 1953, he received instructions from a Nationalist agent named Bai, then a G-2 employee at Taegu. Bai told Li to organize his men once in Pusan to ferret out Communist Party members and officers. In Pusan, the prison authorities allowed Li to establish a Prison Guard (PG), or monitor, squad—a prisoner-staffed security organization that maintained order in the POW camps with clubs and fists. Defector Tang Jusheng became one of the first seven members. Li and his PG squad successfully uncovered several Communists and more than a dozen officers. In June, Li received another job title, "sanitation inspector," which allowed him to roam across various compounds freely.[9]

With G-2's permission, Li entered the processing section and searched registration cards for suspected Communists. Party member Wang Zhaojun was informed on and brought to the PG tent. He immediately crumpled and signed a confession with a fingerprint in blood. Wang went on to expose his company leader, Liu Guang, who had been assessed by his interrogator as "a fanatic communist" who "lied freely" and was "very uncooperative." Liu had even boasted to fellow prisoners that he planned to escape.[10] Liu was tied up, suspended, and beaten—the same kind of torture Li had gone through in Communist prisons in China. The torturer was none other than his former subordinate Wang. Once he had crossed the Rubicon, Wang became one of Li's henchmen.[11]

Li Da'an eventually became the most infamous Chinese prisoner—the "devil incarnate" (*huo yanwang*)—a scourge to fellow prisoners, Communists and anti-Communists alike. Rough (*cu*) and tempestuous (*mang*) were Li's defining characteristics, his allies recalled. His quick temper was legendary: "When he agreed with others, anything was fine; in case of a falling-out, the only outcome was 'white knife in, red knife out.' There was absolutely no room for compromise."[12] Rank-and-file prisoners feared Li. "Sporting a cowboy hat, with a wooden club dangling on his hip, Li Da'an kicked prisoners with his boots or hit them with the club at will, often for no apparent reason," recalled doctor Zhang Yifu. Fellow anti-Communist leader Tao Shanpeng also remembered Li's "lawlessness": Whenever the sulky Li saw Communist prisoners, he whacked them twice with a baseball bat.[13]

The Chinese POW Battalion in Pusan

To his surprise, Sun was not executed; instead, he was simply transferred to the nearby Chinese POW Battalion (*dadui*), where more than 1,000 men were held.[14] By the end of April 1951, the total number of Chinese prisoners reached 3,423.[15] While some were in transit and some in hospitals, the majority were interned in the Pusan camp. The authorities appointed Wang Shunqing, the English-speaking former Nationalist officer and CPV medic who had returned three American prisoners to UNC lines in November 1950, as the battalion leader. When Chinese prisoners were shipped to Koje Island in May, Wang was "in firm control" of 3,400 men.[16]

Within the Chinese Battalion, Sun was interned in the Officers Company consisting of dozens of officers with the rank of platoon leader and above. The company leader was Liu Bingzhang, the ex-Nationalist captain and CPV staff officer who defected hours before the Second Offensive. Another ex-Nationalist captain, Wei Shixi, the CPV training instructor who defected the night before the Third Offensive, was Liu's deputy.[17] "Commissar Sun," Wei received Sun politely with a smile. "Please remember that one has to follow American regulations here. It's not permitted to spread Communist propaganda."[18]

The Chinese anti-Communist prisoners had gained a following early on when they expelled the North Korean prisoners from their camp. This came about as a result of a fight over food. Initially the Koreans were in charge of ladling out food. They routinely asked the queuing prisoners in Korean, "Chinese or Korean?" Chinese prisoners always received less food than the Koreans. One day, Yang Shuzhi and Li Da'an led more than two hundred Chinese prisoners in a violent clash with the Koreans. The UNC intervened and let the Chinese have their own separate compound—thus creating the Chinese Battalion—and control their own food.[19]

Now isolated from the North Koreans, Sun faced a new problem: he knew few other officer prisoners from other units. He had no choice but to lie low and bide his time. Slowly he gathered around him a small coterie of committed Communists, including Liu Guang, who had been tortured by Li Da'an. Sun feigned illness and frequented the prison hospital, where he liaised with North Korean underground leaders. In mid-May 1951, the North Koreans, eagerly anticipating the liberation of the south by advancing CPV and KPA forces, planned a mass uprising on May 27. Sun pledged his participation.[20]

As he was covertly building his network, Sun was approached by Tan Xingdong, the demoted PLA assistant battalion commander who had defected in March. In his thick northern Jiangsu accent, Tan claimed that he was a veteran of the Communist New Fourth Army, which was true, and that he had been a CPV regimental propaganda section chief before his capture, which was false. Tan moved to sleep next to Sun in their crowded tent, so that they could whisper after dark. A tearful Tan implored Sun not to leave him out if Sun was to join the uprising. Tan's story seemed so credible, his emotion so genuine, that Sun almost believed him. But Sun did not let his guard down completely.[21]

As the Chinese Fifth Offensive faltered, the much-anticipated Communist advance to Pusan never materialized. In the meantime, the Korean prisoners were moved to Koje Island. The uprising fell through. Sun was interrogated for allegedly conspiring with the North Koreans. His doubts about Tan now seemed justified. Although he failed to nail Sun, Tan had already informed on more than twenty party members and officers.[22] Few Communist prisoners knew that he was a defector from the 38th Army. Tan would soon come out and show his true colors.

An Influx of Prisoners of the Fifth Offensive

On May 27, at gunpoint, Zhang Zeshi, the 180th Division propaganda officer, and fellow prisoners plodded down from the mountain near the 38th parallel where they had been running and hiding. Before him, Zhang saw a winding line of Chinese captives, tattered and despondent. Swathed in blood- and dirt-stained bandages, many of the injured were leaning on makeshift canes made of tree branches.[23]

"Stop! Or you'll be killed!" shouted one GI, and a shot rang out. Zhang saw a captive breaking ranks and running with hands holding his pants. Zhang yelled in English, "Don't shoot! He has dysentery." With his English ability revealed, Zhang was immediately taken to see an officer.

The prisoners were marched into a "POW stockade," a flat area surrounded by barbed wire with armored vehicles guarding the four corners. When South Korean civilian workers carried baskets full of barley balls toward the main entrance, the some two hundred dejected prisoners got up to their feet and swarmed toward the gate. The US officer asked Zhang to restore order. Zhang obliged.

After the meal, another officer took Zhang to a truck's cabin for a chat. He introduced himself as Captain Joseph Brooks. He said that he was born in Kunming to an American missionary father and a Chinese mother. His godfather was a banker in Chongqing.[24] Zhang could not tell Brooks was half Chinese, but his eyes appeared sincere. After learning of Zhang's Tsinghua background, Brooks said, "If you agree to work in our Eighth Army HQ, we can remove your POW status, and hire you as a civilian. Once the war is over, I can send you to study in America." Startled by this proposition, Zhang imagined getting on a plane to broadcast on the front lines. He came up with a reply, "But I have a fiancée waiting at home. I can't break my vow." The disappointed Brooks wrote a note and handed it to Zhang. "Keep this reference letter. Any time you change your mind, show it to the guards. They'll take you to the HQ promptly. Since we're battling the Chinese Communists, competent Chinese interpreters like you are very much in demand."

When Zhang returned to his stockade, he saw a young soldier sobbing in the corner. The boy was eighteen-year-old Jiang Ruipu, who had made a suicide charge on US tanks the day before. Seeing Zhang in a clean CPV uniform, which was unusual for prisoners, who were mostly in tattered clothes after weeks of combat, Jiang wasn't sure if he was a Chinese or American officer. When Zhang comforted Jiang, Jiang said that he was slapped by a US interrogator when he said that all Chinese soldiers were Communists, and there were 450 million of them in China—the entire population.[25]

Before dawn the next morning, Zhang and nearly a thousand other prisoners were loaded onto trucks and sent to Suwon, where Zhang went through his first interrogation. He gave his actual name, age, and unit number, as well as details about his family origins and education, but he lied when he said that he was an enlisted man and a Christian. He parried questions about the names of regimental leaders, claiming that he was too junior to know their names. Then the interrogator opened up a booklet in English. Zhang was stunned to see all the officers' names were already accurately recorded.[26] Most likely this booklet was a product of Nationalist interpreters Huang Tiancai, Lu Yizheng, and Zheng Xian, all of whom had been serving under Captain Brooks, the leader of the 163d Military Intelligence Service Detachment (163 MISD) attached to the 1st Marine Division.[27]

The camp commander offered Zhang a job as an interpreter, which came with perks, such as a better tent and food, the same as those for American soldiers, and perils, such as being called a *hanjian* (traitor) behind his back.[28] Similarly, when Lin Xuebu, a Sichuan University English major and a POW interrogator in the 180th Division HQ, interpreted for the guards and issued instructions, a former comrade thought to himself, "How could a man change so fast! Now he's serving the Americans."[29]

The anti-Communists, however, did not see Zhang Zeshi as one of their own. When Tao Shanpeng, the former Nationalist captain and CPV deserter of the 12th Army, arrived at the Suwon camp still feeling giddy about his escape, he sized Zhang up. After Zhang translated Tao's questions to the Americans, Tao, who did not understand English, nonetheless concluded, "Once this handsome young man opened his mouth, he sounded and smelled like a Communist."[30]

Zhang Zeshi was one of the very few Communist officers who volunteered to serve as a POW trusty. Even the non-Communists tried to avoid this job, lest they be interrogated. Gao Jie, a graduate of the Northwest Associated University who had volunteered to serve in the CBI theater in World War II, tried to hide his identity as the chief POW interrogator in the CPV 12th Army HQ, claiming to be a propaganda actor. His fluent English was exposed in the hospital, however, when he, outraged by an American surgeon using a scalpel to remove maggots from the festering wound of a prisoner, blurted out: "You don't have the basic humanitarian spirit of a doctor!" Soon Gao was assigned to be a POW interpreter.[31]

Communists in Hiding

In early June, Zhang spotted the first high-ranking officer he knew, Du Gang, the deputy chief of staff of his 538th Regiment. He had to suppress his excitement until they could meet out of sight. Zhang, who had been expelled from the party in 1950 and readmitted "on the front line" soon before his capture, had finally found a senior party member.[32] Zhang's warm welcome must have been equally heartwarming for Du, since he had been snubbed by his erstwhile staff officer, former Whampoa cadet Gao Wenjun, just a few days before in the frontline stockade. When Du told Gao not to reveal Du's identity and to keep track of other prisoners, Gao coldly replied, "I don't know that many people. You'd better find someone else." Du warned, "I hope you will reconsider! Watch out!" Gao simply found Du's wish to conceal his identity ludicrous, as many prisoners knew Du.[33] Nevertheless, Du stuck to his line that he was a cook, befitting his older age, just as commissar Wu Chengde would do a year later when he was finally captured. Du reminded Zhang Zeshi to keep the secret.

Toward the end of May, every day hundreds of Chinese captives arrived at detention centers in Suwon and Seoul. They were shipped by the trainload to Pusan, the central transit depot for POWs. When Cai Pingsheng, the cultural instructor in the 179th Division, first arrived in Pusan, he recognized Zhao Zuoduan, formerly the political director of the 60th Army Attached School before becoming the 538th Regiment's commissar. Zhao signaled for Cai not to reveal his identity. Cai quietly obliged.[34] For this well-known high-ranking officer, however, it soon proved futile to hide under his new identity—Wang Fang the quartermaster. UNC interrogators must have been amused by the large number of self-proclaimed cooks and quartermasters in the CPV.

The traumatic experience of being taken prisoner also produced its fair share of the deranged, demented, and deaf, both real and feigned. In Pusan's Compound 10, where the authorities appointed Zhang Zeshi the leader, there was a certain Cao You, a scout in the 40th Army and one of the very few CPV soldiers captured in Unsan in the First Offensive.[35] After he recovered from severe head injuries, Cao became mentally unstable. Often Cao would spontaneously laugh, sing, and dance, sometimes babbling in English and Japanese. Zhang observed this young man from a distance. Cao had a willowy body, slightly curly hair, and dreamy deep eyes. Zhang suspected his supposed insanity. One night, when the two moved to sleep next to each other in their tent, Cao gingerly asked Zhang to sing for him. In Zhang's sorrowful melody from *The White-Haired Girl*, a popular Communist opera, tears rolled down Cao's face. With the floodgates of emotion burst open, down came the protective mask of insanity. Cao's father, an underground Communist, was executed two weeks after his birth. After his mother fled, he was raised by his grandmother. He joined the PLA at the age of nineteen. After that night, Cao became another member of Zhang's "patriotic small group." Zhang instructed Cao to continue to act crazy in order to learn information from "traitors" working for G-2.[36]

For Xu Yisheng, the organization section chief of the 179th Regiment, 20th Army, the deaf-muteness he affected became resolutely permanent. He was impervious to hard labor, hunger, beating, and any form of humiliation. He never talked to anyone, let alone complained. Legend has it that when his interrogator cocked his pistol behind his head, Xu acted unperturbed and no one could detect that his ears slightly moved. Xu developed these extraordinary skills as a long-time underground Communist agent working in Nationalist-controlled areas. As if it were his second nature, his highest principle was to "never expose his true identity." For more than a year, Xu acted deaf to perfection, until he arrived in safety to the Communists-controlled camp in April 1952.[37]

While male prisoners attempted to conceal their rank, the only known Chinese woman prisoner, Yang Yuhua, an assistant nurse in the 180th Division field hospital, went on a hunger strike and refused to answer questions in Pusan's Compound 7 for female prisoners. Nationalist DAC interrogator Gao Qingchen was impressed by this recalcitrant sixteen-year-old girl. He lamented that "Yang had been poisoned by Communist propaganda since she was little; she has shown no sign of awakening." In fact, however, Yang had only joined the Communist army in November 1950.[38] A Chinese prisoner witness reported that every time Yang saw another Chinese, she would cover her face and cry, "I have no face to see any Chinese. I want to die."[39] Eventually, the prison authorities brought in Zhang Zeshi and Cao You to persuade Yang to end her hunger strike. They comforted her with the news of impending peace talks: "Soon you'll will be able to go home to see your mom." This only made her cry harder, "I've had no mother since I was little. I grew up with my grandma. When I joined the army, I didn't even tell her."[40]

Their American captors probably found Chinese prisoners' visceral sense of shame and reflexive attempt to conceal their identity incomprehensible. A captured document entitled "Temporary Regulations for Wartime Military Law and Discipline" issued by the CPV 9th Army Group sheds some light on the grave implications of allowing oneself to be taken prisoner. The punishment was death if one committed any of the nineteen listed offenses, including "surrender to the enemy or desertion on the front line" (items 1 and 16), "desertion with a weapon" (item 4), "revealing military information" (item 7), and "disclosing military secrets" (item 10).[41] At this point in Pusan, nearly every Chinese POW had already committed one or more capital crimes. This partly explains Chinese prisoners' silence and evasion.

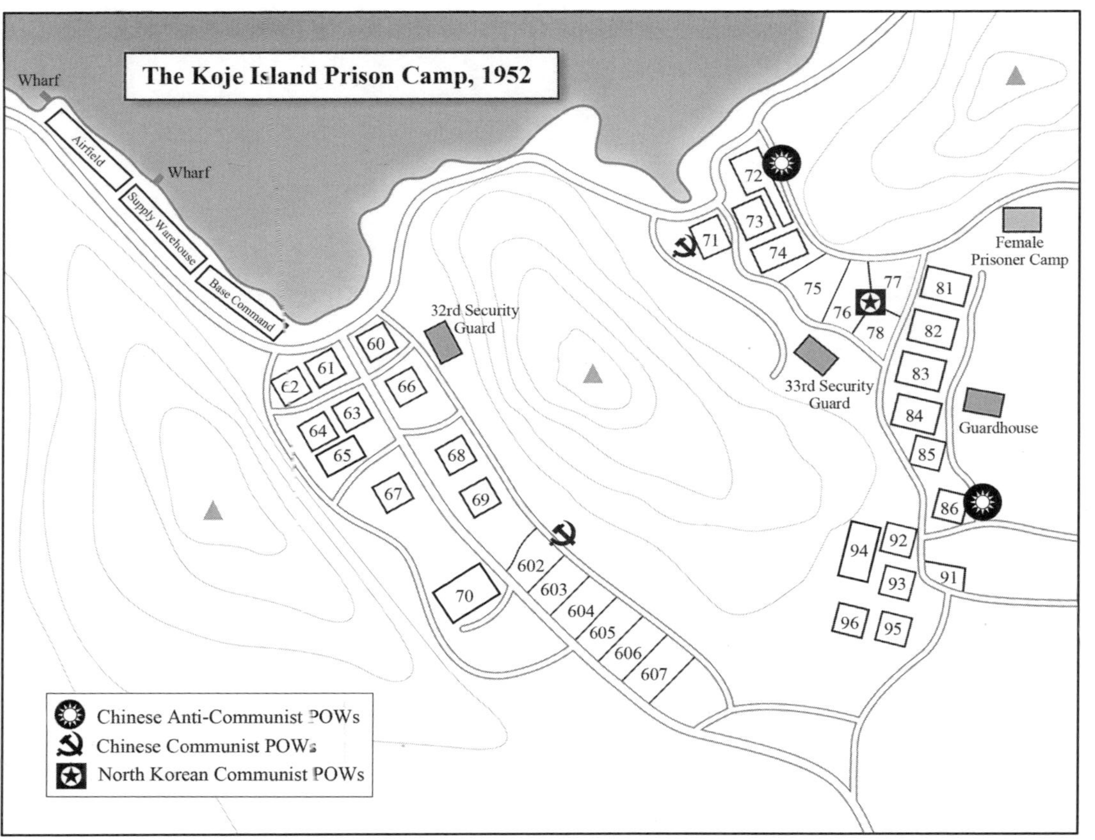
The Koje Island Prison Camp, 1952
Wharf
Airfield
Wharf
Supply Warehouse
Base Command
32rd Security Guard
33rd Security Guard
Female Prisoner Camp
Guardhouse
60
61
62
63
64
65
66
67
68
69
70
71
72
73
74
75
76
77
78
81
82
83
84
85
86
91
92
93
94
95
96
602
603
604
605
606
607
Chinese Anti-Communist POWs
Chinese Communist POWs
North Korean Communist POWs

MAP 4. Koje POW Camp, 1952

Since most Communists were hiding in fear and in shame, some rank-and-file prisoners wondered, "How did the cadres and party members become mute?"[42] Only a few stepped forward, but only in a gray capacity, such as Zhang Zeshi, who served as the leader of Compound 10 in Pusan.

After a brief period in Pusan, most of the more than 14,000 prisoners of the Fifth Offensive were transferred to Koje Island in June and July. They were in for a shock.

Koje Island

Prison construction had begun in February 1951 on Koje Island, Korea's second-largest island at 155 square miles, located roughly twenty miles southwest of Pusan. When the Communists launched the Fifth Offensive, the UNC accelerated moving prisoners from Pusan, South Korea's wartime capital, to Koje. By the end of May, 115,884 of the 154,734 POWs held by the UNC had been relocated, and the number grew "at the staggering rate of 2,000 per day," reported the US Army. By the end of June, 146,000 POWs were on Koje, while Pusan's prisoner population dwindled to less than 10,000. Koje's POW population would reach 155,000 in early 1952. In this massive tent city, the twenty-eight newly constructed compounds, mostly square-shaped enclosures roughly 650 feet long on each side, were designed for a capacity of 4,500 but soon each quickly became "overcrowded by as much as 100 percent." Outside the barbed wire, there were many local residents and refugees.[43]

The US Eighth Army, a field army primarily committed to prosecuting the war along the 38th parallel, was saddled with handling prisoners. Koje Island's population increased "beyond US organizational capacity to handle," the US Army later admitted. While the recommended ratio of guards to prisoners was 1 to 20, the actual ratios were 1 ROK guard to 26 POWs and 1 US guard to 156 POWs as of May 1951, and 1 ROK guard to 33 POWs and 1 US guard to 188 POWs as of September 1951.[44]

Exacerbating the manpower shortage problem were the dismal quality and poor discipline of UNC troops on Koje. Many of the guards were misfits or rejects from combat units, left sulking on this thankless island. Days after Xie Zhiqi and Lin Mocong arrived on Koje, they witnessed an American GI having sex with a South Korean woman outside their compound in broad daylight, in plain view of the prisoners. Indignant prisoners shouted, "Animal (*chusheng*)! Animal!" Other villagers walked by, going about their business nonchalantly. A US officer nearby, instead of intervening, gave a thumbs up and made faces at the prisoners. "Down with American imperialism!" the prisoners exploded in rage.[45]

Most prisoners had limited interaction with their ROK or US guards, who were posted on watchtowers and along the compound perimeter. Only two unarmed US sergeants entered the compound during the daytime to make roll calls and to assign work details. Given the shortage of troops and linguists, the prison authorities had to rely on cooperative prisoners to govern the camps. "Chinese prisoners of war are controlled by a thin veneer of PW trustees not freely elected by the prisoners whom they control, but appointed by US Army camp authorities on the basis of ostensible anti-Communism," observed Philip W. Manhard, the US embassy official who had led the State Department interrogation team in Pusan and also interrogated prisoners on Koje from July to December 1951.[46]

"These trustees exercise discriminatory control over food, clothing, fuel and access to medical treatment for the mass of Chinese prisoners," Manhard continued.[47] A rigid hierarchy of food rationing was established in two camps. Compound leaders customarily enjoyed separate small-stove cooking, very much similar to the Communist system instituted in Yan'an. Other leaders could eat their full; staff such as clerks, PG squad members, and CIE instructors were given a full bowl of food, while rank-and-file prisoners received only half a bowl.[48]

Time magazine glowingly described prisoners' nutrition: "They are fed three times a day—rice, beans, fish, pepper mash, soy sauce. This is a nourishing, 2,800-calorie diet, on which many prisoners have gained weight."[49] However, Communist prisoners disputed the authorities' claim that "each prisoner's daily ration consisted of one pound of food." They reported, "in reality, it never reached that level after it was skimmed at various levels" by anti-Communist trusties. Meat was a rarity. "One pound of meat was allocated for every fifty prisoners, and it usually came as dried squid. Under normal circumstances, prisoners had only two meals a day, each consisting of a fist-sized rice-ball or a half-bowl of barley, and a bowl of clear soup dotted with a few vegetable leaves and drops of cooking oil. If they were lucky, prisoners occasionally found bits of meat or fish in their soup."[50] In fact, most rank-and-file anti-Communists were also left hungry. Whampoa cadet Gao Wenjun recalled, "Our staple diet was not rice, but mostly barley. Side dishes such as dried fish, canned food, and vegetables were normally absent, so we just had 'crystal clear soup' made of water and salt." Fellow cadet Ma Furui reported, "We were constantly hungry, but not to the point of starving to death."[51]

The prison authorities first issued bright red uniforms in July, but were forced to withdraw them days later after prisoners protested vehemently. Then they supplied a khaki jacket, a T-shirt, a pair of long pants, and a blanket—all used—to each prisoner. As fall gave way to winter, only an additional shirt was issued. No underpants or socks were provisioned. To fend off the island winter's damp cold, prisoners wrapped themselves in their blanket all day—some doing so even while working. Some prisoners stuffed newspapers or packaging paper into their pants and others wrapped tattered gunny-sacks round their waists. Since leaders and trusties had the first pick when supplies arrived, they were dressed in new or like-new wool sweaters, jackets, and boots.[52]

Prisoners were quartered in large tents about thirty feet long and sixteen feet wide, each accommodating fifty to eight prisoners. Inside the tents were two rows of sleeping areas on recently leveled rice-paddies and a ditch in the middle as a walkway. As each compound interned twice as many prisoners as designed, the quarters became so crowded that prisoners had to sleep flipped-spoon fashion, head to foot in alternating rows on the ground. With only five to six inches of space per person, prisoners had to sleep on their sides. If they wanted to turn, they had to ask their leaders for permission. If permission was given, all prisoners had to turn in unison. Normally two prisoners shared their blankets and ponchos, one set under their bodies and on top of the straw matt to stay dry, and another set over their bodies as a blanket to keep warm.[53]

Communist prisoners later reported that "none of them had ever had a bath during their captivity, for there was no water in the 'bathhouse' installed in the various camps." Instead, these bathhouses often became "torture chambers where prisoners were hung up and flogged."[54] Among the more than eighty prisoners interviewed by this author, only Dr. Meng Ming recalled a hot bath—a rare treat offered by Li Da'an, Compound 72's deputy leader, after Meng gave Li some sought-after medicine.[55]

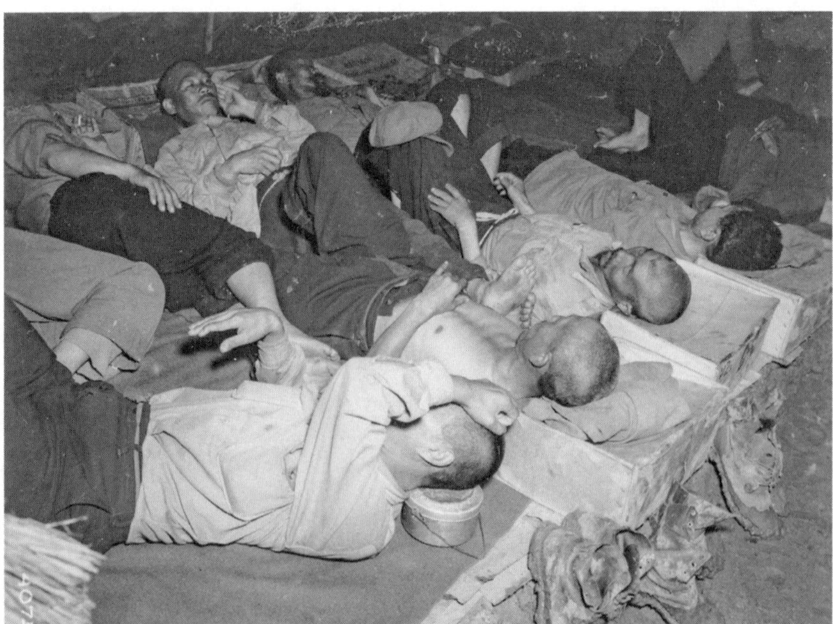

FIGURE 8.1. Prisoners sleep in a flipped-spoon fashion in overcrowded tents. US National Archives.

Roughly 1,300 prisoners shared one outdoor latrine, which contained ten honey buckets—55-gallon oil drums cut in half and covered with wooden seats. As few northerner prisoners had ever used a toilet, some squatted on the seats. "Damn it!" the American sergeant would curse the prisoners, recalled Wu Chunsheng. Trusties were posted to watch the latrine to keep it clean. Every morning after breakfast, each compound dispatched about three hundred prisoners to carry the buckets to the sea.[56]

While physical deprivation and hardship made prisoners' lives miserable, incessant strife—between the Communists and the anti-Communists, between various anti-Communist factions, and between a Sichuanese secret society and the Nationalists—rendered their lives precarious. The civil war continued in POW camps.

Compound 72

After the Chinese Prisoner Battalion in Pusan was transferred to Koje in May and June, the prison authorities expanded it into three battalions in Compound 72—the 4th, 5th, and 6th—with the 1st, 2nd, and 3rd battalions consisting of Korean POWs. Each battalion (*dadui*), with 1,200–1,400 prisoners, consisted of companies (*zhongdui*), platoons (*xiaodui*), and squads (*ban*).[57]

FIGURE 8.2. Prisoner details carry "honey buckets," made of 55-gallon oil drums cut in half, to be emptied into the sea off Koje Island. Large pits were built later. Dimitri Boria collection, MacArthur Memorial Archives.

The former Chinese Officers Company now grew to the 4th Battalion; anti-Communist Wei Shixi was appointed its leader. An incident, however, triggered a regime change. On June 2, Frederick Bieri, a delegate of the International Committee of the Red Cross (ICRC), accompanied by a group of US officers, visited the compound. A US colonel asked Wei to identify the highest-ranking prisoners. Wei pointed to Sun and two other prisoners who were busy digging dirt, and said, "They were a CPV battalion commander, commissar, and deputy commander, all equivalent to majors." Surprised, the colonel said, "If they are field-grade officers, why are they doing labor? Shouldn't they be the leaders here?" Sun quickly responded in English, "Yes. I'm the highest-ranking officer. I should be the leader." With American blessings, Sun proclaimed himself the battalion leader. He immediately appointed his Communist allies to all key posts, sidelining the anti-Communists.[58]

The Nationalists, however, were no pushovers. The day after the bloodless coup, Wei Shixi and a group of ex-Nationalist officers gathered in secret to establish the June 3rd Branch of the Nationalist Party—a name chosen to commemorate the day it was set up, which also happened to be Youth Army Day. The latter was significant as many members were Youth Army veterans, including Meng Ming, the defected CPV doctor, and Yuan Pengying, who had deserted with Tang Jusheng in March. Former Communist Tan Xingdong, the only member with no prior Nationalist affiliation, became the group's "investigator," befitting his recent success as a snitch.[59]

Communist strength received another boost on June 16, when the first 3,000 prisoners captured in the Fifth Offensive, including Zhao Zuoduan, arrived in Compound 72. Sun secretly approached the higher-ranking Zhao and pledged to follow his leadership.[60] On June 18, the Korean officer prisoners in Compound 72 staged a mass hunger strike. The next day, they threw rocks, hitting US guards, and "started rushing the gate, screaming 'Banzai.'" US officers and ROK guards opened fire and killed three prisoners and wounded eight. The authorities cracked down on Korean Communist prisoners, but also arrested Sun, Zhao, and five other top Chinese Communists, apparently acting on tips from the Nationalists. With American backing, Wei Shixi returned to power. The Communist reign in the 4th Battalion had lasted only seventeen days. During their detention, however, the Chinese Communist leaders were pleasantly surprised to meet top Korean leaders Pak Sang-hyon and Lee Hak-koo.[61]

In the wake of this first camp incident involving mass defiance, all Korean prisoners were removed from Compound 72. All six battalions were soon filled by newly arrived Chinese POWs. Like their officer counterparts in the 4th Battalion, non-officer prisoners in the other five battalions had been planning to establish their own organization. On May 28, Li Da'an, Yang Shuzhi, Wu Jiansheng, and Yin Ruliang, most of whom happened to be truck drivers who had defected during the Fourth Offensive, and others decided to establish what they called the Anti-Communist

National-Salvation Youth League in Compound 72. As rumors of the armistice talks abounded, anti-Communist prisoners became increasingly agitated. On June 27, they gathered in a traditional ceremony for sworn brothers, drinking liquor mixed with drops of their own blood. On July 2, 179 men met to formally establish the league. Yin Ruliang became the chair and Li Da'an his deputy. Wu Jiansheng was the general secretary and Yang Shuzhi the investigation section chief.[62]

When Zhao and Sun were released by the prison authorities and returned to the 4th Battalion in late July, the Nationalists had firmly established control. The new leader, Wang Youmin, announced new regulations forbidding any type of private gathering and even conversations among prisoners without permission. Most Communist prisoners were cowed. Zhao made a desperate move one day by shouting outside his tent, "Party members and cadres of the 538th Regiment step out to overthrow Wang!" His rallying cry was met with dead silence. PGs quickly seized him and tortured him. That was Zhao's first and final act of open defiance. In mid-August, he was transferred to Pusan for interrogation, where he cooperated with the Americans in the hope of staying away from Compound 72 as long as possible. He was not sent back until late December.[63]

PG squad leader Li Da'an and his henchmen wreaked violence on not only Communists but also non-Communists. When Whampoa cadets Gao Wenjun, Ma Furui, and Yan Chongfu first arrived, they were shocked by the "menacing-looking PGs." While they were whispering among themselves, PG Yuan Pengying approached them. "I'm also a Manchurian," Yuan said. "Let me give you a survival tip: Keep your mouth shut, even if you feel you're being mistreated. If you talk, you'll be sorry." Gao and Ma heeded the advice; Yan complained and was beaten by the PGs.[64]

Even some anti-Communist leaders did not escape Li's wrath. When Captain Liu Bingzhang returned from Tokyo in the summer, he found himself marginalized after a four-month absence. On one occasion, Li Da'an arrested and tortured him for alleged "badmouthing." Only after fellow leader Yang Shuzhi intervened was Liu released.[65]

Compound 72's top position went to Wang Shunqing in early September 1951.[66] The former leader of the Chinese Battalion at Pusan had been transferred to Tokyo in May to participate in a secret G-2 project involving psychological warfare leaflets (see Chapter 6). "A shrewd leader and organizer in the traditional mold," Wang "was regarded by Americans throughout the period of internment as the most effective and consistently cooperative of the Chinese PW leaders." In Compound 72, he oversaw the rapid buildup of anti-Communist forces.[67] With his deputy Li Da'an performing much of the violent work, Wang usually did not get his hands dirty. However, a CIE report noted that Wang, nicknamed Little Caesar by American soldiers, "exercised a personal monarchy, . . . exacting subservience and personal privileges and indulging in personal violence on a scale not reported in any other compound."[68]

Thanks to Wang's shrewd leadership and Li's iron fist, Compound 72 became a cooperative model POW camp in the eyes of the prison authorities. Even a visiting Swiss official with the ICRC was impressed, noting that "morale is excellent: nobody is idle" and "no complaints were made."[69]

Compound 86

In sharp contrast to Compound 72, the second Chinese compound, No. 86, established a mile away in mid-June to house the influx of new prisoners captured in the Fifth Offensive, was a liberal haven—until October 1951. While prisoners in Compound 72 were forbidden to have private conversations without permission, prisoners in 86 openly sang Communist songs. Its leaders were a group of former Whampoa cadets and educated youths who appeared to be neutral or non-ideological but were secretly pro-Communist or at least pro-repatriation. Although the nominal compound leader was Ying Xiangyun, a Nationalist veteran and truck driver, most power was in the hands of three POWs who directly liaised with the Americans: Ying's deputy, Yang Wenhua, and chief clerk Guo Naijian, both of whom had been cadets in Whampoa's 23rd class (1949), and chief interpreter Gao Jie. Similarly, a number of men who had been cadets in Whampoa's 24th class, and had not finished boot camp when they surrendered to the PLA in December 1949, served as clerks and other important positions throughout the camp. They were known as the clerk faction. Furthermore, the six battalions and the PG squad were power centers of their own. While the 2nd Battalion was led by openly anti-Communist Bai Peiming, the 4th was led by a non-ideological Dai Yushu.[70]

Dai, a native of Chengdu and a former Nationalist platoon leader, led more than a thousand prisoners. In late July, he established a brotherhood (*dixionghui*) based on Sichuan's Gowned Brothers (*paoge*) secret society. In a ceremony of drinking liquor mixed with members' blood, Dai and several hundred mostly Sichuanese prisoners swore: "To return home together, and fulfill our duty of filial piety to our parents, we become brothers today. We will live and die together."[71] The Brothers were non-ideological, even though a few were members of the Communist Party or the Youth League, such as the eighteen-year-old Zhong Junhua. As Dai and his Brothers wanted to return to China, their cause aligned with that of the Communists and came into conflict with the anti-Communists who advocated "returning to Taiwan." With a number of pro-repatriation Whampoa cadets holding key positions throughout the compound and the Brothers controlling three of the six battalions, the anti-Communists appeared to be the underdogs.

Remarkably, Communist prisoners played a minor role in Compound 86. Since all officers were supposed to be interned in the Officers Battalion in Compound 72, Communist officers often tried to hide their rank so that they could be assigned to the less repressive Compound 86. When Guo Zhaolin, chief of the 180th Division's artillery section and a regimental-level officer, was first captured on May 29, his attempt to adopt a fake identity was foiled by interrogators.[72] However, he managed to change his name and identity in Pusan and arrived in Compound 86 as an enlisted man.[73] When approached by deputy compound leader Yang Wenhua, Guo pretended he didn't know him, although they both had worked in the divisional HQ. Giving up his thought of having Guo as a leader behind the scene, Yang told his associates, "Guo is merely a country bumpkin irregular Communist (*tubalu*). He can't lead. It's better to let him go." With the aid of Yang and a North Korean POW doctor, Guo was soon transferred out to the Pusan hospital, which was deemed the safest haven for Communists.[74]

The contrasting strength of the pro-repatriates in the two Chinese compounds became evident in July, when the prison authorities issued short-sleeve and short-trouser summer uniforms, dyed bright red. The North Koreans, recalling that only convicts wore red under the Japanese occupation of Korea, staged violent protests. Three prisoners were killed in the crackdown. The authorities reported that Chinese prisoners accepted the uniforms "without appreciable reaction." "Red being one of their favorite colors," the CIE's chief instructor John Benben went as far as claiming, "they accepted the uniform with enthusiasm." However, such reports are inaccurate. While Chinese anti-Communist leaders ingratiated themselves with the authorities by accepting the garb and rank-and-file prisoners in Compound 72 and in certain battalions of Compound 86 dared not protest, many prisoners in Compound 86, egged on by chief interpreter Gao Jie, protested, threatening a hunger strike. Eventually, the authorities replaced the uniforms with khakis.[75]

A few days later, the pro-repatriates scored another victory: their candidate won the compound spokesman election by a wide margin. Some compounds, which Benben considered "pockets of democracy," had "requested and were granted permission to hold elections for spokesmen." While no evidence indicates elections ever took place in Compound 72, Compound 86 held a competitive election. Although it was claimed that the "details of the election procedure were meticulously followed," the secret ballot procedure adopted in Compound 86 was Chinese Communist style: the so-called "bean voting method" experimented with in Communist base areas before 1949. Clerk Wu Chunsheng recalled: six candidates, one from each battalion, sat in a row, each with a bucket behind him. Each of the roughly 8,000 prisoner-voters filed by, dropping a corn kernel—in place of a bean—into the bucket of his preferred candidate. The winner with the largest number of corn kernels was Xiao Shujun, a Brother favored by the clerk faction and supported by the Communists. The pro-repatriates secured another important position that guaranteed direct access to the Americans.[76]

In mid-July, US Army Chaplain Earle Woodberry and his Korean assistant Pastor Han began proselytizing in Compound 86. Despite a cold initial reception and jeers, the chaplains persisted, and they entered tents to confer with receptive—often anti-Communist—prisoners. Days later, three top compound leaders—Ying Xiangyun, Yang Wenhua, and Guo Naijian—were transferred to Pusan for interrogation. Pro-repatriates suspected collusion between Woodberry, the authorities, and the anti-Communists.[77] While no available evidence supports this particular allegation, camp records show that Woodberry later informed the authorities in January 1952 that a "Chinese officer was posing as an enlisted man in compound 72" and "was forming a communist cell."[78] No doubt, Woodberry was no simple preacher.

Most threateningly, Li Da'an, Compound 72's deputy commander, was named by the authorities to replace Yang Wenhua—clear proof of the authorities' collusion with and reliance on anti-Communists to tame the unruly Compound 86. On August 2, Li led thirty men into Compound 86, and immediately conferred with the two anti-Communist battalion leaders, Bai Peiming and Wang Futian—Wang had recently returned from Tokyo. It looked as if Li was about to replicate his iron rule in Compound 72. That night, however, Dai Yushu's three Brothers attacked Li. "You son of a turtle (*gui'erzi*). How dare you even think of grabbing power from our Big Brother! We'll beat you to death!" Badly pummeled, Li limped back to Compound 72 the next morning, trailed by Wang Futian and Bai Peiming.[79]

Ten days later, however, 244 prisoners, mostly Communists and Youth League members, were transferred to Pusan for interrogation. Communist prisoners suspected that the authorities, in collaboration with G-2, the US Army's Counter Intelligence Corps, the chaplains, and anti-Communist POWs, made a well-timed move to weaken the ranks of the pro-Communists.[80]

Another major development occurred on August 6, when the Civilian Information and Education Section (CIE) initiated an "emergency program" in Compounds 72 and 86. The program "was carried on . . . by a company-grade officer who had a limited knowledge of the Chinese language, an enlisted assistant, and POW teachers," as "Chinese civilian personnel were not made available for use" on Koje until November 1951. Given its patently anti-Communist agenda, only reliably anti-Communist prisoners qualified as POW teachers.[81] Once former Nationalist policeman Cheng Liren heard the news that CIE was hiring teachers, he "immediately rushed to sign up and eagerly asked a bunch of questions." After passing an exam, he was appointed the principal of the CIE school in Compound 86. He happily left the 4th Battalion, where he had risen from a clerk to deputy leader, and moved to the CIE's office.[82]

Coinciding with the arrival of the chaplains and the CIE, Wang Zunming, Cheng Liren, Tao Shanpeng—all deserters from the CPV 12th Army—and others founded the Anti-Communist and Resist Russia Patriotic Youth Alliance (*Fangong Kang'E aiguo qingnian tongmenghui*).[83] As introduced in Chapter 2, former Nationalist Captain Wang Zunming was natural-born leader, whose military bearing and "air of authority and conviction" impressed American social scientists.[84] He was "tall, handsome, and a great basketball player," recalled a pro-Communist prisoner. Wang had an extraordinary ability to relate to men of diverse origins. He often told people, "I was born in Shaanxi, grew up in Henan. My godfather was from province A; my godmother was from province B." Cultivating the image of a caring elder brother (*dage*), he often claimed, "When I was in Pusan, I boiled hot water for our fellow brothers."[85]

Although it first operated covertly, the Alliance's ranks quickly swelled. Huang Changrong and Jin Yuankui, the two peasant boys drafted by the Communists using a hoax, voluntarily joined the group, vowing never to return to Communist China.[86]

The showdown came on October 9, 1951, the eve of the Nationalist National Day, for which the anti-Communists planned a flag-raising ceremony. Earlier that day, Communist officer activist Zhang Chengyuan and chief interpreter Gao Jie both feigned illness and went to the hospital. With the Communists in hiding or bailing out and the clerk faction on the sidelines, a battle between the Brothers and the anti-Communist ensued. After nightfall, the Brothers first attacked the anti-Communist battalions, which had been prepared for the clash. More than a thousand prisoners plunged in the melee, swinging clubs and throwing rocks and punches. According to

FIGURE 8.3. Anti-Communist prisoners hold a flag-raising ceremony in Compound 86 to celebrate the ROC's Double Tenth National Day. October 10, 1951. US National Archives.

Nationalist sources, Wang Zunming, Cheng Liren, and other leaders "steadfastly held their positions and calmly directed the battle."[87] Tao Shanpeng, the 3rd Battalion's deputy leader, threw rocks from a safe distance. Li Yueming, a Sichuan native in the anti-Communist 2nd Battalion, defended his position in the church building with a long tent pole with a steel tip. "They didn't hit me," he proudly recalled, "but I hit them." The most ferocious fighter, Li believed, was Chen Yonghua, the muscular Taiwanese honcho in charge of work detail assignments in Compound 86.[88]

Armed guards soon intervened, ordering all prisoners to return to their tents. The Brothers let down their guard and went to sleep. Guided by anti-Communist trusties, however, US troops then arrested more than a hundred Brothers. The youngest detainee was the nineteen-year-old Zhong Junhua. He recalled that the CIE principal Cheng Liren led troops to arrest him. As a small honcho in charge of work detail assignment in his company, Zhong had used various excuses to resist CIE teaching and thus angered Cheng. After his arrest, however, honcho Chen Yonghua urged Zhong to recant, promising to vouch for him. Zhong simply turned away. Zhang Zeshi, who had arrived from Pusan in August, interpreted for the detainees and decided to stick with them in the cell instead of returning to the compound.[89] Brother Wang Shaoqi, also a Communist Youth League member, was beaten to death by trusties.[90] Separately, Dai Yushu was seized and delivered to Compound 72, where Li Da'an tortured him ruthlessly in revenge.[91]

On October 10, both Compounds 72 and 86 raised the Nationalist flag and "held [a] festival in celebration of the 40th anniversary of the Chinese Republic," noted CIE officer Captain Bernard Booth.[92] Embassy official Manhard observed that "every facility was extended to alleged pro-Nationalist to celebrate Oct 10 with banners, three-ring circuses, speeches, etc."[93]

Despite the Nationalist triumph, many prisoners still secretly yearned to return home to China. Yang Wenhua, now stripped of his position after his return from Pusan, became a thorn in the side of the anti-Communists since he often expressed his wish to return. Instead of directly attacking Yang, Cheng Liren asked Yang's friend, fellow Whampoa cadet Wu Chunsheng, to pass a message. After giving Wu an "extremely warm reception" in his CIE office, Cheng said, "You went to the military academy; I went to the police academy. No matter what, we're loyal to President Chiang Kai-shek. I can't forget my roots." He continued, "but if you don't want to go to Taiwan, I won't stop you, since we're free to do what we want." Cheng asked Wu to tell Yang not to "make trouble," sabotaging the anti-Communist cause. He walked Wu to the door and tried to reassure him: "It takes time to know a man. One day you'll know, I'm different from the others."[94]

Cheng was the brains of the Anti-Communist Alliance and Wang Zunming always listened to him, Wu observed. Unlike crude anti-Communists, Cheng never appeared aggressive or menacing. "Cheng was anti-Communist, but of a very sophisticated kind," Wu noted. "Like an octopus," Cheng's organization won many adherents in Compound 86.[95]

"Use Communist methods to control the Communists" was Cheng's motto. Instead of using outright violence, the CIE combined persuasion and indoctrination with forced participation. Like Communist meetings, some CIE classes involved "speaking bitterness" (*suku*) sessions where prisoners denounced the evils of Communism. The CIE also organized skits dramatizing the violence of the Communists' land reforms, during which landlord families were buried alive. "It was very effective," Wu concluded.[96]

Soon the clerk faction decided to bail out. When Pusan's hospital compound requested more than a hundred orderlies, chief clerk Guo put together a list filled with faction members, including Wu. After the departure of the clerks and the arrest of key Brothers and Communists, the remaining Brothers, including the elected compound spokesman Xiao Shujun, were soon dominated and absorbed by the anti-Communists.[97]

As the contest for power among prisoner factions became increasingly ideological in nature and violent in practice, all prisoners were forced to take sides. In anti-Communist camps, even non-ideological prisoners had to adopt the rhetoric of democracy, freedom, and anti-Communism to meet more practical and immediate needs, namely food, shelter, and physical safety.

By the end of December 1951, Compound 72's population grew to 8,560 and Compound 86's reached 7,981. Together, the two compounds accounted for 80 percent of the 20,600 Chinese POWs at the time.[98]

Compound 71: "Little Yan'an"

On November 8, Sun Zhenguan led 148 pro-Communist officers out of Compound 72. This was indirectly enabled by Manhard. On November 2, Manhard came to Compound 72 to interview Sun, Wei Lin, and Zhang Fuqing to learn about "Chinese prisoners' psychology." The three men, having been segregated and closely watched by trusties, were allowed to stay together during the lunch break. They immediately decided to launch a petition campaign. In the next few days they collected more than two hundred signatures and protest letters. On November 7 and 8, the Communists openly confronted the trusties by staging a sit-in in the compound's yard, and the number of protesters grew from thirty to more than a hundred. The camp authorities arrested seven top leaders on November 8, but soon decided to give in to their demand for a separate enclosure. They were allowed to move across the road to Compound 71, which was occupied by Korean POWs. Before the trusties shut the gate, 148 men pushed their way out.[99] Among them was Chen Qingbin, the Taiwanese and a member of the Chinese Communist Party, from the 12th Army.[100]

Three days later, the eighty-one prisoners arrested on October 9 in Compound 86, including Zhang Zeshi and Zhong Junhua, entered Compound 71, after they threatened to commit mass suicide when the authorities attempted to force them into Compound 72. As the two groups of pro-Communist prisoners joined forces, Compound 71 became known as "Little Yan'an." In the next six months only twenty-five additional POWs were allowed to move to Compound 71, and only after extraordinary efforts. Thanks to Manhard's personal intervention, the two highest-ranking Communist officers, Zhao Zuoduan and Du Gang, escaped from the Li Da'an's clutches in Compound 72 and moved to 71.[101]

Others were less fortunate. On January 4, 1952, fourteen prisoners returning from the Pusan hospital refused to enter Compound 72 as ordered; they demanded to move to 71 across the road. US guards opened the gate of Compound 72; PGs swooped down on the fourteen men and dragged them in. Li Da'an and his henchmen tortured them that night. Li put a red-hot iron to the chest of Tang Yao, the Zhejiang native and a clerk at the 12th Army HQ. Manhard reported that he "interrogated several tattooed Chinese and one branded who confessed they submitted under prisoner intimidation." That branded prisoner was Tang Yao. He told Manhard, "This place is inhumane. I want to protest!" He was transferred to 71.[102]

While Chaplain Woodberry and the CIE teachers were sympathetic toward anti-Communists, Manhard was apparently partial to the Communists. He introduced himself as American reporter Philip and befriended Chinese prisoners, especially the Communists, who nonetheless suspected him of being a CIA spy. Interpreter Gao Jie remembered Philip's "beautiful spoken Chinese" and his contempt for the ingratiating prisoner guards, whom Manhard taunted, "Are you still Chinese?" Poking fun at the mini–Statue of Liberty erected in Compound 72, Manhard compared the torch to the clubs prisoner guards wielded.[103] Years later, Colonel Zhao recalled wistfully, "After talking to him, I often felt that the imperialists were not a monolith." Manhard helped bring tangible improvement to their lives. He provided books and stationery, which were used to write protest letters. Most importantly, he recorded Communist POWs' views and reported them to the camp authorities, the embassy, and the State Department, even though this had little impact on Washington's policy.[104]

Evidently impressed by the caliber of the Communist leaders, especially Sun, Manhard reported to Washington in March 1952: "If allowed freedom to choose a PW compound under the leadership of pro-Nationalists or pro-Communists, I believe many would flee their present compounds to pro-Communist ones in the hope of escaping intimidation and the denial of minimum human freedoms by trusties whose behavior has commanded the respect of very few POWs."[105] However, before the full-scale screening in April 1952, prisoners were not afforded such a choice.

Compound 71's population never exceeded 254, or a little over one percent of the some 21,000 Chinese POWs.

Ironically, however, despite his contempt for the anti-Communists, Manhard's interrogation of Communist prisoners was only made possible by the former, who had uncovered Communist officers and delivered them to Manhard for interrogation. Without the help of the anti-Communists, the Americans would not have even identified the Communists.

In return, anti-Communist POWs found natural allies in G-2, the CIE, chaplains, and DAC interpreters. The CIE provided the institutional and ideological platform for anti-Communist trusties to influence and control fellow prisoners.

The CIE: "Sign[ing] Their Own Death Warrants"

Later remembered as "anti-Communist schools" by pro-Communists or the "school of democracy" by anti-Communists, the CIE schools in Compounds 72 and 86 were not quite the seemingly innocuous "informational programs carried on in the camps" as "part of the recreational activities which are sanctioned by the Geneva Conventions," that the US State Department claimed when the British prime minister Anthony Eden inquired about them in 1952.[106] Nor were they simply "an orientation program during which prisoners of war, on a voluntary basis, attend lectures on the history of Korea and China" and where prisoners would acquire vocational skills such as carpentry and metalworking.[107]

"It was patently a political indoctrination program, reasonably idealistic in nature and content, and was assigned the highest priority in the entire program," an official US Army history boasted. It aimed to "inculcate a more favorable attitude among POWs toward western and democratic ways and to instill distrust of communist ideology."[108]

The CIE curriculum revealed the ideological nature of the program. The centerpiece of the CIE program was a 30-week mandatory classroom training that covered six subjects, including the background of the Korean War, the contrast between democracy and totalitarianism, and the lives of people in the nations of the free world. One of the six themes taught in Chinese compounds included the following issues:

1. What is the purpose of labor unions?
2. What is the Communist propaganda about the life of farmers in the central districts of China?
3. What kind of life have our brethren been leading under the Communists in China?
4. Why did the Chinese farmers oppose the Communists?[109]

If these questions sound somewhat academic, the following slogans plastered in classrooms by POWs were undoubtedly ideological:

- United Nations is the bulwark of the world peace.
- Destroying of red thieves, and recapture of Chinese mainland.
- Bring about the three principles of people in China.
- Establish of free China.
- We shall go back Formosa, in any circumstance.
- We shall revenge to red thieves by the name of people who live beyond the iron curtain.
- The whole world peace could not realize without the complete destroying of red thieves.
- Learning is the preparation for counterattack to Chinese mainland.[110]

No doubt, the content of CIE teaching was blatantly anti-Communist and pro-Nationalist.

As explained in Chapter 6, the CIE was originally established by MacArthur to democratize Japan through education and propaganda. Three days before his dismissal, MacArthur ordered the creation of a CIE field group in Korea to reindoctrinate Chinese and North Korean POWs. When the first group of twenty US officers landed on Koje in May 1951, only two had training and experience in education. The chief instructor, John Benben, had taught education at Northwestern University. The only Chinese-speaking officer, Captain Bernard Booth, was assigned to Compounds 72 and 86.[111]

To meet the shortfall of CIE teachers, many prisoners served as instructors. In some Korean compounds, Communists held sway. CIE director Monta Osborne observed that prisoner teachers were "in many, if not all cases, directly under the control of the POW's in the compounds." They did not "dare say anything that does not meet with the approval of the clique which rules a particular compound." While American CIE personnel retreated from the compounds at night, these prisoner instructors had to remain in the compound, where they were "subject to beating" and were afraid of "adverse reports that may go to the North Korean and Chinese Communist authorities." Most outrageously, some instructors had referred to the Communist nations as "new democracies."[112] However, that was a Korean problem only.

In the Chinese Compounds 72 and 86, there had been "no cases . . . of Communist POWs getting on the teaching staff as there have been in some of the Korean compounds," reported CIE's Chinese Language Material Branch chief W. E. Stout. "The teachers in compounds 72 and 86 appear to enjoy considerable prestige among their fellow POWs."[113] The CIE principals, teaching directors, and teachers were mostly former Whampoa cadets, graduates, or college students, including Cheng Liren, Gao Wenjun, and Ma Furui.[114] Manhard observed, the teachers were "mostly self-appointed POW instructors who tried [to] emphasize anti-Commie polit[ical] indoctrination" that "often requir[ed] POW participation by force."[115]

Soon the CIE become a third power center in the camps, next to compound leaders and the PG squads.

While initially the CIE's teachers were POWs, Mandarin-speaking teachers were hired in Hong Kong, Taipei, and Tokyo as DACs, and they arrived in November 1951.[116] William C. Bradbury and Samuel M. Meyers, social scientists contracted by the US Army to conduct research on prisoner behaviors on Koje Island, reported that 23 Chinese were hired from Formosa. They concluded, "their mere presence in the compounds stimulated pro-Nationalist, anti-repatriation sentiment among the PW's. There is considerable scattered evidence that, both in the classrooms and outside, some of the Chinese teachers functioned, in effect if not by intent, as agents of the Chinese Nationalist government."[117] Similarly, when General Haydon L. Boatner took command of the Koje prisons in May 1952, he concluded that CIE activities were "a major source of unrest."[118]

It is worth noting that while Nationalist teachers did not join the CIE programs on Koje until November 1951, some of the first 73 Nationalist interpreters hired in early 1951 were transferred to Koje to serve as interpreters for the prison authorities, after the surge in the Chinese prisoner population after May 1951. Although Huang Tiancai remained on the 38th parallel, he reported that some of his fellow Nationalist interpreters went to Koje.[119] Therefore, the arrival of the 23 Nationalist teachers only augmented the preexisting Nationalist presence in the prison camps. Unlike earlier interpreters who arrived in Korea before the surge in the number of Chinese POWs, however, these teachers most likely had received specific instructions regarding prisoners. And most probably they worked as agents of the Nationalist government. One of the teachers, Ma He, later wrote that he had received three days of training by Chiang Ching-kuo before leaving Taiwan.[120] DAC interpreter Huang Tiancai recalled that Ma smelled and acted like a special agent.[121] No doubt, CIE instructors from Taiwan were instrumental in the rise of the anti-Communists.

Despite the CIE's overt anti-Communist agenda and its reliance on Nationalist personnel, CIE instructors, like all other US personnel, were not allowed to promise prisoners that they would be sent to Taiwan. The program operated under the implicit assumption that the prisoners would be repatriated to Communist China. As Benben explained to the *New York Times*, the CIE instruction "was sowing seeds of independent thinking and would make good ambassadors of the prisoners when they returned to their homes."[122]

Many CIE personnel recognized the inherent moral hazard of their mission: when prisoners were repatriated, the very achievement of the CIE's objectives in converting prisoners into anti-Communists "may mean death to those individuals who have accepted what has been taught." The CIE's interim report in January 1952 noted: "All

CIE Section personnel assigned to the program are apprehensive that a considerable number of POWs actually have signed their own death warrants by anti-communist behavior while on Koje-do."[123]

Petitions, Tattoos, and Torture

The UNC's self-contradictory POW policy of prisoner reindoctrination only heightened the prisoners' fear. First, as discussed in previous chapters, the UNC indiscriminately treated willing defectors and the captured as POWs. Anti-Communist prisoners felt they had been misled by UNC propaganda. Some had willingly surrendered under the false impression that Nationalist troops were fighting on the UNC side. Many had been misled by the ambiguous language of psychological warfare leaflets promising safety and asylum. They began to lose faith in the Americans.

Second, throughout their long captivity, the UNC made no explicit guarantee that prisoners would be relocated to Taiwan. Both Communist and anti-Communist prisoners understood that Washington might repatriate most—if not all—Chinese POWs to China in an exchange for UNC prisoners. To declared anti-Communists, repatriation would mean death or severe persecution, which many had witnessed in land reform or various other violent political campaigns under the Communists. The stakes for anti-Communist prisoners were extremely high. They had lived in constant fear and uncertainty.

FIGURE 8.4. Chinese prisoners display tattoos of Nationalist flags and anti-Communist slogans. Courtesy of Huang Tiancai.

When news about various peace proposals began to circulate in prison camps in spring 1951, anti-Communist prisoners panicked. When armistice negotiations began in July, it was widely expected that an agreement would be reached quickly, involving the repatriation of all prisoners in an exchange according to the Geneva Convention. Anti-Communist prisoners felt compelled to take more drastic actions.

In the summer of 1951, Chinese anti-Communist prisoners began the practice of writing petition letters in blood and tattooing anti-Communist slogans on their own bodies to demonstrate their determination to resist repatriation. Some of the letters were submitted to the UNC, which remained mute and gave no assurance to prisoners. Other petitions were smuggled to the Nationalist embassy in Pusan through Nationalist interpreters and CIE instructors. Ambassador Wang Dongyuan reported in January 1952 that about half of the 20,740 POWs were former Nationalist troops, and of these 70–80 percent did not wish to return to Communist China. About 3,000 were "resolute in their determination to return to Taiwan," as evidenced by their tattoos and activism, and the rest had not "made their attitude known." Because the American authorities tried to prevent contact between the Nationalist embassy and the prisoners, Wang pursued indirect channels—which presumably meant interpreters and CIE teachers—to instruct the prisoners "to continue their petition campaign, expressing the anti-repatriation stance with absolute determination." Wang asked Taipei to publicize their petitions to the world.[124]

What ensued in the prison compounds was a propaganda drive that was "reaching a climax with use of brutal force to obtain signatures," Manhard reported in March. "With encouragement from Formosan Chinese assigned to PW work by GHQ Tokyo, the trustees have for several months conducted a drive to collect petitions for transfer to Formosa."[125] When a truce seemed imminent, thousands of prisoners petitioned the UNC and world media, imploring that they not be repatriated to China. In tandem with escalating tattooing campaigns, anti-Communist prisoner leadership collected rounds of petition letters written or signed in blood. Nationalist DACs and US chaplains smuggled pictures of mass tattooing and blood petition letters to Taiwan and Western media. "Back to Taiwan or die" and "*Hui Taiwan*" (return to Taiwan) became their rallying cry.[126]

The intensity of this campaign startled American observers. Behavioral scientists Bradbury and Meyers commented that this "aggressive loyalty to . . . Nationalist China" and this kind of "mass resistance to repatriation has been almost unknown in modern warfare until very recent times."[127] Manhard provided an explanation: "The trusties maintain control over the Chinese compounds by means of force and coercion."[128] Corroborating Manhard's observations, another US embassy official named Bennett reported:

> Actions Chinese prisoner signing petitions in blood and tattooing themselves not (rpt not) completely voluntary protest against repatriation to Commie territory. Chinese Nationalist faction of prisoners is in control of Chinese prisoner compound and these leaders have forced some prisoners tattoo themselves and print petitions as part of effort to convince UN auths most Chinese prefer go Formosa.[129]

Various forms of physical punishment and torture were used by the trusties to force prisoners to renounce repatriation, sign petitions, and tattoo their bodies. The most common was to force a prisoner to maintain a plank position—on his fingers and toes—over extended periods of time. In Compound 72, Zhao Yingkui's tormentors scattered map pins on the ground under his body, needles facing upward. Whenever he got tired and raised his hips or his body sagged, the trusties stomped on his back with their boots, pushing his body to the ground to be impaled by the needles. After being repeatedly tortured, Zhao gave in. Luo Jiecao, who could not even sit still for long because his right buttock had been blown off by a shell, suffered a similar ordeal in Compound 86, but with a twist: he was forced to hold a downward dog position above a latrine bucket made of an oil drum cut in half. As Luo was short and crippled, his mouth was barely inches above the overflowing human excrement. Whenever his strength flagged, he risked falling on the jagged drum edge or sinking into the human waste.[130]

One of the most gruesome tortures involved forcing a water hose into the victim's rectum. Torturers then pumped water using a fire extinguisher. Communist prisoners reported that when Zheng Donghai refused to be tattooed, Compound 86's trusties pumped hot chili pepper liquid into him and then tortured him to death with a "red-hot iron bar." Sun Wenqing was killed when boiling water was pumped into his anus. When Liu Youcai, also of Compound 86, put a negative mark under the question "Communism is totalitarianism" on a CIE examination paper, the trusties forced water into his stomach and then stomped on his swollen abdomen until water mixed with blood burst from his nose and mouth.[131] Tao Shanpeng, discipline section chief of the Anti-Communist Alliance in Compound 86, confirmed that he witnessed an allegedly high-ranking CPV officer being killed this way. "We all hated the Communists," Tao explained. "Some people just went out of control, acting just like thugs (*baotu*)."[132] Under the threat of violence or even death, many prisoners were tattooed.

Bennett estimated that, if given a free choice, no more than a quarter of the Chinese prisoners would elect to go to Formosa, because most prisoners were convinced they would be impressed into the Nationalist Army again and many were tired of fighting. Around another 10 to 15 percent, Bennett believed, were "indoctrinated Commies" who would elect to return to China. Finally, Bennett thought that a good many of the remainder, perhaps 5,000 of the 20,000 total, would choose to return to China and "take their chances on Communists, because of love [for] their homeland, family ties, etc."[133] Perhaps Cai Pingsheng belonged in the last group. He later recalled, "I didn't know much about Communism. And I didn't care much about it. I just wanted to return home to see my parents."[134]

Thanks to Manhard's frequent reports from Koje, US ambassador Muccio understood the camp struggle as "a free-for-all between Chinese Nationalists and Chinese Communists." He asserted, "What went on within those compounds was never known or understood by the US military."[135] Although the camp dynamics was never fully understood by policymakers in Washington or even US personnel on Koje, Manhard and Bennett came to the same conclusion as Ambassador Wang had that the majority of prisoners were in the middle. Intimidation and coercion at the hands of the anti-Communist trusties were directed at the majority to prevent them from choosing repatriation.

This development was an unfortunate but logical outcome of the US twin policies of prisoner reindoctrination and voluntary repatriation. While the former policy led anti-Communist POWs to "sign their own death warrants" by participating in anti-Communist activities, the latter induced violent behavior.

While CIE personnel in the field were apprehensive about their reindoctrination work, civilian and military leaders in Washington and Tokyo showed no such moral scruple. In essence, Washington's ill-conceived prisoner reindoctrination policy, while serving no practical purpose, had boxed Chinese prisoners into a deathtrap.

As the next chapter will explain, voluntary repatriation, which was introduced in truce talks in January 1952, meant that to be considered a non-repatriate, a prisoner had to demonstrate that he would forcibly resist repatriation. This was an open invitation to violence. Facing the prospect that the Americans might agree to repatriate them, anti-Communist prisoners sought to control a large number of fellow prisoners and demonstrate their collective will against repatriation, even if that involved violent methods.

As the next two chapters will demonstrate, the intertwining of the two separately developed policies would further ensnare Chinese anti-Communist prisoners, whose only way out was to hijack as many fellow prisoners as possible. By doing so, they would soon hijack the war.

9

The Debate over Prisoner Repatriation in Washington, Panmunjom, and Taipei

IN THE AFTERMATH of the Fifth Offensive debacle, Communist forces retreated to a defensive line above the 38th parallel, except at its western end. By late May and early June 1951, Mao and his generals came to terms with the fact that their earlier ambition of driving the UN forces off the Korean peninsula was unrealistic. Nevertheless, having pushed the Americans back from the Yalu River to a line near the 38th parallel, China could already claim a great victory.[1]

By the time Chinese leaders moderated their war aims and sought a respite on the battleground, American leaders had long abandoned their initial goal of rolling back Communism in North Korea—the policy objective of the secret NSC-81/1 of September 1950. On April 18, 1951, a week after MacArthur's dismissal, Acheson made a major policy address, asserting that a peaceful settlement in Korea was not appeasement.[2] At the MacArthur hearings on June 2, Acheson said that a settlement at or near the 38th parallel would be acceptable.[3] In Korea, General Ridgway halted the UNC's advance in June along the Kansas Line slightly above the 38th parallel, believing that "more real estate" was not worth more expenditure in lives and treasure, nor did it warrant the risk of shortening enemy supply lines and extending his own.[4] Truman and Acheson concurred. The unification of Korea, Acheson believed, should be left to "time and political measures." To his great satisfaction, "the White House, the State Department, the Pentagon, and the Supreme Command in Tokyo found themselves united on political objectives, strategy, and tactics for the first time since the war had started."[5] It appeared both the Communists and the Americans would accept an armistice that restored the status quo antebellum along the 38th parallel.

Like "a pack of hounds searching for a scent," Acheson's emissaries sought contact with the Russians and the Chinese.[6] Charles B. Marshall of the State Department's Policy Planning Staff (PPS), who had been in contact with a phantom-like Chinese "third party" in Hong Kong in January 1951, went back in May and "made himself available for contacts, but with no success."[7] At John Paton Davies's suggestion, Acheson asked George Kennan, former PPS head, on leave working at the Institute of Advanced Studies of Princeton University, to approach Soviet representative to the UN Yakov Malik and "speak with authority and in confidence for the Government."[8] Kennan's two meetings with Malik on May 31 and June 5 yielded only the "sibylline" remark that Washington should directly approach the Chinese and the North Koreans.[9]

On June 13, Stalin gave Mao the go-ahead for negotiations, saying that "an armistice is now advantageous." Mao immediately informed Kim Il-sung of his willingness to accept the restoration of the border at the 38th parallel. Reversing his earlier hard-line position, Mao now decided the PRC's seat in the UN should not be a precondition for an armistice. The question of Taiwan should be raised "in order to bargain" with the Americans, but China would be ready to make a concession.[10]

Malik surprised the world in a UN radio address on June 23, calling for "a cease-fire and an armistice providing for the mutual withdrawal of forces from the 38th parallel," with none of the usual litany regarding the withdrawal of foreign troops from Korea, Taiwan's status, or China's UN seat. President Truman responded two days later: "We are ready to join in a peaceful settlement in Korea now, just as we have always been."[11] Negotiations began on July 10 at Kaesong, the ancient capital of Korea located slightly below the 38th parallel but several miles within Communist-held territory.

Two crucial developments took place from May to July. First, the UNC's tactical situation improved dramatically, putting the enemy on the defensive. The Americans stiffened their attitude toward the Chinese. Second, while the number of North Korean prisoners increased by a mere 2,000 to 145,122, the number of captured Chinese surged fivefold from 3,423 in April to 17,182 in June.[12] The significance of the second event was not apparent to anyone at the time, as no one could have anticipated that the debate over Chinese prisoners would dominate much of the talks.

China's First Team versus America's Third Team

Likely emboldened by Ridgway's stunning military turnaround, Truman and Acheson decided not to accord equal status to Communist China, which had first rebuffed their conciliatory gestures in 1949 and then repeatedly humiliated and staggered them. Now they shunned political contact, something they had earnestly sought merely two months earlier. They left the negotiations exclusively in the hands of military men—a peculiar arrangement considering that soldiers, who were trained to defeat the enemy on the battlefield, now were tasked with reaching a compromise at the negotiating table. UNC delegates were told that the talks were to be "severely restricted to military questions," thus barring the discussion of "political issues" such as "a final settlement" in Korea, Taiwan's status, and China's UN seat.[13]

Ridgway, who had served in Tianjin, China, in the 1920s—with the US 15th Infantry Regiment nicknamed "The Old China Hands"—and had some knowledge of the "Orientals," suggested a remedy: to station Ambassador Muccio and William Sebald, US political advisor (the de facto ambassador) to occupied Japan, at the UNC delegation's base camp in Munsan-ni, 22 miles north of Seoul. Washington promptly rejected the idea out of fear that the presence of diplomats would "invite [the] impression" of potential political talks. "The time for political participation is after conclusion of armistice," the JCS emphatically exhorted.[14] Washington's studied separation of military and political matters would prove self-deceiving and self-defeating.

Leading the UNC delegation was Vice Admiral C. Turner Joy, commander of US Naval Force Far East. The South Korean delegate was Major General Paik Sun Yup, commander of the ROK I Corps.[15] Paik's presence was "purely for show," Chinese negotiators soon concluded, as Joy often passed notes over Paik to other American delegates.[16] On the Communist side, General Nam Il, KPA chief of staff and the nominal head of the Sino–North Korean delegation, initially appeared to be the "dominant figure," as he "kept notes [to] himself and talked directly from notes without prior consultation [with] other delegates." In contrast, Chinese delegates Deng Hua, CPV deputy commander, and Xie Fang, CPV chief of staff, "appeared as junior and silent partners." Joy, however, would soon realize that the Chinese had the "ultimate authority" and Nam was a "figurehead."[17] The Koreans' junior-partner status was mirrored on both sides.

Unknown to the world throughout the war, however, the real Communist authority at Kaesong and Panmunjom was a secretive "leading group" located sometimes a stone's throw from the negotiation room.[18] Its leaders were Red China's spymaster Li Kenong, first deputy foreign minister and intelligence director of the Central Military Commission, and Qiao Guanhua, deputy director of the Policy Committee and director of the International Press Bureau of the Foreign Ministry.[19] Both Li and Qiao had substantial experience in dealing with the Americans. Li was a major Communist representative parleying with General George Marshall's mediation mission during the Civil War in 1946. Qiao, a Tsinghua graduate who went on to receive a PhD in German philosophy from Tübingen University, had been Zhou Enlai's most able diplomat in Chongqing during World War II. Qiao and his wife, Gong Peng, had befriended American journalists and officials alike, including John King Fairbank, then an OSS and Office of War Information officer and later the doyen of China studies in America.[20] In late November and early December 1950, Qiao accompanied General Wu Xiuquan to the UN General Assembly in New York to make Communist China's diplomatic debut. Qiao was clearly the "brains" of the group, Indian diplomats observed.[21] Qiao and Li were assisted by Pu Shan, a Harvard economics PhD trained by the renowned political economist Joseph A. Schumpeter.[22] Harvard undergraduate student Ji Chaozhu would join the delegation in mid-1952.[23] Ji would later become Mao's and Zhou's interpreter; Qiao would rise to the position of foreign minister in the mid-1970s. No doubt, Mao and Zhou assembled their most trusted and most capable intelligence officials and diplomats for the negotiations—they were China's first team.

Most critically, Mao and Zhou took the negotiations extremely seriously. On June 30, Stalin entrusted Mao to take charge of the negotiations, humbly adding that "the most we can give is advice on various questions."[24] The next day, Mao and Zhou summoned Li and Qiao and gave them lengthy instructions regarding the talks. After a farewell dinner with hard liquor, Mao cabled General Peng and Kim Il-sung at 4 a.m. on July 2, informing them that Li and Qiao would leave Beijing for Korea that evening. Mao instructed Peng to ensure the safety of the conference site, so that "nothing should go wrong." Delving into minute details, he ordered special quarters to be arranged for Li and Qiao, somewhere "one or two kilometers from the conference site."[25] Once in Kaesong, Li and Qiao set up their advanced post only three hundred feet away. When Communist negotiators were in doubt, liaison officer Chai Chengwen slipped out from the negotiating room to see Li and Qiao, and bring back their instructions on a piece of paper.[26] After each session of negotiations, delegates conferred with Li and Qiao; then Li cabled Mao and Zhou the same day by midnight. Mao and Zhou, both inveterate night owls, usually replied to Li and forwarded his report to Stalin with their comments before dawn. Stalin often replied, in his typically terse and supportive style, by the end of the next day.[27] In addition, with Soviet help, a hotline was set up linking Zhou's bedside phone with Li and Qiao, who were authorized to call anytime.[28] Mao and Zhou—and to a certain degree Stalin, especially initially—monitored the negotiations on a daily basis with intense interest.

The UNC delegation, composed entirely of military officers, enjoyed no support from senior intelligence officials or diplomats at hand. None of the US delegates had any substantive experience with or knowledge of China, let alone the Chinese Communists. The delegation's principal Chinese-speaking member throughout the twenty-five-month truce talks was a lowly interpreter, Kenneth Wu, a warrant officer and later a lieutenant. An ethnic Chinese born in Burma, Wu joined the US Army in Kunming, China, in 1943. Before Kaesong, he was the chief of the Chinese POW interrogation team in Pusan, where very likely he had interrogated Communist POW leader Sun Zhenguan (see Chapter 8).[29] The Korean language interpreter, Lieutenant Richard F. Underwood, was a third-generation missionary offspring who only spoke "street Korean." On July 7, he was abruptly removed from his POW interrogation duty in Pusan. In Tokyo he met Wu and another Korean interpreter. The party flew to Seoul the next day and immediately proceeded to Kaesong by helicopter for a preliminary meeting with Communist liaison officers.[30]

Wu later earned Chinese negotiators' respect for his integrity ("sense of justice"), but his Chinese language ability was not quite up to the task, especially in the beginning. When he encountered difficulties, Wu had no choice but to "make forced translations and then stared at" the Chinese delegates, waiting for reactions.[31] Wu later admitted that his southern dialect "caused problems for the Chinese delegates, all northerners."[32] Apparently unable to handle written translation work that required a high degree of precision, Wu selected two Nationalist interpreters to help. These two were among the first eighteen DACs who had arrived in February.[33] Most likely they had worked with Wu in his interrogation team in Pusan.

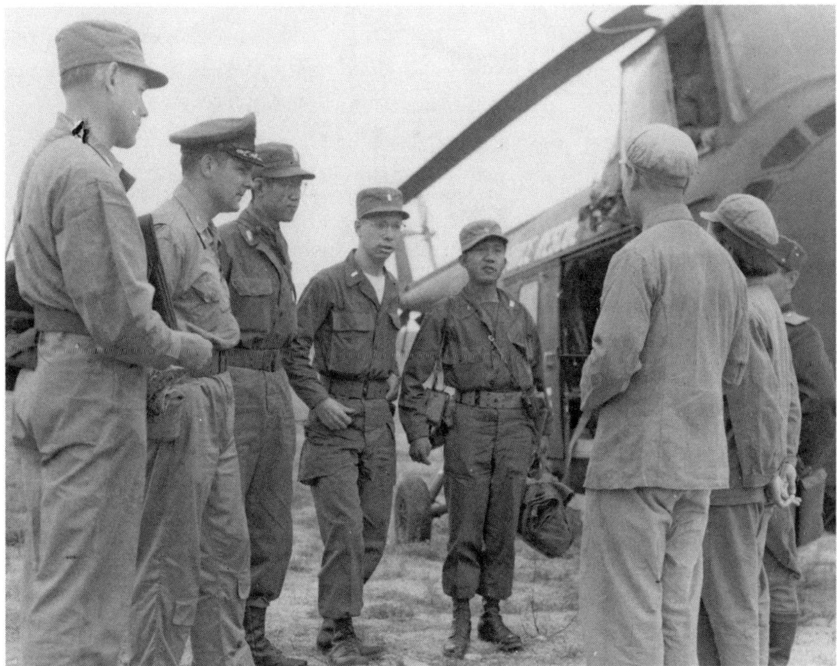

FIGURE 9.1. UNC liaison officers meet their Communist counterparts, who will escort them to the site of the armistice talks at Kaesong. UNC's Chinese interpreter Kenneth Wu and Korean interpreter Richard Underwood stand next to the helicopter. July 8, 1951. US National Archives.

Philip Manhard, probably the only Chinese-speaking Foreign Service Officer stationed in Korea, played no part in the negotiations. Even had he participated, he could not have supplanted Nationalist interpreters due to his limited Chinese language training. The American negotiators knew little about their enemies, while the Chinese knew their opponents very well. Facing off with China's first team was America's third team or the nth team. The battle at the negotiating table was heavily lopsided from the outset.

In sharp contrast to Mao and Zhou's hands-on approach, Truman and Acheson paid scant attention to the negotiations and showed a poor grasp of the complexity involved. The UNC delegation had no direct line of contact with them. The delegation's reports were relayed through Ridgway in Tokyo and from there to the JCS in Washington, where State and JCS officials held regular—but not daily—meetings to discuss replies. Acheson did not participate in meetings at this level; the highest-ranking State officials were Deputy Under Secretary of State for Political Affairs H. Freeman Matthews and PPS director Paul H. Nitze. Only when these officials could not agree did they consult with Acheson and Truman.

Acheson was the president's most trusted advisor and his words carried the most weight in the administration. During the armistice talks, however, Acheson was visibly absent, as he fully occupied himself with building the Western European alliance through the North Atlantic Treaty Organization (NATO). True to his Eurocentric reputation, as the secretary of state he made eleven trips to Europe but none to East Asia.[34] At two critical junctures—when Truman made the initial and final decisions on POW policy—Acheson was either in Europe or had barely returned from there.

Compounding the problem of inattention at the highest level, the UNC delegation was staffed by lackluster personnel. Chinese negotiator Chai observed: "As soldiers, they were not inferior to us. In terms of their work ethic and professionalism, however, they were way behind us." While Chinese and North Korean staff officers made detailed preparations before each meeting, their American counterparts often showed up poorly prepared.[35] At all levels of the US government and military, contempt for the Chinese was manifested in the Americans' arrogance and negligence, which would soon cost them dearly.

Chinese Compromises and American Ambivalence, July–October 1951

Given that Washington had made the initial move to sue for peace and Acheson had indicated that the United States accepted the 38th parallel as the armistice line both before and after Malik's speech, Beijing assumed that an agreement could be reached quickly. In a message to Stalin on July 2, Mao predicted that the "preparations for and conducting of negotiations . . . will occupy approximately ten to fourteen days." He ordered that maximum effort be made to transfer personnel, arms, and ammunition into North Korea within ten days, lest an armistice prohibit future transfers.[36] He told Qiao Guanhua on July 1 that "three to five weeks will be enough" to reach an agreement.[37] Qiao in turn told the Australian leftist journalist Wilfred Burchett that the negotiations would last for "about three weeks." He invited Burchett to tag along, adding, "Take the minimum of gear, for we must travel very light."[38] So light was their gear that none of the Chinese delegates took winter clothing to Korea.[39] No one could have imaged that "three weeks" would turn into two years—in the case of Burchett, two and a half years, until the very end of the POW saga in January 1954.

On July 10, the first session of the negotiations began. General Nam Il quickly laid out the Communist agenda: to establish the 38th parallel as the demarcation line, to create a 20-kilometer-wide demilitarized zone, to "talk over the exchange of prisoners," and to secure the withdrawal of all foreign troops from the peninsula.[40] General Peng told the delegates that the primary issue was the withdrawal of all foreign troops, followed by the restoration of the 38th parallel as the line of demarcation. "Other issues, such as prisoner exchange," Peng declared, "are of technical or minor nature."[41] Despite the hugely disproportionate number of prisoners held by the two sides, Communist leaders anticipated little trouble over prisoner exchanges.

The Communists' optimism had a basis in both fact and law. First, since Acheson had publicly accepted the 38th parallel, the only major unresolved issue would be the withdrawal of foreign troops. Second, the Geneva Convention of 1949, the governing international law on prisoner exchange, was signed by the United States, although not yet ratified by the Senate, and both the UNC and the Communists had pledged to adhere to its provisions. Up to this point the Americans had not once raised the prisoner issue. Therefore the Communists expected a quick exchange. Mao drew up a six-point draft agreement dated July 5 that included a provision that all prisoners should be exchanged within three months after the cease fire.[42] His assumptions soon proved wrong.

Despite bickering for two weeks over minor issues such as protocol, both sides agreed on an agenda on July 26 that placed the POW question as item 4—the final substantive item before a vaguely worded item 5, "recommendations to governments of countries concerned on both sides," which was a face-saving device to cover the Communist agreement to drop the withdrawal of foreign troops from the agenda. Joy proposed that the negotiations proceed item by item and Nam agreed. Item 4 would only be discussed after the resolution of item 2, the "demarcation line," and item 3, "ceasefire arrangements."[43] Acheson was greatly surprised by the apparent Communist capitulation, calling the agreement "a phenomenal feat."[44] The Communists appeared sincere in their desire for a quick truce. The same, however, could not be said of the Americans.

As noted earlier, the UNC's military position had improved markedly between May and July. No longer hat in hand, Washington now not only "had no intention of giving up the strong positions of the Kansas line" mostly north of the 38th parallel, but "hoped to improve them," Acheson admitted.[45] On July 27, the first day of substantive negotiations, Joy rejected the 38th parallel as the demarcation line and advanced "a novel approach"—in the words of official US military historian Walter G. Hermes—arguing that the UNC "should be compensated" with additional territory for "giving up great advantages" in the air and sea.[46] Communist forces would have to retreat north from their current position by 38 to 68 kilometers, ceding some 12,000 square kilometers of land.[47] "Joy's speech was arrogant and preposterous nonsense," Mao fumed in a telegram to Li. "It was not a call for peace, but a clamor for war."[48]

In fact, Ridgway had planned to keep up unrelenting military pressure on the Communists even as the talks began. On July 30 and August 14, the US Air Force bombed Pyongyang, demolishing parts of the capital.[49] On August 18, a limited ground offensive was launched. Leading the assault was General Paik, who had represented South Korea in the truce talks at Kaesong in July.[50]

In the face of the UNC offensive and a string of incidents at Kaesong, the Communists suspended the talks on August 23. Senior Delegate Deng vented his frustration to Peng: "I deeply felt that our timing for the talks was very inopportune." He attributed the Americans' "bullying" arrogance to their tactical advantages on the battlefield and Chinese compromises at the negotiating table. To reach an armistice, Deng argued, the CPV must first fight back.[51] Like his counterpart Paik, Deng resumed his role as a fighting general. As the battles resumed, the talks were suspended.

Mao's and Deng's anger was understandable. Acheson and his colleagues admitted three years later: "The Russians and Chinese could well have been surprised, chagrined, and given cause to feel tricked" when US negotiators rejected the 38th parallel as the armistice line. Acheson conceded that the morass "was of our own making and occurred at the very beginning," though this was "unsuspected by me at the time." The Communists "could never imagine that what appeared to be trickery was wholly inadvertent on our part," he asserted.[52]

In addition to the military's desire to retain a strong tactical position, Washington had other reasons to backpedal. When the Communists showed a surprising willingness to compromise, the Truman administration became wary of a quick armistice, which would prematurely end the massive defense buildup mandated by NSC-68, commonly known as the "blueprint for Cold War militarization," approved by Truman in September 1950. Secretary of Defense George Marshall considered this prospect the worst danger to the country.[53] Washington still wanted a settlement, but was no longer in a hurry. This ambivalence was not lost on Li Kenong, who wryly remarked, "The Americans are no longer as eager as they were when Kennan called on Malik."

The Chinese delegates derided the Americans for "wishing for talks when fighting, but wishing for war when talking."[54]

Peace talks resumed on October 25 at Panmunjom, an outpost in no-man's-land six miles east of Kaesong—a move that was in itself a Chinese compromise. Ready to make another major concession, Mao and Zhou instructed Li to propose using the current battle line—instead of the 38th parallel—as the armistice line.[55] When this new offer was made on November 6, Washington immediately instructed Ridgway to accept it in principle. Ridgway, however, preferred the line of contact "at the time of the signing of the armistice." He asserted that "more steel and less silk, more forthright American insistence on the unchallengeable logic of our position, will yield the objectives for which we honorably contend."[56] But he was overruled. The UNC delegation accepted the Communist proposal on the 17th with the condition that a full agreement would be signed within thirty days.[57] Both sides fixed the demarcation line and ratified item 2 on the 27th.[58] All in all, while the Communists abandoned their insistence on the highly symbolic 38th parallel, the Americans only had to give up their outlandish demand of territorial compensation for air and naval superiority.

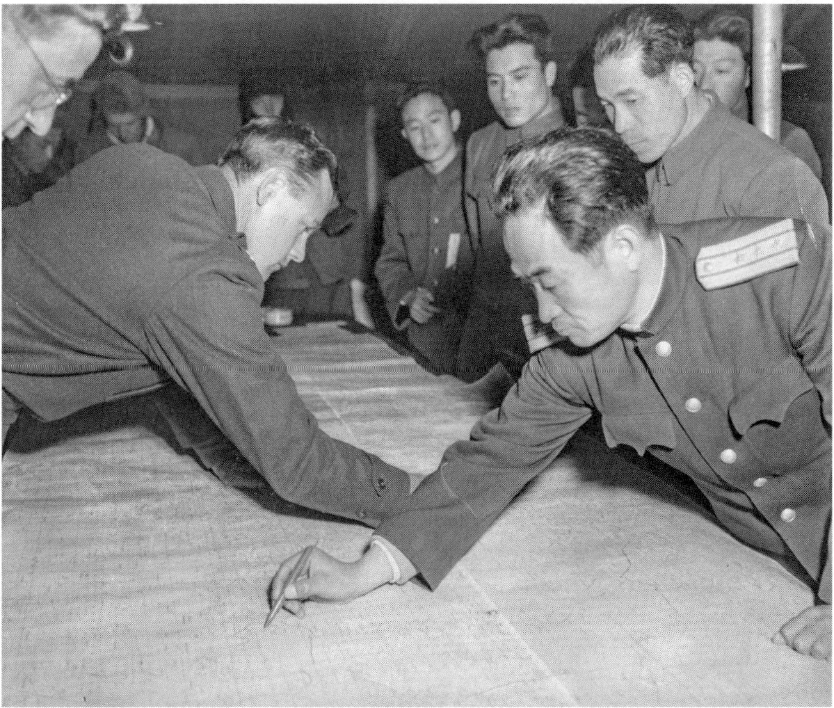

FIGURE 9.2. UNC and Communist liaison officers initial a map showing the 145-mile line of demarcation on which agreement had been reached. November 27, 1951. CPV Colonel Chai Chengwen stands behind the North Korean colonel (right). US National Archives.

Eager to move the negotiations forward and resolve the last major issue—prisoner exchange—Mao cabled Stalin on November 14 to explain his plans. Although China was prepared for the war to continue for another six to twelve months, Mao vowed that "we will strive to achieve an armistice within this year"—in other words, in the next month and a half. Having been informed by Soviet intelligence that the UNC would propose exchanging prisoners on a one-for-one basis, Mao decided to preempt this development by pressing for an all-for-all formula. "I believe," he asserted, "it will not be difficult to reach an agreement on this issue." Stalin replied, "Your position on prisoner exchange is completely correct, and it will be very difficult for the enemy to dispute it."[59] Upon receiving Mao's instruction, the Sino-North Korean delegation held a joint conference on November 20. Li Kenong and most members were optimistic; only Qiao Guanhua voiced his apprehension over the POW issue.[60] Events would soon prove Qiao prescient.

On November 25, Mao sent Li Kenong two telegrams underscoring his opposition to a one-for-one exchange.[61] At the same time, the Americans were also eager to probe the Communist position on POWs. Joy fired the "opening gun" on the 27th, asking Nam Il to exchange POW names before plunging into a discussion of agenda item 3. Nam evaded the request. On December 4, Joy proposed setting up two subdelegations to discuss items 3 and 4 concurrently; the Communists again stalled.[62]

When the item 4 subdelegation finally convened on December 11, Washington was still unsure of what position to adopt: one-for-one, all-for-all, or voluntary repatriation. In the following three weeks, as they awaited instructions from Washington, UNC delegates evaded the question of exchange. Finally, on January 2, 1952, the UNC put forward a voluntary repatriation proposal, which was immediately dismissed by the Communists as a conspiracy to detain prisoners in South Korea or send them to Taiwan. The Chinese overestimated the Americans' deviousness and foresight. Voluntary repatriation "was placed in a strange position—neither in nor out of UNC planning," noted Hermes.[63] Its evolution from a rejected idea to a "final and irrevocable position" of the US government demonstrates American policymakers' lack of foresight, planning, leadership, and understanding when it came to the POW issue.

One-for-One Exchange: The US Military's Position since December 1950

International law on POW repatriation was clear and simple. The Geneva Convention of 1929 took compulsory repatriation for granted as it was generally accepted that prisoners would return home as soon as the fighting stops. After World War II, the Soviet Union detained large numbers of German and Japanese POWs in forced labor camps for years. Designed to prevent such practices, Article 118 of the 1949 Geneva Convention stipulates: "Prisoners of war shall be released and repatriated without delay after the cessation of active hostilities."[64] There is no legal ground for partial repatriation—either one-for-one or voluntary repatriation.

Voluntary repatriation, in essence, was a partial exchange packaged in humanitarianism and emotionalism. Given the proposal's poor legal grounds, Washington resorted to reinterpreting the law, arguing that "the *spirit* of the Geneva Conventions was to protect the best interests of prisoners" and voluntary repatriation would do just that.[65] In fact, the invocation of humanitarianism was an afterthought to justify a stance driven mainly by military concerns; however, it would soon assume a life of its own and take precedence over military calculations.

The one-for-one formula appeared as early as December 12, 1950, when UN forces were reeling from the Chinese onslaught and several UN member states called for a cease-fire. In a memorandum to Secretary Marshall, the JCS laid out its terms and conditions "essential to any ceasefire arrangement," including that POWs "shall be exchanged on a one for one basis." Since a euphoric Mao rejected the cease-fire appeal in January, the JCS's terms were not disclosed. In March 1951, when Ridgway decisively turned the tide and Washington began to ponder the cease-fire question again, Acheson asked Marshall if these terms were still valid. The JCS revised certain terms, but left the one-for-one formula unchanged. On June 30, eleven days before the armistice talks began, the JCS gave Ridgway detailed instructions approved by the State-Defense committee, reprising its March position that POWs "shall be exchanged on a one-for-one basis as expeditiously as possible."[66]

The one-for-one formula was engendered by the military's concern about enemy strength. As the UNC held "some 15,000 Chinese and some 135,000 North Koreans" against fewer than 10,000 UN prisoners in enemy hands, an all-for-all repatriation of POWs "would virtually restore intact to North Korea forces equivalent to the number it possessed at the time of the aggression and thus entirely change the military situation," explained Dean Rusk.[67] UNC negotiators later argued that returning all prisoners was equivalent to giving "the enemy an advantage of 12 divisions."[68] This argument, however, was misguided, in that it was premised on a war against North Korea alone. Since late 1950, the UNC's primary enemy had been China, which had nearly unlimited manpower. A hypothetical return of all Chinese prisoners to the ranks of the CPV would not tip the balance in any meaningful way. China's intervention had wholly altered the situation, but Washington did not adjust its policies accordingly. Much like the prisoner reindoctrination policy discussed earlier, the one-for-one exchange formula, once written into a policy paper, became firmly entrenched.

As the UNC held more than ten times as many prisoners as the Communists did, on the face of it the numerical advantage seemed too great to be given away in an all-for-all exchange. Washington decided to peddle the one-for-one formula—despite its illegality—in order to extract other concessions from the Communists. Unwilling to pay the high price in lives and treasure on the battlefield, as evidenced by the UNC's unilateral halt in the aftermath of the Chinese Fifth Offensive debacle in early June, Washington and Ridgway hoped to gain concessions from the enemy by taking a hard line in negotiations—without fighting real battles. The Chinese, however, were determined not to let the Americans gain at the conference table what they could not on the battlefield.[69]

Despite acknowledging "great difficulty," Washington harbored the illusion that the Communists might accept the one-for-one formula. On June 30, the JCS instructed Ridgway to begin talks with a set of initial positions "more favorable to us than the minimum conditions." One of the nine "essential" minimum conditions was a one-for-one prisoner exchange.[70] How could there be any position more favorable than a one-for-one exchange that would allow the UNC to retain a huge number of prisoners while the Communists would quickly free all UNC prisoners in their hands—thus giving away all leverage they once had? It was a nonstarter. Nevertheless, Washington made it an "essential" minimum position.

The JCS warned Ridgway not to "engage US prestige in a negotiating position as to make retreat to our minimum terms impossible."[71] However, US prestige would be soon staked on the one-for-one exchange when it was rebranded as voluntary repatriation, making any kind of retreat impossible.

Voluntary Repatriation Proposal Nixed by Acheson, August 1951

The concept of voluntary repatriation was first proposed by Brig. Gen. Robert A. McClure, the US Army's chief of psychological warfare, on July 5, five days before the armistice talks began.[72] McClure made his case on humanitarian and propaganda grounds. He argued that many Chinese and North Koreans would be "severely punished, sentenced to slave labor, or executed" upon repatriation, as many Soviet prisoners had been after World War II. He suggested repatriating some Chinese POWs to Taiwan, which was officially the Republic of China.[73]

McClure's proposal was received positively by the JCS, which recommended to Marshall on August 8 that "subject to adequate safeguards for UN prisoners in Communist hands, the UNC be authorized to repatriate to Formosa all Chinese prisoners of war who are found to be acceptable to the Chinese Nationalist Government and who claim to be ex-Nationalists or Nationalists at heart and elect such repatriation." The JCS's justifications included both humanitarian and utilitarian considerations. First, there was "grave likelihood" that Communist prisoners might "be executed or condemned to slave labor." Second, "in the conduct of psychological warfare in Korea, the UN commander promised safety and *asylum*" to Communist soldiers "who would voluntarily surrender." Forced repatriation would be "in violation of his promise." Third, the policy would establish "the principle of United Nations asylum from terrorism." Finally, "the effectiveness of future U.S. psychological warfare programs would be enhanced by the adoption of this policy." While recognizing that the matter transcended the military, on balance, the chiefs were inclined to favor voluntary repatriation because of "its extreme importance to the effectiveness of psychological warfare."[74]

Acheson, a well-regarded lawyer, rejected the McClure proposal on legal grounds. He warned Marshall on August 27 that "the State is seriously concerned over the possibility that the proposed policy might jeopardize the prompt return of all UN and ROK POWs," which should be the "overriding consideration." He concluded: "U.S. interests in this and future conflicts dictate . . . strict observance of the provisions of the Geneva Convention." In the next breath, however, Acheson suggested a compromise: "In order to achieve in so far as possible the desired psychological warfare and humane objectives, prior to the reaching of an armistice agreement, individuals who have rendered outstanding assistance to the UNC or whose return to the Communists would, in all probability, result in their deaths, might be paroled as provided for in the Geneva Convention."[75] Remarkably, Acheson rejected and supported voluntary repatriation at the same time: he rejected McClure's "plan but not its goals," as historian Barton Bernstein has observed.[76]

Acheson's view differed from McClure's in two key aspects. First, while McClure specified Taiwan as Chinese POWs' destination, Acheson made no provision for their disposition. Second, Acheson apparently had a restrictive definition of prisoners eligible for early parole and non-repatriation, whereas McClure had a more expansive criterion designed to encourage mass defection. In essence, Acheson supported a very limited version of voluntary repatriation: an early parole of selected prisoners before the prisoner exchange—i.e., a fait accompli—without specifying their final disposition.

Acheson's seemingly self-contradictory position can be best explained by his loathing for Chiang Kai-shek. While both the one-for-one formula and McClure's plan violated the Geneva Convention, Acheson did not oppose the former in the preceding months. Only McClure's Taiwan reference jolted Acheson's lawyerly mind into action.

Swayed by Acheson's logic, the military quickly reversed its position on prisoner repatriation. Leading the charge for change was Robert A. Lovett, who succeeded the seventy-one-year-old Marshall as secretary of defense on September 17. A week into his job, Lovett questioned the assumption that the Communists might accept a one-for-one exchange. He argued that the UNC should be "authorized to agree to an overall exchange, if such action were deemed necessary in order to effect the release of our own prisoners of war." At the senior NSC staff meeting on the 27th, the Psychological Strategy Board was tasked to review the policy. On October 15, the JCS "accede[d]" to Acheson's views. It also suggested the POW issue be settled by the JCS with State and Defense "without further reference to the National Security Council."[77] Nipped in the bud by Acheson, McClure's plan apparently never reached the president.

All-for-All Exchange Ruled Out by Truman, October 29–December 10, 1951

On October 25, the day armistice talks resumed at Panmunjom, Acheson sailed aboard the SS *America* "for more restful days en route to Le Havre," France. He led an eighty-one-person US delegation for the sixth regular session of the UN General Assembly in Paris. He did not return stateside until December 12 aboard SS *Independence* from Naples, Italy—a remarkable forty-nine-day trip in the age of air transport.[78] During Acheson's long absence, Truman inadvertently injected himself into the prisoner repatriation debate, giving voluntary repatriation a second life.

Ridgway cabled the JCS on October 27, challenging the June 30 directive. He declared that the "basic objective" in any POW exchange was to achieve the early release of the maximum number of UN prisoners. "Secondary and subj[ect] always to the basic objective" was the psychological warfare aims designed to "injure the cause of Communism." In order to secure the basic objective and to prevent a breakdown of negotiations, he requested authorization to "agree to exchange in bulk, including all-for-all." Taking one step further, Ridgway rejected Acheson's limited early parole for individuals who had "voluntarily aided [the] UNC." He predicted that a "premature release of PW through parole or any other medium would be regarded by the Communists as a breach of faith," thus jeopardizing the return of UN prisoners.[79] Ridgway, who had not been an enthusiastic supporter of voluntary repatriation but made the initial mistake of saying "the concept had definite merit" in July, now categorically opposed voluntary repatriation in any shape or form.[80]

Apparently unable to make a decision, Acting Secretary of State James E. Webb took the question to the White House on October 29 during Truman's regular Monday meeting with State officials. In this thirty-minute meeting, whose main agenda was scientific cooperation with India, Truman read a bare-bones three-paragraph memorandum on "the basic situation in the cease-fire talks," then quickly concluded, given the UNC's vast advantage in the number of prisoners held, an all-for-all exchange was not "equitable." Moreover, he did not "wish to send back those prisoners who surrendered and cooperated with us" because he believed they "will be immediately done away with" once repatriated. Webb tried to emphasize the ominous prospect that "a final settlement might rest on exchange of prisoners," and he listed a number of risks involved in any non–all-for-all formula. Unpersuaded, Truman simply "reced[ed] to the extent of saying that he certainly would not agree to any all for all settlement unless we received for it some major concession which could be obtained in no other way."[81]

"As far as I was concerned," Truman later wrote in his memoirs, prisoner repatriation "was not a point for bargaining!"[82] In reality, he had entertained bargaining—at least that was the takeaway message from the meeting. It is a truism that Truman was motivated by both humanitarianism and ideological calculations.[83] There is no need to doubt Truman's humanitarianism. However, when humanitarian principles, which were not supposed to be negotiable, became entangled with horse-trading of prisoners and propaganda calculations, the former were inevitably compromised.

The most astonishing aspect of the event was how little information Truman had and how little time he took to reach a decision. In a matter of minutes, he ruled out an all-for-all exchange, but dangled the idea that his position was negotiable if the Communists would make some unspecified "major concession." This muddled decision placed the onus on US negotiators to perform the unthinkable: first stake a claim to a new human right—voluntary repatriation or asylum from Communism—regardless of the risks involved; then be ready to retreat from the principle if the Communists would offer a good deal.

After reading Webb's memorandum, U. Alexis Johnson, deputy assistant secretary of state for Far Eastern affairs, wrote: "We should consider how to educate Pres. a little on PW problem."[84] Before that education could take place, Truman embarked on a month-long vacation to Key West, Florida.[85] Similarly, Acheson was mostly tuned out of Korean affairs during his forty-nine-day trip to Europe. Remarkably, the two highest-ranking American leaders took extended diplomatic and leisure trips far away from Washington, where and when their leadership was needed the most.

As the Panmunjom talks progressed rapidly and the discussion on POWs seemed imminent, Ridgway bombarded the JCS with repeated calls to rescind its June 30 directive on a one-for-one prisoner exchange. Taking issue with the JCS claim made in August that the UNC had offered "asylum" to enemy troops in its psychological warfare program, Ridgway asserted that the UNC only promised food, medical care, and good treatment. Regarding the Chinese, it had only "proffered the chance to save their lives"—not asylum.[86] Therefore, an all-for-all exchange would break no UNC promise.

Persuaded by Ridgway, the JCS reversed itself, informing Lovett on November 15 that the UNC had "scrupulously avoided the subject of non-repatriation and, further, has held forth no promise of asylum." Rejecting Acheson's early parole idea, the JCS drafted a new directive: while a one-for-one formula "should be sought initially for purpose of negotiation," Ridgway was authorized to agree to an all-for-all exchange in order to "secure the release of all, or a maximum number" of UN prisoners. However, as Bradley and Lovett had gone to Europe to join Acheson in NATO meetings, the directive apparently remained unapproved.[87]

Ridgway made another desperate plea on November 28, arguing that it was "essential to authorize" the UNC delegation "to agree to an all-for-all exchange, even though it would mean turning over to Communist control all prisoners of war," including, among others, "individuals who have voluntarily aided UNC" and "the majority of Chinese POWs many of whom have submitted petitions claiming they are loyal ex-Nationalists impressed into Communist Forces."[88]

On December 3, the JCS formally recommended all-for-all exchange to Lovett, explicitly rejecting Acheson's early parole mechanism for prisoners who had "rendered outstanding assistance" to the UNC.[89] Nearly a year after first demanding a one-for-one exchange, the JCS had completed a 180-degree turn. Its earlier considerations about enemy troop strength and psychological warfare had fallen by the wayside; now it rejected anything short of an all-for-all exchange. If Acheson had killed McClure's voluntary repatriation plan but allowed for a limited early parole mechanism, the JCS seemed determined to eliminate that altogether.

A State-JCS meeting on December 5 "revolved principally around the questions of forced versus voluntary repatriation, one-for-one versus all-for-all exchange." Although Truman was in Key West, his presence was felt. "The President has a strong personal interest in the POW problem," said H. Freeman Matthews, deputy under secretary of state. He repeated Truman's admonition that an all-for-all exchange would not be "equitable." General Bradley added, "I have also been informed by the President that he wants any directive on POWs cleared with him. It looked to the President as though there had been some fuzzy thinking on this problem."[90] Truman's reprimand immediately quenched the JCS's new-found enthusiasm for an all-for-all exchange. The JCS and State had jointly smothered McClure's proposal before it ever reached Truman, but they could not do the same to Truman's own idea.

Apparently cowed by Truman, the JCS made no mention of all-for-all exchange in their draft directive of December 7 instructing UNC negotiators to seek one-for-one exchange initially. If that failed, the "only practical possibility" appeared to be an agreement to screen all POWs. Prisoners refusing repatriation would be permitted to remain without "involving any commitment on part of captor as to future disposition of such POWs." Strangely, there was no mention of the next step if the Communists reject the terms.[91] In essence, the JCS deliberately evaded the issue of the final disposition of prisoners refusing repatriation, tacitly leaving the door open for an eventual all-for-all exchange. It is probably unfair to single out the JCS for fudging the issue. In fact, other than McClure, none of the top policymakers ever discussed the question. While Taiwan was the only realistic destination for Chinese anti-Communist prisoners, sending them to Chiang Kai-shek's embrace seemed to be a taboo subject in the Truman administration.

The draft directive was sent to Truman—who was cruising aboard presidential yacht *Williamsburg* in Key West—for approval. On December 9 Truman returned to

Washington ahead of schedule and summoned the JCS the next morning. The president gave his chiefs a dressing-down: "Our negotiators in Korea had been a little too conciliatory. . . . They [the enemy] had been making the demands and we the concessions." Politely pointing out that the enemy had actually "made very big concessions," Bradley argued that making tradeoffs "was preferable to all-out war with China." He lamely explained why the draft directives "looked bad": these proposals "were only efforts to give a final position to our negotiators." Then the meeting veered off into a long discussion of whether Washington should issue a strongly worded statement warning China against future armistice violations—as if an armistice agreement was at hand. Admiral William M. Fechteler, chief of Naval Operations and the naval member of the JCS, objected, noting that "making a threatening statement would not make much of an impression on China"—an unvarnished, accurate prediction. Concerned about domestic morale, Truman ended the inconclusive meeting with a warning against any letdown.[92]

Inexplicably, in this two-and-a-half-hour meeting, the POW issue was not broached even once, although it had been a major bone of contention between the JCS, State, and the president in the preceding days and weeks. Truman did not ask, and the Joint Chiefs did not tell—they dared not make a case for an all-for-all exchange that they had advocated a week earlier. Both sides beat around the bush, evading the tough issue.

After the meeting, the JCS formally rescinded its June 30 directive. The new December 10 directive was identical to the December 7 draft, except for the opening statement, which now read: "POW exchange on a one-for-one basis should be sought initially for purposes of negotiation and negotiators should vigorously maintain that position as long as possible without precipitating a break in negotiations." The second half of the sentence was added by the State Department "in order to meet the views of the President."[93] Knowing that the Communists would most probably reject a one-for-one exchange, JCS-State officials nevertheless adopted a half-baked policy of a "one-for-one exchange and POW screening without final disposition" in order to accommodate Truman, who knew very little about the complexities involved and had been shielded from dissenting voices. Failing to take a principled stand and lay out opposing views before the president, the JCS put the burden on UNC negotiators to meet conflicting demands simultaneously—an impossible task.

Subdelegation on POWs Convenes on December 11, 1951

The subdelegation on item 4 (POWs) finally convened on December 11. Rear Admiral Ruthven E. Libby and Colonel George W. Hickman represented the UNC; across the negotiating table were KPA Major General Lee Sang-cho and CPV Colonel Chai Chengwen—two of the ablest Communist negotiators in American eyes.[94] Lee and

Chai promptly announced their "simple principle" that "both sides release all POWs" after the armistice—an unconditional exchange of all prisoners. The UNC delegates evaded the issue and countered with two conditional principles: an "early regulated exchange of POWs on a fair and equitable basis and under suitable supervision," and provisions "to insure humanitarian treatment, safety, and comfort of prisoners preceding and during exchange." To implement such principles, the UNC demanded an exchange of POW data and the admission of representatives of the International Committee of the Red Cross (ICRC) to the POW camps. Communist negotiators dismissed these measures as "technical matters" contingent on the UNC's acceptance of an all-for-all exchange. At the end of the day, Joy noted his deep sense of foreboding: "Indications from 1st day are that subsequent sessions will focus primarily on question of all for all versus one for one, or any other arrangement."[95] By broaching "a fair and equitable basis," the UNC implicitly rejected an all-for-all exchange, as Mao had long feared.

Ridgway reported to the JCS the next day that "it is highly improbable that the Communists would agree to any formula for exchange, which involves individual expressions of opinion from prisoners in UNC custody." Ultimately, he predicted, he might have to agree to "an all-for-all exchange to include the forced exchange of those POWs not desiring return to Communist control."[96]

On December 15, the JCS instructed Ridgway to seek a one-for-one exchange initially. "If it becomes clear to you that agreement cannot be reached on anything short of all-for-all exchange, you may then proceed to negotiate on all-for-all basis," provided that "any position requiring forced return of personnel held by UNC must have prior approval by Washington." Remarkably, this reply allowing an all-for-all exchange—a sharp departure from the December 10 directive—was reviewed by Acheson and Army chief of staff Collins, and approved by Truman. Three days after his return from his long trip to Europe, Acheson made his first recorded engagement with the POW issue since August 27. Like Truman, Acheson believed the UNC enjoyed a strong "bargaining position . . . because of large number of POWs we have in comparison with Communist holdings."[97] Little did they realize that the numerical advantage was instead a trap.

In the next few days in Panmunjom, the Communists pressed UNC delegates to accept the all-for-all basis. Both sides traded sharp barbs and colorful metaphors. Chai ridiculed the UNC's insistence on exchanging POW data first as an act of "putting the cart before the horse." UNC negotiators retorted that they could not "buy a pig in a poke. Must negotiate with eyes open." The UNC wanted an armistice, but not at the price of "everything for nothing."[98] The verbal sparring allowed the UNC delegates to stall for time, as Joy had become uneasy with the JCS directive requiring a one-for-one exchange as the initial position. To take that approach, the "UNC would be exposing itself uselessly to adverse propaganda," Joy warned Ridgway on December 14. To avoid this "trap the enemy has set for us," Joy suggested introducing voluntary repatriation directly or a combination of one-for-one and voluntary repatriation, as their "negotiatory and propaganda advantage . . . appear to be great."[99] Since the Communists had effectively branded a one-for-one exchange as inhumane horse trading or slave trading, voluntary repatriation with its attractive "individual option feature" could turn enemy propaganda on its head by invoking humanitarianism, even though both schemes involved partial repatriation.

Apparently intrigued by Joy's analysis, Ridgway flew to Munsan-ni on December 17 to discuss a response to the JCS. UNC delegates worked past midnight preparing a draft. The next morning, joined by Ambassador Muccio and Eighth Army commander Van Fleet, Ridgway held a conference in Joy's tent. The four highest-ranking American officials in the Far East reviewed and agreed on a lengthy memorandum. It began the section on POWs with an acknowledgment that an all-for-all exchange "offers best chance for maximum recovery of our military POWs" and a flat rejection of the one-for-one formula on propaganda and legal grounds, admitting that the Geneva Convention "tends to support their [the enemy's] all-for-all argument." Then it warned against voluntary repatriation, which "may establish a dangerous precedent that may react to our disadvantage in later wars with Communist powers." In case the enemy held more POWs and claimed "none of our POWs wanted to be repatriated, . . . we will have no recourse." More importantly, voluntary repatriation "that extends the institution of asylum to POWs is so appealing to humanitarian sentiment, that once it is announced and publicized, the demand by our people to stand or fall on this proposal may preclude ultimate abandonment of this position." Nevertheless, it concluded, "there appears to be only one practicable way to proceed": using a combination of one-for-one and voluntary repatriation "as a club" to secure the acceptance of an all-for-all exchange of UN-held POWs for Communist-held POWs and civilian prisoners.[100] After all, the UNC was prepared to drop its "club" to make a deal.

Soon after Ridgway left Munsan-ni on the afternoon of December 18, Libby returned from Panmunjom with POW lists—another concession the Communists had just made. Libby had asked the Communists for a recess to study the information. "Of course the real reason for delaying to meet again is that it is essential to wait for an answer to our msg to JCS," Joy admitted.[101] The JCS's approval came the next day: "Actual exchange of POW by UNC for POW and listed civilians by Communists, would be on a one-for-one basis, until prisoners and listed civilians held by enemy are exhausted. Release of remaining POW would be in accordance with principle of voluntary repatriation."[102]

The proposal and the directive were masterpieces of self-contradiction. As Joy and Ridgway had long known that the Communists would reject either one-for-one or voluntary repatriation out of hand, how could they possibly accept a doubly insulting one-for-one plus voluntary repatriation? The new strategy bundled the concept of a supposedly humanitarian voluntary repatriation with a naked one-for-one scheme—a concoction that would only make the UNC appear callous and unprincipled. Clearly, the Americans did not expect the Communists to acquiesce; they merely hoped to give the enemy a bloody nose if "a large number of former Communist soldiers refuse to return to their homeland." But their plan of using mass defection as leverage was extremely risky, as public opinion would preclude any retreat from voluntary repatriation. Therefore, its success hinged on secrecy. Ridgway suggested that the UNC delegates should explore the issue "with as little publicity as possible."[103]

The hope for secrecy was immediately torpedoed by a seemingly coincidental development also on December 18. "Free China Objects to Exchange of POWs against Own Will," the Associated Press reported from Taipei. "Harvard and Cambridge educated Foreign Minister" George Yeh declared that it would be "undemocratic" and "un-Christian" to "send back to the clutches of Communist tyranny these Chinese and North Korean prisoners of war who have come to learn the meaning of freedom." Yeh exhorted, "We must allow ourselves to be guided only by the concept of human rights and the dignity of the human freedom affirmed in the charter of the UN and reaffirmed in the Human Rights Declaration."[104] For the first time, the principle of voluntary repatriation was raised publicly—two weeks before the UNC delegates did so in Panmunjom.

The UNC's dogged resistance to announcing its position on POW exchange frustrated not only the Communists; it also alarmed Chiang Kai-shek. Fearing the fate of prisoners who had signed petitions to "return to Taiwan," Chiang wrote in his diary: "The United States, will abandon justice and morality, and ignore our protests. ~~With an evil heart, certainly the United States will repatriate these men~~ [crossed-out in the original but still legible] and they will be slaughtered by the Communist bandits." He asked rhetorically, "Is there any humanitarianism and justice still in America? How heartbreaking!"[105] Little did Chiang know that his nemesis Truman had so far almost single-handedly prevented an all-for-all exchange.

The Americans Show Their Hand, January 2, 1952

The numbers of POWs reported by the two sides were heavily lopsided. The Communists, having previously boasted of the capture of more than 65,000 UNC prisoners, now furnished a list of 11,559 prisoners, including 7,142 South Korean, 3,198 American, 919 British, and 274 Turkish POWs, as well as a number of men of other nationalities. The UNC's list included 132,474 POWs, including 20,700 CPV and 111,774 KPA prisoners, and 37,000 civilian internees who were defined as prisoners of South Korean origin. While the Communists had claimed that

188,752 of their troops had gone missing or been captured, the UNC reported 169,000 enemy prisoners in custody. In contrast, the reported 11,559 UNC POWs fell considerably short of the UNC claim of 88,000 ROKs and 11,500 Americans captured or missing in action (MIAs). When pressed to explain the discrepancy, Communist negotiators asserted that most of the UNC captives had been "re-educated and released at the battle front," to which UNC delegates retorted, "exactly 177 POWs were so released."[106]

Talks on POWs continued daily throughout late December, despite the expiration of the December 27 deadline on the provisional cease-fire line. While the Communists tenaciously pressed for an all-for-all exchange, the UNC delegates equivocated. They questioned the quality of POW data and continued to demand that ICRC be allowed to visit the camps, arguing that an all-for-all exchange meant a swap of "120,000 men in good condition for 11,000 in unknown condition."[107] As before, the UNC was using such diversionary tactics to stall for time. It was yet to formulate a coherent strategy approved by the JCS. Approval in fact was not forthcoming since Washington was essentially shut down for the Christmas holiday. Ridgway sent multiple cables to the JCS every day, including at least five on Christmas Day, but received no reply.[108]

Forced to improvise, Ridgway devised a seven-phase negotiating plan, using the UNC's one-for-one and the Communist all-for-all positions "as the extreme poles." On December 23, he told Joy to start with one-for-one, as it would allow the UNC to retain "maximum bargaining power for further negotiations" and "make each successive position appear to be a concession."[109] Incredibly, Ridgway thought the UNC's supposedly humanitarian position was divisible into slices to be traded one by one. There was no chance the Communists would follow his script.

Finally, on January 2, 1952, the UNC unveiled a six-point proposal that boiled down to two key items: "POWs who elect repat[riation] shall be exchanged on a 1 for 1 basis until one side has exchanged all such POWs held by it," and "all POWs not electing repat shall be released from POW status and shall be paroled." Libby argued that the Communists had already practiced voluntary repatriation when ROK prisoners were "reeducated and released at the front" and then joined the KPA—as the Communists had claimed. Lee Sang-cho immediately requested a recess.[110] After months of hiding its position and weeks of stonewalling, the UNC finally showed its hand—one-for-one plus voluntary repatriation.

The next day Lee categorically rejected the proposal as a "barbarous formula and a shameful design" to detain POWs on the pretext of "voluntary repatriation." He declared, "The release and repatriation of prisoners of war is not a trade of slaves," nor was the twentieth century a "barbarous age of slavery." Chai Chengwen castigated the proposal as "not only shameful but dangerous." Citing UNC newspaper reports of Chinese POWs demanding to go to Taiwan, Chai called voluntary repatriation a sham that "would be only [an] expression of [the] will of Chiang Kai-shek." UNC negotiators lamely insisted that their proposal made no reference to Taiwan. Two weeks later, however, Libby announced that since China was a country with two governments, prisoners would be allowed to choose between Communist China and Nationalist China. This two-China formula provoked Chai to declare, "If anybody dares to hand over any of the personnel of the CPV . . . to the deadly enemy of the Chinese people, the Chinese people will never tolerate it and will fight to the end."[111]

Was voluntary repatriation a cover for a conspiracy to detain Chinese POWs and transfer them to Taiwan? The Chinese Communists believed so. They rightly pointed out that CIE instructors from Taiwan were active in POW camps, aiding the rise of anti-Communist organizations.[112] Libby admitted that the UNC had "employed many people of Chinese extraction" since the start of the war. However, he asserted, most of those employed in POW camps were "translators and instructors of elementary education, sanitation, health, and skilled trades." The prisoners were taught "the fundamental concepts of democracy . . . the basic principles of democratic life, freedom of speech, freedom of worship, freedom from want, freedom from disease, and freedom from fear." He concluded, "There is nothing in this procedure which remotely savors of coercion or intimidation."[113] In view of the evidence discussed in proceeding chapters, Libby was either being disingenuous or had been misinformed—the latter being more likely.

Libby was not the only one unaware of the conditions in the UN prison camps; none of the American policymakers, from Truman and Acheson in Washington down to Ridgway in Tokyo and Joy in Panmunjom, had good information. Strikingly ignorant of what was transpiring in the camps, they had made a series of decisions that maneuvered the United States into the policy of voluntary repatriation—which would quickly become "final and irrevocable," making a mockery of Ridgway's elaborate seven-phase negotiating plan.

US Military's "Rearguard Defection," January–Early February 1952

Four days after the voluntary repatriation proposal was introduced at Panmunjom, British prime minister Winston Churchill asked Acheson about the prospect of an armistice. Acheson replied, "I would guess that it would come about toward the end of January."[114] Coincidentally, Mao was also very optimistic, but for a different reason. In a cable to Stalin on January 31, Mao dismissed voluntary repatriation as a "rash demand." Claiming that "the enemy in principle cannot oppose the liberation of all prisoners of war," he believed "the negotiations cannot be dragged out for a long time."[115] As it turned out, they dragged out for another eighteen months. Both Acheson and Mao were to be surprised by their opponent's intransigence—and the complexity of the prisoner repatriation issue.

As the Communists vehemently rejected voluntary repatriation, the talks hit an impasse. Apparently anticipating an inevitable retreat, Ridgway cabled the JCS on January 12: "It is imperative that I know soonest the final positions upon the exchange of civilians and voluntary repatriation which will be acceptable to the U.S."[116] After Acheson and other top State officials decided against "forced repatriation," the JCS informed Ridgway on the 15th: "As a final position . . . you are authorized to agree to an all-for-all exchange of mil[itary] POWs except that no forceful return of POWs would be required." Admitting that the government "might find it necessary to further modify our stand," they told Ridgway to "act *as if* current position were final position," noting that the admission was "strictly for your own guidance."[117] After all, there was nothing final about this "final position," which was essentially the same as the December 15 directive that authorized an all-for-all exchange in principle but required Washington's clearance on forcible returns. An all-for-all exchange without forcibly returning anti-Communist prisoners was simply self-deceiving.

As for State officials' hope to poll prisoners to obtain "a definite number to offer to" the Communists, the JCS asked Ridgway for his view. Seeing polling as a prelude to Acheson's early parole mechanism, Ridgway reacted strongly in his reply on January 19. He asserted that choice should only "be expressed by each POW at exchange point." Arguing that the enemy would never accept the results of a poll, he postulated that the Communists did not "have any real concern as to [the] numbers who may choose not to return" since the principle of individual choice was anathema to them.[118] Ridgway would soon find out how wrong he was. Following the Marxist law that quantitative changes lead to qualitative changes, the Communists valued numbers as much as principles.

Unsure of the number of POWs the UNC could deliver, the State Department belatedly sought to tweak the principle. On January 22, it cited Article 6 of the Geneva Convention that allowed for "other special agreements" for POWs as long as they were "not deprived of their rights under the rest of the convention." Since the "spirit" of the convention was to protect POWs' individual rights, it argued that voluntary repatriation did not violate the convention.[119]

On the same day, the State Department established a working group chaired by U. Alexis Johnson to examine "all possible methods" to obtain the Communists' agreement to voluntary repatriation and, if negotiations broke off on this issue, to obtain maximum domestic and international support. Its objectives clearly indicated the top echelon's support for voluntary repatriation.[120] Even though he had rejected McClure's original voluntary repatriation plan designed to encourage mass defection to Taiwan, Acheson had consistently recommended an early parole mechanism for prisoners who had aided the UNC or whose return would result in their deaths—essentially a limited-scale voluntary repatriation without specifying the final destination for parolees. Another major advocate of voluntary repatriation was State Department counselor Charles E. Bohlen. A Soviet expert, Bohlen had personally witnessed the "enormous difficulties, trauma, and bloodshed" involved in forcibly returning Soviet citizens from Western Europe to the Soviet Union after World War II. Many committed suicide rather than return to Stalinism. Tens of thousands of repatriates were "subsequently killed, imprisoned, or sent to Siberia." He did not want the country to commit the same mistake in Korea.[121]

At the working level, however, there were dissenting voices. PPS official Charles Stelle, a former OSS officer and a member of the Dixie Mission to Yan'an in 1944–1945, argued: "In the first place, whether we like to remember it or not, the law is on the Communist side." Citing firsthand reports from Koje Island, Stelle highlighted the unsavory fact that "our prison camps for Chinese in Korea are violently totalitarian, and that the thugs who run them are the people, aside from our own US prisoners, that are the actual objects of our concern in the POW issue." To achieve a quick armistice, Stelle urged making "as graceful as possible a withdrawal" from voluntary repatriation, even if that entailed the "unpleasant business of handing over some 3,000 Chinese to be shot (regardless of the fact that practically all of them well deserve it), and painful necessity of handing over possibly some 30,000–40,000 Koreans to be shot (who probably don't deserve it)."[122] Charles B. Marshall, the PPS official who had been secretly dispatched to Hong Kong in May 1951 to seek contact with the Chinese Communists but returned empty-handed, supported voluntary repatriation for Korean POWs, as the issue "gets at the heart of the contention between Communism and the tradition we live by. It bears on the rights of men to make choices and to claim protection." However, "we are not in Korea to protect a Chinese regime or to protect Chinese. We could force them back without sacrificing our case as to Korea."[123]

These middle-level State officials' objections were easily brushed aside, but the military's stubborn resistance posed a greater challenge. "The military were," Acheson later recalled, "understandably enough, primarily concerned with getting back their men. . . . The Pentagon favored the return of North Korean and Chinese prisoner and civilian internees regardless of their wishes."[124] As Joy explained, "'voluntary repatriation' placed the welfare of ex-Communist soldiers above that of our own UNC personnel in Communist prison camps, and above that of our UNC personnel still on the battle line in Korea."[125]

In sharp contrast to his earlier disengagement, from late January Acheson took an active role, "coming down with both feet for Truman's position," in Robert Beisner's words.[126] Between January 28 and February 1, Acheson had four meetings to discuss the issue: two at Foggy Bottom and another two at the Pentagon. Acheson managed to secure the military's acquiescence with non-forcible repatriation and early parole of prisoners, "thus facing the Communists with a fait accompli."[127]

On February 4, Johnson drafted a memorandum to Truman on behalf of Acheson and Lovett, somberly announcing that "the question of voluntary repatriation of prisoners of war will shortly become the sole remaining fundamental issue in the Korean armistice negotiations." Admitting that it was "not probable" that the Communists would accept voluntary repatriation, Johnson still concluded that "the only course of action that seems to offer any reasonable possibility of carrying out this policy requires the taking of irrevocable actions at the beginning of its implementation *regardless* of the ultimate consequences to prisoners held by the Communists or to the conclusion of an armistice." The "irrevocable action" was to screen out anti-repatriation prisoners, remove them from the POW lists, and present a fait accompli to the Communists.[128]

When the memorandum reached the Pentagon, "a serious rearguard defection" erupted, Johnson recalled. Lovett expressed "serious doubts" and hoped to find a better solution using "Yankee ingenuity." Admiral Fechteler "entirely withdrew his previous concurrence." General Hoyt Vandenberg, the Air Force chief of staff, firmly opposed the position. Unfazed by the military's about-face, Acheson and State leaders decided to stand firm. On the seventh, Acheson, Matthews, Bohlen, Nitze, and Johnson revisited the Pentagon. With the exception of Lovett and two other Defense officials, "there was a clear disposition to agree to return all prisoners of war held by the UNC, including even, if necessary, the 44,000 ROK personnel who had been reclassified to civilian internee status, to achieve an armistice." No wonder Bohlen later called the military "callous." To placate the military, a revised memorandum removed any mention of screening or a fait accompli. Lovett still refused to endorse it, but said that he "would not oppose it and would be prepared to discuss the matter" with Truman the next day.[129]

On February 8, between a cabinet meeting from 11:00 a.m. to 12:00 p.m. and another appointment immediately after, Acheson and Lovett brought the matter to Truman, who "went over the memorandum." In the document, Acheson declared that POW repatriation was "a question of the utmost gravity." He argued: "Any agreement in the Korean armistice which would require United States troops to use force to turn over to the Communist prisoners who believe they would face death if returned, would be repugnant to our most fundamental moral and humanitarian principles on the importance of the individual, and would seriously jeopardize the psychological warfare position of the United States in its opposition to Communist tyranny." While recognizing that the fate of some 3,000 Americans and 8,000 UN prisoners in enemy hands hung in the balance, he recommended adhering to nonforcible repatriation. In the meantime, Acheson claimed "it was possible, but not certain" to devise a solution that would not require the United States to accept forcible repatriation or the Communists to accept voluntary repatriation.[130] That unwritten solution was Acheson's screening and fait accompli approach.

Reluctant to challenge a more powerful Acheson, Lovett did not make a countercase. Sounding diffident and muddled, he started off by saying he did not oppose Truman's approval of the memorandum. He acknowledged Acheson's persuasiveness and noted the Pentagon's lack of consensus. He asked if the document should not be regarded as "definitive"—or "final and irrevocable." Finally, he said that "we could go ahead at once in implementing the memorandum." Upon hearing this, Truman signed "Approved Feb. 8, 1952 Harry S. Truman" on two copies and handed one to Lovett.[131] With a flourish of his pen, Truman sent an unmistakable message on where he stood. The deed was done, probably within a few minutes.

The Far East Mission, Mid-February, 1952

With Truman firmly opposed to forcible repatriation, officials faced a seemingly insurmountable challenge: how to devise a policy that would simultaneously fulfill three conflicting objectives: (1) to adhere to non-forcible repatriation, (2) to "minimize the recognized jeopardy to prisoners of war held by the Communists," and (3) to obtain the Communists' agreement that would "lead to [a] successful conclusion of an armistice." On February 11, Johnson and General John E. Hull, Army vice chief of staff, left for Japan and Korea to "explore and discuss the problem on the spot."[132]

Johnson and Hull spent three full days in Tokyo conferring with Ridgway, Joy, and other officers. General Doyle O. Hickey, UNC chief of staff, reported that "based on guesswork," 15,900 Communist POWs "would [violently] oppose return," including 11,500 Chinese—or 55 percent of the Chinese POWs.[133] Although feeling "he was in no position to question these estimates," Johnson later confided to the JCS that he "felt that the Chinese figure might be high."[134] His doubt apparently arose from the discrepancies between estimates made by Hickey and the "State Dept interrogation team" in Pusan, which was led by Manhard and included Larry Chin (see Chapter 6). In November 1951, Muccio had reported that "maximum one-fourth Chinese POW's in camp here are reluctant return mainland; possibly 15 percent appear genuinely pro-Nationalist."[135] Since then, however, these estimates had become obsolete, as anti-Communist trusties had driven out hardcore Communist POWs and established near total control over some 15,000 Chinese prisoners on Koje.

Johnson and Hull flew to Koje on February 17 for a "brief inspection" of the POW camps to "get a feel of the situation." The "incipient anarchy, the smell of mutiny in the air, frankly shocked me," recalled Johnson. Philip Manhard, the US embassy political officer active on Koje, told Johnson, "For POWs the war was not over." Coincidentally, a riot broke out in Compound 62 the very next day, leaving seventy-seven Korean prisoners and one US guard dead.[136]

Johnson observed a litany of problems: "second-rate facilities and officers," overcrowded barracks, and inadequate rations. Most disturbingly, with "almost no officers who could speak the prisoners' languages or really follow what they were up to," self-styled anti-Communist trusties had "assumed almost complete control over internal administration and judicial powers, removed rivals by informing authorities of alleged communist plots, doled out food, clothing, fuel and access to medical treatment to reinforce their powers, and conducted 'reorientation' programs emphasizing anti-communist indoctrination in which POWs were compelled by force to participate."[137] Clearly, the Communists' allegations about camp conditions were not baseless; UNC negotiators had been disingenuous.

Hull and Johnson met with UNC delegates at Munsan-ni on February 18. All negotiators "expressed strong disapproval" of the fait accompli approach. They saw it as "an act of bad faith" that would "inevitably result in reprisal against prisoners held by the Communists." Joy considered it "dishonorable." Calling it "underhanded and dishonest," Libby declared that he would "not associate himself with such a procedure." However, these strong words were filtered out in Johnson's final report, which merely noted their "strong opposition" and emphasized that the dissenters "were unable to suggest any possible solutions other than forcibly returning . . . all POWs."[138]

Truman's Final Decision, February 27, 1952

Upon returning to Washington, Johnson "privately" told the joint chiefs that "the camps were out of control and required overhaul." In a fifteen-minute meeting with Truman on February 25, however, Hull and Johnson apparently omitted this ominous observation. They neither conveyed to Truman the UNC negotiators' view that Washington had made "the original mistake of insisting on voluntary repatriation," nor did they mention Ridgway's strong opposition. Instead, they told the president what he had largely decided: "there was no feasible method of handling the problem" other than a "unilateral screening" of all POWs, which Ridgway could "accomplish within the daylight hours of a single day"—thus presenting the Communists with a fait accompli.[139]

Despite Johnson's misgivings about Hickey's estimates "based on guesswork," Johnson and Hull relayed them to Truman—with a slight adjustment—that 5,000 North Korean and 11,500 Chinese POWs could be expected to violently resist repatriation. They added, "qualitatively as well as possibly quantitatively, the problem of [Chinese] POWs and possible Communist reactions thereto was much more difficult than that of Korean POWs."[140] However, they did not explain—apparently they themselves did not realize at the time—the significance of these figures: while only 5 percent of the North Korean POWs were expected to violently resist repatriation, more than half of the Chinese would do so.

They were not the only ones who underestimated China's sensitivity. By this time, UNC negotiators had long recognized that the Chinese held the ultimate sway on the Communist side. Libby accurately predicted that "there was no possibility of the Communists accepting the principles of non-forcible repatriation"; but Joy told Johnson that there was a fifty-fifty chance. In Johnson's report, however, Joy's estimate became "some chance."[141] In reality, the chance was little. While Truman believed American prestige was at stake, Mao perceived the large number of Chinese defectors as a major humiliation for his young regime. The scenario of more than half of the Chinese prisoners refusing to return home would strike at the heart of the Communist claim to legitimacy that rested on purported popular support. Like Truman, Mao could not afford to appear weak under pressure.

Also on February 25, Foreign Minister Yeh announced Taiwan's readiness to accept anti-Communist prisoners, complete with an emotional appeal to Americans: "Save them so others may live."[142] Chiang had preempted Truman once again.

Probably sensing that his dissent had not reached Truman, Ridgway cabled the JCS on February 27, vehemently protesting the fait accompli approach, which he called a "subterfuge" and "a breach of faith." Such a policy would "leave ourselves open to the accusation of treachery and deceit which have consistently characterized Communist dealings" and could "result in retaliation against our prisoners." Once again, he demanded Washington to give the "final position on the POW question."[143] Truman gave his answer hours later on the same day.

At 10:30 a.m., Acheson's plane landed in Washington. Truman was at the airport to greet his secretary of state, who had spent two weeks in Europe, first in London for King George VI's funeral, and then in Lisbon for NATO meetings. They immediately proceeded to the White House for a meeting with State and Defense officials to discuss Ridgway's telegram. Except for Admiral Fechteler, all participants expressed their support for non-forcible repatriation—another major reversal for the military men. Deputy Under Secretary of State Matthews misleadingly reported that none of "our key allies" had "indicated any disagreement," even though the Canadians had. Truman concluded that "the final U.S. position should be that the U.S. would not agree to forcible repatriation of POWs." Hours later, Truman signed off on a JCS telegram to Ridgway: "US govt will not accept any agreement which would require use of force to repatriate to Commies POWs held by UNC who would violently oppose such repatriation and whose lives would be endangered thereby." Implicitly reprimanding Ridgway, the JCS pointedly asserted, "We believe this position can be maintained without use of any subterfuge."[144]

Remarkably, the seventy-five-minute conference on February 27 was Truman's first dedicated to the POW issue—all previous discussions were brief, informal exchanges squeezed between other scheduled events. It was also the first meeting on POWs that both Truman and Acheson attended. But neither man was fully informed. Before the decision was made, it was nearly impossible for Johnson to brief Acheson on the explosive prison conditions and the huge disparity in the percentage of Chinese and

North Korean POWs refusing repatriation. Even if he had been briefed, Acheson most unlikely would have opposed Truman. In a meeting with so many "firsts," a "final and irrevocable" decision was made.

"The Chinese Have Influenced the Course of Events in Koje-do and at Panmunjom"

Also on February 27, Ambassador Muccio sent an ominous cable to Washington, confessing that "I personally have a hunch that the Chinese have influenced the course of events in Koje-do and at Panmunjom." Recounting the rising influence of "a lot of the Chinese . . . interpreters, translators and CI&E personnel" hired by the US military and "a recently greatly augmented Chinese Embassy, military attaché and air attaché organization," Muccio lamented his embassy's inability to monitor Nationalist overt and covert activities. If pro-Chiang politicians took power in South Korea, Muccio feared that "we may as well turn the peninsula over to Taipei."[145] While his warning on Chiang's influence in Korean domestic politics sounded alarmist, Muccio's assessment of Taiwan's impact on the course of events in Koje and Panmunjom was accurate. Ironically, while the CPV was pounding UNC troops on the 38th parallel and Communist negotiators were berating Americans at Panmunjom, the Chinese Nationalists had infiltrated both the POW camps on Koje and the truce tents at Panmunjom, throwing a monkey wrench into the truce talks.

This outcome was not the result of any well-planned conspiracy, as events in Koje and Panmunjom developed too rapidly and haphazardly to follow any script. The unexpected rise of the anti-Communist POWs outraged the Communists, staggered the Americans, and heartened the Nationalists. Like Truman and Acheson, Chiang Kai-shek was motivated by both humanitarianism and ideological/propaganda calculations. What distinguished the Nationalists from the other two players was that they were not only among the first to recognize the propaganda potential of anti-Communist POWs, but also the first to take immediate action. Enabled by their direct access to on-the-ground intelligence through DAC interpreters, interrogators, and CIE teachers, they made a series of well-calibrated moves to insert Taiwan into the Korean War over POWs.

As explained in Chapter 6, when more than seventy interpreters were first hired from Taiwan in February and March 1951, there were so few Chinese POWs that no one could have foreseen a controversy over repatriation. After the CPV's Fifth Offensive defeat, the number of Chinese POWs increased fivefold in May and June. Anti-Communist POWs soon emerged, and they asked interpreters from Taiwan to relay their pleas to Taipei, which responded quickly but secretly.

It was perhaps pure coincidence that on July 7, 1951, two days after General McClure proposed sending Chinese prisoners to Taiwan, General Lai Mingtang, director of Nationalist G-2, made a similar proposal to Chiang Kai-shek.[146] The Ministry of

Defense concluded on August 9 that accepting prisoners was "necessary" given its "political and human resources" benefits.[147] While career diplomats raised concerns over legal constraints and feared some of the POWs might be Communist infiltrators posing as anti-Communists, the new ambassador to South Korea, Wang Dongyuan, a former general and senior political operative, assured doubters that a collective responsibility system (*lianbao lianzuo*) could eliminate infiltrators.[148] Chiang Kai-shek and Chiang Ching-kuo apparently agreed. Taipei's policy objective soon became clear: to bring bona fide anti-Communist POWs to Taiwan.

By early July 1951, the Nationalist mission in Tokyo had transmitted to Taipei prisoners' petitions smuggled out by interpreters.[149] The embassy in Korea reported on July 25 that a group of prisoners knelt before interpreters, pleading for Taiwan's intervention.[150] In September, the embassy received a petition by former Nationalist Party and Youth League members, vowing to fight Communism once they were sent to Taiwan. "If we are left to languish in despair," they declared, "the only way out is to commit mass suicide."[151]

The subject of POWs first appeared in Chiang's diary on October 28, one day before Truman ruled out an all-for-all exchange. "Upon reading the blood letters signed by Yin Liangwen, Li Da'an, and more than one thousand prisoners in Korea, pledging allegiance to the [Nationalist] Party and the country," Chiang wrote, "I feel all the more ashamed and uneasy for [failing to protect] my former troops."[152] Rescuing prisoners and bringing them to Taiwan became a deeply personal project for Chiang.

Given the legal constraints, Taipei first proceeded quietly, "without overt actions or public pronouncements."[153] Government-controlled news outlets selectively published prisoners' petitions. To conceal the role of DAC interpreters and the embassy, it was claimed that the petitions were mailed from POW camps, which was impossible in practice. In the meantime, Nationalist representatives in Korea, Tokyo, and Washington approached US officials, seeking to gauge the US position on prisoner exchange, but they were rebuffed.[154] In early November 1951, an alarmed US government ordered Counter Intelligence Corps agents to investigate links between the Nationalist embassy and the POWs.[155] Muccio reported to Acheson on November 12 that it was "not impossible Taipei circles have had access [to] such petitions for some time." Highlighting the new Chinese ambassador Wang's personal involvement, Muccio concluded that the developments "may indicate increasing efforts [by] Chinese Nationalists to influence foreign opinion re disposition [of] Chinese POW's."[156] Muccio's realization came several months too late. The Chinese Nationalists had taken the lead in the propaganda game.

As with the UNC's apparatus on Koje Island and elsewhere, the UNC truce delegation did not escape infiltration. Wu Jiwu, one of the two Nationalist DACs that UNC interpreter Kenneth Wu relied on for translating written statements to be delivered to the Communists, admitted decades later that when off duty, "sometimes we requested a jeep to go shopping at the Army post exchange in Seoul; we also gave secret materials to our military attaché at the embassy, including armistice terms."[157]

On December 18, when POW data were exchanged at Panmunjom, Taipei announced its objection to forcible repatriation—publicizing the principle two weeks before the UNC delegates introduced it. On February 25, 1952, the day Hull and Johnson reported their findings to the president two days before Truman made his "final decision" on voluntary repatriation, Taipei declared its readiness to welcome anti-Communist prisoners. Such impeccable timing was inconceivable without access to insider information. Commanding both superb intelligence and the moral high ground, Chiang preempted Truman time and time again.

Underestimation, Guesswork, and Wishful Thinking

Dismissed as a non-player, Taiwan was entirely excluded from the truce negotiations. To the Americans' shock and chagrin, the US government's control over the truce agenda—and, by extension, the war agenda—was effectively wrested away by Chinese anti-Communist prisoners and Chiang. This was not the result of a coordinated conspiracy, but it was enabled by the ineptitude, neglect, and arrogance of American policymakers and their ill-advised policies.

The earliest prisoner exchange policy—a one-for-one exchange—first developed by the JCS and approved by Secretary of Defense Marshall in late 1950, was blatantly illegal and outlandish, a guaranteed non-starter. It was rejected out of hand by the Communists—although they could have counter-proposed an exchange on a proportional basis, which would have easily erased the UNC's numerical advantage in the number of prisoners held. For almost ten months, the US military held on to this idea, showing little concern over probable retaliation against UNC prisoners in enemy hands. Once that prospect dawned on them, the JCS, Lovett, and Ridgway made a whiplash reversal, advocating an all-for-all exchange, even if that meant sending back defectors who had "rendered outstanding assistance" to the UNC, such as Liu Bingzhang and Wang Shunqing. Humanitarian and psychological warfare considerations were heedlessly cast aside.

Although Acheson nixed McClure's voluntary repatriation proposal ostensibly on legal grounds, he said nothing about the illegality of one-for-one exchange. More alarmed by McClure's plan to send prisoners to Taiwan than about the principle of voluntary repatriation, Acheson suggested voluntary repatriation lite—an early parole mechanism for selected prisoners. However, as he was fully occupied with NATO buildup and spent much time in Europe, he did not follow up and paid little attention to the Panmunjom talks until January 1952.

In Acheson's absence, Truman, in a gut reaction, ruled out the all-for-all exchange favored by the military, arguing that it was "not equitable" and inhumane. Cowed by the president and at their wits' end, the JCS and State cobbled together a half-baked one-for-one plus voluntary repatriation, which was doubly insulting to the Communists, who duly rejected it.

With the war stalemated and truce talks deadlocked, Acheson belatedly turned his attention to POW repatriation in January 1952. He managed to cajole Lovett not to oppose voluntary repatriation before Truman. Others also failed to inform or "educate" the president, as Johnson had vowed to do in October 1951. In their report to Truman on February 25, 1952, Johnson and Hull withheld unwelcome information about the dire conditions on Koje Island. Despite their near universal opposition to voluntary repatriation, none of the joint chiefs, with the exception of Fechteler, dared to challenge Truman.[158] That was dereliction of duty.

Had Truman relented for a moment on voluntary repatriation, the generals would have jumped at the first opportunity to sell anti-Communist prisoners down the river by agreeing to an all-for-all solution. Truman stood firm, but without the benefit of full information or careful analysis. Intellectually incurious and decisive by nature, bordering on the impulsive, Truman made decisions quickly based on highly condensed and filtered information presented by his top advisors—without asking many, if any, questions.[159] Shielded from the unsavory complexities of the POW issue, Truman was spared the wrenching moral dilemmas he otherwise would have faced.

Acheson's early parole concept was in fact humanitarian and sensible, but it made no provision for the disposition of non-repatriates. Even though Taiwan was the only possible destination, Acheson's loathing for Chiang Kai-shek and his extended absence in Europe precluded policy deliberation. From August to December, five months were squandered, during which time the Panmunjom talks resolved nearly all other major issues until hitting an impasse on the question of POW repatriation, and anti-Communist prisoners emerged and dominated Chinese camps. The degree of their dominance was greatly underestimated by the Americans, who at no point could ascertain how many prisoners would violently resist repatriation. In the end, the best estimates Truman received were "based on guesswork." Then he made a momentous decision. The president had been poorly served by his advisors.

When Acheson and Johnson advocated voluntary repatriation or early parole, their unspoken assumption was that the number of prisoners refusing repatriation would be limited, so that the Communists would eventually accept it after some arm-twisting. "At most, they thought, they were adding only a few months, not more than a year, to the war," as Barton Bernstein has noted.[160] Despite their misgivings about the policy, the military men went along, because they assumed they could bomb the Communists into submission. Both assumptions turned out to be wishful thinking.

10

Screening

"Voluntary Repatriation" Turns Violent

DESPITE TRUMAN'S "FINAL DECISION" in favor of "voluntary repatriation" on February 27, debate continued to seethe in Washington. In a JCS-State meeting on March 19, a general asked, "Will they [the US public] advocate leaving our boys in Communist hands or will they want to insist on the principle of no involuntary repatriation?" Admiral Fechteler remarked that "a number of fellows in Tokyo and Korea felt that if Washington would only give up its altruistic concern for a lot of worthless Chinese, there wouldn't be any problem about POWs." There was "nothing altruistic about our position," Bohlen countered, arguing that any retreat from the policy "would be interpreted as a real sign of Western weakness."[1]

Admiral Fechteler was not alone in wishing to dispose of these "worthless Chinese." Kim Il-sung felt the same way about the Chinese POWs who had been "Chiang Kai-shek's brigands." However rigid the American and Chinese views, after months of wrangling, the North Koreans began to show some flexibility, as they became tired of a war they had no chance of winning. On January 16, 1952, Kim's foreign minister Pak Hon-yong visited Peng Dehuai and told him that "the Korean people throughout the country demand peace and do not want to continue the war," but added that this was "purely his personal opinion."[2] Contrary to his disclaimer, Pak's statement was clearly a trial balloon sent by Kim, who told Soviet ambassador V. N. Razuvaev in early 1952 that "expending a lot of effort on them [POWs] is somewhat meaningless."[3] On March 27, the Communist delegation at Panmunjom made a major compromise, dropping the repatriation requirement for KPA prisoners of South Korean origin. Its continued demand for the return of prisoners of North Korean origin was a largely perfunctory position designed to cover the deepening Sino–North Korean schism. The real point of contention at Panmunjom became the Communist—in fact, Chinese—demand for "complete repatriation of all non-Korean prisoners."[4] The North Korean POWs had become a nonissue in the peace talks. From the beginning of 1952 on, the Korean War was fought over Chinese prisoners.

A "Round Figure" of 116,000 Prisoners

With the Communists showing some flexibility, the negotiations seemed to forge ahead, switching into secret sessions to iron out final differences. Repeatedly pressed by the Communists, the UNC scrambled to come up with a "round number" of prisoners it could repatriate, but its staff actually had "no idea as to just how many prisoners would refuse repatriation." UNC chief of staff Hickey made an estimate "based on guesswork" that 116,000 POWs would eventually choose to return. Among the 20,000 Chinese, he thought that over half would "use every means at their disposal to present a solid block of opposition" to repatriation, "since they were well organized, disciplined, and controlled by strong leaders with Nationalist sympathies."[5]

As if Hickey's folly of wishful thinking and guesswork was not enough, on April 1 the UNC delegation's staff officer Colonel George Hickman made an offhand mistake. The Communist negotiators began the session by attacking the UNC's vagueness: "Your side is even unwilling to express your opinion about a round figure." Hickman replied to his Chinese counterpart, Colonel Chai, that roughly 116,000 of the 132,000 POWs would be "the magnitude of the exchange."[6] Failing to mention that half of the Chinese would refuse repatriation, Hickman was heedlessly insensitive to the Chinese Communists' intense desire to recover most, if not all, Chinese prisoners—a fact that should have become glaringly apparent to UNC negotiators. He unwittingly misled Chai into thinking that China and North Korea would recover approximately 116,000, or roughly 81 percent, of their POWs. More critically, without disclosing the drastically higher percentage of Chinese non-repatriates, Hickman misled Chai into assuming the percentage of Chinese and North Korean repatriates to be more or less the same. Hickman's error had colossal consequences.

The Chinese found the number of 116,000 sufficiently face-saving. "The number of POWs whom your side should repatriate to our side should not be far from the figure of 132,000," Chai declared on April 2. Postponing an argument over principles, Chai suggested that both sides "immediately check their lists"—a tacit acquiescence to the screening of the prisoners on their repatriation choices. Joy realized the importance of delivering that number, particularly for the Chinese. To produce such an outcome, Joy recommended to Ridgway that a "minimum standard" be used in the screening process.[7]

It was only after the Communists had agreed to screening that the Koje prison commandant Francis Dodd was summoned to Munsan-ni to confer with Ridgway, Joy, and Van Fleet on April 3. Dodd broke the bad news: only about half of the POWs, or 85,000 men, would want to return—falling 31,000 short of 116,000.[8] But it was too late. Ridgway, who had recently opposed screening and denied that the "Communists have any real concern as to numbers," now made an about-face. On April 4, he informed the JCS that "the question of the numbers and nationalities of the POWs to be returned rather than the principles involved appears to be the controlling issue," and he advocated an immediate screening. Given the "potentially explosive atmosphere" on Koje, he concluded, "the longer we wait, the longer we delay the return of our own POWs, the more we risk armistice failure and the greater is the danger of serious outbreaks on Koje-Do." Washington approved his screening plan at once.[9]

Apparently knowing that he had given the Communists unrealistic hopes, Hickman asked Chai on April 4 to provide an amnesty statement to reassure the prisoners that they would not be punished after repatriation. Although Chai made the obligatory protest, claiming it would be unnecessary, on April 6 he furnished a statement written in the names of Kim Il-sung and Peng Dehuai. In the declaration, Kim and Peng "wholeheartedly welcome the return of all our captured personnel to the arms of the Motherland." Specifically highlighting the fact that some prisoners "have had their arms tattooed or have written certain documents or committed other similar acts," they vowed, "we are deeply aware that such acts have certainly not been done out of their own volition and that they should not be held responsible for these acts." They further guaranteed that "all captured personnel shall, after their repatriation, rejoin their families to participate in peaceful construction and live a peaceful life." The message was broadcast repeatedly in all prison compounds through the public announcement system.[10] Clearly, hopes were high for the Communists, as they believed most "volunteers" would naturally choose to return home. By asking for and broadcasting the amnesty statement, the UNC tried hard to maximize the number of prisoners who might choose repatriation.

In addition to disseminating the Kim-Peng declaration, the UNC also repeatedly broadcast its own announcement in POW camps from April 6 and on. The UNC first cautioned prisoners that their upcoming decision "is a most important one, possibly the most vital one you will ever be called upon to make." It implored, "You must make your own decision and for your own safety." In an apparent move to insulate prisoners from the influence and intimidation of the trusties, the UNC warned:

> It is essential that you do not discuss this matter with others and above all that you let no other person, even your best friend, know what your decision will be prior to the time you are asked for it by the interviewer.

"Your decision in this matter will be considered final" and "irrevocable," the UNC emphasized. It guaranteed that "prisoners of war who are not violently opposed to repatriation" would be returned at the time of prisoner exchange. Prisoners "who refuse to go back to their own people," the UNC warned, could expect "no guarantee whatever as to the[ir] ultimate fate." It continued, "You must consider the effect of your decision on your family" and that "you may well never see your family again." If these warnings were not enough to deter resistance to repatriation, the UNC ominously concluded:

> If your final decision is that you are violently opposed to repatriation, you may undoubtedly be held in custody here on Koje-do for many long months. However, the UNC cannot house and feed you forever. The United Nations Command can make no promises regarding your future. In particular, the UNC cannot and will not guarantee to send you to any certain place. This is a matter which you should consider most carefully.[11]

That "certain place" was an unmistakable reference to Taiwan. Contrary to anti-Communist trusties' claims, the UNC now officially told prisoners there was no guarantee that they could go to Taiwan. Further dampening their hopes, the UNC removed all Taiwanese interpreters and instructors from the camps by early April, as Joy had recommended in late January and the Communists had long insisted.[12] Knowing that it had overpromised to the enemy, the UNC was desperate to deliver as many repatriates as possible.

It appeared both the Communists and the UNC were working together to achieve the magic "round number" of 116,000, which held the key to concluding the armistice talks. Overestimating the Americans' control over and knowledge of the prisoners, Peng Dehuai postponed his trip to Beijing to remove a tumor, because in case an armistice was reached in April, he needed to accompany Kim Il-sung to Kaesong to sign the agreement.[13] Similarly, in Washington, Acheson was so optimistic that he made a "wild guess" on April 3 that a settlement would be reached in a month or so.[14]

Such hopeful scenarios would have come to pass if not for the Chinese anti-Communist prisoners who dominated Compounds 72 and 86.

Compound 86, April 7–8

On the ground things were not so simple. On April 6, the camp authorities summoned representatives from the four Chinese compounds—70, 71, 72, and 86—to a meeting at Compound 72, announcing that the screening would take place within the next two to three days.[15] When anti-Communist representatives learned that CIE instructors recruited from Taiwan would not conduct the screening interviews, they protested, but to no avail.[16] When loudspeakers rumbled the Kim-Peng declaration the next day, anti-Communist prisoners in Compounds 72 and 86 had been prepared. Once the broadcast began, anti-Communist leader Tao Shanpeng immediately "knew what it was all about," even though he "could not hear it clearly." Pro-Communist

Lin Mocong believed that the trusties had got wind of the broadcast in advance, so that they ordered all prisoners to stay in their tents and "sing one song after another all day long," drowning out the loudspeaker. "We didn't hear the broadcast at all," Lin recalled. Neither did Xie Zhiqi of Compound 86 nor Li Dezhi of Compound 72. However, some prisoners, such as Jiang Ruipu in Compound 72, quickly registered the broadcast's main point despite the interruptions and noise.[17]

Even though he did not hear the broadcast, Lin received a secret letter passed along by an old friend, who had become an anti-Communist trusty but nevertheless remained sympathetic, and had learned of the imminent screening. Lin immediately proceeded to contact members of his underground "repatriation small group" composed mostly of young students. As Compound 86 was not as tightly controlled as 72, Lin was able to roam around different tents to call out his friends to go to the latrine together, where he divulged information. This time, however, he was tagged and then seized. After a round of random beating, the PGs lashed him with thick wooden clubs wrapped in sheet metal for several minutes, until he bled and passed out. He was dragged to the 2nd Battalion HQ and was kicked and punched again. His friend, who passed the message, stoically watched on. "Beat him to death, this little Commie bastard!" shouted the chief clerk, who actually did not join the beating. Remembering a fellow resister's words that "the pain only lasts the first two minutes," Lin gritted his teeth and toughed it out. He did not betray his friend as the source of the information.[18]

Lin was one of the few prisoners who had so far managed to resist tattooing. Tao Shanpeng, deputy leader of Compound 86's 3rd Battalion and also the discipline committee chair of the Anti-Communist Resist Russia Alliance responsible for the tattoo campaign in the entire compound, recalled that more than 80 percent of the prisoners had been tattooed by April. As for resisters, "I didn't force it on them," he recalled.[19] His claim was perhaps partially true for the period before April, given Compound 86's less repressive reputation in contrast to 72's. But it was not the case on the night of April 7–8.

Li Jintu, having been physically punished numerous times but still refused to be tattooed, again stood firm on April 7. After being hit by more than thirty blows of the heavy club, he spat blood and blacked out. Presumed to be dying, he was covered with a straw matt.[20] While some prisoners stood their ground and refused tattooing, many others were beaten and forcibly tattooed. Hours after he was pinned down and tattooed, Chen Ronggui asked his friend to slice off his tattooed flesh in secret.[21]

Shortly after midnight, the body of prisoner Zuo Wengang "was found hanging from a rafter in the bathhouse" in Compound 86. Nine hours later, Qi Zhongtang's body "was found hanging in an empty tent," whose interior was festooned with flags of the Allied nations, with a banner bearing the characters *ziyou* (freedom) hanging above his corpse. In a nearly identical fashion, both had died from "suffocation by strangulation." In separate UNC investigations, witnesses provided nearly identical accounts: the deceased had expressed a fear of being returned to "the Communist party zone." When asked "Do you think he hung himself?," the answer was uniformly "Yes." Both investigations concluded that there was "no evidence of foul play," and that each man had "commit[ted] the crime of suicide by taking his own life by hanging himself."[22] Communist prisoners, however, claimed that Zuo, Qi, and at least two other prisoners were murdered in Compound 86 on the night of April 7–8.[23]

Tao Shanpeng, when interviewed, admitted to beating only. He recalled a confrontation where he told his men: "If you're true anti-Communists, do something to these commies flaunting their determination to return to Communist China!" His men dragged the pro-repatriates out and beat them indiscriminately (*luanda*). Tao had warned his men not to beat prisoners in the open, lest the Americans intervene. But the mayhem became so out of control that the US sergeant, accompanied by the compound leader Ying Xiangyun, rushed in. Ying upbraided Tao: "Why are you troublemakers beating people?" Tao replied: "Did you hear me giving them the order? How do I know what they're are doing out there?"[24]

After daybreak, as UNC personnel entered the compound, the beating stopped. The screening began around eight in the morning. As chief clerk Guo Naijian recalled, a uniformed ethnic Chinese interviewer asked compound leader Ying, "Are you ready?" Ying replied, "Yes. No more than a hundred men will get out"—that is, choose to return to China. Guo's duty was to hand POW tags to prisoners, who walked individually into one of the several interview tents newly erected in the compound plaza.[25]

The screening per se was designed to encourage repatriation, "making the maximum number available for return to Communist control, reduced by those who present reasonable evidence that they would forcibly oppose return to Communist control," Ridgway reported.[26] As Taiwan personnel had been removed, the UNC selected about twenty Chinese-speaking Americans, mostly "missionary brats," to conduct the interview. Captain Harold Whallon, the son of Presbyterian missionaries in North China, where he was born, raised, and educated, was transferred from GHQ G-2's China section in Tokyo for the task. He recalled, prisoners entered the interview booth one by one, and "the others would be out of earshot a good fifty feet away."[27]

The interviewers asked prisoners seven questions in Chinese:

1. Will you voluntarily be repatriated to Communist China?
2. Will you forcibly resist repatriation?
3. Have you carefully considered the impact of such actions on your family?
4. Do you realize that you may remain here at Koje-do long after those electing repatriation have returned home?

5. Do you realize that the United Nations cannot promise that you will be sent to any certain place?
6. Are you still determined that you would violently resist repatriation?
7. What would you do if you were repatriated in spite of this decision?

These questions were asked one at a time, and the interviewer waited for a reply before asking the next question. If at any time a prisoner expressed a decision to accept repatriation the questioning ceased and he was taken to a separate area. If at any time the POW mentioned "suicide, fight to death, escape, braving death or similar information," he was segregated with those who would resist repatriation.[28] Prisoners' accounts largely confirm Ridgway's report.

It was sunny on April 8, recalled Xie Zhiqi of the "crippled company" of the 1st Battalion, the first unit to be screened. And Xie was the first interviewee. Having noticed a row of UNC semitrailer trucks parked outside the compound entrance, Xie knew the screening was for real. He moved quickly on crutches, and entered the first booth, where four Americans sat and four ethnic Chinese interviewers stood behind four desks. Xie eagerly announced at the first desk: "I want to return to China!"

FIGURE 10.1. POWs are interviewed regarding their repatriation choices. Koje Island, April–May, 1952. US National Archives.

The interpreter translated to the American, who made a mark on the POW tag and handed it back to Xie. Xie eagerly moved toward the main gate. The MP checked his tag and directed him into the area between the compound's double layers of fences. While Xie was wondering why he wasn't directed to the trucks, anti-Communist leader Wang Futian shouted, "Help that crippled comrade! He is going to Taiwan!" Realizing that he had made a mistake by saying "China" instead of "Communist China," Xie rushed toward his old unit for help. His friends pulled the inner fence up, allowing him to crawl underneath and reenter the compound. As he sprang back toward the interview booth, Xie shouted to fellow prisoners: "Remember, say 'Communist China'!" He told the interviewer, "I want to return to Communist Mainland China!" With a new mark on his tag, he vaulted out of the compound. Once he got on the truck, he found more than forty fellow prisoners, including some members of the Anti-Communist Alliance. The trusties were furious with these crippled defectors; they threw rocks at the open-top trucks. As the rocks rained down, the newly liberated prisoners had nowhere to hide. In defiance, Xie, a former propaganda officer, led the group singing "Go, Go with Mao Zedong" and "Unity Is Power."[29]

Once Fang Xiangqian walked out of the compound, he vented his pent-up anger by pointing his finger at the PGs: "You running dogs and traitors!" Rocks flew; Fang and others were hit on the head and bloodied.[30] As the open-top trucks—each holding a hundred prisoners—were so crowded, when "the barrage of stones" fell, the prisoners "could not stoop for cover," CIE head instructor John Benben recalled. Later fewer men were loaded and the trucks were covered with tarpaulins.[31]

Captain Whallon recalled that his first interviewee was a boy on crutches who "had been beaten up the night before, and now wanted protection from his anti-Communist buddies." The distance from the interview tent to the compound gate was about 100 feet, but "sometimes there was a little fracas" between anti-Communist POWs and the MPs who were trying to get a repatriate out unscathed. The US personnel went into the compound unarmed, for fear the anti-Communists would take the arms and "use them on the Communists." Whallon admitted, "Sometimes it was a little heartbreaking to have to punch a good Nationalist to protect a Communist but we played it straight that way."[32]

Luo Jiecao, another crippled prisoner, limped into an interview booth. "Where do you want to go?" asked an ROK interviewer in perfect Chinese. "The mainland," Luo said, and then added, "the Communist mainland." The interviewer marked "Go" on his tag and said, "Don't show it to anyone except the Americans at the gate." Luo ignored the trusties trying to corral him into the area between double fences—for non-repatriates—and walked straight out of the gate.[33]

As the first two battalions with more than two thousand prisoners had finished their screening, hundreds of prisoners had walked out of the compound and were whisked away. Now there was little doubt that the screening was real. The remaining prisoners became agitated. Chief Clerk Guo heard that fighting had erupted in some tents and someone had been killed—in fact, Qi Zhongtang was found dead at 10:30 a.m. Guo handed all tags to the 3rd Battalion leader and pretended to go to the latrine. He walked straight into an interview booth and declared his wish to return. He briskly moved past anti-Communist trusties near the main gate, who were at first stunned by their chief clerk's defection and then tried to seize his cap with the Nationalist emblem. Guo tossed it away, pulled out a nondescript cap from in his pocket, put it on, and marched out.[34] Tao Shanpeng wasn't surprised by this Whampoa cadet's decision. "Because he probably wasn't even tattooed, I knew he wasn't steadfast," Tao recalled. "He respected me, and I respected him," Tao reckoned, "but we weren't the same type."[35]

When he was screened, Tao found his overseas Chinese interviewer very "fair, strict, and straightforward." After Tao declared that "I won't return [to China], absolutely not," the interviewer warned, "The UN may not provide you with food or clothing." Tao replied, "I don't need them. I can strip off my clothes and return them to the UN right now!" When former Whampoa cadet Wang Houci refused repatriation, the Japanese-looking interviewer smacked the table and threatened, "Why don't you go back? The UN won't feed you if you don't!" Taken aback by the performance, Wang nevertheless stuck to his position. Tao and Wang were two of the more than 7,000 POWs in Compound 86 who rejected repatriation.[36]

By contrast, 1,128 of the roughly 8,600 prisoners in the compound, including some who had declared themselves anti-Communist, had been quietly waiting for this opportunity and took it. Li Mingquan, who had voluntarily tattooed himself in March, told his leader on April 7, "Let's see who gets to Taiwan first!" He chose China the next day.[37] The sight of hundreds of fellow prisoners, including the chief clerk, being escorted out of the compound emboldened more prisoners to express their wish to return home than the trusties had anticipated. The failure of Compound 86's trusties to control prisoners' choices probably gave their counterparts in Compound 72 a heightened sense of threat and vulnerability. Compound 72, already under more repressive and violent control, descended into a living hell on the night of April 8–9.[38]

"Hell" in Compound 72, April 8–9

While Guo Naijian successfully left Compound 86, his friend and fellow Whampoa cadet Yang Wenhua was languishing in a special tent in Compound 72. Yang, the former deputy commander of Compound 86, had been stripped of his power and transferred to the work detail in Compound 70, where he plotted with several Communists to seize power from the anti-Communists but was arrested by the prison authorities.[39] In a stark display of the practice of "using the Chinese [anti-Communists] to control the Chinese [Communists]," the authorities immediately transferred Yang and five other alleged Communist ringleaders, including the nineteen-year-old Jiang Ruipu, to the dreaded Compound 72 on March 15. From then until April 8, the six men were detained in a PG tent and tortured daily by Li Da'an and his gang. In addition to beating them with clubs, Li whipped their heads with water-soaked tent ropes, leaving no skull fractures, only bruises and concussions. Forbidden to talk to each other or sleep on the ground, they were forced to huddle in the narrow ditch-like walking path in the middle of the tent, piled on each other, Jiang recalled. Among the six "Communist diehards," only three, Han Zijian, Li Quanyou, and Zhang Chengyuan, were party members; Yang Wenhua was a Youth League member; Jiang Ruipu and Xu Gongdu were neither. If one relented and agreed to be tattooed and go to Taiwan, his torment could end immediately, but none gave in.[40]

When the prison authorities began broadcasting the coming screening, the 254 pro-Communist prisoners in Compound 71, separated by a narrow road from Compound 72, started shouting slogans, singing songs, and calling out to prisoners in Compound 72 to choose repatriation. To drown out the Communists and the UNC announcement, anti-Communist trusties launched a shouting match: they ordered prisoners to stay in their tents and sing nonstop. When "diehard" Jiang Ruipu went to the latrine, his comrades in Compound 71 spotted him and shouted his name, urging him to be strong. Still followed by PGs, Jiang could not respond. "Damn it!" he cursed to himself. "It's easy for you guys to sing. But I'm getting tortured everyday." On the eve of the screening, PGs tightly patrolled the compounds; trusties launched another drive to get POWs to pledge allegiance to Taiwan and renounce Communism. The six diehards sensed that a life or death moment was imminent.[41]

After dark on April 8, the more than 7,000 prisoners in Compound 72 assembled for small-unit meetings. In the officers' 4th Battalion, Cai Pingsheng's company leader announced, "Tomorrow the UNC will carry out a screening. If you want to return to the mainland, step out now. Tomorrow there'll be no chance." While most Communist veterans and officers remained still, Youth League member Cai sprang up without a second thought. He was dragged away by two club-wielding PGs to a special enclosure, where he and forty-seven other men were tortured and interrogated.[42]

In the 3rd Battalion, Zhao Yingkui was not fooled by his leader, since he had learned his lesson in a similar hoax earlier. In fact, most of the fifty prisoners in his 22nd Company, a manual labor unit composed of Communist officers, had been cowed. Only five or six men raised their hands to express their wish to return. They were not immediately punished, but were dragged out from their tents around midnight and beaten outside with baseball bats and tent poles. An officer's leg was broken. Even though he did not raise his hand, Zhao was picked up as a potential "waverer" and slapped in the face twice.[43] Zhang Yifu heard the sound of the beating and howling after midnight, but he "dared not go out to take a look." If he had, he would have become a suspect and been beaten himself.[44]

Two interpreters for the UNC armistice delegation by the names of Wu and May—Wu was most likely Kenneth Wu—were dispatched to Koje as observers. They later told Admiral Joy that on the eve of the screening, anti-Communist leaders in Compound 72 "asked those who wished to return to step forward. Those doing so were either beaten black and blue or killed."[45] Their account, however, only captured the very beginning of the harrowing night.

While Cai Pingsheng was being tortured, Fu Tietao, his former classmate in the PLA Attached School and now a battalion clerk, approached him: "Why are you so stubborn? Once you agree to go to Taiwan, your pain will end immediately." Cai retorted, "Each man has his own will. My parents are in China; my home is in China." Two PGs ripped off Cai's shirt and pressed him down to the ground. Fu used a razor to slice a large piece of skin off Cai's left forearm bearing the English word "Anti-Red," which had been forcibly tattooed in January. Then Fu sprinkled salt as an "antiseptic" onto the open wound. Dripping in blood, the removed skin was tossed into a steel bowl, which was filled with the skin of other victims, and made the rounds in tents throughout Compound 72.[46]

Cai was one of the forty-eight so-called "turncoats," who had pledged to go to Taiwan and been tattooed but openly professed their will to return to China on the eve of the screening. According to a Nationalist account, their reversal angered the "true anti-Communists," who in revenge "peeled off the traitors' tattooed skin until a bowl was filled."[47] The Communist tallies, however, were much graver: while more than a thousand prisoners were "beaten up" and 560 were "seriously wounded," more than 250 men "had pieces of flesh cut off."[48] Doctor Meng Ming, head of the compound dispensary and an anti-Communist, recalled that "many prisoners had some skin sliced off. Some of them came to the dispensary with pieces of their skin. I stitched them back. Some came without; I bandaged them up and gave them a penicillin shot." He reflected, "It was extremely cruel."[49]

"Devil incarnate" Li Da'an played a central role in the violence. A Nationalist hagiographic account dramatizes Li's act: "Li pulled out his knife, sliced off tattooed characters from the arms of these traitors, piece by piece." In front of fellow prisoners, "as if nothing had happened, he swallowed these bloody slices of skin."[50] Li was not the only cannibal. Tan Xingdong, the PLA assistant battalion commander turned defector and anti-Communist leader, mixed the slices of skin with two cans of beef stew to concoct a large bowl of soup that he shared with other trusties. "Nothing less could have demonstrated his hatred of the Communists," it was reported.[51]

One of the forty-eight "turncoats" was Lin Xuebu, a Sichuan University English major, Communist Youth League member, and one of only twelve students in the university to volunteer for the CPV in 1950. As the main interpreter at the 180th Division HQ, Lin had interrogated several American prisoners in late May 1951.[52] On Koje, Lin initially interpreted at Compound 72's HQ, where he taught trusties English and developed a phrase book for them. However, the well-educated Lin soon became openly critical of the heavy-handed control by compound leaders, especially Li Da'an. Because of Lin's closeness with the Americans, leaders suspected him of reporting on their activities. He was demoted to a labor platoon for enlisted men.[53]

Communist prisoners claimed that Lin joined their underground network after his demotion in early 1952. Forcibly tattooed by trusties, Lin nevertheless remained defiant. On April 8, he became one of the first victims of Li Da'an's wrath. Lin's postmortem indicates "avulsion of the skin over the lateral surface of the left arm for an area measuring 12 × 7 cm." Before midnight, Lin, with his arm still bleeding, was paraded onto the stage in the CIE hall, which had become a torture chamber for Communist diehards, turncoats, and waverers. Brandishing a knife, Li gave Lin a final chance to recant. "I live as a Chinese man; I will die as a Chinese ghost," rasped Lin. As Li's knife drew closer, Lin cried out: "Long live the Chinese Communist Party! Long live Chairman Mao!"[54]

Before Lin could shout more slogans, Li stabbed him in the chest. Li cut out Lin's heart and displayed it to the horrified crowd, a witness in the crowd recalled.[55] The autopsy conducted by the US 64th Field Hospital revealed "two perforating wounds of the left thorax and left abdomen" that resulted in massive hemorrhage and ultimately Lin's death; there was no mention if Lin's heart was intact. Additional injuries, including "ecchymoses of both eyes" and "bleeding from both nares," suggested severe beatings.[56]

When Yang Shuzhi, the former Nationalist paratrooper captain and now the 1st Battalion leader, arrived at the CIE hall, Lin Xuebu was already dead, lying on the ground. Lin had served as Yang's interpreter, and the two men had good rapport, despite Lin's not-so-subtle pro-Communist tendencies. In one incident, Lin announced to the trusties that the US sergeant prohibited all political slogans on compound walls. Yang asked which sergeant; Lin muttered a reply. Yang had tried to persuade Lin to go to Taiwan, but Lin said that he wanted to go home to join his college sweetheart. On this fateful night, once he heard about Lin's detention and torture, Yang rushed to save him, but it was too late.[57]

After killing Lin, Li Da'an's PGs continued to thrash the other twenty to thirty prisoners, their arms tied behind them. Yang saw a young man shouting, "Long live Chairman Mao!" Li and his thugs hit him with baseball bats until his brain splattered out. Perhaps on Yang's heels, "waverer" Zhao Yingkui was dragged into the CIE hall to watch the spectacle. He also heard the scream "Long live the Communist Party! Long live Chairman Mao!" before entering the hall. Once inside, he saw two corpses on the ground. The second victim, Zhao later heard, was a CPV scout, who was most probably Zhang Zhenlong, who deserted during a mission on September 1, 1951, and became the first prisoner from the 139th Division, 47th Army. Little is known about him. Zhang's autopsy indicates that he died of a "severe beating."[58]

As prisoners watched in horror and some in tears, Compound 72's commander Wang Shunqing pointed at the dead and warned the survivors: "If you want to return to China, if you refuse tattooing, this is the consequence!" He added, "We killed them. And we can kill you. So what?" Zhao Yingkui was taken back to his company, where an additional tattoo was forced on him—this time, a Nationalist flag on his forearm. When Zhao demurred about the dirty ink and needles, the trusties said, "Why worry? Everybody is getting tattooed, not just you!" The infected wound later festered and left Zhao with permanent scars.[59]

While the trusties forced additional tattoos onto those suspected of wavering, they removed the tattooed skins of "turncoats," whose torment was far from over. Their arms still bleeding, Cai and other "turncoats" were sent to the special tent where Jiang Ruipu and five other "diehards" had been held. The six men had been stripped naked and lay in the ditch pathway. Having been tortured daily by Li Da'an over the preceding twenty-two days, they were largely neglected on the night of April 8–9, as Li was busy beating people all over the compound. Several club-toting PGs watched over the six men. Anyone who moved without permission received a beating. "In the stuffy tent dimly lit by two gas lamps," Jiang recalled, "naked, bruised bodies piled on each other in the ditch, and guards towered above us, menacingly wielding clubs. It was a scene from hell."[60]

Prisoners were dragged in and out of the tent, beaten in the open space outside lit by camp perimeter lights. Around 3 or 4 a.m., Li Da'an struck Cai Pingsheng with a baseball bat until Cai blacked out. Cai was awakened by Fu, who said: "Can you hear it? We're digging a grave for you. This is your last chance. If you recant, you'll be safe." At a point so close to death, Cai's mind went blank. He uttered, "Say no more." Fu stormed away with a roar: "You just wait and die!"[61]

Finally, Li Da'an came for the six diehards around 6:00 a.m. After a round of random beatings in the tent, Yang Wenhua was singled out and taken outside. For ten minutes or so, Jiang Ruipu heard the heavy thuds of clubs striking Yang. The victim's gasping groans soon weakened to whimpers, until he gave out. Li Da'an re-entered the tent, brandishing a bloody chunk of flesh, and said, "Yang has already gone back to China!" Some prisoners claimed that it was Yang's heart, but Jiang couldn't see it clearly as it was too dark, it happened too fast, and he was too traumatized. The remaining five diehards thought they were the next to be killed. Suddenly, the heavyset former company leader Li Kaiquan shouted: "You can't beat people!" Taken aback, the overwrought PGs blew whistles. As a large number of PGs ran toward the tent, the commotion alarmed the US guards. Armed troops entered Compound 72 and ordered all prisoners to stay put in their tents. Daybreak arrived and with it the atrocity finally came to an end.[62]

Yang's postmortem shows that his skull was "fractured being separated at all the sutures," and there was "a depressed fracture" of the left jaw and "many recent contusions of the face and scalp." However, "the thoracic and abdominal viscera are grossly normal," suggesting that his heart was intact.[63] While some prisoners claimed that Li Da'an killed Yang, the main perpetrator was Lu Lu, Yang's Whampoa classmate and one-time close friend. Both the Communists and anti-Communists remembered Lu's delicate and fine look (*qingxiu*) and intellectual-like manner.[64] In a violent frenzy, Lu murdered Yang.

On the morning of April 9, when the prisoners in Compound 72 went for breakfast, they saw three naked corpses lying in the trash pile near the kitchen. One prisoner recalled, "Lin Xuebu's mouth was stuffed with dirt; his nostrils, arms, and belly were covered in blood. Black bruises were all over his thighs."[65] US guards arrived and reported that Lin's neck "bore rope burns" and his upper left arm "had been peeled of skin"; "a short length of rope was also found around the neck" of Zhang Zhenlong, whose face "appeared very blue"; Cao Lixing's "unclothed body" had "bruises about

FIGURE 10.2. Mutilated bodies of Lin Xuebu, Zhang Zhenlong, and Cao Lixing lie in a garbage dump in Compound 72, as fellow prisoners walk by before the screening on the morning of April 9, 1952. US National Archives.

the face, ears and thighs." When prisoner Wu Zengwen went to the latrine, he saw Yang Wenhua's body lying next to a concrete trough.[66]

Yang, Lin, Zhang, and Cao were four of the five officially reported deaths in Compound 72 on the eve of the screening.[67] The 1st Battalion leader Yang Shuzhi, however, heard that ten or eleven men had been killed.[68] Perhaps no one knew the exact number of deaths across the large compound, but it was apparent to all prisoners that during the reign of terror throughout the night the prison authorities did nothing to curtail the widespread violence. While UNC guards in watchtowers or outside the barbwire could hear victims howling, they did not intervene until daybreak.

The lawless mayhem was not unique to Compound 72 or 86. The CIE's chief instructor John Benben described the horrific scene on Koje:

> Throughout the processing, fights took place during the night, screams charged with torture broke above the night's din, and injured crawled to the gate on all fours, many to drop exhausted before reaching it. Others broke suddenly from the barracks and the darkened spaces between barracks to run for the gate or to scramble up the high barbed-wire fence. Some gained their objectives; others were pulled down dragged away [by trusties].[69]

BASIC PERSONNEL RECORD
(Prisoner of War - Enemy Alien)

1. ARM OR SERVICE: Signal
LAST NAME - FIRST NAME - MIDDLE INITIAL: YANG TIEN HUA
3. RANK: Pvt
4. INTERNMENT SVC NO.: 134K 704886
HOSTILE SERIAL NO.: Unk
6. PLACE OF BIRTH: San Seong Yang Hyen San Kai Si
7. DATE OF BIRTH (Day, Month, Year): 4 Aug 1933
FATHER'S NAME: Yang Jin Tai
9. MOTHER'S MAIDEN NAME: Yang Lee Sheu
10. POWER SERVED: NK
NAME AND ADDRESS OF PERSON TO BE NOTIFIED OF CAPTURE OR INTERNMENT: Yang Lee Sheu (M) Same as 6
ADDRESS TO WHICH MAIL MAY INITIALLY BE SENT INTERNEE OR PW: UN PW Camp 1 APO 59
PW'S HOSTILE UNIT: 60 Corps 180 Div 538 Regt
14. PLACE OF CAPTURE: North of Han River
15. DATE OF CAPTURE: 27 May '51
PW'S PERMANENT HOME ADDRESS: Same as 6
17. NATIONALITY: Chinese
PHYSICAL DESCRIPTION
a. HEIGHT: 5-8
b. WEIGHT: 118
c. EYES: Brown
d. HAIR: Black
e. SKIN: Brown
f. SEX: Male
g. RELIGION: None
h. PHYSICAL CONDITION: Good
i. DISTINGUISHING MARKS, SCARS, ETC.: None

3NK704886 2 JUNE 51
K704886

FIGURE 10.3. POW record card of Yang Wenhua, who was killed before dawn on April 9, 1952. US National Archives.

This unchecked violence traumatized many prisoners, leading them to believe that the UNC was behind all the violence and the screening was only a ruse to round up all the pro-Communists and execute them, as the trusties had asserted. In a state of heightened horror and apprehension, many prisoners yearning to return home dared not choose repatriation.

Screening in Compound 72, April 9

It was a sleepless night for many in Compound 72. So, too, it was for the 254 pro-Communist prisoners in Compound 71 across the road. They redoubled their shouting and singing to urge prisoners in Compound 72 to choose repatriation. Since the 4th Battalion was close to Compound 71, officer prisoners, including diehard Jiang Ruipu, heard their comrades' messages clearly. But Zhao Yingkui, located in the more distant 3rd Battalion, did not.[70]

On the morning of April 9, more than thirty unarmed UNC interviewers and troops entered Compound 72, while more than a hundred armed soldiers were posted around the perimeter. Like the setup in Compound 86 one day earlier, a number of tents were erected in the main square. Only one battalion at a time, numbering more than a thousand, was assembled in the plaza, and prisoners went into the interview booths individually. Other battalions were ordered to remain in their tents.[71]

Although the poll questions were designed to encourage repatriation and no Nationalist personnel participated in the polling, UNC interpreters Wu and May observed that at the polls "the majority of the POWs were too terrified to frankly express their real choice. All they could say in answer to the questions was 'Taiwan' repeated over and over again." They concluded that this was a clear indication of "the terrifying dominance of their pro-Nationalist leaders."[72] Out of the more than 7,000 prisoners, only some 700 chose repatriation.

Zhao Yingkui was greeted by a uniformed ROK interviewer who spoke Chinese with a Manchurian accent. "If the screening is real, the interviewer should come from China," Zhao reckoned. Fearing that it was another ruse just like the one hours earlier, Zhao said he wanted to go to Taiwan. He explained, "I've been tattooed so much, I'm afraid of returning to China." Zhao was sent back to Compound 72.[73]

In contrast, Li Dezhi, also in the 3rd Battalion, took a chance and became the thirty-seventh prisoner in Compound 72 to choose repatriation. Li, a former telephone lineman, had followed the maxim that "a wise man knows better than to fight when the odds are against him." He had kept his mouth shut and acquiesced to tattooing, and as a result avoided torture.[74]

When the 4th Battalion was finally screened late in the afternoon, Cai Pingsheng practically crawled into the tent, his left arm swollen nearly twice as large as his right. A Chinese American interviewer asked, "They beat you?" Cai replied, "Yes. I want to return to the mainland." The officer wrote down "Go" on his POW tag, and called in four GIs. Cai was carried out of the compound gate and loaded onto a truck. Anti-Communist prisoners behind the barbwire erupted into cursing and started throwing rocks at Cai. The US soldiers had to shout back at the prisoners to stop the attack.[75]

Unlike the inexperienced, idealistic young student recruit Cai, most Communists in Compound 72 had resigned themselves to their fate and offered little resistance up to this point. Under pressure, Wu Zengwen, a machine gun platoon leader of the 180th Division, had twice signed the petition to go to Taiwan. On April 6, he renounced his party membership. On the night of April 8, however, he heard the shouting from Compound 71 across the road, "Don't be fooled by the trusties. Choose to return to China tomorrow!" Strictly forbidden to talk to each other, Wu secretly wrote the character *hui* (return) on the leg of Liu Yi, the Korean interpreter with whom he shared the same blanket and mat like a pair of flipped spoons head to foot. Without saying a word, Liu replied in kind.

When Wu entered the interview booth, his heart was pounding. He declared, "I want to return to the mainland," and then added, "to the Chinese Communists." After the interviewer marked his tag, a tall black GI grabbed Wu by the collar and took him away. "I was so relieved," Wu recalled. "The GI was like my guardian god (*baohushen*). I knew I wasn't going to die." The distance between the interview booth and the main gate was only about 150 feet, but club- and knife-wielding PGs threatened to attack people choosing to return. Protected by the Americans, Wu boarded a truck covered with a newly installed canvas that shielding prisoners from rocks thrown by trusties.[76]

Wu's friend Wang Dengyun, a 180th Division propaganda officer, believed he was one of the last prisoners in Compound 72 to be screened. A few days earlier, he had decided to pledge allegiance to Taiwan after witnessing the bloody excision of tattoos. He asked Huang Shaorong, a former subordinate and now an anti-Communist trusty, to vouch for him. He became an orderly in the 4th Battalion HQ, where he was safe but had to endure the abuse of washing the battalion leader's clothes, including his underwear. On the screening day, taking advantage of his job as an orderly, Wang managed to move about and discreetly observe the screening throughout the day. He recalled that order was well maintained during the screening of the 1st Battalion, but deteriorated soon as more prisoners chose repatriation and PGs began grabbing them. Wang and Huang were the last prisoners to be interviewed, and they went into two booths simultaneously. "I am going to the People's Republic of China," Wang declared. After receiving his marked tag, Wang hesitated to leave the interview booth, until two black GIs took him by the arms. Trusties shouted, cursed, and threw rocks at him. When he boarded the truck, other repatriates were surprised: "We thought you were going to Taiwan."[77]

When all other prisoners had been screened, Jiang Ruipu and the four other diehards were still waiting in the plaza. Their names were never called because their POW tags were missing. As it was getting dark, the five men became agitated, knowing that they could not survive another night in Compound 72. They rushed into the interview booth and shouted in simple English, "How about me?" The interviewers pulled out several blank sheets of paper and began the interview. Jiang said, "I want to return to my homeland (*zuguo*)." The interviewer asked, "The mainland or Taiwan?" Jiang said the mainland. Then the interviewer wrote "Go" on the paper. After the five diehards were escorted by GIs out of the compound and onto the truck, their first thought was, "We came out alive, finally." The anti-Communists cursed behind barbwire, "Don't get excited too early! Wait until you return to the mainland. You will suffer!"[78]

Gao Jie, the former chief interpreter of Compound 86 who had left on the eve of the clash on October 9, 1951, for the 64th Field Hospital, was screened in the hospital. When he declared he wanted to return, the interviewer—none other than Captain Joseph Brooks—cautioned, "Have you considered the consequences? How can you prove to the Communists that you didn't collude (*goujie*) with the Americans, given your interpreter duties?" Gao said, "I didn't collude with you Americans, and I have nothing to prove." Brooks warned, "If you return, the Communists will chop your head off (*kantou*)!" Gao replied, "If that happens, so be it. It's none of your business." Brooks relented, "If you insist, I'll let you go."[79]

Also on April 9, all 254 prisoners in Compound 71 chose repatriation. On April 10, in Compound 70, where the anti-Communists did not have total control, 1,217 out of some 1,400 men chose repatriation, after its influential PG squad leader Gao Pan suddenly announced his own wish to return home.[80] After the first four days of screening, as of April 12, 1952, 14,126, or roughly 80.3 percent of the 17,593 Chinese prisoners screened to that point, declared they would forcibly resist repatriation to China.[81]

From April 16 and on, 1,306, or 71.3 percent, of the 1,832 Chinese prisoners in the Communist-dominated hospital compound in Pusan, including Wu Chunsheng and Guo Zhaolin, chose repatriation.[82] In Pusan's Compound 10, 288 out of 296 prisoners (97 percent) chose to return.[83] Clearly, the outcome of the screening in each compound was largely predetermined by the dominant faction. Most of the anti-repatriates were from Compounds 72 and 86, which had a combined population of roughly 16,000.

The number of anti-repatriates surpassed the earlier Nationalist estimate that 8,000 to 10,000 tattooed prisoners would reject repatriation. Ambassador Wang Dongyuan attributed this outcome to the "well-selected" Nationalist interpreters, who had laid the foundation for a favorable screening result despite their last-minute removal by the UNC. He contrasted the outcome to the Korean case. Despite the presence of ROK interpreters, only half of the North Koreans screened up to that point rejected repatriation.[84]

TABLE 10.1. *Screening results in major Chinese POW compounds, April 1952*

COMPOUND	CONTROL	NO. OF POWS	REPATS		ANTI-REPATS	
			Number	Percent	Number	Percent
72	Anti-Com	7,000~	700~	10%	6,300~	90%
86	Anti-Com	8,600~	1,128~	13%	7,472~	87%
70	Neutral	1,400~	1,217	87%	183~	13%
71	Communist	254	254	100%	0	0%
Pusan Hospital	Communist	1,832	1,306	71%	526	29%
Total		**19,086~**	**4,605~**	**24%**	**14,481~**	**76%**

SOURCES: *FRUS 1952–1954*, 15:144, 163; "Dashiji," 22; FGSL, 1:233–34; He, *Zhongcheng*, 37–39; White, *Captives of Korea*, 188.

NOTE: "~": approximate figures.

To Rescreen or Not

When the screening results first reached Tokyo and Washington, all American generals and civilian officials involved were dumbfounded by the large number of anti-repatriates. Their first reaction was to question the screening procedure. Joy summoned UNC interpreters Wu and May, who had observed the screening on Koje, to Tokyo on April 12. They painted a picture that was "not pretty." They suggested that "the compounds with pro-Nationalist leaders were completely dominated by those leaders, to such an extent that the results of the screening were by no means indicative of the POWs real choice." They believed that "the removal of these leaders, coupled with a period of indoctrination of the POWs, would bring the percentage in those pro-Nationalist dominated compounds of those wishing to return to the enemy up from 15 to 85%"—flipping the screening result. Six weeks of indoctrination "would be required to wean them over to a point where they would feel free of the terror that presently gripped them," they opined.[85]

Alarmed by their reports, Joy brought Wu and May to see Ridgway the next morning. They convinced Ridgway enough to order the removal of anti-Communist trusties and a rescreening of anti-repatriates when they were to be relocated from Koje to the mainland or Cheju Island. Eighth Army commander Van Fleet, however, argued that "it was futile to attempt a rescreening at this time chiefly because of the bloodshed that would ensue." Van Fleet and Dodd also correctly pointed out the impracticality of a rescreening: it was impossible to remove anti-Communist leaders because these people could not be identified and the nominal leaders were not necessarily the real ones.[86]

In Washington, JCS and State officials found the screening result to be "a very big problem." In a joint meeting on April 14, General Collins wondered "if there is any way to reduce that number." Bradley said he had "thought it would be about a 50–50 split." Bohlen, who had recommended the removal of "Formosan Chinese" earlier, wondered out aloud if that was done. Before the meeting, he had told Acheson that "we seem to have won an important skirmish in the battle for men's minds and now we are alarmed at the victory we have won." The situation, however, was much more dire. Nitze feared that the United States could be "caught in a trap." In reality, it had already been trapped.[87]

A rescreening was quickly ruled out for three reasons. First, with the UNC lacking the necessary manpower to control the prison camps, there was a risk that rescreening might result in ugly resistance and bloodshed. Second, and more critically, if a rescreening were to invalidate the original numbers, it would "throw doubt on the whole process," Bohlen reasoned.[88] A large increase in the number of prisoners choosing repatriation would undoubtedly play into the hands of the Communists, who had repeatedly alleged that the UNC had employed brutal force to dissuade prisoners from choosing repatriation. Lastly, a retreat from the original screening result would certainly invite a domestic onslaught from the Republicans and the China Lobby, the influential pro–Chiang Kai-shek special interest group consisting of politicians, business people, and missionaries.

As a thorough rescreening proved unrealistic, the default solution was a half-measure—a rescreening without removing the trusties. On April 16, Van Fleet submitted his plan for rescreening. Chinese and North Korean anti-repatriates were to "be given one more opportunity to consider their decision prior to departure" from Koje Island. A statement would be read to them:

> You are now to be shipped to a new camp. This is your final opportunity to return to control of auth[orities] representing Chinese Volunteer Army (or NKPA as applicable) at the time POWs are exchanged. If you elect to return you will be moved to a new compound immediately, where you will be protected and housed only with those who make the same decision.[89]

Also on April 16, Chinese anti-repatriates in Compounds 72 and 86 received the order to move to new camps on Cheju Island. Suspicious of the UNC's intent, especially given the UNC's apparent encouragement of prisoners to choose repatriation during the screening, anti-Communist trusties refused to cooperate. Only after Nationalist teachers and Chaplain Woodberry returned to guarantee their safety did the prisoners agree to move.[90] On April 19, more than 13,000 prisoners boarded UNC trucks heading for the pier. The trucks made a surprise stop midway, and prisoners were rescreened.[91]

More than 200 prisoners took this final chance to return home.[92] Quartermaster Wang Guanhu, who had not chosen repatriation during the initial screening as he had renounced his membership in the Communist Party and had been tattooed, chose to return. However, it appeared that not all anti-repatriates were rescreened. Zhao Yingkui recalled no such opportunity was afforded him.[93]

As Van Fleet and Dodd had expected, the rescreening produced a negligible improvement in the number of repatriates. State and JCS officials' default position was to stick with the current screening results and maintain the existing policy, however compromised and mistaken either might have been in the first place. They agreed it was important to keep the screening results "out of the press," lest a leak "create a very serious problem."[94]

"Duped and Led into a Propaganda Trap"

When armistice talks resumed in Panmunjom on April 19, the Chinese Communist negotiators, anxiously awaiting a result near the "round number" of 116,000, were in for a shock. At the staff officers' meeting, Hickman "calmly" informed Chai Chengwen that "7,200 civilian internees, 3,800 ROK prisoners, 53,900 North Koreans, and 5,100 Chinese—a total of 70,000 men—would be available for repatriation." Chai was stunned "speechless, overcome with emotion." When he finally regained his composure, Chai requested a recess "ostensibly to study the figures." The next day, Chai declared that it was "completely impossible for us to consider" these figures and that "you [the UNC] flagrantly repudiated what you said before." Understandably, the Chinese negotiators felt that "they had been duped and led into a propaganda trap." The official US Army historian Walter Hermes concluded that "the screening process which momentarily seemed to be a way to break the deadlock had merely resulted in increasing it."[95] The war was set to continue, until the Communists, more precisely the Chinese, were willing to accept this humiliating propaganda defeat.

Fully aware that the Chinese would not accept the screening result, Washington nonetheless instructed UNC negotiators to introduce a package deal: the UNC would allow the Communists to rebuild their airfields; in exchange, the Communists would drop their insistence on Soviet membership on the Neutral Nations Supervisory Commission that would supervise and enforce the armistice agreement and make concessions on POW repatriation. By bundling three items into one, Washington sought to obfuscate the reality that only one item prevented an armistice: the POWs. Knowing that this trick would not fool the Communists, who were likely to reject it and call for a recess, the JCS argued that it was more advantageous "having [a] recess occur with three items open rather than merely the issue of POW's." It appeared that the main purpose of the ploy was to confuse the American people at home. The package deal was introduced in a secret session on April 28. As expected, the Communists agreed to the first two items but rejected the third—the repatriation of 70,000 POWs.[96] They were not easily fooled.

The Communists demanded a thorough rescreening with no Nationalist personnel present and anti-Communist prisoner leaders segregated. In Taiwan, Chiang Kai-shek sensed a grave crisis. In his mid-April diaries, he wrote almost daily about the urgency of mobilizing world opinion to condemn the "injustice and inhumanity" of a potential American betrayal of prisoners.[97] The China Lobby shifted into high gear. Holding up psychological warfare leaflets on the Senate floor, Senator Knowland asserted the United States had promised asylum to surrendering Communist soldiers. "I hope," he pronounced, "that the Government . . . is not going to consider turning over a single soldier . . . who has surrendered under those guarantees."[98] Although legalistically speaking, these leaflets promising safety and "good treatment" did not amount to a guarantee of asylum, Knowland's moral argument was powerful.

Truman, evidently uninformed of the compromising conditions before and during the screening processes, felt he could not sound a retreat. Too much of America's moral prestige and his own legacy were at stake. The US government had no choice but to stand by the voluntary repatriation principle, and the screening results.

On May 7, Truman made his first and only public statement on the POW question, announcing that the truce talks had reached an impasse.

> There shall not be a forced repatriation of prisoners of war—as the Communists have insisted. To agree to forced repatriation would be unthinkable. It would be repugnant to the fundamental moral and humanitarian principles which underlie our action in Korea. To return these prisoners of war in our hands by force would result in misery and bloodshed to the eternal dishonor of the United States and of the United Nations. We will not buy an armistice by turning over human beings for slaughter or slavery.[99]

This proclamation effectively foreclosed any possibility of a compromise on prisoner repatriation.

Ironically, the screening, which was originally devised to present the Communists with a fait accompli, generated such a hugely lopsided result that it in fact presented Washington with a fait accompli. Mounting public pressure and Truman's own conscience precluded any possibility of rejecting the result of the screening, let alone abandoning the non-forcible repatriation policy. In addition, practically speaking, there was no way the UNC could repatriate the core group of die-hard anti-Communist prisoners without using brutal force on the very men whom the United States had purportedly converted into anti-Communists. Men like Li Da'an, Wang Shunqing, and Wang Zunming, if repatriated to China, would face certain death. They would rather be killed by the Americans than the Communists. Certainly, that was not an outcome Washington could entertain.

After Truman's pronouncement, however, more damaging reports came from Korea. On May 12, State Department official A. Sabin Chase, chief of the Division of Research for the Far East, whom, along with Philip Manhard, had been sent to interview selected Chinese POWs, reported to Acheson. Based on senior linguist, China expert Lt. Aoa Meisling's "own observations and harrowing experiences as active participant" in the prescreening orientation phase, it was evident that pro-Nationalist trusties in Compounds 72 and 86 dominated both the orientation and screening processes "through violent systematic terrorism and physical punishment," including "severe beatings, torture, some killings." Meisling estimated "this factor reduced Chinese POW's choosing repatriation by upward 2000." On May 23, Chase confirmed that "the screening results reflected local factors"—the Nationalists' dominance—rather than a referendum on the popularity or "the strength of the People's Republic of China."[100]

The findings came too late. The president had spoken. The course had been set. There was no turning back. Not surprisingly, State and JCS officials decided to cover up the embarrassing conditions in the prison camps, which Paul Nitze described as "firecrackers under the table," namely two items: "(a) Chinese Nationalist influence prior to the screening of the Chinese POW's. (b) Prisoner-to-prisoner brutality proceeding and during the course of the screening."[101]

Despite US allies' demands, a consensus emerged in Washington against a thorough rescreening that would most likely increase the number of repatriates, thus invalidating the original screening results. On May 28, Bohlen argued that "the lack of confidence in the validity of our screening on the part of our Allies isn't sufficient to justify the necessity for such a rescreening." The ever-recalcitrant Admiral Fechteler declared, "I am against any rescreening by anybody at any time." His solution: "Just break off negotiations and wait for them to agree."[102]

In Panmunjom, UNC chief delegate Joy gave his farewell address on May 20, declaring that "there is nothing more for me to do. There is nothing left to negotiate." Despite his strong private misgivings about the policy of voluntary repatriation, Joy went on to lecture the Communists for the last time: "Apparently you cannot comprehend that strong and proud and free nations can make costly sacrifices for principles because they are strong . . . and can speak honestly because they are free and do not fear the truth." Then he turned over his "unenviable job" as the UNC senior delegate to Major General William K Harrison, who would lead the UNC delegation until the signing of the armistice agreement fourteen months later.[103]

Chiang Kai-shek's "Unexpected Victory"

Believing that "the conspiracy to end the Korean War was completely smashed," Chiang Kai-shek saw the screening result as "the only satisfying event in this year's work." It was "a victory that came unexpectedly."[104]

On the day of Truman's declaration, North Korean prisoners kidnapped UN prison commandant Brigadier General Francis Dodd (this episode will be examined in detail in the next chapter). To secure his release, Dodd's successors signed an agreement on May 10, effectively admitting that there had been brutality in the camps. In addition to castigating the Americans for murdering POWs and lying, the Communists launched another propaganda offensive, alleging that the United States conducted germ warfare in North Korea and North China.[105] The Communists seemed to have turned things around in the moral battle and gained the high ground.

An exasperated Truman flew into a rage. In his diary he asked rhetorically: "What has happened to the 1,000,000 German prisoners the Soviets hold or have they been murdered as the Poles were murdered at Katyn? Where are the million Japs who surrendered to the Russians?" In a language strikingly similar to Chiang's, Truman lambasted the Communists: "You have no morals, no honor. . . . Your whole program at this conference has been based on lies and propaganda." Finally, Truman wanted the Communists to read Confucius, the Buddha's code, the Declaration of Independence, and the Bible.[106] Ironically, Truman's nemesis, Chiang, not Mao, read Confucius and the Bible.

At this point, it seemed that Chiang's prophecy of ten months earlier was coming true. When the armistice negotiations began in July 1951, Chiang assessed the Communist truce offer as the same kind of gambit they played in 1946 when Marshall mediated the civil war between the Communists and the Nationalists. "The armistice negotiations are only the beginning of retribution for Marshall's deeds. The Americans have not had a true taste [of Communist negotiating tactics], but that is to come."[107] Now, Chiang and Truman had more than mutual contempt in common. Finally, they were on the same page on one issue.

By late May 1952, Chiang Kai-shek had completely regained his confidence. In April, the Nationalist government and Japan had signed the Sino-Japanese Peace Treaty (Treaty of Taipei), in which Japan renounced sovereignty over Taiwan. In Washington, Dulles made a policy announcement supporting Nationalist China. In his diaries, Chiang Kai-shek recalled Dulles's suggestion of UN trusteeship two years earlier, and contrasted it to the new policy of helping "Nationalist China restore its independence and not abandoning Taiwan to its fate."[108] Greatly encouraged, Chiang noted that "the respect accorded to the yellow race is something that people could not have dreamed in the past two thousand years." Sure of his survival and hopeful about his future, Chiang did not spare his detractors. He saw Taiwan's survival as "the biggest lesson for Marshall, Acheson, and other hero dogs (*gonggou*) of the Communist bandits." Chiang exclaimed, "How can sparrows understand the ambitions of a swan?"[109]

In retrospect, it is no exaggeration to conclude that by April and May 1952, in the aftermath of the prisoner screening and Truman's public announcement on May

7, voluntary repatriation had become a "final and irrevocable" US policy, and the breakdown of armistice negotiations and continued fighting had become inevitable. This was anticipated and welcomed by Chiang Kai-shek since it would guarantee the survival of the Nationalist government on Taiwan. This decisive moment occurred half a year before Eisenhower's election in November 1952, and one year after MacArthur's dismissal in April 1951. Chiang Kai-shek and his son Ching-kuo seized a thin thread, first presented by the outbreak of the Korean War and MacArthur in 1950, and ran with it. Despite the sacking of MacArthur, once he had inducted the Nationalists into the psychological warfare in Korea, the Nationalists quickly found leverage on the POW issue, and surreptitiously but forcefully inserted Taiwan into the course of the war. Perhaps the Nationalists finally found the spirit that Madame Chiang had once preached: "God helps those who help themselves."

Stalin and Mao Overrule Kim

For both the Americans and the Chinese Communists, prisoner repatriation had become a matter of both face and principle. Both governments knew the results of the screening were severely compromised by anti-Communist indoctrination and coercion inside UNC prison camps. Especially humiliating to Mao was that a much greater percentage of the Chinese POWs refused repatriation than the North Koreans. Apparently seeking to divide the Chinese–North Korean coalition, UNC chief delegate Harrison pointedly observed that China, with its population of 400 million, sought to prolong the war over a few thousand prisoners while casually ignoring the suffering in North Korea, which had a small population and few resources.[110]

On July 13, the UNC delegation made an improved offer: it increased the total number of Chinese and North Korean repatriates from 70,000 to 83,000, including 6,400 Chinese—an increase of 1,300. The Sino–North Korean delegation was inclined to accept the deal. Li Kenong, the secret head of the Chinese delegation, cabled Mao the same night: "This figure is actually higher than our estimate, not far below our bottom line of 90,000." Given the fact the UNC would not bargain over the figure, "it would be meaningless to continue to fight over numbers." Mao immediately rebuked Li, "Our comrades are too naïve." The key issue was the hugely divergent repatriation ratios: while 80 percent of the North Korean POWs would be repatriated, only 32 percent of the Chinese would.[111] Mao complained to Stalin on July 15: "The percentages of repatriates among the Chinese and North Korean prisoners diverged so much. The enemy's provocative and seductive scheme is designed to drive a wedge" between China and North Korea.[112]

The Sino–North Korean rift over prisoners continued to escalate over the summer. It became so severe that Zhou Enlai took the issue to Stalin in Moscow on August 20. Zhou complained about Kim Il-sung's alleged defeatism, particularly his intention to retreat from the all-for-all prisoner exchange formula. Zhou said the North Koreans had "not considered the crafty game that America is playing here—out of the 83,000 only 6,400 are Chinese, and the rest Koreans. In truth, they are supposed to return another 13,600 Chinese volunteers." He warned, "This clearly shows that they are . . . trying to drive a wedge between China and Korea."[113]

Although the number of Chinese repatriates was a matter of principle for China, Zhou suggested, China was open to more negotiations "if the US agrees to make some concessions, even if they are not major ones." In essence, Mao and Zhou wanted a more face-saving ratio of repatriates to non-repatriates than the ratio of 1 to 2. "Mao Zedong is right," Stalin declared, apparently relishing the stand-off in Panmunjom and the continued Sino-American hostilities. He exhorted the Chinese to stand firm: "Chinese comrades must understand this: if the Americans do not lose this war, China will never recover Taiwan." Brushing aside Kim's repeated entreaties for a compromise on POWs in order to end the war, Stalin said, "The North Koreans have lost nothing, except for casualties."[114]

As Stalin sided with Mao to overrule Kim for the express objective of regaining Chinese prisoners, the negotiations made little headway. After the Communists rejected the improved offer of 83,000 repatriates, the United States found it impossible to offer any more. Finding itself hemmed in morally and practically, it had no choice but to dig in its heels on voluntary repatriation. The war continued.

11

General Dodd's Kidnapping and General Boatner's Crackdown

AFTER THE SCREENING in April 1952, pro- and anti-Communist prisoners were finally separated. The former moved into Compound 602 on Koje; the latter decamped for Cheju Island on April 19. Many pro-Communists, having just escaped from their tormentors in Compounds 72 and 86, thought that a time of peace and recuperation had finally arrived and bloodshed would come to an end. They yearned for a respite from political struggles and violence, but there was none. Life-and-death incidents, including suicides, murders, riots, and massacres, punctuated the prisoners' precarious existence in an alien, confusing, and ever-changing environment under an information blockade. The war in the POW camps was not over.

"Continuous Struggle"

On April 18, the Communist leadership in Compound 602 established a unified party organization called the Communist Solidarity (*gongchanzhuyi tuanjiehui*), a name designed to attract non-party members who had bravely resisted the Nationalists. All other organizations, including various Communist cells, native-place groups, and the Brotherhood, were ordered to cease activities. Zhao Zuoduan, Sun Zhenguan, Wei Lin, and Du Gang became the top leaders. While most leaders' identities and positions remained secret, Sun Zhenguan served as the nominal compound leader. Of the more than 5,000 prisoners, 500 "core members" (*gugan*) who had "passed the test in struggles" against the Nationalists were admitted in the first batch—another 1,700 would be admitted in later stages. While many party members were not initially inducted, a number of non-party members held key positions in the Communist

Solidarity. Zhang Zeshi, who had been expelled from the party before the war, and Gao Jie, a non-party member, served as interpreters. Tang Yao, who was branded by Li Da'an, became one of the four secretaries dealing with confidential works. The nineteen-year-old Zhong Junhua, a Communist Youth League member who had joined the Brotherhood, now headed the communications section. Through clandestine channels, the Solidarity's Central Committee ordered all prisoners to carry out three tasks: "unify, study, and struggle."[1]

"We are all sinners! We can only wash away our shame through struggle. We, dishonored men, must fight to restore our honor!" Such slogans were prisoners' "heartfelt cries," notes PLA writer Yu Jin in *Eyun* (Nightmare), which is still considered by many returnees to be by far the most balanced and well-researched account of their struggle. Within one month, all of the some 2,000 tattooed prisoners had "performed surgery of some sort" to remove the anti-Communist tattoos on their arms. One young male nurse, having performed so many removals with his scalpel that he suffered constant nightmares, begged to be relieved of this job. Zhang Zeshi, the compound interpreter, once implored fellow prisoners not to perform such self-mutilation. One prisoner stood up in front of hundreds and raised his voice, "Party, please don't worry. We're not going to carry these shameful marks back to the motherland." Before everyone's eyes, he sliced his own arm with a homemade blade.[2]

As physical self-cleansing was underway, a political movement to touch every soul gathered steam. While on a work detail unloading rice from a Japanese cargo ship, several POWs found a crumpled copy of the Chinese newspaper *Jiefang ribao* (Liberation Daily) featuring articles on the Three-Anti and Five-Anti campaigns on the front page. "Follow the motherland's footsteps!" the leaders exhorted. A POWs' "Three-Antis campaign" began: "anti-compromise, anti-treason, and anti-right-leaning vacillation."[3] Those who once dreamed of a respite were forced to engage in "continuous struggle" against the enemy. As anti-Communist POWs had been shipped away to Cheju in April, the only enemies the Communist could struggle against on Koje now were the Americans without and traitors within. Soon enough, the North Korean POWs provided a role model.

General Dodd's Kidnapping—"The Biggest Flap of the Whole War"

Since the beginning of May, Brigadier General Francis Dodd, the commandant of the Koje prison camp, had been under pressure from UNC negotiators in Panmunjom to "complete an accurate roster and identification of all the remaining prisoners of war on Koje-do," a task that required the prisoners' cooperation.[4] To accomplish the task, Dodd sought to reduce tension and went out of his way to accommodate the prisoners. On May 6, Dodd "successfully" ended a hunger strike in Compound 602, after he went to the compound gate to negotiate with representative Sun Zhenguan through interpreter Zhang Zeshi. At the time neither Dodd nor Sun and Zhang knew that this exercise was a ploy to lure Dodd into a trap set by the North Korean underground leadership, which, without revealing their plan, had instructed the Chinese to stage the hunger strike.[5]

In the meantime, the Koreans in Compound 76 also demanded to meet with Dodd to "discuss matters of importance," intimating that "they would be willing to let themselves be listed and fingerprinted if Dodd would come and talk to them." Dodd, having so far failed to screen the North Korean Communist prisoners, thought "the chance to win a bloodless victory was too good to be missed." So he went to the compound gate for a talk. The prisoner representatives stood behind the main gate made of a wooden frame and barbed wire, through which they delivered their familiar list of complaints. On the outside of the gate, Dodd listened, US guards standing behind him. As the discussion dragged on, a work detail, after carrying latrine buckets to the sea, returned to the sally port. The main gate was swung open. Trying to avoid the stench, Dodd and his guards stepped aside. Suddenly, the last dozen or so work detail members, the strongest of all, lunged forward, seized Dodd, and dragged him into the compound. Within minutes, the POWs hoisted a large banner with stilted English: "We capture Dodd. As long as our demand will be solved, his safety is secured. If there happen brutal act such as shooting, his life is in danger."[6]

Holding Dodd hostage, the North Korean prisoners demanded the prison authorities bring representatives from all pro-Communist compounds to Compound 76 so that they could collectively negotiate with Dodd. The authorities complied. In the afternoon, Sun Zhenguan and Zhang Zeshi were transported to 76. On the next day, Compound 602's chief clerk Li Ziying (under the alias Fu Zhiheng) and Korean interpreter Liu Yi were also brought to 76.[7]

While the Korean and Chinese representatives from various compounds bitterly recounted a litany of American atrocities in the two-day marathon denunciation meeting (*kongsu dahui*) with Dodd, Ridgway swiftly ordered a tank battalion from the frontline to Koje, as a part of "the killing machinery on hand to do a thorough job" of crushing the prisoners' resistance.[8] Before the tanks' arrival, however, on May 10 Brigadier General Charles F. Colson, Dodd's successor, signed an agreement with the prisoners without proper clearance from his superiors in Pusan and Tokyo. The agreement contained the following lines:

> I do admit that there has [*sic*] been instances of bloodshed where many PW have been killed and wounded by UN Forces. I can assure in the future that PW can expect humane treatment in this camp according to the principles of International Law. I will do all within my power to eliminate further violence and bloodshed. If such incidents happen in the future, I will be responsible.[9]

In effect, Colson's signature on this document was an official admission that there had been brutality in the Koje POW camp, especially during the screening.

Brandishing the Colson agreement, Communist negotiators in Panmunjom castigated the Americans for murder and lying. Feeling the rug had been pulled from under him, UNC chief negotiator Admiral Joy knew that "I am certainly going to take a beating over this at the conference table."[10]

It was the "biggest flap of the whole war," lamented General Mark W. Clark, who had just arrived on May 7 to take over the UNC, as Ridgway was leaving for Europe to replace Eisenhower as the commander of NATO forces. As Ridgway walked up the plane ramp with "a broad smile on his face" and waved good-bye on May 12, Clark visualized Ridgway throwing him "a blazing forward pass." Since Clark had not been briefed in Washington about Koje and the POW mess, he wished he could "catch a plane . . . and get out fast."[11]

Clark promptly repudiated Colson's statement, asserting that it was made under duress. He fired Colson, who had held the commandant job for just five days. He summoned Brigadier General Haydon L. Boatner, the assistant commander of the US 2nd Infantry Division, from the middle of his R&R (rest and recuperation) to Tokyo and ordered him to fly to Koje within two hours.[12]

"Old China Hand" Boatner

After graduating from West Point in 1924, Boatner served in the US 15th Infantry Regiment in Tianjin, China, from 1928 to 1930. Coincidentally, Generals George C. Marshall, Joseph W. Stilwell, and Matthew B. Ridgway had also served in this regiment, nicknamed the "Old China Hands." Boatner then became a US military Chinese language officer based in Beiping, where he met scholar John King Fairbank. Boatner earned an MA degree from the California College in China in 1934. After Pearl Harbor, Boatner returned to Asia in 1942 as Stilwell's commanding officer of the forward echelon in Lashio, Burma, where he witnessed the collapse of the Allied defense. In 1942–1945, he was chief of staff for the Chinese forces in India and Burma. In Fairbank's words, Boatner and Stilwell were "the only two American officers appointed directly under Chiang Kai-shek." Boatner also enjoyed the distinction of being "the only General officer to stay through it in China up to the surrender in October 1945."[13] He represented the United States in two important Japanese surrender ceremonies: first in Zhijiang, Hunan, on August 21, then in Nanjing on September 9.[14] Boatner's eleven years of Asia experience and his knowledge of the "Asiatic mentality" made him an obvious choice as the Koje commandant.[15]

"Restore order" was Clark's simple instruction. Boatner stated that bloodshed might be required to restore order; Clark concurred. Boatner requested the assignment of a judge advocate (military lawyer) knowledgeable of the Geneva Convention, noting that no military lawyer had ever been posted on Koje, "even when the POW population totaled over 160,000." Clark agreed.[16]

On May 13, Boatner flew to Pusan, where he had dinner with the newly released Dodd. The next day, he flew to Koje and met with the outgoing Colson. In his new job, Boatner received the first shock not from the prisoners, but his own men. His staff, "completely oblivious to the international implications and seriousness" of the mess, offered to give him a cocktail reception. Boatner was appalled by the quality of his subordinates. "The Military Police officers, as a group, and the enlisted men were the poorest quality of American soldiers with whom I had ever served. . . . The men and officers were largely culls and rejects from the combat units and other logistical units and headquarters." Within the first ten days, Boatner fired three of the four senior officers, including Col. Maurice J. Fitzgerald, former commandant and then Dodd's deputy, and two of the four senior staff officers. Soon 400 substandard US troops were sent back to the Korean mainland.[17]

FIGURE 11.1. Koje POW camp commandant Haydon Boatner (left). July 1952. US National Archives.

Another person Boatner fired on his second day was a Chinese interpreter—most probably a Nationalist DAC. The CIE officers, unaware of Boatner's Chinese language ability, volunteered to provide him an interpreter, whom Boatner found "dangerous, inflammatory, propagandist and intellectually dishonest." Through this incident, Boatner "stumbled into" investigating the CIE's operations. He "concluded after a very few days" that the CIE was "the cause of many riots and was being irresponsibly run." He shut it down over the protests of its officers. He "never received a reaction" from above.[18] After the closure of CIE programs and the removal of Nationalist instructors, some Nationalist DAC interpreters remained on Koje. Boatner later issued a stern warning to all US officers and men: "We must be careful that interpreters perform their duties properly *but* only the duties of interpreters."[19]

While he was cleaning the house in his first few days on Koje, Boatner found "it was necessary to take unbelievable and disgraceful abuse from the prisoners." While he avoided "taking any action or talking to POW representatives or giving any orders to the POWs," he "sat tight" to assess the situation quietly from a distance. He observed that the inmates, who had "gradually been allowed more than their 'rights' as POWs," were "regularly holding mass demonstrations—marching and waving communist flags, singing, and shouting in unison. Inside were statues of Stalin and Kim Il-sung, along with tall flagpoles with communist flags flying." In each compound, prisoners set up "an observation post on a barracks roof-top from which semaphore messages were sent and received."[20]

The prison enclosures were "in shambles." The outer fences were made of "twisted barbed wire strung on rotten sapling poles." The POWs "would crowd against the perimeter fences and curse our Korean guards outside," Boatner noted. Yet, the guard towers were built inside the perimeter fences, a design endangering the guards. Boatner concluded, "It was what any reasonable soldier would call an unholy mess."[21]

The Killing of a Prisoner and His Funeral

Boatner had his first encounter with the prisoners three days after his arrival. On May 16, 170 Chinese POWs on a latrine bucket work detail returned to the gate of Compound 602. Charlie E. Ainsley, a black sergeant, ordered a body search of the prisoners, who refused and kept singing. According to the Army's investigation report, after warning the prisoners three times, but to no avail, Ainsley "brought two prisoners forward and demonstrated how they would be searched. Prisoner Wang Huayi grabbed his honey bucket pole and attempted to strike Sgt Ainsley," who in turn "shot Wang three times in self-defense." Irrespective of the accuracy of the "self-defense" characterization, the simple fact is that a Chinese prisoner was killed in full sight of many of his comrades. In protest, "the detail team were singing and shouting. Also the prisoners inside the compound were next to the fences and were singing and shouting," an ROK guard recalled. [22] Very soon the neighboring North Korean

Compounds 603, 604, 605, 606, and 607 also demonstrated in a show of solidarity. These protests "went on day and night." [23]

On learning of the incident, Boatner's first reaction was to "stay away," but he quickly recognized the "grave inadequacy" of his staff in dealing with the situation "due entirely to their inexperience with Chinese," while he "had more than 10 years previously with them as friend, ally and enemy." He went to the site discreetly. The scene flabbergasted him:

> The POWs were assembled on their central parade ground, in military formation, waving flags and chanting in unison. Several off-duty US soldiers had rushed to the surrounding fences and were jeering at and taunting the Chinese. It reminded me of a home-side big neighborhood fire. My God!

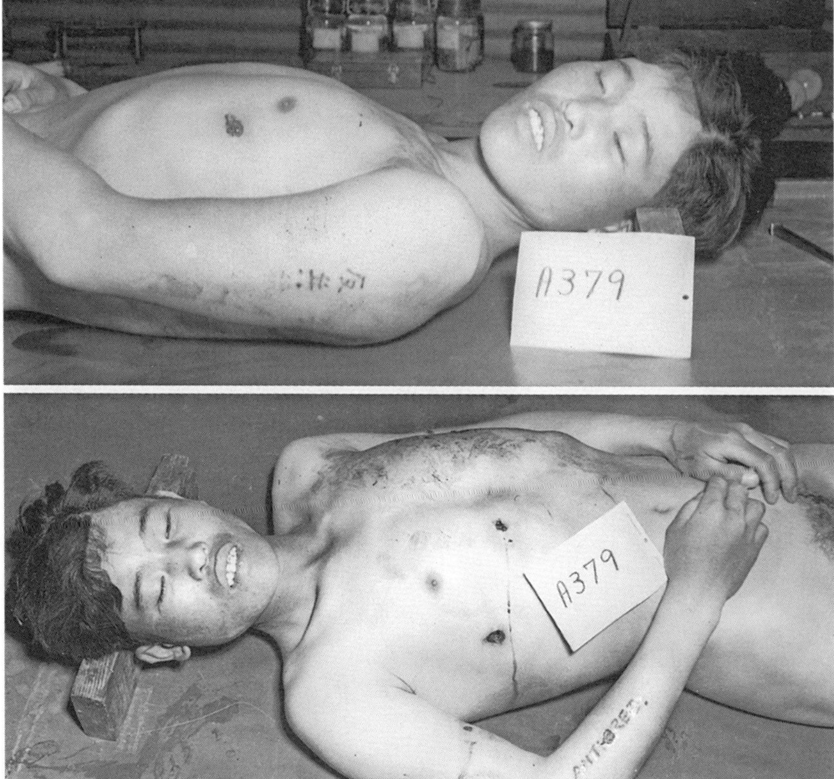

FIGURE 11.2. Postmortem photographs of Wang Huayi. Tattoos of anti-Communist slogans in Chinese have been completely removed from his upper right arm and partially removed from his upper left arm, but "Anti-Red" in English on his right forearm remains intact. Bullets had pierced his chest and his right arm. May 1952. US National Archives.

Soon, that "mob of Americans" was ordered away. Boatner made sure that such scene was never repeated.[24]

Boatner invited Compound 602's new representative Wei Lin, who had succeeded Sun Zhenguan after Sun's transfer to Compound 76, to his office on May 20. Through POW interpreter Gao Jie, Wei made his case, reciting a series of issues and events, including the Panmunjom talks and the Geneva Convention, which Boatner thought was "a lot of bunk!" When Wei finished, Boatner said in Chinese, "Na shi na'er de hua?" (What kind of talk is that?). Wei "almost fainted from surprise." Boatner went on to tell Wei his long connection with China: he had served for two years in Tianjin, where his son was born. He had lived in Beijing and traveled throughout the country. After finding out Wei was from Fenzhou, Shanxi, Boatner said that he had once hunted there, and he knew the famous medical missionary Dr. Lewis there. Invoking his experience in training and commanding Chinese troops as Stilwell's chief of staff in World War II, Boatner told Wei: "You are a soldier, and I am a soldier. And we don't know anything about things like the Panmunjom talks. All I know is what you know: one of your POW colleagues has been killed." Promising an investigation only if the prisoners stopped demonstrating, Boatner concluded, "I will do nothing until they act like the fine Chinese soldiers I have known." Wei and Gao returned to Compound 602, and the demonstration soon ceased.[25]

FIGURE 11.3. A sketch by prisoner Wu Chunsheng depicting a funeral in Compound 602 commemorating prisoners who died in the screening. Courtesy of Wu Chunsheng.

Wang Huayi's funeral was held on the following day. Boatner arranged the supply of twenty rolls of white toilet paper and one quart of Mercurochrome, which were made into funeral flowers.[26] "Shortly after dawn," *Time* magazine reported, "a P.W. band using beer-can bugles, bamboo flutes and drums made of oilcans struck up an eerie cacophony. Twelve Chinese carrying flowers made of G.I. toilet paper shuffled out of the compound to the camp cemetery."[27] Gao Jie recalled a larger group of about a hundred Chinese prisoners participated in the funeral procession, accompanied by Chinese, North Korean, and Soviet flags, three large homemade drums, and fifteen small ones. At the funeral, after Wei and other prisoners made speeches, the US officer read out a eulogy drafted by Boatner, vowing that a similar incident would not occur again. On their way back, all prisoners were in high spirits, singing and shouting. "It was the first time since our capture we vented our anger (*chuqi*)," Gao recalled, "though it was at the cost of Wang Huayi's blood." He added, "It was also the first time that Chinese prisoners had experienced fair treatment" from the Americans.[28]

Both sides claimed victory. Boatner boasted, "Never after that did the Chinese compound give me trouble." The Chinese believed that they had scored a major victory by negotiating face-to-face with the American general, who had recognized their organization. Their perception was not baseless. General Paul F. Yount, Boatner's boss and the commander of the 2nd Logistics Command, ordered him to "utilize the POW Association authorized in the recent negotiation to the fullest extent you find feasible." Boatner, however, disagreed: "I never negotiated with the POWs and never once recognized their association. These were grave errors that in my opinion were largely responsible for the riots." Instead, he announced: "POWs don't negotiate."[29]

In the meantime, a board of officers investigated Wang Huayi's killing. Sgt. Ainsley asserted that Wang had raised his pole in a threatening manner so he shot him. Seven Chinese prisoner witnesses were called in, with Captain Brooks serving as their interpreter. The Chinese invariably claimed that the body search was "illegal." "There was no reason to search us," insisted prisoner Pu Xuelin, who was later shot in the genitals in another incident.[30] The investigators, however, learned that the troops had received a new order to conduct body searches as part of the "get tough" program. The MP company officer had told his troops three days before the incident: "If any prisoner showed any acts of violence or of cursing after us[,] to shoot him. . . . We were to warn them first and if they did not obey[,] to shoot them."[31]

The board ruled on May 29 that Ainsley should be "absolved of any guilt," as the killing was "justifiable homicide."[32] Not without misgivings, Boatner recalled in 1966: "Conditions were such then that I did not think it in the best interest of the US to have a full investigation and resultant court-martial—so I had that soldier returned to the mainland." Communist Fang Xiangqian revealed in 2014: "At the time, our leaders were looking for trouble. Otherwise how could we demonstrate our determination to return home?" It was under such circumstances of "high-voltage tenseness and belligerence," as Boatner described it, that a purposefully confrontational prisoner was killed by a trigger-happy guard who was authorized to shoot.[33]

"Prisoners Don't Negotiate"

Boatner admitted that he "had many many advantages" over his fourteen hapless predecessors. First of all, "on the priority lists, Koje rose from the bottom to the top."[34] Consequently, the troop level shot up drastically. Reinforcements included a Canadian, a British, and a Greek company. Most importantly, the 187th Airborne Regiment was flown in from Japan.[35] Joining forces with the Netherlands Battalion and ROK troops already on Koje, they formed a six-nation tank and infantry force of 14,820 men, almost one division strong.[36] While Dodd never had more than 1,000 US troops, who had to guard more than 160,000 prisoners, Boatner had 14,000 soldiers to guard 80,000 POWs on Koje, as anti-Communist prisoners had been shipped to the mainland and Cheju Island by the time of his arrival. He replaced all ROK perimeter guards with better-disciplined US troops. "Dodd could not do so as he did not have enough US troops," Boatner admitted.[37]

With the arrival of construction materials, US troops started "working on a 24-hour basis" building new 4,000-man compounds, each with eight smaller 500-man sub-compounds.[38]

To cut off contact between prisoners and villagers around the compounds, Boatner ordered the removal of more than 6,000 villagers from the camp area and off the island. Village huts were set ablaze and razed to the ground by tanks. The village had long served as "a key center in the communication network established by General Nam Il's men with the prisoners." Communist agents and guerrillas living in the village had mingled with the ROK guards. According to Clark, the agents' method of communication with prisoners was "so simple as to be elementary." These agents dropped notes where prisoners on work details could find them, and vice versa. Then agents would slip through the zigzagging Koje coastline in fishing boats. The Americans alleged, what transpired in Panmunjom was quickly transmitted to the North Korean Communist prisoner leadership; what occurred in prison camps was readily transmitted to Nam Il at Panmunjom.[39]

General Van Fleet inspected Koje in late May. He found "everything looked fine and dandy, as it has all along to him." As a combat general preoccupied with the war front near the 38th parallel, Van Fleet apparently missed the political significance and operational complexity of the POW issue. After Dodd's kidnapping, Van Fleet had griped, "There'd be no incident down there if the Communists would only behave." Now, once Boatner began implementing a "get tough" policy, Van Fleet announced,

"I don't think there will be any more trouble." Boatner, however, disagreed: "We can't get into those compounds. . . . We can't take a roll call. We don't know what they're plotting."[40]

Boatner's greatest horror was that "the POWs would attempt a mass breakout during which several hundred might be shot." To prevent this, Boatner tightened discipline step by step. First, all UN troops were "put into combat fatigues and constantly armed." Troops practiced bayonet fighting and were issued gas masks. Central to Boatner's riot-control technique was the use of weapons other than bullets: bayonets, tear gas, concussion grenades, and flamethrowers—the last one potentially lethal and arguably more brutal than bullets. Professing his philosophy that "it is far better to intimidate the mob, intentionally, than to kill or wound some of them unintentionally," Boatner emphasized the need to avoid firing bullets, which should only be used as the last resort. Standing on a table to welcome the Canadian troops, Boatner told them not to kill unless absolutely necessary: "If you get into a fight, slash him, use the butt of your rifle, give him the knee in the groin." Boatner later explained that he "went to extremes to prevent brutality to POW's" which was "a very natural thing for unthinking combat soldiers to do."[41]

An increasingly confident Boatner tightened the screws on prisoners. Timing his disciplinary measures with the construction of the new compounds, Boatner began giving orders to the POWs, starting with those he could enforce within a specific timeframe. Boatner ordered prisoners to take down their flags, banners, and statues of Communist leaders. As in the past, no compound complied.[42]

A banner strung on the barbwire fence read in stilted English: "USA imperialists responsible for violating the human rights of PWs and the international law! Secure the human rights of PWs by the international law!" Purposely placed right next to a row of latrine buckets, another banner read: "Prohibit right now, So-called the forced crime of free repatriations instruction with threat and . . . PWs of Korea People's Army."[43] The prisoners carried on their defiance outside their compounds as well. "Even the garbage detail openly defies U.N. orders." A *Life* reporter observed a work detail "flaunting [the] North Korean flag—made from a rice bag—as it marches alongside a bayonet-carrying US guard." It was exactly the same type of prisoners on a honey bucket detail who had seized Dodd on May 7.[44]

Both sides flexed their muscles. Shirtless paratroopers of the 187th Airborne jogged on the roads between compounds. Out of the eyesight of the prisoners, other UNC troops wearing gas masks were rehearsing riot-control tactics with bayonets and rifle butts. In broad daylight, the North Korean prisoners practiced fighting with spears made of tent poles, with instructors openly demonstrating "battle tactics to use on guards."[45] It seemed that a final showdown might be decided by person-to-person close combat.

Boatner chose the Chinese Compound 602 as his "first real test case." He ordered Chinese prisoners to "take down the Communist flag and tear down the statue of a Communist leader . . . at 12 noon" on June 2. Boatner had learned from his World War II experience commanding Chinese troops that "*verbal* orders were no good. . . . They would obey them only if they chose to. But they would obey a written order, if and only if, (1) There was an official seal (chop) on it and (2) There was a time limit for compliance." Therefore, the order was in writing and also broadcast so that "all the POWs, not just the leaders, knew the entire situation." As expected, the Chinese prisoners ignored this order.[46]

Boatner quietly rehearsed his troops for their roles. The 9th Infantry Battalion marched from its staging area to the compound gate and noted the elapsed time. The same was separately done with two tanks. At exactly noon, June 2, infantrymen with two tanks arrived at the compound gate. The gates "were thrown open by guards." The troops, "wearing gas masks, formed a ring of bayonets to keep the prisoners at bay while one of the tanks battered down a fifty-foot flagpole." They "tore down a Communist flag and burned five insulting banners." Evidently "surprised by the suddenness and clockwork precision" of the UNC troops, the prisoners, who were having lunch, did not have time to lower their red flag and hide it, as they had done in the past. They offered no resistance. In less than five minutes, the job was done and the troops moved out.[47]

Similar operations were carried out in other compounds. On June 4, infantrymen of the 38th Regiment supported by two tanks moved quickly into Korean Compounds 85 and 96. They destroyed the flagpoles and burned banners. During these operations, dozens of prisoners escaped from their Communist tormentors and asked for UN protection. Compound 60 was also subdued. "Not a single casualty was suffered by either side during these quick strikes," claims an official US military history.[48]

Aside from flags and banners, POWs' "annoying practices" were also put to an end. Boatner ordered the signalmen on barrack rooftops to be off by a specific date. Again, they ignored the order, "until the first shotgun load of No. 8 shot was fired into one man's legs. . . . All then came down and stayed down." The next order forbade the POWs from leaning on the perimeter fences and established five yards as the closest they could come to the fence. This time they complied.[49] To check for escape tunnels suspected of being constructed by prisoners, British infantrymen used tear gas to move a mob, so engineers could dig the ground.[50]

The 6,400-man-strong Compound 76, however, remained defiant. To intimidate the inmates, Boatner staged a rehearsal using tanks and flamethrowers in an empty compound next door. The prisoners, however, "answered by digging chest-deep trenches and continuing to turn out steel-tipped spears and other crude weapons on their hidden forge."[51]

Inside 76, the North Korean leaders held an emergency meeting to prepare for the worst—a massacre. Sun Zhenguan, Zhang Zeshi, and two other Chinese stuck in 76, witnessed the mobilization.[52] Zhang recalled that the entire compound conducted battle drills, with dare-to-die squads practicing suicidal attacks. Their main weapons were spears with blades cut from gasoline barrels fastened onto shafts made of tent poles. Prisoners also made Molotov cocktails, using gasoline provided by the camp as cooking fuel. The four Chinese prisoners dug trenches, gave pep talks, sang songs, and performed skits for their Korean comrades.[53]

Communist mobilization entailed more than motivational speeches, songs, and labor; it also involved "self-criticism" sessions for all prisoners and "public trials" of suspected traitors in kangaroo courts. In Compound 85, a "1,000-man 'jury' on June 6, 1952, conducted a 'self-criticism' of prisoners and sentenced one to death." The executed was charged with plotting to kill compound leaders.[54] Although he did not personally witness such executions during his stay in Compound 76, Zhang Zeshi acknowledged that as a general rule, before "major battles" executions did occur in both Chinese and Korean camps.[55] Before long, the final breakup of 76 would yield concrete evidence.

Operation Breakup, June 10, 1952

When the new camp construction was done, Boatner was ready to move the prisoners. On June 9 he witnessed the completion of three new compounds—each with eight 500-man sub-enclosures—bringing the total capacity to 12,000. He trained his sights on Compound 76, "the toughest of them all," because prisoners in 76 had kidnapped Dodd and had Communist representatives from other compounds, including the four Chinese. Boatner believed, "if No. 76 can be moved the others would follow suit peacefully."[56]

The "final and crucial test" came on June 10, exactly one month after Dodd's release. At 5:15 a.m., Boatner went to Compound 76 and summoned its representative, Colonel Lee Hak-koo, whom Boatner described as "a dumb, cowardly, fat stooge," to assemble his men in groups of 150 in the center of the compound and prepare for movement at six o'clock.[57]

At 5:45 a.m., messages broadcast over loudspeakers informed the prisoners that they were to be moved to new areas, and that they would not be harmed if they cooperated. Instead of forming into groups to be moved, the prisoners took their positions in the trenches, arming themselves with spears, knives, and other handmade weapons. From his command post on a hill overlooking the camp, Boatner "could see the POW leaders and their henchmen prevent any of their colleagues from assembling as ordered."[58]

At 6:15 a.m., Boatner sent two battalions of the 187th Regiment to break up the compound. All hell broke loose. "With split-second timing, troops covering the initial assault sent rockets of tear gas arching over the barbed wire into the heart of Compound 76. Within a few seconds, the five-sided enclosure was covered with dirty clouds of gas. Another barrage of percussion grenades exploded in a series of crimson flashes inside the tents and long rows of huts. . . . Some of the grenades were lobbed squarely into hidden stores of gasoline inside the enclosure, and the wooden buildings erupted in smoke and flame." The billowing wave of tear gas "soon was so thick that, several hundred yards away on the top of a hill, from where General Boatner commanded the over-all operation, everyone in the sand-bagged post gasped and wiped away tears."[59]

Down in the compound, wire-cutting teams snipped the barbed wire, and nine flame-throwers burned two gaping holes. Then 750 paratroopers stormed into the barricade. They outflanked the POWs by surprise, since the prisoners seemed to have been looking for an attack through the main gate and had manned trenches in preparation for a frontal assault. The paratroopers in masks charged the trenches and bayoneted resisters.[60] A reporter observed, "Cowboy yells from the Americans and an eerie chant from the Communists mixed with the popping of concussion grenades, the swish of tear gas rockets and the heavier explosions of Communist gasoline dumps."[61]

Twenty-year-old Private Thurman J. Nichols of the Reconnaissance Company, US 3rd Infantry Division, recalled: "We were issued live ammo and then we had to go in with fixed bayonets and flame-throwers to get control." As a young but battle-tested soldier, who had been wounded in the Battle of Chosin Reservoir in November 1950, he confessed, "I was never so scared in my whole life." Once troops charged into the compound, a prisoner "came running out of a tent with what looked like a gun." Nichols saw the soldier next to him "tak[ing] aim with his M-1 rifle and shoot him right between his eyes. It looked like his whole head exploded." He continued, "A bunch of prisoners were held up in a sheet metal building. We didn't know if they were armed or not. Someone called in for flame-throwers. I could hear them screaming inside and the tin just melted."[62]

Meeting little resistance, the troops advanced to the middle of the compound. Some prisoners broke ranks from trenches, tents, or huts, ran toward the main gate and assembled in the central yard as ordered. "Hot dog, look at them run," Boatner yelled out. "I think we've got them licked."[63] As planned, the troops halted in the central yard "long enough to allow the POW resistance to crumble." However, it did not. Although "most prisoners quickly quit and squatted in abject surrender," including Colonel Lee Hak-koo, who quit after only twenty minutes, "the diehards fought savagely and when cornered were sometimes seen to stab their own would-be deserters."[64] From a distance, Boatner "could see them being killed and maimed with long spears and barbed-wire whips by other POWs."[65]

The last 1,500 prisoners retreated to a corner of the compound.[66] They fought back with spears and Molotov cocktails—more than a thousand of which were used. Driven out of the trenches, they crowded into huts, locking themselves inside. They had to be driven out by grenades. "I had never thought they would do that," Boatner watched in awe, adding, "That takes a lot of guts."[67] Nevertheless, Boatner ordered tanks to close in on these final resisters. "After all this is war," he noted.[68]

Six M48 Patton tanks rumbled into the compound, training their guns on the holdouts, but held fire.[69] They rammed the buildings, breaking holes in the concrete and mud walls.[70] The paratroopers, "swinging axes, punched holes in the sides of the buildings, then forced in concussion grenades upon the tightly packed prisoners. . . . Many were killed or seriously injured in this manner." In less than an hour, "all forty-five Communist tents were in smoking ashes and many of the twenty-five low wooden buildings had been leveled."[71]

By 8:45 a.m., the fight was over. Compound 76 was "a flaming shambles, . . . and the paratroopers were in control."[72] The camp's grounds were "covered with bayonet-torn captives and wounded soldiers, most of them also weeping from the effects of the gas."[73] Among them were the four Chinese, who had been ordered by the Koreans to hide in an underground bunker and did not join the fighting. When they were flushed out, Zhang Zeshi saw that the entire compound had been "razed to the ground, with burning tents and uniforms everywhere." And "tanks were still burning from the damage done by Molotov cocktails. . . . Martyred and injured comrades were lying on the ground, and wounded GIs were being carried away on stretchers."[74]

The captives were ordered to squat or sit in the center of the camp. Eighteen representatives from other compounds who had come for the negotiations over Dodd a month earlier were identified by a roll call. Zhang Zeshi recalled, "We were herded onto a huge truck, whose tires were taller than a man and whose top was covered by barbed wire. At bayonet point, we were forced to crouch on the floor, with both hands behind our heads."[75] Behind them was "another vehicle with guns ready to discourage any attempt to escape."[76]

At the end of the two-and-a-half-hour battle, 31 prisoners were found dead and 139 wounded.[77] However, *Life* reported, "of 30 dead prisoners 12 had been killed by their own comrades." Some of the wounded later died in hospitals, bringing the final death toll to 41.[78] American casualties included one dead from spear wounds and 14 injured.[79]

A search of Compound 76 turned up "3,000 spears, 4,500 knives, 1,000 gasoline grenades, and a large number of clubs, hatchets, barbed wire flails, and hammers."[80] Also discovered were "three live women, a map blueprinting an escape plan and a tunnel leading toward nearby Compound 77."[81] In fact, these women were representatives from the women's compound, who had been moved by the authorities to 76 to negotiate Dodd's release.[82]

North Korean Communist prisoners in the neighboring Compounds 77 and 78 witnessed the crackdown and took the lesson to heart. By noon 6,800 POWs marched out of Compound 78 in an orderly fashion. The leaders in Compound 77 requested an overnight delay in moving out to which Boatner agreed. After the POWs marched out the next day, UNC troops found "in ditches, wells and oil drums the fresh corpses of 16 anti-Reds tried and murdered by kangaroo courts during the night." Nevertheless, the final bastions of Korean Communist resistance were finally crushed. "Resistance definitely is on the ebb and I believe the worst is over," Boatner declared.[83]

Calling his troops' discipline "superb," Boatner claimed, "Not one shot was fired by US troops throughout the entire operation"—perhaps an exaggeration as it is contradicted by Private Nichols's account. Boatner asserted, "Those killed or wounded were hurt by their own colleagues using spears or by the concussion grenades."[84] Notwithstanding the likelihood of shooting in this crackdown, the troops largely maintained good discipline. Had shooting been ordered, the prisoners' death toll would have been much larger in this two-and-a-half hour battle between more than 6,400 prisoners and 750 troops and 6 tanks. Under the title of "Right Way at Koje," the *Washington Post* lauded Boatner's "extraordinary finesse in cleaning up the prisoner mess."[85]

Having subdued the belligerent Korean Communist prisoners, Boatner faced challenges from an unexpected source—the Chinese Communist POWs, who had "made comparatively little contribution to incidents of violence during the first two years."[86] Several China Hands—old and new—came to Koje and later Cheju Islands, hoping to gain control over the prisoners. Instead, the two sides moved onto a collision course.

12

China Hands on Koje and Cheju

IN THE IMMEDIATE AFTERMATH of Boatner's crackdown on Compound 76, Communist prisoners were rendered powerless to stage any organized confrontation. By July, the authorities achieved unfettered access to all compounds. Clark remarked, "Compound inspection by camp authorities, impossible in some of the enclosures in the past, were made daily in every compound. The POWs no longer were able to declare any part of the camps off limits to UN troops."[1]

The Chinese Communist prisoners in Compound 602 were transferred to Compound 70 without incident on June 17.[2] The Korean Communist Compound 62, the site of Koje's bloodiest riot four months earlier, was broken up on June 19.[3] Finally, the UNC screened all Korean Communist prisoners, who previously had held out in their compounds refusing to be screened.[4] At last, all Communist and anti-Communist Korean prisoners were segregated. All Korean anti-Communist prisoners were transferred to the Korean mainland, leaving Communist POWs on Koje.

The screening and segregation of Chinese POWs had been largely accomplished by April 19, when some 14,000 Chinese anti-Communist POWs were moved to Cheju Island. The approximately 5,600 pro-Communist prisoners were to follow in July.

Manhard Reports from Koje

The camps on Koje opened their doors not only to UNC troops, but also to an old regular—Philip Manhard. On June 5, Acheson signed off a cable to Manhard, requesting "all statistical lists," "trusty and party lists," and "sketch showing your understanding [of] location [of] screening tents in the several compounds in relation [to] compound fence exit." He specifically required the "soonest possible" report via "secret air pouch addressed [to] my name."[5] Apparently aware of the allegations of violence during the screening process, Acheson sought to understand the cause of the large number of anti-repatriates. Lacking confidence in US military reports, Acheson turned to his Foreign Service Officer.

Two days after Boatner's breakup of Compound 76 on June 10, Acheson anxiously instructed Ambassador Muccio: "In view [of] critical importance [of] POW issue, if you could spare Manhard for [a] brief trip Koje." The purpose was to interview "two top Chi[nese] Commie POW leaders . . . regarded [as] promising sources" on the basis of earlier State Department interrogations conducted by Manhard and others. The two men were none other than Sun Zhenguan and Zhang Zeshi, Compound 602's chief representative and interpreter, who had been stuck in Compound 76 from May 7 to June 10, and subsequently held in Koje's maximum-security prison. In fact, the ever-proactive Manhard had arrived on Koje around June 3 "at General Boatner's invitation."[6]

Even though his focus was on Chinese POWs and he only spoke Chinese, Manhard cited a CIE report based on interviews with Korean anti-Communist POW leaders that confirmed the allegation of violence during the screening. Former leaders of Compound 83 "freely admitted beatings at time of polling," claiming that it was justified to beat "enemies" who wanted to return to North Korea. The report boasted that half of the Korean anti-repatriates had been swayed by the CIE.[7] Such phenomena were not unique to the Korean compounds.

Manhard sent a flurry of reports to Washington, beginning with his notes on his interview with Sun, his evaluation of the April screening, and his assessment of the CIE program, and ending with his proposal for improvements in prison management. Sun's "interview highlights" listed verbatim Communist prisoners' main complaints and their criticism of the screening. In this report, the main targets of the pro-repatriation prisoners' grievances were not the US authorities, but rather the anti-Communist prisoner trusties, who had used "info[rmation] blockade," "deception," and "physical terror including organized murders, beatings, threats, before and even during [the] polling process" to deter prisoners from choosing repatriation. In addition, many pro-Communist Chinese POWs asserted the "American chaplain and his Korean assistant"—Woodberry and Han—"played [a] major role in deterring Chinese from choosing repatriation between [the] first and second polling in 72 and possibly in 86." Sun questioned the lopsided screening result by pointing to the opposite outcome in Compound 70, where 1,200 out of 1,400 Chinese POWs chose repatriation. This Sun attributed to "the weakness of pro-Nationalist POW leadership [in] that group and lack [of] physical violence." He maintained that the ideological composition of Compound 70 was typical of the majority of Chinese POWs.[8]

Sun's cogent analysis free of the typical Communist bombast convinced Manhard and Ambassador Muccio that it warranted the reading of Acheson. Most strikingly, Manhard's own evaluation and assessment in ensuing reports closely resembled those of Sun's. The Communist prisoners had long asserted that the result of the April screening was skewed by pro-Nationalists' control in most compounds, and there was no significant demographic difference between those who chose repatriation and those who opposed it.

On June 29, Manhard finally sent Acheson a sketch of Compound 72 during the screening and, more importantly, "statistics obtained last two weeks on 3,200 of 5,300 pro-repatriation Chinese [on] Koje-do, comparable with those on anti-repatriation Chinese [on] Cheju-do." Although he was "still unable [to] get [a] complete roster directly from [the] POWs[,] figures on 3,200 developed from old master lists are considered [a] fairly reliable majority sample. Remaining 2,100 [are] made up of about 1,000 amputees and comparatively recent captures."[9]

Comparing the statistics of pro- and anti-repatriates, Manhard concluded that "most outstanding is [the] percentage similarity [in] almost every statistic." Manhard observed that the "only major differences" between the two groups were that the more anti-repatriates tended to be professional soldiers with longer service in the Nationalist army than in the Communist forces, and a higher percentage of them were from the southwest.[10] The differences could be partially explained by the fact that the CPV 3rd Army Group from the southwest contributed the largest number of Chinese POWs. When the southwest was "liberated" at the end of 1949, the army group absorbed numerous former Nationalist troops but had yet purged all "unreformed Nationalist elements" when it was dispatched to Korea.

A fundamental question remains: What influenced Chinese prisoners of largely similar backgrounds to make opposite decisions when it came to repatriation? Manhard basically agreed with Sun that the UNC's reorientation program, the CIE, played a major role in aiding the rise of anti-Communist trusties and consequently swaying prisoners against repatriation.

Manhard maintained that the screening in April had failed to achieve its designed purpose of applying "objective criteria to determine bona fide anti-Commies." He argued:

> Polling actually appeared as choice between two political allegiances for POW's from divided countries. Polling procedure superimposed on background of extreme coercion and intimidation over long period of both pro- and anti-Commie leaders Korean compounds, anti-Commie leaders Chi[nese] compounds. Physical safety [of] all POW's immed[iately] before and during polling process [was] not guaranteed due [to] lack internal control of compounds by UN guards. Honest naiveté [in] polling questions resulted in involuntary repatriates and many involuntary non-repatriates, choice being made in atmosphere of fear and uncertainty.[11]

Manhard left out Chinese Communist leaders in his charge of "extreme coercion and intimidation over long period" perhaps for a simple reason: Compound 71, the only Communist-controlled enclosure, was established very late and remained very small—it had only 254 prisoners at the time of the polling.

Manhard advised against an immediate rescreening, as it would "probably produce little if any numerical shift," given the "continuing influence [of] previous pro and anti-Commie POW leaders" and the "resumption [of] CIE reorientation activities in present anti-repatriation camps."[12] If the Chinese POWs were to be rescreened, Manhard listed a number of preconditions. The three most important were:

- Separate judicial detention for all POW trusties of former compounds 72 and 86 in Koje-Do against whom evidence exists of subversion of purpose of original polling.
- Rigorous suppression of all PW-appointed "guards" and camp supervised election of new POW reps for smaller units of 500–1000 only.
- Cessation of all polit[ical] indoctrination activities such as CI and E 'reorientation' features and polit[ical] sermons and other non-religious activities by camp chaplains, whether American Chinese or Korean.[13]

These measures were exactly what the Communist prisoners had been demanding. Manhard's proposal amounted to an indictment of the CIE program and the pro-Nationalist prisoner leaders.

TABLE 12.1. *Major differences between pro- and anti-repatriation POWs*

	Pro-repatriates	Anti-repatriates
Total number	14,325	3,247
No CNA military service history	40%	33%
Some CNA service history	60%	67%
More CCF than CNA service	56%	42%
More CNA than CCF service	27%	39%
Common prewar occupation	Farmer	Soldier
North China natives	25%	11%
Southwest China natives	26%	35%

SOURCES: Muccio to Acheson, June 29, 1952, 695A.0024, RG 59, NA; Bradbury et al., *Mass Behavior*, provides the total numbers (343n).

NOTE: CCF: Chinese Communist Forces; CNA: Chinese Nationalist Army.

Manhard further suggested reclassifying bona fide "political defectors from communism . . . no longer POWs" and granting them "asylum from Commie control."[14] Without being privy to high-level discussions in Washington, Manhard's idea is very similar to Acheson's limited early parole scheme, which had been abandoned early on, as explained in Chapter 9. Not surprisingly, Manhard heard no response from Washington.

While Manhard was most critical of the anti-Communist trusties and their CIE sponsors, he held no punches when criticizing the prison authorities. Lamenting "camp command has had difficulty enforcing discipline among US and ROK troops," he noted, "Stones, songs and insults have on occasion been silenced by bullets and bayonets." Moreover, POWs' "authorized personal possessions . . . [are] frequently confiscated by other POWs, ROK and US personnel."[15] These were exactly the same grievances that the Communist prisoners had raised, but to no avail.

Manhard reported a universal complaint: "Amount and type of food ration subj[ect to] constant complaint among practically all Chi[nese] POWs regardless of polit[ical] attitude, and presumably among many Korean POWs."[16] "Since original diet established," Manhard wrote, "rice ration lowered in quality, two-thirds replaced by inferior grains often indigestible for many POWs and requiring more fuel to prepare. Stomach and digestive diseases long chronic among large number POWs."[17]

"Food bulk below non-combat standards of Commie forces" contributed to "previous POW resistance to camp authorities [on] Koje-do," Manhard argued. To remedy the situation, he recommended "modification of food ration to include more rice and vegetables in closer approximation [of] POW eating habits which will conserve fuel [to] cook unmilled grains and reduce medical expense."[18]

Manhard's suggestions, however, did not lead to any tangible improvement. In fact, the situation worsened after Chinese prisoners' move to Cheju. While rice was supplied on Koje, the main staple became unmilled barley and wheat on Cheju, which caused widespread diarrhea. Anti-Communist prisoners sought help from Chaplain Woodberry, who procured a small ox to power a mill. But the mill only flattened the wheat and failed to grind it. Chaplain Woodberry petitioned on the prisoners' behalf. Finally, rice was once again supplied in the anti-Communist camps.[19] Communist prisoners charged that after their move to Cheju in July, their main staple consisted of "unmilled barley, wheat or very roughly ground barley with a moldy smell." Even in his old age, Zhong Junhua still recalled with disgust the nearly indigestible diet. Only after the Communist prisoners launched a hunger strike in early August did the authorities resume supplying ground flour.[20]

If Manhard appeared sympathetic to the plight of Chinese prisoners, particularly the Communists, he nonetheless warned about the danger of allowing the "undisputed control" of compounds by "intractable pro-Commie POW leaders" after the screening.[21] To wrestle control away from them, Manhard suggested having them segregated from the rank and file, the same approach he had recommended for anti-Communist leaders.

On July 5, Manhard sent Boatner a detailed proposal, "by which maximum control could eventually be gained over the mass of POWs while minimizing the influence of hard-core Commie agitators." Designed to improve prison management and intelligence gathering, it "involved a careful and detailed screening for personal background by which segregation could be carried out based on rank, degree of political indoctrination, length of service and literacy." Once segregation was achieved, a prisoner would be exploited for three purposes: "1. Strategic intelligence. 2. Propaganda. 3. Political reorientation (away from Communism to understand and support democratic principles and practices)." Ultimately, his program aimed for "maximum effectiveness in exploiting POWs to our own advantage—to get the biggest pay-off on our investment in care and protection of POWs."[22] Unfortunately, Manhard suffered from the same blind spot that had plagued policymakers in Washington: they all failed to see the inherent moral predicament of indoctrinating prisoners. How could the United States convert prisoners to anti-Communists one day and then send them back into the hands of the Communists the next?

Manhard's proposal entailed not only a significant restructuring of the prison system but also a significant commitment of resources. The proposed "careful and detailed screening" required a large number of experienced Chinese linguists, who were in dire short supply throughout the war. As the only readily available source of linguists was Taiwan, bringing more Nationalist personnel to POW camps would only exacerbate the conflict in the camps. For all of these reasons, Manhard's proposal was inherently impractical.

More fundamentally, by the time Manhard furnished his reports to Washington in late June and early July 1952, a rescreening had been out of the question for the United States. The failure of a junior diplomat in a far-flung island outpost to effect policy changes in Washington is hardly surprising.

Nor did Boatner have strong incentives to implement Manhard's recommendations, despite the two men's frequent interactions. Having fought some of the most grueling battles of the war—at Bloody Ridge, Heart Break Ridge, and Mundung-ni near the 38th parallel—from December 1951 to April 1952 and restored order on Koje in June, Boatner perhaps looked forward to winding down his Asia tour.[23] With Boatner eyeing an exit, Manhard's influence diminished. Two other China Hands entered the scene.

Captain Joseph Brooks and Father Thomas O'Sullivan

Joseph Brooks of the 163rd Military Intelligence Service Detachment attached to the 1st Marine Division had interrogated many Chinese prisoners along the 38th parallel, including Zhang Zeshi (see Chapter 8). After his transfer to Koje, Brooks and chaplain Father Thomas O'Sullivan exercised "a great deal of immediate influence over the policies of handling this particular group of [pro-Communist] Chinese POWs since July" 1952, Manhard reported.[24]

Compared to Boatner and Manhard, Brooks and O'Sullivan were a different type of "China Hand." Both Boatner and Manhard had received formal Chinese language training.[25] In contrast, Brooks and O'Sullivan learned their Chinese "from the masses." Father O'Sullivan claimed he spoke three dialects after having lived among the Chinese from 1936 to 1949 and having spoken the language daily.[26] Brooks learned Chinese as a US Army officer attached to the Chinese Nationalist army from 1945 to 1949. He boasted that he had traveled to twenty-one of the country's twenty-eight provinces and spoke three major dialects—Mandarin, Shanghainese, and Cantonese. In addition, he was "familiar" with less common dialects in central, western, and southwestern China.[27]

Manhard doubted Brooks's language ability: "Although he claims to be a 'Chinese linguist' his vocabulary is limited to coolie lingo and he is almost completely illiterate in the written language."[28] Huang Tiancai, the DAC interrogator-interpreter, however, vouched for Brooks, under whom Huang had served in the 163rd Military Intelligence Service Detachment attached to the 1st Marine Division. "Among all

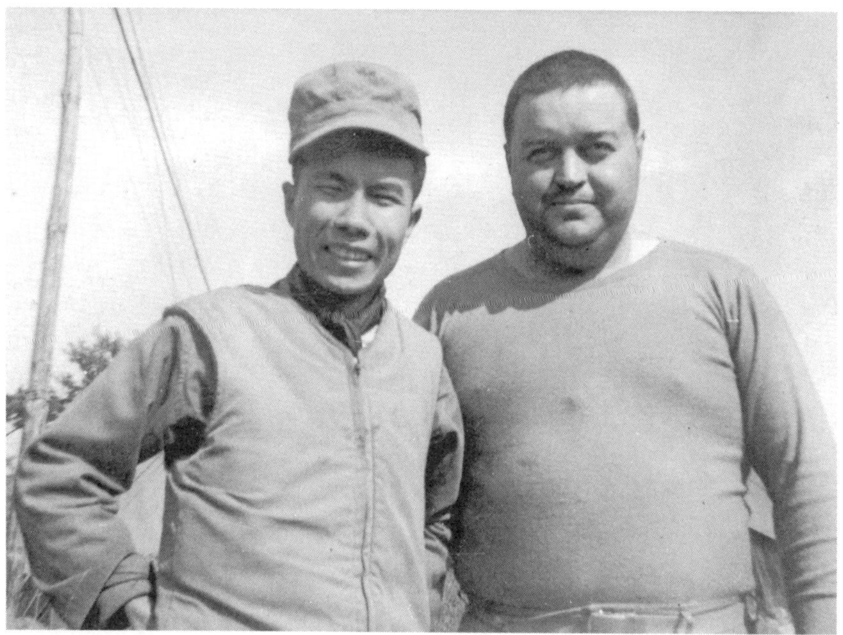

FIGURE 12.1. Captain Joseph Brooks and Department of the Army Civilian (DAC) interpreter Huang Tiancai, 164th Military Intelligence Detachment, attached to the 1st Marine Division. Spring 1951. Courtesy of Huang Tiancai.

the Chinese-speaking American officers I had met Brooks spoke the most authentic Mandarin," Huang recalled. "He had been to many places in China and he could understand a number of dialects."[29] When it came to interrogating Chinese prisoners speaking various dialects, Brooks was much more effective than American interpreters who were university-trained in standard but bookish Chinese.[30]

Zhang Zeshi was one of the few Chinese prisoners who had talked to both Brooks and Manhard. He recalled that in terms of spoken Chinese, the two men were at a comparable level; but Manhard's pronunciation was superior. "In terms of temperament/demeanor (*qizhi*), however, Brooks was no match for Philip."[31] Evidently, the tall, slender, and urbane Manhard, a graduate of the University of Southern California, impressed Zhang much more than the short, portly, and uncouth Brooks ever did. Moreover, the lasting negative image of Brooks was sealed during their final encounter, which took place in Koje's maximum-security prison. As a result, Zhang's impression of Brooks deteriorated from that of a friendly and simple American to a surly imperialist bully.

Interned in Koje's maximum-security prison, Sun Zhenguan, Zhang Zeshi, and another Chinese prisoner, Li Ziying, decided to hold a one-day hunger strike on July 1, 1952, to commemorate the founding of the CCP in 1921. On June 30, Zhang

FIGURE 12.2. Captain Joseph Brooks graces a UNC surrender leaflet that reads: "Surrendered comrades are smiling as they have received good treatment." Spring 1951. Vatcher papers, Hoover Archives.

drafted a protest letter addressed to Boatner. The next day, Brooks came to Zhang's cell, along with a doctor. They had not seen each other for over a year, since they first met in the POW stockade on the 38th parallel on May 27, 1951. After expressing sympathy for Zhang, Brooks told Zhang that he had been sent by Boatner to end the hunger strike. When Zhang refused to cooperate, Brooks threatened, "If you don't follow this order, I'll give you an injection to make your stomach burn!" Zhang noticed the doctor was carrying a tray with a syringe covered by gauze. In the end, Brooks did not carry out his threat; instead, he yelled at Zhang, "I'll keep you locked up here for good!"[32]

As far as Zhang was concerned, this Brooks on Koje was not the same man he had met a year earlier, when Brooks offered the newly captured Zhang a job as a civilian translator for the US Army and had told him that he could go to America to study physics after the war. Little did Zhang know that Brooks would soon become enemy number one of the Chinese Communist POWs on Cheju Island—the most-hated and most-wanted man, reviled as Dog Captain Brooks (*gou dawei Bulukesi*).

What differentiated Brooks and O'Sullivan from Boatner and Manhard was their open antagonism toward Communist prisoners. Boatner had a long and rich

FIGURE 12.3. Sun Zhenguan and Zhang Zeshi were confined in a maximum-security cell on Koje, similar to the one shown here, used for Communist leaders and "troublemakers." US National Archives.

relationship with the Chinese. In his writings, Boatner maintained a largely balanced view of China and the Chinese, and he displayed no particular hostility toward the Communists. In fact, privately he admitted he "never could become an enthusiastic supporter of the principle of voluntary repatriation," which "seemed like a propaganda exercise" to him.[33] In dealing with Chinese prisoners, Boatner was tough but reasonable. Manhard had witnessed the Communist "liberation" of Beiping first hand in early 1949 and stayed on as a deputy consul in Tianjin until the final evacuation of US diplomats in April 1950. He had had his share of difficulties in Communist China, but apparently he did not develop a hatred of the Chinese Communists.

After thirteen years in China, the Irish Franciscan Father O'Sullivan ended his mission in 1949.[34] Most likely he was deported. In view of the larger context of the Chinese Communists' expulsion of missionaries and persecution of Catholics, O'Sullivan could hardly be a friend of the Communists.

Brooks's hatred was much more visceral: his wife and child had been killed by the Communists. Brooks claimed that he first went to China with the Marshall Mission in 1946 and later served in the US Military Advisory Group. He met and married the sister of a Chinese colleague in 1947. They had a baby boy named Willy. When Brooks suffered from a severe case of jaundice, he returned stateside for treatment. He recovered in 1949, but by then China had fallen to the Communists. He had no information about his wife and child, except for hearsay that while fleeing south, they were captured and presumably killed by the Communists.[35] Brooks's story was so dramatic, so hapless at so many turns, that some people found it suspicious. Manhard asserted, "His claim that his Chinese wife and child were killed by the Chinese Commies in 1949 is open to doubt." Even Brooks's subordinate, the interrogator Huang Tiancai, had his doubts. Regardless of the truth, Brooks attitude toward the Communists was "characterized by vicious hatred and a burning desire for 'revenge,'" Manhard noted.[36]

Some prisoners, however, remembered Brooks as a man of honor. When Zhang Yifu's friend regimental deputy commissar Liu Guanglin was first captured, Brooks interrogated Liu. He took Liu's Russian-made wristwatch "for safekeeping," saying that it would only be confiscated or invite trouble in the prison camps. Two years later, Brooks tracked Liu down on Cheju and returned the watch.[37]

Arresting Colonel Zhao Zuoduan

If Brooks and Manhard had anything in common, it was their agreement on the need to segregate Communist leaders from rank-and-file POWs. In Manhard's view, "the majority of the pro-repatriation Chinese POWs" were different from their die-hard Communist leaders, as they were "certainly not fanatic, hard-core Communists."[38] The screening of April 1952 had one unintended consequence: it "allow[ed] Communist

POW leaders to take uncontested control over almost all prisoners choosing repatriation, the practical effect of which was to deny [the] exploitation of this group for intelligence and propaganda."[39] With their leaders removed, Manhard argued, the United States could begin "exploiting POWs to our own advantage" in the areas of "strategic intelligence, propaganda, and political reorientation."[40]

The Chinese Communists' top leader, also their highest-ranking officer on Koje, was Zhao Zuoduan, commissar of the 538th Regiment, 180th Division. Although Manhard had effectively saved Zhao's life half a year earlier by facilitating his transfer from Compound 72 to 71, he played a key role in Zhao's arrest in June, when Zhao was masquerading as a quartermaster. Manhard admitted that "the POW Command was unaware of his identity or rank until I suggested to General Boatner that he be segregated."[41]

Curiously, Zhao had long before been identified by G-2. In his interrogation report dated September 11, 1951, Zhao's full name ("Chao, Tso Tuan") and identity had been established. Significantly longer than usual, this fifteen-page report featured a full personal chronology of Zhao, along with detailed sociological, political, and military information, replete with multiple organizational charts of the Communist government and military.[42] Thus, it is evident that not only did G-2 know his identity, but that Zhao cooperated in the interrogations. Prior to this in-depth interrogation in Pusan, Zhao, disguised as quartermaster Wang Fang, had been uncovered by his former subordinates in Compound 72.[43] Already exposed, he decided to cooperate with his interrogators, so that he could stay away from Compound 72 as long as possible. Zhao rationalized his action in an interview in 1983: "If I'd refused to be interrogated, I would have been sent right back to 72," where he had been routinely tortured.[44]

If Zhao's identity had been known to G-2 in September 1951, how could the POW Command be unaware of his identify or rank in 1952? How could Zhao return to Koje using the alias Wang Fang? The answer to the first question lies in the peculiar dysfunction of the US military authorities; the key to the second question reveals the Chinese Communists' peculiarly secretive approach to underground struggle.

Manhard's claim that the POW Command was unaware of Zhao's identity was probably correct. He later lamented the lack of information sharing between various US military and government agencies, whose "interrogation teams have usually reported their information exclusively through their own, separate channels, while the camp command has had no access to certain information." Moreover, the "coordination of high-level policy and field-level operation between interested government agencies has been largely lacking, one result of which has been to deprive the camp command of information and advice necessary for efficient operation while embroiling it in internecine conflict with various field units having separate chains of command."[45] In Zhao's case, his interrogation was conducted in Pusan by ATIS under the Far East Command G-2 headquartered in Tokyo.

The POW Command's prisoner records were woefully inadequate, to the point of being "near useless" in Manhard's words. The US Army admitted that "the difficulty of translation of Korean and Chinese names into English made the few available records of little value," and fingerprints were "for the most part, of mediocre quality." Calling the situation "sad, embarrassing," Manhard concluded that the "UNC has never been able to develop, and does not now have, anything resembling adequate POW records." The US authorities had "almost no knowledge of the most elementary information about the prisoners." If it had some information, it was often unreliable. "Records do not match the prisoners and vice versa. The majority have assumed false names and ranks, [and] frequently switch or change internment numbers." The records of the Communist POWs were "probably in even worse condition than those of the anti-repatriates." The army conceded that "multiple identifications of single individuals frequently existed."[46]

The second question, however, remains: After Zhao was transferred to the small pro-Communist Compound 71 and became its de facto leader, why did he continue to use an alias? First, Zhao and the Communists might have detected the poor coordination between US agencies, and decided that since Zhao could get away with his alias, he should continue to use it. Second, by using the alias, the underground party organization could protect its leader from traitors. To an underground Communist, especially a leader, the most dangerous threat is not from the enemy in the open, but from within. Therefore, Zhao operated behind the scenes, while Sun Zhenguan, the third or fourth in the chain of command, acted as the nominal compound leader. In a similar arrangement, the famed Lee Hak-koo was a mere figurehead of the Korean Communist POWs; their actual leader was Pak Sang-hyon, a former provincial party secretary operating under deep cover in Compound 76. Pak was not identified and segregated until some time after the June 10 breakup of Compound 76.[47]

Once informed of Zhao's identity, Boatner decided to segregate him. This seemingly simple task turned out to be difficult. While Operation Breakup and the subsequent transfer of Korean prisoners to the newly built 500-man sub-enclosures had subdued the Koreans, more than 5,000 pro-Communist Chinese prisoners still lived in one large unsegregated compound, No. 602, until June 16. At this point, the UNC had completed the construction of 500-man pens on Cheju Island.[48] Before moving the Chinese pro-Communists to Cheju, Boatner decided to segregate Zhao.

Boatner proceeded methodically. On June 17, the POW Command announced that the Chinese prisoners were to move to Compound 70 near the pier, a step in preparation for the transfer to Cheju. "In view of the bloody massacre in Compound 76," the POW leadership decided to comply, as a means to "conserve strength." The POWs were moved without incident.[49]

The next day, a broadcast vehicle announced the order to have "Wang Fang" turn himself in at the gate. Zhao and other leaders decided to ignore the order. "The loudspeaker blared out the order all day long" in the ensuing days, yet the prisoners remained unmoved. In the meantime, Zhao summoned the Central Committee of Communist Solidarity to prepare for the worst. They decided to expand the Central Committee and branch committees to include four echelons of replacement leaders. This meeting turned out to be the last Central Committee meeting Zhao chaired.[50]

Twelve days would elapse before Zhao's final arrest on June 30. In the old days when anti-Communist prisoners were in charge of Compounds 72 and 86, the authorities could arrest any prisoner they wished. The rough and tough anti-Communist trusties would quickly deliver any suspected Communist. After the screening, the POW Command lost its eyes, ears, and arms. Manhard observed that "one result [of] repatriation polling placed intractable pro-Commie POW leaders in undisputed control [of] many large compounds without internal control by UN."[51] Now, the authorities even had trouble entering the Chinese compound, not to mention arresting its leader, who was heavily protected and in disguise. This was a situation similar to that of the Korean Compound 76 before the June 10 crackdown.

"These [Chinese POW] leaders," Manhard pointed out, "possibly fear being killed or punished whether or not they follow camp orders."[52] In fact, they were justifiably wary of the intentions of the POW Command. Exacerbating their suspicion, their representative Sun and chief interpreter Zhang had not been seen since May 7, when they were taken to Compound 76. Understandably, no leader would voluntarily turn himself in.

To single out a prisoner from a mass of more than 5,000 men presented a major challenge. Even if US troops forcibly entered the compound and subdued all the prisoners, they still needed to identify the single man they wanted. Although the authorities had one-inch headshots of prisoners on file, such small photographs would be of little help. The saying that "to a white man all Chinese looked the same" may well be a flippant cliché, but there was some truth to it in the POW camps. For example, prisoners managed to swap identities and enclosures through a simple means: when two work detail teams from different enclosures crossed paths, prisoners would create a commotion and switch teams. The US guards, unable to communicate with the prisoners, were powerless to prevent this.[53]

Certainly, Manhard could easily have identified Zhao. But no one could realistically expect him to finger Zhao, whom he had befriended and helped in the past. Therefore, unless someone else who knew Zhao stepped forward to literally do the finger pointing, Zhao could never be segregated. That person would have to be a "traitor," and one was yet to emerge.

In his next move, Boatner split the Chinese prisoners into two camps. On June 28, approximately 3,000 Chinese prisoners were forcibly segregated and transferred to Compound 66. To accomplish this, "the US troops threw more than forty tear gas bombs into the crowd of Chinese prisoners."[54] On June 30, after tear gas attacks, the remaining 2,000-plus Chinese prisoners in Compound 70 were forced to leave their compound and assemble on the seaside. They were made to walk single file before a "traitor," a former machine gun platoon leader in Zhao's regiment. This led to Zhao's arrest.[55]

Zhao was held in Koje's maximum-security prison for ten days only. During his absence, with the aid of tear gas, the authorities transported the 3,000 prisoners in Compound 66 to Cheju Island on July 3. On July 9, the 2,000-odd prisoners in Compound 70 resisted their scheduled move. They demanded to see Zhao to make sure he was still alive. Yielding to their demand, the POW Command released Zhao from the maximum-security prison and sent him along with this group of prisoners to Cheju.[56]

Downplaying his own role in Zhao's arrest, Manhard claimed that Zhao's "solitary confinement since around July first apparently on the recommendation of Brooks." He continued, "No formal charge has ever been made, but the apparent attitude of the local Army officials is that he is a 'potential trouble-maker' being a hard-core Communist." Manhard asserted, "I, of course, did not intend that he be given unnecessarily cruel and unusual punishment for committing no illegal act."[57]

With the benefit of hindsight, however, Manhard should not have felt so sorry for Zhao. First, although certainly uncomfortable, Zhao's ten-day solitary confinement on Koje was not so much a "cruel and unusual punishment" when compared to the frequent torture he had suffered at the hands of anti-Communist prisoners on Koje.[58]

Second, whether Zhao committed any "illegal act" was a matter of perspective and time frame. After his final meeting with Zhao in early July, Manhard met Sun Zhenguan and Zhang Zeshi for the last time on August 3 in Koje's maximum-security prison, where he gave them two Chinese books and copies of *Time* and *Reader's Digest.* To procure these books for "his old friends," Manhard said, he had flown to Pusan on the previous day.[59] There is no indication that Manhard visited the Chinese prisoners in their new camps on Cheju. Apparently he lost direct contact with Chinese prisoners. More importantly, the Chinese Communist prisoners were no longer the same disorganized underdogs as on Koje. They were in total control of the ten subcompounds in their camp. Their organizational capability on Cheju was far greater than Manhard realized. Their ingenuity in clandestine communications far exceeded anyone's imagination, as did their cruelty in struggles against suspected traitors and the prison authorities.

Ensconced in the relative safety of the Close Confinement Stockade, Zhao and other top Communist leaders directed a resistance movement and mobilized the prisoners to rise up against the authorities.

POWs "Worked Over Frequently" on Cheju

While Manhard failed to recognize the strength of the underground Communists, he correctly pointed out the responsibility of the other side in the dangerous confrontation on Cheju. He reported that "according to a CIC officer who spends a great deal of time in the Chejudo camps and is well qualified in written and spoken Chinese, the pro-repatriation Chinese POWs on Chejudo have been worked over frequently . . . with various 'riot control' techniques."[60] These techniques, having been practiced since Boatner's arrival in May, were applied with increasing intensity and frequency on Cheju. In response, the prisoners upped the ante.

Shortly before their move from Koje to Cheju, on July 1, 1952, the 31st anniversary of the founding of the CCP and the day after Zhao's arrest, "two traitors were promptly uncovered and executed the same night" by the Communist underground, according to the "Chronology of the People's Volunteers Prisoners' Struggles in US Concentration Camps" ("Dashiji") compiled by Communist POW leaders.[61]

Once the pro-Communist prisoners arrived at Camp 3A on the outskirts of the city of Cheju, they were held in the newly built 500-man enclosures, which were ironically built by their anti-Communist brethren in May and June. Each of the ten enclosures was surrounded by three layers of four-meter-high barbed wire fences; the larger overall compound was surrounded by another three layers of fences.[62]

Contrary to the POW Command's hope that this new enclosure layout would end the prisoners' resistance, tensions escalated. On July 7, prisoner Guo Zhihua was bayoneted and wounded on a work detail. The next day, the 3,000 Chinese prisoners in various enclosures held coordinated mass demonstrations. In response, the authorities cut off their food and water.[63] This confrontation soon led to the first POW fatality on Cheju.

On the night of July 9, Chaplain Thomas O'Sullivan accompanied a US officer to Enclosure 2, where the prisoners had been digging near the fence. Claiming that they were thirsty, the prisoner representative argued, "We will stop digging the hole if you give us water." O'Sullivan shouted back, "Step back! Everyone away from the fence and the hole." All prisoners scattered and went back to their tents, where "singing and rhythmic clapping of hands began within a few minutes." O'Sullivan told the US officer, "They are singing Communist songs." He suspected the noise was designed to cover "some special plans on foot."[64]

While O'Sullivan and US troops were waiting and watching, a lone prisoner emerged from a tent and approached the hole. O'Sullivan recalled,

> When he came to the hole he hesitated a moment. A shot rang out. . . . Evidently he was not shot. . . . Within another four or five minutes a prisoner of war appeared [in] the same direction as the last prisoner of war. . . . Another shot rang out. He moved

slightly. Another shot rang out. He turned quickly, bent a little, ran about three steps, stumbled at the entrance as if he tripped on the tent ropes.[65]

The next morning, the corpse of prisoner Zhang Donghai was taken to the compound gate. A postmortem examination revealed that he had been shot point-blank "through the head." A bullet went into his right temple and out from his left temple, where "brain tissue exuded" and "the perforation is jagged and measured 8 cm in diameter."[66] Without calling any prisoner witnesses, the board of investigators nevertheless concluded that his death "was non-intentional, and was not due to the culpable negligence" of the guard who fired the shot. No one was punished.[67]

The message the US military conveyed to the prisoners seemed to boil down to "Obey orders, or get shot!" Communication between the authorities and prisoners had been reduced to orders from the authorities and POWs' protests as answers. The POW Command's reliance on O'Sullivan for day-to-day interpretation work between the guards and prisoners only exacerbated the tension instead of reducing it.

Furthermore, the POW Command imposed an information blockade on the Chinese prisoners. Although in the old days on Koje the Chinese Communist prisoner leaders regularly communicated with their Korean counterparts via underground channels, on Cheju they were totally cut off from any friendly sources of information. Facing increasingly hostile authorities and unsure of their intentions, the Chinese Communist prisoners became ever more desperate and agitated. With their leaders being rounded up, replacement leaders stepped forward with ever more combative countermeasures. Camp 3A was becoming a cauldron of frustration, anger, hate, intrigue, and, eventually, war.

On the same day that Zhang Donghai was shot, July 9, Zhao Zuoduan and the last batch of some 2,000 prisoners temporarily held in Koje's Compound 70 were shipped to Cheju. Hours after their arrival at Camp 3A, Zhao was taken to the nearby Close Confinement Stockade, where he was to remain until his repatriation fourteen months later. The ranks in this special enclosure for top leaders and "troublemakers" eventually swelled to over sixty—so many that they later formed their own party branch.[68]

With their top leader cut off from the main compound and other Central Committee members scattered in different enclosures, each roughly a hundred meters apart, communication among prisoners across compounds became an urgent challenge. Ingenious prisoners rose to the occasion. Only three days after Zhao arrived on Cheju, a semaphore-like system consisting of simple and inconspicuous hand gestures was devised. When prisoners were transmitting between compounds, prison guards initially thought they were practicing calisthenics.[69] As all ten enclosures and the Close Confinement Stockade were within sight of each other, orders, instructions, and reports were transmitted in relays between the Central Committee and various enclosures. The "Chronology" boasts that with the invention of these code transmission techniques in mid-July, "the prisoners in all of Camp 3A acted in a concerted and unified manner."[70]

Other methods were also employed. Prisoners slung rocks to the next compound with coded messages on paper tied to the rocks. Between the two compounds farthest apart, relaying a message via rock-slinging required only one hour, while via semaphore it took more than two hours.[71] As the Korean prisoners had done on Koje, the Chinese prisoners on work details hid messages behind rocks near the pier, which were retrieved by comrades from other compounds. Prisoners also hid messages in food delivery trucks, which made the rounds to multiple enclosures.[72] When required, prisoners entered different enclosures by crawling under fences at night or swapping work detail teams when walking past each other during the day.[73]

When it became absolutely necessary for face-to-face communications with their leaders confined in the special stockade, prisoners picked fights with US guards. As punishment, they were taken to the troublemakers' stockade, which was separated from Zhao's cell by a wall. A small hole had been drilled in the wall, through which they could talk at night.[74]

All these clandestine communications were controlled by the underground Communist leadership. Immediately after the creation of the semaphore system, the Central Committee ordered the creation of branch committees in all ten enclosures.[75] Three echelons of replacement leadership teams were prepared in each branch. Therefore, whatever happened, new leaders could step forward to take charge.[76] Like the standard structure of the Communist Party, each branch committee had a number of functional units, including organization, propaganda, logistics, and security sections. The most critical was the security section, since it controlled communications and enforced discipline.

As the Chinese Communists were perfecting their organization, the prison authorities clamped down.

Boatner: "Shoot to Kill"

On August 4, Boatner was promoted from a brigadier to a major general. Clark hailed Boatner's performance on Koje, on top of his superior combat record as assistant commander of the 2nd Infantry Division during "some of the hardest fighting in Korea."[77] Ten days later, Boatner was promoted to lead the newly established Prison of War Command under the Korean Communications Zone (KCOMZ), a new UNC unit created by Clark to relieve the Eighth Army of all non-combat responsibilities in Korea.[78] While he was responsible for all prisons on the Korean mainland, Koje, and Cheju, Boatner trained his sights on the increasingly belligerent Chinese Communist prisoners in Camp 3A.

Camp 3A's underground leadership first flexed its muscle on August 1, PLA Day. Prisoners raised improvised red flags in all ten enclosures. When US troops entered the compounds, the prisoners managed to lower the flags and concealed them. Troops could only destroyed the flagpoles. Riding high on their first success on Cheju, the POWs proceeded to launch yet another struggle in early August, staging a hunger strike to protest the "abusive" diet consisting mostly of unmilled barley. During the protest, prisoners briefly "restrained" a sergeant and forced him to "eat green wheat which had been distributed and had caused diarrhea." In response, the Camp 3A's commander, Colonel William F. Due, made four prisoners "kneel on the ground in front of the compound all the rest of the day." Nevertheless, the authorities eventually agreed to provide ground grain. The prisoners claimed another victory.[79]

The second flag-raising demonstration was staged on August 15, V-J Day. As Camp 3A was located on the outskirts of the city of Cheju, prisoners pointedly raised a North Korean flag "to have a bigger impact." This time, however, the POW Command reacted with force. US and ROK troops entered compounds, removed flags, destroyed flagpoles, and placed compound leaders in solitary confinement. The prisoners charged, "US troops threw tear gas grenades into all ten enclosures. Four prisoners and four UNC guards were injured."[80]

Clark was livid. Calling the events "embarrassing and harmful to our position in the Eyes of the Free World," he reprimanded KCOMZ commander Thomas W. Herren: "it is incomprehensible to me how prisoners could have in their possession Red Flags for demonstrations, or how they could seize a member from the security forces and force him to eat a POW ration." Herren relayed the message to Boatner and added, "No one in this command has ever been criticized, censored or disciplined by me for using too much force." He declared, "Prisoners who throw or attempt to throw rocks at guards should be shot while in the act." In addition, "prisoners must salute [US officers] as prescribed." On August 20, Herren and Boatner flew to Cheju to hold a conference with officers. They recommended "shoot to kill" when shooting was required. Herren announced that he would accept "POW threw rock at UNC personnel, POW shot dead" as "a satisfactory example of an incident report." Boatner followed up with a special order the next day: "If any incident where POWs are observed hitting, striking, kicking, biting, or in any other ways observed doing injury or maiming or threatening to injure or maim UN personnel, such POW will be shot at that moment."[81]

Hours after the meeting, a prisoner, while on a work detail in the prison office, stole a note taken during Boatner's and Herren's speeches. The message was translated from English to Chinese, to code, and then transmitted to Colonel Zhao Zuoduan in his stockade. Zhao read the message as: "the POW Command must use force, and should not refrain from eliminating [*buxi xiaomie*] the most diehard Reds."[82] When this understanding was transmitted back to other underground Communist branches for discussion, it was read as "it is permissible to find pretexts to massacre prisoners."[83] Fear for their own personal safety precipitated the leaders' decision to take bolder actions.

Before August 20, the Communist leadership had already ordered all compounds to launch "counterattacks from the periphery." Prisoners on work details were instructed to wage "small-scale struggles," such as holding strikes and even "seizing guns from the guards."[84] It is worth noting that the UN prisons observed the Geneva Convention, which exempted officer prisoners from labor. Thus, conveniently all known officers were spared from direct actions.

In late August, prisoners from Enclosure 3 had two clashes with guards during work details. They went on strike to protest against "soldiers beating prisoners for no reason." The authorities cut off food and water for two hours in one instance and a full day in the other. And the prisoners were forced to stand in the rain. In yet another occurrence, they were ordered out of their tents and left outdoors overnight. Furthermore, three prisoners suffered bullet wounds. In Enclosure 10, the tuberculosis patients' compound, the prisoners "gave the US officer and sergeant a good beating after they insulted and beat their Enclosure Representative" and drove them off the premises. The authorities withheld water and food for a day and arrested the "representative" and two other prisoners.[85]

After learning of the "shoot to kill" order by Herren and Boatner, the Communist leaders decided to take more immediate and drastic action. On August 26, Wei Lin, the first in command after Zhao's arrest, had two ethnic Korean POWs escape from the camp in order to contact Korean guerrillas on Cheju. The two prisoners managed to make it as far as Mount Halla at the center of Cheju Island, but before long they were apprehended and taken back. Wei was arrested on August 31 and put in the Close Confinement Stockade. US troops searched Wei's former enclosure for contraband, but found nothing.[86]

On August 28, Boatner, only two weeks into his job as the head of the POW Command, turned over his command to his deputy, Colonel Charles V. Caldwell, recently provost marshal of the Eighth Army. He would return to the United States to serve as the deputy commander of the Fourth Army at San Antonio, Texas.[87]

Clark presented an Oak Leaf cluster to Boatner's Distinguished Service Medal on September 1, praising him for the "exercise of strong leadership," which "permitted security troops to obtain complete jurisdiction over more than 160,000 war prisoners."[88] A day later, *People's Daily* sent the "Old China Hand" a farewell indictment:

"Although he has already left, he should be put on trial as a war criminal." It blustered, "these executioners will not escape the punishment they deserve. The noose of justice awaits them!"[89]

Exactly one month after Boatner's departure, Camp 3A would descend into a bloodbath, where more prisoners were killed than in Boatner's crackdown of Compound 76.

13

October 1 Massacre on Cheju

"FANATIC REDS RIOT on Cheju; 52 Slain: G.I.'s Quell Chinese P.W.'s in First Mass Uprising" screamed the October 2, 1952, *New York Times* headline. The final death toll of 56 made this riot on October 1 the second most deadly prison incident of the war, surpassing the 41 deaths incurred in the widely publicized breakup of Korean Compound 76 on June 10. Although the reason for the outbreak was "not clear," the report mentioned that "the Chinese were celebrating the third anniversary of the Peiping Communist regime" on October 1. The UNC promptly issued an official statement blaming the prisoners for attempting a mass prison breakout and "reverting to former patterns of violence." The *Times* report, however, noted "it was the first time that Chinese prisoners had engaged in a mass disorder. Earlier large-scale disturbances in the prison compounds had been confined almost entirely to fanatical North Korean Communists."[1] Similarly, US embassy official Manhard commented in an internal report, "The history of this group of POWs shows that they have degenerated from an almost completely cooperative behavior in May and June to an attitude of defiance rapidly becoming unanimous." He highlighted the fact that "of an approximate total of 500 POWs in this compound about 11% were killed and 25% wounded."[2] At Panmunjom, General Nam Il called the event "a barbarous yet cowardly massacre."[3]

Was this incident a mass prison break or a deliberate massacre?

"Time for Bloodshed"

Following the pro-Communist prisoners' flag-raising demonstrations on August 1 and 15, both the POWs and the prison authorities anticipated a similar demonstration on October 1, the PRC's National Day. The prisoners knew that the authorities would definitely intervene, as they had done before. In August, when troops forcibly entered the enclosures to confiscate the flags, the prisoners either hid or surrendered the flags. The demonstrations ended quickly without fatalities. This time, however, the POW leaders decided that the prisoners must defend the flags to the death. They considered bloodshed inevitable and a price worth paying—it was just a matter of how much.

A price in blood for what, exactly? First of all, the Communist leaders sought to create a major incident to demonstrate the Chinese prisoners' determination to return to China, as they believed that "US delegates at Panmunjom had repeated the claim that 'Korean and Chinese prisoners do not wish to be repatriated' to justify their policy of 'voluntary repatriation.'"[4] While the anti-repatriation voice of their anti-Communist foes had been amplified at Panmunjom, the Communist POWs patriotic voice had been absent. They felt duty-bound to make their voices heard.

Colonel Zhao Zuoduan later explained that "to demonstrate to the whole world our determination to return to our motherland, to expose our enemy's barbarity, and to rip apart its claim to represent 'freedom and democracy,' we collectively decided to commemorate our National Day on October 1."[5] The POW leaders calculated that a sufficiently large protest on Cheju would draw the world's attention; and a sufficient amount of bloodshed would lead the world to question the morality of "voluntary repatriation."

While the professed goal of aiding the Panmunjom talks seemed elusive, a major incident on Cheju would serve a more immediate purpose: to mobilize and unify the prisoners through constant struggle against the enemy. Since their transfer from Koje to Cheju in July, the Chinese Communist prisoners had been cut off from their North Korean comrades. Manhard, the more or less friendly Chinese-speaking American, was no longer in contact. Their daily encounters with the likes of Brooks and O'Sullivan added nothing but hostility and mistrust. The only information they could glean was from the mouths of friendly US guards and scraps of newspapers such as the US Army newspaper *Stars and Stripes* they stole while on work details.[6] Not surprisingly, their calculations of the situation in Cheju and the war were based on very little information, much speculation, and a great deal of zeal.

In September 1952, the impasse at Panmunjom nearly led to a breakdown in the negotiations. Bits and pieces of the news of the deadlock reached Chinese prisoners on Cheju. "A negative mood of frustration, exhaustion and desperation began to spread slowly" among the rank-and-file prisoners.[7] They began to doubt the purpose and efficacy of their daily struggle against the Americans. Prisoner Cai Pingsheng recalled his sentiment at the time: "Had we just cooperated with the Americans, and waited for repatriation, there would have been no trouble."[8]

To reverse this dangerous tide of "right-leaning passivity," the underground Central Committee held an emergency meeting. "Is bloodshed necessary while we are waiting to be repatriated?" the leaders asked. Some argued, "It's time for bloodshed. Living peacefully under the Americans can only weaken our fighting spirit." Others argued, "Without bloodshed and sacrifice, we cannot have an impact on the Panmunjom talks. The question is how much bloodshed." One leader reasoned, "If the sacrifice is too great, we would wrong the masses (*duibuqi qunzhong*); if the sacrifice is too small, there will not be a sufficient international impact. How can we possibly achieve the maximum impact with a minimum sacrifice?" The dominant view that emerged was that "revolutionary soldiers should not be afraid of sacrifices. New China was won at the cost of martyrs' blood. Today, we are all sinners [for being taken prisoner]. Is there anything we cannot forsake?" Via secret code, Zhao Zuoduan weighed in from his cell in the Close Confinement Stockade: "Without bloodshed and sacrifice, we cannot unify the masses. Without paying the price in lives, we cannot demonstrate our steadfast love for the party and the country. The masses will not allow bloodless cooperation. In the future, the motherland and the people will not forgive us!"[9]

In their calculation of risk and return, the leaders' concerns over their own political future weighed heavily. The leaders' reasoning displayed a strong desire to redeem their own sin of being taken prisoner and making compromises under various circumstances. This desire for redemption motivated them to escalate the struggle. However, while they claimed that they were unafraid of death—which may well have been the truth—the implication was that the price in blood was to be mainly paid by the masses. True to the tradition of the Communist underground, the top leaders operated behind the scenes, letting the masses charge at the front and bear the brunt of the repercussions. For the larger cause of the revolution, the leaders were assets too precious to be sacrificed on the front line.

Regardless of the prisoner leaders' deeper psychological motives, the worsening conditions in the prison convinced many of the need for immediate action. On September 19, prisoner Li Xiaoguang in Enclosure 8 scaled the fence and sought protection from the authorities. He returned with troops and had Central Committee member Wang Huaying identified and arrested. On September 21, more than twenty prisoners on work details were bayoneted when they insisted on singing.[10] From September 20 to 25, troops entered five enclosures, removed all prisoners to another area for a strip-search and searched the compounds thoroughly for contraband.[11] The prisoners alleged that during the week, 54 were bayoneted and wounded; more than 600 were denied water and food for over 45 hours when they were removed from their enclosures; more than 1,000 were stripped naked and beaten.[12]

As the POW Command ratcheted up pressure on the POWs, the underground Communist leadership concluded that drastic actions were required. On September 23, the Central Committee issued an order entitled "Strike Back at the Enemy on October 1," calling on all the enclosures to raise the PRC flag on National Day. "In case of enemy intervention, strike back resolutely and protect the flags, even if it requires bloodshed and sacrifice." Two days later, each branch committee began its mobilization of the masses "from inner circles to outer circles," i.e., party members first, trusted non-party members second, and less reliable elements last. Quickly, "the masses were aroused. They expressed their wish to join the dare-to-die squads and the flag protection squads."[13] The dare-to-die squads were tasked with attacking the enemy troops with rocks and tent poles. It was understood that eventually prison guards would prevail and approach the flagpoles, where the flag protection squads were to make a last-ditch effort to safeguard the flags.

Gu Zesheng, the fifth in command and the de facto leader after the arrest of the other top leaders, recalled, "It was obvious to everyone that rocks and clubs could not kill the enemy, but machine gun bullets could kill us."[14] Nevertheless, prisoners volunteered to sign up for these suicide missions. Many exchanged their home addresses with their comrades, in preparation for martyrdom. "Wash away the shame through struggle, fight for honor!" was the call to battle. A few months earlier on Koje, many prisoners, motivated by the same slogans, had operated on their own bodies to remove anti-Communist tattoos. But the profound sense of guilt did not disappear with their removed skin. The indoctrination program of underground Communists constantly reminded the prisoners that they had "committed sin" against the party and Chairman Mao. The guiltiest were those who had allowed anti-Communist tattoos to contaminate their bodies. Aware of the grave danger entailed in protecting the flags on October 1, some prisoners saw this as "an opportunity to finally 'wash away shame and win back honor.'" In religious terms, Li Ziying wrote, "almost like solemnly making sacrifices before the altar, many prisoners were prepared to charge the enemy's guns . . . under the [PRC's] red five-star flag on October 1."[15]

In this atmosphere of anxious expectancy, prisoners began preparations for the looming battle. They stockpiled rocks, which were broken down from large stones originally provided for the construction of kitchens. They stored gasoline that was provided as cooking fuel.[16] They planned to boil hot water and pour it onto approaching troops. The also made spears out of tent poles and fashioned wooden clubs with spikes and barbed wire.[17]

The Central Committee made two important decisions on September 25. First, it had the enclosure representative send a notice to the POW Command, announcing that the prisoners planned to raise flags on October 1 in celebration of the National Day. It was phrased more like an ultimatum than a request for permission. According to Gu Zesheng, the notice stated, "According to the Geneva Convention, prisoners enjoy the freedom of assembly to express political beliefs. Your side must observe the Convention; otherwise, you will be held responsible for whatever negative consequences may result."[18]

To the authorities, this notice sounded preposterous. Few Chinese prisoners had ever heard of the Geneva Convention until they learned about it from their North Korean comrades. "According to the Geneva Convention" soon became their mantra in any argument with the Americans, notwithstanding the fact that no prisoner possessed a copy of the Convention. Gu's reference to the "freedom of assembly to express political beliefs" was probably a misunderstanding or intentional misinterpretation of Article 34, which reads, "Prisoners of war shall enjoy complete latitude in the exercise of their religious duties, including attendance at the service of their faith, on condition that they comply with the disciplinary routine prescribed by the military authorities. Adequate premises shall be provided where religious services may be held."[19] The Communist prisoners believed Communism was their religion.

As expected, the POW Command rejected the prisoners' plan and threatened that "any unusual activity on October 1 will be treated as a 'riot' and dealt with accordingly."[20] The Chinese prisoners often argued that Boatner had agreed to allow them to fly flags to celebrate their holidays if they asked for permission first.[21] They claimed that Boatner sent a memorandum containing such a promise to Compound 602 on June 2, the same day that Boatner sent tanks into 602 to destroy the flagpole and seize the flag.[22] Colonel Richard D. Boerem, the Cheju prison commandant from late September, later stated that he had never heard of such a thing. His deputy, Lt. Col. Charles Helderman, concurred: "I have not seen it. I know of no one who has seen it."[23]

Manhard maintained that "General Boatner established a policy in June whereby pro-Commie POWs would be permitted to display certain prescribed insignia and take the day off on recognized Commie holidays, provided they submitted proper written application in advance and stuck to the approved activities on the day in question."[24] *Time* magazine also reported that Boatner left a policy that "prisoners should be allowed to celebrate Red holidays if they were orderly and obeyed the rules."[25] In his private papers, Boatner said nothing about the alleged memorandum, probably for a good reason. In view of the tragedy on October 1, he certainly would have preferred not to be implicated by giving prisoners false expectations.

Most likely the prisoners misinterpreted Boatner's permission to "display certain prescribed insignia" as a blanket authorization to fly flags. In reality, as noted earlier, Boatner cracked down twice on flag-raising demonstrations, on August 1 and 15. The prisoners' repeated reference to the alleged memorandum was a means to legitimize their claim to rightful political assembly. Ultimately, their decision had been made and they were determined to raise flags regardless of the authorities' response.

Assassinating Americans and Purging "Traitors"

Also on September 25, the prisoner leaders made another bold decision. Gu Zesheng suggested killing one or two American officers to "beat back the American aggression" and boost morale. Du Gang concurred. They decided to kill Camp 3A's commander Colonel William F. Due and Captain Brooks before October 1.[26] Knowing that an attempt on the lives of the prison commander and officers amounted to a suicide mission, the leaders consciously and actively sought bloodshed. They believed that the inevitable violence, and the possible killing of enemy officers, would energize the prisoners before the October 1 demonstration, and this in turn would generate a greater propaganda impact. This decision had raised the stakes extraordinarily high.

The camp commander, Colonel Due, luckily escaped the assassination attempt, as he was replaced by Colonel Boerem, deputy commander of the POW Command, in late September after a "complete investigation" into "incidents of increasing violence."[27] The descent of the deputy commander of the UNC's thirteen POW camps upon Camp 3A attested to the gravity of the situation.

Brooks, the "Dog Captain," had become enemy number one on Cheju, as much bad blood had been building since the arrest of Colonel Zhao. Private First Class Patrick Vigil of Albuquerque, New Mexico, a squad leader in the 35th Regiment, 25th Infantry Division, arrived in Cheju with his regiment on September 16, 1952, and soon witnessed an incident. When he was guarding the main entrance to an enclosure one day, Vigil saw the heavyset MP Captain Brooks and a sergeant speaking to a prisoner representative inside the compound. "Suddenly, he slapped the prisoner across his face. Then wham! A backhand." The prisoner just "stood at attention, straight like a board, stoic," but "seething with anger," as Vigil could tell from the color of his face. Later Vigil heard from fellow soldiers the reason Brooks "slapped the hell out of the prisoner": because the poor man bowed, instead of saluting him.[28] Vigil's comrade, Howard W. Schaeffer of Colo, Iowa, remembered Brooks as "Captain Big," a man "fast with his fists." Schaeffer also saw Brooks "us[ing] his left hand to slap Chinks." Schaeffer remarked, "Boy, he hated them." The source of his venom was that the Communists had "killed his wife and children over in China" in 1949—a story he had told many.[29]

The Communist leadership selected Enclosure 7 to carry out the assassinations. The party secretary there, Han Zijian, held an emergency meeting to develop a plan. Excited by the honor of "fighting as the vanguard of the more than five thousand Chinese prisoners," the leaders concluded that the best opportunity to kill Brooks would be during the Monday roll call, when prisoners were required to assemble and salute him. Another option was to have work detail members kill him outside the compound. Immediately the masses were mobilized, and many wrote pledges to kill Brooks. They secretly made more than a hundred knives from gasoline barrels and metal shanks removed from boots. As the would-be assassins rehearsed their plans, Brooks's death seemed imminent.[30]

In the meantime, the Central Committee issued another order: "To secure victory on October 1, take strict measures to prevent traitors [from escaping]!" Monitors in each enclosure were posted to guard all compound exits, 24/7.[31] A 30- to 50-man-strong monitor squad (*jiuchadui*), roughly equivalent to a PG squad in the anti-Communist compounds, was the crack troop unit of each enclosure. These squads were directed by the secretive security section (*baoweizu*), whose duty entailed protecting leaders and flags, gathering intelligence, and purging traitors.[32]

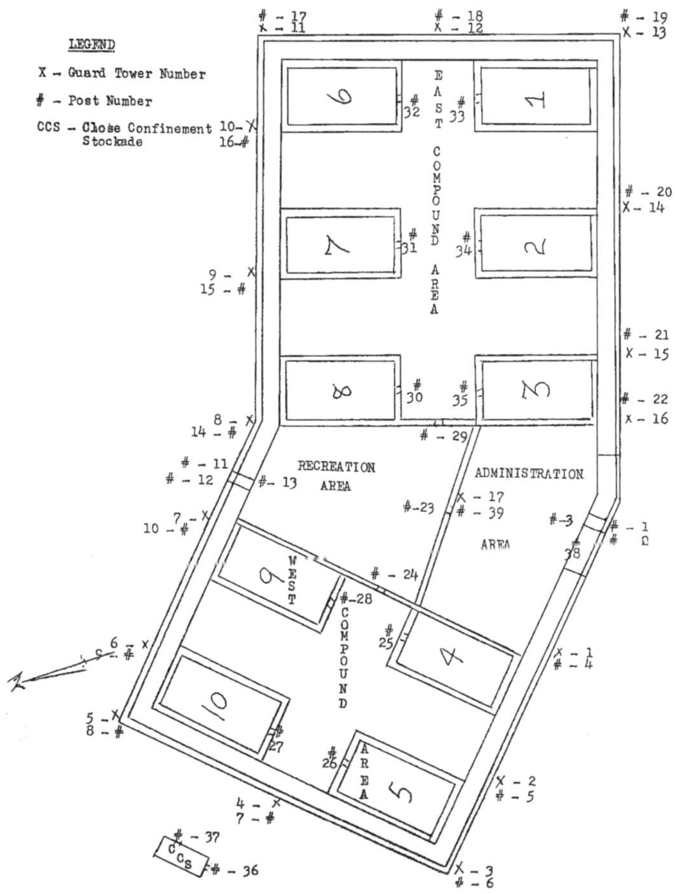

MAP 5. Camp 3A for Chinese Communist POWs, Cheju City
The Close Confinement Stockade (CCS) for POW leaders was located outside the main compound. US National Archives.

Knowing that not every prisoner was enthusiastic about the prospect of imminent bloodshed and probable death, Central Committee member and security section chief Li Xi'er made plans to deal with waverers. Following the Chinese Communist tradition, Li had secretly categorized "the masses" into three tiers: those who could be trusted and relied upon (*yikao*), those who could be "united" with (*tuanjie*), and those who were to be "consolidated" (*gonggu*). The security section assigned its most trusted men to "educate" the targets of consolidation—those who had been pessimistic or cynical about struggle. In the meantime, the monitors prevented them from having any contact with UNC personnel, forbidding them from joining work details or leaving the enclosures. Finally, in a fourth category were traitors, who were no longer considered members of "the masses" or "the people." Li later recalled, "Once concrete evidence was obtained, we overcame great difficulties and eliminated them at all costs."[33] After the armistice, Li reported that a total of seventeen suspected traitors had been put to death by the Communist Solidarity.[34]

In Enclosure 4 for the disabled, a healthy prisoner serving as an orderly had come under close watch by monitors. One day, while moving medicine boxes, he suddenly dashed to the inner fence, scaled it, landed in the area between the two layers of fences, and then ran toward the guard tower. Interpreter Fang Xiangqian immediately rushed to the main gate and yelled at the US guards: "Open the gate! Let me catch this escapee for you!" The guard, a Hispanic soldier whom Fang had befriended, obliged in confusion. Unable to speak English, the escapee received no help from the guards. He was seized by Fang and several monitors. Once he was taken back to a tent, the monitors smashed his head with rocks. When the US guards belatedly realized what had happened, they entered the compound, only to discover the escapee's bloodied body. To everyone's surprise, the man did not die; he recovered. Fang was arrested as a "troublemaker" for his role in seizing the escapee. The Communist prisoners protested day and night, demanding Fang's release. The authorities gave in and returned him to Enclosure 4.[35]

Other individuals trying to escape were not as lucky. A former Nationalist soldier named Zhou in Enclosure 2 howled day and night: "Let me out! I was deceived to come here." Apparently he had gone insane, but the leadership decided to do away with him lest he escape and leak secrets. He was murdered with a corrugated iron sheet and a rope, and then buried under a "collapsed" wall—in a fake accident scene.[36]

In Enclosure 9, two prisoners were executed, recalled pro-Communist activist Lin Mocong. One of them, named Guo, "often talked nonsense." He was first strangled to death, after which a rope was placed around his neck and his body was hung up—a crude suicide scene was created. Another victim was Kim, an ethnic Korean. Distressed by the incessant struggles and demonstrations, he openly professed that he no longer wished to return to China. "I'm Korean," he said, "and I have many relatives in South

Korea." The enclosure leaders decided to kill Kim and report to the Central Committee later. One day when all prisoners were assembled for an outdoor mass meeting, Kim refused to join in and stayed in his tent alone. Three monitors walked in with their hands wrapped in towels. They strangled Kim to death, leaving no fingerprints on his body. Then the leaders declared that Kim had died of acute meningitis—which would account for the fact that his tongue was sticking out. The prisoners wrote a protest letter, faulting the prison authorities for not coming to Kim's aid quickly enough. Then the enclosure initiated a hygiene campaign to eliminate germs or viruses. Other than a handful of insiders, few knew the actual cause of Kim's death.[37]

In September alone, the authorities reported five "'suicides'—real or otherwise."[38] However, other instances of killing went unreported. In Enclosure 7, which was tasked with killing Brooks, the air was especially tense. A Shanghainese prisoner was caught throwing rocks with notes wrapped on them. When questioned, he denied that he was a traitor and pled, "I came here [the pro-repatriation camp] by mistake. I hate struggles. I want democracy. I didn't leak any secrets. I simply asked to leave this camp."[39] When he tried to scream for help, five monitors buried him alive in an unoccupied tent. Coincidentally, four of the five monitors were killed a few days later on October 1.[40]

On the morning of September 25, Cai Xingfu, the college-educated clerk in Enclosure 7, managed to insert himself into the work detail, and marched out. He did not return that evening; he feigned illness and went to the hospital. If he could remain in the hospital for six days, he could avoid the clash on October 1. The doctors, however, found him to be well. Acting upon this intelligence, Brooks interrogated Cai, who cracked and revealed the assassination plot.[41]

The next morning, Colonel Boerem and Brooks led armed troops into Enclosure 7. They first ordered the prisoners to assemble and salute them. Brooks, annoyed by prisoner Wang Fusheng's foot-dragging, punched him from behind and used a confiscated homemade knife to slash at Wang's head behind his ear. Luckily Wang did not bleed, as the blade was too dull. The prisoners were marched into an empty area and strip-searched. More than a hundred homemade knives were seized. So were many written pledges to kill Brooks. Another of Brooks's objectives was to arrest underground leader Han Zijian. Although Cai was not present, he apparently had described Han's facial features to Brooks. Han barely escaped identification, thanks to the medicine he had taken in advance to make his face swell beyond recognition.[42]

Similar scenes were repeated over several days. Boerem entered every compound, and made the prisoners assemble and salute US officers. Boerem described the procedure: the prisoners "were marched into the administrative area under adequate guard, stripped of their clothing, and their clothing searched." In the meantime, "cleared of all PWs," all enclosures were "given a thorough shakedown."[43] PFC Vigil participated in two of these raids. "We went into the compound when they were out, and searched for contraband," he recalled. "We inspected their living quarters, tearing up their beds, but never found anything. They were ingenious [in hiding things]."[44]

In Enclosure 4, interpreter Fang Xiangqian had a run-in with Brooks. Brooks ordered Fang to assemble the prisoners for inspection by Colonel Boerem. "I don't understand!" Fang replied. "We're all cripples. We can't even walk. How can we line up perfectly for inspection?" Irritated by "troublemaker" Fang, Brooks pulled out his pistol and pointed it at him. Fang ripped his shirt open, thrust his chest forward, and dared Brooks to fire: "Come on! Here!" Brooks walked off in a huff.[45]

On September 30, Brooks took "traitor" Li Xiaoguang to Enclosure 6. He made all the prisoners walk past Li in a single file with their mouth wide open. Li identified Du Gang, the second-in-command, whose front teeth had been knocked out by the anti-Communists on Koje a year earlier. "Aha! I caught you finally!" Brooks taunted Du. "Go ahead and raise your flags tomorrow!"[46]

So far, all top four Communist leaders had been arrested. However, Gu Zesheng, the fifth in command, assumed leadership according to plan. Gu, a former battalion commissar in the 20th Army, had been well disguised as a cook in Enclosure 8—he was only identified and arrested shortly before the armistice.[47] That evening, Gu issued the Central Committee's final order: "The flag-raising struggle on October 1 will be carried out as planned. Any instance of cowardice or vacillation will be treated as desertion on the battlefield."[48] Furthermore, "under no circumstances should the flags be seized by the enemy. They should be burned as a final resort."[49] Once again, Enclosure 7 was chosen to be the vanguard of action. This decision was based on three considerations. First, the de facto leader Gu, residing in the neighboring Enclosure 8, could easily monitor any action in 7. Second, as Enclosure 7 was located on slightly higher ground, other enclosures could look to it for signals.[50] And finally, Enclosure 7 had been thoroughly mobilized.

The same evening, Colonel Boerem addressed the assembled officers of two units guarding the camp: the 1st battalion of the 35th Infantry Regiment and the 11th MP Service Company. He went over the battle plan and discussed the methods he desired for the next day. A day earlier, tear gas grenades had been flown in from Pusan.[51] Both sides were ready for the final showdown.

October 1 Massacre

Before dawn on October 1, all Chinese prisoners in the ten enclosures rose quietly and had breakfast earlier than usual. They had planned to raise flags when the US troops were having breakfast so that it would take longer for them to respond.[52] When unarmed administrative sergeants went to all the enclosures at 7:15 a.m. to get head count, the prisoners refused to assemble. Instead, they quickly erected 50-foot-tall flag poles made of 4×4 timbers spliced in sections, notched, and joined together.[53] At 7:30 a.m., nine Chinese national flags and one North Korean flag were hoisted simultaneously.[54] Following the lead of Enclosure 7, buglers in each compound began blasting the national anthem and then the "March of the People's Liberation Army" on their homemade instruments. In the morning sun, prisoners sang, "Forward! Forward! Forward! Forward! Our army faces the sun . . . " Many were in tears.[55]

Captain Brooks rode in his jeep to report to Colonel Boerem and Executive Officer Helderman, who had just finished breakfast.[56] The commanders immediately rushed to the HQ to assemble the troops. At 7:40 a.m., Brooks arrived at Enclosure 7 to broadcast Boerem's prepared message through an interpreter:

> Attention. Attention. Your attention is directed to Article 82 of the Geneva Convention of 12 August 1949. A prisoner of war shall be subject to the laws, regulations and orders in force in the armed force of the detaining power. You will not fly flags of any nature without proper authority. You have not, repeat not, been given that authority. You are ordered to take down all flags at once.[57]

The message was repeated five times. Brooks had a second message handy, but Boerem had instructed him that it "would not be given to the prisoners until the Infantry units were in place." At about 8:00 a.m., the 1st Battalion arrived. Boerem posted tanks to contain the perimeter.[58]

Prisoners behind barbed wire recalled a menacing scene: "Fighters were circling above the prison camp. Eleven tanks rumbled into the administrative area [between the enclosures]. Approximately two battalions of troops in full combat gear, with helmets and gas masks, manned positions at the gates of each enclosure. They were armed with submachine guns, automatic rifles, grenades, various gas canisters, and flamethrowers."[59] As the prison was located adjacent to an airstrip, the prisoners' claim of seeing fighters was most likely an exaggeration. Their impression of the two battalions, however, was probably not wide off the mark. The 35th Infantry was a Regimental Combat Team, a reinforced "elite fighting force" with three battalions, each of which had five companies, according to PFC Vigil.[60] The headcount of the 1st Battalion was probably equivalent to that of two Chinese battalions.

As the 1st Battalion took their positions and were issued tear gas grenades, Boerem claimed, he "personally instructed" troops that "they must not kill people unless attacked" and that they must follow their platoon leaders' commands. Only minutes later, Boerem "heard a small number of shots fired in the vicinity of Compound Number 7."[61] Helderman reported, "Before we got down to the inclosure [*sic*] . . . we heard 8 to 10 to 12 shots, M-1 or carbine."[62] What happened was that when Company B's 2nd Platoon "moved in at high port arms, down to Compound 7 and the rocks were hurled" at the troops, "approximately 5 to 8 men . . . started firing *without being ordered to* before they entered the compound." The company commander and the platoon leader "immediately gave orders to cease fire and fall back."[63]

Boerem stopped at the gate of Enclosure 7 and "decided that it would be the first one to be entered if necessary." At about 8:10 a.m., Boerem ordered Brooks to call the compound representative to the gate. Brooks did "call several times, speaking Chinese. There was no response." At this point, Boerem ordered a Chinese Nationalist interpreter named Sun Teh Chen, to broadcast the second prepared message to the prisoners:

> You have failed to observe a lawful order of the Commanding Officer, to wit, you will take down all flags at once. You are now being notified that in accordance with Article 42 of the Geneva Convention of 12 August 1949 that armed forces and weapons will be used if necessary to effect compliance with this order.[64]

"No!" All prisoners answered in unison. Boerem then ordered the gates to be opened and the troops to move in. As the prisoners had fastened the inner gate with wire and ropes, MP Sergeant Dean Titus brought a wire cutter. Brooks recalled, "While I covered him with a drawn pistol, he . . . had just begun to remove the wire fastener with wire cutter, when the groups of prisoners behind the rock and cement structure which is intended to be their shower room, stood up and began throwing rocks at Titus and myself," who wore no helmets. Firing with his "snub nose 38" pistol, Brooks "shot one prisoner through the head who stood up with a rock in his hand."[65]

As the prisoners hiding behind the shower-room wall rose up, threw rocks—"the air was full of them"—and then ducked back down, the squad of infantrymen fired to keep them down, recalled Helderman. "When the gates were opened, the alert platoon entered. They did not just walk in. They were . . . shooting people throwing rocks. They kept firing." The prisoners "kept throwing rocks from tents, barracks and the kitchen."[66]

Forcing its way into Enclosure 7, the 2nd Platoon "was met with a hail of stones thrown by the prisoners."[67] When PFC Vigil led his squad of six or seven men into the enclosure's lower left corner, "rocks were coming at us, already." When they approached the shower-room wall ten feet away, they could see the prisoners up close with rocks and clubs in their hands. Suddenly Vigil heard firing, "like rapid fire from automatic weapons, carbines." He "just followed up, [and] fired a burst" like "a spontaneous kind of thing." In a few seconds, one clip on his short carbine was expended. He didn't hear an order to fire, but only remembered that "there were huge confusion and fright, from the POWs, running amok, running from us."[68]

Prisoners fought mainly with rocks. Boerem estimated "there were 250 [rocks] in the air pretty steady for a matter of minutes" when he entered the compound with the troops. And he was "personally hit by one of the rocks. . . . five inches in diameter."[69]

The prisoners had made various crude weapons for "close-in, hand-to-hand fighting," but as Brooks noted, "none of these were used except one tent pole . . . which . . . had been sharpened, thrust as a spear, wounding one American soldier in the hand."[70] Since the Americans were firing automatic weapons, there was no chance for hand-to-hand fighting.

Some men nonetheless made suicide attacks without any real arms. Sergeant Titus recalled: "Two PWs charged one platoon on the right with tent poles. . . . They were shot." In another case, "a Chinese prisoner was shot down by one of our men with an M-1 rifle," recounted Colonel Caldwell, "but like a wild beast he rose from the ground after he was shot and still came on at the soldier. He shot him a second time and the prisoner dropped dead within a few feet of the soldier."[71]

Despite their bravery, the prisoners were overwhelmed by UNC firepower. Vigil saw them "trying to run away and hide. But where to hide?" Some prisoners hid behind the short wall. Vigil thought, "They were hiding there to stay out of trouble, not hurting anyone." A fellow soldier from his platoon carrying a Browning Automatic Rifle (BAR)—a type of light machine gun—went around the wall, and "just sprayed at them."[72]

The shooting probably lasted ten minutes, "then it was all over," Helderman recalled.[73] In this rampage, the 2nd Platoon, one of the two that entered the enclosure, alone fired roughly 500 rounds from carbines and BARs.[74] In the end, 56 prisoners had been killed and 96 severely wounded, yet only two of the 80 US soldiers who entered Enclosure 7 were "wounded slightly."[75] Later investigation found that nine troops "received non-serious injuries, consisting of lacerations and bruises."[76]

Among the 56 killed, most were from the 50-man dare-to-die squad, which was nearly wiped out. The flag protection squad lost nine of its twelve members, but it accomplished its mission. The men lowered the flag and had it burned with gasoline, thus denying it to the enemy.[77] Among the 96 wounded was Cai Derong, the 180th Division deputy commander's bodyguard. Cai had been severely wounded during the Fifth Offensive breakout in May 1951, when he opened fire to divert the enemy's attention away from his commander, who succeeded in escaping back to CPV lines. Also wounded was Dai Yushu, the former *Paoge* brotherhood leader in Compound 86 on Koje.[78] When Dai's blood-covered body was taken to the motor pool awaiting air transfer to Pusan's hospital, anti-Communist leader Yang Shuzhi, who was there on a work detail, recognized Dai's face and thought he was dead. Later Yang heard from a UNC interpreter that during the incident, Dai mocked Brooks for his mixed blood, calling him a "mongrel" (*zazhong*). Enraged, Brooks shot him.[79]

Brooks later claimed that, at the very end of the battle, he found "the compound representative and other political leaders hiding in a tent far in the rear, safely behind a large pile of rocks." He boasted, "I utilized the barbwire-wrapped clubs made by prisoners to leave some permanent marks on their bodies."[80]

Indeed, none of Enclosure 7's top leaders were among those killed or severely wounded. Li Weiwen, the head of the dare-to-die squad, survived the bloodbath unscathed, because he made a timely "return to the rear to report to the leaders" between the final two waves of enemy attacks. Zhao Guoxi, a former Whampoa cadet, a probationary CCP member, and the enclosure's organizational chief, had volunteered to join the dare-to-die squad. He was severely wounded.[81]

The Aftermath

On the afternoon of October 1, KCOMZ commander General Herren and POW Command commander Colonel Caldwell flew from Pusan to Cheju. By 2:30 p.m. the next day, an investigation board had completed its questioning of witnesses, including eighteen Americans and four Chinese prisoners. Herren announced to a group of reporters just flown in by the US Army that the crackdown had been a response to "a mass break." He asserted that "5,884 Reds in 10 compounds had planned to use the riot—in compound 7—as a signal for a mass break," with the intention of joining Communist guerrillas in the hills of Cheju. He claimed the prison authorities had learned of the escape plot on August 24, and were "able to move quickly when the decisive hour arrived. . . . US infantry moved in so swiftly and sternly."[82]

FIGURE 13.1. Homemade weapons uncovered after the October 1 massacre in the Chinese Communist compound in the Cheju POW camp: a rock sling, barbed wire flails, and wooden clubs with spikes. US National Archives.

The mass prison break claim, however, was preposterous. Why would thousands of unarmed prisoners choose to break out in broad daylight instead of at night? Why would they raise red flags to attract armed troops and tanks without actually making any move to escape? Manhard observed that the prison authorities offered "no tangible proof" of an attempted mass breakout, "except to point out that the prisoners refused to carry out assigned jobs, raised flags and sang songs on that day." [83] Probably Captain Brooks did not believe it either. When investigators asked him if there were "a sufficient number" of handmade weapons, such as flails and spears, to equip each of the 500 prisoners in Enclosure 7, Brooks replied, "No. I would say approximately 60 or 70 such weapons were found."[84] Obviously, the prisoners were not in any position to launch a prison break in broad daylight with such few weapons.

The prison break idea was so outlandish that the authorities probably did not take it too seriously back in August. They broached it for the first time only after October 1, most likely as a means to justify the excessive casualties inflicted on prisoners. The disproportionate use of force was apparent. After a 15-minute battle between 500 prisoners and 80 troops, the death toll of 56 was staggering. In contrast, in Boatner's crackdown of Compound 76, after a two-hour pitched battle between more than 6,400 prisoners and 750 troops and several tanks, the death toll was 41, including some executed by POWs themselves.[85] Manhard protested to the State Department that the POW Command's "solution calls for bullets as the answer to songs and stones." He continued, "it is absolutely unbelievable that such methods are necessary to achieve adequate security control."[86]

The Board of Officers questioned the sole reliance on bullets in this incident. They noted that while tear gas grenades were available, none were used. Boerem argued, "There was no object to use gas, as the troops were attacked with rocks, handmade pikes, barbed wire flails and other missiles. The PWs continued to attack and attempt to get to our troops, and had to be stopped."[87] Unlike Boatner's days when bullets were considered the last resort, now "shoot to kill" had become the standard operating procedure (SOP) of the POW Command.[88]

Unsurprisingly, the six-member Board of Officers concluded that "the amount of force used by members of the UNC was, under the circumstances, reasonable, and the deaths and injuries inflicted are deemed to be justifiable." Consequently, the board's recommendation was that "no disciplinary action be taken against any member of the UNC."[89] However, one member, Major Richard C. Lyons, signed a written statement expressing reservations about the prevalent interpretation of the SOP: "All extreme actions against prisoners of war, for any action determined to be of an aggressive nature, is within reason and justifiable regardless of the retaliatory measures which may be taken against UN prisoners of war in the hands of the enemy."[90]

When the "Report of Proceedings" reached General Clark's UNC GHQ in Tokyo, Lyons's reservation raised eyebrows. The GHQ struck back with a stern disclaimer:

"This headquarter is unaware of any instructions which may be construed as to mean that *any and all actions* against prisoners of war are within reason merely because they are used to overcome aggressive action by the prisoners." It rejected the report and requested, "Major Lyons be afforded the opportunity to withdraw his 'reservation', if he so desires."[91] Lyons withdrew his reservations, but then he simply stated his dissent from the findings.[92] He remained unpersuaded.

On Cheju, "Prisoners Angry But Obedient," reported the *New York Times*. "The prisoners wore white paper carnations in mourning for their dead but made no other effort to hold a demonstration."[93] In fact, they tried. On October 2, top Communist leaders Zhao Zuoduan, Wei Lin, and Du Gang hung a large protest banner from the barbed wire fence of the Close Confinement Stockade. Captain Brooks led troops to seize the banner and "gave Zhao and his comrades a beating."[94]

The POW leaders achieved their original goals. As Manhard noted, "One of the main objectives of these leaders is to produce anti-American and pro-Commie propaganda in the public press. They are succeeding remarkably well so far."[95] Their success, however, came at a very high cost—56 men dead and 96 wounded, not to mention the suspected traitors executed or maimed before and after the incident. Yet, Zhao Nianzhi, one of the leaders in Enclosure 7, concluded, "The enemy had gained nothing, except killing and wounding 150 to 160 of our men."[96] This sounded strikingly similar to Stalin's words to Zhou Enlai six weeks earlier: "The North Koreans have lost nothing, except for casualties."[97]

All this was small consolation for the Chinese POWs. Although they failed to kill the detested Brooks, they were happy to see him transferred away soon after the October 1 incident.[98] Later, in January 1953, Brooks left the army because he felt "fatigued by army life and the war." He soon started working as a Taiwan correspondent for a San Francisco–based magazine, *Bi-Weekly*. In a September 1953 article in *Xinshengbao* (New Life News), a newspaper run by the Taiwan provincial government, Brooks bragged about his valor on October 1, 1952: "I personally shot two men, then I ordered the troops to enter the compound. We had to shoot approximately 160 of them before order was restored." In a morbid display of his hatred for the Chinese Communists, Brooks claimed, "I still have one of their blood-stained flags covering a 'shrine of hate' in my room. It reminds me of my enemies."[99]

In retrospect, the Chinese Communist prisoners on Cheju Island lived under a prison regime that permitted guards to "shoot to kill" for *any and all* aggressive actions. They were confronted by the obsessively hostile Captain Brooks and Chaplain O'Sullivan. Equally dangerously, they were commanded by a group of Communist leaders who were seeking bloodshed in hopes of scoring a propaganda coup to redeem their own past cowardice. That was a combination too precarious, too deadly for any individual prisoner to survive unscathed.

Breakdown in Panmunjom

It may seem odd that the POW leaders repeatedly claimed that one of their goals was "to support the negotiations in Panmunjom," when they had absolutely no contact with the Chinese Communist government throughout their time in prison. In Pusan and Koje, they had collaborated with their North Korean counterparts, who most likely had contact with the North Korean government via clandestine channels. As if a fitting irony to their acclaimed "Sino-North Korean brotherhood cemented by blood," although the Chinese and North Korean negotiators collaborated daily in Panmunjom in their verbal war against the Americans, Nam Il, the reputed North Korean spy chief in charge of prisoners' underground activities on Koje and the Communists' chief delegate at Panmunjom, apparently did not facilitate communication between the Chinese prisoners and their government. Nevertheless, as the October 1 massacre was widely reported, the news reached Panmunjom.

On October 2, Nam Il lodged a formal protest with his UNC counterpart, General William K. Harrison Jr., lambasting this "bloody incident of a barbarous yet cowardly massacre." Nam concluded that the incident "belies all your fraudulent pretexts for refusing to repatriate war prisoners."[100] On October 8, after Nam rejected the UNC's "final and irrevocable" position of non-forcible repatriation of prisoners, Harrison made a 34-minute speech haranguing the Communists for starting the war and refusing a reasonable settlement. Harrison announced that the UNC negotiators had not come to Panmunjom to merely "listen to . . . abuse and false propaganda." Declaring an indefinite recess, Harrison and the UNC delegation walked out of the conference tent.[101] The negotiations broke down.

Washington's preferred solution was to bomb the enemy into submission. An already savage aerial bombing campaign escalated. The war was to continue until Mao was willing to accept voluntary repatriation, an eventuality that only occurred after Stalin's death in March 1953.

14

Exchanges and "Explanation"

A LITTLE OVER TWO WEEKS after the Panmunjom talks had broken down on October 8, Dwight D. Eisenhower, the Republican presidential candidate, made a dramatic declaration: "I shall go to Korea," a pledge that sealed his landslide victory on November 4, 1952. Fulfilling his promise, Eisenhower visited Korea from December 2 to 5. En route to Korea, JCS chairman Bradley briefed the president-elect on America's "swelling nuclear arsenal." "We had so many atomic bombs now," he later recalled, "that we could spare a considerable number for the Korean War, should it be deemed advisable to use them." Back in 1951, the JCS had recommended using atomic weapons "ONLY in the event" of a major "military disaster" in Korea.[1]

In his State of the Union address on February 2, 1953, Eisenhower declared the end of the neutralization of the Taiwan Strait—a move that was often referred to as the "unleashing" of Chiang Kai-shek's forces to attack the mainland. Chiang, however, did not launch an attack. Similarly, despite Washington's tough talk of escalating the war to force the Communists to capitulate, the new administration had neither the intention of expanding the conventional war nor a silver bullet to end the war expeditiously.[2] In the meantime, the CPV had become increasingly well equipped, well supplied, and well entrenched. Mao, determined to inflict more casualties on UN forces so that he could end the war on favorable terms, declared in February that China was prepared to continue the war "until the American imperialists give in and until the people of China and Korea win a complete victory."[3] Peace was nowhere in sight.

On May 20, 1953, the JCS recommended that "in the event that current armistice negotiations fail," the United States should "extend and intensify military action against the enemy," including "air and naval operations directly against China and Manchuria" and "extensive strategical and tactical use of atomic bombs."[4] Had this plan been carried out, it would have inflicted an American nuclear holocaust on Asia for the second time within a decade. Such a dire eventuality did not occur. Contrary to Eisenhower and Dulles's claim that American nuclear threats intimidated the Chinese into capitulation, it was Stalin's death and the new Soviet leadership's radical change of course that forced the Chinese to make major concessions in the truce talks.[5]

Little Switch, April 20–May 2, 1953

Less than a month after Mao made his combative speech, Stalin suddenly died of a cerebral hemorrhage on March 5. His successors, the ruling troika of Georgi M. Malenkov, Lavrentiy Beria, and Vyacheslav Molotov, quickly launched a peace initiative. When Zhou Enlai attended Stalin's funeral in Moscow, the Soviets told the Chinese to give up their demand that all Chinese prisoners be repatriated. Surprised by this reversal, Zhou protested, "Our struggle over POW repatriation is just. We did not create any trouble, but the enemy did." While Mao and Zhou were reluctant to accept this change, Kim Il-sung was elated. He pointedly told the Russian envoy that North Korean losses "at the front and in the rear (daily nearly 300–400 persons) are very significant and it is hardly advisable to conduct further discussion with the Americans regarding repatriation of a disputed number of prisoners of war."[6] Unlike Stalin, who had strongly backed Mao's hard-line position on POWs and rebuked Kim for his willingness to compromise, the new Soviet leaders sided with the North Koreans. However grudgingly, Mao had to oblige.

A breakthrough occurred on March 28. Kim Il-sung and Peng Dehuai replied to UNC commander Clark's request for the exchange of sick and wounded prisoners. In addition to agreeing to the UNC's proposal, they stated that the exchange of sick and injured prisoners should "lead to the smooth settlement of the entire question of prisoners of war, thereby achieving an armistice in Korea for which people throughout the world are longing." Two days later Zhou Enlai proposed that both sides "should undertake to repatriate immediately after the cessation of hostilities all those prisoners of war in their custody who insist upon repatriation, and to hand over the remaining prisoners of war to a neutral state so as to ensure a just solution to the question of their repatriation." Asserting that most of the so-called anti-repatriation prisoners were intimidated and oppressed, Zhou expressed confidence that once these prisoners heard the explanation made by representatives from their motherlands, their apprehension would disappear and they would choose to return home.[7] In essence, such a two-step approach had been proposed by India back in November, but rejected by Beijing out of hand. Kim Il-sung immediately seconded Zhou's new proposal.

Both sides were ready to resume negotiations. On April 6, the liaison officers met at Panmunjom and quickly got down to business without the usual trade of verbal attacks. An agreement on exchanging sick and wounded prisoners was reached on April 11.[8] On April 14, a group of 770 sick and wounded Chinese POWs, including thirteen litter patients, many of them amputees, was selected as the first shipment. While Xie Zhiqi was selected, fellow crippled prisoner Luo Jiecao was told by his Communist underground superior to stay on Cheju "for future struggles." While eager to return home after nearly two years of captivity, Luo nevertheless complied without hesitation.[9] The POW Command ordered prisoners to exchange their POW uniforms for unmarked new clothing, but they refused. At the time of departure, seventy-two prisoners refused to move until they were permitted to see Wang Fang (Zhao Zuoduan). Tear gas was employed to force their removal.[10]

When an LST arrived in Pusan on the morning of April 15, the group refused to disembark unless a number of their demands were met, including that no photographing be allowed. Colonel Boerem, deputy commander of the POW Command who had overseen the massacre on October 1, 1952, led sixty infantrymen onto the ship. Prisoners capitulated and filed ashore.[11] After the group's arrival in Pusan's processing depot, the prisoners again refused to change into the new garb. They protested "the US Army's conspiracy to cover up its abuse of POWs." It was only after a tear gas attack

FIGURE 14.1. Having discarded their prison uniforms, Chinese Communist POWs shout slogans when they reach the exchange point at Panmunjom. US National Archives.

that they were subdued and agreed to switch uniforms. According to Hermes, some prisoners "went on a hunger strike for several meals," accusing the UNC of poisoning their food. "Seeing braised pork with steamed white rice for the first time in two years," Xie recalled, "we had to swallow our saliva because our underground leaders had instructed us 'not to wear nice clothes and not to eat nice food.'"[12]

On April 19, some 100 Chinese prisoners were bused to the train station before heading north. During the short ride, they "cut or tore buttons from overcoats, removed and discarded shoe laces, cut overcoat belts, and 'urinated on the floor of the bus, acting more like pigs than human beings,'" the US Army claimed.[13] On May 1, however, Xie Zhiqi's group, marched for an hour to reach the train station, where they boarded a train for Munsan-ni, from which point the group headed to Panmunjom in UNC trucks. Braving the early spring chill, the prisoners stripped off their new uniforms, down to just their underpants. At Panmunjom, Xie saw the four large characters, *zuguo huaibao* (the motherland's embrace) emblazoned on an arch, and a welcome crowd. The exchange took place very quickly, "with no ceremony, no warm embraces, and no prolonged handshakes as seen in the movies."[14]

After they changed into brand-new CPV uniforms—without any insignias—Xie noticed a large banner outside: "A warm welcome to CPV returnees! We salute the comrades who tenaciously struggled!" A chill ran down his spine. The banner not so subtly taunted the returnees: "Have you struggled persistently? Do you deserve our salute?" In the afternoon, General Nam Il paid a visit to the Chinese repatriates, and a North Korean song and dance troupe performed for them with great enthusiasm. The next day a Chinese troupe performed, going through the motions with ice-cold faces and no eye contact with the audience, who returned the disdain by not applauding. During their two-day stay at Panmunjom, no Chinese official, even a junior one, came to see the sick and disabled returnees, Xie recalled. A pall was cast over their future.[15]

In Operation Little Switch between April 20 and May 2, the UNC returned 1,030 Chinese POWs, 5,194 North Korean POWs, and 446 Korean civilian internees. The Communist side repatriated 684 UNC POWs, including 149 Americans.[16]

Panic and Infighting among Anti-Communists

Interned at Mosulpo on Cheju Island, the more than 14,200 Chinese anti-Communist prisoners panicked. "A growing atmosphere of dissatisfaction at nonrepatriate Chinese Camp 3 (Mosulpo) led camp authorities to conclude that agitators and pro-Communists were at work in what had previously been considered the model POW camp." The POW Command reported an incident on April 23, when thirty-three Communist suspects were "removed and placed in protective custody for further investigation and disposition. Seven of the 33 had been beaten severely prior to segregation and were placed in the hospital, where 3 subsequently died."[17] Several eyewitnesses, however, disputed the claim that these victims were Communists.

Former Whampoa cadet Wang Houci recounted the event. After breakfast, prisoners in Compound 2, consisting of the first four battalions of Koje's Compound 86, were called to assemble. Roughly five thousand prisoners sat down on the ground facing the CIE hall, not knowing what was to happen. Suddenly the doors were swung open and there emerged more than twenty prisoner leaders, including various battalion, company, and platoon leaders. Most prominent among them was Cheng Liren, now Compound 2's PG battalion leader. They were paraded onto the stage as criminals, with club-wielding guards on both sides of each man. Presiding over the meeting, compound leader Wang Zunming accused Cheng and other arrested leaders of plotting to kill him the night before. After one of Wang's henchmen displayed the alleged weapon—a kitchen knife—Wang asked the crowd, "What should we do with these traitors?" After a minute's silence, some scattered voices emerged, "Beat them! Beat them!" Then the PGs shoved the accused to the ground, and struck their

FIGURE 14.2. Chinese anti-Communist prisoners stage a drama showing the beheading of "Bandit Mao Zedong" with a bucksaw. Mosulpo, Cheju Island. By Dimitri Boria, US National Archives.

legs with tent poles. Sitting near the stage, Wang Houci was shocked by the scene, which reminded him of the Communist struggle meetings in Sichuan in 1950. The blows were so heavy that several tent poles broke. However, these "tough men, who had led the anti-Communist battles on Koje-do, did not moan even once," recalled Wang Houci.[18]

How did Cheng, Compound 86's CIE school principal, become the PG battalion leader? Why did the two former allies, Cheng and Wang Zunming, turn against each other? Liu Chunjian, a prisoner instructor of the CIE, gave a plausible explanation. In late 1952 or early 1953, DAC interpreters and instructors from Taiwan intimated to prisoner leaders that after they arrived in Taiwan, they would receive ranks according to their positions in the POW camps. A compound leader would be ranked as a lieutenant colonel; a battalion leader as a major, and so on. However, there was no mention of the rank for the CIE school principal. Soon, Cheng quit his CIE job and became the leader of the 5th Battalion (the PG battalion). Given that most prisoners were southerners like Cheng, and Wang was a northerner, perhaps Cheng felt that he could replace Wang as the compound leader. Wang preempted Cheng and his allies by arresting them, accusing them of being Communist agents. "Cheng miscalculated," Liu concluded.[19] Cheng was no match for a battle-hardened Nationalist officer who had also survived Communist mental torture and hard labor for a year.

Armistice

Following the positive momentum generated by the Little Switch, the plenary sessions of the armistice negotiations resumed at Panmunjom on April 26. On June 8 both sides signed the Terms of Reference on prisoner exchange. Some of the key clauses were related to the disposition of anti-repatriation prisoners, especially item 8:

> The Neutral Nations Repatriation Commission [NNRC], after having received and taken into custody all those prisoners of war who have not exercised their right to be repatriated, shall immediately make arrangements so that within ninety (90) days after the Neutral Nations Repatriation Commission takes over the custody, the nations to which the prisoners of war belong shall have freedom and facilities to send representatives to the locations where such prisoners of war are in custody to explain to all the prisoners of war depending upon these nations their rights and to inform them of any matters relating to their return to their homelands, particularly of their full freedom to return home to lead a peaceful life.[20]

In essence, the Chinese Communists accepted the principle of voluntary repatriation—the policy they had fought against so bitterly for seventeen months—under the guise of a face-saving procedure, which entailed a period of "explanation" for non-repatriation prisoners under the custody of neutral nations. Clark optimistically informed Washington that an armistice could be signed as early as June 18. A final truce "appeared so tantalizingly close," Clark thought.[21]

At 6:00 a.m. on June 18, Clark was awakened and told that South Korean president Syngman Rhee had ordered ROK guards to release anti-repatriation Korean prisoners from the UNC's prison camps. "All hell broke loose, by Rhee's order," Clark recalled. In two days, 27,000 Korean POWs were "freed in a dramatic, well-planned operation."[22] Amid the chaos, a small number of Chinese prisoners who were interned near Pusan also escaped from their enclosures. While Clark suspected that "Rhee was not interested in them," the South Korean police were nevertheless sympathetic to Chinese anti-Communist prisoners. The US embassy reported, "In [the] past few days about 200 Chinese anti-repatriates have fled camps but most now recovered. Over 40 still AWOL under protection Korean Police."[23] In fact, more than 40 Chinese escapees managed to hide with local Chinese families in Pusan. Soon the Nationalist embassy established contact with them. Eventually, on October 8, two days before the October 10 National Day celebration, 63 Chinese escapees were flown to Taipei. They were the first group of Anti-Communist Heroes to arrive in Taiwan.[24]

Chinese anti-Communist prisoners on Cheju quickly learned of the POW exchange agreement. Defying the authorities' increasingly stringent censorship, Nationalist DAC interpreters and teachers smuggled information into the camps.[25] Understandably, anti-Communist prisoners became frightened, as the agreement required them to listen to Communist "explanations" administered by neutral nations. India, the leading neutral nation and the provider of custodian forces, was far from neutral in the prisoners' eyes, since it was the first non-Communist country to recognize the PRC. "The anti-repatriation Chinese POWs are in a state of considerable agitation and their POW leaders extremely fearful of their fate under a neutral commission," observed US counterintelligence officers. "In recent weeks this camp has seen an upsurge in beating and killings by self-styled anti Communists of those accused of wavering in their attitude toward Formosa."[26]

On June 20, two days after Rhee's release of anti-repatriation Korean POWs, Chinese anti-Communist prisoners on Cheju launched a mass protest. "They demonstrated for equal consideration and immediate release to Formosa and refused [to] perform routine tasks," reported US ambassador Ellis O. Briggs. In response, the authorities "forced compliance by severe gassing of about one-third of total 14,000."[27] The prisoners claimed that on the third day of their protest, fully armed UNC soldiers wearing gas masks entered one of the compounds, drove prisoners out of their barracks with tear gas, and destroyed all anti-Communist decorations.[28] A US Army internal report analyzed the prisoners' psychology: having rejected repatriation in the screening in April 1952, anti-Communist POWs felt that they had proved that they were on the UNC's side; but the UNC still treated them as POWs. Their hope of release to

Taiwan had been built up in the fall of 1952, when a large number of non-repatriate Koreans were reclassified as civilian internees and released. Any prisoner's continued, indefinite internment against the backdrop of the rapid progress at Panmunjom led to "a growing suspicion of the UNC and a recurring fear that the detaining power would sacrifice him by forcing his repatriation for the sake of a truce." The report admitted that the prisoners' "anti-American feeling . . . was held down only by their stronger anti-Communist leanings."[29] No longer cooperative, the Chinese anti-repatriates had become a hindrance to the US government's wish for a clean and rapid resolution of the POW issue. Soon the US government would have to ask Taiwan for help.

On the 38th parallel, the CPV launched its final big push against the UNC on July 9. Armistice talks nonetheless resumed on July 10. Punishing Rhee for his release of prisoners, the CPV concentrated its attack on ROK positions, inflicting near 30,000 casualties.[30] This show of force did not end until July 27, the day the armistice agreement was signed. On that day, UNC commander Clark "gained the unenviable distinction of being the first United States Army commander in history to sign an armistice without victory," as he later noted.[31] The fighting had finally come to an end. The war over Chinese anti-Communist prisoners, however, was to go on. Soon the Chinese Communist government would confront these prisoners directly for the first time.

Big Switch, August 5–September 6, 1953

Soon after the armistice, the exchange of prisoners in Operation Big Switch began. From August 5 to September 6, the UNC transferred 75,823 prisoners, including 5,640 Chinese, to the Communist side at Panmunjom. Able-bodied male prisoners were moved from various island camps by sea to Inchon and subsequently by rail to a 1,800-man transient camp at Yongdungpo. Sick and wounded prisoners and women and children were moved from their island camps by water to Pusan and then by rail to the Munsan-ni transfer point. The US Army reported "numerous harassing incidents, caused mainly by female fanatics," who "displayed Communist flags, chanted, screamed, cried." Rail cars were destroyed, as "every window in the hospital cars was either completely broken out, holes knocked in it, or cracked." Tear gas was used to subdue the female POWs.[32] Yang Yuhua, the only Chinese female prisoner, was loaded onto a railcar with North Korean women and children repatriates on August 8. When tear-gas canisters were thrown into the cabin, Yang tried to protect the children. Exploding canisters burned her arms. Upon her arrival at Panmunjom, General Du Ping, director of the CPV Political Department, warmly shook her hand, promising her that "the motherland will take good care of you just like your mother."[33] Apparently Du was unaware that Yang had been orphaned at a young age.

The 4,328 Chinese Communist prisoners interned in Cheju City were loaded onto LSTs fitted with barbed-wire 60-man cribs and guarded by two officers and sixty infantrymen on each vessel. The operation went "without major incident, though considerable amount of POW clothing and equipment were damaged and destroyed by the prisoners," the US Army reported.[34] The prisoners staged their final struggle, much in the same fashion as their crippled comrades had done three months earlier. Before departure, Fang Xiangqian and fellow prisoners refused to board the ships, demanding that Zhao Zuoduan, Sun Zhenguan, Zhang Zeshi, and the other segregated "troublemakers" to be allowed to join them. As expected, the US guards fired tear gas. As the canisters fell, spitting white, choking smoke, the prisoners quickly grabbed spent shells amidst the pandemonium. Using his newly acquired profanity taught by friendly American sergeants, Fang shouted, "Stop your fucking atrocity!" With evidence of an American atrocity and prisoner resistance in hand, the prisoners boarded the ships without seeing their top leaders.[35]

FIGURE 14.3. Chinese Communist POWs, being transferred to an LST at Cheju Island, are heading to Inchon and Panmunjom for repatriation in "Big Switch." August 3, 1953. US National Archives.

On the last day of Big Switch, September 6, the highest-ranking Chinese prisoner, Wu Chengde, the 180th Division's acting commissar, and some one hundred "troublemakers," including Zhao Zuoduan (Wang Fang), Wei Lin, Sun Zhenguan, and Zhang Zeshi, were repatriated. Pak Sang-hyon, the North Korean underground leader, was also repatriated.[36]

Combined with the 1,030 sick and wounded Chinese prisoners exchanged in April, the total number of repatriated Chinese prisoners reached 6,670, slightly more than the 6,400 offered by the UNC in July 1952.[37] The final number of repatriates in 1953 had largely been determined by the April 1952 screening. Although pro-Communist prisoners believed that they had fought bravely since the screening and thus secured their right to return home, in fact their return to China was never an issue in the peace talks. The UNC never intended to retain the pro-Communist POWs. Rather, the issue in contention over the preceding twelve to fifteen months was over the fate of their anti-Communist compatriots, who had refused to return home. The war was fought over these roughly 14,000 Chinese anti-Communists. And the struggle over their fate was not over yet.

Transfer of Anti-Communist POWs to Panmunjom, September 10–23, 1953

To implement the armistice agreement, the UNC had to transfer anti-repatriation prisoners from the prison camps to the NNRC in the Demilitarized Zone under the Custodial Forces of India. However, the more than 14,000 Chinese anti-repatriates presented a major challenge. Manhard reported that the POW leaders "now maintain they will resist the takeover of the camp by Indian forces—'with words if the Indians use words, with force if they use force.'" They also claimed that they were ready to sacrifice many prisoners' lives "in order to . . . maintain anti-Communist discipline over the mass of prisoners."[38] Basically, they refused to be transferred to Panmunjom and to be placed under India's control. Washington found itself forced to turn to Chiang Kai-shek for help.

US Ambassador Karl L. Rankin called on Chiang on July 28. He first praised Chiang's "helpful attitude during the weeks preceding the signing of an armistice," acknowledging that Chiang "has been under great pressure of public opinion, both at home and abroad, to oppose a truce in Korea." After sweet-talking Chiang by announcing that "the solicitude of the President for the Chinese prisoners of war in Korea who look to him for leadership is fully understood," Rankin asked him to issue a statement to Chinese prisoners "express[ing] confidence in the UNC's assurance that the rights of the prisoners of war will be fully protected, and urg[ing] their full cooperation with the UN forces and with the NNRC." Washington wanted Chiang to promise the POWs that "no coercion or force will be used against them and that they will be free men within a relatively short time." After Rankin assured

Chiang of the "non-exclusion of Formosa as a possible eventual destination of the POWs and the possibility of a visit to the Mosulpo Camp of a Chinese delegation from Formosa," Chiang within forty-eight hours handed the US embassy his statement complete with Chinese text and English translation, a tape recording, and photographs of himself.[39] After the Americans had abused and neglected Chiang for years, suddenly they showered him with accolades. The United States had finally realized that it was impossible to dismount from the tiger of anti-Communist prisoners that its psychological warfare program had nurtured.

TABLE 14.1. *Prisoner exchange in Little Switch and Big Switch, 1953*

NATIONALITY	LITTLE SWITCH	BIG SWITCH	TOTAL
Communist POWs			
North Koreans	5,640	70,183	75,823
Chinese	1,030	5,640	6,670
Total	6,670	75,823	82,493
UNC POWs			
US	149	3,597	3,746
ROK	471	7,862	8,321[a]
UK	32	945	977
Turks	15	229	243[b]
Filipinos	1	40	41
Canadians	2	30	32
Colombians	6	22	28
Australians	5	21	26
Frenchmen	-	12	12
South Africans	1	8	9
Greeks	1	2	3
Netherlanders	1	2	3
Belgians	-	1	1
New Zealanders	-	1	1
Japanese	-	1	1
Total	**684**	**12,773**	**13,444**

SOURCE: Hermes, *Truce Tent*, 514.

[a, b] The numbers—taken from Hermes—do not add up. Since one cannot be certain of the source of the errors, no attempt has been made to correct them.

In his statement on July 30, Chiang urged "anti-Communist compatriots" in Korea to cooperate with the UNC, and vowed to make sure that the UN would fully implement the principle of voluntary repatriation and facilitate the prisoners' eventual repatriation to Free China on Taiwan.[40] By August 5, leaflets bearing a reproduction of Chiang's handwritten appeal had been distributed to each prisoner on Cheju. In late August, two Nationalist delegations flew to Cheju to reassure prisoners that once they completed their "explanation" in the demilitarized zone, the UNC would release them to Taiwan.[41] After meeting with Nationalist officials, anti-Communist prisoner leaders agreed to cooperate with the UNC. Chiang noted in his diary, "The message to anti-Communist prisoners had a major impact. The loyalty displayed by prisoners greatly impressed the Americans. . . . The United States is becoming increasingly firm and proactive in its dealings with the Communist bandits."[42]

Soon the UNC began to transport anti-Communist prisoners from Cheju to Panmunjom. By September 23, the UNC had turned over 22,604 non-repatriates, including 14,704 Chinese, to the NNRC in the Demilitarized Zone under the Indian forces; the Communist side delivered 359 UNC non-repatriates to the NNRC the following day, including 23 Americans, one Briton, and 335 Koreans.[43] Once they were in the prison camp under Indian custody in the so-called Indian Village, the Chinese prisoners could no longer turn to the Nationalist interpreters and teachers for help as they had done on Cheju Island. However, they maintained close contact with the Nationalist intelligence apparatus through clandestine means.

FIGURE 14.4. Chinese anti-Communist prisoners interned in Mosulpo, Cheju Island, salute the visiting Nationalist delegation from Taiwan. Late August 1953. Kuomintang Archives, Taipei.

As early as June, Chiang Kai-shek had given instructions to Chen Jianzhong, deputy director of the Sixth Section of the Nationalist Party Central Committee, which was in charge of counterintelligence and psychological warfare against the Communists.[44] Soon Chen arrived in Korea under the cover identity of Chen Zhiqing, the Nationalist embassy's deputy army attaché. Operating from the old embassy compound in Seoul, Chen directed all Nationalist intelligence efforts related to the POWs. While former CIE teachers and interpreters could not enter the prison camps controlled by the Indian army, they served as UNC interpreters on the periphery of the camps. Ma He, the CIE teacher who had been trained by Chen Jianzhong before coming to Korea in autumn 1951, now worked as an administrator in the US Army hospital near the Indian Village, which operated as an intelligence hub for anti-Communist prisoners and the UNC psychological warfare unit.[45] NNRC chairman General Kodendera Thimayya suspected that the DACs had "organized the prisoners and trained leaders." He noted, "None of the DACs accompanied POWs into our custody, although the Neutral Commission may still believe that they did."[46]

Thimayya was surprised to learn that the POWs had radio equipment. At a party in the Demilitarized Zone one night, an American psychological warfare officer, "inspired by pride and bourbon," bragged to the Indian general that he "broadcast every evening in code to the POWs. Each compound . . . had a receiver, sacks of potatoes were used to smuggle in fresh batteries." When Thimayya unofficially told UNC chief negotiator Harrison what he had learned, the latter "was genuinely shocked."[47] In reality, however, Nationalist sources confirmed that the prisoners had more than ten radio receivers.[48] Was this radio-smuggling scheme merely a random event or a sign of the systematic involvement of the US military in sabotaging the "explanation"?

In fact, before and during the 90-day "explanation" administered by the NNRC, US psychological warfare personnel worked closely with anti-Communist POW leaders and ROK and Chinese Nationalist DACs to derail the process. Unlike the situation during the screening in April 1952, when Washington was keen to maximize the number of repatriates in order to reach a settlement, now in 1953 a large number of alleged anti-Communist prisoners reversing their decision would deal a major blow to the credibility of the screening result of 1952 and to the legitimacy of the principle of voluntary repatriation, with which the United States had so closely identified. It was in the US government's interest to minimize the number of prisoners reversing their decision against repatriation.

On May 25, Brig. Gen. Lionel C. McGarr, the POW Command's commander, ordered the CIE, G-2, and psychological warfare personnel to collaborate and intensify their activities in the camps. He stressed that "you must make maximum use of personnel in each camp to continually explain to the non-repatriate PWs the advantage of adhering to their original decision to forcibly resist repatriation."[49] Colonel Kenneth Hansen, chief of UNC Psychological Warfare (PsyWar), and Monta Osborne, head of the CIE, flew to Cheju Island in July to "talk to the anti-communist enclosure and compound leaders and as many of the prisoners of war themselves as possible." Prisoners rehearsed their lines in mock "explanations," which were designed to "school them on the questions that probably would be asked, and what pressures might be put on them," according to Colonel William R. Robinette of the POW Command. Hansen reported that "the POWs considered every possible angle which might be employed to persuade them to return—and the hero [POW] had an answer to every avenue of approach." Moreover, the CIE instructors, who had been removed by General Boatner in May 1952, now actively coached the prisoners.[50] Clearly, it was official US policy to encourage prisoners to derail the "explanation" and refuse repatriation.

"Explanation," September 24–December 23, 1953

As the anti-Communists had controlled the majority of Chinese prisoners for more than two years, their reign only became more thorough and violent. On their first day under Indian custody, prisoner leaders "planned to nail the skulls of . . . Communist spies to the entrance posts of their enclosures, as proof to the world of their unswerving anti-Communism." Upon learning this plan, Colonel Hansen promptly dissuaded them from carrying it out. The eighty-five suspected Communist spies that the POW leaders had fingered furiously protested the label, professing to be "passionate anti-Communists who would never return" to Communist China. They were segregated in a small compound.[51]

Thimayya was shocked on the first day. In front of the Indians' eyes, a gang of prisoners tried to kill two men attempting to escape and asking for repatriation. Thimayya concluded, "No prisoner was allowed to escape, even for a moment, from the iron discipline imposed by the organization. This discipline, we actually learned, was imposed also for the purpose of preventing any member of the group from choosing repatriation."[52] Facing such organized resistance, the explanation procedures could not possibly proceed smoothly.

By December 23, 1953, when the 90-day explanation period expired, only 10 days had been used for explanations, and, of the total of 22,000 Chinese and Korean POWs, only around 3,500, or 15 percent, had received the explanation. Fewer than 150, or slightly more than 4 percent, asked for repatriation. "This was a much smaller number than the total who sought repatriation by escape from the compounds," Thimayya noted.[53] Only 2,021, or 15 percent of the 14,704 Chinese prisoners, went through "explanation" sessions; only 90 (4.4 percent) chose repatriation. Another 350 Chinese prisoners escaped the clutches of their ruthless leaders by scaling the barbed wire fences or through other perilous means, and were repatriated.[54]

One of the ninety Chinese interviewees choosing repatriation was Zhao Zhidao, a former Whampoa cadet and CPV artillery staff officer. The moment he entered the "explanation" tent and saw Chinese representatives, he broke into tears. The explainer assured him: "The motherland will forgive all past mistakes. Be brave and come back home!" Zhao pulled out a photo of Mao Zedong he had secretly clipped from a newspaper and hidden in his notebook, and shouted, "Long live Chairman Mao! Long live the CCP! Down with the American imperialists!" Three of Zhao's friends also chose to return.[55]

More than 95 percent of the Chinese interviewees rejected the explainers' entreaties. Wan Delin, a thirty-year-old former Nationalist soldier, was the first prisoner in his compound to receive the "explanation." He was escorted by two Indian troops into the explanation tent observed by representatives from five neutral nations, the UNC, and the Communists. Once the Chinese "explainer" began raving about New China's progress and development, Wan talked back as rehearsed. Hailing from a hardscrabble peasant family in Shanxi, he had gone to primary school for merely one month, but he spoke eloquently: "We Chinese have a history of five thousand years. The Communists have destroyed our history and culture." Three minutes later, the "explainer" ended his futile performance. He pointed to the door to China and said, "You come this way to return home." Wan instead chose to exit the way he had entered, and returned to his POW compound. Despite his poor peasant family background, Wan had resented the tight control in the Communist army. On Koje, he had been among the first to join an anti-Communist organization. Now he affirmed his choice for Taiwan.[56]

When Kim Kwan-ok, a North Korean prisoner who was an anti-Communist leader in charge of security, entered the explanation tent, the KPA representative waxed poetic: "This road leads to light; the other leads to the devils." Kim retorted, "The road you're pointing to leads to the devils. And the other leads to light. I'll walk the other road." He returned to his anti-Communist camp.[57]

The largest yield of repatriates occurred on December 31, a week after the "explanation" had ended. During the morning roll call conducted by the Indian guards, nineteen-year-old Liang Guanghui and thirteen of his comrades suddenly dashed toward the compound gate in a planned attempt to escape. Other prisoners also joined them. Taken by surprise, the anti-Communist trusties failed to stem the torrent. In the end, 131 men broke out and requested repatriation.[58]

Under NNRC custody in Panmunjom, fifteen Chinese prisoners died and two went missing. At least two were shot by Indian guards.[59] And a number of suspected waverers were murdered by anti-Communist prisoners. The most infamous case was the murder and dismemberment of Zhang Zilong, which was widely reported in the Communist press and memoirs of repatriated prisoners. It was claimed that Zhang's heart and liver were cut out and eaten by other prisoners.[60] When an escaped witness returned with the Indian guards to identify the perpetrators, he pointed out seven alleged murderers and an additional fifteen or sixteen witnesses. "Oddly enough," Thimayya later found, "every one of the alleged murderers were compound leaders. Every one of the witnesses opted for repatriation."[61] Apparently the witness tried to rescue his friends by identifying them as fellow witnesses.

Following the escapee witness's directions, the investigators dug into the ground where Zhang was allegedly buried, but found no trace of his remains. Kitchen worker Guo Shigao explained that the trusties, having received a tip-off beforehand, had exhumed Zhang's body, dismembered it, and burned it into ashes in the gasoline-fueled stoves. After their arrival in Taiwan in 1954, several trusties received commendations for their killing of "Communist bandit" Zhang Zilong and the burning of his corpse to destroy evidence.[62]

TABLE 14.2. *Disposition of Non-Repatriation Prisoners in late 1953 and early 1954*

DISPOSITION	CHINESE	KOREAN	TOTAL
Returned to Communist control			
Asked for repatriation through "Explanation"	90[a]		
Escaped and asked for repatriation without taking part in "Explanation"	145[b]		
Escaped and asked for repatriation (Dec. 22, 1953–Jan. 20, 1954)	135[c]		
Escaped and asked for repatriation on Jan. 20–21, 1954	70[d]		
Total	**440**	**188**	**628**
Escaped and missing	2	11	13
Died in custody of Custodial Forces of India (CFI)	15	23	38
Went to India with CFI	12	74	86
Returned to UNC control and went to Taiwan	14,235	7,604	21,839
Total	**14,704**	**7,900**	**22,604**

SOURCE: Hermes, *Truce Tent*, 515, unless otherwise noted.

[a, b] Reports of the Neutral Nations Repatriation Commission (UN document A/2641), 108.

[c] 440–90–145–70 = 135.

[d] FGSL, 1:342.

The Final Release and Escape

On January 12, 1954, Lt. Gen. Lai Mingtang, G-2 director of the Nationalist Ministry of Defense, arrived in Korea. Soon 61 Nationalist officers, 20 MPs, and 45 interpreters followed. Lai's mission was to arrange the transfer of more than 14,000 Chinese anti-Communist prisoners to Taiwan after their expected release on January 23.[63] After conferring with UNC officers, Lai reported to Taipei that "internal control among the [anti-Communist] heroes is very tight and no incident is expected." However, he was told, "hidden waverers might be executed by the heroes on the eve of the release, and the UNC will not intervene."[64]

On the morning of January 20, the NNRC began releasing the more than 14,000 Chinese and 7,600 North Korean non-repatriate prisoners and transferring them to the custody of the UNC. Dr. Zhang Yifu was released from Enclosure 6 in the DMZ at 4 p.m. He recalled that prisoners exited from their compound one by one, thirty feet apart. Each was given the final chance to choose China, Taiwan, or a neutral nation. "It was a completely free choice," Zhang said. As a veteran Communist, however, Zhang knew how cruelly the Communists treated traitors and suspected traitors. He had decided long before to follow the majority of prisoners and take his chances on Taiwan.[65]

When it came to his turn to choose, twenty-one-year-old Zhao Huilin decided to follow the lead of chief interpreter Guo, who had secretly told Zhao that he would return to China. When Guo took the path to China, Zhao followed him. At this moment, Zhao heard compound leader Wang Zunming calling him: "Little Zhao, come back this way." Zhao reluctantly turned around and switched course for Taiwan. "Wang, as if he were an elder brother, had treated me well. I didn't feel comfortable in disobeying him," Zhao explained fifty-four years later in his home in Taiwan. However, five or six interpreters Zhao knew chose either China or neutral nations.[66]

While three fellow prisoners in his platoon escaped the anti-Communists' clutches and returned to China, Zhao Yingkui did not have the opportunity. Zhao had been closely watched since his days in Compound 72 on Koje. When the platoon exited from their compound, two monitors sandwiched Zhao, with one man grasping his backpack from behind. Zhao gave up and went with the flow.[67]

During the release and transfer on January 20 and 21, seventy prisoners broke ranks and asked the Indian guards to return them to China. "There is no doubt," Thimayya maintained, "that there were a few more prisoners who would have chosen repatriation if they had an opportunity to do so."[68]

Moreover, 12 Chinese and 76 Korean prisoners chose neutral nations. Although the Nationalist government branded them "Communist agents," two of the 88 men had been prominent anti-Communist leaders.[69] After his torture at Wang Zunming's hands, Cheng Liren and a handful of other prisoners were interned in a small separate enclosure nearby. When the Nationalist delegation led by Fang Zhi flew to Cheju to meet Chinese anti-Communist prisoners in late August 1953, Cheng was still among the prisoner representatives.[70] After the non-repatriates' move to Panmunjom, one morning before dawn Cheng scaled the fence and told the Indian guards he wanted to be sent to a neutral nation. Had he attempted the escape later that day, other prisoners would have stopped him, Cheng believed.[71] Three years earlier, Cheng had made a predawn escape from the Communists in his hometown in Guizhou. Now, in Panmunjom, he made another desperate attempt to escape, this time from fellow anti-Communists. In a similar move, Korean prisoner Kim Kwan-ok used his privilege as security chief to approach the main gate. He spoke to a Japanese-speaking Indian guard, asking for protection.[72]

On February 9, Cheng, along with 11 other Chinese, and Kim, together with 75 other Korean POWs, were taken on board SS *Asturias* sailing toward India.[73] Cheng's life as a desperado running away from both the Communists and anti-Communists finally came to an end. An unknown fate awaited them in India.

When the 14,220 prisoners who had opted for Taiwan, now called "Anti-Communist Heroes," set out for the island by sea and by air, the fiction of Communist soldiers rejecting Communism en masse seemed real. American policymakers could rest assured that the veneer of legitimacy for fighting the second half of the Korean War had been preserved.

Missing from the released POWs—14,220 bound for Taiwan, 70 for China, and 12 for neutral nations—were several hundred men, who were mostly former Whampoa cadets or graduates, Nationalist officers, and anti-Communist leaders, including Yang Shuzhi, Liu Bingzhang, Wei Shixi, Li Da'an, Gao Wenjun, Ma Furui, and Meng Ming. The UNC declared that most of them had escaped, but the Chinese government charged that they had been drafted by US Army intelligence as spies, and some of them had been captured.

15

Prisoner-Agents of Unit 8240

AT 1:43 A.M. on February 19, 1952, a C-46 transport plane took off from K-16 airbase south of Seoul and ascended into the dark winter sky. Soon it crossed the 38th parallel. Onboard were ten Americans, including seven crew members and three US Army personnel, as well as six Chinese in cotton-padded CPV uniforms, each with a rifle tied to his body. When the pilot spotted ground signals near Koksan, a strategic town located 55 miles southeast of Pyongyang, the plane slowed and descended to a low altitude. At 2:30, a red light flashed over the open door near the plane's tail. "Stand up! Hook up!" called Master Sergeant David T. Harrison. As the Chinese lined up, Harrison hooked the clips from their parachutes to the static line running down the roof of the aircraft. He picked a tall Chinese as the last person to jump, so that he could use his body weight to push out the short man before him, in case the latter hesitated. If even that failed, jumpmaster Harrison would act as the "pusher." Right before the moment came, the short Chinese asked Harrison if he could jump last instead. Harrison gave his OK. When the tall man leaped out, the short one reached the door. Suddenly he took a step backward. With his left thumb he pulled the firing pin of a grenade hidden in his hand glove, threw the live grenade deep into the cabin, and then bailed out. The grenade exploded, causing the plane to catch fire and crash in flames two miles down the flight path.[1]

When the grenade-throwing Chinese landed, he checked his watch: it was 2:40 a.m. He immediately proceeded to turn himself in to the Communist forces. He reported that he was Zhang Wenrong, a former wireless operator of the CPV 180th Division HQ captured by the UNC during the Fifth Offensive in May 1951. He claimed that he and four fellow POWs were secretly removed from Compound 72 on Koje Island on December 13, 1951. They were forced to undergo spy training in Tokyo and Seoul before being dispatched on their first airdrop mission into North Korea. Their assignment was to collect intelligence and then return to UNC lines on foot.

The First Chinese POW to Return to China

Among the more than 21,000 Chinese prisoners captured by the UNC in the entire war, Zhang Wenrong had the distinction of being probably the first to return to China—and in a most unexpected fashion. His story was too fantastic to be believed by anyone. Luckily, Harrison and six other Americans survived the explosion, parachuted, and were captured. Their confessions corroborated Zhang's account. Zhang's act destroyed one enemy spy plane, killed three Americans, including an instructor navigator, and led to the capture of seven others. This was possibly one of the most remarkable feats by any single soldier in the entire war. Under normal circumstances, Zhang would become a most decorated hero. But his case was anything but normal.

Zhang's storyline was so extraordinary and his background so complicated—he was one of the 150 Whampoa cadets screened out to join the 60th Army before entering Korea—that the Chinese government took several months to interrogate him and the US crew before publicizing his name on May 8, 1952, hours after President Truman announced that the United States would not forcibly repatriate prisoners. *People's Daily* reported the capture of several "parachuted special agents" who were Chinese POWs. Zhang was described as having "defected to our side."[2] His destruction of the plane, however, was not mentioned. In July, a Xinhua News Agency dispatch entitled "CPV Prisoner Zhang Wenrong Exposes the Americans' Egregious Crime of Forcing POWs to Spy" outlined Zhang's grenade-throwing act in a few brief sentences.[3] Harrison's confession was published in October, detailing his training of Chinese POWs and the fateful explosion.[4] For a Communist mouthpiece known for its vitriolic hyperbole, the reporting of Zhang's case turned out to be measured and factual.

If Harrison's confession cannot be taken at face value, it is bolstered by his recounting of essentially the same story to US Army interviewers after his release in September 1953. Later he was awarded the Bronze Star for his leadership in enemy prison camps.[5] Evidently the US Army did not consider Harrison's confession an act of treason or cowardice. Ed Evanhoe, a former special operations officer during the war and later a historian, interviewed another surviving crew member, whose narrative largely matches Harrison's.[6] Zhang's spectacular act no doubt took place.

Zhang Wenrong was one of the few hundred Chinese prisoners who were secretly removed from POW camps and declared "escaped" by the UNC. They were forcibly trained to serve as agents for a US intelligence unit—the 8240th Army Unit (hereafter Unit 8240). These prisoner-turned-agents were sent into North Korea by land, air, and sea to collect intelligence and then return to UNC lines on foot. More than half of them—probably more than 200—were killed or captured during missions, and some of the captured were executed by the Communists. Fewer than a hundred made a narrow escape from death and eventually went to Taiwan in January 1954.

Allegations and Evidence

The Zhang Wenrong incident provided the Chinese Communists with timely propaganda ammunition in the Panmunjom talks, which had been deadlocked over prisoner repatriation. Zhang's case proved that the Americans had forcibly drafted Chinese POWs as spies, against their will and in violation of international law, thus debunking the American claim that many Chinese POWs voluntarily chose not to return to China. Despite widespread coercion in POW camps, Chinese prisoners still longed to return home, as Zhang had demonstrated. Chinese negotiator Chai Chengwen praised Zhang's heroism: "At a decisive moment, he acted fearlessly and returned to the embrace of the motherland."[7]

Chai and other Communist negotiators reasoned, and perhaps earnestly believed, that "hundreds or thousands of Chinese and Korean prisoners would refuse repatriation is inconceivable." Admittedly, there were "an extremely small number of individuals" who would resist repatriation, but Chai dismissed them as unreformed "former Nationalist officers, army ruffians, and hooligans."[8] As preceding chapters have demonstrated, however, Chai and his colleagues underestimated the number of willing defectors—certainly there were more than several hundred. The Communists' argument was also undermined by their own revelations. Most of the prisoner-agents that were subsequently captured were determined by the CPV to be former defectors or deserters. Zhang Wenrong was an anomaly.

Furthermore, the prisoner-agent allegations were overshadowed by a concurrent propaganda blitz. Also in early 1952, the Communists accused the Americans of waging germ warfare in North Korea, Manchuria, and Shandong. These charges were met with great skepticism outside the Communist bloc.[9] Amid the sensationalism of this imbroglio, the prisoner-agent allegation became sidelined. While the Communists could only produce dubious evidence of its germ warfare allegations, it indeed had a solid case on prisoner-agents. A string of captured agents told similar stories of secret removal from POW camps and forced training.[10] If their confessions alone could not establish the case, UNC blunders gave credence to the Communists' allegations.

After the two sides exchanged prisoner rosters at Panmunjom on December 18, 1951, the Communists protested that the UNC rosters contained nothing more than Anglicized names and UNC-assigned ID numbers. Without names in Chinese or Korean, without unit or rank information, it was impossible to identify prisoners.[11] When the UNC furnished revised rosters on January 28, 1952, the Communists quickly noticed that fifty-two names on the original lists had disappeared.[12] What happened to these prisoners?

The answer delivered itself to the Communists' doorstep three weeks later. When Zhang Wenrong and other captured agents reported their prisoner IDs, it became apparent that they were among the fifty-two vanished POWs. Pressed to explain this discrepancy, UNC negotiators equivocated for months until July 17, when they replied that among the fifty-two missing prisoners thirteen, including Zhang Wenrong, had "escaped" in March and April.[13] These men, however, had been captured before their supposed escape dates. Zhang allegedly escaped on March 21, yet he had blown up the C-46 a month earlier. Three other agents on Zhang's plane were captured on the same day or soon after, yet their "escape dates" were in April. Liu Chenghan, the tall man who jumped before Zhang, was captured on February 25, forty days before his official "escape date" (see Table 15.1).

TABLE 15.1. *Prisoner-agents' alleged escape dates versus actual capture dates*

UNC POW roster records			*People's Daily* reports	
POW NO.	NAME	ESCAPE DATE (1952)	NAME IN PINYIN	CAPTURE DATE (1952)
710482	Jang Won Yoong	Mar. 21	Zhang Wenrong	Feb. 19
702415	Tan Kwong Ching	Apr. 7	Tan Guangqing	Feb. 20
700783	Lyoo Choong Ham	Apr. 5	Liu Chenghan	Feb. 25
710772	Moo Ping Seong	Apr. 15	Mu Bingyun	Feb. 20

SOURCES: UNC POW rosters, Entry 466, RG 389, NA; *Renmin ribao*, May 8, 1952: 1.

63 NK

Internment Serial No.	Name	Rank	Sex	Photographs	F.P.	Sig.	Roster Number	Deceased	Disposition	Remarks
710,482	JANG WEN YOONG	2nd Lt	M	X	X	X	3144			ESCAPED 21 Mar '52
710,483	LEE SEU HUI	2nd Lt	M	X	X	X	3144	[illegible]		SEP.2 1.1953
710,484	MA FU SUI	2nd Lt	M	X	X	X	3144			ESCAPED 27 FEB 53
710,485	KWAN CHUNG FU	2nd Lt	M	X	X	X	3144	TRANSFERRED	TO NNRC:	SEP 21 1953
710,486	LEE KWO CHI	2nd Lt	M	X	X	X	3144			ESCAPED 27 FEB 53
710,487	KOW WON JWIN	2nd Lt	M	X	X	X	3144			ESCAPED 27 FEB 53
710,488	HWANG SEU	1st Lt	M	X	X	X	3144			ESCAPED 23 Apr '52
710,489	WANG DEI LYANG	M/SGT	M	X	X	X	3144		REPATRIATED:	5 Aug 53

FIGURE 15.1. Zhang Wenrong (710482), Ma Furui (710484), Li Guoqi (710486), Gao Wenjun (710487)—all four were Whampoa cadets—and Huang Shi (710488), were declared to have escaped by the UNC. In fact they were drafted by Unit 8240. Huang was captured during a mission; Ma, Li, and Gao survived and went to Taiwan in 1954. US National Archives.

The absurdity was not lost on the Chinese negotiators. Chai asked: "How could your side know back in January that these prisoners would escape in March or April, leading you to eliminate them from the rosters?"[14] The original rosters of December 18, 1951, probably prepared days or weeks earlier, were apparently honest.[15] When Zhang and four other POWs were removed from their camps on December 13, the intelligence unit and the prison authorities somehow failed to alert the UNC delegation to remove their names from the rosters, which in fact included the names of all future prisoner-agents. Between December 18, 1951, and January 28, 1952, the UNC delegation belatedly removed the fifty-two names. But this tampering was too clumsy to escape the eyes of the Communists. The UNC had dug itself into a hole. Unable to account for the discrepancy, the UNC's negotiators simply stonewalled further questions on this issue, until they walked out of the truce tent on October 8, 1952, when the peace talks broke down.

In the following six decades, the US government has never acknowledged the existence of the prisoner-agent program, and related documents remain classified or have been reclassified.[16] Nevertheless, traces in the records of multiple agencies demonstrate their knowledge of the program. In internal documents, "volunteers" seems to be the code word for prisoner-agents. In a telegram from Ambassador Muccio to Acheson dated July 7, 1952, the peculiar phrase "prisoners . . . screened out voluntarily by intelligence agencies" was an unmistakable reference to prisoner-agents.[17] Douglas Dillard, a former officer in charge of airdrop operations, claims that aside from Korean civilians, "other sources of recruits were both captured North Koreans and Chinese volunteers who had been anti-Communists." Another officer, George Gaspard, asserts, "A great number of Chinese POWs volunteered to work for the 8240 on intelligence missions, and participated successfully in many such operations."[18] In reality, they were not volunteers. If they were volunteers, Zhang Wenrong would not have blown up the plane in order to demonstrate his innocence to the Communists, and several others would not have fled into the Nationalist embassy for rescue, as will be shown.

Thanks to recent oral history interviews with surviving agents and newly declassified Nationalist documents in Taiwan, the history of the program and the agents can be revealed.

The Program

In January 1951, MacArthur's FEC GHQ established the Far East Command Liaison Group (FECLG), Unit 8240, to coordinate and conduct intelligence operations in the Far East. A liaison detachment—FEC/LD (K)—was set up in the Eighth Army HQ in Korea.[19] These were umbrella groups of a bewildering array of intelligence and partisan/guerrilla organizations controlled by the US Army, Navy, Air Force, and the CIA. Simultaneously, another umbrella unit was formed: Combined Command Reconnaissance Activities, Korea, Unit 8240 (CCRAK), whose director was appointed by the FEC and deputy director was named by the CIA.[20] Regardless of the ever-changing bureaucratic jurisdiction of these organizations, FEC/LD (K), Unit 8240, and CCRAK all shared the same mission: to insert agents and partisans into North Korea and to have them return on foot with intelligence.

To infiltrate by air, FEC/LD–CCRAK's Operation Aviary flew agents deep into North Korea. Aviary officer Douglas Dillard recalled that "hundreds of clandestine airborne agent and partisan drops were made" during the war.[21] If each flight carried five to ten agents, thousands of agents were parachuted, among which, perhaps hundreds were Chinese. To infiltrate overland, the Tactical Liaison Office attached to each US infantry division sent line-crossing agents to walk several miles behind enemy lines. Line-crossers were more numerous than parachuted agents, but their exact number remains elusive.

The most authoritative information on prisoner-agents is in the dossiers created for each agent, containing "name in English and Kanji, code ID, date joined the organization, nationality, age, height, weight, identifying marks such as tattooing, scars and missing digits, area with which agent is most familiar, education, linguistic ability, marital status, family residence, fingerprints, photograph, and biographical sketch."[22] These dossiers, however, are not available in archives.

Perhaps most officially "escaped" prisoners became prisoner-agents, as it was nearly impossible for Chinese POWs interned on the islands of Koje and Cheju to escape. Therefore, a roster of "escapees" may effectively be considered a roster of agents. The number of Chinese "escapees" came to 188 as of August 1953.[23] Unfortunately, this method is flawed, as some known prisoner-agents were not listed as "escapees," such as Meng Ming and Yang Shuzhi.[24] The UNC's unreliable prisoner records make it impossible to accurately calculate the number of prisoner-agents.

The Chinese Communists claimed that between August 1951 and April 1953, a total of 188 Chinese prisoners in nine batches were drafted for spy training.[25] Perhaps it is a pure coincidence that 188 is the same as the number of "escapees" discussed above. But the two figures cover different time periods. The Communist tally does not include data between May and August 1953, when the UNC transported Chinese anti-Communist prisoners from Cheju Island to Panmunjom and placed them under the custody of the NNRC. During the POWs' final four months on Cheju, the prisoner-agent program continued, and probably accelerated.[26]

Estimates by Nationalist operatives in Korea suggested higher headcounts. Although the top-secret Unit 8240 strictly shunned interactions with Nationalist personnel, Taiwan still got wind of the program through two probable channels: several prisoner-agents who escaped from their safe houses and sought refuge in the Nationalist embassy in Seoul, and Nationalist interpreters employed in less sensitive but related units. As early as January 1952, the Nationalist embassy reported to Taipei that more than a hundred "outstanding prisoners" had been selected by the UNC to serve in various functions: "five in the wireless section in Seoul, eight in the POW interrogation section, three in the intelligence department, five in the ROK intelligence unit, five in the psychological warfare unit, and more than eighty in other units."[27]

Recruitment

In September 1951, US intelligence agencies set up a turncoat program to select North Korean and Chinese POWs for infiltration operations. "When a suitable recruit was found, the potential agent would be taken from POW camps and sent to a safe house for training," former CCRAK officer Ed Evanhoe reports.[28] Apparently based on captured agents' confessions, the Communists provided a breakdown of 188 agents selected between August 1951 and April 1953: the first batch of 14 POWs was taken to Taegu; the second, third, and fourth batches with 74 POWs, including Zhang Wenrong, were trained in Tokyo; 95 prisoners from the fifth to ninth groups were trained on Songap Island, 40 miles off the coast of Inchon; and five others received training in Seoul.[29]

In all likelihood, the selection of the prisoner-agents was closely linked to their interrogation assessment. As all prisoners had been briefly interrogated at the time of capture and some had been re-interrogated in depth, the US military had extensive knowledge of the prisoners, especially the cooperative ones, who in turn became some of the most obvious candidates. In terms of candidate profiles, the program clearly targeted the following types of prisoners: (1) former Nationalist military academy graduates and cadets, especially those with technical expertise, such as artillery majors Gao Wenjun and Ma Furui, and wireless operator Zhang Wenrong; (2) former Nationalist officers, such as Liu Bingzhang and Wei Shixi; (3) former Nationalist Youth Army soldiers, who were relatively well educated, such as Meng Ming; (4) CIE prisoner instructors, who were well-educated and highly intelligent, including Gao Wenjun and Ma Furui, (5) other anti-Communist leaders and activists with sufficient education. Of course, as prerequisites, they had to be physically fit, reliable, and anti-Communist—or at least not have displayed any pro-Communist tendencies. Meeting multiple criteria, the roughly one hundred Whampoa graduates and cadets became prime candidates, and many were drafted.[30]

Once a prisoner was identified as a candidate, intelligence officers approached him, suggesting a vaguely worded opportunity to "serve in the UNC." Enticed by the prospect of leaving the prison camps and making themselves useful to the UNC, many prisoners took the "offer." Many prisoner-agents felt a special affinity for Americans. Some were educated in missionary schools and several majored in English in college. Some had been trained by Americans and fought alongside them in the China-Burma-India theater in World War II. On the battlefield in Korea, many risked their lives to defect.

Pouring their hearts out, they answered interrogators' questions in great detail. Some, such as Captain Liu Bingzhang, offered their advice on how to defeat the Communists. Most probably Liu had been identified as a prime candidate early on.

Prisoners might have had other reasons for wanting to get away from the strife in the camps. When Liu Bingzhang returned from Tokyo after a four-month stint with a UNC psychological warfare unit, he was transferred to the officers' battalion in Compound 72 on Koje Island and soon fell victim to the wrath of Li Da'an, who was then the deputy compound leader. Li perceived Liu and other military academy graduates and cadets as a threat to his power. Both Yang Shuzhi and Gao Wenjun recalled that on several occasions Li and his henchmen—the PGs—staged "Communist-style public trials" to torture Whampoa graduates and cadets, serving as a warning to other Nationalist elites. In one instance, Liu was rescued by Yang.[31] In another session, Li thrashed Liu with a wooden club. Upon hearing the news, Dr. Meng Ming rushed to see Liu, who was lying in bed, severely beaten. Once a "dashingly handsome, upright young man with an air of confidence," now a reticent Liu told Meng to leave quickly and quietly, lest Meng also suffer Li's attack. Soon after, Liu disappeared. Rumor had it that he had volunteered to "serve in a US intelligence unit."[32]

Ironically, anti-Communist prisoners who distrusted the Americans managed to escape the snare. While Sun Zhonggeng, the CIE school principal in Compound 72, was selected by 8240 and later captured by the Communists, his counterpart in Compound 86, Cheng Liren, evaded that fate. During interrogations in 1951, Sun, a former Whampoa cadet, was rated "good" for his cooperation and "fair" for his intelligence and reliability. In contrast, Cheng was rated "fair" for his intelligence and cooperation, but "poor" for reliability and "judgment of distance and measurement, and memory."[33] It is hard to believe that Cheng, a police academy graduate, had a poor memory and poor judgment of distance and measurement. Most probably, he was playing dumb. His poor reliability assessment probably arose from his evasiveness. At the time of his interrogation, the prisoner-agent program had only begun and it was unlikely he had any knowledge of it. His distrust of the Americans was probably instinctive. Cheng's performance fooled his interrogators and spared him the ordeal of becoming a prisoner-agent.

Whampoa cadet Hou Guangming was approached by a Chinese-American interrogator in March 1952 with a proposition: "I can give you a difficult task. If you take it, you can leave the POW camp immediately." Hou thought, "as long as I can leave the camp, I'm willing to do anything, even at the risk of my life." On the morning of March 29, Hou and nineteen other prisoners were taken away in a truck with canvas flaps tightly shut; they were forbidden to look out. Little did they know that they were on the first leg of a trip all the way to Tokyo for spy training. After arriving in Tokyo in total secrecy, Hou noticed two problems. First, they were billeted in a compound where the barbed wire on the walls tilted inward, apparently designed to prevent people from escaping. Second, their training included a course entitled Deception Studies. "What kind of place is this?" Hou asked himself.[34] It was too late.

Training and Missions

Perhaps Liu Bingzhang thought he was being trained for the type of intelligence and psychological warfare work he had experienced in Tokyo, such as interrogation or propaganda-leaflet design. Probably he thought, "How could anything worse happen than being tortured by thugs like Li Da'an?" He was wrong. The last documentary trace of him is the few words typed on his roster sheet: "Escaped, 18 Apr '52."[35] No surviving agents, including his friend Meng, who joined Unit 8240 in the summer of 1952, reported seeing him again. Nor did the Communists report his capture. By 1954, Liu was presumed dead.[36]

Days or weeks after they were selected, the draftees were finally told their mission was to infiltrate into North Korea. A batch of twenty-one prisoners including Gao Wenjun, Wen Chuanji, Lu Lu, and Ma Furui, were horrified when they received their mission in November 1952. "If caught by the Communists," Ma pointed out, "one will be executed for sure."[37] Clearly, this type of special operation was not something they had imagined when they were recruited. Possibly some defectors indeed offered to join the UNC; but probably none of them volunteered for special operations behind enemy lines, which was an entirely different game.

To prepare agents for missions masquerading as CPV personnel, one of the first measures Unit 8240 took was to have a US Army tattoo artist alter prisoners' anti-Communist tattoos. The begonia-shaped map of the Republic of China on Hou Guangming's arm was remade into a crab; the words "Anti-Red" on Ma Furui's arm were covered by a snake.[38] Befitting Dr. Meng's profession, "Anti-Red" was covered by the caduceus—two snakes entwined around a winged rod.[39] Such tricks did little to protect agents, since few Communist soldiers had tattoos in any shape or form.

In terms of training, Evanhoe claims that the turncoat program "included airborne training because most of these people were inserted by air."[40] S. L. A. Marshall, however, described the earliest parachute training for Korean agents—"human material [who] were simple Asiatics who know little of military operations and less about the treachery of a descending silk canopy"—as "stepping from the rear of a speeding jeep, so that they would master the knack of tumble-and-roll."[41] When the war stabilized and supplies became available, Unit 8240 trained some Korean partisans in parachuting.[42]

However, none of the Chinese prisoners reported actual parachute jumps. Even though two of the earliest Chinese agents, Zhang Wenrong and Pan Jie, claimed that they had received "parachutist training" in Kawasaki, Japan, Yamada Zenjiro, a

Japanese cook for the program, recalled the "primitive form" of "exercises on a high tower constructed in the garden behind the house."[43]

Doctor Meng recalled, "Our parachute exercise was such a joke. It was done in three hours on Songap Island, including chute control and landing techniques. No actual practice in the air. . . . We just jumped from a platform."[44]

The Chinese prisoner-agents' maiden jumps were nighttime descents deep into the hostile terrain of North Korea, tens or hundreds of miles north of the 38th parallel. When the parachute malfunctioned, as was reported at least once, the agent crashed to the ground and died instantly.[45] If an agent landed safely, it would take him two to three weeks to return to UNC lines on foot, provided he was lucky enough to evade all checkpoints and survive the crossfire and the minefields in no-man's-land. After capturing some prisoner-agents, the Communists became increasingly adept in uncovering agents, who had invariably been tattooed in the POW camps. Soldiers and militiamen manning checkpoints interrogated suspects, and then suddenly ordered, "Take your clothes off!" In a split second, prisoner-agents had to decide either to resign themselves to their fate and surrender or to wield their gun and fight their way out.[46]

Airdrops proved to be the most deadly method. In the very initial stage of the program, in the summer of 1950, less than half of the men parachuted ever made it back to UNC lines.[47] No doubt the odds were stacked against them. Simple math shows that their chances of survival diminished rapidly with each additional mission. Assuming prisoner-agents had a survival rate of 50 percent on any given mission, their chance of survival rapidly dropped to 25 percent on the second mission, 13 percent on the third, around 6 percent on the fourth, 1 percent on the seventh, and near zero on the eighth. Airborne missions were literally suicidal. Ma Furui observed that no one survived a second parachute mission.[48]

Seaborne operations along the North Korean coast, where prisoners were delivered by boats or submarines at night, were also highly risky. Since the CPV mainly traveled on inland roads and mountain paths, the sudden appearance of men in CPV uniforms on the heavily mined seashore naturally raised suspicion and led to interrogation and often arrest.[49]

Somewhat safer was the land route, or line-crossing, which was short and quick and was the path most frequently used. In Ma Furui's batch of twenty-one men, all four line-crossers, including Ma and Gao, returned safely; only four of the sixteen airborne or seaborne agents came back; and one agent refused to carry out his mission. Not surprisingly, all but one survivor chose line-crossing for a second mission. The agent who chose to be airdropped again did not return. Between November 1952 and January 1954, Ma completed six line-crossing missions.[50] The nineteen-year-old Liao Ting, probably the youngest prisoner-agent, completed ten missions, mostly overland. Most agents, however, did not have such extraordinary luck. Liang

Ji, Liao's best friend and comrade from high school through Unit 8240, was shot by CPV scouts in no man's land. He died in Liao's arms.[51]

"Futile and callous" was the official verdict on airborne partisan operations against enemy supply routes.[52] Disregard for agents' lives was endemic and systemic. In 1952, the FEC conducted an investigation on the high loss rate of parachuted agents. When asked if he was sure agents were dropped in the right drop zone, a second lieutenant with Operation Aviary replied, "It doesn't make any difference if we're off a few miles. The main thing is to get these 'gooks' on the ground. They'll find their way back."[53] While American personnel stayed in relative safety in the sky, landing a few miles off on the ground often meant life or death to agents.

One of the most striking features of the missions is that while Chinese prisoner-agents infiltrated by air or land, they exfiltrated on foot only, regardless of the distance or situation. Occasionally US helicopters dropped agents behind enemy lines to capture enemy soldiers for interrogation. Once the captured intelligence source was hooked up and raised to the helicopter by a winch cable, however, the agents were left to their own devices on the ground.[54]

Yang Shuzhi's Luck and Li Da'an's Fall

Yang Shuzhi, the former Nationalist commando and CPV truck driver, was probably the only agent with prior parachuting experience. In 1945 he had jumped five times in Kunming, Yunnan. When drafted into Unit 8240 in 1953, however, he resisted airborne missions and consistently chose line-crossing. After successfully completing his first line-crossing, Yang led a team to infiltrate into an area near Chorwon and Pyonggang—the Iron Triangle. He hid in the mountains while four other agents went out to gather information on Communist troop deployment. Once they returned with intelligence, Yang quickly coded and transmitted short messages with a tiny Siemens device—all had to be done within twenty minutes. Immediately afterward, his team fled to another hiding place. Once the Communists detected radio signals and located their source, search troops would swoop down to encircle the area. An experienced wireless operator since his Whampoa Academy days (1941–1942), Yang successfully sent three messages to Seoul and Okinawa. Five days later, his team approached the UNC lines after dark. "Hello, Captain Black!" Yang shouted the password. "Come on, come on!" responded US troops. Yang survived his second line-crossing mission unscathed.[55]

Yang's only airborne mission occurred in September or October 1953, when he and Du Wenpu, his long-time sidekick since their CPV days, were parachuted into the mountains near Sunchon, 27 miles north of Pyongyang and 110 miles north of the 38th parallel. They walked back to UNC lines eighteen days later.[56]

Another wireless team did not have such luck. On the night of April 22, 1953, Li Da'an and Wang Qin parachuted into the mountains near Pyoktong, a town on the Yalu

River 200 miles north of the 38th parallel. They carried forged travel documents, a radio transmitter, a codebook, and counterfeit cash. Not a single radio signal was received by the Americans before their capture three days later. Yang commented that Li, having received only two months of wireless training, was probably not up to the task.[57]

What's surprising was not that Li Da'an was captured, but that he managed to hide for three days at all. Pyoktong was where around 5,000 UNC prisoners were held by the CPV. Probably Li was sent to gather information on the POW camp. The Communists, however, had been waiting. Mao had issued an order on January 21: "POW management is of great importance. Cadres and troops must be reinforced and prepared for battles against enemy airborne operations. Not a single POW should be seized by the enemy. If these prisoners are taken away, we will have no capital in prisoners exchange negotiations."[58] Evidently Mao and the CPV were anticipating some kind of substantial rescue operations by US paratroopers. When it came to catching agents like Li and his team, this level of preparedness was overkill. Three other agents dropped in a different zone, Liu Fei, Wang Zhushan, and Wang Huaili, were also caught near Pyoktong. The five men shared one attribute—they were all natives of Manchuria.[59]

It was puzzling that the Americans selected truck driver Li Da'an, who had only four years of elementary school education, to take up this highly technical and risky mission deep into North Korea. While most agents were either Whampoa cadets or graduates, Nationalist officers, or well-educated Youth Army soldiers, Li probably had the least education and military training, having never served in any regular army. Dr. Meng recalled that prisoner-agents of earlier batches "strongly recommended" Li to their American superiors: "Li is very tough. He should join our special operations to fully reach his potential."[60] By urging the Americans to select Li to join their deadly enterprise, these prisoners took their revenge on their erstwhile tormentor.

Li was removed from Cheju and taken to Songap Island for training in late November 1952. Surprised to see dozens of POWs whom he had bullied, Li quickly became a different man, adopting a humble manner. He apologized to Gao Wenjun for his past "inconsideration" and sought tips for surviving behind enemy lines. He ingratiated himself with the English-speaking Dr. Meng, whom he relied on for communicating with the Americans. Gao and Meng comforted Li, "Let the past pass." However, as the training progressed and the inevitable mission loomed, Li became increasingly distressed, as he could not find any agent he could trust with his life. More disturbing news came from Seoul, where several experienced agents went on strike. "If Li Da'an doesn't go on a mission, we won't either," they threatened. Yet, they all refused to team up with Li.[61]

Unit 8240's Captain Fox made an exception for Li, accompanying him to the Cheju POW camp to assemble his own team—it was probably the only time a prisoner-agent returned to a POW camp.[62] One member of Li's team was Liu Fei, "a half White Russian and half Chinese, tall, handsome young man with huge bright eyes just like the Russians," recalled Liu's friend Wang Houci.[63] In 1947, fifteen-year-old Liu left home in Harbin and joined a newly established PLA medical school. Soon he was assigned to the 39th Army, which "liberated" half of China during the Civil War. In May 1951, he and a squad leader deserted near Kaesong and surrendered to the UNC after hiking and hiding for a week.[64] Working in the dispensary of Compound 72, Liu was widely appreciated. Liu's boss, Dr. Han, repeatedly implored a Chinese-American intelligence officer not to select Liu to "serve in the UNC" on the grounds that he was the only son in his family.[65] When Li Da'an returned to the camps, however, Liu was chosen. After his arrival on Songap Island, Liu belatedly learned the nature of his new job. He cried out, "Li Da'an knows he is going to be sent to die; why does he drag me along?!"[66]

A postwar US Army study noted:

> A number of special projects were also planned by the partisan command in the first four months of 1953. These included projects for the penetration of POW camps, the recruiting of partisans in Manchuria and Sakhalin, assassination of Communist officials, the capture of an enemy aircraft, and the use of Chinese partisans for sabotage operations in the Sinuiju-Antung complex. Practically all these were dropped by April, either as unrealistically conceived or for lack of specific intelligence on the operation planned.[67]

Li Da'an, Liu Fei, and other Manchurians became nameless victims of such "unrealistically conceived" projects.

Resistance, Punishment, and Disappearance

Having witnessed the loss of fellow agents and fully aware of the danger associated with each assignment, Chinese prisoner-agents, under the threat of physical punishment and even death, continued to undertake missions into North Korea. Betraying the Americans' distrust, Unit 8240 did not give agents arms until the day of their mission. In response to Zhang Wenrong's sabotage of the plane with a hand grenade, more stringent security measures were put in place. Before parachute missions, jumpmasters made sure agents' weapons were not loaded and their grenades were not accessible in flight.[68] Once they returned to the UNC lines, they were immediately disarmed.[69] Confined to Songap Island or guarded safe houses in Seoul, with no access to newspapers or radios, they were cut off from the outside world.[70] Most critically, there was no exit option. None of the several hundred Chinese prisoner-agents were allowed to quit and return to the regular POW camps.

Zhang Wenrong charged that US intelligence officers frequently threatened to kill agents refusing assignments, citing the case of Guo Baotong. Selected in the first batch in August 1951, Guo received training in Taegu. When he refused a mission, he was reportedly thrown into the sea and drowned. In late 1953 more details emerged: Guo was taken away on the night of November 27, 1951, and was never seen again. His cigarette lighter, however, was seen being used by an ROK employee of Unit 8240.[71] Guo was declared "escaped, 14 Apr 1952"—more than eight months after his actual removal from a POW camp and four months after his disappearance.[72] The fear of being drowned was so strong that prisoner-agents created a code word, *bei shabao*, "carrying sandbags on one's back," to describe the drowning of prisoners tied to sandbags. Even in January 1954, when surviving agents were told that they were to be transported to another island in preparation for their final release, some still feared that it was an American hoax to have them drowned.[73]

Another defiant agent, Wen Chuanji, also went missing. Wen was drafted along with fellow Whampoa cadets Ma Furui and Gao Wenjun in November 1952. After twenty days of simple training on Songap Island, for their first mission, Wen, Mao, and Gao chose line-crossing near the 38th parallel. Just before they set out from the front line, Wen suddenly balked. He asked a US officer in English: "If I complete this mission, do I have to do it again in the future?" The reply: "Of course you will." Wen told the officer, "I'm not going, no matter what!" Wen was left behind as Ma and other agents went on their missions. That was the last time Ma saw Wen. Ma feared Wen had been executed.[74]

Wen was not killed. Instead, he was taken back to Songap. His defiance incurred the wrath of his captors, who stripped him naked and threw him into a cage—the dreaded "monkey house"—in the middle of the yard. The cage was so short that Wen couldn't stand up. Liao Ting and fellow Chinese agents wanted to help Wen but were turned away by the Americans. Finally, late in the night, when the Americans were in bed and the ROK guard looked the other way, Liao rushed to the cage to give Wen a coat. That was all he could do. Liao would never forget that night of heavy snow and subzero temperatures near the end of December 1952. "He's been stuck in my mind all these years," Liao recalled in 2015. The next day, Wen was taken away and was never seen again. It was rumored that he soon died.[75]

The only documentary window to Wen's personal history is his interrogation report, which states that he "answered all questions without hesitation and did not appear to be lying." Hailing from a small town in northern Sichuan, Wen had seven years of high school in the provincial capital of Chengdu.[76] He was one of the very few Chinese agents who spoke fluent English. It is very likely that he had attended missionary schools. In a sense, his direct manner was American.

After the Central Military Academy's surrender in late 1949, Wen became a cultural instructor in the PLA 180th Division. His direct superior, Tian Fangbao, recalled: "Wen was one of the two successfully reformed Whampoa cadets in my company.

His performance was excellent."[77] As discussed in Chapter 7, Wen was taken prisoner during the Fifth Offensive debacle in Korea. He was not a defector.

Once in the Pusan prison camp, however, Wen became a different man. When his boss Tian, now also a prisoner but posing as an enlisted man, ran into him, Wen simply ignored him. Tian lamented, "Now he openly mingled with former Nationalists." Tian's officer identity was soon uncovered and he was arrested for organizing resistance. The interpreter who accompanied the US guards was none other than Wen. Tian had good reason to suspect Wen had informed on him.[78]

A tidbit on Wen's interrogation report reveals his deep pro-Nationalist sentiment. This Sichuan native's home address was recorded as "China, Formosa."[79] Among the more than one thousand Chinese POWs whose interrogation reports are available, other than the three Taiwan natives, Wen was the only person who gave Taiwan as his home address. A year after his interrogation, he was drafted as a spy. Days before New Year 1953, he was thrown in an iron cage and left to freeze. He was declared "escaped 24 February 1953."[80] Wen, who had most probably grown up with a special affinity for America, poured out his heart to his American captors. In the end, he was betrayed and his life destroyed by the very country he had trusted.

Suicides, Escapes, and Strikes

Li Jingqiang, a Whampoa graduate of the 22nd class (1948), attempted suicide in protest. On the evening of April 7, 1952, when Li was equipped and about to depart from his safe house in Seoul for an airborne mission, he fired his pistol into his chest, sending a round through his right lung. Li was taken to hospital after a two-hour delay, during which two US soldiers removed his padded CPV uniform—lest the top secret prisoner-agent operations be exposed. Before the incident, Li had written seven protest letters. One of them read: "Since the USA claims that it protects human rights, why do the US authorities force POWs to serve as a stake in its war gamble?" Remarkably, both Chinese Communist and Nationalist intelligence agents soon learned of the incident from captured and escaped agents respectively.[81]

On the evening of the next day, April 8, agent Wang Naiyong scaled the wall of his safe house in Seoul.[82] He fled to the Nationalist embassy and was put in the penthouse, where he hid for nearly two years, until early 1954.[83] Like Wen Chuanji, Wang was a former Whampoa cadet (1949) and a cultural instructor in the CPV 180th Division. After his surrender to the UNC on May 28, 1951, he was exceptionally cooperative. In a 28-page interrogation report, one of the longest for any individual Chinese POW, Wang detailed the Communists' military tactics, social control mechanisms, and techniques for indoctrinating UN prisoners—different for Caucasians and blacks.[84] When he was interrogated, he did not know that his candidness could endanger him. Luckily he escaped.

A Nationalist intelligence report dated May 3, 1952, reported "Chinese prisoners' frequent escapes" from the spy program without mentioning Wang's name. It also claimed that the US Counter Intelligence Corps posted agents around the embassy and in Chinese diaspora neighborhoods in an attempt to intercept escapees.[85] As the 8240 tightened its control of prisoner-agents, it became increasingly difficult to escape. Most agents continued to carry out missions, while fully aware of the escalating danger associated with each additional mission. In order to persuade Gao Wenjun and his teammates to accept their second mission, the US commanding officer promised that they would be sent to Taiwan after its completion. When they returned, however, the officer denied such a promise had ever been made. Gao and his friends went on strike and were placed in detention. One day, the US officer forced five prisoners to beat three others with baseball bats for alleged offenses. Finally, the prisoners caved in and resumed their missions. The only concession they wrung from the officer was that they would take line-crossing missions only, nothing by air or sea.[86]

When a number of agents had completed four missions, the US officer declared that they would be released and sent to Taiwan after the fifth assignment. This move generated so much enthusiasm that ten seasoned agents and twenty newcomers volunteered. The outcome was devastating: only six of the veterans and ten rookies came back.[87] The survivors demanded that the Americans deliver on their promise, only to find that the officer had been replaced. His successor denied that the promise had any validity.[88]

After the armistice in July 1953, Unit 8240 continued its operations. With no end in sight, Gao Wenjun and twelve other prisoners refused to go on any further missions. On the third day of their strike, a US second lieutenant stormed into their quarters and ordered them to pack up and get ready for a mission immediately. The agents stood firm. All of a sudden, the fuming officer raised his submachine gun and fired into the empty cots, sending the Chinese scrambling for cover. After the incident, the officer was replaced by a soft-spoken Chinese-speaking first lieutenant. Nonetheless, the prisoner-agents had to continue their missions.[89] In another incident, Hou Guangming recalled, the US personnel ordered striking agents to line up on a beach and fired into the sand around them.[90] The fear of being murdered was real.

Liberation

In November 1953, Ma Furui infiltrated into the area north of Panmunjom, observed the movement of Communist troops, and returned to the UN lines two days later. That was his sixth and last mission.[91] While Ma cooperated with the Americans, four of the most experienced prisoner-agents had escaped in October and sought refuge in the Nationalist Chinese embassy in Seoul.[92]

Soon after, two other Chinese prisoner-agents, while out on errands for their safe house in Seoul, entered the embassy. They reported that 400 to 500 Chinese prisoners served in special operations and an unknown number had been killed or gone missing behind enemy lines. Off the top of their heads they recited more than a hundred prisoner-agents' names. Before returning to their safe house, they implored Nationalist officials and reporters to rescue the group to go to Taiwan, which they said was "their holy land and paradise, but out of reach." Chiang Ching-kuo instructed Foreign Minister George Yeh to look into the matter.[93]

Soon the embassy produced a detailed report: from August 1951 to August 1953, eleven batches of Chinese prisoners—241 men in total—were selected and trained as agents. Among them, 143—or 57 percent—had been lost (*xisheng*) in action, 7 had escaped, and 3 had been detained by Unit 8240 and disappeared. The remaining 93 men were located in Seoul and on Songap Island. Some of the survivors had undertaken eleven missions and staged hunger strikes five times, but their request to go to Taiwan had been denied. The embassy suggested bringing these prisoner-agents along with the more than 14,000 non-repatriates to Taiwan.[94]

On January 12, 1954, when Nationalist General Lai Mingtang arrived in Seoul to arrange the transfer of Chinese non-repatriates to Taiwan, he also had a secret mission: to secure the release of the approximately 100 surviving Chinese prisoner-agents. The US Eighth Army agreed to release only 44, claiming that the remaining 56 wished to continue to serve in the US Army. Lai pressed the Americans to allow him to visit the 56 men. The Americans agreed, and at a meeting on January 22, only 8 out of the 56 prisoners wished to stay, including daredevil Yang Shuzhi; most of them were desperate to go to Taiwan. The second batch of 48 prisoner-agents left Korea for Taipei on January 26.[95]

Three days earlier, Gao Wenjun, Ma Furui, and others in the first batch had departed for Taipei. In flight, they switched uniforms. As he put on his new Nationalist uniform, tears streamed down Gao's face. Since he shed his Whampoa cadet uniform in Chengdu in January 1950, four years and twenty-three days had passed. To Gao, this day was his final liberation and homecoming.[96]

The Final Toll

Among the 100 lucky survivors, however, 29 were recent defectors who arrived after the armistice. The UNC kept them in Chunchon near the front line, and 14 were drafted as line-crossers.[97] Aside from these 29 rookies, 71 experienced prisoner-agents survived—a figure close to Gao's estimate that only 65 out of the roughly 400 agents survived.[98] Dr. Meng Ming claimed that more than 250 agents were lost behind enemy lines, not counting those killed by friendly fire or landmines in no-man's-land.[99]

The exact number of prisoner-agents remains impossible to determine. It probably ranges somewhere between 241 and 400—the embassy and Gao Wenjun's estimates respectively. Subtracting the 71 survivors, the number of lost prisoner-agents probably ranges between 170 and 329. These numbers may seem small compared to the total number of more than 21,000 Chinese POWs; however, they are roughly comparable to the total number of Chinese prisoner deaths in UNC custody—325.[100] The 325 deaths were caused by disease, accidents, murder by fellow POWs, and shooting by UNC prison guards, such as the gunning down of the 56 flag-raising pro-Communists on October 1, 1952. That is to say, within two years (August 1951–August 1953), the number of prisoner-agents who died in Unit 8240 alone is comparable to the total number of reported deaths among the entire Chinese POW population over three years (late 1950–August 1953). Moreover, after August 1953, the prisoner-agent program continued, and more agents were killed or captured in North Korea. Although this was not literally the proverbial death rate where "nine perished and only one survived" (*jiusiyisheng*), no doubt these agents had lived at death's door.

The most striking feature of the prisoner-agents program was not its high loss rate, but that it practically destroyed the best educated and most committed Chinese anti-Communist prisoners—with Li Da'an being the outlier. As discussed in Chapter 8, the Nationalist Party June 3rd branch, founded by Wei Shixi, Meng Ming, and others, dominated the Officers' Battalion in Compound 72. Among its 25 listed cadres, 17 (or 68 percent) were drafted by Unit 8240. Only 7 of the 17 survived; 10 were killed or captured, including Wei. The organization chart became a death chart.[101]

"I used to have a great impression of the Americans," remarked Hou Guangming. "Once I came into close contact with them, however, I found them unscrupulous and brutal. They employed vicious methods to coerce us into submission. Powerless to resist, we were their prisoners."[102] Gao Wenjun concluded, "Sometimes we hated the Americans even more than Mao and the Communists. They were the same. They had no humanity, no feelings. They just forced us to die for them."[103]

16

Aftermath

AS OF JUNE 1954, the total number of Taiwan-bound Chinese POWs reached 14,342, including the first 63 Anti-Communist Heroes flown to Taipei on October 8, 1953, the 14,220 prisoners released by the NNRC on January 20–21, 1954, the roughly one hundred prisoner-agents of US Army Unit 8240, and a small number of others. Despite their rallying cry of "Return to Taiwan or Die!," among Taiwan-bound POWs, only two were actually Taiwanese—Chen Yonghua and Wang Yingchang. While Wang remained little known, Chen became a symbol of the Anti-Communist Heroes.

None of the 7,110 POWs who were repatriated to China between April 1953 and January 1954 went directly home. Most of the 1,030 sick and wounded prisoners who returned in April 1953 were interned in Dalai and Fuyu Counties, Manchuria, until January 1954. The approximately 6,000 prisoners who returned after the armistice were held in Manchuria until the summer of 1954. What followed was lifetime stigma and persecution for nearly all the returnees. Those who returned in later stages of their captivity suffered even more. Mao's punishment for repatriated prisoners might have been less severe had their captivity been kept short, but the long road to the armistice prevented that.

Repatriates in the PRC

When a group of well-dressed, solemn-looking doctors from Beijing came to Fuyu to examine the wounded returnees, the prisoners initially thanked Chairman Mao. But soon they realized that the doctors were only interested in evidence of alleged

American medical experiments on prisoners. Xie Zhiqi asked if his numb leg could be treated. The doctor turned a deaf ear.[1]

The wounded prisoners received their final verdicts in early January 1954. As some 700 prisoners assembled in the county theater, PLA soldiers with rifles and fixed bayonet were posted every twenty meters along the perimeter. For his crime of "participating in writing reactionary dramas and songs," Xie was expelled from the army and the Youth League. Most prisoners received similarly severe verdicts, with the exception of a small minority of prisoners who had never been to Compounds 72 and 86 on Koje—and therefore had neither been tattooed nor participated in anti-Communist activities. Five prisoners were arrested on the spot. As they were being tied up and dragged away, they shouted "I've been wronged!" The following day, the rest of the repatriates were sent packing. As a final insult, POWs who were expelled from the PLA, including Xie, were ordered to strip off their green army uniforms and change into blue civilian jackets and pants—a stark reminder of their dishonorable discharge.[2]

The 6,000 prisoners who returned after the armistice were subjected to a yearlong investigation in Changtu, Manchuria, which resulted in the expulsion of 91.8 percent of the 2,900 Communist members' from the CCP, the dishonorable discharge of 4,600 repatriates from the PLA counting from the date of their capture, the expulsion of some 700 men from the PLA, and the arrest of a small number of traitors and suspected spies. No one was allowed to rejoin the PLA.[3]

Cai Xingfu, who had feigned illness to escape expected bloodshed on October 1, 1952, and revealed Communist plans under interrogation, returned to China and went through the "study"-cum-investigation in Changtu. He was expelled from the army. Then an army jeep arrived, and an officer asked, "Who is Cai Xingfu? Get in." He was sentenced to death in 1958.[4]

Also arrested was An Baoyuan. An had been slated for execution by the Communist underground leadership on Cheju, but before the order was carried out, the armistice was reached. He was taken back to China and sentenced to death in 1957. Luckily for him, the verdict was overturned due to insufficient evidence. He escaped execution again and was released. He went on to become a factory worker in Manchuria.[5]

Fan Ligui, a CPV company leader and a party member since 1945, disagreed with the harsh verdict. His investigator hectored him: "You prisoners have no right to speak." He added, "If you write letters to the upper levels to complain, why don't you add a fingerprint in blood?"—an insulting allusion to anti-Communist prisoners' petition practices on Koje Island. Fan was expelled from the party.[6]

Wu Chengde, acting commissar of the 180th Division and the highest-ranking prisoner, was doubly expelled—from the party and the army—for "treason against the party and the country." Similarly, the majority of the 34 leaders of Communist Solidarity were expelled from the party; only three escaped punishment. Wu and the more than 30 regimental- and battalion-commander-level officers were dismissed and assigned to civilian jobs in Manchuria. More than 400 junior officers and some 5,000 enlisted men were discharged and sent home. Unknown to the prisoners at the time, in the sealed envelope that held each man's dossier were secret labels such as "For internal control and monitoring" and "Suspected spy."[7]

If Communist officers were treated severely, former Nationalists could only expect worse. Former Whampoa cadets Guo Naijian and Zhang Jiliang were expelled from the PLA and had to wear blue jackets before their departure. Both men thought they had proved their loyalty to the Communists. Guo, Compound 86's chief clerk, had protected many Communist prisoners. Although Zhang had briefly worked for Chaplain Woodberry on Koje Island, he later interpreted for Colonel Zhao Zuoduan in the Close Confinement Stockade on Cheju. After the prisoner exchange in August 1953, Guo and Zhang, along with twenty-one top Communist POW leaders, stayed in Kaesong to prepare materials for the "explanation" delegation, which recorded Guo's speech urging non-repatriates to return. "I was the chief clerk, and I came back." Guo asked, "What are you afraid of?" A year later, Guo was sent back to his native city, but could not find a job. In the aftermath of the Great Leap Forward and the Great Famine that followed, the government sent millions of urban residents to the countryside. Guo, labeled as a "bad element," was sent to a village in 1962, where he farmed until 1978. Zhang Jiliang's fate was far more tragic. A year after his return to Hunan, he was arrested in the Campaign to Purge Counterrevolutionaries. He soon died in prison.[8]

During the same campaign, Liu Shixiu, a former Nationalist officer and CPV assistant artillery battalion commander, was persecuted. Liu had joined the pro-Communists in POW camps, and returned to China at the age of fifty-one. Placed under "internal control" as a suspected spy, this Sichuan native was relocated to Yingkou, Manchuria, where he jumped into a river, drowning himself.[9]

Gao Pan, the Prison Guard squad leader in Compound 70 who had led 1,217 men in his compound to choose repatriation in May 1952, was expelled from the army and sent home. During the Anti-Rightist Campaign in 1957, Gao was arrested as a "counterrevolutionary" and sent to a labor camp in the northwest wilderness, where he died in 1976.[10]

At Changtu the *paoge* brotherhood in Compound 86 on Koje was declared to be a "reactionary organization." Dai Yushu, the Big Brother who had protected many Communists, drove Li Da'an out of Compound 86, and was nearly killed in the massacre on October 1, 1952, was kicked out of the army. After returning to his hometown of Chengdu, he was forced to relocate to a village, where his wounds deteriorated. Later he resumed his old trade as a cobbler to feed his family of four.[11]

Zeng Dequan, the Brother who had pummeled Li Da'an on Koje Island and executed several "traitor suspects" on Cheju, was also sent to the countryside. To join his wife and daughter living in Chengdu, he became a handcart porter. Brother Chen Zhijun, who also beat Li Da'an, remained in the city but was unable to find a job. He worked as a tricycle porter until he fell ill in 1979.[12]

Between 1957 and 1959, more than half a million Chinese, mostly intellectuals, were branded "Rightists"—political pariahs stripped of their rights as citizens. Many educated repatriates also fell victim. Tricked by a government-planted snitch, Xie Zhiqi privately groused, "The Communists are undemocratic. Their words are no good. Worse than the Americans!" He was arrested. For the next seven years, despite his leg injury, he did hard labor in various camps. Following his release in 1965, he still worked as a coolie until 1981.[13]

Lin Mocong, the tough young activist who risked his life to resist tattooing, received a relatively good verdict: "restoration of military service record," meaning his time in POW camps was recognized as part of his military service. He received a demobilization payment of 100 yuan but no job placement. In 1955, he passed the college entrance examination and entered Sichuan University to study history, but was expelled within three months. He worked as a peasant and then a village teacher near Chengdu. After he cooperated with the cadres in the "Opening your hearts to the party" campaign in 1958, he was fired for his "ultra-rightist thinking." He had to haul a night soil cart to make a living. In the ensuing Great Famine, Sichuan became the worst hit province, where more than ten million people starved to death, including Lin's grandmother and mother.[14] Lin escaped to Yunnan, where the famine was less severe, and became a farmhand hauling night soil. Luckily, now the cart was ox-drawn.[15]

Zhang Zeshi, the Tsinghua student-turned-underground Communist and chief interpreter of Compound 602, received a dishonorable discharge. He became a high school teacher, but was branded a Rightist in 1957. Two years later, his father died in prison. During the Cultural Revolution (1966–1976), Zhang was sent to labor camps and was tortured by student rebels in ways "much more cruel than what I had experienced in American prisons in Korea," he recalled.[16] Crippled prisoner Luo Jiecao escaped the Anti-Rightist Campaign, but not the Cultural Revolution. He was arrested in 1966 for alleged treason, and worked in a labor camp until 1969.[17]

Cai Pingsheng returned to Chengdu but became unemployable. He started a cooperative workshop with others, but was soon arrested for "treason." He worked in labor camps and mines until his release in 1962. Then he was assigned to another no less dangerous, backbreaking job in a brick factory.[18]

Former college graduate and POW interpreter Gao Jie went back to Chongqing only to find that his family had disappeared. He became homeless, then did odd jobs for years, and later became a college instructor. In the Cultural Revolution, he was repeatedly struggled against. Gao recalled Captain Brooks's dire warning during the screening: "How could you prove to the Communists that you had not collaborated with the Americans?" At the time, Gao confidently declared, "I'll have nothing to explain." Years later he lamented, "How true had Brooks' prediction become!"[19]

Similarly, idealistic former student Chen Zhinong paid no heed to the anti-Communist POWs, who had warned him, "If you return to China, roll call will be done with a machine gun. At the minimum, you'll be sent to the labor camps!" Chen chose repatriation nonetheless. He did not know that in the same year his father, a former county assemblyman and wealthy merchant, was arrested for being a "local bully" and received a commuted death sentence. Although Chen did not go to labor camp after his return, his father died in one in 1958.[20]

Chen Qingbin, the Taiwanese who became a Communist in the PLA, found his future wife, the daughter of his host family in Changtu, where he was billeted. They named their first two sons Yong (valor) and Sheng (victory). But the third child, a daughter, was named Yilan, after Chen's birthplace in Taiwan. Placed under "internal control" in Yingkou, Manchuria, Chen was closely watched. During the Cultural Revolution, he was paraded through the streets with a placard hung around his neck, and sent to live in a cowshed. His wife was beaten and driven insane.[21] What Chen experienced was not unusual during the Cultural Revolution, but his dual labels of Taiwanese and POW made him and his family doubly vulnerable.

Some prisoners fared better. He Rui, whose severe wound had kept him away from Koje, received the best possible verdict: double restoration—of party membership and military service history. He went back to Sichuan and survived largely unscathed throughout the years of political tumult that followed.[22] Tang Yao, the Zhejiang native who was branded by Li Da'an, became one of the very few POWs to enter a university and receive a degree. After graduating from East China Normal University in Shanghai, he became a college instructor.[23]

The "Anti-Communist Heroes" in Taiwan

The more than fourteen thousand POWs who arrived in Jilong and Taipei from January 25 to 27, 1954, were greeted by tens of thousands of enthusiastic citizens who poured onto the docks and streets to pay their respects to the Anti-Communist Heroes. After parading through Taipei, however, they were taken to hastily constructed barracks dozens of miles away. The drivers carrying Zhang Yifu's group lost their way after dark; the prisoners climbed off the trucks and trudged along the muddy road in all directions. They did not reassemble until the next morning. All this did not bode well, Zhang thought.[24]

When the National Assembly convened in Taipei on February 19, several thousand POWs were selected to salute Chiang Kai-shek, who was to be reelected president. With the unassuming Chiang Ching-kuo standing behind him, Wang Zunming, the former leader of Compound 86, spoke on behalf of the Anti-Communist Heroes. The sixty-seven-year-old Chiang Kai-shek was moved. "Their enthusiasm brought tears to my eyes," he noted in his diary.[25]

While the Communists held repatriates in two small towns in Manchuria for almost a year, the Nationalists held anti-Communist POWs in four barracks near Taipei for three months. During this so-called counseling (*fudao*) period, prisoners' personally histories were investigated and recorded. On March 18, 4,410 men, or 31 percent of the 14,342 POWs, renounced their membership in the Communist Party and Youth League. Additionally, 609 Communist spies turned themselves in, and fifteen were arrested. Thirty-three others, labeled recalcitrant "troublemakers," were detained for "reformatory training" (*ganxun*)—Taiwan's counterpart to "re-education through labor" (*laojiao*) on the mainland. Following a series of mobilization meetings, 97.4 percent of the prisoners, excluding the sick, wounded, and overaged, "volunteered" to rejoin the Nationalist military.[26] Despite the fanfare surrounding this supposedly spontaneous demonstration of patriotism and anti-Communism, in fact this was coerced reenlistment of former POWs, who had been exhausted by years of fighting and captivity. This became a source of resentment. During their visit to Cheju in August 1953, the Nationalist delegates had promised the prisoners that they could freely choose their future career in Taiwan. Now the POWs felt cheated.[27] While the Communists allowed no POW to reenter the PLA, the Nationalists practically spared few healthy POWs from reenlisting in the Nationalist military so that these ex-Communist soldiers could be closely monitored.

Not only was the rank-and-file loath to rejoin the military, but so too was Wang Shunqing, the Little Caesar of Compound 72 and one of the two or three highest-ranking POW leaders. He went AWOL soon after arriving in Taiwan. A year later, he was charged with beating another prisoner and desertion.[28] Little else is known about him.

Wang Houci, former Whampoa cadet, was arrested on charges of being a Communist spy. To gather evidence against him, an interrogator wired a fellow prisoner, eighteen-year-old Wang Zirong, to a field telephone, and cranked it up, administering excruciating shocks. Zirong was tortured all night, but still refused to declare his friend a Communist. "Wang Houci," he simply said, "had been a resolute anti-Communist since our days on Koje." Without any solid evidence, Houci was nevertheless detained for three years, including several months on the dreaded Green Island, a tiny isle off Taiwan's east coast, where political prisoners were held. After his release, he became an elementary school teacher.[29]

In June 1954, all enlisted men were distributed to various military units across Taiwan and on the Nationalist-controlled islands near China's coast, including Jinmen and Mazu. Officer POWs were formed into an Anti-Communist Fighter Regiment (*Fangong yishi zhandou tuan*). "This period was the most terrifying," recalled Dr. Zhang Yifu, now a lieutenant. "People who spoke carelessly during the day disappeared at night. We heard news of people committing suicide by jumping into wells or hanging themselves. One couldn't trust anybody." A POW friend wrote Zhang a postcard with the phrase "your fellow sufferer" (*nanyou*). For this, his friend was jailed for half a year. Zhang recalled, "We had no freedom of speech. Our every move was watched."[30]

Zhao Yingkui, the young Communist who had been forcibly tattooed in Compound 72, remembered that merely a week after arriving in Taiwan a former college student, whose hope of getting out of the army and leading a civilian life dashed, hanged himself. Three other POWs in his unit also committed suicide in that first summer in Taiwan. The dead were all branded "desperate Communist spies." In 1955, Zhao was arrested for "conspiring to overthrow the government" and concealing his membership in the Communist Party. After three years of interrogation, sometimes involving torture, two alleged ringleaders were sentenced to death; Zhao and two others received life imprisonment. Their crime was their one-time discussion of becoming sworn brothers, exchanging photos and home addresses in China, and grumbling that when the Communists attacked Taiwan, they should turn their guns on Chiang Kai-shek. After spending two years on Green Island, Zhao received an early parole, but he was interned for five more years at a "vagrants detention center" because he could not find two guarantors to vouch for him until 1965. He later worked in factories, ran a noodle shop, and eventually became a Mongolian barbeque chef.[31]

Notwithstanding the White Terror that engulfed Taiwan under Chiang Kai-shek and Chiang Ching-kuo and the general distrust of the former POWs, the Nationalists' authoritarian government treated the prisoners as valuable human resources, whereas Mao's totalitarian regime classed them as political pariahs. While China-bound POWs were met with systematic stigmatization and persecution, their counterparts in Taiwan, especially former Nationalists, enjoyed opportunities that were unimaginable on the mainland.

To expose the "Communist tyranny" in China and shore up support for Taiwan in the West and in the Chinese diaspora, the Nationalist government selected five groups of Anti-Communist Heroes to tour America and Europe, Japan, the Philippines, Vietnam, and Thailand in 1954.[32] Gao Wenjun and five other ex-prisoners toured in the United States, Canada, Cuba, and Western Europe. Gao was baptized at the Vatican. Tao Shanpeng and Chen Yonghua went on a speech tour in Japan. Later, Gao, Tao, and Wang Futian joined the Nationalist Party Central Committee's

Sixth Section (in charge of psychological warfare against the mainland). Gao served until 1972, when he went to America to study law. As of 2017, Gao remained an active member of the Nationalist Party and a leader of Nationalist veterans in San Francisco.[33]

While China-bound repatriates were openly mistreated, former POWs in Taiwan, though secretly monitored and not trusted, enjoyed the semblance of normal life and work. Chen Wenji, a former Nationalist Youth Army soldier and CPV ammo bearer, retired from the army in 1968. He became an accountant in the comptroller's office in the Political Warfare Department located on the fifth floor of the Presidential Palace, where he worked until 1992.[34]

When Taiwan's economy began to take off in the 1960s, ex-POWs benefited from increasing opportunities. Yan Tianzhi, the student refugee from Hubei, had learned English from the American guards in the POW camps, a skill he put to good use in Taiwan. After serving in the army in Taiwan for five years, he passed the highly competitive college entrance examination, aided by a 20 percent boost in scores for military applicants. He went on to receive a master's degree in 1968. In the following two decades, Yan participated in the making of the "Taiwan economic miracle" as an economist on the powerful Economic Planning Council. After retiring from the government, he taught at National Chengchi University until the age of seventy.[35]

Yu Rongfu joined a construction company after his military service and took part in building Taiwan's expressways. Dr. Meng Ming interpreted for the US Military Assistance and Advisory Group until 1973. Later he became a successful English teacher.[36] Dr. Zhang Yifu served with a Nationalist special forces unit in Laos and Burma in 1960–1961. When he left the army in 1974, he started his own clinic, where he practiced until 2013.[37]

Because of the need to accommodate the 14,000 ex-POWs, Chiang Kai-shek and Chiang Ching-kuo inadvertently left an important institutional legacy. Taking a lesson from his gross failure to care for veterans on the mainland, Chiang Kai-shek ordered Ching-kuo to set up the Employment Assistance Council for Anti-Communist Heroes shortly before their arrival. Although it became a misnomer, as most POWs were pressed into the army, it was soon renamed the Veterans Employment Council, and eventually morphed into today's Veterans Affairs Council. It provided vocational, educational, and health care services to former POWs and later veterans in general. The government confers upon veterans with ten years of military service the title of "honored citizens" (*rongmin*). Slightly over half of the 14,000 POWs qualified as *rongmin*, and enjoyed retirement benefits, including full health care. As of 2013, 485 surviving POW-*rongmin*, including some of the men interviewed for this book, lived in government-run retirement homes.[38]

Fates

Daredevil Yang Shuzhi, the former Nationalist paratrooper and CPV truck driver, returned to Taiwan in 1955 after a year of additional service in Korea with the US special forces Unit 8240. He joined the Nationalists' special operations. Between 1955 and 1958 he and his teammates commandeered mainland fishing boats in the Taiwan Strait, and once infiltrated the mainland coast at night. His luck never ran out. After a falling-out with his boss, he quit the military and ran a Sichuanese restaurant. He remained healthy and active as of 2017. At the age of ninety-five, Yang still runs a restaurant in Taipei with two younger partners, multitasking as a cashier and a chef. He still loves driving, a skill he learned from his World War II American allies in Ramgarh, India.

Yang's colleague in Unit 8240 Li Da'an did not have such luck. In June 1958, five years after his airdrop and capture near Pyoktong, North Korea, the infamous Li was sentenced to death by a military court in Beijing. A bullet to the back of his head ended his life.[39]

One day in 1962, Tian Fangbao, the repatriated former CPV political instructor, was summoned to the main office of his factory in Jiaozuo, Henan. Two officials from Beijing No. 2 Prison, one in a PLA uniform, asked him: "Do you know who betrayed your identity to the Americans when you were in the POW camp in Pusan?" Tian hesitantly replied, "I don't know." The officer put a photo on the desk. Tian was shocked, saying, "I suspected him! But I didn't have any hard evidence." It was Wen Chuanji, the former Whampoa cadet and cultural instructor under Tian. Apparently Wen was not killed by the Americans as fellow prisoner-agents in Unit 8240 Ma Furui and Liao Ting had assumed. Nine years after his ordeal in a "monkey house" and subsequent disappearance, he was parachuted into Fujian Province at a time when Chiang Kai-shek clamored to retake the mainland in the wake of the Great Famine. Unsurprisingly, Wen was captured. He confessed to betraying Tian in the UN prison in 1951. The Beijing prison officials came to Henan to verify Wen's account.[40]

What transpired in the nine years between Wen's disappearance on New Year's Eve 1952 and his capture in 1962 is unknown. Was he held by the Americans in Okinawa, Saipan, or Guam? Had he ever set foot on Formosa, a place where he probably had never been to but that he once put down as his home address? What happened to Wen in the end? None of these questions can be answered here.

In 1968, Foreign Service Officer Philip Manhard, now a senior US advisor in Hue, South Vietnam, was captured by the Vietnamese Communists in the Tet Offensive. He was held in solitary confinement in Hanoi for five years. After his release in 1973, he received the State Department's Award for Valor. He served as ambassador to Mauritius from 1974 to 1976.[41]

In 1980, four years after Mao's death, the Communist Party Center issued Document 74, "Opinions on the Reinvestigation and Treatment of Returned CPV Prisoners." Most repatriates' verdicts were reviewed and revised, provided they had survived the twenty-two years of Maoist rule after their repatriation.[42]

Lin Xuebu, who was murdered by Li Da'an before the screening in April 1952, was posthumously honored as a "revolutionary martyr" in 1982. His name along with those of other revolutionary alumni of Sichuan University was inscribed on a stele on the campus. But none of his family members were present at the ceremony. His father, a Nationalist elected official, had been executed by the Communists in 1952, the same year Lin was brutally murdered by anti-Communist Li Da'an in Korea.[43]

In Taiwan, the Nationalists finally lost power in 2000, when Chen Shuibian of the Democratic Progressive Party was elected president of Republic of China. Victims of the White Terror were compensated for their sufferings. Zhao Yingkui, for his ten years of incarceration, received an amount roughly equivalent to US$65,000.[44]

In June 2000, a PLA officer of the Beijing Military Region traveled to Liaozhong, Manchuria. His mission was to hand-deliver a letter to Zhang Wenrong, the former Whampoa cadet and prisoner-agent who destroyed the C-46 spy plane in early 1952. Zhang had been released in 1958 after a six-year investigation. He was sent home with 800 yuan, a large sum at the time, but without any formal recognition of his deed. The decision to rehabilitate him entailed recognizing Zhang's military service, issuing him a demobilization certificate, and making a retroactive demobilization payment. Zhang, however, had died three months earlier at the age of seventy-four.[45] He did not live to see his honor restored.

Cai Derong, the 180th Division commanders' bodyguard who was wounded when he attracted enemy fire to enable the commanders to escape, was severely wounded again during the October 1, 1952, massacre when he tried to protect the flag. After repatriation, he was expelled from the party, and his military service was considered terminated on the day of his capture, May 27, 1951. Physically unfit to farm, he became a Chinese medicine doctor through self-study. In 2010, when this author, accompanied by Zhang Zeshi, met Cai, he was bedridden and unable to speak. His wife said that his greatest regret in life was that the government did not recognize him as a "disabled soldier."[46] That summer, I found in the US National Archives a document that reads: "Chai Deo Yoong, 63 NK-711825. Wound posterior scalp. Incurred in riot, 1 October 1952, POW Camp 3A."[47] Then came the news that Cai had just passed away.

Conclusion

IN THE LAST TWO YEARS of the Korean War, from the time the truce talks began in July 1951 to the armistice in July 1953, 12,300 US soldiers were killed on the battlefield. And for the better part of those two years, the contest was over the repatriation of Chinese prisoners, or more precisely the some 14,000 allegedly anti-Communist Chinese prisoners. Finally, on January 20, 1954, the UNC handed 14,220 Chinese prisoners to Nationalist Taiwan.

Admitting that "thousands of casualties had been suffered . . . in the fight to protect the defectors from communism," US army historian Hermes contends, "the UNC had kept faith with the nonrepatriate prisoners and won a psychological victory." He asserts that although "disobedience, riot, and rebellion [among Communist POWs] had taken some of the luster from this victory," voluntary repatriation was "bound to have an influence upon future conflicts and their settlement."[1] Similar hyperboles had been made in the immediate aftermath of the Korean War.

"The principle of nonforcible repatriation for which the United Nations fought so long has been firmly established," declared UNC commander John E. Hull upon the release of the last anti-Communist prisoners on January 23, 1954. "From this day on," he promised, "all soldiers of every Communist army may know of a certainty they may seek and find sanctuary in the Free World."[2] Four months later, in a rare reference to enemy POWs, President Eisenhower, who had pointedly deleted the mention of enemy prisoners in his televised speech announcing the signing of the armistice agreement in July 1953, proclaimed that "a new principle of freedom"—voluntary repatriation—"had been inaugurated" and "its impact on history . . . may weigh more than any battle of our time."[3]

To end the United States' next war in Asia, however, National Security Advisor Henry Kissinger demanded each party "return all captured persons . . . without delay" once the fighting ended in Vietnam. Article 6 of the Protocol to the Paris Peace Accords in 1973 reads: "The detaining parties shall not deny or delay their [POWs'] return for any reason."[4] So much for the talk of a new human right having been established. Although the policy of voluntary repatriation was never formally repudiated, it was never brought up again by the US government.

Voluntary repatriation and prisoner reindoctrination, twin US policies in the second half of Korean War—the war over the prisoners—were major failures, as they achieved none of their original objectives and denied the rights of the majority of prisoners while protecting only the minority.

Denying the Rights of the Majority While Protecting the Minority

The "defection" of some fourteen thousand Chinese prisoners to Taiwan was a propaganda coup for Chiang Kai-shek, but not the United States. If two-thirds of the Chinese POWs had genuinely rejected Communist China, it would have played right into the hands of the pro-Chiang China Lobby, which had accused the Truman-Acheson administration of "pulling the rug from under" the Nationalist government while it was "still stubbornly squirming with life" in its epic civil war against the Communists from 1945 to 1949.[5] On the other hand, if the widespread violence and coercion in UN prisons became known to the world, the Communists' allegations would have been validated, the justification for the final two years of the Korean War would have crumbled, and the prestige of Truman and America would have been damaged. It was a lose-lose situation.

After the war, the US government deliberately avoided mentioning the defection of anti-Communist prisoners, let alone profiting from it. "For obscure reasons the case of the Chinese and Korean prisoners who chose freedom has not been given the type of exploitation which it deserves," remarked a psychological intelligence analyst in the NSC, especially given the fact "the liberation of these people is almost all that we have to show for our Korean effort."[6] Evidently, he failed to comprehend Washington's predicament. After all, having nothing to show was preferable to inviting unwanted scrutiny of a dubious victory.

If the supposed propaganda victory was a flop, proponents of voluntary repatriation and prisoner reindoctrination might still argue that the two policies served a military objective: to "cause defection of enemy troops in the field," as stated in NSC-81/1, and to deter future Communist aggression. The Joint Chiefs were initially inclined to favor voluntary repatriation "because of its extreme importance to the effectiveness of psychological warfare."[7] This envisaged effectiveness, however, proved to be illusory. "There have been no wholesale defections," admitted Admiral Joy. And Communist expansion in Indochina and the threat to Taiwan went undeterred.[8]

In fact, very few Chinese troops defected or surrendered after voluntary repatriation was introduced in January 1952. The vast majority of the Chinese prisoners (74 percent) had been captured during the disastrous Communist Fifth Offensive in April, May, and June 1951. The number of Chinese prisoners in UNC hands only grew from 20,773 in January 1952 to its peak of 21,106 in January 1953—a meager increase of 333 men in a year.[9] Other than a minority of willing defectors and deserters, the majority of Chinese prisoners had surrendered in 1951 only because they had been out of food and ammunition for days and found themselves hopelessly encircled by overwhelming UN forces.

Even though the psychological warfare value of voluntary repatriation was practically nil on the battlefield, Washington could still argue that moral and humanitarian reasons alone justified America's costly defense of the prisoner's right not to be repatriated. "Strong and proud and free nations can make costly sacrifices for principles," Joy lectured Communist negotiators in his farewell performance on May 20, 1952, although in private he had vehemently opposed the policy.[10] This same sort of rhetorical flourish was echoed in President John F. Kennedy's inaugural address nine years later: "We shall pay any price, bear any burden, meet any hardship, support any friend, oppose any foe to assure the survival and success of liberty."[11] It has become widely known that Kennedy's commitment to South Vietnam proved to be ill-advised and ill-fated. Less known is the history of the US commitment to voluntary repatriation in the Korean War, a policy no less poorly conceived, disastrously executed, and morally compromised.

Apologists may still argue that the US commitment at least protected a sizeable number of prisoners who refused repatriation. General Boatner, however, questioned the very concept of voluntary repatriation, which, he argued, "had no lasting or realistic benefits to the individuals concerned." He asked rhetorically, "Is it not crass hypocrisy for the United States to restrict immigration in times of peace when men are relatively free, yet take pride in the conversion of our erstwhile enemies to 'our side' by their 'free choice'? Especially when they were in fact in our prisons, subject to our indoctrination and therefore not free to make a 'free choice.'"[12]

It is true that US policy protected the interests of a sizeable minority, especially the roughly 3,000 diehard anti-Communists—an estimate shared by Communist, Nationalist, and American intelligence. Bona fide anti-Communists, such as Gao Wenjun, Yu Rongfu, Jin Yuankui, Huang Changrong, and Wang Zunming, were saved from repatriation and certain persecution. But this last redeeming purpose was also heavily compromised. As discussed in Chapter 15, approximately 150 to 300, or 5 to 10 percent, of the some 3,000 genuinely anti-Communist Chinese prisoners—often the most committed, best educated, and most fit—never made their way to Taiwan in the end. They had been drafted by US military intelligence units and squandered in futile and callous operations by air, by sea, and by land. Most of them never returned, and were simply listed as "escaped" by the UNC. While a total of 325 Chinese prisoners died under UNC custody from all types of causes, a comparable number of prisoners were listed as "escaped." Only about seventy prisoner-agents survived and went to Taiwan in 1954. Wiped out were the most committed anti-Communist POWs, for whose freedom the United States supposedly fought the second half of the Korean War.

The United States and its allies paid a steep price for voluntary repatriation and prisoner reindoctrination. "Fifteen months were required to impose our principle of voluntary repatriation on the Communists," Joy lamented. "It was a long year for Americans on the battle line in Korea. It must have been a painful year for Americans in Communist dungeons."[13] These policies endangered the lives of some 12,000 UNC prisoners in Communist custody, including more than 3,000 Americans. In effect, the United States adopted a voluntary repatriation that promised freedom to Communist prisoners but prevented the early return of its own prisoners and a timely conclusion of the war. Its prisoner reindoctrination policy only served to polarize and agitate prisoners, encouraging the dominance of Chinese anti-Communist POWs, whose vehement rejection of repatriation took the US government by surprise and subsequently hijacked the armistice talks agenda. No one had anticipated the price for paying lip service to fighting the Chinese Communists—with propaganda and psychological warfare—could be so dear.

Alternatives?

Most American historians consider President Truman's decision to uphold voluntary repatriation to have been based on the high-minded principle that the interests of Chinese prisoners had to be protected, even at the cost of American lives. However, few have asked what the alternatives were or if there were any viable alternatives at all. Although the screening process was originally devised to present the Communists with a fait accompli, it generated such a hugely lopsided result that in effect it presented a fait accompli to the US government. From a moral standpoint, how could the United States possibly return these POWs to China after its psychological warfare program had succeeded in converting them into "avowed anti-Communists"?

From a practical standpoint, how could the UNC forcibly return thousands of prisoners who had declared themselves to be anti-Communist? Admittedly, only a minority of the 14,000 alleged anti-Communist prisoners were diehards. If we accept the minimum estimate of 3,000 diehards, it would have been equally difficult for the UNC to forcibly return 3,000 or 14,000 prisoners.[14] This would have become a propaganda nightmare. In fact, many prisoners announced that they preferred to be killed by the Americans in Korea rather than by the Communists in China.

Two insiders, Manhard and Joy, had argued that after the removal of the anti-Communist trusties coupled with a period of indoctrination to relieve prisoners of fear and clear up any misunderstanding, the Chinese prisoners should be re-screened, which most likely would have led to more of them choosing repatriation. However, without adequate manpower, especially a sufficient number of linguists who were not Nationalist Chinese, it is doubtful this scheme would have worked. It was precisely on this ground that Ridgway sided with Van Fleet, and dropped the idea of a thorough rescreening. Instead, a half-hearted surprise rescreening was carried out, producing a paltry 415 cases of Chinese prisoners reversing their repatriation decisions.

In fact, by the time the United States belatedly realized that the anti-Communist prisoners could pose a threat to the armistice talks, it was already too late. These POWs had dominated Compounds 72 and 86 by October 1951, two or three months before the policy of voluntary repatriation was first broached at Panmunjom and half a year before the screening in April 1952. Their dominance was aided by G-2, the CIE, and the prison authorities, all of which relied on the anti-Communists to control the uncooperative Communists.

Therefore, regardless of the motivation behind Truman's insistence on voluntary repatriation, there was practically no way the United States could have forcibly returned a large number of Chinese prisoners without bloodshed. Some US military leaders' frequent attempts to backtrack from this policy only demonstrate their lack of clear thinking or indifference to potential bloodshed.

In retrospect, there were two possible ways of extricating the United States from this quagmire. First, the UNC could have prevented the anti-Communists from dominating the other prisoners, had it segregated bona fide defectors from the outset. When Chinese defectors trickled in, the UNC could have separated them instead of lumping all prisoners together in the same camp.

In reality, however, the UNC utilized some defectors for psychological warfare operations; G-2 relied on anti-Communist trusties to identify Communist officers for interrogation; and the prison authorities depended on them to administer the camps and control the unruly Communists. While the UNC utilized anti-Communist POWs for various purposes, it treated them as regular prisoners who were supposed to be exchanged as soon as there was an armistice. Not surprisingly, anti-Communist prisoners felt cheated and insecure. Consequently, they were compelled to organize and control as many prisoners as possible, even through violent means. Had the UNC segregated the small number of bona fide anti-Communist defectors early on and promised them asylum, much of the intra-camp violence could have been avoided. The number of anti-repatriates would definitely have been much smaller than 14,000, and more acceptable to the Communists.

Even in later stages, Washington could still have employed a novel approach to resolving the POW issue. The UNC could have told prisoners that only, say, three thousand or X number of "bona fide anti-Communists" would be given asylum and sent to Taiwan, and required the trusties to produce such a roster. With the assurance of asylum and the incentive to reduce the ranks of non-repatriates, the trusties most likely would have quickly come up with a short list, from which the waverers would gladly be left out. As shown in Chapter 10, had the percentage of Chinese non-repatriates been close to that of the North Koreans', Beijing would have been amenable to accepting a partial repatriation in July 1952. The armistice could have been reached one year earlier.

However, none of these steps was taken; in fact, none was even discussed. Throughout Truman's presidency, his administration did not debate the final destination of Chinese anti-repatriates—McClure's proposal to send prisoners to Taiwan was nipped in the bud by Acheson—even though it could only be Taiwan by default, as neither the United States nor South Korea would accept them. If Washington had never intended to send prisoners to Taiwan, why did it expand the reindoctrination program to convert Chinese POWs into "avowed anti-Communists" who were to be sent back to China as "ambassadors of independent thinking"? No one in Washington noted the glaring contradiction: the very success of the conversion program would lead prisoners to reject repatriation—a situation that would certainly prevent a quick armistice. Why was Washington so blind to this obvious contradiction?

The answer lies in American policymakers' deep-rooted arrogance toward the Chinese people and their ignorance of the Chinese Communists.

Arrogance toward the Chinese and Ignorance of the Chinese Communists

Truman as a young man once professed to his future wife that he "hate[d] Chinese and Japs," which was hardly extraordinary given the racism prevalent in early twentieth-century America. He wrote, "I think one man is just as good as another so long as he's honest and decent and not a nigger or a Chinaman."[15] The outwardly cosmopolitan Acheson had traveled to China and Japan when he was young, but as the secretary of state he made eleven trips to Europe but none to Asia. His biographer Robert Beisner notes that Acheson "condescended to Mao's nation." Early in the Korean War, when US planes accidentally bombed Chinese territory, Acheson joked that "the Chinese don't know the difference between a bomb and a rocket anyway. They both make an awfully big bang."[16]

George Kennan, the early architect of the containment strategy, was equally dismissive. Around the time when Mao proclaimed the founding of the People's Republic in October 1949, Kennan remarked, "China doesn't matter very much. It's not very important. It's never going to be powerful."[17] When the CPV began pummeling UN forces in Korea, China Hand John Paton Davies said that the Chinese would "do no critical damage."[18] How wrong they were.

American policymakers' arrogance toward and contempt for the Chinese and the Korean people were manifested in their cavalier attitude toward negotiations and their proclivity for using force. When armistice negotiations began July 1951, Mao and Zhou assembled China's first team—their most trusted and most capable intelligence officials and diplomats—to direct the negotiations from behind the scenes in Kaesong and later Panmunjom. They maintained daily communication with the delegation. In sharp contrast, Truman and Acheson paid scant attention to the negotiations. To maintain the self-deceiving fiction of a purely military negotiation, the UNC delegation was composed entirely of military officers, who enjoyed no support from senior diplomats or intelligence officials at hand and had no direct line of contact with the president or secretary of state.

None of the military delegates had any substantive experience with or knowledge of China, let alone the Chinese Communists. The delegation's principal Chinese-speaking member throughout the twenty-five months of truce talks was a lowly interpreter, Kenneth Wu. Unable to handle complex written Chinese, Wu had to rely on two interpreters from Taiwan, who frequented the Nationalist embassy. It is dumbfounding that the United States could not furnish its most important military-diplomatic endeavor in the war with a single qualified Chinese linguist. Philip Manhard, the only Chinese-speaking US diplomat in Korea, was excluded from the Panmunjom negotiations. A junior political officer who had only begun learning Chinese in 1948, Manhard made astute observations of the Koje prison conditions but had little policy impact.

In Washington, Truman devoted little time to consider the armistice negotiations. The intellectually incurious president made important decisions often on the fly, based on highly condensed and filtered information presented by his top advisors without asking many, if any, questions. His most trusted advisor, Secretary of State Acheson, was preoccupied with rebuilding Western Europe through NATO. Mostly absent from Washington in the fall of 1951, Acheson was in Europe when Truman made the initial decision on prisoner repatriation and he had barely returned from Europe when Truman made the final and irrevocable decision.

Senior officials on the State-JCS joint committee, and perhaps Acheson as well, withheld unsavory facts and complex policy implications—as well as their own mistakes and misjudgments—from the president. Shielded from the full facts and spared the difficult moral dilemma he otherwise would have confronted, Truman made morally righteous but severely flawed decisions. Nevertheless, the top civilian officials went along, hoping that the Chinese Communists would somehow cave in. The top brass hid their vehement opposition to voluntary repatriation once Truman's preference became known. They assumed that they could bomb the Communists into submission, and bomb their way out of the mess they had helped create. The result of their dereliction of duty was the near doubling of the length of the war and the unnecessary deaths of thousands of American GIs in the second half of the war. Most of the approximately 280,000 North Korean civilians who were killed in US bombing raids in this period.[19] American policymakers demonstrated a callous indifference to the lives of "Asiatics"—and of their own men on the front line and in enemy hands. In the name of protecting American prestige, policymakers protected themselves by hiding their own mistakes and doubling down on misguided policies.

The US military's unthinking expansion of the prisoner reindoctrination program, with Washington's approval, to cover Chinese prisoners reflects a gross ignorance about the Chinese Communists. The Soviet Union's cruel treatment of repatriate POWs after World War II had been well known to American leaders, including Truman. Some policymakers, especially Charles E. Bohlen, had come to regret the American role in forcibly returning Soviet citizens. Why didn't they consider the consequences of reindoctrinating Chinese POWs and then sending them back to Communist China? As explained in Chapter 8, CIE personnel in the field had recognized the inherent moral hazard of their mission: successful conversion meant death or severe persecution to those converts after repatriation. And General Boatner suspended the program immediately after he took command on Koje. But civilian and military leaders in Washington and Tokyo showed no concern over or even awareness of the program.

Other than indifference, one plausible explanation was that few could have anticipated the cruelty of the Chinese Communist government in treating repatriates, given the prevalent assumption among American policymakers that the Chinese Communists were the "so-called Communists"—not real Communists like the Soviets. In fact, even most repatriated Chinese prisoners did not anticipate the severity of the punishment they were to receive, as they had dismissed anti-Communist prisoners' dire predictions as scaremongering propaganda.

Some may argue the ignorance about the Chinese Communists was the unfortunate consequence of the McCarthyite purge of the China Hands from the State Department before and during the Korean War. They were considered "some of America's most able and best qualified China specialists."[20] Unfortunately, the experiences of the China Hands precisely exemplified Americans' ignorance about the Chinese Communists.

"The Chinese Communists Are Not Communists"

The US policy of prisoner reindoctrination makes little sense if viewed in isolation as a Korean War policy. It can only be explained in the larger context of the United States' rapidly changing Cold War strategy against Communism and its peculiar China policy, which had become increasingly out of sync with the former. Many American policymakers, from Roosevelt to Marshall to Acheson and Davies, had assumed that the Chinese Communists were not real Communists, so that they could be detached from the Russians through a wedge policy.

During the Yalta Conference in early February 1945, Roosevelt told Stalin that he blamed the Nationalists and Chiang Kai-shek more than the "so-called communists" for the sorry state of their united front against the Japanese.[21] Stalin and his foreign minister V. M. Molotov had repeatedly assured US ambassador to the USSR Averell Harriman and Roosevelt's special envoy to China Patrick Hurley that the "so-called Chinese Communists are not in fact Communists at all," dismissing them as "Margarine Communists." They swore that the Soviet Union was not supporting the Chinese Communists.[22] None of these claims was true. Roosevelt fell victim to one of the most successful and consequential hoaxes of the twentieth century.

While Stalin coined the term "Margarine Communists" in 1944, American diplomats and reporters had long called the Chinese Communists "so-called Communists." As early as October 1939, US Ambassador Nelson Johnson reported that many Americans had the impression that the beliefs of these "so-called Communists" resembled "far more American democratic concepts" than those of the Soviets. He attributed the popularity of the Chinese Communists in the United States to Edgar Snow's book *Red Star Over China* published in 1937.[23] Johnson, however, did not know that Snow, the American leftist reporter, had been handpicked and cultivated by Soong Qingling, Sun Yat-sen's widow and a Communist International (Comintern) agent. Another American reporter, Agnes Smedley, was bypassed precisely because of her openly pro-Communist reputation—in fact, she was a Comintern agent.[24] In 1936 Snow became the first Western journalist to enter the Communist base area in northern Shaanxi and interview its leaders. Mao, "a Lincolnesque figure" who impressed Snow, had long conversations with Snow and he carefully edited and reedited Snow's writings. A large portion of the book focusing on Mao's life and struggle was in effect co-authored by Mao and Snow. The Chinese Communists Snow portrayed were decidedly indigenous agrarian reformers.[25]

As the Chinese Communists remained the underdog in the struggle against the Nationalists until 1948, the Americans tended to view them with sympathy. The French historian Lucien Bianco judiciously observes that "in the eyes of a good many reporters and most outsiders who dealt with the ingratiating Chou En-lai, the party's grand master of public relations, the Chinese Communists were nothing more than agrarian reformers." The Americans were prone to "impute to the Communists views that conformed to their own ideal." But this notion, Bianco concluded, was an illusion.[26]

Zhou Enlai's first major prize was John Davies, the US embassy second secretary detailed to General Stilwell as his political advisor. After Stilwell walked out from the jungles in the wake of his disastrous First Burma Campaign in May 1942, Zhou told Davies "half jokingly, half seriously" that if Chiang would permit, he would lead Communist troops in a campaign to retake Burma and "I would obey General Stilwell's orders!"[27] Strangely, Zhou's costless and worthless verbal pledge became the basis of Stilwell's conviction that the Communist army had committed to follow his orders. This contributed to his increasingly acrimonious feud with Chiang Kai-shek, which reached a climax in September 1944 when Roosevelt signed off an ultimatum drafted by Marshall demanding Chiang give Stilwell "unrestricted command of" the entire Chinese military. In the meantime, Stilwell was pushing for arming the Chinese Communists.[28] The idea of America arming the Chinese Communists had been first proposed in January 1943 by John (Jack) Service, a Davies protégé in the US embassy. It would be "both vicious and stupid" to "play both sides in a foreign country" in danger of a civil war, warned Stanley Hornbeck, a senior State Department official.[29] Now, the Americans' plan to seize power and Stilwell's demand to arm the Communists proved to be the last straw for Chiang.

After much agonizing and wavering, Chiang stood firm and demanded Stilwell's recall, and Roosevelt relented. Stilwell's recall in October 1944 marked the turning point in the Nationalist government's standing with the American public. The *New York Times* declared that it represented the "political triumph of a moribund antidemocratic regime" that was "unenlightened, cold-hearted, and autocratic."[30] The Chinese Communists had succeeded in driving a wedge between the United States and the Nationalists.

While the Chinese Communists subverted the Nationalist government "from below" during World War II, Davies later readily boasted, the Americans threatened it "from above" through "Roosevelt's insistence that Stilwell be given control over all Chinese armed forces" and that a US Army Observation Group (Dixie Mission) be stationed in Yan'an—the latter was first proposed by Service in January 1943.[31] The day after Stilwell's recall from China, Davies flew to Yan'an. In sharp contrast to his doom-and-gloom assessment of the Nationalists, Davies reported that the Communists were "the toughest, best organized and disciplined group in China." Despite noting that they "still acclaim the infallibility of Marxian dogma and call themselves Communists," he declared that they were ideological "backsliders" who had "become indulgent of human frailty" and "deviated so far to the right." He asserted "agrarian democracy as their immediate goal, socialism as their distant one." The reasons for their moderation? Because "they are Chinese"; "they are realists"; and "they are nationalists."[32] Davies and his fellow China Hands seemed impervious to the possibility that one can be both Chinese and Communist, and simultaneously nationalistic and Communist.

The spell of the notion that "the Chinese Communists are not Communists" was so powerful that weeks before his death, Roosevelt met with Edgar Snow to discuss China's political future. "I have been working with two governments there," Roosevelt said. "I intend to go on doing so until we can get them together."[33]

The very idea of a Nationalist-Communist coalition government was first introduced by Roosevelt to Chiang at Cairo in November 1943, as the historian Lü Xun has delineated. In fact, the Chinese Communist leaders "had been lagging behind the Americans in contemplating how to reorganize the [central] government," Mao admitted in September 1944.[34]

Operating under the assumption that "the so-called Chinese Communists are not Communists," Hurley tried in vain for a year to bring Chiang's and Mao's parties together to form a coalition government. Out of frustration, Hurley abruptly resigned in November 1945. Instead of changing course, Truman raised the stakes by appointing the "greatest living American" General George Marshall, the newly retired army chief of staff, to carry out the same quixotic task. In a directive prepared by John Carter Vincent, director of the Office of Far Eastern Affairs and a China Hand, Marshall's objective was to "bring in to bear . . . the influence of the United States" to "encourage concessions by the Central Government, by the so-called Communists, and by the other factions."[35]

The only weapon at Marshall's disposal was "the withholding of American aid" to the Nationalist government, observed Dr. Hu Shi, the Cornell and Columbia-educated philosopher and former ambassador to the United States (1938–1942), and it "could only checkmate" the Nationalist government but "had no effect whatever on the Chinese Communists."[36] Soon after the full-scale civil war broke out in mid-1946, at Marshall's suggestion, the United States imposed a ten-month arms embargo on the Nationalists. Even after the embargo ended in May 1947, Marshall and Acheson, then deputy secretary of state, continued to delay arms shipment. "The American aid to Chiang Kai-shek has not been generous," Zhou Enlai reported to fellow Communist leaders in July 1947. "The Chiang government even had major difficulties in purchasing arms and ammunition from private companies." Apparently in reference to the US Marines' departure from North China in early 1947, Zhou noted, "In fact, the US forces have been withdrawing."[37]

While professing friendship for its erstwhile ally, the US government hamstrung the Nationalists' fight for survival. While pretending neutrality, the Soviet Union had provided substantial military aid to the Communists in Manchuria, where the PLA decisively defeated the Nationalist forces in late 1948, heralding its final triumph in 1949.[38]

China Hands Staggered

After his transfer to Moscow in early 1945, Davies found a greater platform for his China expertise, as he became George Kennan's confidant and his "mentor on all things Chinese."[39] When Marshall ended his futile China mission in January 1947, he became the new secretary of state. He tapped Kennan to establish the Policy Planning Staff (PPS), and soon Davies joined the PPS to handle its East Asian portfolio. The two men became the early architects of America's political warfare doctrines and practices. The PPS's preference for cheap nonconventional, nonmilitary measures, that is, covert operations and propaganda, against Communist China was evident in NSC-48/2, which Truman approved on December 30, 1949. The document, titled "Position of the United States with Respect to Asia," notes John Lewis Gaddis, "distilled a series of Policy Planning Staff studies, written mostly by Davies."[40]

When Acheson succeeded Marshall in early 1949, his China policy followed the trajectory set by Davies. Acheson's stubborn hope that a Chinese Titoism would emerge and his obsession with driving a wedge between the PRC and the USSR was still manifest in the *China White Paper*, which was originally advocated by Kennan and Davies and finally published on August 5, 1949. Designed to exculpate the administration for the loss of China to the Communists, it turned out to be a masterpiece of self-contradiction. "Egged on by Davies," Acheson lashed out against the Chinese Communists in his fifteen-page "letter of transmittal," denouncing them for having "forsworn their Chinese heritage." Acheson warned against "basing our policy on wishful thinking," but in the same breath professed his belief that "ultimately the profound civilization and the democratic individualism of China will reassert themselves and she will throw off the foreign yoke." Robert Beisner notes that it was a "remarkable position trying to divide Chinese from Russian communists by describing the former as fanatics subservient to the latter."[41] The term "democratic individualism of China," however, was no longer a reference to "the so-called Chinese Communists," but rather an elusive third force, on whom Acheson and Davies pinned their last hope. This lingering hope for a non-Communist China was the intellectual origin of the Korean War prisoner reindoctrination program.

"The *White Paper* is a record of the bankruptcy" of American imperialism, Mao Zedong declared in his famous article "Farewell, Leighton Stuart!," mocking the ambassador's departure from China as "a symbol of the complete defeat of the U.S. policy of aggression."[42] Mao had announced on June 30 that his new China "must lean to one side"—the Soviet Union—assuring Stalin that he would not become an Asian Tito.[43]

It seemed to Acheson, Kennan, and Davies that Mao "failed to follow the script," Gaddis has observed. Kennan was "no China expert," as laid bare by his failures. "Surprises, for experts, can be unsteadying," Gaddis notes, "and on China both

Kennan and Davies were staggering. Thanks to them, Acheson was too."[44] Apparently furious with Mao's embrace of Stalin, which made a mockery of his earlier "agrarian democracy" and "nationalistic" assessment of the Chinese Communists, Davies swung violently to the other extreme. A week after Mao's "Farewell, Leighton Stuart!" was published, Davies proposed to explore forms of punitive action to compel China's leaders "to respect the United States and moderate their behavior." He began his PPS paper with a frank admission of three "nevers": "Never in the history of U.S. relations with China has the predominant regime of that country viewed us with such uncompromising enmity. Never has the prestige of the United States in China been so low. And never have we been so apparently at a loss to make our influence felt in China." Claiming that "we have put up with enough misbehavior on their part," Davies made the case for "selective bombing" on "installations in Manchuria" in order to "belie the role of 'paper tiger' attributed to us." The proposal was so hawkish that the State Department's China Division chief Philip D. Sprouse remarked, "Maybe I'm old-fashioned, but this has to be read to be believed."[45]

Davies's strident language sounded not much different from that of the Republicans and MacArthur. Yet, at the same time, he remained virulently anti-Nationalist. In early July 1949, when Chiang Kai-shek was moving troops and treasures to Taiwan, Kennan proposed that the United States should act with "resolution, speed, ruthlessness, and self-assurance" to evict the 300,000 Nationalists troops already there, in "the way that Theodore Roosevelt might have done it." This move would have "an electrifying effect in this country and throughout the Far East." Apparently having second thoughts, he withdrew this recommendation the same day. Years later Kennan attributed the idea to Davies, who, when interviewed by Gaddis, denied his role in making such a "totally implausible" plan that bordered on a "mad act." Nevertheless, Gaddis concludes, "Kennan's eviction scenario grew out of a Policy Planning Staff study Davies had helped prepare."[46] As the early architect of American covert operations overseas, Davies was privy to many secret, outlandish plans.

Although Washington was determined to check the spread of Communism in Europe and everywhere else in Asia, by means of containment and even rollback, it was equally determined *not* to counter the Chinese Communists militarily, either on the Chinese mainland or Taiwan, until the outbreak of the Korean War necessitated a policy reversal on Taiwan, and Taiwan only.

By the time the Korean War POW issue emerged in the armistice talks in late 1951, Davies had been transferred to Germany and played no further role in policy making. However, his contribution to the most consequential NSC document in the war, NSC-81/1, reverberated in Korea, as the rollback collapsed and the prisoner reindoctrination program backfired.

The Korean War prisoner reindoctrination program was a natural offshoot of the political/psychological warfare programs that Kennan and Davies had first advocated. Although Davies's propaganda scheme for China did not materialize on his watch, Chinese POWs in Korea became the subject of a similar program. His hope for "the democratic individualism of China," as expressed in the *China White Paper*, motivated Washington to reindoctrinate Korean War prisoners so that they could become "ambassadors of independent thinking" after repatriation.

His concept of recruiting refugee-agent for the USSR was also carried out in Korea—with Korean and Chinese POWs substituting for Russian refugees, and North Korea substituting for the USSR as the drop zone. And, as Chapter 15 has shown, it led to the death of hundreds of Chinese and perhaps many more Korean prisoners.

Hindsight

While the Chinese Volunteers were pummeling American troops in Korea in December 1951, Marshall belatedly related to Truman and British prime minister Attlee that during his mediation of the Chinese Civil War in 1946, Zhou Enlai told Mrs. Marshall "at the dinner table with great emphasis that there was no doubt they were Marxist Communists and he resented people referring to them as merely agrarian reformists. They made not the slightest attempt to conceal their Moscow affiliations." When he visited Yan'an in March 1946, he saw "pictures of Stalin and Lenin were everywhere." He concluded, "They regarded the Russians as co-religionists."[47] Testifying before the Senate in the MacArthur hearing in May 1951, Marshall asserted, "When I got out to China and looked the ground over, from the very start, there was no doubt that the leadership of this group [the CCP] were Marxist Communists, and they so stated in my presence, and insisted, in my presence, that they were."[48] Most likely, Marshall was dissembling. Had he grasped in Yan'an in March 1946 that the Chinese Communists were real Communists bent on seizing power militarily, he would not have squandered another ten months trying to foist a coalition government on China and imposed an arms embargo on the Nationalists. Marshall came to understand the significance of Zhou's statement and what he saw in Yan'an five years too late.

"The Communists disdain to conceal their views and aims," Marx and Engels declared in the *Communist Manifesto* in 1848. "They openly declare that their ends can be attained only by the forcible overthrow of all existing social conditions."[49] "A revolution is not a dinner party," Mao Zedong famously pronounced in 1927. "A revolution is an insurrection, an act of violence by which one class overthrows another."[50] True to their credo, the Chinese Communists never once renounced their ideology. "The Chinese Communists themselves never at any time made claim to being anything but revolutionaries—period," recalled Colonel David D. Barrett, head of the Dixie Mission.[51]

In hindsight, Barrett confessed in 1970 that he was "naïve" and "woefully wrong" to believe the Chinese Communists were "Chinese first and communists afterwards."[52] Davies admitted in the 1980s that he had ascribed the "misnomer" of "democratic force" to the Chinese Communists. But he still lamely insisted "they were a popular force . . . and only in that sense, they were democratic."[53] In his autobiography *China Hand*, published posthumously, he conceded that his "idea of politically capturing the Chinese Communists was unrealistic." His hope of detaching the Chinese Communists from the Russians, he acknowledged, reflected his "underestimation of the Communists' commitment to ideology."[54]

The very source for this "wishful thinking" (*yixiang qiangyuan*) on the part of American policymakers—from young diplomats like Davies and Service to President Roosevelt—was that they knew little of the Communist Party's history and theories, argues the historian Yang Kuisong.[55] Most of the China Hands could speak Chinese, but few could actually read it, observed Lin Yutang, the leading liberal writer, who was educated at Harvard and Leipzig Universities. They never bothered to check the actual Communist Party documents in Chinese, but relied instead on "what the Communists say through their interpreters to foreigners on a conducted tour."[56] They made their conclusions "based primarily upon personal remarks of Chinese Communist leaders," noted the political scientist Tang Tsou in his 1963 classic *America's Failure in China, 1941–50*. This endemic ignorance was exemplified by John Carter Vincent, who admitted in a 1952 hearing that he had not read any works of Mao. Nor had he read the *Communist Manifesto* by Marx and Engels or other representative works of Lenin and Stalin.[57]

Many leading Chinese liberals and some Nationalist officials were well educated—some had advanced degrees from elite American and European universities. They warned the Americans that the Chinese Communists were "more Communist than the Communists," only to be dismissed.[58] Why couldn't they persuade the China Hands?

K. P. Chen, the Wharton-educated banker who negotiated US loans for China before Pearl Harbor, astutely pointed out that Stilwell and other China Hands had "bathed themselves in the ease and luxury of the decadent life" in Beijing in the 1920s, when the Beijing government's foreign policy was to "please and give in to foreigners in every way." During World War II, whenever Chinese "showed resentment to this insufferable Occidental superiority complex," the China Hands "quickly became irritated and violently anti-Chinese." While they "profess their love and admiration of the Chinese people," Chen concluded, they meant "the Chinese people who obey and please them as in those 'Good Old Days.'"[59]

Despite Stilwell's instance that he loved the "common man in China," John Pomfret argues he exhibited "an inflated self-confidence born of his sense of himself as a superior white man among the heathens." Similarly, Service, who "routinely expressed his love for the country, "was one in a long line of Americans who believed that he could mend China if only everyone would listen."[60]

When Nationalist officials and Chinese liberals, many of them well educated or even better educated than most China Hands, disagreed with the Americans, they threatened the sense of racial, moral, and intellectual superiority enjoyed by the latter, who in turn become hostile toward the Nationalists. The China Hands' criticism of the Nationalists became increasingly strident with a moralizing overtone.

In all seriousness, Jack Service reported to Washington the lurid tales of Chiang Kai-shek's "not particularly monogamous . . . sexual life," while he, with his wife stateside, kept a Chinese mistress in Chongqing, China's wartime capital.[61] Colonel Barrett, a professed lover of Chinese culture and people, once shouted "God damn you! I didn't say please!" to a young Chinese interpreter on stage in front of more than a thousand officers at the Kunming Infantry Training Center in 1943, when the nervous rookie interpreter inadvertently added "please" to Barrett's instruction "Give me your attention."[62]

That hapless interpreter, Wen Chao Chen, reflected in 2012: "The attitude of the 'Old China Hands' towards the Chinese was kind-hearted but condescending, feeling sorry for the poor helpless souls who are obviously inferior but innocent, who needs us (the good, noble Americans) to protect and guide them." He continued, "What Stilwell and friends saw in the Chiang government and army was quite true. They were a mess, even I as a small fry could see it." However, "their mistake was in mistaking the problems as signs of the Chiang group's wickedness instead of the state being in a society rendered helpless and almost hopeless by war. That Chiang was able to hold it together at all should have been lauded. [That it was] instead being defamed was the tragedy." Moreover, "Stilwell and friends weren't the only ones who failed to see Mao Zedong's true color in the 1940s; many others were fooled by the way the CCP foot soldiers behaved during the war years."[63]

The more the Americans came into close contact with the Nationalists, the more they became disillusioned with each other. The Communists, however, had the advantage of being distant and novel. Communist leaders Zhou Enlai and Mao Zedong ingratiated themselves with the China Hands, liberally promising submission to American leadership in war and economic cooperation in peace. With little knowledge of Communist history, ideology, and actual practice, the China Hands were taken in.

The consequence of the China Hands' arrogance—or paternalistic racism—and ignorance was grave: they urged the United States government to abandon the Nationalist government, an ally that had never threatened US national interest other than hurting some China Hands' sense of superiority or propriety, and to accommodate an armed rebel group, the Chinese Communists, whose declared mission was to overthrow the capitalist world order by force. More than a hundred years of American investments in China—political, economic, missionary, and cultural—were wiped out within a few short years.

Reassessing the Chinese Civil War and the Early PRC

The US government's incoherent and self-contradictory prisoner policies in Korea were an extension of its failed China policy in World War II and the Civil War. Throughout the POW fiasco, Washington did not understand the deeply divided Chinese prisoner population, just as it had failed to understand the divided Chinese society during the Civil War from 1945 to 1949. Assuming the dust had settled in China with the defeat of the Nationalists on the mainland, Acheson and other policymakers could not imagine that a sizeable minority of the Chinese prisoners might actually want to go to Taiwan to rejoin Chiang Kai-shek, whom Acheson had dismissed as thoroughly corrupt, incompetent, illegitimate, and moribund. Truman and Acheson were completely blindsided by the rise of Chinese anti-Communist prisoners, whose sheer numbers, tenacity, and desperation seemed beyond comprehension. The Chinese prisoners' war in the UN prison compounds in Korea was another Chinese civil war that the Americans failed to understand and manage.

As easy as it is to blame MacArthur for all the things that went wrong in Korea, it is just as easy to blame Chiang Kai-shek for all the things that went wrong in China, especially for "losing" China to the Communists. In the case of Korean War POWs, Chiang again became a scapegoat for US policy failures. Ambassador Muccio attributed much of the prison camp chaos to the seventy-five "Chiang Kai-shek's Gestapos" brought to Korea as "camp guards" by MacArthur. As demonstrated in Chapter 6, this charge was misguided.

From a larger geo-political perspective, Nationalist Taiwan's quiet shift from a non-player and a non-factor in the Korean War to that of a victor and a beneficiary signaled a profound reversal of its political fortunes. Once regarded as the "orphan of Asia" and on the brink of collapse, it became a bastion of the Cold War anti-Communist crusade.

The POW episode raises a fundamental question regarding Chiang Kai-shek's and the Nationalist government's legitimacy in China. The prevalent view is that Chiang's loss of popularity among intellectuals and peasants led to his regime's defeat in the Civil War. The Americans have long attributed the outcome to Nationalist corruption and ineptitude. As the UNC forces suffered humiliating defeats at the hands of the Chinese Communist forces in North Korea and were later checkmated, could similar charges be leveled at the US government and its leaders? Clearly, corruption and ineptitude cannot sufficiently explain the regime change of 1949.

The late Chinese historian Gao Hua observed that Chiang's loss on the mainland was primarily a military defeat, from which all other failures stemmed. In fact, he noted, throughout the civil war, no single major city fell as a result of a popular uprising. Cities only fell before the advancing PLA, sometimes after many months of brutal sieges.[64] Once the Communists took a territory and controlled its population, they mobilized and—demanded—popular support. As demonstrated in this book, with each military victory, the Communists effectively commanded the submission and even support of some former Nationalist personnel, not to mention the common people or young students.

However, beneath the veneer of complete submission and ideological conversion, at least a portion of the population still identified with Chiang and the old regime. If the prisoner population—3,000 of the 21,000 POWs were bona fide anti-Communists—can be seen as a very rough proxy, as much as 15 percent of the Chinese population, or one in every seven people, were anti-Communist. As the Communists moved to persecute supporters of the Nationalist government, some sought to escape, and being taken prisoners in Korea afforded them such an opportunity. Given a similar opportunity, how many people in Communist China would choose to escape? While it is impossible to provide a definitive answer, it is safe to conclude that as Mao's political campaigns escalated, more people yearned to escape. But in the meantime, as Mao's regime became consolidated, the opportunity for escape soon disappeared.

The early years of the People's Republic have been traditionally called a "golden age" or a "honeymoon period," during which the Communists supposedly enjoyed a more or less harmonious relationship with the populace in a common effort to rebuild the nation—in sharp contrast to the catastrophic Great Leap Forward and the Cultural Revolution that followed.[65] As recent scholarship has uncovered the extent of violence and suppression in the early 1950s, the notion of a "honeymoon" has become increasingly untenable.[66] Roderick MacFarquhar reduces the "honeymoon" to the period between the founding of the PRC on October 1, 1949, and the start of the Korean War in June 1950 or China's entry into the war in October.[67] As Chapter 3 has demonstrated, however, this one-year "honeymoon" is still an illusion, especially for many people in the southwest, from where the largest number of Korean War prisoners hailed. For them, it was a bloody "honeymoon."

"Without the freedom to criticize, there can be no true praise" (*Sans la liberté de blâmer, il n'est pas d'éloge flatteur*), wrote the French playwright Beaumarchais in *Figaro*. I would suggest: Without the freedom to dissent, there can be no true support. When dissent became a crime in China, the notion of the Communists' popularity became a myth.

By early 2018, Russia's meddling in the 2016 US presidential election has become widely known, although the extent of its interference remains difficult to measure. Only after the Russian information war hit America hard did some Americans realize the vulnerability of their democracy. Few Americans are aware that eight decades earlier, another Russian information war had sabotaged America's World War II ally, the Republic of China.

In March 2018, the *Economist* pronounced that "the West's 25-year bet on China has failed." The *New York Times* lamented China's "unabashed charting [of] its own course—one that diverges rather than converges with the liberal democracies and market economies of the West." Kurt M. Campbell, former assistant secretary of state for East Asian affairs, advocates "doing away with the hopeful thinking that has long characterized the United States' approach to China."[68] In reality, America's wishful thinking about the Chinese Communists was not merely twenty-five years old, but almost eighty, since the time of Edgar Snow, Joseph Stilwell, George Marshall, and Franklin Roosevelt.

The first casualty of the Americans' misunderstanding of the Chinese Communists was Nationalist China, which was subverted by the Communists in 1949. Although America's century-long political, economic, missionary, and cultural investments in China were obliterated within a few short years, US policymakers could comfort themselves as Americans paid a negligibly small price in blood in the process. To explain the loss of China to the American people, Acheson and the China Hands claimed innocence while pinning all the blame on Chiang Kai-shek. "The ominous result of the civil war in China was beyond the control of the government of the United States," Acheson declared in the *China White Paper*. "Nothing that this country did or could have done within the reasonable limits of its capabilities could have changed that result; nothing that was left undone by this country has contributed to it."[69]

Upon reading the above two sentences, Dr. Hu Shi wrote on the margin: "Matthew 27:24." The verse reads: "When Pilate saw that he could prevail nothing, but that rather a tumult was made, he took water, and washed his hands before the multitude, saying, I am innocent of the blood of this just person: see ye to it." The US government, Hu believed, "was not 'innocent of the blood' of fallen China, because of the betrayal of China at Yalta, because of its withholding of effective aid to China at crucial times."[70] The American people, however, for the most part cared less who was to blame for the fate of China, as long as no American blood was spilled there.

Merely a year later, however, Chinese Communist troops bloodied Americans in the mountains and valleys in Korea. The United States finally paid a punishing price in Korea for its arrogance toward the Chinese people and its ignorance of the Chinese Communists in the preceding decade.

This lesson remains to be learned.

Acknowledgments

It has been an amazing journey to meet and get to know men and women of an extraordinary generation, who had lived through, and often fought in, World War II and the Chinese Civil War before fighting in the Korean War. On either side of the Taiwan Strait or in neutral nations they survived battles, captivity, and postwar political vicissitudes. I am deeply indebted to them all for the inspiration of their stories of courage, perseverance, hope, and humor.

The genesis of this book can be traced back to the connection between my late grandfather Chang Shouheng (1914–2004) and the first Chinese prisoner of war I met, Zhang Zeshi. Both were graduates of Oberlin Shansi Memorial School (Mingxian), but they enrolled some ten years apart and never met. The school ceased to exist soon after 1949, but many alumni and their children have sought to revive the school and its spirit since the 1980s. At my father's urging, I visited Zhang in Beijing in 2007. That meeting kindled my interest in the Korean War POW issue, though I was somewhat skeptical of repatriated prisoners' accounts. Alerted by Jeremy Brown to the trove of POW-related documents at the US National Archives, I went there and found numerous documents confirming their extraordinary stories. I once told Zhang that I would devote the next five to ten years on POW research. It has turned out to be more than ten years.

In the past eleven years, my research has taken me to cities and villages across the Taiwan Strait—the most memorable being a night spent with Shi Xinggui in his spartan cave dwelling in Shanxi—and to the United States, Argentina, and Brazil. More than ninety former POWs opened their homes, diaries, photo albums, and memories to me. I am unable to quote from every interview, but the images evoked by their stories bring that war-torn era to life in my mind when I write. I owe a special debt to Zhang Zeshi, who directly or indirectly introduced me to all interviewees in China; Zhong Junhua, my main contact person in Sichuan; Wu Yuezheng, the son of POW Wu Tenghai, who accompanied me on my travels to various places in Shanxi; and Wu Jinfeng, a Korean War veteran and the former *PLA Arts and Literature* editor-in-chief. In Taiwan, my special gratitude goes to Zhang Yifu, Yang Shuzhi, and Veteran Affairs Commission officials Chao Yu-hsin, Fang Chin-kuo, Li Ling, and Sun Hsin-hsia. In the United States, I thank former POW Gao Wenjun, American guard Patrick Vigil, and interpreter James Bard. In Argentina, I thank Cheng Liren and Kim Kwan-ok. In Brazil, I thank Lim Kwan-tae.

A number of interviewees have passed away. Zhao Huilin, one of my first interviewees in Taiwan, died in 2010. In the same year, Tang Yao passed away in Shanghai a few months after our second interview. The feisty Tian Fangbao of Henan died of flu one month after our interview in 2014. . . . Frequent hospital visits and occasional funerals became part of the research experience. Their withering away gives me a greater sense of urgency to record their voices. My greatest wish is to publish a Chinese version of this book, so I can present it to the survivors.

I have benefited from the works of other scholars, on whose shoulders I stand. I am especially indebted to William Stueck and Barak Kushner, who reviewed the manuscript and whose critique made this book much stronger; to Joseph Esherick, Lü Xun, and Wang Chenyi, who read the entire manuscript and gave incisive comments; and to other colleagues who gave perceptive comments on individual chapters: Joshua Derman, Frank Dikötter, James Gao, Madeline Hsu, Sheila Miyoshi Jager, Monica Kim, Peter Perdue, Yiching Wu, Yafeng Xia, and Wen-hsin Yeh. Military historians Jiyul Kim and Renee Hylton saved me from embarrassing errors. Charles Young generously shared photos. John Pomfret shared important documents.

I owe the greatest intellectual debt to Paul Pickowicz and Joseph Esherick, my mentors at University of California, San Diego. Their intellectual rigor, dedication, and tolerance set very high standards, which I aspire to meet. I also thank Suzanne Cahill, Takashi Fujitani, Weijing Lu, Sarah Schneewind, and Ye Wa. My early work also benefited from critiques by fellow PhD students: Emily Baum, Angie Chau, Maggie Greene, Jenny Huangfu, Justin Jacobs, Judd Kinzley, Jun Lei, Jomo Smith, and James Wicks. I was fortunate to have the advice and support of senior students: Jeremy Brown, Matt Johnson, Zheng Xiaowei, Dahpon Ho, Miriam Gross, Brent Hass, and Jeremy Murray. At Stanford University, Matthew Sommer and Gordon H. Chang have been great teachers and advocates. Hsiao-ting Lin of the Hoover Archives has provided tremendous help over the years. I also owe a special debt to Lucien Bianco, whose teaching at Stanford in 2005 inspired me to become a historian.

The best and most courageous scholarship on modern China comes from China. The late Gao Hua (1954–2011) was my teacher and friend in the last three years of his life, and will forever remain an inspiration. I have had the privilege of receiving generous help from leading historians Shen Zhihua, Li Danhui, Yang Kuisong, Zhang Jishun, Wang Haiguang, and Feng Xiaocai—all from East China Normal University. Jean Hung (Xiong Jingming) of the Chinese University of Hong Kong has been an unfailing mentor and advocate. Qian Gang and Yu Jin have been a great inspiration. I owe them all a special debt of gratitude.

In Taiwan, I made the Institute of Modern History, Academia Sinica, my intellectual home from 2009 to 2011. I thank Chang Peng-yuan, Chen San-ching, Chen Yung-fa, Chak Chi-shing, Yu Miin-ling, Chang Su-ya, Chang Jui-te, Chang Li, Hu Kuo-tai, Huang Ko-wu, Lo Jiu-jung, Yu Chien-ming, and Wu Zhe. Chou Hsiu-huan of Academia Historica shared many documents with me. Huang Tiancai and Chang Show-foong shared their memories of the Korean War era. My gratitude goes to them.

While POW research remains taboo in China and largely ignored in Taiwan, I have been fortunate to collaborate with like-minded scholars in Korea and Japan: Jung Keun-sik, Jung Byung Jung, Jen Gap-Saeng, Kang Sunghyun, Lee Sunwoo, and Sato Yoshifumi. I look forward to seeing our collaboration bear fruit in the coming years.

Xiaojing Du of the Voice of America, who is a first-rate researcher in his own right, generously shared his research findings and documents with me. Li Yongfeng and Zhang Dongpan shared their photo collections with me. I am deeply grateful.

My home institution, the School of Humanities and Social Sciences at the Hong Kong University of Science and Technology (HKUST), has provided a wonderful research environment. I thank my supportive colleagues, in particular Li Bozhong, James Lee, Billy So, Kellee Tsai, Christian Daniels, Cameron Campbell, Cai Yongshun, Chang-tai Hung, Liu Zaifu, Liu Jianmei, Wu Shengqing, and Yan Lianke.

I have been blessed with motivated, brilliant student research assistants at HKUST, who have transcribed hundreds of hours of interviews conducted in various Chinese dialects into a text of more than one million characters. Zhao Yanling and Wang Caiyu transcribed half of them. Others include Chu Chau Yuet, Deng Weisi, Du Yumeng, Gu Wenxin, Guo Zijian, Han Wenfei, Lau Hiu-kwan, Lee Wing-tung, Li Kang, Lin Zhuyun, Liu Yishan, Man Tingjun, Shen Ruiqing, Wang Yiqiao, Wong Wing-man, Xia Mengyao, Xie Xinyi, Xue Yuyuan, Yang Chunpu, Yeung Tsz-wang, Zhang Wenjing, and Zhao Liang. Claudius Kim translated a Korean prisoner's speech into Chinese. Kim and HC Leung also read the manuscript and gave helpful comments.

I owe a great deal to librarians and archivists who have tremendously aided my research. He Jianye, UC Berkeley's East Asian librarian, has been incredibly resourceful. James Zobel of the MacArthur Memorial Archives introduced to me Dimitri Boria's photos.

Financial support has come, over the years, from Hong Kong's Research Grants Council, Fulbright-IIE, a University of California Pacific Rim Research Fellowship, the Chiang Ching-kuo Foundation, and the Center for Chinese Studies in Taiwan.

I thank Margo Irvin and Jessica Ling of the Stanford University Press for their steadfast support. This narrative history also owes a great deal to Sandra Ward's deft and meticulous copy editing. Angie Chau and Janet L. Chen also gave excellent editorial help.

Friends and family sustained me over the last decade. While I traveled across China for interviews, my family and friends opened their homes to me. I thank my late maternal grandparents Li Xingzhong and Liu Shuhua, my uncles Li Lujun and Li Luwen, and my best friends Chen Zhenbo and Huo Zhigang.

My parents, Chang Qinlin and Li Luqiong, and my sister Lan Chang showed unwavering faith in me through the years. If not for my father's exhortation, I would not have visited Zhang Zeshi. I am eternally grateful to them. I met my wife, Ines Peihua Lee, during my research in Taipei. Since then we have traveled together across Taiwan, China, and North and South America in search of documents and interviewees. Her talent and resourcefulness constantly amaze me. She identified and located several key interviewees, especially Cheng Liren and Yang Shuzhi. She was my Spanish interpreter in Argentina. She is also an excellent interviewer, photographer, videographer, and cartographer—this book's highly customized maps are her work. As this manuscript entered the home stretch in January 2018, our child Tenzin Zhicheng's arrival brought great joy. I thank them for pulling me over the finish line.

Appendix

"POW Population by Month," Box 1, Statistical Reports Relating to Enemy POWs, 1950–53, Office of the Provost Marshal, RG 554, NA.

PRISONER OF WAR POPULATION
BY MONTH

1950	NK	CCF	TOTAL
July			39
August			1,753
September			10,829
October			62,697
November			98,176
December	135,930	1,245	137,175
1951			
January	136,090	1,360	137,450
February	138,247	1,550	139,797
March	142,400	1,672	144,072
April	142,217	3,423	145,640
May	143,929	8,643	152,572
June	145,122	17,182	162,304
July	145,206	17,605	162,811
August	145,749	17,711	163,460
September	147,723	18,214	165,941
October	148,693	19,741	168,434
November	115,949	20,505	136,454
December	111,392	20,674	132,068
1952			
January	111,485	20,773	132,217
February	111,484	20,775	132,259
March	111,490	20,794	132,281
April	112,826	20,728	133,517
May	112,844	20,740	133,584
June	112,846	20,800	133,646
July	112,958	20,880	133,827
August	112,983	20,905	133,793
September	112,956	20,903	133,996
October	102,744	20,985	123,732
November	101,702	21,083	122,791
December	101,557	21,102	122,659
1953			
January	101,620	21,106	122,726
February	101,598	21,063	122,661
March	101,539	21,063	122,599
April	98,762	20,369	119,131
May	96,367	20,031	116,398
June	69,072	20,071	89,143
July	69,018	20,109	89,127

Abbreviations

CCF	Chinese Communist Forces
CCP	Chinese Communist Party
CIA	Central Intelligence Agency, US
CIC	Counter Intelligence Corps, US Army
CIE	Civilian Information and Education Section
CNA	Chinese Nationalist Army
CPV	Chinese People's Volunteers Army
DAC	US Department of Army Civilian
DMZ	Demilitarized Zone
FEC	Far East Command, US
GHQ	general headquarters
G-2	army intelligence
ICRC	International Committee of the Red Cross
JCSUS	Joint Chiefs of Staff
KCOMZ	Korean Communications Zone
KMT	Kuomintang/Chinese Nationalist Party
KPA	Korean People's Army
NATO	North Atlantic Treaty Organization
NNRC	Neutral Nations Repatriation Commission
NSC	National Security Council (1947–present)

OSS	Office of Strategic Services (1942–1945)
PG	prison guard
PPS	Policy Planning Staff, US State Department (1947–present)
ROK	Republic of Korea (South Korea)
UNC	United Nations Command
USIS	United States Information Service
VFW	Veterans of Foreign Wars

ABBREVIATIONS IN NOTES

"Andeshe"	Wu Jinfeng, "Andeshe biji: guoguo zhanfu zishu ji"
ATIS	Entry 17A (Allied Intelligence Division Translators & Intelligence Service, Records of the Assistant Chief of Staff, G-2, Far East), RG 554, US National Archives II
CKSD	Chiang Kai-shek Diaries, Hoover Archives, Stanford, CA
CWIHPB	*Cold War International History Project Bulletin*
CZED	Shen Zhihua, ed., *Chaoxian zhanzheng: Eguo dang'anguan de jiemi wenjian*
"Dashiji"	Li Ziying, "Zhongguo renmin zhiyuanjun beifu renyuan zai meijun jizhongying douzheng dashiji"
FFDS	Fangong yishi fendou shi bianzuan weiyuanhui, ed., *Fangong yishi fendou shi*
FFTL	Zhou Xiuhuan, Zhang Shiying, and Ma Guozheng, *Hanzhan fangong yishi fangtanlu*
FGSL	Zhou Xiuhuan, ed., *Zhanhou waijiao shiliao huibian: Hanzhan yu fangong yishi pian*
FRUS	United States Department of State, *Foreign Relations of the United States*, State Department Document Series
KZZJ	Zhongguo junshi bowuguan, ed., *Kangmei yuanchao zhanzheng jishi*
KZZS	Junshi kexueyuan junshi lishi yanjiubu, *Kangmei yanchao zhan zheng shi*

MISDI	Entry 39 (Assistant Chief of Staff, G-2, MIS (D/A) Intelligence Division Translators & Intelligence Service), RG 554, US National Archives II
NA	National Archives II, College Park, MD
NYT	*New York Times*
PRC Database	Song Yongyi, ed., *Zhongguo wushi niandai zhongqi de zhengzhi yundong shujuku*
RG	Record Group
RMRB	*Renmin ribao* [*People's Daily*]
TL	Harry S. Truman Library, Independence, MO
TWGFB	Ministry of Defense Archives, Taipei, Republic of China
TWGSG	Academia Historica, Taipei
TWJSS	Archives of the Institute of Modern History, Academia Sinica, Taipei
TWNA	National Archives Administration, Taipei

Notes

INTRODUCTION

1. The following description of the event is based on multiple sources: *NYT*, Jan. 20–21, 1954; *Chicago Daily Tribune*, Jan. 20, 1954; *South China Morning Post*, Jan. 21, 1954; *Time*, Feb. 1, 1954; *Life*, Feb. 1, 1954, 8–11; Lai Mingtang, "Report by Liaison Team for the reception of Non-repatriates in Korea," in *FGSL*, 1:324–45, 375–78; Fang, *Wo sheng zhi lu*, 109.

2. *Time*, Feb. 1, 1954.

3. Ibid.; *NYT*, Jan. 20, 1954, 1; *Life*, Feb. 1, 1954, 8–11; *FFDS*, 221.

4. *FFDS*, 221.

5. *FGSL*, 1:336.

6. Chang, "Zhang Yifu's Oral History Records," 148.

7. Chen Juntian interview, June 4, 2015.

8. Ibid.

9. Nationalist embassy to Taipei, telegram, Jan. 20, 1954, 633.43-0008-532805, TWJSS.

10. CKSD, Jan. 20, 1954.

11. *FGSL*, 1:337–38.

12. Ibid., 344. In a separate collision in Inchon, twenty-eight US Marines were drowned and killed. See *Time*, Feb. 1, 1954.

13. *NYT*, Jan. 23, 1954.

14. The number of North Koreans is from *Time*, Feb. 1, 1954.

15. *FGSL*, 1:341–42.

16. Ibid., 339–40.

17. Chiang Ching-kuo to Chiang Kai-shek, June 1954, 00012389000090052w, TWGFB.

18. Hermes, *Truce Tent*, 514–15. On "Explanation," see Chapter 14.

19. *FGSL*, 1:342.

20. Acheson, *Present at the Creation*, 652. The Chinese death figure is a minimum estimate that equals half of the total deaths of 180,000 (see Xu, "Zhongguo xisheng," 83). The Korean civilian death toll is a minimum estimate that equals half of the total deaths of 280,000 (see Memorandum by USSR embassy to North Korea, Mar. 1954, in *CZED*, 1341).

21. CKSD, Jan. 24, 1954.

22. *FGSL*, 1:384.

23. *Lai Mingtang Oral History* (Taipei: Academia Historica, 1994), 169.

24. *FFDS*, 234. In 1928, Beijing ("Northern Capital") was renamed "Beiping/Peiping" ("Northern Peace") by the Nationalist government, whose capital was Nanjing/Nanking ("Southern Capital").

25. Taylor, *The Generalissimo's Son*, 219.
26. CKSD, Jan. 24, 1954.
27. *FGSL*, 2:327.
28. *FRUS 1952–1954*, 15:1730.
29. *RMRB*, Jan. 25, 1954.
30. Ibid., Jan. 30, 1954.
31. Ibid., Apr. 30 and May 5, 1954; *Chaoxian wenti wenjian huibian*, 2:290–432.
32. After mid-1954, the Korean War POW issue rarely was mentioned in *People's Daily*. The last time was October 27, 1957.
33. *FRUS 1969–1976*, 17:774.
34. *FGSL*, 2:336–37.
35. Yeh's speech, Sept. 27, 1954, 633.05-0006-445388, TWJSS. Yeh inflated the percentage.
36. Ibid.
37. *NYT*, Jan. 23, 1954, 1.
38. Truman, *Memoirs*; Acheson, *Present at the Creation* and *The Korean War*.
39. Truman, "Statement by the President on General Ridgway's Korean Armistice Proposal," May 7, 1952, in Woolley and Peters, *American Presidency Project*, http://www.presidency.ucsb.edu/ws/?pid=14108.
40. Johnson, *The Right Hand of Power*, 130.
41. Eisenhower, "Radio and Television Address to the American People Announcing the Signing of the Korean Armistice," July 26, 1953, in Woolley and Peters, *American Presidency Project*, http://www.presidency.ucsb.edu/ws/?pid=9653; Eisenhower, *Mandate for Change*, 190–91.
42. The expression is from NSC staffer Mallory Browne, "The Strategic Significance of Involuntary POW Repatriation in Korea," Feb. 1952, Psychological Strategy Board Files, TL, cited in Young, *Name, Rank, and Serial Number*, 177.
43. Joy, *How Communists Negotiate*, 152.
44. Acheson, *Present at the Creation*, 652.
45. Joy, *Negotiating While Fighting*, vii.
46. Major works focusing on the POW issue include, Bernstein, "The Struggle over the Korean Armistice"; Foot, *A Substitute for Victory*; Young, *Name, Rank, and Serial Number*. Other works that contain chapters on the issue: MacDonald, *Korea*; Stueck, *The Korean War*. In *Brothers at War*, Jager devotes a chapter to the Korean as well as UN POWs; Morris-Suzuki, "Prisoner Number 600,001"; Kim, *The Interrogation Rooms of the Korean War*.
47. Nietzsche, *The Genealogy of Morals*, 57–58, quoted in Cumings, *Origins of the Korean War*, 2:767.
48. Cumings, *Origins of the Korean War*, 2; Shen, "Sino-Soviet Relations and the Origins of the Korean War"; Halberstam, *Coldest Winter*.
49. Cumings, *The Korean War: A History*, 229.
50. *FRUS 1952–1954*, 15:35.
51. Ibid., 1506.
52. Bernstein, "The Struggle over the Korean Armistice"; Foot, *A Substitute for Victory*; Stueck, *The Korean War*; Young, *Name, Rank, and Serial Number*.
53. Foot, *A Substitute for Victory*, 108–18; Robin, *The Making of the Cold War Enemy*, 124–61; Tovy, "Manifest Destiny in POW Camps."
54. According to Nationalist statistics, 4,628 Taiwan-bound POWs renounced their membership in the Communist Party or the Youth League (Whiting, "The New Chinese Communist," 593). Of the 7,110 POWS repatriated to China, 2,900 were CCP members (He, *Zhongcheng*, 138).

55. Joy, *How Communists Negotiate*, 140.
56. Joy, *Negotiating While Fighting*, 333.
57. Ibid., 335.
58. Glavin to McClure, Feb. 28, 1951, Box 19, Special Warfare, RG 319, NA.
59. Joy, *How Communists Negotiate*, 141, 151.
60. Haydon L. Boatner, "Prisoners of War: Have U.S. Policies Protected Americans in Asia?" (c. 1967), unpublished typewritten draft, 19, Box 2, Boatner Papers, Hoover Archives.
61. Bernstein, "The Struggle over the Korean Armistice," 282; MacDonald, *Korea*, 144; Foot, *A Substitute for Victory*, 126–29; Young, *Name, Rank, and Serial Number*, 177.
62. Gordon Gray, "Preliminary Report on the Situation with Respect to Repatriation of Prisoners of War," Oct. 19, 1951, CIA-RDP80R01731R003200010023-5, CIA-FOIA files.
63. "Andeshe."

CHAPTER 1: FLEEING OR EMBRACING THE COMMUNISTS IN THE CHINESE CIVIL WAR

1. Yang Shuzhi (Xinlin) interview, Jan. 27–28, 2014; Xu, *Naduan yinglie de rizi*, 307.
2. Zhong, "Guomingdang sanbing jianshi," 588.
3. Yang Shuzhi, ATIS KG 446, Aug. 31, 1951, 1.
4. Yang interview, Jan. 27–28, 2014; United States War Department, *War Report*, 456; Liu, *Luoye chengni*, 34–37.
5. Yang Shuzhi interview, Jan. 27–28, 2014.
6. *Guangzhou ribao*, Aug. 31, 1945.
7. Li, "Guangzhou shouxiang," 483.
8. *Evening Independent* (Massilon, OH), Aug. 22, 1945.
9. *RMRB*, Sept. 9, Dec. 24, 1952, and Aug. 19, 1953.
10. *Mao Zedong nianpu* (1893–1949), 3:13.
11. Chang, "Zhang Yifu's Oral History Records."
12. Shi, "Yanjun qiangzhan Shangdang," 18.
13. Chen, "Dongbei anye du xingjun," 242; Chen Yonghua, ATIS 3943, Mar. 12, 1951.
14. Chen Guimei interview, July 7, 2013.
15. Chen Qingbin, ATIS KT 514, May 27, 1951; Chen Guimei interview, July 7, 2013.
16. Wang Yingchang, ATIS KG 781, Oct. 20, 1951.
17. Chen, "Dongbei anye du xingjun," 243
18. He, "Bukanhuishou de huishou," 21; Huang Yujin interview, Jan. 23, 2014.
19. Chen, "Dongbei anye du xingjun," 244; Chen Yonghua, ATIS 3943.
20. Chen, "Dongbei anye du xingjun," 242–43; Chen Yonghua, ATIS KG 443, Aug. 31, 1951.
21. Chen, "Interview," in *Taiji laobing de xuelei gushi*, 73.
22. Chen Qingbin, ATIS KG 443, Aug. 31, 1951. Yutai is near Xuzhou.
23. Wang Yingchang, ATIS KG 781, Oct. 20, 1951.
24. Chen, "Dongbei anye du xingjun," 244–46; Chen Yonghua, ATIS 3943, 1.
25. Lü, *Da qiju zhong de guogong guanxi*, 150–53, 165–66.
26. Wang, *Zhongguo jindai tongshi*, 376.
27. Zhang, *1949*, 10.
28. Ibid., 11. Oberlin Shansi relocated from Shanxi to Sichuan during the war with Japan.
29. Ibid., 20, 26.
30. Ibid., 45, 57–62.
31. Ibid., 72–75; Zhang interview, Nov. 21, 2018; Zhonggong Beijing shiwei dangshi yanjiushi, *Kangyi Meijun zhuhua baoxing yundong*, 700.

32. Zhonggong Beijing shiwei dangshi yanjiushi, *Kangyi Meijun zhuhua baoxing yundong*, 6.
33. Ibid., 8.
34. Zhang, *1949*, 86, 108–13.
35. Ibid., 130–32.
36. Ibid., 145–50.
37. Ibid., 170–76, 188–90, 220.
38. Ibid., 225–27.
39. Yu Rongfu, ATIS KG 169, July 30, 1951; Yu Rongfu interview, July 4, 2010.
40. Gao, *Hanzhan yiwang*, 35–36.
41. Zhonggong zhongyang wenxian yanjiushi, *Chen Yun nianpu*, 425–26.
42. Lü, *Da qiju zhong de guogong guanxi*, 116–19.
43. Huang, ed., *Luo Ronghuan nianpu*, 458–59.
44. Wang, *Zhongguo jindai tongshi*, 55.
45. The Soviet Union had formally transferred Shenyang to the Nationalist government on December 27. However, the Nationalist army did not arrive until January 15, 1946 (Yang, "Nanyi queding de duishou (1917–1949)," 129).
46. Yu Rongfu interview, July 4, 2010.
47. Ibid.
48. Gao, *Hanzhan yiwang*, 36–37.
49. Ibid., 37; Gao Wenjun interview, Jan. 10, 2010. His parents passed away in the 1960s; he returned home for the first time in 1992.
50. Gao, *Hanzhan yiwang*, 37–38; Yu Rongfu, ATIS KG 169, July 30, 1951.
51. Zhongguo renmin jiefangjun junshi kexueyuan, *Zhongguo renmin jiefangjun jiefang zhanzheng shi*, 4:215.
52. Chen Yonghua, ATIS 3943, Mar. 12, 1951; Chen, "Dongbei anye du xingjun," 247.
53. Chen, "Dongbei anye du xingjun," 248.
54. Zhang, *1949*, 207–11.
55. Chen, "Dongbei anye du xingjun," 248.
56. Ibid., 249.
57. Zhongguo renmin jiefangjun junshi kexueyuan, *Zhongguo renmin jiefangjun jiefang zhanzheng shi*, 4:362.
58. Wang Yingchang, ATIS KG 781, Oct. 20, 1951.
59. Chen Qingbin, ATIS KG 443, Aug. 31, 1951.
60. Mao, *Mao Zedong junshi wenji*, 5:548.
61. Ibid., 591–92.
62. Ibid., 471, 495–96, 513–16.
63. Tang Yao interview, Nov. 21, 2009, May 26, 2010; Tang Yao, ATIS KT 187, May 27, 1951.
64. Chen Qingbin, ATIS KG 443, Aug. 31, 1951.
65. Yan Tianzhi interview, May 5, 2010.
66. Yu Rongfu interview, July 4, 2010; Gao Wenjun interview, Jan. 10, 2010; Gao, *Hanzhan yiwang*, 38.
67. Yu's estimate was 15,000 cadets; Gao's was more than 10,000. Other estimates are around 30,000 (Yao, "Wo yu junxiao," 177).
68. Gao, *Hanzhan yiwang*, 39–41.
69. Yu Rongfu interview, July 4, 2010; Gao Wenjun interview, Jan. 10, 2010; Gao, *Hanzhan yiwang*, 38–39.
70. Yao, "Wo yu junxiao," 183–85.
71. Gao, *Hanzhan yiwang*, 41–43; Wang, *Zhongguo jindai tongshi*, 513.

72. Gao, *Hanzhan yiwang*, 41–43.

73. He, "Bukanhuishou de huishou," 2–29; He Rui interviews, Oct. 21, 2009, Jan. 16, 2013. The rest of the section uses the same sources.

74. It was a PLA custom to serve lavish meat dishes before major battles. See Chang, "Zhang Yifu's Oral History Records," 132.

75. Zhong Junhua interview, Sept. 13, 2007.

76. Ibid.

77. Bai and Xu, *Fengyan rensheng*, 3:494, 498.

78. Cai Pingsheng in ibid., 1:354–55; Cai interview, Sept. 2007.

79. Cai Pingsheng in Bai and Xu, *Fengyan rensheng*, 1:354–55; Cai interview, Sept. 2007.

80. Lin Mocong interview, Nov. 1–2, 2009; Dec. 11–16, 2012.

81. Ibid., Dec. 11–16, 2012.

82. Ibid.

83. Ibid.

84. Ibid.

85. Yang Yuhua, ATIS KT 1376, Aug. 28, 1951; Yu, *Eyun*, 39.

86. Zhang, *1949*, 366–68.

87. Zhang Zeshi in "Andeshe," 2:59; Zhang, email to the author, May 28, 2011; Zhang interview, Nov. 21, 2018.

88. Lin interview, Nov. 1–2, 2009.

CHAPTER 2: REFORMING FORMER NATIONALISTS

1. Chengdushi zhengxie wenshi ziliao yanjiu weiyuanhui, *Sichuan wenshi ziliao xuanji*, 18:195–98.

2. Chen, *Muse Huangpu*, 214; Wu Chunsheng interview, Aug. 12, 2011; Yu Rongfu interview, July 4, 2010.

3. Wang, *Wang Xinting huiyilu*, 436, 447; Deng, *Deng Xiaoping zishu*, 128–31.

4. Wang, *Wang Xinting huiyilu*, 435–36.

5. Mao, *Mao Zedong junshi wenji*, 5:513–14.

6. Wang, *Wang Xinting huiyilu*, 437–38.

7. Chengdu difangzhi bianzuan weiyuanhui, *Chengdushi zhi*, 239.

8. Wang, *Wang Xinting huiyilu*, 439; Chengdu difangzhi bianzuan weiyuanhui, *Chengdushi zhi*, 240.

9. Luo Shiqing, ATIS KG 565, Sept. 15, 1951.

10. Chengdu difangzhi bianzuan weiyuanhui, *Chengdushi zhi*, 239–40.

11. Ibid., 239.

12. Gao, *Hanzhan yiwang*, 43–44.

13. Yu Rongfu interview, July 4, 2010; Chen, *Muse Huangpu*, 220, 223.

14. Gao, *Hanzhan yiwang*, 44.

15. Chen, *Muse Huangpu*, 218–19.

16. Kou Weicheng, ATIS KG 336, Aug. 23, 1951; Guo Yadong, ATIS KG 094, July 18, 1951; Guan Chongfu, ATIS 355, Aug. 22, 1951.

17. Guan, ATIS 355, Aug. 22, 1951.

18. Gao, *Hanzhan yiwang*, 45.

19. Guan, ATIS 355, Aug. 22, 1951.

20. Ibid.; Chen, *Muse Huangpu*, 221.

21. Chen, *Muse Huangpu*, 219, 223; Gao, *Hanzhan yiwang*, 47–48; Gao interview, Jan. 6, 2010.

22. Gao, *Hanzhan yiwang*, 51–52; Gao interview, Sept. 8, 2009.

23. Bradbury et al., *Mass Behavior*, 137–38.
24. Liangshan (Liangping) is 100 miles northeast of Chongqing.
25. Bradbury et al., *Mass Behavior*, 138.
26. Luo, ATIS KG 565, Sept. 15, 1951.
27. Ibid.
28. Ibid.
29. Qian Shungui, ATIS no. 5107, April 26, 1951, 102.
30. Li Guhua, ATIS KG 331, Aug. 31, 1951.
31. Gao, *How the Red Sun Rose*, 453.
32. Wang Tsun-ming (Wang Zunming), in Bradbury et al., *Mass Behavior*, 141.
33. Chen, *Muse Huangpu*, 224.
34. Gao, *Hanzhan yiwang*, 53.
35. Lin interview, Dec. 11–12, 2011.
36. Li Guhua, ATIS KG 331, Aug. 31, 1951.
37. Kou Weicheng, ATIS KG 336, Aug. 23, 1951; Chen, *Muse Huangpu*, 219–20, 225–26.
38. Guan Chongfu, ATIS KG 355, Aug. 22, 1951.
39. Chen, *Muse Huangpu*, 227.
40. Kou Weicheng, ATIS KG 336, Aug. 23, 1951.
41. Zhang, *Kaoyan*, 334.
42. Guo Naijian in "Andeshe," 2:160.
43. Yu Rongfu interview, July 4, 2010.
44. These social scientists were contracted by the Human Resources Research Office (HumRRO) to study Communist soldiers' behavior (Bradbury et al., *Mass Behavior*, xx, 122). HumRRO was affiliated with the US Department of Defense.
45. Ibid., 121.
46. Wang Tsun-ming (Wang Zunming) interview in ibid., 123–24; Wang, ATIS KG 562, Sept. 15, 1951, 1. While his interview offers more details, the chronologies in both interviews and the ATIS are consistent.
47. Wang Houci interview, Apr. 22, 2010.
48. Wang Zunming's biography in this section is drawn from Bradbury et al., *Mass Behavior*, 124–53, unless noted otherwise.
49. Wang, ATIS KG 562, Sept. 15, 1951.
50. Wang Tsun-ming in Bradbury et al., *Mass Behavior*, 146.
51. Wang, ATIS KG 562, Sept. 15, 1951.

CHAPTER 3: DESPERADOES AND VOLUNTEERS

1. Cheng Liren, ATIS KG 633, Sept. 24, 1951; Cheng interview, Aug. 14, 2014.
2. Mao, *Jianguo yilai Mao Zedong wen'gao*, 1:661–62.
3. *KZZS*, 2:97.
4. Cheng Liren interview, Aug. 14, 2014.
5. "POW Population by Month," July 1953, Box 1, Statistical Reports Relating to Enemy POWs, 1950–53, Office of the Provost Marshal, RG 554, NA. See Appendix, 391.
6. Yang, *Zhonghua renmin gongheguo jianguo shi yanjiu 1*, 184.
7. Yan, "Gaige kaifang qian," 1.
8. Luo Ruiqing's report to the Second National Public Security Conference, Oct. 16, 1951, in *PRC Database*.
9. CCP Southwest Bureau report, Nov. 10, 1950, in *PRC Database*.
10. Mao, *Jianguo yilai Mao Zedong wen'gao*, 1:663–64.

11. Mao's cables to regional leaders, Jan. 17 and 30, 1951, in *PRC Database.*

12. Mao Zedong, "Dui Zhenfan sharen bili de zhishi," Apr. 20, 1951, in *PRC Database.*

13. Deng Xiaoping, "Guanyu san si yuefen gongzuo xiang Mao Zhuxi de baogao," May 9, 1951, in *PRC Database.*

14. Luo Ruiqing, "Zai disanci quanguo gong'an huiyi de baogao," May 10, 1951, in *PRC Database.*

15. Luo Ruiqing, "Zai disici quanguo gong'an huiyi de baogao," Sept. 11, 1951, in *PRC Database.*

16. Yang, *Zhonghua renmin gongheguo jianguo shi yanjiu 1*, 217n.

17. "Wenjiang diqu san xian shanzi chujue renfan de jiantao zhaoyao baogao," June 28, 1951, in *PRC Database.*

18. "Guizhou shengwei guanyu zhenya fangeming wenti de baogao," Mar. 31, 1951, in *PRC Database.*

19. Mao, "Dui Zhenfan sharen bili de zhishi."

20. Yang, "Reconsidering the Campaign to Suppress Counterrevolutionaries," 120. Yang argues that the actual toll is much higher. Song Yongyi makes a similar argument (see the preface to *PRC Database*, http://www.chineseupress.com/chinesepress/promotion/DCPC/DCPC_e.htm#b*).*

21. Yin, "Mao Zedong yu disanci quanguo gong'an huiyi," 5.

22. Junshi kexueyuan junshi lishi yanjiubu, *Zhongguo renmin jiefangjun zhanshi*, 403.

23. Luo Ruiqing, "Zai gesheng, shi, zizhiqu dangwei wuren xiaozu huiyi shang de zongjie fayan jiyao," Nov. 27, 1956, in *PRC Database.*

24. Luo Ruiqing, "Zai disanci quanguo gong'an huiyi de zongjie," May 14, 1951, in *PRC Database.*

25. Cheng Liren, ATIS KG 633, Sept. 24, 1951; Cheng interview, Aug. 14, 2014.

26. Deng Xiaoping, "Guanyu san si yuefen gongzuo xiang Mao Zhuxi de baogao," May 14, 1950, in *PRC Database.*

27. He, *Guizhou dangdai shi*, 20.

28. Cheng Liren, ATIS KG 633, Sept. 24, 1951.

29. Cheng Liren interview, Aug. 14, 2014.

30. *Si'nan xian zhi*, 388–89.

31. Ibid., 282–83.

32. Ibid., 313. It is not clear if the two Chengs were related.

33. Cheng interview, Aug. 14, 2014.

34. Yin, "Mao Zedong yu disanci quanguo gong'an huiyi," 5.

35. Deng Xiaoping et al., "Guanyu 1950 Jiaofei qingkuang xiang Mao Zhuxi ji junwei de zonghe baogao," Jan. 6, 1951, in *PRC Database.*

36. Cheng Liren, ATIS KG 633, Sept. 24, 1951; Cheng interview, Aug. 14, 2014.

37. Yang Shuzhi interview, Jan. 27–28, 2014; Yang Shuzhi, ATIS KT 21, Apr. 17, 1951, and KG 446, Aug. 31, 1951. The timeline is corroborated by both sources. Details are from interviews.

38. On Chinese forces' transit through Kowloon, see Sun, *Wu guo er zhong*, 89–97.

39. Yang interview, Jan. 27–28, 2014; Zhong, "Guomingdang sanbing jianshi," 589; Liu, *Luoye chengni*, 56–58.

40. On the Temporary 1st Army, see Cao, *Zhongguo Guomingdang jun jianshi*, 3:1907.

41. Yang interview, Jan. 27–28, 2014, June 3, 2015.

42. The Southwest Service Corps reached Chongqing on December 8, 1949 (Zhonggong zhongyang wenxian yanjiushi, *Deng Xiaoping zhuan*, 791).

43. Northern Sichuan Party Committee, "Guanyu zhenya fangeming feishou eba de baogao," Feb. 13, 1951, in *PRC Database*.

44. Li Da'an, ATIS KG 486, Sept. 3, 1951; Yu, *Eyun*, 76–77. Li was recaptured by the Communists in 1953, and was sentenced to death in 1958. PLA writer Yu Jin read Li's confessions, in which the basic outline of events matches that in ATIS KG 486. The details here are based on a combination of the two sources.

45. Yu, *Eyun*, 76–77.

46. *FFDS*, 34, 52.

47. Zhang Ruiqi, in *FFTL*, 360; Qi, *Juliuhe*, 563. Qi's older cousin Qi Zhengwu joined the PLA in January 1949, because he was "constantly nagged by the town's officials." See Qi Zhenwu, ATIS no. 2766, Nov. 29, 1950. Their accounts are also corroborated by PLA writer Zhang Zhenglong's interview in Zhang, *Xuebai xuehong*, 219–20.

48. Huang Changrong interview, July 8, 2013, Jan. 24, 2014.

49. Ibid.

50. Ibid. Similar mutual surveillance is also reported by Liu Chunjian in his interview, March 26, 2015.

51. Huang interview, July 8, 2013, and Jan. 24, 2014.

52. Tian Fangbao, ATIS KG 135, Mar. 12, 1952, 15.

53. Jin Yuankui interview, Feb. 8, 2010, Dec. 27, 2012.

54. Ibid, the same source in the following three paragraphs.

55. Zhou, *Zhou Enlai junshi wenxuan*, 4:159.

56. Tan Xingdong, ATIS no. 4649, Apr. 11, 1951.

57. Tan Xingdong, ATIS no. 4036, Mar. 12, 1951; no. 4649, Apr. 11, 1951.

58. Wang Shunqing, ATIS 164-MISDI-1276, Dec. 1, 1950.

59. Zhou, *Zhou Enlai xuanji*, 1:315; Jin, *Zhou Enlai zhuan*, 884.

60. Bradbury et al., *Mass Behavior*, 343; Chiang Ching-kuo, report to Chiang Kai-shek, June 1954, 00012389000090057w, TWGFB.

61. Yan Tianzhi interview, Apr. 5, 2010.

CHAPTER 4: CHIANG, MACARTHUR, TRUMAN, AND NSC-81/1

1. Taylor, *The Generalissimo's Son*, 185; Yi, *Wo de huiyi*, 142.

2. Truman statement, Jan. 5, 1950, TL, http://www.trumanlibrary.org/publicpapers/index.php?pid=574&st=&st1.

3. *FRUS 1950*, 6:261.

4. Ibid., 258n.

5. CKSD, "Reflections on works in 1950," Dec. 31, 1950.

6. CKSD, Jan. 9, 1950. Chiang repeated his criticism of the Marshall mediation (e.g., diary entries of July 28, 1951, May 24 and June 10, 1952).

7. Marshall's decision is described in Walter Mills, ed., *The Forrestal Diaries* (New York: Viking, 1951), 534, quoted in Lyman P. Van Slyke, "Introduction," in United States Department of State, *China White Paper, August 1949*, page 4 of the "Introduction," which is not paginated. Dean Acheson, "Letter of Transmittal," in *China White Paper, August 1949*, xiv, xvi.

8. CKSD, Dec. 31, 1950.

9. *FRUS 1950*, 6:316.

10. Ibid., 561.

11. Ibid., 330, 336.

12. Ibid., 340.

13. Ibid., 342–43.

14. Strong, May 22, 1950, Cooke Papers, Hoover Archives.
15. *FRUS 1950*, 6:351.
16. Ibid., 346n.
17. Ibid., 348–49.
18. Ibid., 367.
19. This language would eventually become the quasi-legal grounds for the future Taiwan independence movement.
20. Koo diary entry, June 27, 1950, Wellington Koo Papers, Columbia University, NY.
21. Koo and Dulles note of a conversation, July 25, 1950, 004170100420301w, TWGFB.
22. Chang Su-Ya, "Pragmatism and Opportunism," 77–78.
23. Qu, Xiao, and Ye, *Zhonghua minguo shishi jiyao*, 912.
24. CKSD, June 28, 1950.
25. Koo and Dulles note of a conversation, July 25, 1950, 004170100420302w, TWGFB; "The U.S. Tragedy in Formosa," *Time*, July 17, 1950.
26. CKSD, June 28, 1950.
27. Koo and Dulles note of a conversation, 004170100420302w, TWGFB.
28. "The U.S. Tragedy in Formosa," *Time*, July 17, 1950.
29. CKSD, June 28, 1950. Here "Taiwanese" refers to Taiwan's local population.
30. *FRUS 1950*, 7:158, 179–80.
31. *FRUS 1950*, 6:367–68.
32. Ibid., 380–81.
33. *FRUS 1950*, 7:276–77; Acheson, *Present at the Creation*, 412.
34. Acheson, *Present at the Creation*, 422.
35. *FRUS 1950*, 7:162; Acheson, *Present at the Creation*, 405–6.
36. Lin, *Accidental State*, 159–62.
37. *FRUS 1950*, 7:165.
38. Bradley and Blair, *A General's Life*, 527, 530, 549.
39. List of MacArthur's party, July 31, 1950, 000005030001 0012w, TWGFB.
40. Manchester, *American Caesar*, 562.
41. *FRUS 1950*, 6:410–11.
42. Huang, *Wo zai 38 du xian de huiyi*, 58.
43. Acheson, *Present at the Creation*, 422.
44. MacArthur, *Reminiscences*, 339.
45. Acheson, *Present at the Creation*, 422.
46. Bradley and Blair, *A General's Life*, 549.
47. *FRUS 1950*, 6:428–30.
48. Ridgway, *The Korean War*, 37–38.
49. *FRUS 1950*, 6:486.
50. Ibid., 534.
51. Ibid., 437.
52. Ibid., 416.
53. Ibid., 452–53.
54. Ibid., 454.
55. Bradley and Blair, *A General's Life*, 551.
56. Ibid.; Margaret Truman, *Harry S. Truman*, 479–80.
57. Margaret Truman, *Harry S. Truman*, 480–81.
58. Bradley and Blair, *A General's Life*, 556–57.
59. CKSD, Dec. 31, 1950.

60. "POW Population by Month," see Appendix, 391.

61. Willoughby and Chamberlain, *MacArthur*, 375.

62. Blair, *Forgotten War*, 337. This total unpreparedness for Chinese intervention was a woeful replay of the disaster four months earlier. When North Korea attacked in June, there were only two Korean linguists on MacArthur's G-2 staff (Finnegan, *Military Intelligence*, 115).

63. Charles A. Willoughby, "Intelligence in War: A Brief History of MacArthur's Intelligence Service 1941–1951," Reel 918, RG 23 (Willoughby Papers) (Norfolk, VA: MacArthur Archives, 2006), 23–24.

64. Bradley and Blair, *A General's Life*, 561.

65. Willoughby, *MacArthur*, 381.

66. Blair, *Forgotten War*, 337.

67. Margaret Truman, *Harry S. Truman*, 483; Truman, *Off the Record*, 196, 210.

68. Acheson, *Present at the Creation*, 456.

69. Truman, *Off thee Record*, 200.

70. Manchester, *American Caesar*, 589–90.

71. Truman, *Memoirs*, 2:364–65; Truman, *Off the Record*, 200; Addendum to notes on Wake Conference, Oct. 15, 1950, Secretary of State File, Acheson Papers, TL.

72. Substance of Statements Made at Wake Island Conference, Oct. 15, 1950, Secretary of State File, Acheson Papers, TL.

73. Ibid.

74. Rusk and Papp, *As I Saw It*, 168–69.

75. Substance of Statements Made at Wake Island Conference.

76. *NYT*, Oct. 16, 1950.

77. Ibid.

78. *Newsweek*, Oct. 23, 1950.

79. Substance of Statements Made at Wake Island Conference.

80. Addendum to Notes on Wake Conference, Oct. 15, 1950, Acheson Papers, TL.

81. Bradley and Blair, *A General's Life*, 559; *FRUS 1950*, 7:716–17.

82. Acheson, *Present at the Creation*, 445.

83. Cumings, *Origins of the Korean War*, 2:709–11; Bradley and Blair, *A General's Life*, 558.

84. Several scholars have studied the prisoner reindoctrination aspect of the NSC-81/1 without fully recognizing its impact, e.g., Tovy, "Manifest Destiny in POW Camps."

85. *FRUS 1950*, 7:718.

86. Cumings argues that NSC-81 and the rollback strategy "caused the Chinese intervention, and not the subsequent arrival of American troops at the Yalu River" (*The Korean War*, 25).

87. *FRUS 1950*, 7:718.

88. Ibid., 715n.

89. MacArthur to Dept. of the Army, "Reorientation Program for North Korean Prisoners of War," Feb. 28, 1951, Box 19, Top Secret Correspondence, Special Warfare, RG 319, NA.

90. Bradley and Blair, *A General's Life*, 564–65 (emphasis added).

91. US Army, *Handling*, 5, 102; MacArthur to Dept. of the Army, "Reorientation Program for North Korean Prisoners of War," Feb. 28, 1951, Box 19, Top Secret Correspondence, Special Warfare, RG 319, NA; *FRUS 1950*, 7:857, 1007–10, and passim.

92. *FRUS 1950*, 7:919.

93. Cumings, *Origins of the Korean War*, 2:709–11; Cumings, *The Korean War*, 22, 229; Beisner, *Dean Acheson*, 395–99.

CHAPTER 5: DEFECTORS AND PRISONERS IN THE FIRST THREE CHINESE OFFENSIVES

1. Bradley and Blair, *A General's Life*, 577.

2. Ibid. Truman's schedule discussed in the following paragraphs is also from Bradley and Blair, *A General's Life*.

3. *KZZS*, 1:326. Also confirmed by PW interrogation (*FRUS 1950*, 7:1047).

4. Blair, *Forgotten War*, 357.

5. *KZZS*, 1:326–29.

6. Substance of Statements Made at Wake Island Conference, Oct. 15, 1950, Secretary of State File, Acheson Papers, TL.

7. Appleman, *South to the Naktong*, 670–71.

8. *KZZS*, 1:365–66, 398.

9. Paik, *From Pusan to Panmunjom*, 86.

10. Ibid., 86–87; Appleman, *South to the Naktong*, 675–77.

11. Appleman, *South to the Naktong*, 676, 752.

12. Blair, *Forgotten War*, 377.

13. Paik, *From Pusan to Panmunjom*, 87.

14. Li Xinlin, 164-MISDI-1166, Oct. 28, 1950.

15. Syng Chong San, 164-MISDI-1165, Oct. 26, 1950, Entry 39, RG 554, NA (MISDI hereafter). Syng claimed that he was unable to write his own name.

16. Yan Shuzheng, 164-MISDI-1167, Oct. 28, 1950.

17. Appleman, *South to the Naktong*, 752–53. CCF: Chinese Communist Forces.

18. Ibid., 751–53.

19. Ibid., 687–88. Beijing was known as Beiping between 1928 and 1949.

20. Halberstam, *Coldest Winter*, 431–32, 439. Halberstam considers the phrase as reflecting "pure racism."

21. Appleman, *South to the Naktong*, 687.

22. Blair, *Forgotten War*, 377.

23. Ibid., 370, 377.

24. Muccio, "Oral history interview" (TL, 1971), 72, 74.

25. Blair, *Forgotten War*, 377 (italics original).

26. Appleman, *South to the Naktong*, 751–54.

27. Mao, Oct. 23, 1950, in *Jianguo yilai Mao Zedong junshi wen'gao*, 281.

28. Sun Hou Chin (Sun Houjin), ATIS 4567, Jan. 9, 1951, 114–15; Syng Chong San, 164-MISDI-1165, Oct. 26, 1950, 4; Hwang Chin Tai, 164-MISDI-1170, Oct. 31, 1950, 2, Entry 39, RG 554, NA.

29. Yang Wanfu interview, Jan. 3, 2010.

30. Appleman, *South to the Naktong*, 688. A deserter confirmed these features on Chinese uniforms. See Hwang Chin Tai, 164-MISDI-1170, Oct. 31, 1950.

31. Hastings, *The Korean War*, 130; see also Manchester, *American Caesar*, 600.

32. *FRUS 1950*, 7:1046–47.

33. Hwang Chin Tai, 164-MISDI-1170, Oct. 31, 1950. If attached units were included, the estimate was not a wild exaggeration.

34. Appleman, *South to the Naktong*, 761–63.

35. *KZZS*, 1:345.

36. Appleman, *South to the Naktong*, 770–71.

37. Ma Yufu, ATIS 4632, Jan. 22, 1951, 35–40.

38. Appleman, *South to the Naktong*, 767n59.

39. Ibid., 743n29. The following details are based on his interview in Bradbury et al., *Mass Behavior*, 48–53, and multiple interrogation reports: Wang, Fu Tien (Wang Futian), ATIS 4614, Dec. 28, 1950, 1–27; ATIS 4016, Mar. 5, 1951, 35–37; ATIS 3022, Jan. 26, 1951, 61; ATIS 3733, Mar. 2, 1951, 72–75.

40. Bradbury et al., *Mass Behavior*, 48.

41. The special force operated under Chiang Kai-shek's spymaster Dai Li with support from SACO (the Sino-American Cooperative Organization).

42. On the Transport Police, see Cao, *Zhongguo Guomingdang jun jianshi*, 1439–40.

43. Bradbury et al., *Mass Behavior*, 51.

44. Ibid., 52.

45. Ibid., 52–53.

46. Appleman, *South to the Naktong*, 742–44; *KZZS*, 1:403.

47. ATIS 3022, Jan. 26, 1951, 61.

48. *KZZS*, 1:396, 403.

49. Appleman, *South to the Naktong*, 754.

50. *KZZS*, 1:466, 471.

51. Appleman, *South to the Naktong*, 763, 754–55.

52. *FRUS 1950*, 7:1175.

53. Appleman, *South to the Naktong*, 774; Blair, *Forgotten War*, 432;

54. Blair, *Forgotten War*, 432; Manchester, *American Caesar*, 606.

55. Blair, *Forgotten War*, 434; Manchester, *American Caesar*, 606–7; MacArthur, *Reminiscences*, 373.

56. Futrell, *The United States Air Force in Korea*, 229–30.

57. *FRUS 1950*, 7:1175.

58. Marshall, *The River and the Gauntlet*, 1, 14.

59. *KZZS*, 1:476, 483–84, 488–95, 501; Mossman, *Ebb and Flow*, 72–83.

60. Mossman, *Ebb and Flow*, 127.

61. *KZZS*, 1:540–43.

62. Ibid., 547.

63. Truman and Acheson, *Affection and Trust*, 115. Bull Run was the first major battle of the American Civil War in 1861, in which the Union forces were defeated by the Confederates.

64. Mossman, *Ebb and Flow*, 149.

65. Qi Zhenwu, ATIS 2851, Nov. 27, 1950, 4; ATIS 2776, Nov. 29, 1950, 90. Qi was the cousin of writer Chi Pang-yuan (Qi Bangyuan). See Qi, *Juliuhe*, 563–64.

66. Wang Shunqing, 164-MISDI-1276, Dec. 1, 1950, 1–4, Entry 39, RG 554, NA. The following details are from 164-MISDI-1276, unless otherwise noted.

67. His rank is from Xiao Lixing, in *FFTL*, 428. On the 63rd Army, see Cao, *Zhongguo Guomingdang jun jianshi*, 1825. As Hainan was "liberated" in early May, perhaps Wang was in hiding.

68. *KZZS*, 1:481–82.

69. Liu Bingzhang, ATIS 2842, Nov. 26, 1950, 130–31, 135; ATIS 2737, Dec. 7, 1950, 126.

70. Mossman, *Ebb and Flow*, 72; *KZZS*, 1:483–90.

71. *KZZS*, 1:494, and map of the Second Offensive in appendix.

72. Liu Bingzhang, ATIS 2758, Nov. 29, 1950, 49, 57.

73. Ibid., 53.

74. Ibid., 2745, Dec. 17, 1950, 144.

75. Ibid., 144–46. "Poison gas" (*duqi*) was used quite liberally by the PLA. It often simply meant tear gas.

76. *FFDS*, 41–42.
77. *FRUS 1950*, 7:1237–38.
78. Ibid., 1253.
79. Truman used the epithet in a 1958 letter (Truman, *Off the Record*, 368).
80. *FRUS 1950*, 7:1243.
81. Stueck, *The Korean War*, 138–39.
82. *FRUS 1950*, 7:1243.
83. Hastings, *The Korean War*, 165.
84. Margaret Truman, *Harry S. Truman*, 495–97.
85. *FRUS 1950*, 7:1262.
86. Ibid., 1337.
87. Ibid. 1321.
88. Ibid., 1312.
89. Ibid., 1324–25.
90. Ibid., 1326.
91. Ibid., 1385.
92. Ibid., 1367–68.
93. Ibid., 1397.
94. Ibid., 1406–7.
95. Ibid., 1367–69.
96. Ibid., 1411–12.
97. Ibid., 1532.
98. Ibid., 1469.
99. Ibid., 1588.
100. Ibid., 1606.
101. Ibid., 1616.
102. Ibid., 1630–31.
103. *FRUS 1951*, 7:42.
104. *KZZS*, 1:476–77, 536; Mossman, *Ebb and Flow*, 147–48; Montross, Canzona, and Bauer, *U.S. Marine Operations in Korea*, 3:382.
105. "War: Retreat of the 20,000," *Time*, Dec. 18, 1950.
106. Hastings, *The Korean War*, 154; Mossman, *Ebb and Flow*, 89–91; *KZZS*, 1:516.
107. Montross, *U.S. Marine Operations in Korea*, 3:152, 161; *KZZS*, 1:517.
108. Mossman, *Ebb and Flow*, 92, 102–3; *KZZS*, 1:518–20; Sun Zhenguan, ATIS 4773, Feb. 25, 1951, 10.
109. Mossman, *Ebb and Flow*, 140; *KZZS*, 1:532–33; Sun, ATIS 4773.
110. *KZZS*, 1:534–35.
111. Mossman, *Ebb and Flow*, 142–45.
112. *KZZS*, 1:535.
113. Sun, ATIS 3613, Jan. 15, 1951, 51.
114. The following details are from Sun, in "Andeshe," 1:3–4.
115. Mossman, *Ebb and Flow*, 145.
116. Sun's capture is also recorded in Appleman, *Escaping the Trap*, 350.
117. Sun in "Andeshe," 1:3–4, and 2:1.
118. Mossman, *Ebb and Flow*, 177–78.
119. Ridgway, *The Korean War*, 93–94.
120. Wei Shixi, 164-MISDI-1298, Dec. 31, 1950, Entry 39, RG 554, NA; ATIS 5172, May 12, 1951, 13; ROC Embassy to Ministry of Defense, "A partial list of Chinese Communist POWs with the rank of platoon leaders or above," May 7, 1951, 0004146700010005w, TWGFB.

121. Wei, 164-MISDI-1298.
122. Yu, *Eyun*, 127.
123. *KZZS*, 1:625–27; Mossman, *Ebb and Flow*, 188.
124. *KZZS*, 2:115.
125. Ibid., 1:632.
126. Mossman, *Ebb and Flow*, 208.
127. Fang Xiangqian interview, April 19, 2014; Lu Xuewen interview, Jan. 24, 2014.
128. *KZZS*, 1:636–37, and 2:3, 50.
129. Ibid., 1:637.
130. "POW Population by Month," see Appendix, 391. In the 1980s, PLA writer Wu Jinfeng studied the dossiers of more than four hundred repatriated prisoners and found that none were captured in the Third Offensive ("Andeshe," 1:4).
131. *RMRB*, Jan. 5, 1951; *KZZS*, 2:7; Peng Dehuai zhuan bianxiezu, *Peng Dehuai zhuan*, 261.
132. Bradley and Blair, *A General's Life*, 623.
133. *FRUS 1951*, 7:102–5.

CHAPTER 6: RIDGWAY'S TURNAROUND, MACARTHUR'S EXIT, AND TAIWAN'S ENTRY

1. *KZZS*, 2:1–2, 6.
2. Ibid., 5, 9.
3. *KZZS*, 2:51–53; Mossman, *Ebb and Flow*, 237–42.
4. *KZZS*, 2:3, 50; Mossman, *Ebb and Flow*, 243–44.
5. Mossman, *Ebb and Flow*, 243.
6. *KZZJ*, 74.
7. *KZZS*, 2:54–57; Peng Dehuai zhuanji zu, *Peng Dehuai quanzhuan*, 940.
8. *KZZS*, 2:59.
9. Ibid., 65–67; Peng Dehuai zhuanji zu, *Peng Dehuai quanzhuan*, 943.
10. Lu Xuewen interview, Jan. 24, 2014.
11. Ibid.
12. *KZZS*, 2:67–68.
13. Fang Xiangqian interview, Apr. 19, 2014.
14. *KZZS*, 2:68.
15. Wu Jiansheng, ATIS no. 3738, Feb. 24, 1951; Gao, *Kongzhan*, 241.
16. *KZZS*, 2:75–84.
17. Mossman, *Ebb and Flow*, 300.
18. Ibid., 308–10.
19. *KZZS*, 1:385, 540–41, 632; *KZZS*, 2:83–84.
20. Chen Yonghua, ATIS no. 4103, Feb. 28; no. 4120, Mar. 2; no. 3943, Mar. 5; no. 5307, June 15, 1951.
21. Peng Dehuai zhuanji zu, *Peng Dehuai quanzhuan*, 957.
22. Mossman, *Ebb and Flow*, 321.
23. Fang Xiangqian interview, Apr. 19, 2014; *KZZS*, 2:111–12.
24. *KZZS*, 2:112.
25. Appleman, *Ridgway Duels for Korea*, 342.
26. *FFTL*, 402–5, 431.
27. Lu Xuewen interview, Jan. 24, 2014.
28. *KZZS*, 2:113–14.

29. Tan, ATIS 4036, Mar. 12, 1951; ATIS 4649, Apr. 11, 1951. On Tan's background, see Chapter 3.

30. Hallim University Asia Culture Institute, *Han'guk*, 3:332.

31. Shi Wenxuan, ATIS 5322, June 18, 1951; Yuan Pengying, ATIS 5265, June 5, 1951.

32. ROC Embassy to MoF, May 7, 1951, 0004146700010008w, TWGFB. The following details are from my interview of Meng Ming, Jan. 1–2, 2013.

33. *KZZS*, 2:24, 59, 114–15.

34. Ibid., 122; Mossman, *Ebb and Flow*, 343.

35. Li Da'an, ATIS KG 486, Sept. 3, 1951.

36. *FFDS*, 86.

37. Li's confession is cited in Yu, *Eyun*, 77. Li was later drafted by US intelligence and parachuted into North Korea, where he was captured. See Chapter 15.

38. Mossman, *Ebb and Flow*, 372–73.

39. Yang Shuzhi, ATIS KT 21, Apr. 17, 1951; Yin Ruliang and Du Wenpu, ATIS KT 23, Apr. 17, 1951; Yang Shuzhi interviews, Jan. 19, 2014, and Mar. 24, 2015.

40. "POW Population by Month," see Appendix, 391.

41. Zheng Zheng'an interview, Apr. 26, 2010.

42. Bradley and Blair, *A General's Life*, 623.

43. Ibid., 616.

44. *FRUS 1951*, 7:146, 146n.

45. Mossman, *Ebb and Flow*, 305; Ridgway, *The Korean War*, 109–10.

46. Mossman, *Ebb and Flow*, 319; *NYT*, Mar. 8, 1951.

47. Blair, *Forgotten War*, 746.

48. *FRUS 1951*, 7:265–66.

49. Truman to Elsey, Apr. 16, 1951, quoted in James, *The Years of MacArthur*, 3:588.

50. Margaret Truman, *Harry S. Truman*, 513.

51. *FRUS 1951*, 7:299; Truman, *Off the Record*, 210–11.

52. Truman, *Off the Record*, 210 (italics in the original).

53. MacArthur, *Reminiscences*, 395; Manchester, *American Caesar*, 645.

54. Ridgway, *Soldier*, 223.

55. Jager, *Brothers at War*, 177.

56. MacArthur, *Reminiscences*, 395.

57. Chiang to He Shili, Apr. 12, 1951, 002-010400-00017-008, TWGSG; Chiang to MacArthur, Apr. 12, 1951, 002-010400-00017-007, TWGSG.

58. CKSD, May 10, 1952. Ridgway was close to Marshall, to whom he dedicated his *The Korean War* (1967).

59. *FRUS 1951*, 7:1627–30.

60. Truman diary, June 21, 1951 (*Off the Record*, 213).

61. CKSD, June 2, 9, 18, 1951.

62. Bradley and Blair, *A General's Life*, 640.

63. Huang, *Wo zai 38 du xian de huiyi*, 61.

64. Chiang to MacArthur, Apr. 12, 1951, 002-010400-00017-007, TWGSG.

65. US Army, *Handling*, 103.

66. Ibid., 102–3; GHQ FEC to DoA [Dept of the Army], "Reorientation Program for North Korean Prisoners of War," Feb. 28, 1951, Box 19, Top Secret Correspondence, Special Warfare, RG 319, NA.

67. GHQ FEC to DoA [Dept of the Army], "Reorientation Program for North Korean Prisoners of War," memo for record, Mar. 16, 1951.

68. Nishi, *Unconditional Democracy*, 2, 143.

69. McClure, "Reorientation Program for Prisoners of War," Mar. 19, 1951, and Collins to MacArthur, Mar. 22, 1951, both in Box 19, Top Secret Correspondence, Special Warfare, RG 319, NA.

70. Ridgway to DoA [Dept of the Army], Apr. 16, 1951, Box 19, Top Secret Correspondence, Special Warfare, RG 319, NA; US Army, *Handling*, 102–5.

71. Ridgway to CIE, Apr. 23, 1951, Box 309, 383.6 TS, RG 319, NA.

72. *FRUS 1951*, 7:397–98, 487, 646n (italics added).

73. Glavin to McClure, Feb. 28, 1951, Box 19, Top Secret Correspondence, Special Warfare, RG 319, NA.

74. US Army, *Handling*, 106–7.

75. CIE UNC, "Interim Report," Jan. 10, 1952, 4, Box 309, 383.6 TS, RG 319, NA.

76. Ridgway, *Soldier*, 205, 216.

77. Hatch and Benson, *The Korean War*, 11.

78. Willoughby, "Intelligence in War: A Brief History of MacArthur's Intelligence Service 1941–1951," 20, Reel 918, RG 23, MacArthur Archives.

79. *NYT*, Mar. 7, 1951.

80. Ibid.

81. Gao, *Kongzhan*, 231–33.

82. Ibid., 233–35.

83. Presidential Office to MoD, Feb. 21, 1951, 00042798000200013w, TWGFB.

84. Gao, *Kongzhan*, 237–38.

85. Dept of State to GHQ, FEC, Mar. 13, 1951, Box 45, RG 9, MacArthur Archives. According to the *New York Times*, Mar. 7, 1951, the salary ranged between $230 and $260 a month. The local salary in Taiwan was equivalent to about $15 a month (see Huang, *Wo zai 38 du xian de huiyi*, 128).

86. Huang, *Wo zai 38 du xian de huiyi*, 11–25, 39–47; Huang interview, July 14, 2010.

87. Chu, Lü, and Huang, *Chu Songqiu xiansheng fangwen jilu*, 54–55; Chiang Ching-kuo to Lei Yanjun, June 1, 1951, 002-080200-00641-081, TWGSG. Chu served as Chiang Kai-shek's press secretary from 1954 to 1958.

88. He Shili to Chiang Ching-kuo, June 1, 1951, 002-080200-00663-061, TWGSG; Wang, *Wenxue jianghu*, 187.

89. Shao to Chiang Kai-shek, Feb. 7, 1951, 002-080200-00663-003, TWGSG. "Bandit" was a standard Nationalist epithet for the Communists.

90. Shao to Chiang Kai-shek, Feb. 21, 1951, 00042798000200013w, TWGFB.

91. Gao, *Kongzhan*, 238–41.

92. Dept of State to GHQ, FEC, Mar. 13, 1951, Box 45, RG 9, MacArthur Archives. Certain Air Force officers were in "mufti cover" (see *NYT*, Mar. 7, 1951).

93. *FFDS*, 39–42; Gao, *Kongzhan*, 246.

94. Yu, *Eyun*, 96.

95. Gao, *Kongzhan*, 238.

96. Shao to Chiang, May 7, 1951, 00041467000100004w, TWGFB.

97. Gao, *Kongzhan*, 242–43.

98. Chu to Chiang, June 29, 1951, 005-010100-00053-039, TWGSG.

99. US Army, *Handling*, 103.

100. Du, *Zai Zhiyuanjun zongbu*, 341; *FFTL*, 427.

101. Robin, *The Making of the Cold War Enemy*, 153.

102. *FRUS 1950–55, Intelligence*: 2, 45.

103. GHQ Chief of Civil Affairs, "Summary of three conferences held on the subject of Reorientation-Reeducation in North Korea," Nov. 1950, and Department of State, "Reorientation Plan for Korea," Nov. 1950, both in Box 18, 319.5, RG 319, NA.

104. *FRUS 1951*, 7:374.

105. Manhard, interview by Marshall Green, Dec. 1, 1988, Association for Diplomatic Studies and Training Foreign Affairs Oral History Project, http://hdl.loc.gov/loc.mss/mfdip.2004man01.

106. Webb to US embassies in Pusan, Taipei, and Hong Kong, Sept. 5, 1951, and Muccio to Acheson, Oct. 5, 1951, both in 695A.0024, RG 59, NA. On Chin's arrest in 1985 and his trial and suicide in a prison cell in 1986, see *NYT*, Feb. 22, 1986. Chin was convicted on seventeen counts of espionage and other crimes. According to court records, his primary alleged crime was providing PRC agents with intelligence "concerning the location of Chinese POWs in Korea and the information that the American and Korean Intelligence Services were seeking from the Chinese POWs." The information that Chin had access to, however, was non-military in nature, as Manhard stated in his affidavit. Chin's intelligence, contrary to allegations, could not have had an impact on the course of the war, because by mid-1952, when the transmission took place in Hong Kong, China had captured a number of prisoner-agents drafted by US military intelligence to infiltrate North Korea, and had obtained extensive knowledge of UN POW camps. See Chapter 15.

107. Foot, *A Substitute for Victory*, 115.

108. Muccio oral history, TL.

CHAPTER 7: THE FIFTH OFFENSIVE DEBACLE

1. Zhang, *Wo de Chaoxian zhanzheng*, 4; *KZZS*, 2:97.
2. Zhang, email correspondence with author, June 26, 2011.
3. *KZZS*, 2:97; Xie, "Zuinie," 24–28.
4. Ibid., 93–97; Li, *China's Battle for Korea*, 82; Yan, *Wei Jie gushi*, 134.
5. Yan, *Wei Jie gushi*, 106–7.
6. Zhang, *Kaoyan*, 175; "Andeshe," 1:37.
7. Jiang Ruipu interview, June 24, 2014.
8. Wei Jie, interviewed by Wu Jingfeng, May 24, 1984, in "Andeshe," 1:28.
9. Zhou, *Zhou Enlai xuanji*, 1:315; Jin, *Zhou Enlai zhuan*, 884.
10. Zhang, *Kaoyan*, 175.
11. *KZZS*, 2:97.
12. Chen, *Muse Huangpu*, 227.
13. Cheng Liren, ATIS KG 633, Sept. 24, 1951; Cheng interview, Aug. 14, 2014.
14. Sun Xiuhe, ATIS KG 797, Oct. 24, 1951.
15. *KZZS*, 2:97.
16. Sun Xiuhe, ATIS KG 797, Oct. 24, 1951.
17. Chang, "Zhang Yifu's Oral History Records," 135.
18. Huang Changrong interview, July 8, 2013.
19. Li Yueming interview, Feb. 26, 2010; He Rui interview, Jan. 16, 2013.
20. Yu, *Eyun*, 19; Liu, *Liuxue dao tianming*, 6.
21. Zhang Zeshi, Zhong Junhua, and Cai Pingsheng interviews, Aug. and Sept. 2007.
22. *KZZS*, 2:97.
23. Chang, "Zhang Yifu's Oral History Records," 136.
24. Xie, "Zuinie," 38–39.
25. Hallim University Asia Culture Institute, *Han'guk*, 3:263.

26. *KZZS*, 2:97–98.

27. Appleman, *Ridgway Duels for Korea*, 378–80.

28. *KZZS*, 2:96; Jiang Ruipu interview, June 24, 2014; Lin Xuebu, ATIS KT 665, June 28, 1951; Zhang, *Wo de Chaoxian zhanzheng*, 4.

29. Ma Furui in *FFTL*, 232–33.

30. Wu Xiaozong interview, Aug. 17, 2011.

31. Zhang, *Wo de Chaoxian zhanzheng*, 5–6.

32. Ma Furui in *FFTL*, 234.

33. He Rui interview, Jan. 16, 2013.

34. Zhang, *Wo de Chaoxian zhanzheng*, 7.

35. Wang, *Shujuan renfeng*, 73–74.

36. Ma Furui in *FFTL*, 233–34.

37. Tao Shanpeng, ATIS KG 415, undated; Tao interview, Jan. 22–23, 2015.

38. *KZZS*, 2:96–98.

39. Du, *Zai Zhiyuanjun zongbu*, 161; Hong, *Kangmei yuanchao*, 138.

40. Wang, *Peng Dehuai nianpu*, 487–88; Du, *Zai Zhiyuanjun zongbu*, 162; *KZZS*, 2:188.

41. Yang, *Zai Zhiyuanjun silingbu*, 129.

42. *Mao Zedong nianpu (1949–1976)*, 1:310.

43. Yang, *Zai Zhiyuanjun silingbu*, 128–30.

44. Ibid., 128.

45. *KZZJ*, 41.

46. Hong, *Kangmei yuanchao*, 141; Du, *Zai Zhiyuanjun zongbu*, 165–66; Wang, *Peng Dehuai nianpu*, 488.

47. Hong, *Kangmei yuanchao*, 148–50; Du, *Zai Zhiyuanjun zongbu*, 172–73; Yang and Wang, *Beiwei 38 du xian*, 322–23.

48. For a detailed operational history of the Fifth Offensive, see Li, *China's Battle for Korea*.

49. Du, *Zai Zhiyuanjun zongbu*, 164; Yang, *Zai Zhiyuanjun silingbu*, 131. But the tank units were not used in this offensive (*KZZS*, 2:191n; Appleman, *Ridgway Duels for Korea*, 458).

50. *KZZS*, 2:193.

51. Wang, *Peng Dehuai nianpu*, 490–92; *KZZS*, 2:190–92.

52. Wang, *Peng Dehuai nianpu*, 492.

53. Appleman, *Ridgway Duels for Korea*, 446, 448, 457.

54. *KZZS*, 2:192–93.

55. Yang, *Zai Zhiyuanjun silingbu*, 129–32; Hong, *Kangmei yuanchao*, 153.

56. Zhang and Liu, *Zhongguo renmin zhiyuanjun*, 4.

57. Ye, *Zhongguo renmin jiefangjun di 60 jun*, 195–96.

58. Yang, *Zai zhiyuanjun silingbu*, 133; *KZZS*, 2:221.

59. Li, *China's Battle for Korea*, 113.

60. Millett, *The War for Korea*, 429; Mossman, *Ebb and Flow*, 436.

61. *KZZS*, 2:209, 217; Wang, *Peng Dehuai nianpu*, 493.

62. Yu, *Eyun*, 19; Jiang Ruipu interview, June 24, 2014.

63. Ye, *Zhongguo renmin jiefangjun di 60 jun*, 201–4.

64. Chen Shihuan, 164-MISDI-1916, 1944, May 2, 3, 1951.

65. Tao Shanpeng, ATIS KG 415, undated; Tao interview, Jan. 23, 2015.

66. *KZZS*, 2:219–20; Mossman, *Ebb and Flow*, 437.

67. Wang, *Peng Dehuai nianpu*, 495.

68. *KZZS*, 2:223–27; Wang, *Peng Dehuai nianpu*, 494.

69. *KZZS*, 2:232; Mossman, *Ebb and Flow*, 438.

70. Blair, *Forgotten War*, 873.
71. Mossman, *Ebb and Flow*, 443; Appleman, *Ridgway Duels for Korea*, 502–4; Zhang Wenxing, ATIS KT 464, May 14, 1951, and ATIS KT 2248, Oct. 23, 1951.
72. Mossman, *Ebb and Flow*, 444.
73. *KZZS*, 2:224–25, 233–36; Blair, *Forgotten War*, 874.
74. *KZZS*, 2:233–35; Mossman, *Ebb and Flow*, 445.
75. Mossman, *Ebb and Flow*, 450.
76. Zhang and Liu, *Zhongguo renmin zhiyuanjun*, 7.
77. Xie, "Zuinie," 46.
78. *KZZS*, 2:235–37; Yang, *Zai Zhiyuanjun silingbu*, 143.
79. Appleman, *Ridgway Duels for Korea*, 520–22, 528; *KZZS*, 2:242.
80. Appleman, *Ridgway Duels for Korea*, 533.
81. *KZZS*, 2:237–38.
82. Ibid., 240–41; Wang, *Peng Dehuai nianpu*, 496–97.
83. *KZZS*, 2:243–45.
84. Appleman, *Ridgway Duels for Korea*, 535.
85. Ibid., 524; Mossman, *Ebb and Flow*, 470–73; *KZZS*, 2:245, 253.
86. *KZZS*, 2:254, 263; Yang, *Zai Zhiyuanjun silingbu*, 143–44. According to Yang, the return date was May 27.
87. Wang Zunming, ATIS KT 190, May 28, 1951.
88. Sun Xiuhe, ATIS KG 797, Oct. 24, 1951.
89. Cheng Liren, ATIS KG 633, Sept. 24, 1951; Cheng interview, Aug. 14, 2014, Oct. 14, 2016.
90. Zhang and Liu, *Zhongguo renmin zhiyuanjun*, 11.
91. Chen Qingbin, 164-MISDI-2103, May 27; ATIS KG 443, Aug. 31, 1951.
92. Xie, "Zuinie," 23, 35, 50–53. The exact circumstances of Chen's surrender remain impossible to verify. Nonetheless, Chen later chose to return to Communist China, not his native Taiwan, to the surprise of many.
93. Tang Naiyao (Tang Yao), ATIS KT 187, May 27, 1951; Tang interview, May 26, 2010.
94. Gao Jie and Feng Zequn in "Andeshe," 1:7; Feng Jiaji (alias), ATIS KT 270, June 1, 1951.
95. Zhou, *Zhou Enlai junshi wenxuan*, 4:159; Jin Yuankui interview, Feb. 8, 2010, and Dec. 27, 2012. See Chapter 3.
96. Jin Yuankui interview, Feb. 8, 2010, and Dec. 27, 2012.
97. *KZZS*, 2:246.
98. Hong, *Kangmei yuanchao*, 158; Yan, *Wei Jie gushi*, 133.
99. *KZZS*, 2:251; Yan, *Wei Jie gushi*, 133, 147; Wei Jie in "Andeshe," 1:28; Ye, *Zhongguo renmin jiefangjun di 60 jun*, 214.
100. Ye, *Zhongguo renmin jiefangjun di 60 jun*, 213.
101. *KZZS*, 2:251; Yan, *Wei Jie gushi*, 133–35.
102. *KZZS*, 2:251; Yan, *Wei Jie gushi*, 133, 138–40.
103. *KZZS*, 2:251–52; Yan, *Wei Jie gushi*, 142.
104. Millett, *The War for Korea*, 451; "Andeshe," 1:31.
105. *KZZS*, 2:252–53; Ye, *Zhongguo renmin jiefangjun di 60 jun*, 221–25.
106. Appleman, *Ridgway Duels for Korea*, 528; Mossman, *Ebb and Flow*, 472.
107. Appleman, *Ridgway Duels for Korea*, 538; Mossman, *Ebb and Flow*, 476–77.
108. *KZZS*, 2:252; Yan, *Wei Jie gushi*, 143–44.
109. Mossman, *Ebb and Flow*, 477.
110. *NYT*, May 26, 1951; Appleman, *Ridgway Duels for Korea*, 538; Mossman, *Ebb and Flow*, 478. The distance has been measured with Google Earth, as the *NYT* report exaggerates it.

111. Cai Derong in "Andeshe," 1:52; "Lishi de huiyin" bianshen weiyuanhui, *Lishi de huiyin*, 286–88 (hereafter cited as *Lishi de huiyin*).

112. Liu Chunjian interview, Mar. 26, 2015.

113. Xu, *Cuojue*, 110–11.

114. Zhang, *Wo de Chaoxian zhanzheng*, 18–19; Ye, *Zhongguo renmin jiefangjun di 60 jun*, 226–27; Ping Zhanfang interview, Feb. 26, 2010.

115. Mossman, *Ebb and Flow*, 478.

116. Ye, *Zhongguo renmin jiefangjun di 60 jun*, 227–28; Yan, *Wei Jie gushi*, 146–47; *Lishi de huiyin*, 279.

117. *KZZS*, 2:252–53; Ye, *Zhongguo renmin jiefangjun di 60 jun*, 227–28.

118. Yang, *Zai Zhiyuanjun silingbu*, 140–41.

119. Yan, *Wei Jie gushi*, 146–47; Mossman, *Ebb and Flow*, 478–79.

120. Yan, *Wei Jie gushi*, 147.

121. He Rui in "Andeshe," 1:131; He Rui interview, Jan. 16, 2013.

122. *KZZS*, 2:261–62; Yan, *Wei Jie gushi*, 148–50; *Lishi de huiyin*, 272–75.

123. Appleman, *Ridgway Duels for Korea*, 551; Xu, *Cuojue*, 116.

124. Jiang Ruipu interview, June 24, 2014; *Lishi de huiyin*, 304–5; Yan Minfu, Du Gang, and Xue Shanwa in "Andeshe," 1:39, 57, 61, 92.

125. *Lishi de huiyin*, 305.

126. Jiang Ruipu interview, June 24, 2015.

127. *KZZS*, 2:262; Yan, *Wei Jie gushi*, 151; *Lishi de huiyin*, 272, 275–76.

128. Yang, *Zai Zhiyuanjun silingbu*, 149; Hong, *Kangmei yuanchao*, 165.

129. Wei Jie, interviewed by Wu Jinfeng, May 24, 1984, in "Andeshe," 1:28; Cai Derong in "Andeshe," 1:52; *Lishi de huiyin*, 322–23; Wen, *Wen Xiaocun zizhuan*, 110.

130. *Lishi de huiyin*, 272, 276.

131. *KZZS*, 2:262–63; Yan, *Wei Jie gushi*, 151–52; *Lishi de huiyin*, 272, 275–76, 322–24.

132. Yang, *Zai Zhiyuanjun silingbu*, 149–50; Wu Chengde, interviewed by Wu Jinfeng, May 24, 1984, in "Andeshe," 1:25–27.

133. Du Gang, Zhang Shi'an, and Tian Fangbao in "Andeshe," 1:39, 115, 120.

134. *Lishi de huiyin*, 322–24; "Andeshe," 1:32, 43, 100.

135. *KZZS*, 2:262–63; *Lishi de huiyin*, 322–24; Guo Zhaolin in "Andeshe," 1:32.

136. Wu Chengde, Zhang Chengyuan, and Xue Shanwa in "Andeshe," 1:24, 54, 92.

137. Wu Jingfeng and Hao Mingchang in "Andeshe," 1:6, 83.

138. Cai Derong in "Andeshe," 1:53; *Lishi de huiyin*, 324–25.

139. Zhao Zuoduan and Du Gang in "Andeshe," 1:36–39; Zhao, ATIS KG 537, Sept. 11, 1951.

140. Liu Pushan in "Andeshe," 1:97.

141. Li Zhenhuai and Qiao Shouyi in "Andeshe," 1:80, 117.

142. Chen Yuanlai in "Andeshe," 1:117–18.

143. Li Shaoliang in "Andeshe," 1:99.

144. Jiang Ruipu in "Andeshe," 1:120; Jiang interview, June 24, 2014.

145. Jiang Ruipu, ATIS KT 546, June 1, 1951.

146. Ma Furui (Qungen) in *FFTL*, 242–45; Guo Zhaolin, ATIS KT 545, June 1, 1951.

147. Zhao Yingkui interview, Dec. 21, 30, 2012.

148. Zhang, *Wo de Chaoxian zhanzheng*, 23–24.

149. Cai in Bai and Xu, *Fengyan rensheng*, 1:356; Cai, ATIS KG 837, Nov. 5, 1951.

150. Appleman, *Ridgway Duels for Korea*, 542, 545.

151. Zhang Qize and Chai Wanfu in "Andeshe," 1:121–22; Yang, ATIS KT 517, May 29, 1951.

152. Du, *Zai Zhiyuanjun zongbu*, 217.

153. Zhang, *Kaoyan*, 25; Wang, *Shujuan renfeng*, 81.

154. Liu, *Liuxue dao tianming*, 225. Liu Lang's prisoner ID number, 710608, matches Liu Ruyu's. Liu Ruyu, ATIS KG 608, Sept. 20, 1951.

155. Yu Rongfu interview, Jan. 2, 2013; Yu, ATIS KG 169, July 30, 1951.

156. Li Zhiyuan in "Andeshe," 1:113.

157. Wen, ATIS KG 834, Nov. 3, 1951.

158. Gao, *Hanzhan yiwang*, 148–53; Gao, ATIS KG 402, Sept. 3, 1951.

159. Liu, *Liuxue dao tianming*, 66; Huang, *Wo zai 38 duxian de huiyi*, 80; Zheng Zheng'an interview, Apr. 26, 2010; Bradbury et al., *Mass Behavior*, 52–53.

160. Yan Tianzhi interview, May 5, 2010.

161. Zhao Yingkui interview, Dec. 21, 30, 2012.

162. Guo Shigao interview, Mar. 1, 2010.

163. Yu Dehai interview, Jan. 24, 2014.

164. *FRUS 1951*, 7:792.

165. Liu, *Liuxue dao tianming*, 225.

166. Wang, *Peng Dehuai nianpu*, 501–3.

167. Peng, *Peng Dehuai zishu*, 262.

168. Wang, *Peng Dehuai nianpu*, 504.

169. Xu, *Cuojue*, 184.

170. Zhang and Gao, *Chongwei*, 132.

171. *KZZS*, 2:263.

172. Wang, *Peng Dehuai nianpu*, 503–4.

173. Ibid., 506.

174. *Mao Zedong nianpu (1949–76)*, 1:350–51.

175. Hong, *Kangmei yuanchao*, 159.

176. *KZZS*, 2:219, 241, 272.

177. Appleman, *Ridgway Duels for Korea*, 549–51.

178. Du, *Zai Zhiyuanjun zongbu*, 186.

179. Hong, *Kangmei yuanchao*, 166; Yang, *Zai Zhiyuanjun silingbu*, 152.

180. Appleman, *Ridgway Duels for Korea*, 551.

181. "POW Population by Month," see Appendix, 391.

182. Matsushita, ATIS KT 258, May 27, 1951. For Matsushita's life after his capture, see Morris-Suzuki, "Prisoner Number 600,001." Pyongchang was the site of the 2018 Winter Olympics.

183. Tao Shanpeng, ATIS KG 0415, undated.

184. Wang Yingchang, ATIS KG 781, Oct. 20, 1951.

185. Wen Qingyun, KT 3402, June 23, 1952; Wen, *Wen Xiaocun zizhuan*, 115; Wu Chengde in "Andeshe," 2:56.

186. US embassy to Acheson, Oct. 17, 1952, 695A.0024, RG 59, NA.

187. Wu Chengde, ATIS KT 3680, Sept. 2, 1952.

188. US embassy to Acheson, Nov. 13, 1952, Box 3026, 695A.0024, RG 59, NA.

189. Zhang, *Kaoyan*, 41; 0001671500050087w, TWGFB.

190. US embassy to Acheson, Nov. 13, 1952, 695A.0024, RG 59, NA. Dean hid for thirty-five days before he was captured.

CHAPTER 8: CIVIL WAR IN THE POW CAMPS

1. Yu Qingde in "Andeshe," 2:185; Fang Xiangqian interview, Apr. 19, 2014; Yu, *Eyun*, 96, 99–100.

2. Sun Zhenguan in Zhang, *Kaoyan*, 52, and in "Andeshe," 2:1.

3. Sun's "united front" skills were acknowledged by friends and foes alike (*FFDS*, 71).

4. Sun Zhenguan in "Andeshe," 2:1, and in Zhang, *Kaoyan*, 49.

5. Sun in Zhang, *Kaoyan*, 46–52, and in "Andeshe," 2:1. Sun was interrogated by Wu in both ATIS 3613, Feb. 15, 1951, and ATIS 4773, Feb. 25, 1951.

6. Fang Xiangqian interview, Apr. 19, 2014.

7. Sun in "Andeshe," 2:2, and in *Kaoyan*, 53; Fang Xianqian interview, Apr. 19, 2014.

8. Yu, *Eyun*, 100.

9. Ibid., 103.

10. Ibid., 103–4; Wang Zhaojun, ATIS KT 275, Apr. 25, 1951; Liu Guang, ATIS KT 240, Apr. 23, 1951.

11. Yu, *Eyun*, 103–4.

12. *FFDS*, 84–85.

13. Chang, "Zhang Yifu's Oral History Records," 141; Tao interview, Jan. 22, 2015.

14. Sun in "Andeshe," 2:2, and in Zhang, *Kaoyan*, 53.

15. "POW Population by Month," see Appendix, 391.

16. Bradbury et al., *Mass Behavior*, 256.

17. Sun in "Andeshe," 2:2, and in Zhang, *Kaoyan*, 53.

18. Yu, *Eyun*, 122; Sun in "Andeshe," 2:2.

19. Yang interview, Jan. 25, 2014; *FFDS*, 19–20, 86–87.

20. Sun in "Andeshe," 2:2.

21. Yu, *Eyun*, 124–26.

22. Ibid., 126–27; Sun in "Andeshe," 2:2–3.

23. Unless otherwise noted, the details in the next four paragraphs are from Zhang, *Wo de Chaoxian zhanzheng*, 25–30.

24. Zhang Zeshi, email correspondence with the author, June 4, 2008.

25. Zhang, *Wo de Chaoxian zhanzheng*, 30; Jiang Ruipu, interview, June 24, 2014. Zhang had changed into a clean uniform after his capture.

26. Zhang, *Wo de Chaoxian zhanzheng*, 32.

27. Huang, *Wo zai 38 du xian*, 64–70, 157; Huang interview, July 3, 2010. After the war, both Huang and Lu became journalists. Huang later became the head of the Central News Agency; Lu joined the foreign service and served as Taiwan's last ambassador to South Africa from 1990 to 1996.

28. Zhang, *Wo de Chaoxian zhanzheng*, 33–34.

29. Wang Tielong interview, Apr. 18, 2014.

30. Tao interview, Jan. 22, 2015.

31. Gao in "Andeshe," 2:187.

32. Zhang, *Wo de Chaoxian zhanzheng*, 37.

33. Gao, *Hanzhan yiwang*, 152.

34. Cai, in Bai and Xu, *Fengyan rensheng*, 1:357.

35. Cao You, ATIS no. 3701, Feb. 22, 1951.

36. Zhang, *Wo de Chaoxian zhanzheng*, 48; Yu, *Eyun*, 109–10.

37. Yu, *Eyun*, 107–8.

38. Gao, *Kongzhan*, 242; Yang Yuhua, ATIS KT 1376, Aug. 28, 1951.

39. Confession by recaptured prisoner-agent Luo Baorong, in Yu, *Eyun*, 113.

40. Ibid., 113–14.

41. Hallim University Asia Culture Institute, *Han'guk*, 3:316–17.

42. Yu, *Eyun*, 105.

43. US Army, *Handling*, 12–14; Muccio to Acheson, Feb. 2, 1952, 695A.0024, RG 59, NA; Bradbury et al., *Mass Behavior*, 256; *FFDS*, 25–27.

44. US Army, *Handling*, 14, 19.

45. Xie, "Zuinie," 58; Lin Mocong interview, Dec. 11–12, 2011.

46. *FRUS 1952–1954*, 15:98–99.

47. Ibid.

48. *FFDS*, 87; Zhang, *Kaoyan*, 113; Ma Furui in *FFTL*, 252.

49. "Beggars' Island," *Time*, Jan. 28, 1952.

50. Zhang, *Kaoyan*, 4–5.

51. Gao, *Hanzhan yiwang*, 157–58; Ma Furui in *FFTL*, 252.

52. Red Cross Society of China, *Atrocities of the U.S. Armed Forces*, 10; Xie, "Zuinie," 67.

53. Red Cross Society of China, *Atrocities of the U.S. Armed Forces*, 11; Xie, "Zuinie," 67.

54. Red Cross Society of China, *Atrocities of the U.S. Armed Forces*, 12.

55. Meng Ming interview, Jan. 1–2, 2013.

56. Red Cross Society of China, *Atrocities of the U.S. Armed Forces*, 12; Xie, "Zuinie," 58; Wu Chunsheng interview, Aug. 11–12, 2011.

57. *FFDS*, 28.

58. Sun in "Andeshe," 2:3; Liu Guang in "Andeshe," 2:11; *FFDS*, 29, 65.

59. Yu, *Eyun*, 163–65; Meng Ming interview, Jan. 1–2, 2013; *FFDS*, 65–67; Sun in "Andeshe," 2:4.

60. "Dashiji," 2.

61. US Army, *Handling*, 15–16; "Dashiji," 3; Zhao in Zhang, *Kaoyan*, 179–80.

62. *FFDS*, 26–27, 52–53.

63. "Dashiji," 4; Zhao in Zhang, *Kaoyan*, 181–87; Zhao Zuoduan and Li Ziying in "Andeshe," 2:19, 63; Zhao, ATIS KG 537, Sept. 11, 1951.

64. Ma Furui in *FFTL*, 250.

65. Yang interview, Jan. 25, 2014.

66. "Dashiji," 6.

67. Gao Wenjun and Xiao Lixing in *FFTL*, 305, 408–10, 428.

68. Bradbury et al., *Mass Behavior*, 256, 329.

69. White, *Captives of Korea*, 139.

70. Wu Chunsheng in Zhang, *Kaoyan*, 125–27.

71. Ibid., 133–34; Yu, *Eyun*, 153–54. For the most authoritative and up-to-date study of paoge, see Chapter 10 of Wang Di's *Violence and Order on the Chengdu Plain: The Story of a Secret Brotherhood in Rural China, 1939–1949*.

72. Guo Zhaolin, ATIS KT 545, June 1, 1951.

73. Guo in "Andeshe," 2:22.

74. Wu Chunsheng interview, Aug. 11–12, 2011.

75. US Army, *Handling*, 16–17; Benben, "Education of Prisoners of War on Koje Island, Korea," 165; Xie, "Zuinie," 58–59; Fang Xiangqian interview, Apr. 19, 2014; Wu Chunsheng interview, Aug. 11–12, 2011; Yang Shuzhi interview, Jan. 27, 2014.

76. Benben, "Education of Prisoners of War on Koje Island, Korea," 167; Wu Chunsheng in Zhang, *Kaoyan*, 134–35; Wu Chunsheng interview, Aug. 11–12, 2011. On "bean elections," see Crook and Crook, *Revolution in a Chinese Village*, 94.

77. Wu Chunsheng in Zhang, *Kaoyan*, 134.

78. 94th MP Battalion daily journal, Jan. 11, 1952, PW Camp 1 Command Reports, Box 373, Entry 37042 (8238th AU), RG 338, NA.

79. "Excerpt from the Deposition of Special Agent Li Ta-an," in Red Cross Society of China, *Atrocities of the U.S. Armed Forces*, 66; Wu Chunsheng in Zhang, *Kaoyan*, 135; Wu interview, Aug. 11–12, 2011; Yu, *Eyun*, 156–58; "Dashiji," 4–5; Tao Shanpeng interview, Jan. 22, 2015.

80. "Dashiji," 5.

81. CIE UNC, "Interim Report on Progress of Educational Program for POWs," Jan. 10, 1952, Box 309, 383.6 TS, RG 319, NA; *FFDS*, 98.

82. Cheng interview, Aug. 14, 2014.

83. *FFDS*, 54–64.

84. Bradbury et al., *Mass Behavior*, 122.

85. Wang Tielong interview, Apr. 18, 2014; Wang Houci interview, Mar. 3, 2010.

86. Jin interview, Feb. 25, 2010; Huang interview, July 8, 2013.

87. *FFDS*, 54–55, 90–91.

88. Tao Shanpeng interview, Jan. 22, 2015; Li Yueming interview, Feb. 26, 2010.

89. Zhong interview, Sept. 13, 2007; Zhong, "Wuwei suiyue," in Bai and Xu, *Fengyan rensheng*, 3:239.

90. "Dashiji," 8.

91. Dai Yushu in "Andeshe," 2:176.

92. CIE weekly report, Oct. 12, 1951, Box 3, Entry 103, RG 554, NA.

93. Manhard, "Chinese POW Incident, Chejudo, Oct 1," in Muccio to Acheson, Oct. 20, 1952, 695A.0024, RG 59, NA.

94. Wu Chunsheng interview, Aug. 11–12, 2011.

95. Ibid.

96. Ibid.

97. Wu in Zhang, *Kaoyan*, 317–18; Bradbury et al., *Mass Behavior*, 262.

98. CIE weekly report, Dec. 28, 1951, Box 3, Entry 103, RG 554, NA.

99. Zhang, *Kaoyan*, 152–57; PW Camp 1 Command Report, Nov 1951, Box 374, 8238th Unit, RG 338, NA; CIE weekly report, Nov. 9, 1951, Box 3, Entry 103, RG 554, NA.

100. Chen Zhinong interview, Apr. 17, 2014.

101. Zhang, *Kaoyan*, 159.

102. Tang in Zhang, *Kaoyan*, 171–72; Tang Yao, ATIS KT 187, May 27, 1951; Tang interview, May 26, 2010; "Dashiji," 14; Muccio to Acheson, Feb. 2, 1952, 695A.0024, RG 59, NA.

103. Gao Jie in "Andeshe," 2:191–92.

104. Yu, *Eyun*, 162.

105. *FRUS 1952–1954*, 15:99.

106. *FFDS*, 98; Red Cross Society of China, *Atrocities of the U.S. Armed Forces*, 14; Young to Johnson, May 22, 1952, 695A.0024, RG 59, NA.

107. State Department to ICRC, July 3, 1952, 695A.0024, RG 59, NA (underlining original).

108. US Army, *Handling*, 106–7.

109. CIE weekly report, Sept. 14, 1951, Box 3, Entry 103 (CI&E), RG 554, NA.

110. Ibid., Sept. 7, 1951. Original translation.

111. Benben, "Education of Prisoners of War on Koje Island, Korea," 160–64; *NYT*, Nov. 20, 1951.

112. Osborne memo, Aug. 14, 1951, Entry 103, RG 554, NA.

113. Ibid., Stout memo, Aug. 31, 1951.

114. Gao, *Hanzhan yiwang*, 161.

115. *FRUS 1952–1954*, 15:369.

116. CIE weekly report, Nov. 16, 1951, Box 3, Entry 103, RG 554, NA.

117. Bradbury et al., *Mass Behavior*, 259.

118. Boatner to the Adjutant General, Jan. 31, 1967, Box 2, Boatner Papers, Hoover Archives; White, *Captives of Korea*, 112.

119. Huang Tiancai interview, July 13, 2010.

120. Ma, "Hanzhan yu qianfu douzheng," 443.

121. Huang Tiancai interview, July 13, 2010.

122. *NYT*, Nov. 20, 1951.

123. CIE UNC, "Interim Report on Progress of Educational Program for POWs," Jan. 10, 1952, 23, Box 309, 383.6 TS, RG 319, NA.

124. Wang Dongyuan to Yeh, Jan. 08, 1952, 633.43-530946–530951, TWJSS.

125. *FRUS 1952–1954*, 15:99.

126. *FFDS*, 39.

127. Bradbury et al., *Mass Behavior*, xviii.

128. *FRUS 1952–1954*, 15:99.

129. Telegram, Muccio to Acheson, Feb. 2, 1952, 695A.0024, RG 59, NA. Rpt not: repeat not; auths: authorities.

130. Zhao Yingkui interview, Dec. 21, 2012; Luo Jiecao interview, Apr. 16, 2014.

131. *RMRB*, Dec. 8, 1953; Red Cross Society of China, *Atrocities of the U.S. Armed Forces*, 14–15, 26–27.

132. Tao interview, Jan. 22, 2015.

133. Muccio to Acheson, Feb. 2, 1952, 695A.0024, RG 59, NA. Bennett's rough guess that a quarter of the prisoners in Compounds 72 and 86 were hardcore anti-Communists was actually larger than Ambassador Wang's estimate of 3,000 made in January 1952.

134. Cai interview, Sept. 1, 2007.

135. Muccio, interview by Jerry N. Hess, Feb. 18, 1971, 101–2, TL.

CHAPTER 9: THE DEBATE OVER PRISONER REPATRIATION IN WASHINGTON, PANMUNJOM, AND TAIPEI

1. Chen, *Mao's China*, 97.

2. *FRUS 1951*, 7:368.

3. Ibid., 497.

4. Ridgway, *Soldier*, 219.

5. Acheson, *Present at the Creation*, 529.

6. Ibid., 532.

7. Stueck, *The Korean War*, 206–7; *FRUS 1951*, 7:1476–1503.

8. Stueck, *The Korean War*, 205.

9. Acheson, *Present at the Creation*, 533.

10. Telegram from Roshchin conveying message from Zhou to Soviet government, Dec. 07, 1950; telegram from Stalin to Mao, June 13, 1951; handwritten letter from Mao Zedong to Gao and Kim, June 13, 1951, *CWIHPB*, no. 6–7 (Winter 1995–1996): 52, 60–61.

11. *FRUS 1951*, 7:547.

12. "POW Population by Month," see Appendix, 391.

13. *FRUS 1951*, 7:598.

14. Ibid., 640.

15. Hermes, *Truce Tent*, 17.

16. Chai and Zhao, *Banmendian tanpan*, 127.

17. *KZZS*, 2:362; Joy, *How Communists Negotiate*, 12, 17; Joy, *Negotiating While Fighting*, 17–18.

18. Chai and Zhao, *Banmendian tanpan*, 124, 168.

19. *KZZS*, 2:361.

20. Fairbank, *Chinabound*, 271–72.

21. *FRUS 1950*, 7:1299.

22. "Harvard Graduate Acts as Red Envoy at Peace Talks," *Harvard Crimson*, Apr. 10, 1952; Chai and Zhao, *Banmendian tanpan*, 119.

23. Ji, *The Man on Mao's Right*, chaps. 11–12.

24. Mao to Filippov [Stalin]; Filippov to Mao, June 30, 1951, *CWIHPB*, no. 6–7 (Winter 1995–1996): 64–65.

25. Qiao, "Guanyu Chaoxian zhanzheng yu tingzhan tanpan," 29; Mao to Peng and Kim, July 2, 1951, *Mao Zedong nianpu (1949–1976)*, 1:367.

26. Chai and Zhao, *Banmendian tanpan*, 168.

27. Telegrams between Mao and Stalin, July 10–Aug. 20, 1951, *CZED*, 1 & 2:860–983. Mao regularly made his replies to Li at 3:00 or 4:00 a.m. See *Mao Zedong nianpu (1949–1976)*, 1:367, 370, 372–75, 378–80, and passim.

28. Qiao, "Guanyu Chaoxian zhanzheng yu tingzhan tanpan," 32.

29. Hermes, *Truce Tent*, 22, 31; Janisch and Palumbo, "The House Armed Services Committee National Defense Specialists," 47. Captain Bertrand Brinley of the UNC HQ described Wu as "the only constant link of understanding" between the UNC and the CPV for twenty-five months, in *Life*, Aug. 31, 1953, 9.

30. Millett, *The War for Korea*, 461–62. Underwood's grandfather Horace G. Underwood founded a school that became Yonsei University.

31. Chai and Zhao, *Banmendian tanpan*, 132.

32. Li, Millett, and Yu, *Mao's Generals*, 194–95, 260n13–14.

33. Guxiweng, "Canjia Banmendian tanpan de Wu Tingqia," *Shijie ribao* [World Journal], Oct. 18, 2004, 2F; Gao, *Kongzhan*, 246.

34. Beisner, *Dean Acheson*, 174.

35. Chai and Zhao, *Banmendian tanpan*, 175–77.

36. Mao to Stalin, July 3, 1951, *CWIHPB*, no. 6–7 (Winter 1995–1996): 67.

37. Qiao, "Guanyu Chaoxian zhanzheng yu tingzhan tanpan," 29.

38. Burchett, *At the Barricades*, 161.

39. Chai and Zhao, *Banmendian tanpan*, 150–51.

40. *FRUS 1951*, 7:650.

41. *KZZJ*, 144.

42. *CZED*, 2:856.

43. *FRUS 1951*, 7:740.

44. Acheson, *Present at the Creation*, 535.

45. Ibid.

46. Hermes, *Truce Tent*, 36; Joy, *Negotiating While Fighting*, 22.

47. Chai and Zhao, *Banmendian tanpan*, 167.

48. Mao to Li, July 28, 1951, *Mao Zedong nianpu (1949–1976)*, 1:380.

49. Bernstein, "The Struggle over the Korean Armistice," 269.

50. Hermes, *Truce Tent*, 83.

51. *KZZJ*, 162; Wang, *Peng Dehuai nianpu*, 515.

52. Acheson, *Present at the Creation*, 535–36.

53. Stueck, *The Korean War*, 211.

54. Chai and Zhao, *Banmendian tanpan*, 131, 142, 152.
55. *KZZJ*, 181.
56. *FRUS 1951*, 7:1091–93, 1128–30.
57. Ibid., 1147.
58. Ibid., 1172, 1186n.
59. *CZED*, 3:1054, 1103, 1108.
60. Chai and Zhao, *Banmendian tanpan*, 179–83.
61. *Mao Zedong nianpu (1949–1976)*, 1:423–24. Nearly all telegrams were drafted by Zhou.
62. *FRUS 1951*, 7:1186–87; Joy, *How Communists Negotiate*, 148; Joy, *Negotiating While Fighting*, 108–15.
63. Hermes, *Truce Tent*, 139.
64. Ibid., 135; "Geneva Convention Relative to the Treatment of Prisoners of War," adopted on August 12, 1949, https://www.icrc.org/applic/ihl/ihl.nsf/Treaty.xsp?documentId=77CB9983BE01D004C12563CD002D6B3E&action=openDocument.
65. Joy, *How Communists Negotiate*, 153 (italics original).
66. *FRUS 1950*, 7:1530; *FRUS 1951*, 7:285–88, 598–600.
67. *FRUS 1951*, 7:596, 618.
68. Ibid., 1422.
69. Chai and Zhao, *Banmendian tanpan*, 166.
70. *FRUS 1951*, 7:598–600.
71. Ibid.
72. Hermes, *Truce Tent*, 136.
73. Bernstein, "The Struggle over the Korean Armistice," 276; Foot, *A Substitute for Victory*, 87–88.
74. *FRUS 1951*, 7:792–93 (italics added).
75. Ibid., 857–58.
76. Bernstein, "The Struggle over the Korean Armistice," 277.
77. Gordon Gray, "Preliminary Report on the Situation with Respect to Repatriation of POWs," Oct. 19, 1951, CIA-RDP80R01731R003200010023-5; "Report on the Situation with Respect to Repatriation of POWs," Oct. 22, 1951, RDP80R01731R003200010024-4, CIA-FOIA.
78. *FRUS 1951*, 3:1312; Acheson, *Present at the Creation*, 576–78.
79. *FRUS 1951*, 7:1068–71.
80. Hermes, *Truce Tent*, 137.
81. Truman's daily appointments, TL; *FRUS 1951*, 7:1073. Truman's belief that repatriated prisoners would be "done away with" was informed by the Allies' forcible repatriation of 5.2 million Soviet citizens after World War II. See Elliott, *Pawns of Yalta*; Applebaum, *Gulag*, 435–38.
82. Truman, *Memoirs*, 460.
83. Stueck, *The Korean War*, 264; Jager, *Brothers at War*, 203.
84. *FRUS 1951*, 7:1073.
85. Truman's travel log, Nov. 8–Dec. 9, 1951, TL; *FRUS 1951*, 7:1276–81.
86. Hermes, *Truce Tent*, 138.
87. *FRUS 1951*, 7:1168–71, 1184n1, 1189.
88. Ibid., 1197–98.
89. Ibid., 1224–27.
90. Ibid., 1244.
91. Ibid., 1276–78.
92. Truman's daily appointments, TL; *FRUS 1951*, 7:1290–96.

93. *FRUS 1951*, 7:1276, 1296.

94. Hermes, *Truce Tent*, 139.

95. Joy, *Negotiating While Fighting*, 115–16; *FRUS 1951*, 7:1311.

96. *FRUS 1951*, 7:1316–17.

97. Ibid., 1340–41. Curiously, Truman's daily appointments show no meeting with Acheson or Collins on Saturday, December 15, TL.

98. Joy, *Negotiating While Fighting*, 122; *FRUS 1951*, 7:1330.

99. Joy, *Negotiating While Fighting*, 126.

100. Ibid., 132–37; *FRUS 1951*, 7:1366–72.

101. Joy, *Negotiating While Fighting*, 138.

102. *FRUS 1951*, 7:1380.

103. Joy, *Negotiating While Fighting*, 136–37; *FRUS 1951*, 7:1366–72, 1380.

104. *FGSL*, 1:172–73; Yeh statement, 633.43-530944, TWJSS.

105. CKSD, Dec. 21, 1951.

106. *KZZS*, 3:148; Hermes, *Truce Tent*, 141–43; Joy, *How Communists Negotiate*, 104, 107–8; Joy, *Negotiating While Fighting*, 138, 151–52, 155; *FRUS 1951*, 7:1434.

107. *FRUS 1951*, 7:1422.

108. Ibid., 1401–73.

109. Ibid., 1423–25.

110. Joy, *Negotiating While Fighting*, 174–79.

111. Ibid., 179–82, 199; Hermes, *Truce Tent*, 144.

112. Joy, *Negotiating While Fighting*, 191.

113. Transcript of proceedings, Jan. 12, 1952, in Sin, *Nam-Pukhan kwan'gye saryojip*, 5:532.

114. Acheson, "Memorandum of Conversation at British Embassy, Jan. 6, 1952," Jan. 7, 1952, Acheson Papers, TL.

115. Mao to Stalin, Jan. 31, 1952, History and Public Policy Program Digital Archive, APRF, f. 45, op. 1, d. 342, ll, 73–77, http://digitalarchive.wilsoncenter.org/document/113020.

116. *FRUS 1952–1954*, 15:18.

117. Ibid., 22, 25 (italics added).

118. Ibid., 27.

119. Hermes, *Truce Tent*, 147; Bernstein, "The Struggle over the Korean Armistice," 279.

120. *FRUS 1952–1954*, 15:32–33; Stueck, *The Korean War*, 259.

121. Johnson, *The Right Hand of Power*, 133; Johnson oral history, 71–72, TL; Bohlen, *Witness to History*, 300.

122. Stelle to Nitze, Jan. 24, 28, 1952, in National Defense Force History Research Institute, *Records of the Policy Planning Staff of the Department of State*, 1–6. The US Army Observation Group (the Dixie Mission) was the US military intelligence and liaison unit stationed in Yan'an, the Communist headquarters, from July 1944 to March 1947. Captain Stelle, who was born and educated in Beijing, believed the Communists "were outstripping" the Nationalists in fighting Japan—which was inaccurate. See Carter, *Mission to Yenan: American Liaison with the Chinese Communists*, 33; Carter, "Mission to Yenan: The OSS and the Dixie Mission," 312.

123. Marshall to Nitze, Jan. 28, 1952, in National Defense Force History Research Institute, *Records of the Policy Planning Staff*, 11; Beisner, *Dean Acheson*, 424–26.

124. Acheson, *Present at the Creation*, 653.

125. Joy, *How Communists Negotiate*, 152.

126. Beisner, *Dean Acheson*, 438.

127. *FRUS 1952–1954*, 15:32–34.

128. Ibid., 35–37 (italics added).

129. Johnson, *The Right Hand of Power*, 135; Bohlen, *Witness to History*, 300; *FRUS 1952–1954*, 15:41–42.

130. *FRUS 1952–1954*, 15:43–45; Truman's daily appointments, Feb. 8, 1952, TL.

131. *FRUS 1952–1954*, 15:44–45.

132. Ibid., 45, 76.

133. Hermes, *Truce Tent*, 169; Bernstein, "The Struggle over the Korean Armistice," 275n40.

134. *FRUS 1952–1954*, 15:113.

135. Muccio to Acheson, Nov. 12, 1951, 695A.0024, RG 59, NA.

136. *FRUS 1952–1954*, 15:77–78; Johnson oral history, 76–77, TL; Johnson, *The Right Hand of Power*, 136–37; Hermes, *Truce Tent*, 239.

137. Johnson, *The Right Hand of Power*, 136–37.

138. Joy, "Discussions held 18 Feb 1952 at Munsan-ni," Joy Papers; *FRUS 1952–1954*, 15:78.

139. *FRUS 1952–1954*, 15:58–59; Johnson, *The Right Hand of Power*, 136–37; Joy, "Discussions held 18 Feb 1952 at Munsan-ni," Joy Papers; Truman's daily appointments, TL.

140. *FRUS 1952–1954*, 15:58–59; Johnson, *The Right Hand of Power*, 136–37.

141. Joy, "Discussions held 18 February 1952 at Munsan-ni," Joy Papers; *FRUS 1952–1954*, 15:78.

142. *FGSL*, 1:208–10.

143. *FRUS 1952–1954*, 15:66–67.

144. Truman's daily appointments, TL; Acheson, *Present at the Creation*, 610, 623; *FRUS 1952–1954*, 15:68–71.

145. Muccio to Johnson, Feb. 27, 1952, *FRUS 1952–1954*, 15:64–66.

146. Lai Mingtang to Chiang, July 7, 1951, 00041598000010004w, TWGFB.

147. Zhou Zhirou to Chiang, Feb. 1, 1952, 00041598000040023w, TWGFB.

148. Wang Dongyuan to Taipei, Jan. 23, 1952, 633.43-530882, TWJSS.

149. Chu Songqiu to Chiang Ching-kuo, June 29, 1951, 005-010100-00053-039, TWGSG.

150. Zhou Zhirou to Chiang, Aug. 21, 1951, 00041598000100011w, TWGFB.

151. Wang Dongyuan to Ye Gongchao, Nov. 11, 1951, 633.43-530890, TWJSS.

152. CKSD, Oct. 28, 1951. Yin Liangwen was most likely Yin Ruliang's pseudonym.

153. Zhou Zhirou to Chiang, Aug. 21, 1951, 00041598000100012w, TWGFB.

154. He Shili to Yeh, Nov. 23, 1951, 633.43-530905–6, TWJSS.

155. Wang Dongyuan to Yeh, Nov. 6, 1951, 633.43-530891, TWJSS.

156. Muccio to Acheson, Nov. 12, 1951, 695A.0024, RG 59, NA.

157. Wu, "Banmendian tanpan wo zaichang"; Chi-Wu Wu obituary, Restland, accessed Aug. 16, 2017, http://www.restlandfuneralhome.com/obituaries/Chi-Wu-Wu/#!/Obituary. A World War II veteran who served under Stilwell, Wu received training at the US Armor School in Fort Knox from 1947 to 1948. He eventually rose to the post of the Nationalist deputy chief of staff in the 1970s.

158. Stueck finds it "difficult to condone" their failures; see *The Korean War*, 263.

159. On Truman's tendency for "premature cognitive closure," see Deborah W. Larson, *Origins of Containment: A Psychological Explanation* (Princeton, NJ: Princeton University Press, 1985), 146–47. Henry Wallace noted, "Everything [Truman] said was decisive. It almost seemed as though he was eager to decide in advance of thinking" (cited in Foot, *A Substitute for Victory*, 89, 234n30).

160. Bernstein, "The Struggle over the Korean Armistice," 282.

CHAPTER 10: SCREENING

1. *FRUS 1952–1954*, 15:103–4.

2. Mao to Stalin, Feb. 8, 1952, *CWIHPB*, no. 6–7 (Winter 1995–1996): 75; *CZED*, 3:1152–53.

3. Shen, "Sino-North Korean Conflict," 19.

4. Hermes, *Truce Tent*, 168; Vishinsky to Molotov, July 7, 1952, *CZED*, 3:1183; Du, *Zai Zhiyuanjun zongbu*, 333.

5. Joy, *Negotiating While Fighting*, 343; Hermes, *Truce Tent*, 169; *FRUS 1952–1954*, 15:136.

6. Hermes, *Truce Tent*, 169.

7. Joy, *Negotiating While Fighting*, 346–47.

8. Joy, *Negotiating While Fighting*, 349–50.

9. *FRUS 1952–1954*, 15:27, 136–38.

10. Hermes, *Truce Tent*, 169; *FRUS 1952–1954*, 15:160–64.

11. *FRUS 1952–1954*, 15:160–64.

12. Ibid., 127; Tao Shanpeng interview, Jan. 22, 2015.

13. Wang, *Peng Dehuai nianpu*, 526.

14. Foot, *A Substitute for Victory*, 130.

15. "Dashiji," 19.

16. Benben, "Education of Prisoners of War on Koje Island, Korea," 171.

17. Tao interview, Jan. 22, 2015; Li interview, June 27, 2014; Lin interview, Dec. 11–12, 2011; Xie, "Zuinie," 71; Jiang interview, June 24, 2014; *FRUS 1952–1954*, 15:360.

18. Lin Mocong interview, Dec. 11–12, 2011.

19. Tao interview, Jan. 22, 2015; *FFDS*, 59–64.

20. Li Jintu in "Andeshe," 2:210. Li chose repatriation.

21. Wu Yongfang, Ren Yangjie, Zhang Guanghua, and Chen Ronggui in "Andeshe," 2:196, 205–10. They all chose repatriation.

22. "Report of Proceedings by Board of Officers," Cases 120 and 121, Entry 224, RG 554, NA (hereafter "Proceedings").

23. *RMRB*, Dec. 8, 1953.

24. Tao interview, Jan. 22, 2015.

25. Guo Naijian in "Andeshe," 2:213.

26. *FRUS 1952–1954*, 15:160.

27. White, *Captives of Korea*, 184–87.

28. *FRUS 1952–1954*, 15:160–62.

29. Xie, "Zuinie," 72–72.

30. Fang interview, Apr. 19, 2014.

31. Benben, "Education of Prisoners of War on Koje Island, Korea," 171.

32. White, *Captives of Korea*, 186–87.

33. Luo interview, Apr. 16, 2014.

34. Guo Naijian in "Andeshe," 2:213.

35. Tao Shanpeng interview, Jan. 22, 2015.

36. Ibid.; Wang Houci interview, Mar. 3, 2010.

37. Li Mingquan in "Andeshe," 2: 195.

38. Wang, *Shujuan renfeng*, 102.

39. Huang Shaorong statement, Yang Wenhua files, Box 11, Entry 1005, RG 389, NA.

40. Jiang Ruipu interview, June 24, 2014.

41. Wang, *Shujuan renfeng*, 100; Jiang Ruipu interview, June 24, 2014.

42. Cai Pingsheng interview, Oct. 7, 2009.

43. Zhao Yingkui interview, Dec. 21, 2012.
44. Chang, "Zhang Yifu's Oral History Records," 143–44.
45. Joy, *Negotiating While Fighting*, 355. For more on Kenneth Wu, see Chapter 9.
46. Cai Pingsheng interview, Oct. 7, 2009; Fu Tietao, ATIS 386, Aug. 24, 1951.
47. *Lianhebao* (Taipei), Jan. 27, 1954.
48. *RMRB*, Dec. 8, 1953; Red Cross Society of China, *Atrocities of the U.S. Armed Forces*, 27.
49. Meng Ming interview, Jan. 2–3, 2013.
50. *FFDS*, 88, 126.
51. *Lianhebao* (Taipei), Jan. 27, 1954.
52. Zhang, *Kaoyan*, 331; Lin Xuebu, ATIS KT 633 & 665, June 25 and 28, 1951.
53. Ma, "Fangong, konggong, kongguo?," 133; Xiao Lixing in *FFTL*, 426; Meng Ming interview, Feb. 19, 2018.
54. Zhang, *Kaoyan*, 330–34.
55. Yu, *Eyun*, 267; *RMRB*, Dec. 8, 1953.
56. "Proceedings," Case 117.
57. Yang Shuzhi interview, Jan. 27, 2014.
58. Ibid.; Zhao Yingkui interview, Dec. 21, 2012; Zhang Zhenlong, ATIS KT 1545, 1554, Sept. 4 and 6, 1951; "Proceedings," Case 117; Yu, *Eyun*, 264.
59. Zhao Yingkui interview, Dec. 21, 2012.
60. Jiang Ruipu interview, June 24, 2014.
61. Cai Pingsheng interview, Oct. 7, 2009, Oct. 16, 2010.
62. Jiang Ruipu interview, June 24, 2014.
63. Postmortem, Case 136, Entry 224, RG 554, NA.
64. Liu Tonghe (alias) in *FFTL*, 329; Zhang, *Kaoyan*, 336–37; Yu, *Eyun*, 273; Tao Shanpeng interview, Jan. 22, 2015.
65. Yu, *Eyun*, 266–67.
66. Cases 117 and 136, Entry 224, RG 554, NA; Wu Zengwen interview, Aug. 20, 2011.
67. Muccio to Acheson, June 28, 1952, 695A.0024, RG 59, NA.
68. Yang Shuzhi interview, Jan. 27, 2014.
69. Benben, "Education of Prisoners of War on Koje Island, Korea," 171. However, Benben's claim that "very little trouble occurred in the two Chinese compounds" is false, contradicted by the account of UNC interpreters Wu and May.
70. Jiang Ruipu interview, June 24, 2014; Wu Zengwen interview, Aug. 20, 2011; Zhao Yingkui, interview, Dec. 21, 2012.
71. Wang, *Shujuan renfeng*, 103.
72. Joy, *Negotiating While Fighting*, 355.
73. Zhao Yingkui interview, Dec. 21, 2012.
74. Li Dezhi interview, June 27, 2014.
75. Cai Pingsheng interview, Oct. 7, 2009.
76. Wu Zengwen interview, Aug. 20, 2011; Wu in "Andeshe," 2:160.
77. Wang, *Shujuan renfeng*, 103–4.
78. Jiang Ruipu interview, June 24, 2014; Xu Gongdu in "Andeshe," 2:179.
79. Gao Jie in "Andeshe," 2:188.
80. He, *Zhongcheng*, 37–39.
81. *FRUS 1952–1954*, 15:143–44.
82. Ibid., 163.
83. Joy, *Negotiating While Fighting*, 365.
84. *FGSL*, 1:233–34.

85. Joy, *Negotiating While Fighting*, 355. Here the term "indoctrination" means a period of reeducation to free the prisoners of the fear instilled by the anti-Communist leaders in these compounds.

86. Ibid.

87. *FRUS 1952–1954*, 15:145–52.

88. Ibid., 157.

89. Joy, *Negotiating While Fighting*, 361. NKPA: North Korean People's Army.

90. Tao Shanpeng interview, Jan. 22, 2015; Benben, "Education of Prisoners of War on Koje Island, Korea," 171.

91. *FFDS*, 105–6.

92. *RMRB*, Dec. 8, 1953; Wang Dianwu and Liu Sandai in "Andeshe," 2:147, 159,

93. Wang Guanhu interview, June 29, 2014; Zhao Yingkui interview, Dec. 21, 2012.

94. *FRUS 1952–1954*, 15:149.

95. Hermes, *Truce Tent*, 171–72.

96. Bernstein, "The Struggle over the Korean Armistice," 273–74.

97. CKSD, Apr. 9–12, 1952.

98. Foot, *A Substitute for Victory*, 99–100.

99. Woolley and Peters, *American Presidency Project*, http://www.presidency.ucsb.edu/ws/?pid=14108.

100. *FRUS 1952–1954*, 15:192–3.

101. Sargeant to Acheson, May 20, 1952, 695A.0024, RG 59, NA.

102. *FRUS 1952–1954*, 15:257–9.

103. Joy, *Negotiating While Fighting*, 436–37; Hermes, *Truce Tent*, 265.

104. CKSD, Apr. 30, 1952.

105. For the most up-to-date study of the germ warfare controversy, see Jager, *Brothers at War*, 242–57.

106. Truman, *Off The Record*, 250–51.

107. CKSD, July 28, 1951.

108. Ibid., May 22, 1952.

109. Ibid., May 23, 1952.

110. Du, *Zai Zhiyuanjun zongbu*, 350; Hermes, *Truce Tent*, 276.

111. Du, *Zai Zhiyuanjun zongbu*, 349–50.

112. Shen, "Sino–North Korean Conflict," 19–21; *CZED*, 3:1186.

113. Stalin-Zhou conversation, Aug. 20, 1952, *CWIHPB*, no. 6–7 (Winter 1995–1996): 12.

114. Ibid.

CHAPTER 11: GENERAL DODD'S KIDNAPPING AND GENERAL BOATNER'S CRACKDOWN

1. Zhang, *Kaoyan*, 199–201; "Dashiji," 23–24. The total membership reached 2,200 before the armistice. See He, *Zhongcheng*, 155.

2. Yu, *Eyun*, 326–27.

3. Ibid., 326.

4. Hermes, *Truce Tent*, 244–45.

5. Zhang, *Wo de Chaoxian zhanzheng*, 130–32.

6. Ibid., 136–37. Zhang's account, based on what he heard from his Korean comrades, offers more details than Hermes, *Truce Tent*, 244–45.

7. Zhang, *Wo de Chaoxian zhanzheng*, 132–42.

8. Ibid., 139–42; Ridgway, *Soldier*, 233.

9. Hermes, *Truce Tent*, 252.

10. Clark, *From the Danube to the Yalu*, 39.

11. Ibid., 36, 45.

12. Boatner, "Haydon's letters," July 1, 1952, Box 1, Boatner Papers, Hoover Archives.

13. Boatner to Johnson, Jan. 4, 1966, and Fairbank to Service, Sept. 9, 1971, both in Box 1, Boatner Papers, Hoover Archives.

14. *NYT*, Aug. 23 and Sept. 8, 1945.

15. "Asiatic mentality" is frequently evoked in Boatner's writings, e.g., Boatner to Johnson, Jan. 4, 1966.

16. Boatner, "Military Control of Riot and Koje-Do," circa 1971, Box 1, Boatner Papers.

17. Boatner, "Haydon's letters," July 1, 1952; Boatner to Johnson, Jan. 4, 1966; Boatner to DoA [Dept of the Army], "Comments on *Truce Tent and Fighting Fron*t," Jan. 31, 1967, Boxes 1 and 2, Boatner Papers, Enclosure. Boatner did not name Fitzgerald in this letter.

18. Boatner to Johnson, Jan. 4, 1966; Boatner to DoA [Dept of the Army], "Comments on *Truce Tent*."

19. Boatner to enclosure and compound commanders and their subordinates, June 21, 1952, Box 368, Entry 37042, RG 338, NA.

20. Boatner, "Military Control of Riot and Koje-Do," circa 1971; Boatner, "Comments on *Truce Tent*"; Boatner, "Haydon's letters," July 1, 1952.

21. Boatner, "Military Control of Riot and Koje-Do"; Boatner, "Comments on *Truce Tent*"; Boatner, "Haydon's letters," July 1, 1952.

22. Letter to the commanding general and "Report of Proceedings by Board of Officers," Case 106, Entry 224, RG 554, NA (hereafter "Proceedings").

23. Gao Jie interview by Lin.

24. Boatner to Tower, Feb. 4, 1970, Box 1, Boatner Papers; Boatner, "Comments on *Truce Tent*"; Boatner, "Military Control of Riot and Koje-Do."

25. "Dashiji," 30; Fehrenbach, *This Kind of War*, 408; Boatner, "Comments on *Truce Tent*"; Boatner to Tower, Feb. 4, 1970; Boatner to Johnson, Jan. 4, 1966. Boatner did not mention Wei and Gao by name; that he was referring to them can be inferred from Gao in "Andeshe," 1:7, and Gao Jie interview by Lin.

26. Boatner to Tower, Feb. 4, 1970; Fehrenbach, *This Kind of War*, 408.

27. "Trouble at Koje," *Time*, June 2, 1952.

28. Gao interview by Lin.

29. Boatner to Tower, Feb. 4, 1970; Boatner, "Comments on *Truce Tent*."

30. "Proceedings," Case 106, 3, 5, and Exhibit G; *RMRB*, Dec. 8, 1953; "Andeshe," 2:176.

31. "Proceedings," Case 106, 5.

32. Ibid., 8.

33. Boatner to Johnson, Jan. 4, 1966; Boatner, "Military Control of Riot and Koje-Do"; Fang Xiangqian interview, Apr. 19, 2014.

34. Boatner, "Military Control of Riot and Koje-Do"; Boatner, "Haydon's letters," July 1, 1952.

35. Clark, *From the Danube to the Yalu*, 227.

36. Korea Institute of Military History, *The Korean War*, 370.

37. Boatner, "Comments on *Truce Tent*"; Boatner, "Military Control of Riot and Koje-Do"; Boatner, "Haydon's letters," July 1, 1952.

38. Boatner, "Haydon's letters," July 1, 1952.

39. US Army, *Handling*, 35; Clark, *From the Danube to the Yalu*, 57, 65–66; Boria photo collection, MacArthur Archives.

40. "Trouble at Koje," *Time*, June 2, 1952; *Life*, May 26, 1952, 23.

41. Boatner, "Military Control of Riot and Koje-Do"; "Prisoners: Ticklish Job," *Time*, June 9, 1952; Boatner, "Comments on *Truce Tent*."

42. Boatner, "Haydon's letters," July 1, 1952.

43. Boria photo collection, MacArthur Archives.

44. *Life*, June 9, 1952, 35.

45. Ibid., 34.

46. Boatner, "Comments on *Truce Tent*"; Boatner, "Military Control of Riot and Koje-Do" (underlining original).

47. "Dashiji," 30; *NYT*, June 2, 1952, 3; Boatner, "Comments on *Truce Tent*"; Boatner, "Military Control of Riot and Koje-Do"; Fang Xiangqian interview, Apr. 19, 2014.

48. Hermes, *Truce Tent*, 259.

49. Boatner, "Military Control of Riot and Koje-Do."

50. *Life*, June 16, 1952, 34.

51. "Hands Up," *Time*, June 16, 1952.

52. The existence and operation of the North Korean Communist underground headquarters are recorded in Clark, *From the Danube to the Yalu*, 60–62, and corroborated by Zhang Zeshi, *Wo de Chaoxian zhanzheng*, 139.

53. Zhang, *Wo de Chaoxian zhanzheng*, 155.

54. Clark, *From the Danube to the Yalu*, 62.

55. Zhang, email to the author, Feb. 20, 2011.

56. Boatner, "Haydon's letters," July 1, 1952; Boatner, "Military Control of Riot and Koje-Do."

57. Boatner, "Haydon's letters," July 1, 1952, 2; Hermes, *Truce Tent*, 259.

58. Boatner, "Military Control of Riot and Koje-Do," 8.

59. *NYT*, June 10, 1952, 3.

60. Ibid., 1, 3.

61. *Los Angeles Times*, June 10, 1952, 1.

62. Thurman J. Nichols's memoirs, Aug. 2010, *Korean War Educator*, accessed Mar. 1, 2011, http://www.koreanwar-educator.org/memoirs/nichols_thurman/index.htm#Kojedo.

63. *NYT*, June 10, 1952, 3.

64. *Life*, June 23, 1952, 30.

65. Boatner, "Military Control of Riot and Koje-Do."

66. *Washington Post*, June 11, 1952, 1.

67. *Times* (London), June 11, 1952, 6. Xinhua claimed that "the US fired roughly 1,000 flame bombs" (*RMRB*, June 11, 1952, 1).

68. *NYT*, June 10, 1952, 3.

69. *Washington Post*, June 11, 1952, 1.

70. *Times* (London), June 11, 1952, 6.

71. *NYT*, June 10, 1952, 3.

72. *Life*, June 23, 1952, 30.

73. *NYT*, June 10, 1952, 3.

74. Zhang, *Wo de Chaoxian zhanzheng*, 156.

75. Ibid.

76. *Life*, June 23, 1952, 30.

77. Hermes, *Truce Tent*, 259.

78. *Life*, June 23, 1952, 30–31.

79. Hermes, *Truce Tent*, 259.

80. Ibid.
81. *Life*, June 23, 1952, 30.
82. Zhang Zeshi, email to the author, Feb. 22, 2011.
83. *Life*, June 23, 1952, 30.
84. Boatner, "Military Control of Riot and Koje-Do."
85. *Washington Post*, June 11, 1952.
86. US Army, *Handling*, 35.

CHAPTER 12: CHINA HANDS ON KOJE AND CHEJU

1. Clark, *From the Danube to the Yalu*, 65–66.
2. *NYT*, June 17, 1952, 4; "Dashiji," 31.
3. *NYT*, June 19, 1952, 4.
4. Boatner, "Haydon's letters," July 1, 1952, Boatner Papers, Hoover Archives.
5. Acheson to Muccio, June 5, 1952, 695A.0024, RG 59, NA.
6. Acheson to Muccio, June 12, 1952, and Muccio to Acheson, June 13, 1952, 695A.0024, RG 59, NA.
7. Muccio to Acheson, Tel. 1476, June 28, 1952, 695A.0024, RG 59, NA.
8. Muccio to Acheson, Tel. 1474, June 28, 1952, *FRUS 1952–1954*, 15:360–61.
9. Muccio to Acheson, June 29, 1952, 695A.0024, RG 59, NA.
10. Ibid.
11. Muccio to Acheson, July 5, 1952, *FRUS 1952–1954*, 15:379.
12. Ibid.
13. Muccio to Acheson, Tel. 19, July 2, 1952, 695A.0024, RG 59, NA.
14. Muccio to Acheson, July 5, 1952, *FRUS 1952–1954*, 15:379.
15. Muccio to Acheson, Tel. 18, July 2, 1952, *FRUS 1952–1954*, 15:369–70.
16. Ibid.
17. Ibid.
18. Muccio to Acheson, Tel. 20, July 2, 1952, 695A.0024, RG59, NA.
19. Zhao Yingkui interview, Dec. 21 and 30, 2012.
20. Zhang, *Kaoyan*, 4–5; Zhong Junhua interview, Oct. 17, 2009; "Dashiji," 34.
21. Muccio to Acheson, Tel. 18, July 2, 1952, *FRUS 1952–1954*, 15:370.
22. Manhard, "Chinese POW Incident, Chejudo, Oct 1," Oct. 20, 1952, and enclosed memo, July 5, 1952, 695A.0024, RG 59, NA (hereafter "Chejudo")
23. Boatner, "Haydon's letters," July 1, 1952.
24. Manhard, "Chejudo."
25. Manhard, interview by Marshall Green, Dec. 1, 1988, transcript, Association for Diplomatic Studies and Training Foreign Affairs Oral History Project, Library of Congress, http://hdl.loc.gov/loc.mss/mfdip.2004man01.
26. "Report of Proceedings by Board of Officers," Exhibit A, 7, Case 158, Entry (A1)224, RG 554, NA (hereafter "Proceedings," cases may vary).
27. "Proceedings," Case 154, 16.
28. Manhard, "Chejudo."
29. Huang, *Wo zai 38 du xian de huiyi*, 154.
30. Huang Tiancai interview, Oct. 8, 2010.
31. Zhang, email to the author, Mar. 21, 2011.
32. Zhang, *Wo de Chaoxian zhanzheng*, 168–69.
33. Boatner, "Prisoners of War: Have US Policies Protected Americans in Asia?," circa 1968, 19, Box 2, Boatner Papers, Hoover Archives.

34. *Life*, June 15, 1953, 132.

35. *Zhongyang ribao*, Sept. 3, 1953. *Zhongyang ribao* (Central Daily) was the Nationalists' equivalent of the *People's Daily*.

36. Huang interview, Oct. 8, 2010; Manhard, "Chejudo."

37. Chang, "Zhang Yifu's Oral History Records," 140.

38. Manhard, "Chejudo" (underlining original).

39. Manhard, "Reappraisal of POW Concept in Light of Korean War Experience," enclosed in memo to Dept of State, Feb. 2, 1953, 695A.0024, RG 59, NA.

40. Manhard, "Chejudo."

41. Ibid.

42. Zhao, ATIS KG 537, Sept. 11, 1951.

43. Zhang, *Kaoyan*, 180.

44. Zhao in "Andeshe," 2:20. He asserted, "I only told public information, nothing secret."

45. Manhard, "Chejudo."

46. Manhard to Briggs, "Recent developments in the UNC POW camps," June 16, 1953, 695A.0024, RG 59, NA; US Army, *Handling*, 23.

47. Zhang, *Wo de Chaoxian zhanzheng*, 139; White, *Captives of Korea*, 192–97.

48. *FFDS*, 111.

49. Zhang, *Kaoyan*, 191; "Dashiji," 31; *NYT*, June 17, 1952.

50. Zhang, *Kaoyan*, 191.

51. Muccio to Acheson, July 2, 1952, 695A.0024, RG 59, NA.

52. Ibid.

53. Zhong Junhua interview, Oct. 17, 2009. Similarly, according to interrogator-interpreter Huang Tiancai, it was quite possible that Nationalist agents assumed the identity of US-hired Taiwanese interrogator-interpreters or teachers, and infiltrated the camps. Huang interview, Oct. 8, 2010.

54. "Dashiji," 31.

55. Zhang, *Kaoyan*, 191.

56. Ibid., 192–93.

57. Manhard, "Chejudo."

58. Zhang, *Kaoyan*, 193–94.

59. Zhang, *Wo de Chaoxian zhanzheng*, 175–76.

60. Manhard, "Chejudo."

61. "Dashiji," 31–32.

62. *FFDS*, 111.

63. "Dashiji," 32.

64. "Proceedings," Case 158, Exhibit A, 7.

65. Ibid.

66. Ibid., Exhibit B.

67. Ibid., Exhibit A, 2.

68. Zhang, *Kaoyan*, 192–96.

69. Ibid., 213.

70. "Dashiji," 33.

71. Zhang, *Kaoyan*, 214.

72. "Dashiji," 33.

73. Zhong Junhua interview, Oct. 17, 2009.

74. Zhang, *Kaoyan*, 194.

75. "Dashiji," 33.

76. Gu Zesheng in "Andeshe," 2:16.
77. *NYT*, Aug. 5, 1952.
78. US Army, *Handling*, 38.
79. "Dashiji," 34: US Army, *Handling*, 43.
80. "Dashiji," 34; US Army, *Handling*, 43.
81. US Army, *Handling*, 42–45.
82. "Dashiji," 35; Zhang, *Kaoyan*, 195.
83. "Dashiji," 35.
84. Ibid., 34–35.
85. Ibid., 35–36.
86. Ibid., 36–37.
87. *NYT*, Sept. 1, 1952.
88. Ibid.
89. *RMRB*, Sept. 2, 1952.

CHAPTER 13: OCTOBER 1 MASSACRE ON CHEJU

1. *NYT*, Oct. 2, 1952.
2. Manhard, "Chinese POW Incident, Chejudo, Oct 1," in Muccio to Acheson, Oct. 20, 1952, 695A.0024, RG 59, NA.
3. *NYT*, Oct. 3, 1952; *RMRB*, Oct. 3, 1952.
4. Zhang, *Kaoyan*, 237.
5. Ibid., 195.
6. Fang Xiangqian interview, Apr. 19, 2014; Zhang, *Kaoyan*, 214.
7. Yu, *Eyun*, 371.
8. Cai Pingsheng interview, Aug. 6, 2007.
9. Yu, *Eyun*, 371.
10. "Dashiji," 38.
11. Boerem testimony, 22, in "Report of Proceedings by Board of Officers," Case 154, Entry 224, RG 554, NA (hereafter "Proceedings").
12. "Dashiji," 38.
13. Zhang, *Kaoyan*, 237.
14. Gu Zesheng in "Andeshe," 2:38.
15. Zhang, *Kaoyan*, 237.
16. Ibid.
17. Yu, *Eyun*, 380.
18. Gu in "Andeshe," 2:17.
19. Fang Xiangqian interview, Apr. 19, 2014; "Geneva Convention Relative to the Treatment of POWs."
20. Yu, *Eyun*, 373.
21. Chin testimony in "Proceedings," 6.
22. "Dashiji," 30.
23. Helderman testimony in "Proceedings," 40.
24. Manhard, "Chejudo."
25. "Death in Compound 7," *Time*, Oct. 13, 1952.
26. Du Gang in "Andeshe," 2:29; Zhang, *Kaoyan*, 237; Yu, *Eyun*, 372.
27. US Army, *Handling*, 46.
28. Ibid.; Vigil interview, Aug. 26–27, 2014, May 22, 2016.
29. Howard Schaeffer's letter to Patrick Vigil, Nov. 29, 1993, Vigil personal papers.

30. Yu, *Eyun*, 373; Zhang, *Kaoyan*, 238.
31. Yu, *Eyun*, 374.
32. Zhang, *Kaoyan*, 210–11.
33. Ibid., 212.
34. Yu cites Li Xi'er's report to the PLA headquarters upon his repatriation in 1953 (*Eyun*, 367). See also Li Xi'er in "Andeshe," 2:85.
35. Fang interview, Apr. 19, 2014.
36. Yu, *Eyun*, 353.
37. Lin Mocong telephone interview, Sept. 21, 2010.
38. US Army, *Handling*, 44.
39. Yu, *Eyun*, 354.
40. Ibid., 354–55.
41. Ibid., 375–76.
42. "Dashiji," 39; Yu, *Eyun*, 375–76; Wang Fusheng in "Andeshe," 2:272.
43. Boerem testimony in "Proceedings," 22.
44. Vigil interview, Aug. 26, 2014.
45. Fang interview, Apr. 19, 2014.
46. Du Gang and Wang Daoxi in "Andeshe," 2:29, 289.
47. Li Ziying in "Andeshe," 2:69.
48. Zhang, *Kaoyan*, 238.
49. Yu, *Eyun*, 380.
50. Gu Zesheng in "Andeshe," 2:16.
51. Boerem testimony in "Proceedings," 22.
52. Gu Zesheng in "Andeshe," 2:39.
53. Yu, *Eyun*, 381; Titus testimony in "Proceedings," 36.
54. Chin testimony in "Proceedings," 4.
55. Yu, *Eyun*, 381.
56. Boerem testimony in "Proceedings," 19.
57. Brooks testimony, 12, and Boerem testimony, 18–19, in "Proceedings."
58. Chin testimony, 4; Brooks testimony, 12; Boerem testimony, 18–19, in "Proceedings."
59. Zhang, *Kaoyan*, 239.
60. Vigil interview, Aug. 26–27, 2014, and May 22, 2016.
61. Boerem testimony in "Proceedings," 19.
62. Helderman testimony in "Proceedings," 37.
63. Lyons testimony, 58, and Fitzgerald testimony, 60 (italics added), in "Proceedings."
64. Brooks testimony, 12, and Boerem testimony, 19, in "Proceedings."
65. Zhao Guoxi in "Andeshe," 2: 276. Helderman testimony, 37; Brooks testimony, 12; Titus testimony, 34–35, all in "Proceedings."
66. Helderman testimony in "Proceedings," 38.
67. Lyons testimony in "Proceedings," 57.
68. Vigil interview, Aug. 26–27, 2014, and May 22, 2016.
69. Boerem testimony in "Proceedings," 21.
70. Brooks testimony in "Proceedings," Case 154, 16–17.
71. Manhard, "Chejudo."
72. Vigil interview, Aug. 26–27, 2014, and May 22, 2016.
73. Helderman testimony in "Proceedings," 38.
74. Lyons testimony, 58, and Hesse testimony, 44, in "Proceedings." 154.
75. *Los Angeles Times*, Oct. 2, 1952.

76. Findings of Fact, in "Proceedings," 100.
77. Zhang, *Kaoyan*, 240.
78. Certificate of the injured, Exhibit I-2, 3, in "Proceedings"; "Dashiji," 41.
79. Yang interview, Jan. 27–28, 2014.
80. Wang Liwen [Brooks's Chinese name], *Xinshengbao* (Taipei), Sept. 5, 1953.
81. Zhao Guoxi, ATIS KG 939, July 8, 1951; Certificate of the injured, Exhibit I-2, 3, in "Proceedings"; Zhao in "Andeshe," 2:275–77.
82. *NYT*, Oct. 3, 1952; *Los Angeles Times*, Oct. 3, 1952.
83. Manhard, "Chejudo."
84. Brooks testimony in "Proceedings," 16–17.
85. "Death in Compound 7," *Time*, Oct. 13, 1952.
86. Manhard, "Chejudo."
87. Boerem testimony in "Proceedings," Case 154, 20.
88. Judge Advocate's report, in "Proceedings," Case 154, 16–17.
89. "Proceedings," Case 154, 100–101.
90. Review, Dec. 17, 1952, in "Proceedings," Case 154, 1 (underlining original).
91. UNC GHQ to Herren, Dec. 1, 1952, Supplementary Proceedings, Case 154 (italics added).
92. Review, in "Proceedings," Case 154, Dec. 17, 1952.
93. *NYT*, Oct. 2, 1952, 2.
94. Zhang, *Kaoyan*, 241.
95. Manhard, "Chejudo."
96. Zhao in "Andeshe," 2:37.
97. Stalin-Zhou conversation, Aug. 20, 1952, *CWIHPB*, no. 6–7 (Winter 1995–1996): 12.
98. "Andeshe," 2:77.
99. Wang Liwen, *Xinshengbao* (Taipei), Sept. 5, 1953.
100. *NYT*, Oct. 3, 1952; *RMRB*, Oct. 3, 1952.
101. Hermes, *Truce Tent*, 281.

CHAPTER 14: EXCHANGES AND "EXPLANATION"

1. Bradley and Blair, *A General's Life*, 649, 656–58.
2. Hermes, *Truce Tent*, 408.
3. *RMRB*, Feb. 8, 1953.
4. *FRUS 1952–1954*, 15:1062–63.
5. Foot, "Nuclear Coercion"; Weathersby, "Stalin, Mao, and the End of the Korean War"; Shen, *Lengzhan zai Yazhou*, 282–83; Jager, *Brothers at War*, 272–75. However, Chen Jian emphasizes that Beijing also took the initiative in ending the war. See *Mao's China and the Cold War*, 115–16.
6. Shen, *Lengzhan zai Yazhou*, 288; Telegram from Kuznetsov and Fedorenko in Pyongyang, March 29, 1953, USSR Archive of Foreign Policy, Fond 059a, Opis 5a, Delo 5, Papka 11, Listy 120–122, Wilson Center Digital Archive, translated by Kathryn Weathersby, http://digitalarchive.wilsoncenter.org/document/117036.
7. Hermes, *Truce Tent*, 412–13.
8. Ibid., 414–15.
9. Luo Jiecao interview, Apr. 16, 2014.
10. US Army, *Handling*, 64–65.
11. Ibid., 65.
12. Xie, "Zuinie," 92; Hermes, *Truce Tent*, 416.

13. US Army, *Handling*, 66.
14. Xie, "Zuinie," 92–94.
15. Ibid., 94–95.
16. Hermes, *Truce Tent*, 417–19.
17. US Army, *Handling*, 68.
18. Wang Houci interview, Apr. 25, 2010; Wang, *Hanzhan shengshi lian*, 7. Huang Mo, Cheng Liren's subordinate in the PG battalion, also described the same incident in his affidavit made in 1969 for an unrelated case in Taiwan, A305000000C/0053/1571/4020/4/003, TWNA.
19. Liu Chunjian telephone interview, Mar. 28, 2017.
20. Hermes, *Truce Tent*, 534.
21. Clark, *From the Danube to the Yalu*, 276–81.
22. Ibid., 279.
23. Ibid., 281; Briggs to Dulles, June 29, 1953, 695A.0024, RG 59, NA.
24. CKSD, Oct. 8, 1953.
25. *FFDS*, 129.
26. Manhard to Briggs, "Recent developments in the UNC POW camps," June 16, 1953, 1, 695A.0024, RG 59, NA.
27. Briggs to Dulles, June 29, 1953, 695A.0024, RG 59, NA.
28. *FFDS*, 130–33.
29. US Army, *Handling*, 81.
30. Hermes, *Truce Tent*, 477.
31. Clark, *From the Danube to the Yalu*, 1.
32. US Army, *Handling*, 87.
33. *RMRB*, Aug. 11, 1953.
34. US Army, *Handling*, 85–89.
35. Fang interview, Apr. 19, 2014.
36. *RMRB*, Sept. 8, 1953; Zhang, *Wo de Chaoxian zhanzheng*, 197–99.
37. Hermes, *Truce Tent*, 274.
38. Manhard to Briggs, June 16, 1953, 695A.0024, RG 59, NA.
39. Rankin to State Dept, Aug. 5, 1953, 1–2, 695A.0024, RG 59, NA.
40. Chiang's speech, accessed July 8, 2011, www.chungcheng.org.tw/thought/class07/0027/0006.htm.
41. *FFDS*, 141–46; Ni Wenya report, Sept. 24, 1953, 020-000021-0057A, TWGSG.
42. CKSD, Aug. 31, 1953.
43. Hermes, *Truce Tent*, 515.
44. CKSD, June 3, 1953.
45. This charge was made by alleged anti-Communist prisoners who escaped or chose repatriation during the explanation. He, *Jianzheng*, 206.
46. Thimayya, *Experiment in Neutrality*, 124.
47. Ibid., 127–28.
48. *FFDS*, 215; *FGSL*, 1:335.
49. McGarr memo, May 25, 1953, Box 1656, Entry (A-1)224, RG 338, NA.
50. White, *Captives of Korea*, 249; Hansen, *Heroes*, 145–46. Also in *RMRB*, Dec. 4, 1953; *FFDS*, 145–46.
51. White, *Captives of Korea*, 245. For the most recent in-depth study of the "Explanation," see Kim, *Interrogation Rooms*, chap. 6.
52. Thimayya, *Experiment in Neutrality*, 122.

53. Ibid., 189–90.

54. Hermes, *Truce Tent*, 515; Reports of the Neutral Nations Repatriation Commission (UN document A/2641), 108.

55. Zhao Zhidao in "Andeshe," 2:306; "Andeshe," 3:42.

56. Wan Delin interview, Jan. 22, 2014.

57. Kim Kwan-ok, interviewed by Lee Sunwoo and the author, Feb. 6, 2017.

58. Reports of the NNRC (UN document A/2641), 122; Prasad, *History of the Custodian Force (India) in Korea, 1953–54*, 79; Yu, *Eyun*, 412–13.

59. Hermes, *Truce Tent*, 515; *FFDS*, 187–88.

60. *RMRB*, Oct. 16, 1953; Yu, *Eyun*, 413–15.

61. Thimayya, *Experiment in Neutrality*, 201–2.

62. Guo Shigao interview, Dec. 12, 2012; Shen, *Yiwansiqian ge zhengren*, 207; Dept. of the Army commendation list, Apr. 1, 1954, 00016715000050100w, 00016715000050122w, TWGFB.

63. *FGSL*, 1:334.

64. Lai to Zhou Zhirou, Jan. 14, 1953, 00012388001301 22w-25w, TWGFB.

65. Chang, "Zhang Yifu's Oral History Records," 147–48.

66. Zhao Huilin interview, Sept. 11, 2008.

67. Zhao Yingkui interview, Dec. 30, 2012.

68. Thimayya, *Experiment in Neutrality*, 205.

69. *FFDS*, 219.

70. Fang, *Wo sheng zhi lu*, 106.

71. Cheng interview, Oct. 14, 2016.

72. Kim Kwan-ok, interviewed by Lee Sunwoo and the author, Feb. 6, 2017.

73. US Army, *Handling*, 98; Singh, *Indelible Reminiscences*, 230–32.

CHAPTER 15: PRISONER-AGENTS OF UNIT 8240

1. Details in this section are from the Red Cross Society of China, *Atrocities of the U.S. Armed Forces*, 87–89; *RMRB*, Dec. 8, 1952, 4; Evanhoe, *Darkmoon*, 142–44; Dillard, *Tiger Hunters*, 87–88.

2. *RMRB*, May 8, 1952, 1.

3. *RMRB*, July 23, 1952, 1.

4. Ibid., Oct. 23, 1952, 4.

5. Dillard, *Tiger Hunters*, 88–89.

6. Evanhoe, *Darkmoon*, 143–44, 186.

7. Chai and Zhao, *Banmendian tanpan*, 231.

8. Ibid., 234.

9. For an up-to-date account, see Jager, *Brothers at War*, 242–57.

10. *RMRB*, Mar. 27, 1952, 1, and May 8, 1952, 1.

11. *KZZJ*, 198.

12. *RMRB*, July 21, 1952, 1.

13. Ibid.; Chai and Zhao, *Banmendian tanpan*, 230.

14. Chai and Zhao, *Banmendian tanpan*, 230.

15. UNC delegates first put the POW roster "on table" at Panmunjom on the December 16, 1951 (see *FRUS 1951*, 7:1347).

16. Dillard, *Tiger Hunters*, 332. This author encountered reclassified files such as Command Report, Combined Command for Reconnaissance Activities, Korea (CCRAK), Jan to May 1953, Entry 95D, RG 554, NA. This author's requests made under the Freedom of

Information Act (FOIA) have received no response. Documents in the US National Archives are often incomplete, heavily filtered, and redacted.

17. Muccio to Acheson, July 7, 1952, 695A.0024/6-2952, RG 59, NA.

18. Dillard, *Tiger Hunters*, 36, 273.

19. Evanhoe, *Darkmoon*, 14–15. Tessa Morris-Suzuki and Catherine Churchman provide the most up-to-date study of the prisoner-agents and the covert program in chapters 7 and 8 of *The Korean War in Asia: A Hidden History*.

20. Haas, *Apollo's Warriors*, 18.

21. Dillard, *Operation Aviary*, 77.

22. 8242d AU to FEC/LD (K), Apr. 20, 1953, Entry 95D, RG 554, NA.

23. UNC POW Rosters, Entry 466, RG 389, NA.

24. Yang interview, Mar. 24, 2015; Meng interview, Mar. 31, 2015. A captured agent reported that he had seen Yang undergoing wireless training in Seoul in November 1953 (*RMRB*, Jan. 22, 1954, 4).

25. *RMRB*, Dec. 8, 1953, 4.

26. Gao, *Hanzhan yiwang*, 268.

27. Seoul to Taipei, Jan. 28, 1952, 633.43-0004-530986, TWJSS.

28. Evanhoe, *Darkmoon*, 91.

29. *RMRB*, Dec. 8, 1953, 4.

30. Ma, "Fangong, konggong, kongguo?," 173–74.

31. Yang interview, Jan. 25, 2014; Gao interview, Aug. 12, 2015.

32. Meng interview, Mar. 31, 2015.

33. Sun Zhonggeng, ATIS KG 393, Aug. 25, 1951; Cheng Liren, ATIS KG 633, Sept. 24, 1951.

34. *FFTL*, 286–87. The Communists also accused the FECLG of teaching agents deception skills (see *RMRB*, Dec. 8, 1953, 4).

35. UNC POW Rosters, Entry 466, RG 389, NA.

36. *FFDS*, 42.

37. *FFTL*, 261.

38. Ibid., 261, 289.

39. Meng interview, Jan. 3, 2013.

40. Evanhoe, *Darkmoon*, 91.

41. Marshall, *The River and the Gauntlet*, 3.

42. Dillard, *Tiger Hunters*, 115–19.

43. Red Cross Society of China, *Atrocities of the U.S. Armed Forces*, 83–88; Tessa Morris-Suzuki, "The United States, Japan, and the Undercover War in Korea," in *The Korean War in Asia*, 184.

44. *FFTL*, 263; Meng, "Hanzhan dihou," 60.

45. Gao, *Hanzhan yiwang*, 248.

46. Zhou Zhirou to George Yeh, Nov. 14, 1953, 0042-633.43 (9)/533038, TWNA.

47. Marshall, *The River and the Gauntlet*, 4. Aviary officer Captain Bob Brewer estimated that the survival rate of airdropped agents, at least in the first year of the war, was around 70 percent (see Haas, *Apollo's Warriors*, 19).

48. *FFTL*, 266–67.

49. Ibid., 346–47.

50. Ibid., 266–69.

51. Liao interview, Mar. 24, 2015.

52. Cleaver, *UN Partisan Warfare in Korea*, 94.

53. Evanhoe, *Darkmoon*, 89.
54. Zhou Zhirou to George Yeh, Nov. 14, 1953, 0042-633.43 (9)/533037, TWNA.
55. Yang interview, Mar. 24, 2015.
56. Ibid.
57. Daying, *Zhiyuanjun zhanfu jishi*, 204; Yu, *Eyun*, 431; Yang interview, Mar. 24, 2015.
58. *KZZJ*, 311.
59. Yu, *Eyun*, 432.
60. Meng interview, Jan. 3, 2013.
61. Ibid.; Gao interview, Aug. 12, 2015; Liao interview, June 3, 2015.
62. Daying, *Zhiyuanjun zhanfu jishi*, 204; Gao, *Hanzhan yiwang*, 247.
63. Wang Houci interview, Mar. 25, 2010.
64. Liu Fei, ATIS KG 128, July 24, 1951.
65. Wang Houci interview, Mar. 25, 2010.
66. Gao interview, Aug. 12, 2015.
67. Cleaver, *UN Partisan Warfare in Korea*, 64.
68. Dillard, *Tiger Hunters*, 89.
69. Gao, *Hanzhan yiwang*, 249, 255.
70. Ibid.
71. *RMRB*, July 23, 1952, 1, and Dec. 8, 1953, 4.
72. UNC POW Rosters, Entry 466, RG 389, NA. Ironically, Guo, a former Nationalist air force captain and a CPV truck driver, was a defector. After their trucks was strafed and destroyed by UNC planes on April 20, 1951, he and three other drivers walked south for twenty-two days until they surrendered to UNC troops in Chunchon (Guo Baotong, ATIS KG 300, Aug. 14, 1951).
73. *FFTL*, 288, 270.
74. Ibid., 265.
75. Liao interview, Mar. 24, 2015; *FFTL*, 287; *RMRB*, Dec. 8, 1953, 4.
76. Wen Chuanji, ATIS KG 834, Nov. 3, 1951.
77. Tian interview, June 30, 2014.
78. Ibid.
79. Wen Chuanji, ATIS KG 834, Nov. 3, 1951.
80. UNC POW Rosters, Entry 466, RG 389, NA.
81. Gu Zhenggang to George Yeh, May 3, 1952, 0042-633.43 (9)/531068–70, TWNA; Red Cross Society of China, *Atrocities of the U.S. Armed Forces*, 34; *RMRB*, Dec. 8, 1953, 4. The Communists mistook his name as Li Liqiang.
82. *RMRB*, Dec. 8, 1953, 4.
83. Gao, *Hanzhan yiwang*, 269.
84. Wang Naiyong, ATIS KG 420, Aug. 28, 1951.
85. Gu Zhenggang to George Yeh, May 3, 1952, 0042-633.43 (9)/531068–70, TWNA.
86. Gao, *Hanzhan yiwang*, 254–56. Ma Furui also reported a similar incident involving beating with baseball bats (*FFTL*, 268).
87. Gao, *Hanzhan yiwang*, 263.
88. Meng, "Hanzhan dihou," 62; Ma Furui in *FFTL*, 269.
89. Gao, *Hanzhan yiwang*, 267; Meng Ming, "Hanzhan dihou," 61; Hou Guangming in *FFTL*, 292.
90. Hou Guangming in *FFTL*, 292.
91. Ma Furui in *FFTL*, 269.
92. ROC embassy in Seoul to Taipei, Nov. 22, 1953, 0042-633.43 (9)/533045, TWNA.
93. Zhou Zhirou to George Yeh, Nov. 14, 1953, 0042-633.43 (9)/533065–8; Chiang Ching-kuo to Yeh, Nov. 20, 1953, 0042-633.43 (9)/533052–3, TWNA.

94. ROC embassy in Seoul to Taipei, Nov. 22, 1953, 0042-633.43 (9)/533045, TWNA. Admittedly, not all 143 agents lost in action were killed, as some were captured; nor were all captured agents necessarily executed by the Communists. Nevertheless, even those who were not executed would certainly face a long prison term and lifetime persecution in China.

95. *FGSL*, 1:342–43; Yang Shuzhi interview, Mar. 24, 2015.

96. Gao, *Hanzhan yiwang*, 277–78.

97. ROC Embassy to Taipei, Jan. 8, 1954, 0042-633.43 (9)/533072, TWNA.

98. Gao, *Hanzhan yiwang*, 275.

99. Meng, "Hanzhan dihou," 62.

100. This number is calculated by counting all prisoners listed as "deceased" on UNC POW rosters (Entry 466, RG 389, NA). Using three death lists provided by the UNC at different times, the Communists arrived at a higher death toll—482—which perhaps involved some double-counting (*RMRB*, Aug. 25, 1953, 4).

101. *FFDS*, 66; Ma, "Fangong, konggong, kongguo?," 173–74.

102. Hou Guangming in *FFTL*, 292.

103. Gao, *Hanzhan yiwang*, 255, 257.

CHAPTER 16: AFTERMATH

1. Xie, "Zuinie," 108; Zhang, "Wo fengming jieshou Zhiyuanjun bingshang zhanfu," 22–24.

2. Xie, "Zuinie," 108–10.

3. He, *Zhongcheng*, 138.

4. Yu, *Eyun*, 378–79; Zhong Junhua interview, Sept. 13, 2007.

5. He, *Zhongcheng*, 176–78; Guo in "Andeshe," 3:51.

6. Fan Ligui in "Andeshe," 3:80.

7. He, *Zhongcheng*, 138–39.

8. Ibid., 147, 186; Guo in "Andeshe," 3:51.

9. Liu Shixiu, ATIS KG 530, Sept. 10, 1951; "Andeshe," 3:32.

10. He, *Zhongcheng*, 179.

11. Ibid., 153–54; Dai in "Andeshe," 3:98.

12. Zhang, *Wo de Chaoxian zhanzheng*, 67; He, *Zhongcheng*, 260; Zeng and Chen in "Andeshe," 3:94.

13. Xie, "Zuinie," 123–200.

14. Yang, *Mubei*, 253.

15. Lin Mocong interview, Nov. 11, 2009; He, *Zhongcheng*, 381.

16. Zhang, *Wo de Chaoxian zhanzheng*, 299–300.

17. Luo interview, Apr. 16, 2014.

18. Cai in "Andeshe," 3:91.

19. Gao Jie in "Andeshe," 2:163–64; "Andeshe," 3:100; He, *Zhongcheng*, 363.

20. Chen interview, Apr. 17, 2014; Chen in "Andeshe," 3:95.

21. Chen Qingbin, letter to Zhong Junhua, Mar. 14, 1982, Zhong's private collection.

22. He Rui interview, Oct. 21, 2009.

23. Tang Yao interview, Nov. 21, 2009.

24. Zhang Yifu interview, Dec. 26, 2012.

25. *Zhongyang ribao*, Feb. 20, 1954; CKSD, Feb. 19, 1954.

26. Chiang Ching-kuo to Chiang Kai-shek, June 1954, 00012389000060028w–51w, TWGFB.

27. Zhao Yingkui interview, Dec. 21, 2012.

28. Zhandoutuan to MoD, July 1, 1954, 00016716000080097w, TWGFB; MoD report, Oct. 28, 1955, 00041265000050041w, TWGFB.

29. Wang Houci interview, Mar. 3, 2010.
30. Chang, "Zhang Yifu's Oral History Records," 150.
31. Zhao Yingkui interview, Dec. 21, 2012.
32. *FGSL*, 3:1–378; *FFDS*, 273–84; *NYT*, Sept. 15, 1954.
33. Gao, *Hanzhan yiwang*, 282–333; Tao interview, Jan. 22, 2015.
34. Chen Chaoxun (Chen Wenji's son), email to the author, Mar. 20, 2018.
35. Yan interview, May 5, 2010.
36. Yu interview, July 4, 2010; Meng interview, Feb. 19, 201.
37. Chang, "Zhang Yifu's Oral History Records," 151.
38. Taipei rongyu guomin zhijia, *Jueze*, 13.
39. Daying, *Zhiyuanjun zhanfu jishi*, 205.
40. Tian Fangbao in "Andeshe," 3:67; Tian interview, June 30, 2014.
41. White House press release, Sept. 7, 1976, Box 30 of press releases, Gerald R. Ford Library, Ann Arbor, MI.
42. Zhang, *Wo de Chaoxian zhanzheng*, 326.
43. Zhang, *Kaoyan*, 333; Yu, *Eyun*, 270.
44. Zhao Yingkui interview, Dec. 21, 2012.
45. Zhang and Gao, *Chongwei*, 187.
46. Author's meeting with Cai, June 4, 2010.
47. See Chapter 13.

CONCLUSION

1. Hermes, *Truce Tent*, 432.
2. *NYT*, Jan. 23, 1954, 1.
3. Eisenhower, "Address at the Columbia University National Bicentennial Dinner, New York City," May 31, 1954, in Woolley and Peters, *American Presidency Project*, http://www.presidency.ucsb.edu/ws/?pid=9906.
4. Beisner, *Dean Acheson*, 438; Gettleman, *Vietnam and America*, 481.
5. Quoted by Lyman Van Slyke, "Introduction" to United States Department of State, *The China White Paper, August 1949*, unpaged.
6. Quoted in Young, *Name, Rank, and Serial Number*, 175.
7. *FRUS 1951*, 7:793.
8. Joy, *How Communists Negotiate*, 152.
9. "POW Population by Month," see Appendix, 391.
10. Joy, *Negotiating While Fighting*, 436.
11. Kennedy, "Inaugural Address," Jan. 20, 1961, in Woolley and Peters, *American Presidency Project*, http://www.presidency.ucsb.edu/ws/?pid=8032.
12. Boatner to General Harold K. Johnson, Jan. 4, 1966, Box 1, Boatner Papers, Hoover Archives, 6; Boatner, "Prisoners of War for Sale," 40.
13. Joy, *How Communists Negotiate*, 160.
14. Xu, *Diyici jiaoliang*, 290.
15. Quoted in Peraino, *A Force So Swift*, 36.
16. Beisner, *Dean Acheson*, 92, 399.
17. Quoted in Cumings, *Origins of the Korean War*, 2:55.
18. Beisner, *Dean Acheson*, 415.
19. *CZED*, 2:1341.
20. Van Slyke, "Introduction" to *The China White Paper*, unpaged.
21. *FRUS 1945, Malta & Yalta*, 771.

22. *FRUS 1944*, 6:97; United States Department of State, *The China White Paper, August 1949*, 93.

23. *FRUS 1939*, 3:308–9.

24. Yang, *Minguo renwu guoyan lu*, 363–65; Price, *The Lives of Agnes Smedley*, 190, 274–75.

25. Thomas, *Season of High Adventure*, 138.

26. Bianco, *Origins of the Chinese Revolution*, 76.

27. Davies, *Dragon by the Tail*, 247.

28. Lü, *Da qiju zhong de guogong guanxi*, 57–61; Davies, *China Hand*, 202.

29. *FRUS 1943*, China: 201.

30. *NYT*, Oct. 31, 1944.

31. Davies, *Dragon by the Tail*, 318.

32. *FRUS 1944*, 6:669–70; *FRUS 1945*, 7:336.

33. Snow, *Journey to the Beginning*, 348.

34. Lü, *Da qiju zhong de guogong guanxi*, 45–48.

35. *FRUS 1945*, 7:761.

36. Hu, "Introduction" to John Leighton Stuart, *Fifty Years in China*, xviii.

37. Lü, *Da qiju zhong de guogong guanxi*, 184, 225–26.

38. Ibid.; Yang, "Guanyu Jiefang Zhanzheng zhong de Sulian junshi yuanzhu wenti," 285–306.

39. Gaddis, *Kennan*, 279.

40. Ibid, 387.

41. Beisner, *Dean Acheson*, 187–88; United States Department of State, *The China White Paper, August 1949*, xvi. For more on Davies's role, see Davies's paper, July 7, 1949, *FRUS 1949*, 7:1147–51.

42. Mao, "Farewell, Leighton Stuart!," 433–39.

43. Lü, *Da qiju zhong de guogong guanxi*, 302–3.

44. Gaddis, *Kennan*, 358.

45. *FRUS 1949*, 9:536–40.

46. Gaddis, *Kennan*, 357–58.

47. *FRUS 1950*, 7:1369.

48. US Congress, *Military Situation in the Far East*, 377.

49. Marx and Engels, "Manifesto of the Communist Party," 500.

50. Mao, "Report on an Investigation of the Peasant Movement in Hunan," 28.

51. Barrett, *Dixie Mission*, 47.

52. Ibid., 46.

53. Davies in Sue Williams's documentary film, *China: A Century of Revolution* (1989), 01:27:00.

54. Davies, *China Hand*, 232.

55. Yang, "Mei Su lengzhan de qiyuan ji dui Zhongguo geming de yingxiang," 7–9.

56. Lin, "China and Its Critics," 324.

57. Tsou, *America's Failure in China, 1941–50*, 208–9, 221–22.

58. *FRUS 1944*, 6:652.

59. Pomfret, *The Beautiful Country and the Middle Kingdom*, 283–84; K. P. Chen, "My Reflections on Chinese Attitude towards Britain," Feb. 1, 1945, Kwang Pu Chen Papers.

60. Pomfret, *The Beautiful Country and the Middle Kingdom*, 284, 288, 326.

61. Service and Esherick, *Lost Chance In China*, 93–96; Pomfret, *The Beautiful Country and the Middle Kingdom*, 326.

62. Wen Chao Chen interview, Mar. 26, 2012, Kalamazoo, Michigan.

63. Wen Chao Chen, email to the author, May 26, 2011. Chen came to the United States for training in early 1945. He later became a professor of political science at Kalamazoo College and served as its vice president.

64. Gao, *Lishi biji*, 1:273; Gao interview, Dec. 20, 2008.

65. Perry, "Shanghai's Strike Wave of 1957," 1–2; Fairbank and Goldman, *China: A New History*, 352; Cheng and Selden, "The Origins and Consequences of China's Hukou System," 646.

66. Strauss, "Paternalist Terror"; Brown and Pickowicz, eds., *Dilemmas of Victory*; Dikötter, *The Tragedy of Liberation*.

67. MacFarquhar, "Background and Research Context of the Databases of Chinese Political Campaigns in the 1950s," 67.

68. Campbell and Ratner, "The China Reckoning"; Kevin Rudd, "What the West Doesn't Get about Xi Jinping," *NYT*, Mar. 20, 2018; "How the West Got China Wrong," *Economist*, Mar. 1, 2018.

69. United States Department of State, *The China White Paper, August 1949*, xvi.

70. Hu, "Introduction" to Stuart, *Fifty Years in China*, xx.

Bibliography

ARCHIVAL SOURCES

Academia Historica (Guoshiguan) (TWGSG), Taipei.

Archives of the Institute of Modern History, Academia Sinica (TWJSS), Taipei.

Archives of the Kuomintang, Taipei.

Archives of the Ministry of Defense (TWGFB), Taipei.

Boatner, Haydon L. Papers. Hoover Archives, Palo Alto, CA.

Chen, Kwang Pu. Papers. Rare Book and Manuscript Library, Columbia University, NY.

Chiang Kai-shek Diaries (CKSD). Hoover Archives, Palo Alto, CA.

Foreign Ministry Archives, Beijing.

Joy, C. Turner. Papers. Hoover Archives, Palo Alto, CA.

Koo, Wellington. Papers. Rare Book and Manuscript Library, Columbia University, NY.

National Archives Administration. National Development Council (TWNA), Taipei.

Shanghai Municipal Archives, Shanghai.

Shanxi Provincial Archives, Taiyuan.

Sichuan Provincial Archives, Chengdu.

Truman Library (TL), Independence, MO.

United Nations Archives, New York.

University Service Centre for China Studies. Chinese University of Hong Kong.

US National Archives II, College Park, MA (NA). Record Group 59: General Records of the Dept. of State, 1950–54; Record Group 319, Records of the Army Staff (G-3 Operation); Record Group 338, Records of Army Operational, Tactical, and Support; Record Group 389: Records of the Office of the Provost Marshall General; Record Group 554: Records of General Headquarters, Far East Command, Supreme Commander Allied Powers, and United Nations Command, 1945–57.

USSR Archive of Foreign Policy of the Russian Federation. Wilson Center Digital Archive, Washington, DC.

Vatcher, William H. Papers. Hoover Archives, Palo Alto, CA.

Willoughby, Charles A. Papers. MacArthur Memorial Archives, Norfolk, VA.

INTERVIEWS

All interviews are by the author unless otherwise noted.

Bard, James S., 2013, Sacramento, CA, USA.

Cai Derong 蔡德榮, 2010, Taiyuan.

Cai Pingsheng 蔡平生, 2007, 2009, 2010, Chengdu.

Cao Yueqiao 曹月喬, 2010, 2014, Beijing.

Chen Guimei 陳貴美, 2013, Yilan, Taiwan.

Chen Juntian 陳君天, 2015, Taipei.
Chen, Wen Chao 陳文昭, 2012, Kalamazoo, MI.
Chen Zhinong 諶志農, 2014, Chengdu.
Cheng Liren 程立人, 2014, 2016, Buenos Aires, Argentina.
Fang Xiangqian 方向前, 2014, Chongqing.
Gao Hua 高華, 2008, Shanghai.
Gao Jie 高子. Interview by Lin Mocong 林模叢, circa 1990s. Unpublished interview transcript.
Gao Wenjun 高文俊, 2009, 2010, 2011, 2013, San Francisco, CA, USA.
Guo Shigao 郭仕高, 2010, 2012, Taipei.
He Rui 何瑞, 2009, 2013, Chengdu.
Huang Changrong 黃昌榮, 2013, 2014, Jiayi, Taiwan.
Huang Tiancai 黃天才, 2010, 2017, Taipei.
Huang Yujin 黃玉金, 2014, Tainan.
Huang Zhi 黃直, 2010, 2012, 2018, Taipei.
Jiang Ruipu 姜瑞溥, 2014, Beijing.
Jin Yuankui 金元奎, 2010, 2012, Taipei.
Kim Kwan-ok 金冠玉, 2014, 2016, Buenos Aires, Argentina; 2017, São Paulo, Brazil.
Li Dezhi 李德智, 2014, Taiyuan, Shanxi.
Li Yueming 李月明, 2010, 2012, Taipei.
Liao Ting 廖汀, 2015, Taipei.
Lin Mocong 林模叢, 2009, 2011, Kunming.
Liu Chunjian 劉純儉, 2015, Jilong, Taiwan.
Lu Xuewen 盧學文, 2014, Tainan, Taiwan.
Luo Jiecao 羅節操, 2014, Chengdu.
Manhard, Philip. Interview by Marshall Green, Dec. 1, 1988. Association for Diplomatic Studies and Training Foreign Affairs Oral History Project, Library of Congress.
Meng Ming 孟明, 2013, 2014, 2015, 2016, 2018, Taipei.
Muccio, John J. Interview by Jerry N. Ness, 1971. Harry S. Truman Library.
Ping Zhanfang 平占芳, 2010, 2012, Taipei.
Tang Yao 唐耀, 2009, 2010, Shanghai.
Tao Shanpeng 陶善鵬, 2015, 2018, Taipei.
Tian Fangbao 田方保, 2014, Jiaozuo, Henan.
Vigil, Patrick, 2014, 2016, Albuquerque, NM, USA.
Wan Delin 萬德林, 2014, Gangshan, Taiwan.
Wang Guanhu 王官虎, 2010, 2011, 2014, Wenxi, Shanxi.
Wang Houci 王厚慈/Wang Beishan 王北山 (alias), 2010, 2011, Taoyuan, Taiwan.
Wang Tielong 王鐵龍, 2013, 2014, Chongqing.
Wu Chunsheng 吳春生, 2011, Anyang, Henan.
Wu Jinfeng 吳金鋒, 2008, Beijing.
Wu Xiaozong 吳孝宗, 2010, 2011, Taiyuan, Shanxi.
Wu Zengwen 毋增溫, 2011, 2013, Pingyao, Shanxi.
Xie Zhiqi 謝智齊, 2012, 2014, Chongqing.
Yan Tianzhi 嚴天秩, 2010, Taipei.
Yang Shuzhi 楊樹芝, 2014, 2015, 2016, 2018, Taipei.
Yang Wanfu 楊萬福, 2010, 2012, 2018, Taipei.
Yu Dehai 余德海, 2014, Tainan, Taiwan.
Yu Rongfu 于榮福, 2010, 2013, 2015, Taipei.
Zhang Yifu 張一夫, 2012, 2013, 2014, 2015, Taoyuan, Taiwan.

Zhang Zeshi 張澤石, 2007, 2010, 2011, 2012, Beijing; 2018, Hong Kong.
Zhao Huilin 趙會林, 2008, Zhongli, Taiwan.
Zhao Yingkui 趙英魁, 2012, Taipei.
Zheng Zheng'an 鄭正安, 2009, Taipei.
Zhong Junhua 鍾俊驊, 2007, 2009, 2010, 2014, Chengdu.

BOOKS, ARTICLES, AND DOCUMENTARY FILMS

Acheson, Dean. *The Korean War*. New York: W. W. Norton, 1971.

———. *Present at the Creation: My Years in the State Department*. New York: W. W. Norton, 1969.

Applebaum, Anne. *Gulag: A History*. New York: Anchor Books, 2003.

Appleman, Roy E. *Escaping the Trap: The US Army X Corps in Northeast Korea, 1950*. College Station: Texas A & M University Press, 1990.

———. *Ridgway Duels for Korea*. College Station: Texas A & M University Press, 1990.

———. *South to the Naktong, North to the Yalu, June–November 1950*. Washington, DC: Center of Military History, 1961.

Armstrong, Charles K. *Tyranny of the Weak: North Korea and the World, 1950–1992*. Ithaca, NY: Cornell University Press, 2013.

Bai Juntao 白鈞陶 and Xu Lianbing 許聯炳, eds. *Fengyan rensheng* 烽烟人生 [Lives in war]. Vol. 1, 2003; vol. 3, 2007. Chengdu: unofficial publication.

Barrett, David D. *Dixie Mission: The United States Army Observer Group in Yenan, 1944*. Berkeley: Center for Chinese Studies, University of California, 1970.

Beisner, Robert L. *Dean Acheson: A Life in the Cold War*. New York: Oxford University Press, 2006.

Benben, John S. "Education of Prisoners of War on Koje Island, Korea." *Educational Record* 36, no. 2 (Apr. 1955): 157–73.

Bernstein, Barton J. "The Struggle over the Korean Armistice: Prisoners of Repatriation?" In *Child of Conflict: The Korean-American Relationship, 1943–1953*, edited by Bruce Cumings, 261–307. Seattle: University of Washington Press, 1983.

Bianco, Lucien. *Origins of the Chinese Revolution*. Stanford, CA: Stanford University Press, 1967.

Blair, Clay. *The Forgotten War: America in Korea, 1950–1953*. New York: Random House, 1987.

Boatner, Haydon. "Prisoners of War for Sale." *American Legion* (Aug. 1962): 14–15, 38–41.

Bohlen, Charles E. *Witness to History, 1929–1969*. New York: W W. Norton, 1973.

Bradbury, William C., Samuel M. Meyers, Albert D. Biderman et al. *Mass Behavior in Battle and Captivity: The Communist Soldier in the Korean War*. Chicago: University of Chicago Press, 1968.

Bradley, Omar Nelson, and Clay Blair. *A General's Life: An Autobiography*. New York: Simon and Schuster, 1983.

Brown, Jeremy, and Paul Pickowicz, eds. *Dilemmas of Victory: The Early Years of the People's Republic of China*. Cambridge, MA: Harvard University Press, 2007.

Burchett, Wilfred G. *At the Barricades: Forty Years on the Cutting Edge of History*. New York: Times Books, 1981.

Campbell, Kurt M., and Ely Ratner. "The China Reckoning: How Beijing Defied American Expectations." *Foreign Affairs* 97, no. 2 (2018): 60–70.

Cao Jianlang 曹劍浪. *Zhongguo Guomingdang jun jianshi* 中國國民黨軍簡史 [A concise history of the Nationalist forces]. 3 vols. Beijing: Jiefangjun chubanshe, 2010.

Carter, Carolle J. *Mission to Yenan: American Liaison with the Chinese Communists, 1944–1947*. Lexington: University Press of Kentucky, 1997.

———. "Mission to Yenan: The OSS and the Dixie Mission." In *The Secret War: The Office of Strategic Services in World War II*, edited by George C. Chalou, 302–17. Washington, DC: National Archives and Records Administration, 1992.

Chai Chengwen 柴成文 and Zhao Yongtian 趙勇田. *Banmendian tanpan* 板門店談判 [Panmunjom negotiations]. 2nd ed. Beijing: Jiefangjun wenyi chubanshe, 1992.

Chang, Su-Ya. "Pragmatism and Opportunism: Truman's Policy toward Taiwan, 1949–1952." PhD diss., Pennsylvania State University, 1988.

Chang Cheng 常成 [David Cheng Chang]. "Zhang Yifu's Oral History Records" 張一夫先生訪問紀錄. *Koushu lishi* 口述歷史 13 (2013): 121–52.

Chaoxian wenti wenjian huibian 朝鮮問題彙編 [Selected documents of the Korean problem]. Vol. 2. Beijing: People's Press, 1959.

Chen, Jian. *Mao's China and the Cold War*. Chapel Hill: University of North Carolina Press, 2001.

Chen Yonghua 陳永華. "Dongbei anye du xingjun—Chen Yonghua" 東北暗夜獨行軍•陳永華 [Nightly lone march in the northeast]. Interview by Lin Jintian 林金田, July 7, 1994. In *Shanghen xie lei: zhanhou yuan taiji guojun koushu lishi* 傷痕血淚—戰後原台籍國軍口述歷史 [Scars, blood, and tears: Oral history accounts by Nationalist soldiers of Taiwanese origins in the post–World War II era], edited by Lin Jintian, 241–54. Nantou, Taiwan: Guoshiguan Taiwan wenxianguan, 2006.

———. Interview by Xu Shaorong 許紹榮 and Xue Hongfu 薛宏甫, April 26, 2006. In *Taiji laobing de xuelei gushi* 台籍老兵的血淚故事 [Blood and tears: Oral history accounts by Nationalist soldiers of Taiwanese origin], edited by Xue Hongfu, 52–77. Gaoxiong: Gaoshi Wenxianhui, 2009.

Chen Yu 陳宇. *Muse Huangpu: Huangpu junxiao zai dalu de zuihou yiqi xiezhen* 暮色黄埔: 黄埔軍校在大陸的最後一期寫真 [The Whampoa Military Academy's final class on the mainland]. Beijing: Jiefangjun chubanshe, 2013.

Cheng, Tiejun, and Mark Selden. "The Origins and Consequences of China's *Hukou* System." *China Quarterly* 139 (Sept. 1994): 646–68.

Chengdu difangzhi bianzuan weiyuanhui 成都市地方志編纂委員會, ed. *Chengdushi zhi: junshi zhi* 成都市志 · 軍事志 [Chengdu gazetteer: Military gazetteer]. Chengdu: Sichuan daxue chubanshe, 1997.

Chengdushi zhengxie wenshi ziliao yanjiu weiyuanhui 成都市政協文史資料研究委員會. "Chengdushi renmin relie huanying Jiefangjun rucheng" 成都市人民熱烈歡迎解放軍入城 [People of Chengdu warmly welcomed the PLA to enter the city]. In *Sichuan wenshi ziliao xuanji* 四川文史資料選輯 18, 195–201. Chengdu: Chengdushi zhengxie wenshi ziliao yanjiu weiyuanhui, 1979.

Chu Songqiu 楚崧秋, Lü Fangshang 呂方上, and Huang Kewu 黄克武. *Chu Songqiu xiansheng fangwen jilu: lanjin cangsang bashi nian* 楚崧秋先生訪問紀錄: 覽盡滄桑八十年 [Records of interviews with Mr. Chu Songqiu: Eighty years of life]. Taipei: Zhongyang yanjiuyuan jindaishi yanjiusuo, 2001.

Clark, Mark W. *From the Danube to the Yalu*. New York: Harper, 1954.

Cleaver, Frederick W. *UN Partisan Warfare in Korea, 1951–1954*. Chevy Chase, MD: Operations Research Office, Johns Hopkins University, 1956.

Crook, Isabel, and David Crook. *Revolution in a Chinese Village: Ten Mile Inn*. London: Routledge, 2010.

Cumings, Bruce. *The Korean War: A History*. New York: Modern Library, 2010.

———. *The Origins of the Korean War*. Vol. 2, *The Roaring of the Cataract, 1947–1950*. Princeton, NJ: Princeton University Press, 1990.

Davies, John Paton, Jr. *China Hand: An Autobiography*. Philadelphia: University of Pennsylvania Press, 2012.

———. *Dragon by the Tail: American, British, Japanese, and Russian Encounters with China and One Another*. New York: W. W. Norton, 1972.

Daying 大鷹 [Jin Daying 靳大鷹]. *Zhiyuanjun zhanfu jishi* 志願軍戰俘紀事 [CPV POWs' stories]. 2nd ed. Beijing: Jiefangjun wenyi chubanshe, 1998.

Dean, William F. *General Dean's Story as Told to William L. Worden*. New York: Viking, 1954.

Deng Xiaoping 鄧小平. *Deng Xiaoping zishu* 鄧小平自述 [In Deng Xiaoping's own words]. Beijing: Jiefangjun chubanshe, 2005.

Dikötter, Frank. *The Tragedy of Liberation: A History of the Chinese Revolution, 1945–1957*. New York: Bloomsbury, 2013.

Dillard, Douglas C. *Operation Aviary: Airborne Special Operations—Korea, 1950–1953*. Victoria, B.C.: Trafford, 2003.

———. *Tiger Hunters: Airborne and Ground Special Operations*. Bloomington, IN: Xlibris, 2010.

Du Lin, Li Su, and Sasha Gong, eds. *Zhiyuanjun zhanfu* 志願軍戰俘 [CPV POWs]. Documentary film. Washington, DC: Voice of America Chinese-language program, 2015–2016.

Du Ping 杜平. *Zai Zhiyuanjun zongbu* 在志願軍總部 [At the CPV GHQ]. Beijing: Jiefangjun chubanshe, 1989.

Eisenhower, Dwight D. *Mandate for Change, 1953–1956: The White House Years*. Garden City, NY: Doubleday, 1963.

Elliott, Mark. *Pawns of Yalta*. Urbana: University of Illinois Press, 1982.

Evanhoe, Ed. *Darkmoon: Eighth Army Special Operations in the Korean War*. Annapolis, MD: Naval Institute Press, 1995.

Fairbank, John King. *Chinabound: A Fifty-Year Memoir*. New York: Harper & Row, 1982.

Fairbank, John King, and Merle Goldman. *China: A New History*. Cambridge, MA: Belknap Press of Harvard University Press, 2006.

Fang Zhi 方治. *Wo sheng zhi lu* 我生之旅 [My journey through life]. Taipei: Dongda tushu, 1986.

Fangong yishi fendou shi bianzuan weiyuanhui 反共義士奮鬥史編纂委員會, ed. *Fangong yishi fendou shi* 反共義士奮鬥史 [The history of the anti-Communist fighters' struggles]. Taipei: Fangong yishi jiuye fudao chu, 1955.

Fehrenbach, T. R. *This Kind of War: The Classic Korean War History*. Washington, DC: Brassey's, 2000.

Finnegan, John Patrick. *Military Intelligence*. Army Lineage Series. Washington, DC: Center of Military History, United States Army, 1998.

Foot, Rosemary J. "Nuclear Coercion and the Ending of the Korean Conflict." *International Security* 13, no. 3 (1988): 92–112.

———. *A Substitute for Victory: The Politics of Peacemaking at the Korean Armistice Talks*. Ithaca, NY: Cornell University Press, 1990.

Futrell, Robert F. *The United States Air Force in Korea: 1950–1953*. Revised ed. Washington, DC: Office of Air Force History, 1983.

Gaddis, John Lewis. *George F. Kennan: An American Life*. New York: Penguin, 2011.

Gao Hua 高華. *How the Red Sun Rose: The Origins and Development of the Yan'an Rectification Movement, 1930–1945*. Translated by Stacy Mosher and Guo Jian. Hong Kong: The Chinese University Press, 2018.

———. *Lishi biji* 歷史筆記 [Notes on history]. Vol. 1. Hong Kong: Oxford University Press, 2014.

Gao Qingchen 高慶辰. *Kongzhan fei yingxiong* 空戰非英雄 [The non-hero of the air war]. Taipei: Maitian chuban, 2000.

Gao Wenjun 高文俊. *Hanzhan yiwang: yuxue yusheng hua renquan* 韓戰憶往: 浴血餘生話人權 [Remembering the Korean War: Discussing human rights after surviving the bloodbath]. Taipei: Shengzhi wenhua chubanshe, 2000.

Gettleman, Marvin E. *Vietnam and America: A Documented History*. New York: Grove, 1995.

Gu Weiun 顧維鈞 [VK Wellington Koo]. *Gu Weijun huiyilu* 顧維鈞回憶錄 [Wellington Koo's memoirs]. Vol. 8 Trans. by Zhongguo shehui kexueyuan jindaishi yanjiusuo. Beijing: Zhonghua shuju, 1989.

Haas, Michael E. *Apollo's Warriors: US Air Force Special Operations during the Cold War*. Honolulu: University Press of the Pacific, 2002.

Halberstam, David. *The Coldest Winter: America and the Korean War*. New York: Hyperion, 2007.

Halliday, Jon. "Anti-Communism and the Korean War, 1950–1953." *Socialist Register* 21 (1984): 130–63.

Hallim University Asia Culture Institute, ed. *Han'guk chŏnjaenggi Chunggonggun munsŏ* 韓國戰爭期中共軍文書 [Captured documents of the Chinese Communist Forces]. 3 vols. Chunchon, ROK: Hallim University Press, 2000.

Hansen, Kenneth K. *Heroes Behind Barbed Wire*. Princeton, NJ: D. Van Nostrand, 1957.

Hastings, Max. *The Korean War*. New York: Simon & Schuster Paperbacks, 1987.

Hatch, David A., and Robert Louis Benson. *The Korean War: The SIGINT Background*. [Fort George G. Meade, MD]: Center for Cryptology History, National Security Agency, 2000.

He Changfeng 何長鳳 et al., eds. *Guizhou dangdai shi* 貴州當代史 [Contemporary history of Guizhou]. Chongqing: Xi'nan shifan daxue chubanshe, 1995.

He Ming 賀明. *Jianzheng: Chaoxian zhanzheng zhanfu qianfan jieshi daibiao de riji* 見證: 朝鮮戰爭戰俘遣返解釋代表的日記 [Witness: Diaries of an "Explanation" representative during the POW repatriation in the Korean War]. Beijing: Zhongguo wenshi chubanshe, 2001.

———. *Zhongcheng: Zhiyuanjun zhanfu guilai renyuan de kanke jingli* 忠誠：志願軍戰俘歸來人員的坎坷經歷 [Loyalty: The difficult experiences of repatriated POWs of the Korean War]. Beijing: Zhongguo wenshi chubanshe, 1998.

He Rui 何瑞. "Bukanhuishou de huishou" 不堪回首的回首 [A past too sad to recall]. Unpublished memoir, 2001.

Hermes, Walter G. *Truce Tent and Fighting Front*. Washington, DC: Center of Military History, U.S. Army, 1966.

Hong Xuezhi 洪學智. *Kangmei yuanchao zhanzheng huiyi* 抗美援朝戰爭回憶 [Recollections of the War of Resisting America and Aiding Korea]. Beijing: Jiefangjun chubanshe, 1990.

Hu Shih 胡適. "Introduction" to Liu Shaw-Tong, *Out of Red China*, xi–xiv. New York: Duell, Sloan and Pearce, 1953.

———. "Introduction" to John Leighton Stuart, *Fifty Years in China: The Memoirs of J.L. Stuart, Missionary and Ambassador*, xix–xx. New York: Random House, 1954.

Huang Tiancai [Hwang Tien-tsai] 黃天才. *Wo zai 38 duxian de huiyi* 我在三十八度線的回憶 [My memories at the 38th parallel]. Taipei: Ink Book, 2010.

Huang Yao 黃瑤, ed. *Luo Ronghuan nianpu* 罗荣桓年谱 [Chronology of Luo Ronghuan]. Beijing: Renmin chubanshe, 2002.

International Committee of the Red Cross (ICRC). "Geneva Convention Relative to the Treatment of POWs," adopted August 12, 1949. https://www.icrc.org/ihl.

Jager, Sheila Miyoshi. *Brothers at War: The Unending Conflict in Korea*. New York: Norton, 2013.

James, D. Clayton. *The Years of MacArthur*. Boston: Houghton Mifflin, 1985.

Janisch, Ricky, and Donna Palumbo. "The House Armed Services Committee National Defense Specialists." *Armed Forces Journal International* 115 (May 1978): 36–49.

Ji, Chaozhu. *The Man on Mao's Right: From Harvard Yard to Tiananmen Square, My Life Inside China's Foreign Ministry*. New York: Random House, 2008.

Jin Chongji 金沖及. *Zhou Enlai zhuan* 周恩來傳 (1898–1976) [A biography of Zhou Enlai, 1898–1976]. Beijing: Zhongyang wenxian chubanshe, 2008.

Johnson, U. Alexis. *The Right Hand of Power*. With Jef Olivarius McAllister. Englewood Cliffs, NJ: Prentice Hall, 1984.

Joy, C. Turner. *How Communists Negotiate*. New York: Macmillan, 1955.

———. *Negotiating While Fighting: The Diary of Admiral C. Turner Joy at the Korean Armistice Conference*. Edited by Allan E. Goodman. Stanford, CA: Hoover Institution Press, 1978.

Junshi kexueyuan junshi lishi yanjiubu 軍事科學院軍事歷史研究部. *Kangmei yuanchao zhanzheng shi* 抗美援朝戰爭史 [History of the Resist America and Aid Korea War]. 3rd ed. 3 vols. Beijing: Junshi kexue chubanshe, 2014.

———. *Zhongguo renmin jiefangjun zhanshi, quanguo jiefang zhanzheng shiqi* 中國人民解放軍戰史 全國解放戰爭時期 [History of the PLA, the Liberation War period]. Beijing: Junshi kexue chubanshe, 2000.

Kim, Monica. *The Interrogation Rooms of the Korean War: The Untold History*. Princeton, NJ: Princeton University Press, 2019.

Korea Institute of Military History. *The Korean War*. Vol. 3. Lincoln: University of Nebraska Press, 2002.

Lai Mingtang 賴名湯. *Lai Mingtang xiansheng fangtan lu* 賴名湯先生訪談錄 [Lai Mingtang oral history]. Taipei: Academia Historica, 1994.

Li Hanzhong 李漢沖. "Guangzhou shouxiang jieshou yu sujian jishi" 廣州受降接收與肅奸紀實 [Receiving surrenderers and purging traitors in Guangzhou]. In *Guangzhou kangzhan jishi* 廣州抗戰紀實 [The War of Resistance in Guangzhou], 477–99. Guangzhou: Guangzhou renmin chubanshe, 1995.

Li, Xiaobing. *China's Battle for Korea: The 1951 Spring Offensive*. Bloomington: Indiana University Press, 2014.

Li, Xiaobing, Allan R. Millett, and Bin Yu, trans. & eds. *Mao's Generals Remember Korea*. Lawrence: University Press of Kansas, 2001.

Li Ziying 黎子穎. "Zhongguo renmin zhiyuanjun beifu renyuan zai meijun jizhongying douzheng dashiji" 中國人民志願軍被俘人員在美軍集中營鬥爭大事記 [Chronology of the People's Volunteers prisoners' struggles in US concentration camps]. Unpublished draft: original draft, POW Returnees' Management Bureau, Changtu, Liaoning, January 1954; revised draft, Changshou, Sichuan, June 1990.

Lin, Hsiao-ting. *Accidental State: Chiang Kai-Shek, the United States, and the Making of Taiwan*. Cambridge, MA: Harvard University Press, 2016.

Lin Yutang. "China and Its Critics." *The Nation* 160 (Mar. 24, 1945).

"Lishi de huiyin" bianshen weiyuanhui 《歷史的迴音》編審委員會. *Lishi de huiyin: 180 shi shizhanlu* 歷史的迴音:180師實戰錄 [The echo of history: The 180th Division's battle history]. Beijing: Xiandai chubanshe, 2015.

Liu Lang 劉朗. *Liuxue dao tianming* 流血到天明 [Bleed until dawn]. Hong Kong: Yazhou chuban youxian gongsi, 1955.

Liu Zhongyong 劉忠勇. *Luoye chengni: Zhonghua minguo sanbing zuozhanshi 1945–1953* 落葉成泥: 中華民國傘兵作戰史 [Fallen leaves: An account of some overlooked stories of the Chinese paratroopers]. Taipei: Jinglun tianxia chubanshe, 2011.

Lü Xun 吕迅. *Da qiju zhong de guogong guanxi* 大棋局中的国共关系 [English title: *Butterfly and Dragonfly: From the Civil War to the Cold War, 1944–1950*]. Beijing: Shehui kexue wenxian chubanshe, 2015.

Ma Guozheng [Ma Kuo-Cheng] 馬國正. "Fangong, konggong, kongguo? Hanzhan lai Tai Zhiyuanjun zhanfu wenti zhi yanjiu" 反共、恐共、恐國？韓戰來台志願軍戰俘問題之研究 [Anti-Communist, Communist-phobia, Nationalist-phobia? A study on the CPV prisoners who came to Taiwan]. Master's thesis. Jiayi, Taiwan: National Chung Cheng University, 2008.

Ma He 馬和. "Hanzhan yu qianfu douzheng" 韓戰與遣俘鬥爭 [The struggle over Korean War POWs]. In *Caihui rensheng bashi nian—Chen Jianzhong xiansheng bazhi huadan wenji* 彩繪人生八十年: 陳建中先生八秩華誕文集 [Eighty years of colorful life: Essay collections in celebration of the eightieth birthday of Mr. Chen Jianzhong], 441–48. Taipei: Riben yanjiu zazhishe, 1992.

MacArthur, Douglas. *Reminiscences*. New York: McGraw-Hill, 1964.

MacDonald, Callum A. *Korea: The War before Vietnam*. New York: Free Press, 1986.

MacFarquhar, Roderick. "Background and Research Context of the Databases of Chinese Political Campaigns in the 1950s: From Land Reform to the State-Private Partnership, 1949–1956." *Journal of East Asian Libraries*, no. 160 (2015): 65–69.

Manchester, William. *American Caesar: Douglas MacArthur, 1880–1964*. Boston: Little, Brown, 1978.

Mao Zedong 毛澤東. "Farewell, Leighton Stuart!" *Selected Works of Mao Tse-tung*, 4:433–40. Beijing: Foreign Languages Press, 1967.

———. *Jianguo yilai Mao Zedong junshi wen'gao*, shang 建國以來毛澤東軍事文稿 上 [Mao Zedong's writings on the military after the founding of the PRC, vol. 1]. Beijing: Junshi kexue chubanshe, 2010.

———. *Jianguo yilai Mao Zedong wen'gao* 建國以來毛澤東文稿 [Mao Zedong's writings since the founding of the People's Republic of China]. Beijing: Zhongyang wenxian chubanshe, 1987.

———. *Mao Zedong junshi wenji* 毛澤東軍事文集 第五卷 [Collection of Mao Zedong's military papers, vol. 5]. Beijing: Junshi kexue chubanshe and Zhongyang wenxian chubanshe, 1993.

———. *Mao Zedong nianpu (1949–1976)* 毛澤東年譜 [Mao Zedong chronology]. Edited by Pang Xianzhi 逄先知. Beijing: Zhongyang wenxian chubanshe, 2013.

———. "Report on an Investigation of the Peasant Movement in Hunan." *Selected Works of Mao Tse-Tung*, 1:23–59. Beijing: Foreign Languages Press, 1965.

Marshall, S. L. A. *The River and the Gauntlet: Defeat of the Eighth Army by the Chinese Communist Forces, November, 1950, in the Battle of the Chongchon River, Korea*. New York: William Morrow, 1953.

Marx, Karl, and Friedrich Engels. "Manifesto of the Communist Party." In *The Marx-Engels Reader*, edited by Robert C. Tucker, 469–500. New York: W. W. Norton, 1978.

Meng Mingfei 孟明非 [Meng Ming 孟明]. "Hanzhan dihou diebao neimu" 韓戰敵後諜報內幕 [Inside stories of special operations behind enemy lines in the Korean War]. *Zhongwai zazhi* 中外雜誌, Taipei, 33:2, vol. 192 (1983): 59–63.

Millett, Allan R. *The War for Korea, 1950–1951: They Came from the North*. Lawrence: University Press of Kansas, 2010.

Montross, Lynn, Nicholas A. Canzona, and K. Jack Bauer. *U.S. Marine Operations in Korea, 1950–1953*. Vol. 3, *The Chosin Reservoir Campaign*. Washington, DC: Historical Branch, U.S. Marine Corps Headquarters, 1954.

Morris-Suzuki, Tessa, ed. *The Korean War in Asia: A Hidden History*. Lanham, MD: Rowman & Littlefield, 2018.

———. "Prisoner Number 600,001: Rethinking Japan, China, and the Korean War 1950–1953." *Journal of Asian Studies* 74, no. 2 (2015): 411–32.

Mossman, Billy C. *Ebb and Flow: November 1950–July 1951*. Washington, DC: Center of Military History, 1990.

National Defense Force History Research Institute (Korea), ed. *Records of the Policy Planning Staff of the Department of State: Country and Area Files: Korea II (1952–1954)* 美國務部政策企劃室文書. 韓國戰爭資料叢書 [Korean War sources series], vol. 5. Seoul: National Defense Force History Research Institute 國防軍史研究所, 1997.

Nishi, Toshio. *Unconditional Democracy: Education and Politics in Occupied Japan, 1945–1952*. Stanford, CA: Hoover Institution Press, 2004.

Paik, Sun Yup. *From Pusan to Panmunjom: Wartime Memoirs of the Republic of Korea's First Four-Star General*. Dulles, VA: Brassey's, 1992.

Peng Dehuai 彭德懷. *Peng Dehuai zishu* 彭德懷自述 [In Peng Dehuai's own words]. Beijing: Renmin chubanshe, 1981.

Peng Dehuai zhuan ji bianxiezu 彭德懷傳記編寫組. *Peng Dehuai zhuan* 彭德懷傳 [A biography of Peng Dehuai]. Beijing: Dangdai Zhongguo chubanshe, 2006.

Peng Dehuai zhuanji zu 彭德懷傳紀組. *Peng Dehuai quanzhuan* 彭德懷全傳 [A complete biography of Peng Dehuai]. Vol. 3. Beijing: Zhongguo dabaike quanshu chubanshe, 2009.

Peraino, Kevin. *A Force So Swift: Mao, Truman, and the Birth of Modern China*. New York: Crown, 2017.

Perry, Elizabeth J. "Shanghai's Strike Wave of 1957." *China Quarterly* 137 (Mar. 1994): 1–27.

Pomfret, John. *The Beautiful Country and the Middle Kingdom: America and China, 1776 to the Present*. New York: Henry Holt, 2016.

Prasad, S.N. *History of the Custodian Force (India) in Korea, 1953–54*. New Delhi, India: Historical Section, Ministry of Defense, 1976.

Price, Ruth. *The Lives of Agnes Smedley*. Oxford: Oxford University Press, 2005.

Qi Bangyuan [Chi Pang-yuan] 齊邦媛. *Juliuhe* 巨流河 [The great flowing river]. Taipei: Tianxia yuanjian chuban, 2009.

Qiao Guanhua 喬冠華. "Guanyu Chaoxian zhanzheng yu tingzhan tanpan" 關於朝鮮戰爭與停戰談判 [The Korean War and the armistice negotiations]. In *Zhonggong dangshi ziliao* 中共黨史資料 68 (Dec.): 26–33. Beijing: Zhonggong dangshi ziliao chubanshe, 1998.

Qu Shaohua 瞿韶華, Xiao Liangzhang 蕭良章, and Ye Zhongju 葉忠鉅, eds. *Zhonghua minguo shishi jiyao (chugao), 1950* 中華民國史事紀要(初稿), 1950 [Chronology of main events of the Republic of China in 1950]. Taipei: Guoshiguan 國史館, 1994.

Red Cross Society of China. *Atrocities of the U.S. Armed Forces against Prisoners of War in Korea: A Report by the Red Cross Society of China*. Beijing, 1953.

Ridgway, Matthew B. *The Korean War*. Garden City, NY: Doubleday, 1967.

———. *Soldier: The Memoirs of Matthew B. Ridgway, as Told to Harold H. Martin*. New York: Harper, 1956.

Robin, Ron. *The Making of the Cold War Enemy: Culture and Politics in the Military-Intellectual Complex*. Princeton, NJ: Princeton University Press, 2001.

Rusk, Dean, and Daniel S. Papp. *As I Saw It*. New York: W. W. Norton, 1990.

Service, John S., and Joseph W. Esherick. *Lost Chance In China: The World War II Despatches of John S. Service*. New York: Random House, 1974.

Shen Xingyi 沈幸儀. *Yiwansiqian ge zhengren: Hanzhan shiqi "fangong yishi" zhi yanjiu* 一萬四千個證人：韓戰時期「反共義士」之研究 [Fourteen thousand witnesses: A study on the "Anti-Communist Righteous Men" during the Korean War]. Taipei: Academia Historica, 2013.

Shen Zhihua 沈志華, ed. *Chaoxian zhanzheng: Eguo dang'anguan de jiemi wenjian* 朝鮮戰爭: 俄國檔案館的解密文件 [The Korean War: Declassified documents from archives in Russia]. 3 vols. Taipei: Institute of Modern History, Academia Sinica, 2003.

———. *Lengzhan zai Yazhou: Chaoxian zhanzheng yu Zhongguo chubing Chaoxian* 冷戰在亞洲:朝鮮戰爭與中國出兵朝鮮 [The Cold War in Asia: The Korean War and China's intervention]. Beijing: Jiuzhou chubanshe, 2013.

———. "Sino-North Korean Conflict and Its Resolution during the Korean War." *Cold War International History Project Bulletin*, no. 14–15 (2003–2004): 9–24.

Shi Zebo 史澤波. "Yanjun qiangzhan Shangdang de cuobai he 'Xuechi fendou' de huanmie" 閻軍搶佔上黨的挫敗和「雪恥奮鬥」的幻滅 [The debacle of the capture of Shangdang by the Yan forces and the disillusionment of the "Avenging humiliation battle group"]. In *Shanxi wenshi ziliao* 山西文史資料 24:13–20. Taiyuan: Wenshi ziliao yanjiu weiyuanhui, 1982.

Sin Chae-hong 申載洪. *Nam-Pukhan kwan'gye saryojip* 南北韓關係史料集 [A collection documents on North-South Korean relations]. ROK: Kuksa P'yŏnch'an Wiwŏnhoe, 1994.

Si'nan xian zhi 思南縣誌 [Si'nan county gazetteer]. Guiyang: Guizhou renmin chubanshe, 1992.

Singh, Gurbakhsh, and Sudesh Gurbakhsh Singh. *Indelible Reminiscences: Memoirs of Major General Gurbakhsh Singh*. New Delhi: Lancer, 2013.

Snow, Edgar. *Journey to the Beginning*. New York: Random House, 1958.

Song Yongyi 宋永毅, ed. *Zhongguo wushi niandai zhongqi de zhengzhi yundong shujuku: cong Tudi Gaige dao Gongsiheying, 1946–1956* 中國五十年代初中期的政治運動數據庫: 從土地改革到公私合營, 1946–1956 [Database of the Chinese political campaigns in the 1950s: From Land Reform to the State-Private Partnership, 1946–1956]. Hong Kong: Chinese University Press, 2014. <http://ccrd.usc.cuhk.edu.hk/>.

Strauss, Julia C. 2002. "Paternalist Terror: The Campaign to Suppress Counterrevolutionaries and Regime Consolidation in the People's Republic of China, 1950–1953." *Comparative Studies in Society and History* 44, no. 1 (Jan.): 80–105.

Stueck, William W. *The Korean War: An International History*. Princeton, NJ: Princeton University Press, 1995.

Sun Yang 孫揚. *Wu guo er zhong: zhanhou Zhong Ying Xianggang wenti jiaoshe* (1945–1949) 無果而終: 戰後中英香港問題交涉 [Fruitless: Sino-British negotiations on the Hong Kong issue after the war]. Beijing: Shehui kexue wenxian chubanshe, 2014.

Taipei rongyu guomin zhijia 台北榮譽國民之家 [Taipei Honored Citizens' Home]. *Jueze: 14,000 min Fagong yishi tulu* 抉擇: 一萬四千名反共義士 [Choice: 14,000 anti-Communist heros]. Taipei: Veteran Affairs Commission, 2014.

Taylor, Jay. *The Generalissimo's Son: Chiang Ching-Kuo and the Revolutions in China and Taiwan*. Cambridge, MA: Harvard University Press, 2000.

Thimayya, Kodendera Subayya. *Experiment in Neutrality*. New Delhi: Vision Books, 1981.

Thomas, S. Bernard. *Season of High Adventure: Edgar Snow in China*. Berkeley: University of California Press, 1996.

Tovy, Tal. "Manifest Destiny in POW Camps: The US Army Reeducation Program during the Korean War." *Historian* 73, no. 3 (2011): 503–25.

Truman, Harry S. *Memoirs*. Vol. 2, *Years of Trial and Hope*. Garden City, NY: Doubleday, 1956.

———. *Off the Record: The Private Papers of Harry S. Truman*. Edited by Robert H. Ferrell. New York: Harper & Row, 1980.

———. *Public Papers of the Presidents of the United States: Harry S. Truman: Containing the Public Messages, Speeches, and Statements of the President, April 12, 1945 to January 20, 1953*. 8 vols. Washington, DC: U.S. G.P.O, 1961.

Truman, Harry S., and Dean Acheson. *Affection and Trust: The Personal Correspondence of Harry S. Truman and Dean Acheson, 1953–1971*. New York: Alfred A. Knopf, 2010.

Truman, Margaret. *Harry S. Truman*. New York: Morrow, 1973.

Tsou, Tang. *America's Failure in China, 1941–50*. Chicago: University of Chicago Press, 1975.

United States Army Military History Office. *The Handling of Prisoners of War during the Korean War*. San Francisco: Headquarters, U.S. Army, Pacific, 1960.

United States Department of State. *The China White Paper, August 1949*. Originally issued as *United States Relations with China, with Special Reference to the Period 1944–1949*. Stanford, CA: Stanford Univ. Press, 1967.

———. *Foreign Relations of the United States* [*FRUS*]. Washington, DC: U.S. Government Printing Office, 1939–2007.

United States War Department. *War Report of the Office of Strategic Services*. Washington, DC: U.S. Government Printing Office, 1949.

US Congress, Senate Committee on Foreign Relations. *Military Situation in the Far East; Hearings Before the Committee on Armed Services and the Committee on Foreign Relations, United States Senate, to Conduct an Inquiry into the Military Situation in the Far East and the Facts Surrounding the Relief of General of the Army Douglas MacArthur from His Assignments in That Area*. Washington: US GPO, 1951.

Wang Beishan 王北山 [Wang Houci]. *Hanzhan shengshi lian* 韓戰生死戀 [Life, death, and love in the Korean War]. Taipei: Zhiyang chubanshe, 2003.

Wang Chaoguang 汪朝光. *Zhongguo jindai tongshi, di shi juan: Zhongguo mingyun de juezhan (1945–1949)* 中國近代通史, 第十卷: 中國命運的決戰 (1945–1949) [General history of modern China; Vol. 10, The final battle over China's fate]. Nanjing: Jiangsu renmin chubanshe, 2009.

Wang Dengyun 王登雲. *Shujuan renfeng: Wang Dengyun huiyilu* 舒卷任風: 王登雲回憶錄 [Memoirs of Wang Dengyun]. Hong Kong: Huaxia wenhua chubanshe, 2013.

Wang, Di. *Violence and Order on the Chengdu Plain: The Story of a Secret Brotherhood in Rural China, 1939–1949*. Stanford University Press, 2018.

Wang Dingjun 王鼎鈞. *Wenxue jianghu* 文學江湖 [The literature trade]. Taipei: Erya, 2009.

Wang Dongyuan 王東原. *Fu sheng jianshu* 浮生簡述 [A brief autobiography]. Taipei: Zhuanji wenxue chubanshe, 1987.

Wang Xinting 王新亭. *Wang Xinting huiyilu* 王新亭回憶錄 [The memoirs of Wang Xinting]. 2nd ed. Beijing: Jiefangjun chubanshe, 2008.

Wang Yan 王焰, ed. *Peng Dehuai nianpu* 彭德懷年譜 [Chronological biography of Peng Dehuai]. Beijing: Renmin chubanshe, 1998.

Weathersby, Kathryn. "Stalin, Mao, and the End of the Korean War." In *Brothers in Arms: The Rise and Fall of the Sino-Soviet Alliance, 1945–1963*, edited by Odd Arne Westad, 90–116. Stanford, CA: Stanford University Press, 1998.

Wen Xiaocun 文曉村. *Wen Xiaocun zizhuan: cong Heluo dao Taiwan* 文曉村自傳: 從河洛到台灣 [Autobiography of Wen Xiaocun: From Henan to Taiwan]. Taipei: Shiyiwen chuban, 2000.

White, William Lindsay. *The Captives of Korea: An Unofficial White Paper on the Treatment of War Prisoners, Our Treatment of Theirs, Their Treatment of Ours*. New York: Scribner, 1957.

Whiting, Allen S. "The New Chinese Communist." *World Politics: A Quarterly Journal of International Relations* 7, no. 4 (1955): 592–605.

Williams, Sue, dir. *China: A Century of Revolution*. Part 1. Documenary film. New York: Zeitgeist Films, 1997.

Willoughby, Charles Andrew, and John Chamberlain. *MacArthur, 1941–1951*. New York: McGraw-Hill, 1954.

Woolley, John T., and Gerhard Peters. *The American Presidency Project*. Santa Barbara, CA. http://www.presidency.ucsb.edu/index.php.

Wu Jinfeng 吳金鋒. "Andeshe biji: guoguo zhanfu zishu ji" 安德舍筆記—歸國戰俘自述集 [Andeshe notes: Statements by repatriated POWs]. 3 vols. Unpublished ms. (a compilation of interviews by Wu in the mid-1980s and dossier file transcripts), 1986.

Wu Jiwu 伍濟武. "Banmendian tanpan wo zaichang" 板門店談判我在場 [I was there at the Panmunjom talks]. *Dallas Chinese News* 達拉斯新聞, circa Oct. 2004. http://www.dallaschinesenews.com/detail.php?id=4590.

Xie Zhiqi 謝智齊. "Zuinie" 罪孽 [Crime]. Unpublished memoir.

Xu, Jianhong 許劍虹. Naduan yinglie de rizi: Zhong Ri zhanzheng yongshi yusheng lu 那段英烈的日子：中日戰爭勇士餘生錄 [Heroes of the Sino-Japanese War]. Taipei: Jingang chuban, 2017.

Xu Yan 徐焰. *Diyici jiaoliang: Kangmei yuanchao zhanzheng de lishi huigu yu fansi* 第一次較量：抗美援朝戰爭的歷史回顧與反思 [The first duel: A reflection on the War to Resist America and Aid Korea]. Beijing: Zhongguo guangbo dianshi chubanshe, 1990.

———. "Zhongguo xisheng shiba wan Zhiyuanjun" 中國犧牲十八萬志願軍 [The Chinese People's Volunteers Army's death toll is 180,000]. *Wenshi cankao* 文史參考 83 (June 2010): 82–84.

Xu Yipeng 徐一朋. *Cuojue: 180 shi Chaoxian shoucuoji* 錯覺：180師朝鮮受挫記 [Delusion: The 180th Division's setback in Korea]. Nanjing: Jiangsu renmin chubanshe, 1996.

Yan Lebin 晏樂斌. "Gaige kaifang qian wuchanjieji zhuanzheng de duixiang" 改革開放前無產階級專政的對象 [The targets of the dictatorship of the proletariat before Reform and Opening-up]. *Yanhuang chunqiu* 炎黃春秋, no. 8 (2012): 1–9.

Yan Xinning 閻欣寧. *Wei Jie gushi* 韋傑故事 [Wei Jie's story]. Beijing: Jiefangjun chubanshe, 2014.

Yang Di 楊迪. *Zai Zhiyuanjun silingbu de suiyueli: xianwei renzhi de zhenshi qingkuang* 在志願軍司令部的歲月裏：鮮爲人知的真情實況 [My years at the CPV GHQ: Untold true stories]. Beijing: Jiefangjun chubanshe, 1998.

Yang Feng'an 楊鳳安 and Wang Tiancheng 王天成. *Beiwei 38 du xian: Peng Dehuai yu Chaoxian zhanzheng* 北緯三十八度線：彭德懷與朝鮮戰爭 [The 38th parallel: Peng Dehuai and the Korean War]. Beijing: Jiefangjun chubanshe, 2000.

Yang Jisheng 楊繼繩. *Mubei: 1958–1962 nian Zhongguo dajihuang jishi* 墓碑：1958-1962年中國大饑荒紀實[Tombstone: The true story of China's great famine]. Hong Kong: Tiandi tushu, 2017.

Yang Kuisong 楊奎松. "Guanyu jiefang zhanzheng zhong de Sulian junshi yuanzhu wenti—jian tan zhixue taidu bing da Liu Tong xiansheng" 關於解放戰爭中的蘇聯軍事援助問題—兼談治學態度並答劉統先生 [On Soviet military aid during the Civil War—with a discussion of scholarship and a response to Mr. Liu Tong]. *Jindaishi yanjiu* 近代史研究, no. 1 (2001): 285–306.

———. "Mei Su lengzhan de qiyuan ji dui Zhongguo geming de yingxiang" 美蘇冷戰的起源及對中國革命的影響 [The origin of the Cold War and its impact on the Chinese revolution]. *Lishi yanjiu* 歷史研究, no. 5 (1999): 5–22.

———. *Minguo renwu guoyan lu* 民國人物過眼錄 [A glimpse of Republican figures]. Guangzhou: Guangdong renmin chubanshe, 2009.

———. "Nanyi queding de duishou (1917–1949)" 難以確定的對手 [The uncertain opponent]. In *Zhong Su guanxi shigang* 中蘇關係史綱 [History of Sino-Soviet relations, 1917–1991], edited by Shen Zhihua, 3–76. 3rd ed. Beijing: Shehui kexue wenxian chubanshe, 2011.

———. "Reconsidering the Campaign to Suppress Counterrevolutionaries." *China Quarterly* 193 (Mar. 2008): 102–21.

———. *Zhonghua renmin gongheguo jianguo shi yanjiu 1* 中華人民共和國建國史研究 1 [Studies on the founding of the PRC, 1]. Nanchang: Jiangxi renmin chubanshe, 2009.

Yao Guojun 姚國俊. "Wo yu junxiao Guan Linzheng he Zhang Yaoming" 我與軍校關麟征和張耀明 [My relationship with the Military Academy's [presidents] Guan Linzheng and Zhang Yaoming]. In *Sichuan wenshi ziliao xuanji* 四川文史資料選輯, no. 19: 173–79. Chengdu, 1979.

Ye Qingsong 叶青松. *Zhongguo renmin jiefangjun di 60 jun zhengzhan jishi* 中國人民解放軍第六十軍征戰紀實 [Military history of the PLA 60th Army]. Beijing: Jiefangjun wenyi chubanshe, 2006.

Yi Fu'en 衣復恩. *Wo de huiyi* 我的回憶 [My memories]. Taipei: Li-Ching Cultural Educational Foundation, 2011.

Yin Shusheng 尹曙生. "Mao Zedong yu disanci quanguo gong'an huiyi" 毛澤東與第三次全國公安會議 [Mao Zedong and the Third National Public Security Conference]. *Yanhuang chunqiu* 炎黃春秋, no. 5 (2014): 1–5.

Young, Charles S. *Name, Rank, and Serial Number: Exploiting Korean War POWs at Home and Abroad.* New York: Oxford University Press, 2014.

Yu Jin 于勁. *Eyun* 厄運 [Nightmare]. Nanjing: Jiangsu wenyi chubanshe, 1988.

Zhang Chengyuan 張城垣 and Gao Yansai 高延賽. *Chongwei: Zhiyuanjun 180 shi daizhengwei Wu Chengde yu zhanyoumen* 重圍：志願軍180師代政委吳成德與戰友們 [Layers of siege: The People's Volunteer Army 180th Division Acting Commissar Wu Chengde and his comrades]. Beijing: Zhongguo wenshi chubanshe, 2001.

Zhang Mingjin 張明金 and Liu Liqin 劉立勤, eds. *Zhongguo renmin zhiyuanjun lishi shang de 27 ge jun* 中國人民志願軍歷史上的27個軍 [The twenty-seven armies of the CPV]. Beijing: Jiefangjun chubanshe, 2014.

Zhang Yinghua 張英華. "Wo fengming jieshou Zhiyuanjun bingshang zhanfu" 我奉命接收志願軍病傷戰俘 [I was ordered to receive sick and wounded CPV POWs]. *Shiji* 世紀, no. 4 (2012): 22–24.

Zhang Zeshi 張澤石, ed. *Kaoyan: Zhiyuanjun zhanfu Meijun jizhongying qinliji* 考驗：志願軍戰俘美軍集中營親歷記 [Test: Personal accounts of Chinese People's Volunteer Army prisoners in US Army concentration camps]. Beijing: Zhongguo wenshi chubanshe, 1998.

———. *1949 wo buzai Qinghuayuan* 1949我不在清華園 [I was not on the Tsinghua campus in 1949]. Beijing: Dangdai Zhongguo chubanshe, 2003.

———. *Wo de Chaoxian zhanzheng* 我的朝鮮戰爭 [My Korean War]. Beijing: Jincheng chubanshe, 2011.

Zhang Zhenglong 張正隆. *Xuebai xuehong* 雪白血紅 [White snow, red blood]. 3rd ed. Hong Kong: Tiandi tushu, 2012.

Zhong Hanxun 鐘漢勳. "Guomingdang sanbing jianshi" 國民黨傘兵簡史 [A brief history of the Nationalist paratroopers]. In *Wenshiziliao cungao xuanbian, junshi jigou, shang* 文史資料存稿選編 軍事機構 上 [Selected unused literary and historical materials about military organizations, vol. 1], 584–94. Beijing: Zhongguo wenshi chubanshe, 2002.

Zhonggong Beijing shiwei dangshi yanjiushi 中共北京市委黨史研究室, ed. *Kangyi Meijun zhuhua baoxing yundong ziliao huibian* 抗議美軍駐華暴行運動資料彙編 [Collected sources on the movement protesting the US Army's atrocities in China]. Beijing: Beijing daxue chubanshe, 1989.

Zhonggong zhongyang wenxian yanjiushi 中共中央文獻研究室, ed. *Chen Yun nianpu* 陳雲年譜 [Chronological biography of Chen Yun]. Vol. 1. Beijing: Zhongyang wenxian chubanshe, 2000.

———. *Deng Xiaoping zhuan (1904–1974)* 鄧小平傳 下 [Deng Xiaoping biography, vol. 2]. Beijing: Zhongyang wenxian chubanshe, 2014.

Zhongguo junshi bowuguan 中國軍事博物館, ed. *Kangmei yuanchao zhanzheng jishi* 抗美援朝戰爭紀事 [Chronology of the War to Resist America and Aid Korea]. 2nd ed. Beijing: Jiefangjun chubanshe, 2008.

Zhongguo renmin jiefangjun junshi kexueyuan junshi lishi yanjiubu 中國人民解放軍軍事科學院軍事歷史研究部. *Zhongguo renmin jiefangjun quanguo jiefang zhanzheng shi* 中國人民解放軍全國解放戰爭史 [The history of the PLA's liberation of China]. Vol. 4. Beijing: Junshi kexue chubanshe, 1997.

Zhou Enlai 周恩來. *Zhou Enlai junshi wenxuan* 周恩來軍事文選 [Selected military works of Zhou Enlai]. Vol. 4. Zhonggong zhongyang wenxian yanjiushi, ed. Beijing: Renmin chubanshe, 1997.

———. *Zhou Enlai xuanji* 周恩來選集 [Selected works of Zhou Enlai]. Zhonggong zhongyang wenxian bianji weiyuanhui, ed. Beijing: Renmin chubanshe, 1980.

Zhou Xiuhuan [Hsiu-huan Chou] 周琇環 ed. *Zhanhou waijiao shiliao huibian: Hanzhan yu fangong yishi pian* 1–3 戰後外交史料彙編: 韓戰與反共義士篇 1–3 [Documentary collection on the foreign affairs of postwar Taiwan: The Korean War and the Chinese Communist defectors]. 3 vols. Taiwan: Academia Historica, 2005.

Zhou Xiuhuan 周琇環, Zhang Shiying 張世瑛, and Ma Guozheng 馬國正. *Hanzhan fangong yishi fangtanlu* 韓戰反共義士訪談錄 [The reminiscences of Korean War anti-Communist defectors]. Taipei: Academia Historica, 2013.

Index